90997

THE NEW WHITE NATIONALISM
IN AMERICA

Over the past ten years, a new white nationalist movement has gained strength in America, bringing with it the potential to disrupt already fragile race relations. Eschewing violence, this movement seeks to expand its influence mainly through argument and persuasion directed at its target audience of white Americans aggrieved over racial double standards, race-based affirmative action policies, high black-on-white crime rates, and liberal immigration policies. The movement has also been energized, Swain contends, by minority advocacy of multi-culturalism. Due to its emphasis on group self-determination, multiculturalism has provided white nationalists with justification for advocating a parallel form of white solidarity. In addition, as Swain illustrates, technological advances such as the Internet have made it easier than ever before for white nationalists to reach a more mainstream audience. Swain's study is intended as a wake-up call to all Americans who cherish the civil rights era vision of an integrated America, a common humanity, and equality before God and the law.

Carol M. Swain is Professor of Political Science and Professor of Law at Vanderbilt University. She is the author of *Black Faces, Black Interests: The Representation of African Americans in Congress* (1993, 1995), which was selected by *Library Choice Journal* as one of the seven outstanding academic books of 1994. Award of the American Political Science Association, the D. B. Hardeman Prize of the Lyndon Baines Johnson Foundation, and the co-winner of the V. O. Key Award of the Southern Political Science Association.

THE NEW WHITE NATIONALISM IN AMERICA

ITS CHALLENGE TO INTEGRATION

CAROL M. SWAIN
Vanderbilt University Law School

CAMBRIDGE
UNIVERSITY PRESS

PUBLISHED BY THE PRESS SYNDICATE OF THE UNIVERSITY OF CAMBRIDGE
The Pitt Building, Trumpington Street, Cambridge, United Kingdom

CAMBRIDGE UNIVERSITY PRESS
The Edinburgh Building, Cambridge CB2 2RU, UK
40 West 20th Street, New York, NY 10011-4211, USA
477 Williamstown Road, Port Melbourne, VIC 3207, Australia
Ruiz de Alarcón 13, 28014 Madrid, Spain
Dock House, The Waterfront, Cape Town 8001, South Africa

http://www.cambridge.org

First published 2002

Printed in the United States of America

Typeface Sabon 10.25/13.5 pt.   *System* QuarkXPress [BTS]

A catalog record for this book is available from the British Library.

Library of Congress Cataloging in Publication Data
Swain, Carol M. (Carol Miller)
The new white nationalism in America : its challenge to integration /
Carol M. Swain.
p.   cm.
Includes bibliographical references and index.
ISBN 0-521-80886-3
1. White supremacy movements – United States.   2. United States – Race relations.   3.
United States – Ethnic relations.   4. Racism – United States.   5. Hate groups – United
States.   6. United States – Social conditions – 1980–   I. Title.
E184.A1 S966 2002
305.8034′073 – dc21

2001043919

ISBN   0 521 80886 3   hardback

To Robert K. Merton
for his inspiration and support

CONTENTS

CONTENTS

LIST OF FIGURES
AND TABLES

FIGURES

TABLES

xiii

PREFACE

This book explores the development of an emerging white nationalist movement in America that poses a threat, I believe, to the peace and repose of our multiethnic society. Appropriating to its own ends the language of multiculturalism and civil rights activism, this developing social movement, I argue in these pages, has the potential to expand its ranks among ordinary white Americans, who increasingly find themselves frustrated by a host of unresolved public policy issues in the area of ethnicity and race. Often disguising themselves in the mantle of mainstream conservatism, white nationalists have developed skills at packaging their message to conceal the radicalism of their views, and have been successful in recent years in expanding their influence into our homes, our computers, and our schools. This development, I believe, is alarming, and it is a major purpose of this book to draw attention to the danger posed by the growing influence of the white nationalist movement.

White nationalism thrives by its willingness to address many contemporary issues and developments that mainstream politicians and media sources either ignore entirely or fail to address with any degree of openness or candor. These developments include the continuing influx into the country of nonwhite immigrants and the prospect that America in the not-too-distant future will cease to be a white majority nation; the decline in high-paying, low-skill-requisite, industrial jobs as a result of globalization and other structural changes in the American economy; continuing white resentment over affirmative action policies that favor officially designated minority groups over native whites in education and employment; continued white fear of black crime; the continued emphasis on racial identity politics and the fostering of an ethnic group pride on the part of nonwhite minority groups; and the expanding influence and reach of the Internet. When these conditions combine with the rising expectations on the part of racial and ethnic minorities for a larger share of power and influence in American society, the stage is set for increased political conflict and turmoil.

I have written this book to heighten public awareness of the groups and leaders in the white nationalist movement and the issues they use in their recruitment efforts. I have also written it with the special hope that it will provide useful insights into the nature of America's continuing racial problems, especially for people who consider themselves to be liberals on public policy issues, because some of the policies that they support are contributing to a worsening racial climate. By liberals I refer to individuals who favor vigorous government intervention to ensure the advancement of racial and ethnic minorities and to protect them from official and private discrimination. I try here to provide liberals with information that can give them a more informed idea of the tradeoffs involved in continuing down the same path that they have embarked upon since the late 1960s and early 1970s, when our current affirmative action regime was first put in place and when nonwhite immigrants first began pouring into the country in large numbers. Although many liberal activists will probably continue to believe that the benefits for society of the expanded racial and ethnic diversity made possible by current public policies are well worth the price of social unrest, others might use the information in this book to rethink their strategies and to consider how best to help disadvantaged minority populations to improve their lot in life without alienating potential allies frustrated by current government policies. A major goal in writing this book is to inform Americans – and particularly liberal Americans – of what I see as dangers looming ahead, as well as to highlight areas of potential agreement and consensus among racial and ethnic groups where viable multiracial coalitions might be forged.

In earlier presentations of some of the ideas contained in this book, some critics have expressed the fear that in publicizing the views of white nationalists and others on the racist right I am giving them a new and better forum from which to press their claims. Others have stated their concern that in drawing attention to the racial tension caused by current affirmative action policy, I may be giving ammunition to conservative opponents of such policies who seek to eliminate them rather than mend them. To the first group I respond that white nationalists already have a forum, one far more powerful than any I can provide. By exposing their strategies and giving voice to some of their grievances I hope to promote greater racial harmony and to heighten America's awareness of what is at stake. What I would like to see is more scholarly assessment countering the social science data that white nationalists eagerly proffer, and I would like to see open forums on university and college campuses where ideas can be combated with other ideas rather than censored, and where hearts can be opened and perhaps changed.

If the material in this book presents a challenge to liberals, it also, I believe, offers a warning to conservatives. By conservatives I mean those who are suspicious of activist government, particularly in the domestic sphere, and who are often more willing than liberals, at least among themselves, to express criticisms of the behavior of racial minorities. A major contention of this book is that we need a reinvigorated public dialogue in the area of race where well-meaning persons of all political persuasions will not be labeled as racists or antiblack for criticizing social welfare programs, opposing racial preferences, or condemning unhealthy or irresponsible behavior in black communities. I believe there should be a place where a vigorous intellectual conversation can take place about such hot-button issues as affirmative action, black crime rates, racial differences in IQ scores, and the wisdom of racial preference programs that include immigrant minorities and their offspring. However, mainstream conservatism, in my view, crosses the line of acceptable discourse, and enters the destructive territory of white racism and white chauvinism, when it begins to argue that blacks are criminal by nature, that minorities are a menace to the high civilization that white people have created, or that the alleged genetic inferiority of black and brown peoples requires a regime of white separatism or white supremacy to preserve Western culture from degradation and despoilment. Participants in any fruitful dialogue must be united by at least some shared values and beliefs, and in the case of meaningful racial dialogue, both a modicum of goodwill and an affirmation of our common humanity are indispensable prerequisites. It is these latter prerequisites that are missing from the discourse of most of the white nationalists profiled in this book, and their example should serve as a warning to conservatives who share some of their views. One can only say to such conservatives: Don't go there!

PERSONAL REFLECTIONS: THE AUTHOR AS INTERPRETER AND DATA SOURCE

In this book I break with the tradition of impersonal, value-free social science insofar as I do not pretend to be neutral and do not hesitate to interject many personal observations and comments into the body of the text. Because I care so deeply about the future of American race relations and because I have acquired valuable experiences in life that give me some insight into a number of the issues treated in this study, I have reserved for myself the right to explore hunches and draw upon personal intuitions as I interpret and evaluate the data. This is particularly true on the issue of affirmative action.

When I express reservations about certain forms of current affirmative action policy, I do so from the standpoint of a black woman with a firsthand knowledge of what it means to be poor and disadvantaged in America. I was born in rural Virginia into an abusive and impoverished farm household of twelve children with many different fathers. None of my siblings – seven brothers and four sisters – ever graduated from high school. Although I, too, dropped out of school after completing the eighth grade, I nevertheless managed to earn five college degrees from an array of institutions, starting at a community college and ending at an Ivy League university.[1] Over the years, I have been a divorced welfare mother of two sons, both of whom, I am proud to report, managed to avoid most of the serious problems that plague black males in contemporary America. I have worked as an assistant in a nursing home for the aged, as an unskilled worker in a garment factory, as a door-to-door salesperson, and as a library worker at a community college before becoming a successful university professor. My varied experiences at different occupations and class levels have enabled me, I believe, to relate better to Americans from many different racial, economic, and educational backgrounds. I have seen life in

---

[1] My degrees are from the following colleges and universities: Virginia Western Community College (A.A.S, 1978), Roanoke College (B.A., 1983), Virginia Polytechnic Institute and State University (M.A., 1984), University of North Carolina at Chapel Hill (Ph.D., 1989); and Yale University Law School (M.S.L., 2000).

America from the bottom, from the middle, and from the top, and I think I have learned something about just who is in need of special help programs and what sort of programs are likely to work.

I can speak, for instance, of the great value of having race-neutral federal grants and loans, since these were crucial to my own ability to start and continue my education. Despite the existence of affirmative action and the public perception that it supposedly allows blacks to attend colleges on free scholarships, that was certainly not my own experience during the early to mid-1980s. In addition to working, sometimes at a full-time job, I had to borrow heavily from the federal government to complete my education. It was, in fact, my experience of struggling financially at the four-year institution I attended that led me to approach the outside black business community with a proposal to establish a private academic scholarship for minorities.[2] Rather than straightforward racial preferences, I believe that what enabled me to overcome some of the disadvantages of my social background was a combination of both help from concerned mentors and government financial assistance from such programs as Basic Grant.

Some forms of affirmative action, I believe, are harmful to their recipients and can diminish both their efforts to achieve and their self-esteem. I have seen how the very existence of racial preferences can have the paradoxical effect of undermining initiative and self-confidence. In a society with a long history of racial prejudice and discrimination, it is all too easy for members of racial and ethnic minorities to fall into the role of helpless victim or legitimizing token. Racial preference policies, I think, often encourage this kind of behavior. Such policies carry a subliminal message of doubt and uncertainty – a message that says, in effect, that you, as a woman or member of a minority group, are less capable than a white male and will need special preference in order to compete successfully in a world dominated by superior white males. This is particularly the case at the most competitive universities, where affirmative action policies take on the greatest salience. At elite institutions the walls seem to whisper, "white

---

[2] While a senior at Roanoke in Salem, Virginia, I approached the wealthiest black businessman in the city, Lawrence Hamlar, with a proposal to establish a scholarship in honor of his deceased wife, who had served as my teacher and mentor at the community college I attended. In 1994, the Constance J. Hamlar Scholarship endowment exceeded $250,000.

males are superior . . . African Americans and Hispanics are inferior."
Believing that everyone else is more capable than you are, or that the
world is dominated by malevolent forces out to victimize and eliminate you, is hardly conducive to high levels of personal achievement
or high self-esteem.

I felt some of these forces at work while I was on the faculty at
Princeton University. For ten years I was the Department of Politics'
sole African-American faculty member and one of just two blacks in
the Woodrow Wilson School, Princeton University's prestigious public
policy institute. Many times I sat on committees and in meetings in
which I had to listen to patronizing remarks about affirmative action
from my mostly "liberal" colleagues, and suffered the feelings of inad-
equacy that many African Americans experience as they fulfill what is
at best a token and marginalized role in majority white institutions,
where most remain outsiders. Undoubtedly, some of what I can now
see as my ambivalence about being on the faculty of a world-class university was a product both of my rapid change in social class and my
personal insecurities about the role that affirmative action may have
played in my own success story. Despite the fact that when I arrived
at Princeton I had a solid record of scholarly achievement and a book
contract from Harvard University Press – a rarity for a new assistant
professor – I nevertheless worried about whether I was qualified
enough to be there. Even after receiving tenure there was a period when
I felt immobilized by self-doubt despite the fact that I had continued
to publish and received a number of prestigious awards for my scholarly work. Affirmative action policies, I believe, can send a powerful
message to whites and blacks alike that minorities are incapable of
competing on their own, and it has contributed to the continued white
denigration of genuine minority accomplishment.

The way affirmative action programs are administered at many universities is also troubling. It has been my experience that, at least in
academia, the right class pedigree for black scholars is valued by some
institutions just as highly – and in some cases even more highly – than
a record of solid scholarship. This applies to both hiring and tenure
decisions where lower standards sometimes seem to apply to the well
bred. When one considers that the original justification for affirmative
action policies was to give the "shackled runners" (Lyndon Johnson's
metaphor) a boost up after a long life of deprivation and disadvantage,

one sees how perverse this development really is. Some predominantly white institutions seem to be more interested in having a small number of well-bred middle-class minority tokens than minority scholars from more modest backgrounds.

Minority scholars hired under such circumstances often display a degree of class snobbishness that is rarely discussed outside of minority circles. Many affluent African Americans I have encountered in academia act as if all academic positions and awards should go to their group as some kind of special entitlement. They also seem to be made uneasy when minorities from lower-class backgrounds achieve more than individuals from their more privileged backgrounds. Surprisingly, I have even encountered such feelings among middle-class blacks who have achieved much on their own and have received the social recognition that one would suppose would make them feel more secure and less threatened by the achievement of others.

One other effect of affirmative action in academia is to stifle open discussion and dissent about the wisdom of the policy itself, especially among those in the groups intended as its beneficiaries. For a minority scholar to express reservations about affirmative action is to risk all sorts of accusations about one's motivations. "How dare you?" is often the response to any black critic who challenges the white supporters of affirmative action at our elite universities or questions the integrity of their alliances with those they often disdain in private conversations.

In criticizing many aspects of affirmative action policy, I do not, of course, wish to deny the goodwill of at least some of its supporters and the genuine concern that many have for helping those truly in need. Nor do I wish to suggest that grades and test scores should be the only criteria that universities can legitimately use in determining who they accept into their undergraduate or graduate programs. Indeed, I think such an approach can miss a great deal about a person's real accomplishments. Because I transferred with an associate's degree and a solid academic record into a four-year college from a community college that had an open-door admission policy, I was not required to take the Scholastic Assessment Test (SAT) that so many black students score poorly on. And although I graduated magna cum laude from a solid liberal arts college (while working full-time as a community college librarian assistant), my Graduate Record Exam (GRE) scores were unimpressive, despite my having met the academic requirements of the highest honor societies at my undergraduate school. So I can sympathize with students of all races who have had excellent grades and past academic performance but nevertheless fail to score high on standardized tests. In addition, like most of the Americans whose survey responses I analyze later in this study, I believe that what constitutes merit within an academic context can be legitimately expanded to take account of the obstacles an individual has had to overcome in life. But real problems exist with affirmative action programs as they currently exist in academics and elsewhere, and I feel obligated to say what is wrong with them. I would particularly like to see the community college route that gave me a second chance utilized by more students from disadvantaged backgrounds, because it represents an important option rarely discussed in the current affirmative action debate.

So I believe I can speak as an American who has seen this country from many different vantage points and can empathize with the plight of the nation's truly disadvantaged. Over the course of less than twenty years I have moved from an underclass background to my present status as solidly entrenched in the comfortable middle class, and I have also had over this period an enriched religious and spiritual evolution that has taken me from traditional Christianity through the New Age movement and back again to traditional Christianity with what I believe are new insights and expanded perspectives. The biblical teaching that we are all children of God – and all members of one and the same divinely created human race – is one that has conditioned my thoughts on racial issues and guided much of my efforts on this project. I have written this book with a sense of urgency because I believe that America is deeply in trouble regarding its race relations. In the course of researching this study I have gone from being a Pollyanna on race matters to a Cassandra, who warns of an impending and unprecedented level of racial conflict that will stem from America's unresolved policy controversies surrounding not only affirmative action but black-on-white crime and liberal immigration policies as well. My wish is that as many individuals as possible will be challenged, provoked, and perhaps even persuaded in places by reading and reflecting on the material contained in this book. Just as with my first book, *Black Faces, Black Interests*, which generated considerable controversy when published several years ago, I fully expect to be vindicated by the passage of time.

THE STRUCTURE OF THE BOOK

The book is divided into four major parts. Part I consists of five chapters that introduce the new white nationalists and their core beliefs. In Chapters 1 and 2, I try to show that white nationalists are not the sort of people we may think they are. They are not, for instance, to be equated with the members of the older racist right represented by organizations like the Ku Klux Klan or the American Nazi Party. While sharing some of the same ideological beliefs as members of the older racist right, contemporary white nationalists are now part of a movement that has jettisoned most of the images and tactics of the older racist right organizations, as well as many of their more bizarre rituals and beliefs, in an attempt to expand their influence to a larger and more mainstream audience. Chapter 2 presents an overview of some of the literature and ideas that undergird white nationalism and discusses how these ideas might be received in mainstream America. In Chapter 3, I provide a summary of some of the core elements in the traditional white supremacy belief system and discuss movement literature. Chapter 4 covers recent immigration and demographic changes – developments which, if they continue on the same track, will lead to the eventual minority status of white Americans. Chapter 5, the last chapter in Part I, presents data on crime and white nationalists' concerted efforts to heighten Americans' awareness of black-on-white violent crime.

Part II consists of four chapters focusing on different aspects of the affirmative action issue – a high voltage policy controversy that white nationalists seek to exploit in their efforts to woo mainstream whites. Chapter 6 covers the history and politics of the policy, and is followed by a chapter that discusses the importance of media framing in understanding the issue. Chapter 7 also presents data from public opinion polls and presents further material on the affirmative action issue from a series of ethnically homogeneous focus groups consisting of Asian, African-American, Latino, and Euro-American participants. In Chapter 8, I present the views of white nationalists and explain how they frame and describe affirmative action and related issues. Chapter 9 rounds out the material in Part II and focuses on the legal and constitutional history of affirmative action in higher education.

I devote a great deal of effort to discussing affirmative action policy because I believe this issue is one of the most useful grievances for white nationalists seeking to rally support among mainstream Americans. Indeed, surveys and focus groups show that a majority of Americans strongly oppose racial preferences and racial quotas. I believe that resentment over the perceived injustice of affirmative action has the potential to cause many otherwise well-adjusted young white Americans to come to see themselves as victims of reverse discrimination and to displace their anger over this situation to the members of the minority groups who benefit from racial preference policies.

Part III examines the impact that living in a racially charged environment can have on young Americans. In Chapter 10, I present information on the growing competitiveness for college admission and how this affects everyone, and then present case studies of three young white Americans who competed for freshman seats during the latter half of the 1990s. This chapter illustrates different potential modes of adaptation of young people to the new competitive environment, including anger, disappointment, frustration, and resignation. The remaining two chapters in Part III discuss multiculturalism and the recruitment strategies of white nationalists.

Part IV presents three concluding chapters on potential remedies to the unresolved public policy issues that white nationalists seek to exploit in their efforts to build support for their political agendas. In Chapter 13, I show that in the area of affirmative action in higher education, there is considerable agreement between blacks and whites about how colleges should determine who gets admitted to their entering classes. There is a consensus in favor of class-based rather than race-based affirmative action, and a consensus for the determination of merit based on the consideration of handicaps and barriers that an individual has had to overcome to reach a given level of achievement. Chapter 14 discusses the potential of religion to promote racial and social harmony by examining its negative and positive effects on American society. Because I believe that many of America's social problems can be addressed by teaching biblical principles that emphasize brotherly love, a common creator, and equality before the law, I focus on the monotheistic religions as I argue in favor of increased partnerships between religious and political leaders. In addition, this chapter includes a section on African Americans, faith-based approaches to social problems, and the challenge that homosexuality poses to traditional Christians and to the white nationalists who often include gays and lesbians among their targets of hate. Chapter 15, the final chapter, offers two sets of policy recommendations designed to address the kinds of issues and concerns that white nationalists seek to exploit during their interactions with mainstream Americans. The first set is aimed at America's social, political, and institutional leaders, and the second set is geared specifically for African-American leaders.

ACKNOWLEDGMENTS

A book like this could not be written without incurring numerous debts along the way. My first debt is to Lewis Bateman for his courage and tenacity in vigorously pursuing and defending the manuscript that other university publishers found too hot to handle. Lew provided crucial support during a time when many liberal white scholars urged me to abandon the project on the grounds that it might provide a forum for the dangerous ideas of white nationalists as well as a justification for ending racial preferences.

In addition, I would like to thank James McHenry, a Vanderbilt University political science and law student who worked tirelessly on the project, and Russell Nieli of Princeton University, who conducted all the interviews of the white nationalists and helped with the editing of chapters. My thanks go also to my assistant, Kelley Walker, who proofread and offered suggestions for the book cover and for the chapters that she read. Again and again Kelley challenged me with her probing questions and unsolicited advice. Katie Fischer, a Yale University law student, worked on the project during its earlier stages, along with Yale University undergraduates Melanie Harris and Anne-lena Lobb. Vanderbilt University graduate students Eleanor Fleming and Eric Taylor assisted me during the final stages of manuscript preparation, and Eric offered a number of insightful suggestions for the religion chapter. Professor George Graham of Vanderbilt University and the graduate students in his interdisciplinary seminar on social and political thought offered a number of great suggestions for improving the presentation of ideas. Thanks also to Martin Cerjan, Elizabeth Gernert, Renee Hawkins, and Kaleshia Page of Vanderbilt University

Law School for their assistance. Russell Perkins of the Tennessee State Attorney General's Office commented on the religion chapter.

I am especially indebted to my former colleague, Stanley Kelley, Jr., of Princeton University, who read and commented on an earlier draft of this manuscript, and to Kent Syverud, Dean of the Vanderbilt University Law School, for his continuing encouragement and support. Professors Suzanna Sherry of Vanderbilt University Law School and Burke Marshall and Stephen Yandle of Yale University Law School offered invaluable comments. Others who bear special recognition include David Mayhew and Donald Green of Yale University; Richard Fenno of the University of Rochester, who warned me that I had a tiger by the tail; Hugh Douglas Graham of Vanderbilt University; John D. Skrentny of the University of California at San Diego; William J. Wilson of Harvard University; and writer Jim Sleeper of Yale University.

Elvis Brathwaite and Kevin O'Sullivan of the Associated Press; Mark Potok, Tafeni English, and Russell Estes of the Southern Poverty Law Center; Jonathan Tilove of Newhouse Publishing; David Goldman of Harvard University; and David Hillman of Virginia Western Community College have each in his or her own unique way provided invaluable assistance. David Hillman indexed this book and Stephanie Sakson served as copyeditor. Moreover, I am indebted to Princeton University's Woodrow Wilson School and Vanderbilt University for their resources and support.

Others who deserve special recognition as long-term mentors include Fred I. Greenstein of Princeton University, C. William Hill of Roanoke College, William R. Keech of Carnegie Mellon University, Richard D. Shingles of Virginia Polytechnic Institute and State University, Linda L. Fowler of Dartmouth University, Jane Mansbridge of Harvard University, and Ruth Simmons of Brown University.

Finally, I acknowledge the support of my family: Reggie and Sherry Miller and their children, Destiny and Storm, and Benjamin and Roseanna Miller, and granddaughter, Tiara Woodson. My mother, Dorothy Henderson, deserves recognition for her struggles raising twelve children under the distressing conditions of rural southern poverty. Elder George W. Burns, Bishop Sherman Merritt, Bishop Melvin Boyd, Sr., Pastor Wilhemina Redmon, Pastor Walter R. Oliver, and Minister Gaytres Foster are cheerfully recognized for the spiritual nourishment they have provided me over the last couple of years.

The funding for this research came from a number of different sources, including the National Science Foundation, the Carnegie Mellon Foundation, and the Smith Richardson Foundation. It is acknowledged that the final product is quite different from the research proposals that some of the grant makers funded.

INTRODUCTION

This is a revolution. Like Johnny Appleseed, we've sowed the seeds.
I told the FBI in the presence of my lawyer one time. I said: It's too late,
we've done the work, and you can't reverse it. And out there these seeds
we know will grow into apple trees and they'll bear fruit.

> Bob Miles, former Republican Party leader of Flint,
> Michigan, speaking about the government's inability to
> stop the growth of the white power movement[1]

This book is about the growing threats to peaceful and harmonious
race relations in America and the best ways of dealing with them.
During the latter half of the 1990s, a set of converging conditions
developed in the United States that have the potential to fuel a new
and expanded white consciousness movement on the part of those
Americans of European ancestry that for lack of a better term I call
white nationalism. Grown from the roots of the older white supremacy
movement, this emerging white nationalist movement, it is argued here,
has the potential for considerable expansion beyond its present scope
and threatens to disrupt the fragile racial situation in America and
elsewhere.[2]

---

[1] Bob Miles, quoted in James Ridgeway, *Blood in the Face: The Ku Klux Klan, Aryan
Nations, Nazi Skinheads, and the Rise of a New White Culture* (New York: Thunder's
Mouth Press, 1995): 42.

[2] A growing number of sociologists, journalists, and activists have established the
existence of a growing white nationalist and white supremacist movement that gained
momentum in the late 1980s and continues to be a force in American and European
societies. See, e.g., Jeffrey Kaplan and Leonard Weinberg, *The Emergence of a Euro-
American Radical Right* (New Brunswick, N.J.: Rutgers University Press, 1999) (Kaplan
and Weinberg argue that there is a right-wing extremist movement that transcends
national boundaries); Betty A. Dobratz and Stephanie L. Shanks-Meile, "*White Power,*

At least seven conditions threaten to fuel the growth of this new racial consciousness movement. These include: (1) the growing presence of nonwhite immigrants, both legal and illegal, resulting in the prospect that white, European Americans may soon become – or in some places like California have already become – a racial minority; (2) the structural changes in the global economy that have led to a decline in high-wage production jobs for unskilled workers, who must now compete with legal and illegal immigrants for a dwindling share of low-paying employment opportunities; (3) the continuing white resentment and hostility over the perceived unfairness and questionable constitutionality of race-based affirmative action policies; (4) the continued existence of high black-on-white violent crime rates; (5) the growing acceptance of multiculturalism with its emphasis on promoting racial and ethnic group pride and identity politics; (6) the rising expectations of racial and ethnic minorities; and (7) the exponential growth in the number of households connected to the Internet, which provides a means for like-minded people to consolidate their strength, share ideas, and mobilize their resources for political action.

Each of these conditions taken individually is potentially troublesome for many Americans, but collectively they pose a major challenge to a racially integrated and vibrant nation. Scholars have shown that social movements gain momentum when the right combination of political opportunities provides activists with enough grievances to generate what sociologists call "collective action frames" around issues previously viewed as tolerable, but which under changing circumstances have come to be viewed as grossly unfair, immoral, or other-

White Pride!": The White Separatist Movement in the United States (New York: Twayne Publishers, 1997) (Dobratz and Shanks-Meile conducted field research on 125 movement leaders and followers); Jesse Daniels, *White Lies: Race, Class, Gender, and Sexuality in White Supremacist Discourse* (New York: Routledge, 1997) (Daniels provides a content analysis of 369 white supremacy publications); Ridgeway's *Blood in the Face* (a journalistic account of the growth of the white supremacy movement and its linkages to mainstream politics and politicians); Michael Barkun, *Religion and the Racist Right: The Origins of the Christian Identity Movement* (Chapel Hill: University of North Carolina Press, 1994); Howard L. Bushart, John R. Craig, and Myra Barnes, *Soldiers of God: White Supremacists and Their Holy War for America* (New York: Kensington Books, 1998) (Barkun covers the core religion of many traditional white supremacists, whereas Bushart, Craig, and Barnes provide detailed information on a wider spectrum of white nationalists groups and leaders they interviewed).

wise intolerable.[3] A frame, similar to a personal narrative, is a story line that helps groups and individuals perceive and explain the world around them. Crucial to the mobilization of racial group consciousness is a heightened awareness of grievance and the existence of a target of blame for perceived injustices.[4] For white activists seeking to generate greater solidarity and pride among European Americans, racial minorities, Jews, and the federal government all serve as visible and viable targets for the hostility generated by the different conditions mentioned above.[5]

TARGETING A MAINSTREAM AUDIENCE

Of utmost importance to understand in this situation is that the new white nationalist movement, while similar in some important ways, also differs very significantly from the older white nativist and white supremacy movement out of which it in some sense has grown. In terms of similarities, contemporary white nationalism, like such older organizations on the racist right as the Ku Klux Klan and the Nazi Party, seeks to foster a sense of white racial pride and European-American group consciousness. To further this end, it is also interested – again, like the older racist right – in celebrating the great intellectual, artistic, scientific, and political achievements of white people throughout human history. Similarities can also be seen in the personnel of the two movements. For instance, some of the leaders of the new white nationalist organizations that are quoted extensively in this book, including David Duke of the National Organization for European American Rights and Don Black of the Stormfront website, got started in the business of white racial advocacy as members of the older Klan movement.

But the new white nationalist movement is very different from the Klan and Nazi movements of an earlier era – or their contemporary offshoot in the more loosely organized skinhead movement that has

---

[3] For more information about social movements and collective action frames, see Sidney Tarrow, *Power in Movement* (New York: Cambridge University Press, 1994); Enrique Larana, Hank Johnston, and Joseph R. Gusfield, eds., *New Social Movements: From Ideology to Identity* (Philadelphia: Temple University Press, 1994); Doug McAdam, John D. McCarthy, and Mayer Zald, eds., *Comparative Perspectives on Social Movements* (New York: Cambridge University Press, 1996).
[4] Tarrow, 3–4.   [5] Dobratz and Shanks-Meile; Daniels; Ridgeway.

received so much sensationalized publicity in recent years on the TV trash-show circuit – insofar as it is preeminently a movement of discourse, persuasion, and ideas. Rejecting the kind of violence and intimidation once advocated by the older racist right, the new white nationalism seeks to expand its influence mainly through argument and rational discourse aimed at its target audience of white Americans who have become embittered or aggrieved over what they perceive to be a host of racial double standards in the areas of affirmative action policy and crime reporting, as well as over the continuance of large-scale immigration from Third World countries. Unlike the Klan and Nazi movements, white nationalism is aggressively seeking a mainstream audience, and in going mainstream it has found it necessary to abandon most of the tactics, postures, and regalia of the older racist right, which no longer resonate in contemporary America.

The leadership of the new white nationalist movement is also different from that of the older racist right. While some of the leaders of the newer racial advocacy organizations were once active in the Klan and Nazi movements, many of the key personalities involved in the new white nationalism bear little resemblance to the sorts of people we normally tend to associate with Klansmen and Nazis. Most are better educated, more articulate, and in many ways more appealing as human beings than the sorts of people who ran the older racist organizations. Syracuse University scholar Michael Barkun, who has written the best book on the new racist religious right in America, explains the situation well: The leaders of many of the newer white separatist and white advocacy groups, Barkun writes, are "not simply younger than their predecessors but better educated, more polished, and more adroit in shaping their message to a skeptical audience, having learned from David Duke's example how effectiveness, appearance, and manner can deflect hostility."[6] Sociologists Jeffrey Kaplan and Leonard Weinberg make a similar point in their important recent work, *The Emergence of a Euro-American Radical Right*. "The groups and individuals who make up the radical right movement," Kaplan and Weinberg explain, "may have embarked on a destructive path, but they are often more complicated, considerably more personable, and far more nuanced than is suggested by the caricatures."[7]

[6] Barkun, 253.   [7] Kaplan and Weinberg, 2.

Because of these differences, and because of the new conditions that have developed in recent years, I believe that white nationalism poses a much greater threat to racial harmony in America than most people currently realize. To give just one example: In San Jose, California, there is a strong movement among whites to record in government records an official "European-American" or other white ethnic identity as a means of establishing equal status with those adopting an identity as members of one of the officially designated minority groups; and in May 2000 a Stockton, California, school district declared the month of April European American Heritage Day. Journalist Jonathan Tilove argues that what is happening in San Jose and elsewhere is just "one manifestation of white people struggling, consciously or unconsciously, to carve out new identities for themselves, free of guilt or apology, in an era of identity politics that demands everyone be something more than just generic 'Americans.'"[8] Calls for white identity are occuring at a time when many Americans are uncertain about the future, and some have come to see the government as more geared toward advancing the rights of racial and political minorities than those of the undifferentiated mass of white people. Using frames associated with the black civil rights movement and multiculturalism, some ordinary white Americans are making a case for increased white solidarity and white consciousness by employing the same brand of identity politics that minorities have successfully used in the past to further their own group interests and group identities.

Although I cover a number of controversial topics in this study, including immigration, black crime rates, and various racial double standards, a disproportionate amount of attention is devoted to affirmative action policy because I believe that within its politics lie the seeds of increased racial hostility. Although affirmative action policy has been around for more than thirty years and it has never been the catalyst for serious racial unrest, the social and political milieu of the country is changing dramatically in ways that will make the issue ever

---

[8] Jonathan Tilove, "Don't Call Them 'White': European-Americans Demand Recognition and Respect for the Diversity of a Group That Has Been Maligned and Marginalized in the Age of Affirmative Action," *The Plain Dealer*, December 31, 1995, p. 1C; Thomas Lee, "Stockton Celebrates Euro-American Heritage: The First School District to Proclaim Heritage Month," *AsianWeek*, May 4, 2000; Lee's article e-mailed from the Americans Against Discrimination and Preferences, *adp@dnail.com*, May 7, 2000 (no page number).

more problematic in the future. At the same time that white Americans are declining as a percentage of the total population, jobs are going overseas and recent immigrants and their children – many of whom are eligible for racial preferences – are competing with older stock white Americans for a dwindling supply of good jobs, for scarce positions in prestigious colleges, and for governmental contracts under set-aside systems that often favor minorities.

THE NEED FOR HONEST DIALOGUE

What makes some of the newer organizations and individuals in the white nationalist movement such a threat to racial harmony, I believe, is that they address many pressing issues of race and nationality that are usually ignored in more mainstream discourse. On sensitive issues of race, our public discourse has become so inhibited by norms of political correctness and racial taboos that many Americans – particularly white people – feel reluctant to express many of their deepest convictions and concerns. Together with many of my colleagues, I have personally seen this process of silence and self-censorship at work even among many of the university students I have known over the years – people who, one would suppose, would be much less inhibited than older adults to say what is on their minds. Even in such congenial forums as Princeton and Vanderbilt universities, it is not uncommon for white students to preface their comments on such sensitive issues of race as affirmative action with statements such as "my roommate thinks" or "my roommate is upset about," when really they are expressing their own views. White colleagues relate very similar experiences with students who censor themselves, perhaps out of fear of being called racist.

The great danger here is that with few legitimate mainstream arenas in which to discuss some of their deepest anxieties and concerns, many people turn to white nationalist and white supremacist groups, whose Internet pages and chatboards may offer the only forum for candid discussions of race. It is only within such forums that many aggrieved whites feel comfortable sharing with one another the basis of their grievances. This may explain the incredible popularity in recent years of Don Black's Stormfront website, which since its inception in 1995 reports having received more than 3 million visitors, and lately as many as 15,000 to 20,000 per week. White nationalist groups have taken to discussing in an open and candid manner many of the issues that are specifically of concern to white people and that whites feel inhibited from talking about in other public forums.

For their users, of course, the great advantage of the white advocacy websites is that even a distorted or partial truth contains at least an element of truth, which is more than one can elicit from more mainstream forums on topics that have been effectively banned from the public square. The discussions that take place in such forums, however, are inevitably one-sided. Data and statistics are cited on crime, immigration, affirmative action, and so on, which may well be true, but which are almost always of a highly selective nature that creates a distorted impression. Lacking any contrasting viewpoint or alternative data to challenge what they are already inclined to believe, the existing prejudices and beliefs of some participants are only reinforced.

The dangers of racial division and racial extremism emerging out of this kind of situation have been illuminated recently by University of Chicago law professor Cass R. Sunstein. Drawing extensively from recent social psychology literature, Professor Sunstein has explained how the process of group discussion can produce dramatically different results depending on whether the group involved is ideologically homogeneous or whether it contains a variety of contrasting viewpoints. In the latter case, where there are multiple perspectives and competing points of view, people often come to realize through discussion that their own views are overly simplified, parochial, or otherwise in need of significant qualification. Group discussion under such circumstances often encourages people to broaden or moderate their earlier viewpoints or, at the very least, convinces them that certain views that they had previously dismissed out of hand may contain worthwhile insights. However, when group discussion takes place among like-minded people without the benefit of contrasting perspectives, the tendency, Sunstein says, is for the members of the group to become more extreme in their views and more convinced of the rightness of those views. Under such circumstances, the members of an insular group tend to adopt the views of those closest to the fringe.

Sunstein sees this process of group polarization at work in many areas of politics, including the arena of racial and ethnic conflict.[9]

Sunstein's analysis seems to describe something clearly at work among many of the white nationalist leaders interviewed for this study. I believe that one reason why many of the members and potential members of their organizations have such little exposure to alternative viewpoints is because of the overall feebleness and lack of honesty that currently dominates discussion about controversial racial issues in America.

President Clinton talked about this very same problem in a commencement address he delivered at the University of California at San Diego, in June of 1997. After announcing the launching of a new initiative on race to be headed by a distinguished multiracial panel, Clinton explained the purpose of his new initiative as one of expanding public dialogue: "Over the coming year," Clinton said, "I want to lead the American people in a great and unprecedented conversation about race." "I want this panel to help educate Americans about the facts surrounding issues of race, to promote a dialogue in every community of the land to confront and work through these issues." Clinton then went on to explain how difficult things would be at the initial stages of such a dialogue, but that it was important to persevere: "Honest dialogue will not be easy at first. We'll all have to get past defensiveness and fear and political correctness and other barriers to honesty. Emotions may be rubbed raw, but we must begin." He then concluded his remarks on a hopeful note: "But if ten years from now people can look back and see that this year of honest dialogue and concerted action helped to lift the heavy burden of race from our children's future, we will have given a precious gift to America."[10]

Unfortunately, Clinton's "great and unprecedented conversation about race" was by all accounts an abysmal failure, and the race panel's efforts probably had the net effect of tightening the stranglehold that political correctness and racial taboos continue to exert upon open

---

[9] Cass R. Sunstein, "The Law of Group Polarization," John M. Olin Law and Economics Working Paper No. 91 (published by the Law School, University of Chicago, 1999), 1. The paper is available on the Internet from the Social Science Research Network electronic Paper Collection: http://papers.ssrn.com/paper.taf?abstract_id=199668.

[10] William Clinton, Commencement Speech, University of California at San Diego, June 14, 1997. Available on the Internet at http://www.whitehouse.gov/Initiatives/One America/announcement.html.

discussion of controversial racial topics in America. Prospects for expanded dialogue were not helped much by the fact that all the panel members were known to be supporters of race-based affirmative action policy. Worse still, the panel's leader, the distinguished black historian John Hope Franklin, set the tone for the panel's activities early in the panel's deliberation when he announced that the race panel would be interested in hearing the testimony only of people who supported the value of "diversity." When the boundaries of acceptable discourse are set so narrowly in our national conversation about race, it is easy to understand why some aggrieved European Americans turn to white nationalist websites for comfort and direction.

DATA SOURCES

The data I bring to this subject come from diverse sources that include interviews of white nationalists, case studies of three white college students, results of national surveys, and focus group analyses of members of different racial and ethnic groups talking about affirmative action. In addition, I break with social science tradition and interject personal anecdotes and observations into chapters where I think my unusual social background and personal history may offer some valuable insight or perceptions. Of course, in doing this I realize that I can speak definitively only for myself. Only the survey data in this study can be generalized to the wider public.

When I started this research project more than five years ago, it was initially confined to the politics of affirmative action and I was concerned with identifying areas of consensus between whites and blacks on this issue. A hunch about how racist and white supremacist figures outside the mainstream liberal-conservative continuum might be using anger and discontent about racial preferences in their efforts to recruit new members to their cause led to my decision to interview white nationalists. I was especially curious about the social and cultural backgrounds of some of the leaders of the newer white solidarity movements, and suspected – correctly, as it turned out – that they might be different from our stereotypical notions of those on the racist right. All of this led me to decide to commission interviews of select white nationalist and white supremacist leaders and other high-profile individuals espousing racist or racial separatist viewpoints.

As an interviewer I selected Dr. Russell Nieli, an experienced political scientist of Italian descent, who made every effort to approach his subjects in a relaxed, professional, and nonjudgmental manner. Nieli asked our interviewees a variety of questions, including how they became involved in the white nationalist and white advocacy movement, which public policies they liked and disliked, and what were their feelings about the future of American race relations. While many searching questions were posed to our respondents – some of which may have proved unsettling or embarrassing – it was made clear to each of the participants from the outset that the purpose of the interviews was not to debate or condemn those being interviewed but to give them the opportunity to state their beliefs on controversial racial issues in an honest, thorough, and forthright manner. All of the interviews were in the form of tape-recorded telephone conversations that were conducted from Princeton University's Woodrow Wilson School of Public and International Affairs between November 1999 and May 2000. Interviewees were given the opportunity to read over the printed transcript of the interview and make any additions or corrections if they thought such changes would better explain or elucidate various points they were trying to make.[11]

Altogether we interviewed ten people, who were selected on the basis of their national prominence, general articulateness, and the range and content of their specific views. We sought and received the permission of each of the ten interview subjects to publish the interview transcripts, which can be read in their entirety in a companion volume to the present study edited by Dr. Nieli and myself.[12] What we found from interviewing these figures, visiting their web pages, and reading their publications is that these individuals are more intelligent, more sophisticated, and potentially more dangerous than most Americans realize.

Those interviewed included the following: Jared Taylor, the editor of *American Renaissance* magazine, the leading intellectual journal of

---

[11] Michael Levin, Michael H. Hart, and Dan Gayman made extensive changes to the transcript, usually by adding material to better explain ideas they had stated more briefly in the original phone interview. None of the interviewees, however, changed in any significant way the basic substance of the ideas they initially presented.

[12] The interviews are contained in Carol M. Swain and Russell Nieli, eds., *White Pride, White Protest: Contemporary Voices of White Nationalism* (forthcoming, 2002).

contemporary white nationalism; Reno Wolfe, director of the white-advocacy organization the National Association for the Advancement of White People (NAAWP); Michael Levin, a professor of philosophy at the City University of New York and author of the controversial book *Why Race Matters*; David Duke, a former Klan leader and political candidate, who founded the first NAAWP and more recently founded the National Organization for European American Rights (NOFEAR); Don Black, the founder of Stormfront, perhaps the most influential white separatist website; Michael H. Hart, a white separatist Jew and retired astrophysicist who has proposed a widely discussed plan for the four-way partition of the United States; Dan Gayman, pastor of the Missouri-based Church of Israel, who is a leading advocate for a variant of the Christian Identity philosophy that calls for the separation of the races in all intimate social and religious settings; Matthew Hale, the leader of the white supremacist World Church of the Creator; Lisa Turner, the Women's Information Coordinator of the World Church of the Creator; and William Pierce, the head of the neo-Nazi-oriented National Alliance and author of the *Turner Diaries*, which the FBI calls the Bible of the racist right.

Supplementing my interview data and supporting my conclusions are a number of recent sociological studies that document the growth of a white rights and white consciousness movement in the United States.[13] These studies allow me to draw on the research of others who have interviewed large numbers of individuals within the white nationalist movement and have observed them interacting among their members. By drawing on other academic studies, I can argue that there are clear linkages between controversial public policies and the grass-roots activities of white rights and white nationalist organizations with a degree of confidence that personal observations, focus groups, and interview data alone would not permit. The next logical step for the research ideas introduced in this book would be to create a national survey designed to identify developing white consciousness and white identity politics and to explore how well the arguments advanced by white nationalists resonate among ordinary whites. Such a follow-up

---

[13] Kaplan and Weinberg, *The Emergence of a Euro-American Radical Right*; Dobratz and Shanks-Meile; Daniels, *White Lies: Race, Class, Gender, and Sexuality in White Supremacist Discourse* (provides a content analysis of 369 white supremacy publications); Ridgeway; Barkun; Bushart, Craig, and Barnes.

study would allow us to systematically examine whether their arguments are having the desired effect of getting more people to think and act more like the members of other racially self-conscious, self-interested minority groups.

IS THERE CAUSE
FOR ALARM?

THE NEW WHITE
NATIONALISM

The conference brought some of the leading intellectual and political lights of the white far right. . . . They talked about an America that they believe once was and ever ought to be a white, European-American nation. Theirs would be a nation bound by blood and sanctified by genetic scientists who appeared before them as a place where white people might rightly prevail over the black and brown people; a nation where what they consider the natural hierarchy might finally triumph over what they count as the false promise of egalitarianism.

Jonathan Tilove, American Renaissance Conference,
spring 2000[1]

Over the past ten years a new white racial advocacy movement has gained strength in the United States that poses a severe challenge to the ideals of an integrated society. Many of the leaders of this new movement, which is called "white nationalism" here, are very different from the sorts of people we have come to associate with the traditional racist right in America. Cultured, intelligent, and often possessing impressive degrees from some of America's premier colleges and universities, this new breed of white racial advocate is a far cry from the populist politicians and hooded Klansmen of the Old South who fought the losing battles for segregation and white supremacy during the great civil rights upheavals of a generation ago. The new white nationalists differ even more from the small band of misfits and psychopaths who formed the

---

[1] Jonathan Tilove describing the more than 200 participants at the annual American Renaissance Conference in "White Nationalists Seek Respectability in Meeting of 'Uptown Bad Guys,'" *American Renaissance*, http://www.amren.com/newhous.htm.

heart of the ineffectual neo-Nazi movement of that era. While sharing much in common with the older style of white racist and white supremacy movement, and drawing upon important white supremacist beliefs, the new white nationalism is potentially broader in its appeal and a development sufficiently different from the older racist right to be considered a distinct phenomenon. The new white nationalism, in this sense, might be considered a kind of repackaged, relabeled, and transformed white supremacy that is aiming its appeal at a broader and better-educated audience.

In this chapter, I discuss some of the new white nationalists, their political goals, their ideas about racial separatism, and their insistence on calling themselves nationalists rather than white supremacists. I argue here that however educated and nonviolent they may be, we should be as concerned about the new white nationalists and their organizations as we are about individuals in traditional white supremacy and hate groups. The polish and sophistication of some of the new white nationalists, their separatist agenda, and their ability to disguise themselves and move freely within many mainstream institutions poses a major threat to racial harmony, I believe, in our increasingly multiethnic, multiracial society.

SOME CHARACTERISTICS OF THE NEW WHITE NATIONALISM

With some important exceptions, these new racial activists call themselves "white nationalists" or "white racialists" rather than "white supremacists" because they believe that the concept of "racial nationalism" captures their core beliefs in racial self-determination and self-preservation better than any supremacist or segregationist label. Contemporary white nationalists draw upon the potent rhetoric of national self-determination and national self-assertion in an attempt to protect what they believe is their God-given natural right to their distinct cultural, political, and genetic identity as white Europeans. This identity, they believe, is gravely threatened in contemporary America by the rise of multiculturalism, affirmative action policies that favor minorities, large-scale immigration into the United States from nonwhite nations, racial intermarriage, and the identity politics pursued by rival racial and ethnic groups.[2]

Above all, white nationalists are driven by a sense of urgency. America, they believe, is fast becoming a nation dominated by non-white people. Since they believe that it is the white blood and white genes – and the white culture these have created – that are responsible for America's past greatness and success as a nation, this development can have only catastrophic consequences, according to their reckoning. The black and brown peoples of the world, they contend, are morally and intellectually inferior to whites and Asians, and thus the more numerous and influential they become, the more American society will degenerate. The fact that demographic trends project European Americans gradually becoming a minority over the next several decades is viewed with horror. "Our children . . . will live in an America where alien cultures will not simply be present, but will dominate us," warns former Klansman David Duke, who now describes himself as a white nationalist. "This alien influx," he goes on, "is a disaster for our country, our people, our families."[3]

A similar observation is offered by Jared Taylor, the founder and editor of *American Renaissance* magazine, the most important intellectual organ of the new white nationalism. Powerful forces are destroying both "European man and European civilization" on the American continent, Taylor declares. "If we do nothing the nation we leave our grandchildren will be a grim Third World failure, in which whites will be the minority . . . [and Western Civilization, if it exists at all,] will be a faint echo."[4]

Within the white nationalist movement are fresh-faced converts from academia including Professors Michael H. Hart, Michael Levin, J. Philippe Rushton, and Glayde Whitney, who share many of the beliefs of traditional white supremacists, especially their negative assessments of African Americans. These scholars believe the main

[2] Arthur E. LeBouthillier, "Introduction to nationalism," http://www.duke.org/library/potpourii/nationalism.html.
[3] David Duke, "America at the Crossroads," http://www.duke.org/writings/crossroads.html.
[4] Jared Taylor, ed., *The Real American Dilemma* (Oakton, Va.: New Century Books, 1998), 55.

reason black people today are plagued by such high incidence of criminal violence, out-of-wedlock births, poor school performance, and AIDS is rooted in their differential genetic endowment. The process of human evolution, as it has adapted to different ecological circumstances, has produced, they contend, a distinct racial hierarchy in terms of innate intelligence, the ability to delay gratification, to control emotions, and to plan for the future, with North Asians at the top of the hierarchy, white Europeans somewhere below them, Hispanics significantly below the white Europeans, and black Africans and their recent descendants at the very bottom.[5]

Besides their belief in the biogenetically determined inequality of the races, white nationalists believe that race is a legitimate criteria for inclusion within the civil community and that nations are least faction-ridden when a given territory is dominated by a single race or ethnic group. A country that embarks on a policy of encouraging racial and ethnic diversity within its borders through liberal immigration policies is courting national disaster, they contend. To cite Jared Taylor again:

> Up until 1965, we had an immigration policy that was designed . . . to keep the country white. I see absolutely nothing wrong with that. In fact, I think that's a healthy, normal and natural position for a country to take. I think Japan should stay Japanese. I think Mexico should stay Mexican. Some think somehow that it's virtuous of the United States, after having been founded and built by Europeans, according to European institutions, to reinvent itself or transform itself into a non-white country with a Third World population. I think that's a kind of cultural and racial national suicide. . . . Wherever you go, wherever you mix racial groups, you're going to have tensions, you're going to have friction, and to have an immigration policy that imports millions of people of all sorts of different racial and ethnic groups, I think, it's bound to cause racial tension. . . . We're all now more or less obliged to say, "Oh! Diversity is a wonderful thing for the country," whereas, practically every example of tension, bloodshed, civil unrest around the world is due to precisely the kind of thing we're importing – diversity.[6]

---

[5] See, e.g., Michael Levin, *Why Race Matters: Racial Differences and What They Mean* (Westport, Conn.: Praeger, 1998); and Philippe Rushton, *Race, Evolution, and Behavior* (New Brunswick: Transaction Books, 1995).

[6] Jared Taylor, interview, Dec. 21, 1999.

White nationalists recognize that America is already a multiracial, multiethnic society, but given their pessimism about the long-term health and viability of such societies, they believe that drastic measures must be taken to change things. Their solution is usually some form of ethnic separatism based on territorial partition. Racial separation is the obvious next step for people who believe that racial and ethnic minorities are a danger to the personal safety and social values of white Americans. The logic of the separatists' argument is well captured by American Enterprise Institute scholar Dinesh D'Souza in summing up the ideology that pervades *American Renaissance*: "Western civilization is inherently white, America was founded on white norms, immigrants are perennial outsiders, blacks are 'Africans in America,' they are in America but not of America, race determines culture, miscegenation and intermarriage are an abomination, and racial separatism, preferably separate black and white nations, is the answer."[7]

White nationalists will often invoke the statesmen of America's founding generation to support their contention that a multiracial America, one involving the successful integration of blacks and whites, is not a viable option. Indeed, many of the new white nationalists see themselves as true patriots who seek to preserve the kind of European-dominated society that the founding generation bequeathed to posterity but which is now threatened with destruction. They seek to preserve an America – or a segment of America – where white, European Americans would be able to develop freely their common culture and common political life without hindrance from members of other racial groups, particularly the black and brown groups. This, they say, is the kind of America that statesmen like Washington and Jefferson originally envisioned, though their true views, they charge, have long been forgotten or suppressed by those who would force America into a multiculturalist mode.

Don Black, the founder of the Stormfront website, expresses this view very clearly. Black, a former Klansman who, like David Duke, now calls himself a white nationalist, was asked by our interviewer whether or not he accepted the term "white supremacist" as an accurate description of his views. He responded that he was a racial

---

[7] Dinesh D'Souza, *The End of Racism: Principles for a Multiracial Society* (New York: Free Press, 1995), 396–7.

nationalist, not a white supremacist, and that all he and other white nationalists were demanding was the preservation of the kind of white America envisioned by many of the great statesmen of America's past:

> I think [the term "white supremacist" is] an inaccurate description of most of the people that are part of our movement, because white supremacy implies a system, such as we had throughout most of this country through the 50s and 60s, in which there was legally enforced segregation and in which whites were in a position of domination. We did have a supremacist-type government in most states, but today the people who are attracted to the white nationalist movement want separation. . . . We are separatists. We believe that we as white people, as European-Americans, have the right to pursue our destiny without interference from other races. . . . We believe segregation certainly didn't work, and the only long-term solution to racial conflict is separation. As long as races are forced together by government, there will continue to be racial hatred and mutual animosity caused by one side or the other feeling that they are being discriminated against. As Thomas Jefferson said, "Nothing is more certainly written in the book of faith than that these people [i.e., the black slaves] are to be free, nor is it less certain that equally free, they cannot live under the same government. Nature has an opinion. It's drawn indelible lines of distinction between them." . . . Almost all of the founding fathers believed that [an integrated black/white society in America was impossible]. They even founded an organization called the American Colonization Society whose purpose was to free black slaves and repatriate them to Africa. . . . But this part of our history is now hidden from most students going through our school systems today, because it's not politically fashionable.[8]

One of the most influential arguments for the racial partitioning of the United States has been made by Michael H. Hart, a retired professor of astrophysics, who holds advanced degrees in physics, computer science, and law. Hart has argued that a "multiracial state hurts all of us, and it hurts whites in particular." Whites, he says, have to put up with much higher crime rates because of the presence in America of large numbers of nonwhites. They have to put up with higher incidence of many social problems, including illegitimacy, welfare dependency, and declining standards in schools. All this could be avoided,

---

[8] Don Black, interview, April 20, 2000.

Hart claims, by the racial partitioning of America. He has proposed partitioning America into four parts that would provide for a black-dominated state, a white-dominated state, an Hispanic-dominated state, and an integrated, mixed-race state for all those who genuinely prefer a multicultural arrangement.[9]

Hart distinguishes between a nation, in the sense of an ethnically self-consciousness group of individuals who consider themselves to be a distinct people, and a state, in the sense of a centralized government ruling over a territory. "The Norwegians," he writes, "are a nation, and they have their own state, Norway. The Kurds are a nation, but they do not have their own independent state. Rwanda, in Africa, is a state containing two national groups, the Hutu and the Tutsi. India, Nigeria, the former Soviet Union, and the former Yugoslavia are, or were, multinational states." The history of states that contain within their borders more than one nation, Hart believes, is not an encouraging one. "Most binational and multinational states do not work well, but are beset by endless ethnic strife, often quite bloody."[10]

African Americans already behave as if they constitute a separate nation, Hart contends, and it is for this reason that separation is called for. As evidence for a distinct black nation-consciousness Hart cites the African-American middle class's embrace of the black holiday of Kwanza, the existence of a black flag and a black national anthem, demands for Afro-centric curriculums, and demands for quotas in hiring, promotions, and college admissions. When combined with the considerable degree of support that black communities have shown over the years for black nationalist figures such as Marcus Garvey, Elijah Muhammad, and Louis Farrakhan, the case, he believes, is clinched: Blacks constitute a separate and alien nation that cannot be integrated into white America.

Like other white nationalists, Hart is particularly insistent on describing himself as a separatist rather than a supremacist. "I, like most other white separatists," he told our interviewer, "resent being called a white *supremacist*. . . . I have no desire to rule over blacks, or to attempt to rule over blacks, or have someone else rule over blacks

---

[9] Michael H. Hart, interview, April 14, 2000.

[10] Michael H. Hart, "Racial Partition of the United States," 1996, http://Irainc.com/swtaboo/taboo/mhartol.html.

in my behalf. Quite the contrary, I want to have complete independence. All that I – and most white separatists – want is the opportunity to rule ourselves, in our own independent country. Far from wishing to extend our rule, we are quite willing to give up much of the territory that American whites already control. All we want is to live in peace in our own country, and to trade with foreign countries on mutually acceptable terms. . . . I do not want to rule, enslave, or exterminate anyone."[11]

Hart's views are similar to those of other white nationalists, as well as to those of white racists and white supremacists of the older style, many of whom have advocated partitioning the United States into separate nations. The Pacific Northwest is the section of the country that they usually single out as the territory for an all-white nation because of its current low concentration of nonwhites.[12]

A belief that racial integration has not and cannot work in the United States and that racial separatism is the only answer joins many contemporary white nationalists with black nationalists, past and present. "White racism and black racism are now mirror ideologies," Dinesh D'Souza writes.[13] This development, however, is nothing new, as black nationalists and white racists have always shared much in common. Since the days of Marcus Garvey and his back-to-Africa movement in the 1920s, Klansmen and members of other white racist groups have periodically gotten together with members of black nationalist groups to affirm their common goal of preserving racial purity.

WHITES AND ASIANS

The white nationalists' view of Asians and their place in a white America is considerably more complex than their view of black and brown peoples. While the latter are seen as genetically less endowed than whites in terms of intelligence, capacity for future planning, emotional self-control, and several other characteristics that are conducive to high levels of civilization, certain Asian groups are seen by many

---

[11] Michael H. Hart, interview.
[12] For an example of a proposed partition of the nation, see Ridgeway, 168–9.
[13] D'Souza, 429.

white nationalists as somewhat *superior* to whites in terms of these same characteristics. It is for this reason, many white nationalists contend, that certain Asian groups, including the Japanese and Chinese, are better able to assimilate into white American culture. It is also for this reason, they contend, why whites tend to avoid Asians less than African Americans or Hispanics, and why whites intermarry more frequently with Asians. The white nationalist view of Asians is obviously very different than the older style of white supremacy, which held white Europeans to be unequivocally superior to all of the nonwhite racial groups. Many contemporary white nationalists, including Jared Taylor, J. Philippe Rushton, and Michael Levin, express considerable admiration for the general sobriety, law-abidingness, and educational achievement of Asians both in Asia and in America.

Nevertheless, despite their high regard for certain Asian groups, most white nationalists believe that Asians are sufficiently different from white Europeans in their culture, genetics, and physical characteristics to render continued large-scale immigration of Asians into America highly unwise. Asians, they believe, should stay in Asia where they can develop their own ethnically homogeneous cultures. In sufficient numbers, Asians, they argue, would constitute a threat to white European culture, just as any alien, nonwhite racial group would. "If the number of Asians entering the country rivaled the number of blacks who are here," Michael H. Hart remarks, "I think that there would be a lot of trouble." "If sufficiently large numbers of Asian immigrants entered the United States," he says, "we would lose our country."[14]

Some of the more radical white nationalists are not willing to abandon the more traditional white supremacist view that holds white Europeans to be superior to all of the world's nonwhite peoples, including Asians. For these white racial advocates, the undeniable educational and technological achievement of Asians in recent years is acknowledged but explained away as a meritless copying of white creative developments. Lisa Turner, the Women's Information Coordinator of the World Church of the Creator (WCOTC) – an organization that espouses an atheistic and white supremacist philosophy known as Creativity – argues that "Asians are nothing but imitators, copycats.

[14] Michael H. Hart, interview.

... It's monkey-see, monkey-do. They have copied what white Europeans have done, and that's the only reason that Asians have any kind of a civilization at all."[15]

Matthew Hale, the leader of the WCOTC, elaborates further on the copy-cat theme. Asian success in America, in Japan, and elsewhere, Hale contends, is a result of copying the creative technologies and inventions of whites. Hale concedes, however, that Asians work hard – indeed, harder than whites – and he thinks any superiority they show to whites in scientific achievement is a result of this harder work:

> I think that the Asians are a good example of hard work. They work very hard; there's no question about that. But I think if white people worked as hard, they would surpass the Asians without question. . . . The Asians are good at copying and expanding upon things that white people already created. If we were to go back one hundred and fifty years, back before Commodore Matthew Perry sailed into Tokyo Bay, . . . there were almost no technological achievements there at all. So what we have seen is the Asians looking towards the Western white world and choosing to adopt a white culture, to adopt white technology and a white mode of achievement. And they have taken this white technology and run with it – there's no question about that. But if white people spend a little less attention drinking or partying, I think that they would be able to replicate, indeed, surpass, what the Asians have been able to accomplish recently.[16]

A more imaginative attempt to reconcile belief in white, European superiority with current high levels of Chinese and Japanese achievement is offered by David Duke. In his autobiographical book, *My Awakening*, he suggests that the intelligence and creativity of the Chinese may be due to prehistoric incursions of Caucasians into China. "New evidence," he says, "shows early Aryans [i.e., white Caucasians] introduced the wheel and the chariot as well as domesticated horses to ancient Asia." There may well have been, he suggests, "white incursions in the Chinese gene pool" at this time, at least in those provinces where lighter-skinned Chinese reside. There was, he believes, "a line of prehistoric Caucasian migration all the way across China."[17]

---

[15] Lisa Turner, interview, April 28, 2000.
[16] Matthew Hale, interview, Nov. 12, 1999.
[17] David Duke, *My Awakening* (Covington, La.: Free Speech Press, 1999), 510–11.

Lighter-skinned Asians, in other words, may really be descendants of whites.

SPIN, REPACKAGING, EXPANDING THE APPEAL

In his 1995 book somewhat misleadingly titled *The End of Racism*, Dinesh D'Souza concludes that "white racism is not dead, but, as many blacks suspect, it now wears a different face."[18] This is an accurate description of much of the new white nationalism and white racial advocacy. Since the 1980s, much has changed in the world of the racist right. Many former white supremacists such as Don Black and David Duke have changed with the times and reinvented themselves as white nationalists or white civil rights crusaders. With the change to nationalism and civil rights advocacy has come the adoption of new tactics, new symbols, and new language designed to allay the fears of citizens repelled by more extremist approaches characteristic of the older racist right. While the older style of racist right certainly lives on and has its audience, for many middle-class and better-educated Americans it has little appeal.

Much of the new white nationalism, by contrast, is a more sophisticated enterprise that has much greater possibility of winning over large numbers of middle-class, white Americans. Unlike the older racist right epitomized by the 1950s- and 1960s-era Ku Klux Klan, the new white nationalist movement that has emerged in America over the past two decades is preeminently a movement of discourse and ideas. It seeks to expand its audience largely through argument and persuasion directed at its target audience of white Americans who have become angered over race-based affirmative action policy and impending demographic change. In this regard, it is more akin to Leftist and Green parties around the world than to the older style of white supremacy groups. The new white nationalists are skillfully using the rhetoric of civil rights, national self-determination, and ethnic identity politics as they make their case among the many aggrieved whites in America for a white, European-centered nation.

It is important to grasp what a radical makeover this represents, at least in style, from the older racist right movement. The older racist

[18] D'Souza, 396.

and anti-Semitic right, represented by organizations like the Klan and Nazi Party, made its appeal primarily through fiery speeches and emotional rhetoric with minimal rational content. A few well-chosen slogans endlessly repeated and prominently displayed formed the ideological backbone of the movement: "Niggers in Their Place," "White Men Built This Country," "Jews Get Out!," "Segregation Now, Segregation Tomorrow, Segregation Forever." In addition, secret initiations and rituals, flamboyant costumes, and mass parades formed important aspects of the movement's activities that for many members, at least, offered the additional allurement of an intimate fraternal order or esoteric club. There was very little in the way of intellectual content, and not surprisingly, the audience remained largely lower-class and uneducated. Many of the newer white nationalist groups, by contrast, seek a broader and more influential audience, and as Americans have become more educated, their approach has adjusted accordingly.

Unlike the older racist right, the Americans that many white nationalists would most like to recruit as activists are not those at the margins of society. Apparently wary of the ignorant, redneck image, white nationalists and white power advocates today are seeking a more educated class of converts and spokespersons in order to attract a potentially more influential following among the young. Although Joe Six-pack is still welcomed into the ranks of most white nationalist and white racist organizations, he is not being encouraged to appear on talk shows and present himself as the standard bearer of white racial advocacy. Today's white nationalist recruit could just as easily be a graduate of an Ivy League college who wears an expensive suit and sports a Rolex as a high school dropout who works a gas pump at the local filling station. As Mark Potok of the Southern Poverty Law Center has remarked, many of the new recruits to some of the newer white racist and white supremacy groups "are not people who live in trailers. There is a concerted effort . . . to recruit college-bound middle- and upper-middle-class kids."[19]

The rise in the caliber of recruits parallels the rise in the caliber of the new white nationalist leadership. Not only are many leaders of the new white nationalist and white supremacy groups better educated

[19] Potok as quoted in Pam Belluck, "A White Supremacist Group Seeks a New Kind of Recruit," *New York Times*, July 7, 1999, pp. A1, A16.

than their predecessors of a generation ago, but they are often more personable and more appealing as human beings as well. This last point may be difficult to grasp since it has been distorted in many ways by some of the watchdog groups that help keep us informed of what those on the racist right are up to. As Jeffrey Kaplan and Leonard Weinberg explain in *The Emergence of a Euro-American Radical Right*, our image of what is going on among members of the contemporary racist and racial-nationalist right may be influenced heavily by watchdog agencies such as the Simon Wiesenthal Center, SOS Racism, Klanwatch, and the Anti-Defamation League of B'nai Brith. These organizations, Kaplan and Weinberg explain, are intensely hostile to the people and organizations they monitor and they have a tendency to portray them in the worst possible light. The goal of these watchdog agencies, they say, "is to have members of the public regard the racist and anti-Semitic right with the same affection they would the AIDS epidemic or the outbreak of the ebola fever." Kaplan and Weinberg, however, point out the shortcomings of this strategy: "There is a price to be paid for reducing the groups and individuals involved to screen villains straight out of Central Casting. The price is that these efforts distort the reality." The reality, Kaplan and Weinberg explain, is that many of the individuals and groups that make up the contemporary racist right "are often more complicated, considerably more personable, and far more nuanced" than is suggested by the negative stereotypes.[20]

Sociologists Betty Dobratz and Stephanie Shanks-Meile, who conducted participant observations and many interviews with white supremacists, had an assessment similar to that of Kaplan and Weinberg. They found that their subjects deviated considerably from the caricaturist stereotypes of the watchdog agencies and were considerably more personable than expected.[21]

Any attempt to weigh the seriousness of the threat posed by the new white nationalism must take into account how certain groups are transforming themselves in order to widen their appeal. If observers limit themselves to monitoring the more extremist groups or those espousing more virulent forms of racial hatred, the seriousness of the problem currently confronting America will be greatly underestimated. To

[20] Kaplan and Weinberg, 2.   [21] Dobratz and Shanks-Meile.

increase their appeal, some white nationalist groups are disguising themselves and adopting names less racially inflammatory than "Ku Klux Klan" or "Aryan Nations." A growing number of white nationalist and white supremacy groups have adopted innocuous-sounding names such as the Euro-American Student Union, the Institute for Historical Review (a Holocaust denial group), the Conservative Citizens Council, the New Century Foundation, and the National Organization for European American Rights. Such groups can more easily attract Americans who do not think of themselves as racist, but are nevertheless upset over racial preferences, black-on-white crime, and immigration policies that are seen as detrimental to Euro-American interests. Casual listeners are unlikely to be alarmed or tipped off about a friend or colleague's affiliation with such groups since their names raise no red flags.

White nationalist organizations espousing racial hatred or racial separatism can hide among such groups, many of which have been newly legitimized by America's embrace of identity politics and widespread acceptance of ethnic group pride. Groups with names like European/American Issues Forum or the National Organization for European American Rights can more easily find mainstream acceptance in a milieu in which we now have Asian American, Hispanic American, and Welsh American advocacy groups. White identity groups, critics would charge, are the next logical expansion of a multiculturalism run amok.

In an effort to expand their base, certain white nationalists have also broadened their list of issues and concerns to include an array of topics of interest to many mainstream social and religious conservatives. Loretta J. Ross, director for the Center for Democratic Renewal, reports that some white nationalists have combined traditional racist, white supremacist, and anti-Semitic beliefs with opposition to homosexuality, condemnation of abortion, support for family values, and a strong pro-American foreign policy. "This broadening of issues and the use of conservative buzzwords," Ross writes, "has attracted the attention of whites who may not consider themselves racists, but do consider themselves patriotic Americans concerned about the moral decay of their country."[22]

---

[22] Loretta J. Ross, "White Supremacy in the 1990's," *The Public Eye*, http://www.publiceye.org/pra/eyes/whitsup.html, p. 2.

Potential converts to white nationalism can be found among the millions of frustrated white Americans who have supported mainstream conservative political candidates and the conservative racial policies of presidents Richard Nixon, Ronald Reagan, and the elder George Bush. Republicans have repeatedly demonstrated the party's ability to attract a significant majority of white votes whenever it champions racially tinged issues such as welfare and immigration reform, affirmative action, and crime reduction. Many of these Republican supporters have been attracted to the party's racially conservative campaigns and policies out of a concern and belief that the interests of white people are being trampled on by an insensitive government, a theme common among white nationalists.

The ability of white nationalists to pass themselves off as mainstream conservatives is well illustrated by the case of Samuel Francis. Francis, a former journalist for the influential conservative newspaper the *Washington Times*, moved freely in conservative circles until his white nationalist views were first exposed in 1995 in D'Souza's *The End of Racism*. "What we as whites must do," Francis proclaimed at Jared Taylor's first *American Renaissance* conference, "is reassert our identity and our solidarity, and we must do so in explicitly racial terms through the articulation of a racial consciousness as whites." "The civilization that we as whites created in Europe and America could not have developed apart from the genetic endowments of the creating people, nor is there any reason to believe that the civilization can be successfully transmitted to a different people."[23]

Francis's exposure as a racial nationalist eventually led to the loss of his job at the *Times*. Bitter over this, he would later complain that a small number of liberal zealots in America could silence the many white people who sympathized with the white nationalist viewpoint. He seemed to be equally angry with the many white sympathizers who shared his own beliefs and goals regarding race, but remained silent and immobilized for fear of retaliation. He would later write:

> It is fairly commonplace for those of us who speak and write frankly about race and inequality to encounter audiences where the criticisms and hostilities of a handful are triumphant, only to find after the speech that we are approached privately by many sympathizers who have sat silently

[23] D'Souza, 389–90.

throughout the whole proceeding and said nothing but who now rush to our side to assure us that they really agree with us, only they just can't run the risk of saying so. How sweet. I and Jared Taylor and Phil Rushton and Michael Levin are supposed to run the gauntlet, risk our own jobs and even our physical safety, while others secretly and silently – and safely – applaud.[24]

Another factor in the expanding influence of the white nationalist message is the ability of many of the newer groups on the racist right to forge alliances with like-minded whites in Europe, Canada, and elsewhere. As Kaplan and Weinberg explain, common conditions have brought together forces on both sides of the Atlantic, resulting in a united desire to maintain a common racial identity that transcends national boundaries. These conditions include demographic pressures, social dislocations, and economic changes. In addition, U.S. groups have found a ready demand for their racist literature overseas, since such literature often cannot be legally published in Europe, where more restricted views of free speech prevail than in America.[25]

THE INTERNET

The Internet is a technological advancement that has opened new possibilities to groups with unpopular ideas likely to be censored or marginalized by mainstream media organizations. Its importance to the growth of contemporary white nationalism can hardly be understated. In 1995 there was only one website associated with white supremacy, Don Black's Stormfront. By 1999, according to the Simon Wiesenthal Center, there were over 1,800 websites associated with white supremacy groups and individuals espousing various racist and other hate-filled messages.

Stormfront would become a model in many ways for other websites. Don Black expressed the view of many white nationalists who have set up shop on the Internet when he told a reporter that he was "tired of the Jewish monopoly over the news media and the entertainment

---

[24] Samuel Francis, "Equality Unmasked," in Jared Taylor, ed., *The Real American Dilemma* (Oakton, Va.: New Century Books, 1998), 42.
[25] Kaplan and Weinberg, 18.

media" and was looking to provide an alternative medium to disseminate his racially hostile views about blacks and Jews.[26] In a discussion
with our interviewer, Black explained in greater detail the importance
of the Internet to the expansion of the white nationalist movement.

> INTERVIEWER: Five years ago, in March, 1995, you launched the
> Stormfront website. Could you explain what Stormfront is and what
> you hope to accomplish by it?
>
> BLACK: Stormfront is a resource for a movement which we call white
> nationalism. Our purpose is to provide an alternative news media with
> news and information and online forums for those who are part of our
> movement or for those who are interested in learning more about white
> nationalism. . . . Stormfront began in 1991 as an online bulletin board,
> a dial-in bulletin board, during one of the David Duke campaigns – the
> David Duke for U.S. Senate campaign. The purpose of the bulletin
> board system, or BBS, was simply to provide those participants in that
> campaign who had their own computers and modems and knew how
> to use them with the ability to exchange messages and files. At that
> time, we had very few users, because there were very few people who
> had the equipment or were savvy enough to understand how to use it.
> It was the exponential growth of the Internet, which began, I think, in
> '94 or '95, that we first had the opportunity to reach potentially mil-
> lions of people with our point of view. These are people who for the
> most part have never attended one of our meetings or have never sub-
> scribed to any of our publications. We were for the first time able to
> reach a broad audience. And Stormfront, being the first white nation-
> alist website, was able immediately to draw a very large number of vis-
> itors. The response has continued to grow until this day. And in the
> future, with the advent of broadband technology for consumers, we
> hope to be able to compete with television networks themselves by pro-
> viding an alternative video. . . . So the Net has certainly provided our
> movement and other movements like ours with only limited resources,
> the ability for the first time to compete with what we consider to be a
> very biased and controlled news media.[27]

White nationalist websites have been particularly adept at net-
working and linking up with each other. Stormfront has links to many

---

[26] Julie Salamon, "The Web as Home for Racism and Hate," *New York Times*, October 23, 2000.
[27] Don Black, interview.

dozens of other white nationalist and white racist websites, and many of these also feed into Stormfront. David Duke's web page includes Internet links to Stormfront, the *Barnes Review*, *American Renaissance*, *Spotlight Newspaper*, *American Populist Review*, the Institute for Historical Review, and the Institute for Civil Rights Review, among others.

White nationalist websites contain vast amounts of material on all sorts of topics ranging from affirmative action to the alleged Jewish domination of Hollywood. The quality of this material is highly mixed, though some is of a higher quality than one might suppose. Don Black's Stormfront, for instance, contains a slick, in-depth analysis of the life of Dr. Martin Luther King, Jr., that is skillfully designed to discredit him as a moral leader. This professional-looking presentation offers detailed information about the FBI surveillance tapes of King, and the allegations of plagiarism in which selected excerpts from Kings' writings, speeches, sermons, and dissertation are laid side by side with documents from which some scholars say they were taken. Whenever possible, white nationalists will cite mainstream scholars, books, and governmental statistics to support their allegations about minorities and about persons perceived as individual threats to the white nationalist cause.

Since the early 1990s, the growth of the Internet has been exponential, so that by the end of the decade an estimated 100 million Americans were Internet users with access at home, work, school, or their local libraries. The impact of the Internet may be even greater than that suggested by the large number of users, since the affluent and those with white-collar and professional jobs are overrepresented among these.[28] The Internet also enables white nationalists to reach many young people, who are also greatly overrepresented among regular users. As Mark Potok of the Southern Poverty Law Center has remarked, "[t]he Internet is allowing the White Supremacy movement to reach into places it has never reached before – middle and upper middle-class, college bound teens. The movement is terribly interested in developing the leadership cadre of tomorrow."[29]

---

[28] Laurie J. Flynn, "Surprising Geography of America's Digital Divide," *New York Times*, September 25, 2000.
[29] "Hate Groups on the Rise," *Jet*, March 22, 1999.

The Internet has also enabled some of the more radical white nationalist and white supremacist groups with predilections toward violence to pose a considerable danger to public safety. Howard P. Berkowitz, the chairman of the Anti-Defamation League, summed up the problem in testimony before a senate committee in May of 1999: "The Internet is probably the greatest forum for the exchange of ideas that the world has ever seen, but the medium has also allowed extremists unprecedented access to a potential audience of millions – permitting bigots to communicate easily, anonymously, and cheaply to raise money for their activities, and to threaten and intimidate their enemies. . . . The Internet offers both propaganda and how-to manuals for those seeking to act out fantasies of intolerance and violence."[30] By the mid-1990s information obtainable through the Internet included a *Terrorist's Handbook* and an *Anarchist's Cookbook*, with complete instructions on how one can make a bomb similar to the one used in the Oklahoma City bombing in April 1995. Many racial hate crime perpetrators are not active members of hate groups but have reported that on the Internet they found inspiration, validation, and, in some cases, their actual training.[31]

The Internet has served as a great recruiting tool for white nationalist and white supremacy groups that often try to lure the curious or the aggrieved, sometimes with deceptive come-ons. A student researching a term paper under the heading "Holocaust" or "Civil War," for example, might stumble on a white supremacy link designed to change the student's entire outlook on life. Sometimes a group might try to cloak itself in legitimacy by making, for instance, a standard conservative argument opposing affirmative action, but have links to progressively more racist sites to lure the unwary.

---

[30] Howard P. Berkowitz, national chairman of the Anti-Defamation League, as quoted in *U.S. Newswire*, "ADL to Congress: There Is a 'Virus of Hate' on the Internet," May 20, 1999; Stacia Brown and Larry Bellinger provide an excellent discussion of hate groups on the Internet and some of their strategies, *Sojourners* 29 (2000). Stacia Brown, "Virtual Hate," *Sojourners*, www.sojo.net/magazine/index.cfm/action/sojourners/issue/soj0009/article/000910.htm. Larry Bellinger, "You Say You Want a Revolution," *Sojourners*, www.sojo.net/magazine/index.cfm/action/sojourners/issue/soj0009/article/000910a.htm.

[31] Rabbi Abraham Cooper as quoted in Bobby Cuza, "Hate Crimes Increase by 12 Percent," *Los Angeles Times*, July 28, 2000.

DISCUSSION

This chapter has discussed the new white nationalists, their political goals, their ideas about racial separatism, and their insistence on calling themselves nationalists rather than white supremacists. Although the new white nationalists are not lynching blacks or burning crosses on lawns, it has been suggested here that they may be more dangerous than the uneducated participants in the more traditional racist type of organizations because of their greater intellectual prowess, their sophistication in shaping and delivering their message, and their greater access to centers of influence and power.

Because they are presenting themselves as advocates for white civil rights, some members of the new white nationalist movement have the potential to win the allegiance and respect of millions of Americans who do not consider themselves racists and who would never dream of joining an organization like the Ku Klux Klan but are nevertheless upset over current governmental policies, angry with minorities, and worried about the future. When one evaluates the potential growth of the white nationalist movement, it is necessary to take into consideration that survey data often show a majority of white Americans holding very definite and often negative assessments of racial and ethnic minorities, especially African Americans.[32] A 1990 General Social Science Survey conducted by the National Opinion Research Center, for instance, found that a significant majority of whites believed blacks and Hispanics were "more likely than whites to be lazy, violence-prone, less intelligent and less patriotic."[33] White nationalists are seeking to expand their ranks by indoctrinating anyone who will listen with a skewed version of history and a philosophical message that can transform simple anger over such policies as affirmative action or liberal immigration into hatred of racial and ethnic minorities.

Unfortunately, current discussions of controversial racial issues often take place in an atmosphere where political correctness dictates that people either remain silent about their true convictions or engage in dissimulation or subterfuge. Herein, I believe, lies a real danger for the

[32] See, e.g., Mark Peffley, John Hurwitz, and Paul Sniderman, "Racial Stereotypes and Whites' Political Views of Blacks in the Context of Welfare and Crime," *American Journal of Political Science* 41 (1997): 30–60.

[33] "Poll Finds Whites Use Stereotypes," *New York Times*, January 10, 1991.

future of American race relations. Because few legitimate arenas exist for white Americans to discuss openly their genuine fears on such racial issues as black-on-white crime, their impending minority status, and the continued existence of racial preference programs, white nationalists have stepped to the forefront and are encouraging a divisive form of white identity politics that has ominous implications for the future. White nationalists are providing aggrieved white Americans with the only forums where they can openly express their anxieties and fears on racial matters among an attentive and sympathetic audience that will not simply dismiss what they say as the rantings of racist bigots.

What is most needed now, I believe, is for white nationalists to be heard and debated in mainstream forums where their data and ideas can be openly evaluated and subjected to critical assessment. There is a real danger, I believe, when like-minded people get together and discuss only among themselves issues about which they care deeply that cannot be discussed in open forums. Such discussions are certain to lead to one-sided and distorted conversations that in the context of race will inevitably enhance racial polarization and political extremism. A colleague who read the full transcripts of our interviews with white nationalists summed up well, I believe, what is our current dilemma in this regard. "There is enough logic to what they argue," he wrote, "to make [their case] compelling." "Most importantly," he went on,

> they address topics and give voice to views that the mainstream media never allows in the public arena. Since those arguments are never allowed in the mainstream, these leaders are able to make them on the margins without clear and systematic refutation. THAT is a real danger. In the mainstream media, when such views are given voice, they are only dismissed and not refuted. Simply saying that the views are wrong and sending [former] Atlanta Braves pitcher John Rocker for psychological rehabilitation is counter-productive.

In the next chapter, I try to show what happens when people begin to subscribe to a more extremist ideology and become part of a radical racist right that makes no pretense to mainstream respectability and has broken all ties with mainstream American social and political norms.

3

RACIAL HOLY WAR! THE BELIEFS AND GOALS OF THE RADICAL RACIST RIGHT

What a blow *that* was to us! And how it shamed us! All that brave talk by patriots, "The government will never take *my* guns away," and then nothing but meek submission when it happened. . . . We should be heartened by the fact that there were so many of us who had guns . . . after the Cohen Act had outlawed all private ownership of firearms in the United States. It was only because so many of us defied the law and hid our weapons instead of turning them in that the government wasn't able to act more harshly against us after the gun raids. . . . Today it finally began! After all these years of talking – and nothing but talking – we have finally taken our first action. We are at war with the System, and it is no longer a war of words.

Andrew Macdonald, *The Turner Diaries*[1]

In the previous chapter, I discussed the new white nationalist movement that was seeking to expand its appeal to a wider audience by exploiting a number of white grievances and concerns often ignored in mainstream forums. The focus was on the softer or less extreme individuals and organizations that make up the racist right in America that have deliberately sought to strike a tone of moderation and rationality in their appeal for support. In this chapter, I deal with the more radical style of white nationalism and white supremacy that makes no attempt to conform its often hate-filled message to mainstream American values or sensibilities. The organizations and individuals in

---

[1] Andrew Macdonald, *The Turner Diaries*, 2nd ed. (Hillsboro, W.Va.: National Vanguard Press, 1978, 1980), 1.

this category, it is suggested here, have the potential to expand their influence – at least among a suitable niche audience – for much the same reasons that the more moderate groups do. Since many of these groups either actively or passively condone violence, the danger they pose should be apparent.

MOVEMENT LITERATURE

The Turner Diaries

Radical social and political movements often derive much of their energy and inspiration from key writings of activist members and founders that often go on to acquire a certain cult-like status. *The Communist Manifesto*, *Mein Kampf*, and *The Sayings of Chairman Mao* are three better-known examples of such movement-inspiring literature. Among the more radical white nationalist, white supremacist, and neo-Nazi groups in America, certain books have played a parallel role, with the most important of these being William Pierce's futuristic tale of racial apocalypse, *The Turner Diaries*. This book, which the FBI describes as the "Bible of the racist right,"[2] first became known to many Americans when it was revealed that Timothy McVeigh, the Oklahoma City bomber, may have been partially inspired in his murderous deed by his reading of this work. Although the book is by any literary standard very poorly written, it has exercised a powerful fascination for many of the members of the more radical racist right, and particularly for young people.

Pierce, a former university physics professor and head of the influential white supremacist group the National Alliance, published *The Turner Diaries* under the pseudonym Andrew Macdonald in the late 1970s. The novel describes in graphic detail a race war in which white patriots in California (collectively known as the Organization) launch a successful attack against the Zionist Occupied Government in Washington for its crimes against white Americans. Members of the Organization assassinate federal officials, lawmen, and politicians; slaughter Jews, nonwhite minorities, and race traitors; and then launch a nuclear

[2] Robert L. Snow, *The Militia Threat: Terrorists Among Us* (New York: Plenum Trade, 1999), 95.

attack upon the state of Israel with the nuclear arsenal that the Zionist Occupied Government itself had assembled. The author's views on the necessity of violence is well summed up in the conclusion that "there is no way to win the struggle in which we [whites] are engaged without shedding torrents – veritable rivers – of blood."[3]

Particular scorn is heaped upon white women who marry or cohabitate with nonwhites and Jews. The appropriate form of justice for such women is vividly described in the following passage:

> The first thing I saw in the moonlight was the placard with its legend in large, block letters: "I defiled my race." Above the placard leered the horribly bloated, purplish face of a young woman, her eyes wide open and bulging, her mouth agape.... There are many thousands of hanging female corpses like that in the city tonight, all wearing identical placards around their necks. They are the white women who were married to or living with Blacks, with Jews, or other non-White males. There are also a number of men wearing the I-defiled-my-race placard, but the women easily outnumber them seven or eight to one.[4]

Pierce's second novel, *Hunter*, was even more focused on the extermination of whites who marry outside their race. Interracial marriage of this kind is depicted as a heinous crime against nature and a treasonous assault on the integrity and purity of the white race. We were able to interview Pierce, and specifically asked him about the violent message in his novels:

> INTERVIEWER: In one of your two novels, the novel *Hunter*, you depict the killing of interracial couples in a manner that many people have seen as endorsing those kinds of actions. Was it intended as such an endorsement?
>
> PIERCE: Well, if I thought that that could be done on a significant scale today, why then, sure, I would endorse it. But I don't believe so, and actually that wasn't the purpose of the novel. *Hunter*, just like my earlier novel, *The Turner Diaries*, is not about the action in the book. The action is just something to carry the reader along. It's the ideas expressed by the characters which are important in both novels, and I, of course, chose *types* of action which would be attractive or interesting to the type of people I thought I would be able to most easily reach and influence with my ideas. I wasn't trying to reach liberals and make

[3] Macdonald, 79.   [4] Ibid., 161.

liberals understand that they were sick and needed to cure themselves. I was trying to reach people who were basically racially conscious, but simply hadn't really put it all together, didn't have a coherent way of thinking yet, hadn't figured out yet the answers to a lot of things. I wanted to clarify the thinking of people who already were more or less amenable to my message.

INTERVIEWER: But you say that you would advocate killing of interracial couples if it were able to achieve the desired end?

PIERCE: Yes, if it were to accomplish something. But I've never advocated violence or, in fact, any kind of illegal activity, because I don't think it would be productive. I think it would be counterproductive at this time.

INTERVIEWER: But you have no moral opposition to such action?

PIERCE: No, I mean when you're faced with the choice between allowing your race to die, or causing individual members of your race to die who have transgressed against certain basic and very important principles, the choice is easy.[5]

Pierce's novels have been widely distributed both in bound form and over the Internet, and have been important to the radical racist right in providing an alternative vision for the future of the United States. Although Pierce says he does not advocate violence, passages in *The Turner Diaries* describe, down to the last details, how to construct and deliver a truck bomb for maximum damage. These passages, many believe, were used as a model for the bombing of the Murrah Federal Building in Oklahoma City. Philip Lamy, author of *Millennium Rage*, reports that the federal authorities believe that certain pieces of the bomber's plan (such as target, dates, and timing) accord so closely to material in *The Turner Diaries* that the book may have provided both the motive and method in the Oklahoma City bombing. It is known, in fact, that Timothy McVeigh not only read *The Turner Diaries* but sold – or gave away – many copies of the book at gun shows he attended. The notoriety that *The Turner Diaries* received after the Oklahoma City bombing led to Pierce's appearance in 1997 on the popular TV show *60 Minutes*, as well as a segment of CNN.

Despite the brutal violence which the book seemingly endorses, significant numbers of whites who have read *The Turner Diaries* seem to be attracted to its vision of an all-white America purged of the pernicious influence of racial minorities and Jews. Journalist Susan Eastman

[5] William Pierce, interview.

interviewed one such reader of the novel, who referred to herself simply as "a regular white woman," who was captivated by the book's vision of a homogeneous white community. This "regular white woman" had recently attended an all-white barbecue in a coastal town and saw this as a metaphor for the America she and other whites yearned for. The woman explained to Eastman:

> I remembered reading in the *Turner Diaries* at the end where the white people were finally separate. I imagined that this celebration was for that. It seemed so fitting, it looked like the America we long for. I hope one day we can live like that, friendly white people, no one afraid of anything, it was an atmosphere hard for me to describe.[6]

Eastman was amazed – and appalled – that a seemingly ordinary woman could be so attracted to a novel that condones mass violence to achieve its vision of an ethnically purified America. "In her fantasy," Eastman writes, "the 'regular white woman' glosses over the descriptions in the book . . . of the blood revolution where Jews are dispatched on death marches at the rate of a million a day, [and] African Americans and Jews are marched out of captured white enclaves. To get to the all-white world that 'a regular woman' finds so appealing, white separatists bomb buildings, disrupt power to cities, and wind up hanging 55,000 to 60,000 white people from lampposts, power poles, and trees all over Los Angeles on a day called the 'Day of the Rope.' "[7]

Many ordinary people, like this "regular white woman," have read *The Turner Diaries* – the readership is put in the hundreds of thousands – even if most have not reacted so positively to its message. To add a personal note here: During a trip in March 2000 to my hometown of Roanoke, Virginia, I chatted with a used car salesman who had recently read *The Turner Diaries*. The salesman told me of an experience he had had with a customer a few days earlier who explained to him his version of constitutional doctrine and tried to recruit him to a white supremacy group, leaving behind literature explaining how the U.S. government has subverted the Constitution. The salesman expressed his regret and embarrassment at having kept the literature in his desk. Similarly, in 1999, as I sat in a bookstore in Princeton,

---

[6] Susan Eastman, "Divide and Conquer," *Weekly Planet*,
    http://www.weeklyplanet.com/1999/1209/cover1.html.
[7] Ibid.

New Jersey, engrossed in a copy of *The Turner Diaries*, a white man at an adjacent table stopped by to inquire with a look of obvious amusement (of the man-bites-dog type), "Should I be calling the FBI on you?" Clearly, a number of ordinary white Americans have at least heard of *The Turner Diaries*, and the news media has provided the book with much coverage; in fact, one report even stated that the Unabomber had a copy in his library.

The White Man's Bible and *Nature's Eternal Religion*

Other books that have influenced the more radical wing of the white supremacy and white nationalist movements include *The White Man's Bible* and *Nature's Eternal Religion*, both distributed by the neo-Nazi-oriented World Church of the Creator (WCOTC). These texts provide the theoretical foundation for what the WCOTC calls "Creativity," an atheistic and occult "religion" that calls for a Racial Holy War against members of the subhuman "mud races" – a category that includes all nonwhite racial and ethnic groups. The founder of the WCOTC was a man named Ben Klassen, who committed suicide after writing these two foundational books.

Matthew Hale, a graduate of the University of Southern Illinois Law School at Carbondale, is the current head of the WCOTC. He is in his late twenties, calls himself Reverend Hale, and is designated the supreme leader, or Pontifex Maximus, of the Creativity religion. Hale was asked by the interviewer to explain the basic tenets of his Creativity church:

> The World Church of the Creator is a pro-white, racial-religious organization which is dedicated to the survival, expansion, and advancement of the white race and the white race alone. We are not a Christian organization. Instead of basing our views, our ideology, our religion on Christianity, we base it on the eternal laws of nature as revealed through science, logic, history and commonsense. We believe that in a natural state each and every species looks out for its own kind. Each and every subspecies looks out for its own kind. This being the case, it follows that we as white people should look out for our own kind. We should not care about the other races – they can do what they will – but we should focus on our own. The World Church of the Creator in this respect is certainly a very radical organization, and we do not pay homage to Christianity

or to the Constitution or even to America. We are an international organization in scope – we consider all white people, wherever they may be,
to be our brothers and sisters.[8]

A recurring theme in Creativity literature is the beleaguered state of
the white race today. White Americans are depicted as an endangered
species that must wake up and respond to their plight before it is too
late. In *The White Man's Bible*, Klassen warns that "the White Race
is not holding its own in the battle for survival. It is shrinking, while
the mud races of the world are multiplying and breeding like rats."[9]
Nonwhites are consistently referred to with contempt in Creativity
literature as "niggers," "mongrels," "mud people," and the like. Jews
are described in an even worse manner. The Jews, Klassen holds, are
the mortal enemies of the white race because they are race mixers and
polluters who are working toward the "niggerization of America."[10]
They are more dangerous than blacks and browns, he believes, because
they are more powerful and fiendish. Echoing older anti-Semitic literature, Klassen claims that there is a Zionist conspiracy to take over the
world and enslave its entire non-Jewish population.[11] Klassen blames
Jews for affirmative action and for America's inability to solve its
race problem. It is the Jews, he says, who have used the institutions of
American government to perpetuate racial discrimination against
whites in jobs, loans, and immigration:

> The government claims that it is colorblind, and there should be no dis-
> crimination in any activity because of race, color, religion or creed. . . .
> The Jewish controlled government is putting forth a blatant lie. Every law,
> every decision, every activity by our so-called color-blind government is
> loaded against the White race and favors the mud races. In Washington
> . . . a qualified White applicant is passed over for an unqualified nigger in
> the majority of the cases. They call this "filling the quotas" system. . . .
> [The Jews invented affirmative action. The concept of affirmative action]
> blatantly means favoring niggers and other mud races over Whites,
> regardless of qualifications.[12]

---

[8] Matthew Hale, interview.
[9] Ben Klassen, *The White Man's Bible* (Lighthouse Point, Fla.: World Church of the
Creator, 1981), 23.
[10] Ibid., 23.   [11] Ibid., 134.   [12] Ibid., 278–9.

The message of Klassen's writings is uniformly crude, vitriolic, and unequivocal. Whites are threatened around the world by the advances of nonwhites, he says, and unless they awaken to the danger and mobilize against this development, they will be destroyed:

> Your children and their offspring can only survive, live and prosper in the framework of a white society. Were we to be engulfed in a world of billions of niggers, Chinese, and other mud races, your children, grandchildren and their progeny would not only be doomed to extinction, but what mongrelized bastards did survive would be swallowed up in a horrible mass of clawing, starving humanity.[13]

New recruits to the WCOTC, most of whom are under twenty-five years of age, are encouraged to read both *The White Man's Bible* and *Nature's Eternal Religion*, which are available free over the Internet or in bound volumes for only five dollars each. However crude Klassen's works may seem to outsiders, like *The Turner Diaries*, they seem to be able to exert a powerful influence on a suitably susceptible audience. Matthew Hale described to the interviewer the powerful effect that reading Klassen's writings had on him when he first read them as a very young man, and he challenged all white people to discover for themselves the wisdom in Klassen's works:

> INTERVIEWER: Is there anything else that you would like to tell us that you haven't so far, either about your own views or about your organization?
>
> HALE: Well, one thing I would like to say is that for me, the most powerful book I have ever read is *Nature's Eternal Religion*. This is a book available through our organization. I first read it in 1990. To all white men and women I offer this challenge: read this book cover to cover and see if you don't come to the same conclusions that we have. Read this book and judge for yourself the soundness of the principles we espouse. I invite anyone to do this.[14]

Like Hale, Lisa Turner, the WCOTC's Women's Information Coordinator, was also influenced by Klassen's writings. She explained to the interviewer how a reading of *Nature's Eternal Religion* first drew her to the Creativity religion:

[13] Ibid., 134.   [14] Matthew Hale, interview.

My involvement with the World Church of the Creator came about through a contact with Rev. Matt Hale over the Internet. Prior to that time, I had not been a formal member of any pro-white organization, and when I came into contact with him, he introduced me to the racial religion of Creativity. The Creativity religion seemed to express more clearly than anything else I had ever encountered before exactly what I felt the white race should be following and should be adhering to – which is getting away from the Jewish pollution of our race through the biblical fantasies of Christianity, which we believe have led our race to destruction. The central tenets of Creativity really appealed to me. I had never been very interested in being part of what they call the Christian Identity movement, so I started reading the primary books of Creativity, such as *Nature's Eternal Religion*, which is one of the main books that was written by our founder, Ben Klassen, and I was very impressed by what he had to say. I therefore joined the church formally in March of 1998.[15]

Mein Kampf

Given the fact that Hitler's autobiographical *Mein Kampf* was written over seventy-five years ago and addressed a European audience facing problems which were unique to interwar Germany, one might suppose that few Americans today would have much interest in this work except as an historical curiosity. The catastrophic defeat of Hitler's armies at the hands of the American-led Allies, and the subsequent repudiation of Hitler and Hitlerism by most of the postwar generation of German youth, would seem to make it even less likely that Hitler's writings would find any resonance in contemporary America. For mainstream Americans this is largely true, yet many members of radical white nationalist and white supremacy groups report that their reading of *Mein Kampf*, often at a young age, was a watershed event in their lives that changed their entire outlook on the world. Matthew Hale, for instance, explained to the interviewer how he first read *Mein Kampf* when he was only twelve years old, and as a result began to think seriously about issues of race. It was at this time, he says, that he first began reflecting seriously about Jewish influences around the world and the reasons for the general hostility that most peoples have shown toward Jews throughout the ages.

[15] Lisa Turner, interview.

For Lisa Turner, *Mein Kampf* played an even more pivotal role in her early development as a white supremacist. She has described, in fact, her first reading of it as a real turning point in her life that moved her in the direction of radical white nationalism and white supremacy. The interviewer questioned her specifically on this matter:

INTERVIEWER: What was your interest [before joining the World Church of the Creator] in pro-white and white supremacy groups?

TURNER: Well, I had been part of the movement for about ten years or so, even though I had not joined a particular organization. I had had loose affiliations with a variety of organizations very early on – the David Duke organization, which was the NAAWP, the National Association for the Advancement of White People. . . . I contributed money and that type of thing, and of course, I became very interested in Adolf Hitler. I read *Mein Kampf*, which was really a turning point in my life. When I read *Mein Kampf*, it completely opened my eyes to the reality that the white race had been lied to about a number of things, such as the Holocaust, and for a period of time I referred to myself as a National Socialist. So I went through, shall we say, some evolutions, some political evolutions before reaching Creativity. It was a period of about ten years of personal education and growth before I reached the point that I am at now.

INTERVIEWER: What impressed you about Hitler's *Mein Kampf*? Many Americans reading that book today would find it both vulgar and repulsive, but obviously you reacted to it very differently.

TURNER: Yes. I found it to be a very cogent, truthful, and straightforward discussion of what Hitler was seeing in his society. I was obviously not repulsed by what he was saying. It rang a bell with me. I looked around at my own era, and I felt that the Jews, just as in his time, were running our media – newspapers, television. I identified with everything he had to say. I felt that it was not written in an hysterical style. I felt it was a very controlled and highly intelligent – indeed, brilliant – piece of political testimony. So for several years I certainly considered myself a devotee of Adolf Hitler.[16]

The fascination with the personage of Adolf Hitler is pervasive among the more extreme elements in the white supremacy and white nationalist movements, and is not specific to street toughs or skinheads. *Turner Diaries* author William Pierce, for instance, has described Adolf

---

[16] Ibid.

Hitler as "the greatest man of our era." Pierce's fascination with the German Fuhrer seems intimately linked both to the racial policies of the Third Reich (which prohibited Aryan/non-Aryan intermarriages), and to its progressive record in the area of labor relations and public health measures. Hitler's meteoric rise to power from very humble circumstances also seems to be part of the continuing fascination that the life of this man has for many members of the racist right. Pierce revealed all this to the interviewer:

> INTERVIEWER: You once described Adolf Hitler as the greatest man of our era. What did you mean by that?
>
> PIERCE: Well, I meant by that that he had done more than anyone else to show us the way that we need to take in the future. He came up from nothing at the end of the First World War, he was blinded, wounded in a military hospital, he had no friends, no family, both his mother and father were dead. He had no money, he had nothing but a high school education, and without any of these advantages at all, he rose in a few years' time – from the time he was discharged from the army, thirteen years later he was the chancellor of Germany. And he transformed that country. He made it strong and self-confident again. He developed many very healthy, positive institutions in that country for young people, for education, for a relation between labor and management, for the development of natural resources and for the protection of the environment. He was probably the most prominent anti-smoking pioneer in Europe, and in many other ways was a leader for the future. If the Second World War hadn't come along, I think he would have had an opportunity to set an example that would have been followed in many other countries.[17]

RACIAL HOLY WAR: A CALL TO VIOLENCE?

A recurring theme in the literature of the more radical racist right is the impending violent confrontation between whites and the colored peoples of the world. Groups like the Aryan Nations, the National Alliance, and the WCOTC, while they occasionally pay lip-service to nonviolent intentions, employ violent metaphors and incendiary language that essentially condones violence, despite explicit denials. Lisa Turner can once again serve as an example. The interviewer asked her

[17] William Pierce, interview.

how she reconciles the rhetoric of a Racial Holy War used frequently in Creativity literature with denials of violent threats to nonwhites. She began by denying any intent to commit violence but ended saying that nonwhites had already waged war on whites and that whites, in a defensive posture, must fight to save themselves.

INTERVIEWER: You have said in your literature that your organization seeks to operate within the law and does not advocate violence. Yet a main tenet of the Creativity religion seems to be a call to a racial holy war against dark-skinned people and Jews. This racial holy war under the acronym RAHOWA is proclaimed repeatedly in your website and literature. How do you reconcile these two conflicting positions – non-violence and a call to war?

TURNER: Well, for me personally the word RAHOWA does not mean a literal killing or harming of anyone. It is a symbolic battle cry. For instance, when we speak of a war on drugs, does that mean a literal battle in the streets? Not necessarily. It's a motivating cry. It's also a symbolic understanding that unless we as whites turn this situation around, there will be a racial war – not one that we instigate, but one that is going to come about because we are going to have to defend ourselves against nonwhite violence directed against us.

The Women's Frontier and the church are very clear on this subject as far as violence is concerned. We do not advocate going out and killing anyone; we simply say that if there is not a raising of the consciousness of our white people, there will be violence. There will be a racial war. This is something that we want to avoid. We do not want to see this happen, and so I view my position more as being a warning voice, a warning cry, to prevent a racial war in this country.

INTERVIEWER: Who would start this war?

TURNER: We believe that the non-white peoples have *already* started the war against the white race. The daily violence against our people, women being raped, murdered – these are things that occur everyday and aren't even being reported in the press. We are under siege on a daily basis, we consider that a racial war has already been declared against us by the non-whites. The Mexicans, the mestizos, who declare their intention to take back the Southwest – "We will retake your territory," "We are going to kill you, whitey" – we've had years and years of this kind of rhetoric from non-whites. There has clearly been a war against us for many years. So it's already in progress.[18]

[18] Lisa Turner, interview.

Melanie Harris, an African-American research assistant to this project, was asked to visit the WCOTC web page and describe in detail her reactions. Harris found the Creativity website to display the same pattern that the interviewer found in the remarks of Lisa Turner and William Pierce: Lip-service paid to nonviolence coupled with a message from racist "true believers" that is hard to interpret as anything other than an open call to racial violence:

> Each page of the WCOTC site opens with a serene picture of a blond woman gazing off into an alpine landscape. The site seems geared toward a more intellectual audience than does the NAAWP site (though not THAT much more). It is also emotionally driven. . . . What interested me most about this site is that, as I searched more deeply into the links, the tone became more and more blatantly racist and violent. On the front page the group claims not to condone violence and for the first few screens the author refers to non-white races by their "politically correct" names. As I went deeper, however, African Americans became Blacks who became Negroes, then finally, grouped with Jews, mud races. Furthermore, the claims of non-violence were replaced by arguments of the world's over-population dilemma that is threatening the future of the white race. While there is never a blatant call to violence, there are references to Darwinism and thoughts of destruction of other "species" that are taking up the earth's limited resources. This site was particularly disturbing because it was so matter-of-fact. While the NAAWP site offered counter-arguments and then attempted to shoot them down, the WCOTC site simply states its beliefs as fact – as if nothing else makes sense. These people seem so convinced.[19]

RACIAL APOCALYPSE: THE CHRISTIAN IDENTITY MOVEMENT

During the 1960s and 1970s a bizarre and peculiarly American style of religiously oriented white supremacy known as Christian Identity became a significant force on the radical right in America. Some of the foundational themes of Christian Identity can be traced back to a nineteenth-century British movement known as Anglo-Israelism (or British Israelism), which claimed that the Ten Lost Tribes of biblical Israel – that is, the ten tribes spoken of in the Hebrew Bible that did not return

---

[19] Research assistant's account of her visit to the website of the WCOTC.

to Palestine after the Babylonian exile – were to be identified with the Anglo-Saxon and other European peoples. For Christian Identity, as for Anglo-Israelism, the Anglo-Saxon and other "Aryan" races are seen as the dominant part of the true nation of Israel, which, as God's Chosen People, has a special mission to bring godliness and right-eousness into the world.

The peculiar form of the Anglo-Israelite doctrine developed in Christian Identity circles in the United States, however, went well beyond its more benign British precursor to develop a virulently anti-Semitic and antiblack ideology of white racist triumphalism. While Christian Identity is a highly decentralized and in many ways fragmented movement with a variety of often contrasting or conflicting viewpoints, most who would consider themselves part of the Christian Identity fold would adhere to each of the four following statements of belief:

- *Opposition to Racial Universalism.* Not all human beings living today are the descendants of Adam and Eve. Such a view is the product of a pernicious racial universalism which is totally alien to the biblical emphasis on maintaining distinctions of race, ethnicity, and genealogy. Adam and Eve are latecomers to the human scene and are to be understood as the first *white* people.

- *A Pre-Adamite Creation of Inferior Humans.* Long before God brought forth Adam and Eve, there was a Pre-Adamite creation of human-like beings, who were, however, in their morality, godliness and intelligence, inferior to Adam and Eve and their descendants. The current descendants of this Pre-Adamite creation are the black, brown, and other nonwhite peoples of the earth.

- *The Jews as Children of Satan.* The people who today are called Jews, are, for the most part, not the true Israelites spoken of in the Bible with whom God has made his everlasting covenant, but the descendants of Cain. Cain was the product of sexual relations between the Devil (in the guise of the Serpent) and Eve, and would pass on Satan's proclivity for demonic evil to all of his blood line.

- *The Jews as Race Mixers and Polluters.* Cain took as a wife one of the inferior Pre-Adamite peoples thus mating the darker skinned, more animalistic peoples of the earth with the more clever but satanic Jews.[20]

As can be readily seen, Christian Identity theology is an attempt to provide a biblical basis for an extreme form of white racism and anti-Semitism, and in its more militant varieties, it attempts to justify something like a racial holy war against both nonwhites and Jews. Drawing upon apocalyptic themes in the biblical books of Daniel and Revelation, Christian Identity believes that human history is approaching an End Time in which there will be a final battle between the people of Christ, represented by the Anglo-Saxon and other white European peoples, and the forces of Satan, represented by the Jews and their allies. It will be a time of great tribulation in which war, famine, and other disasters will engulf the entire world. A final apocalyptic battle will ensue in which the fate of mankind will be decided and the Kingdom of Christ will ultimately prevail.

Both the tone and content of the Christian Identity message can be readily discerned from the following excerpts taken from the official creedal statement put out by the Identity group known as the Aryan Nations. Led by the former aerospace engineer Richard Butler and headquartered in Hayden Lake, Idaho, the Aryan Nations was perhaps the most influential Christian Identity group in America from the late 1970s until the early 1990s. Its influence has waned in recent years, however, due to Butler's advancing age and ill-health, as well as to the burdens of defending his organization from costly trials and lawsuits.

> We believe that there are literal children of Satan in the world today. These children are the descendants of Cain, who was a result of Eve's original sin, her physical seduction by Satan. We know that because of this sin, there is a battle and a natural enmity between the children of Satan and the Children of The Most High God.
>
> We believe that the Cananite Jew is the natural enemy of our Aryan (White) Race. This is attested by scripture and all secular history. The Jew is like a destroying virus that attacks our racial body to destroy our Aryan culture and the purity of our Race. Those of our Race who resist these attacks are called "chosen and faithful."

[20] The theological beliefs and motivating myths of the Christian Identity movement are discussed most extensively in Michael Barkun's *Religion and the Racist Right* (Chapel Hill: University of North Carolina Press, 1994). These four statements summarize the material in Barkun.

We believe that there is a day of reckoning. The usurper will be thrown out by the terrible might of Yahweh's people, as they return to their roots and their special destiny. We know there is soon to be a day of judgment and a day when Christ's Kingdom (government) will be established on earth, as it is in heaven.[21]

To be prepared for the tribulation that is to come, some Identity groups have gone into survivalist mode. They have moved to isolated rural locations, and tried as best as possible to insulate themselves from what is seen as a corrupted world and to become as self-sufficient as possible in order to endure the inevitable hardship and economic collapse that the period of tribulation is sure to bring. Identity groups have sometimes compared survivalist activities of this kind to the actions of Noah building the Ark.

Other, more militant Identity groups have taken a paramilitary route to preparing for the tribulation. James Ellison's Covenant, Sword and Arm of the Lord (CSA), for instance, purchased 224 acres of land in northern Arkansas in 1976 and used the land for training like-minded Identity Christians in guerrilla warfare and related skills. Ellison's organization, however, was effectively put out of business in 1985 when his Arkansas compound was raided by the Bureau of Alcohol, Tobacco and Firearms. Ellison himself was arrested and sent to prison for acts of arson, bombing, and the manufacture of automatic weapons.[22]

Militant Identity Christians also deny the doctrine of the "rapture," to which most fundamentalist Christians adhere. The "rapture" refers to the belief, based on the first letter of the Apostle Paul to the Thessalonians, that the Christian faithful will be spared from the suffering and ordeal of the final tribulation by being rapt up to the heavens where they will be safe with God ("Then we which are alive and remain shall be caught up together with them in the clouds, to meet the Lord in the air; and so shall we ever be with the Lord".[23] For the more militant Identity Christians, the doctrine of the rapture is a dangerous teaching that will disarm Christians and ill prepare them for the Final Battle against the forces of Satan. "The rapture doctrine," the Identity

[21] From the *Aryan Nations' Creed*, reproduced in Jeffrey Kaplan, *Encyclopedia of White Power* (Lanham, Md.: Rowman and Littlefield, 2000), 469–70.
[22] Barkun, 216.
[23] 1 Thessalonians 4:17, King James Version, 146.

writer Sheldon Emry has remarked, "has done more to disarm and make American Christians impotent than any other teaching since the time of Christ."[24]

DAN GAYMAN AND THE CHURCH OF ISRAEL

Unlike the leaders of the more secularized groups on the racist right, who are usually eager to be interviewed by journalists and scholars, Christian Identity figures generally confine their public speaking to small groups of like-minded believers or to potential converts to their viewpoint. The interviewer tried to interview Richard Butler of the Aryan Nations and Pete Peters, one of the most influential of the younger generation of Christian Identity pastors, but neither responded to repeated requests.

We were fortunate, however, that Pastor Dan Gayman of the Schell City, Missouri-based Church of Israel agreed to an interview. Gayman's views are particularly valuable in order to understand the function of religion in influencing certain groups on the racist right. He gives the impression of one who is theologically sophisticated and generally quite articulate. As a theorist of Anglo-Israelite Christianity, Gayman has few, if any, peers among contemporary Americans. For over thirty years Gayman has influenced important elements within the Christian Identity movement, though in recent times he has sought to distance himself from some of the more extreme views of Christian Identity proponents, especially their espousal of race hatred and support for violent confrontation with the government. His own congregation in Missouri practices racial separation and a quietistic disengagement from what are seen as the corruptions of an ungodly world, but it strongly condemns the mistreatment of minorities and disrespect for the established law. In this sense, Gayman's views can be seen as representative of the more moderate direction in which the Anglo-Israelite philosophy can move, and in some ways resembles the older style of British Israelism of nineteenth-century English writers.

One of the first questions the interviewer asked Gayman concerns the function of the Lost Tribes of Israel in the theology of his church:

[24] Cited in Barkun, 105.

INTERVIEWER: Let's take up the issue of the identification of the lost ten tribes, since that's clearly what distinguished you from the more typical fundamentalist church. Could you explain your views on that?

GAYMAN: Yes, we believe that the identification of the lost ten tribes of Israel is singularly a very important theological belief for the Church of Israel. Now, obviously the very name of the church, Church of Israel, would indicate that the word "Israel" holds a position of great prominence in our belief system. . . . What happened to [the ten lost tribes] at the time of the Assyrian captivity seven hundred years before the birth of Christ becomes of paramount importance to us, because we believe that God has not forgotten the unconditional covenants and pledges made to these people at a time when they were still residing in their separate kingdoms. . . . We know what happened to the southern kingdom, made up of Judah and Benjamin and portions of Levi. A remnant from those tribes returned at the end of the seventy-year Babylonian captivity. However, that does not satisfy the need to know what happened to the greater body of the Israelites, that is, the ten tribes of Israelites [who did not return]. We believe that those people can be identified in history and that their movement across the geographic locations on a map can be fairly well and accurately pinpointed. . . . [We believe that] the ten tribes today are to be identified among the great mass or millions of people who are generally referred to as the Anglo-Saxon and kindred peoples of the earth. . . .

INTERVIEWER: Do you believe that Anglo-Saxons are in some sense morally, spiritually, or intellectually superior to other ethnic groups?

GAYMAN: The Anglo-Saxon people, being the descendants of the twelve tribes of Israel, have a special calling and election to become a blessing to all the other peoples of the earth. In other words, every people that God has created may have their unique calling, but the Israelites have a unique calling and blessing in the election of God to bring the blessings of God to the rest of the world. We believe that a cursory examination of history would confirm very quickly that most of the technological blessings and advances of the last one hundred and fifty years have basically come from the Anglo-Saxon nations of the world [and kindred peoples]. . . . We do not believe that the Anglo-Saxon people are necessarily superior to any other ethnic group, but do believe that their success, their greater prosperity, their higher standard of living are no mere accidents or products of chance. The fact that the Anglo-Saxon people have historically generated the highest standards of living on the planet, we believe, derives entirely from their willingness to apply the principles of the Bible.[25]

The interviewer asked Gayman about nonwhite Christians, and especially about black and Hispanic Christians. Did Gayman believe that nonwhites could be Christians and find salvation through the Christian faith? He replied that nonwhites could benefit from adapting many Christian moral practices but that they could not be true Christians in the way of Anglo-Saxons because they are not part of the Israelite nation that is called by God in the Bible to a special covenant relationship:

> INTERVIEWER: Can nonwhites be Christians in the same way that Anglo-Saxons can be Christians?
>
> GAYMAN: Well, we believe that in order to be a qualifying believer in the Lord Jesus Christ, there is a covenantal standing. In Jeremiah 31:31 the prophecy is given that, "behold, I will make a new covenant," . . . [and] in Jeremiah 31:32–33, it goes on to elaborate that this new covenant, of which the New Testament is the sum and substance, was to be made with the House of Israel and with the House of Judah. We do not believe that the God of the Bible entered into all these special, unconditional covenants with the Israelites, and then all at once universalized these covenants. Nowhere in the Bible do we find where God universalized the unconditional covenants and made them suddenly universally applicable to all the peoples of the earth. So we believe that if there are individuals from the other races that seek to embrace Christianity, they will most assuredly be blessed to the degree and to the measure that they embrace the moral principles and values of Christianity, but in so far as to say that these individuals share in the same covenantal standing or blessing as the Anglo-Saxons and kindred races, we would not be able to say that.[26]

Gayman was asked specifically about why he has sought to distance himself in recent years from the Christian Identity label despite many similarities between Identity views and his own, especially on the question of racial separatism and the special mission of the Anglo-Saxons. He responded at length:

---

[25] Daniel Gayman, telephone interview, May 24, 2000.   [26] Ibid.

INTERVIEWER: Your views are very similar to those of the Christian Identity movement, yet in recent years you have tried to disassociate yourself from the label of Christian Identity, while still acknowledging important similarities between the Church of Israel and the Christian Identity religion. Could you explain what distinguishes your group from Christian Identity?

GAYMAN: Yes. First of all, Christian Identity, to the best of my knowledge, has no structured means by which they identify with historical Christianity. I know of *no* Christian Identity church that embraces creedal Christianity, as we do. We embrace the Apostles' creed, the Nicene creed, the Athanasian creed. I would say also that there is an important difference in, for example, the doctrine of the Trinity. We have been long adherents to the doctrine of the Trinity, while in contrast Christian Identity groups vary in their position on the godhead. Some of them believe in the Trinity; some of them do not. . . .

I would also like to emphasize the fact that in the more than fifty years of the existence of the Church of Israel, there has never been a single racial incident whereby hostility toward other races has ever drawn the attention of law enforcement officers or agencies. So there is a *decided* difference, we believe, in the attitude that the Church of Israel has toward other races and that of certain Christian Identity groups. We believe God is the author and creator of *all* the distinct races, that He placed His mark of ownership upon them all, that He has a unique plan and purpose for every race that He created, and that God relates to every race, and they relate to Him in a manner unique to their own special existence. We believe that is a major contrast between us and Christian Identity. We count God as the author of all races, and we do not believe that there is any room whatsoever in our theology for hatred of any race. God says in Genesis 1:31: "He looked at everything that he made, and behold, it was very good." Therefore, if God called everything that He created very good, we're happy to call it very good also. . . .

INTERVIEWER: So you don't believe in hatred towards any race and you don't believe in violence directed towards any race, but you do believe in ethnic separatism.

GAYMAN: Yes. We have traditionally, throughout the entire history of the Church of Israel, held to a view of ethnic separatism in marriage, in worship, and in social settings. . . . Like the Pilgrims who settled America in 1620, and the thousands of Puritans who followed them as Separatists from England, remnant Christians from the Church of Israel seek to live in marriage, worship, and social settings as *separatists*. We have no problem, however, with the diversity of races in the workplace. Our people have historically worked very well in racially diverse workplaces. . . . But when it comes to the idea of marriage and worship and social settings, we practice ethnic separatism. It would be a violation of our religious conscience to bring the races together in a worship forum.[27]

Gayman went on to cite a number of biblical passages in the Old and New Testaments which he believes make the doctrine of ethnic separatism imperative for biblical Christians "to the very end of history." Aside from the specific scriptural references to ethnic separation, Gayman believes that the separation of the races in social settings is a practical necessity to prevent interracial marriage, which he and the members of the Church of Israel believe is against God's plan for mankind. He explains:

GAYMAN: Aside from specific scriptural problems, the idea that people can come together and worship God in the same building, sitting in the same pews, and not have interracial dating and marriage would be inconceivable. If we bring them together in the church and we are all going to become one family inside the walls of the sanctuary, certainly there will be no question that we will have interracial dating and then marriage, and all that goes with that. So we would be opposed to any kind of multiracial worship. Absolutely.

INTERVIEWER: Why do you oppose interracial marriage so strongly?

GAYMAN: We oppose interracial marriage so strongly because we believe that it . . . basically undermines the whole concept of God's original design and creation. . . . Interracial marriage works against the very nature of all of the orderly design in the creation. Every form in the flora and fauna world that God has created follow the pattern of the law of kind after his kind, a law which is stated no less than ten times in the first chapter of Genesis. . . . And we believe that what interracial marriage really does is that it takes away from every race. We would want every race to retain the original creation design that God intended for that race, and we believe that interracial mixing or marriage tends to take away *from* every race what God intended.[28]

The doctrine of "kind after kind," which in variant forms can be found throughout much of the racist right, including the nonreligious right, was elaborated further by Gayman:

---

[27] Gayman interview.   [28] Ibid.

Let me explain further what we mean by the law of kind after his kind. . . . All of nature surely does witness to the truth of mixing with your own kind. All the birds that fly in the heavens associate with their own kind, and have done so from the day of their creation. Black birds mix only with their kind. All the animals of the forest were programmed by the Creator God to mate among their own kind. . . . This basic law of God and creation is inherent in all of life, including the diverse and distinct races on earth. Within each distinct race is a strong propensity to stay within the perimeters of their own kind. The proclivity for every distinctly created race to stay within its genetic borders is the very reason that the divergent racial stocks have persisted throughout history. The Caucasoid, Mongoloid, and Negroid races were created separate and distinct from one another. The creator programmed within each race an instinctive drive to cohabit within their kind. The survival of every pure race is dependent upon the practice of ethnic separatism. It is only when these divergent races are brought together in the same landscape, places of worship, and educational settings that the law of kind after his kind is broken down. We believe that every race has the responsibility to pre-serve the original design of ethnic distinctions which the Creator God placed there, and that is why we practice ethnic separatism.[29]

Gayman is aware of the fact that most white people today deny the separationist doctrines that the Church of Israel and the various Christianity Identity churches proclaim. He contends, however, that most white Americans believe in their hearts in the doctrine of racial sepa-ratism even if they are too intimidated by its current disfavor in the media and elsewhere to openly acknowledge their beliefs. The Church of Israel, he says, states openly not only what most white people in America believe but, more important, what they actually practice. He criticized, in this context, those who would condemn the kind of ethnic separatism that his church practices as being intolerant of the very diversity they claim to support:

With regard to our racial beliefs, we believe that . . . the primary differ-ence between the Church of Israel and mainstream Christianity, is that most of the white people – and certainly most of the white people in the rural sectors of the United States of America – believe in separation of the races in marriage and in worship, but they are reluctant to make that belief system public. The major difference that separates us from the vast

[29] Ibid.

majority of all Caucasians in America is that we do not hide our belief regarding racial separatism. Just look at America's white suburbs. White people have engaged in a white flight out of the inner cities and have congregated into the suburbs, and as the old suburbs fill up with a racial mix, we find a new white flight out of those suburbs into new all-white or nearly all-white areas. All of those people believe in their hearts what the Church of Israel practices, that is, the separation of the races. And if I were to travel and visit the vast majority of all Anglo-Saxon religious services on a given Sunday morning in the rural villages and hamlets of this country, I would find ethnic separatism from beginning to end. . . .

We believe that racial, ethnic separatism by biblical standards is what God ordained from the beginning of the creation So we practice it. We have no problem with those who choose not to, but at the same time we feel that we are being deprived of *our* civil rights. . . . We find it increasingly more and more difficult to practice *our* definition of ethnic separatism, because in the very country of great religious, racial, and ethnic diversity, in the very country that promises such a democratic and liberal belief system to be practiced within its borders, there seems to be a growing unwillingness to allow Caucasian people to practice their religious differences and uniqueness.[30]

DISCUSSION

In considering the views of Christian Identity and Anglo-Israelite writers, it is important not to confuse their many biblically grounded claims with Protestant fundamentalism or other conservative forms of evangelical Christianity. To be sure, there are significant similarities. Like fundamentalists, Identity Christians claim to believe in a literal interpretation of the Bible, and they believe in the prophetic relevance of the Book of Revelation to explain the contemporary conditions of the world. Like many fundamentalists they also believe that the Last Days may be near, that a period of tribulation and torment must precede the Second Coming of Christ, and that a final apocalyptic battle between the forces of God and Satan will determine the ultimate fate of mankind. These similarities largely account for the fact that most of the recruits to Christian Identity seem to be drawn from the ranks of those brought up in a fundamentalist Christian culture.

---

[30] Gayman interview.

But Christian Identity is a kind of religion radically different from Christian fundamentalism or, indeed, any kind of genuine, biblically based Christianity. Identity Christians read selectively from the Bible and either ignore inconvenient passages and themes or offer wild and thoroughly unsubstantiated claims to defend their biblical interpretations, which have little or no foundation in biblical text or history. Claims that the Anglo-Saxons are the Lost Tribes of biblical Israel, that the darker-skinned peoples of the world are part of a Pre-Adamite creation, that Cain was the offspring of Eve and the Devil are so fanciful and deluded that they are hard to take seriously by anyone who does not have a powerful need to believe them.

In the past, mainstream white fundamentalists most certainly engaged in many forms of antiblack and anti-Semitic bigotry. The history of race relations within the Christian churches is surely not a pretty one to contemplate. Yet in recent years fundamentalists and other evangelical Christians have made a concerted effort to denounce bigotry, to reform their practices, and to make amends for the past. Groups like the Christian Coalition and Promise Keepers, and evangelists such as Jerry Falwell and Billy Graham, have rejected racism and anti-Semitism, and tried hard to recruit nonwhite people into the Christian fold. Christian Coalition activist Ralph Reed has specifically sought repentance for the sin of racism and racial exclusiveness in the white Christian churches, and antiracist sermons can often be heard today from the same conservative white pulpits that a generation ago supported segregation.[31] Moreover, unlike many of their parents and grandparents, most fundamentalist and evangelical Christians today look favorably upon the Jewish people, and see the in-gathering of the Jews in the Mideast and the formation of the state of Israel as part of a divinely ordained plan.

While one can find in the Bible certain "tribal" or ethnicity-based elements, the dominant thrust of contemporary fundamentalist and evangelical Christianity is to focus on the equally or more powerfully universal elements that sensitive Christians throughout the ages have always understood as the dominant message of the Gospels and the letters of Paul. One can hardly read Paul's letter to the Galatians

---

[31] Ralph Reed, *Active Faith: How Christians Are Changing the Soul of American Politics* (New York: Free Press, 1996), 68–69.

without being overwhelmed by its majestic message of universal brotherhood and sisterhood of all Christians regardless of their race or genealogical background:

> But the scripture hath concluded all under sin, that the promise by faith of Jesus Christ might be given to them that believe. . . . For ye are all the children of God by faith in Christ Jesus. For as many of you as have been baptized into Christ have put on Christ. There is neither Jew nor Greek, there is neither bond nor free, there is neither male nor female, for ye are all one in Christ Jesus. And if ye be Christ's, then are ye Abraham's seed, and heirs according to the promise.[32]

If, for a Christian, "there is neither Jew nor Greek," and if all Christians are, by virtue of their faith, of "Abraham's seed," then the Christian Identity claim about ethnic exclusivity and a special Anglo-Saxon status as the chosen people becomes an absurdity. As I attempt to show in the final chapter of this study, adherence to genuine Christian beliefs, and not to the racist doctrines espoused by Identity Christians and Anglo-Israelites, may be one way of overcoming the racial divisions that currently threaten America.

RADICAL WHITE NATIONALISTS AND MILITIA GROUPS ON THE LEGITIMACY OF THE U.S. REGIME

Closely related to the views of those on the racist religious right who would deny the legitimacy of the current U.S. regime are the unorthodox political beliefs of many white nationalists and militia group members, who contend that the United States government has usurped the people's authority and now operates outside the Constitution and laws of the land. Some foundational support for allegations of this kind can be found in the research of liberal scholars such as Yale University law professor Bruce Ackerman, who has written that the "Reconstruction amendments – especially the Fourteenth – would never have been ratified if the Republicans had followed the rules laid down in Article Five of the original Constitution."[33] Similarly, Gary Lawson, Professor of Law at Northwestern University, has argued that the

---

[32] Galations 3:22, 26–29, King James Version, 135.
[33] Bruce Ackerman, *We the People* (Cambridge, Mass.: Harvard University Press, 1991), 44–45.

"post-New Deal administrative state is unconstitutional, and its validation by the legal system amounts to nothing less than a bloodless constitutional revolution."[34] As suggested by these quotations, even mainstream scholars can draw attention to questionable circumstances surrounding both the ratification of the Reconstruction-era constitutional amendments and the emergency powers that President Franklin Roosevelt assumed during the Great Depression.

Militia groups and white supremacy groups use similar sets of facts to challenge the legitimacy of many of the constitutional amendments ratified since the Bill of Rights.[35] Not only do the more extreme white nationalists refuse to recognize the legitimacy of the three Civil War era amendments – the Thirteenth Amendment, which freed the black slaves; the Fourteenth Amendment, which gave former slaves the rights to citizenship; and the Fifteenth Amendment, which gave black men the right to vote – they also refuse to recognize the legitimacy of the Nineteenth Amendment, which gave women the right to vote, and the Sixteenth Amendment, which authorized the federal government to collect an income tax. According to the white supremacy narrative, the U.S. government itself has been operating illegitimately since 1933 when President Roosevelt took office and proclaimed a state of emergency, in effect allowing him to suspend the Constitution and pass a host of regulatory acts of dubious legitimacy. The factual basis for such claims, once again, is something on which a number of mainstream scholars concur.[36]

Many of the more extreme white nationalists harbor an intense hatred for the United States government, which they see not only as illegitimate but as the purveyor of evil policies intended to destroy America or sap it of its strength. Frequently, this hatred of the government is tied to the belief that it is controlled by diabolical Jews who deliberately encourage Third World immigration, miscegenation, and multiculturalism in order to weaken white influence in America.

[34] Gary Lawson, "Symposium: Changing Images of the State: The Rise of the Administrative State," *Harvard Law Review* 107 (1994): 1231.

[35] See also Cass R. Sunstein, "Constitutionalism After the New Deal," *Harvard Law Review* 101 (1987): 448.

[36] Susan P. Koniak, "When Law Risks Madness," *Cardozo Studies in Law and Literature* 65 (Spring/Summer, 1996): 9; William C. Banks and Alejandro D. Carrio, "Presidential Systems in Stress: Emergency Powers in Argentina and the United States," *Michigan Journal of International Law* 15 (1993): 45–46, as cited in Koniak, 9–10.

Lisa Turner of the WCOTC is a typical representative of such extremist views. Like other hard-core white nationalists, Turner believes the federal government is under the control of international Zionist forces bent on the destruction of the Caucasian people. Asked by the interviewer which current policies of the U.S. government she supported and would like to see retained, she replied that the entire government was corrupt and needed to be replaced by a government that looked out for the interests of white people:

> As far as my position on the government, of what I would want to see retained in this government – I would want to see *nothing* retained about this government. As far as I am concerned, this government is the Jewish occupational government. I would dismantle it, destroy it, and reform it into a pro-white government based on nature's racial laws. So there's nothing I would retain of this government.[37]

Members of some militia groups have evolved their own common law and common law courts derived from their understanding of history and their interpretation of the U.S. Constitution.[38] Central to their belief is the distinction they make between Common Law Sovereign Citizenship and Fourteenth Amendment Citizenship. Sovereign Citizenship, they believe, belongs to whites as a birthright and guarantees them freedom from tyranny, which they tend to identify with all current government entities above the local level. Generally speaking, most radical white nationalists believe that the farther a government entity is removed from the control of local white majorities, the more sinister and diabolical it becomes – and the more it is prone to manipulation by Jewish money and the Jewish-dominated news media.

RADICAL MINORITY SCHOLARS PREDICT A FUTURE RACE WAR

In the radical white nationalist, white supremacist, and Christian Identity view of America's future, an elite of race-conscious white patriots

---

[37] Lisa Turner, interview.
[38] Koniak, 71–73; James Corcoran, *Bitter Harvest, Gordon Kahl and the Posse Comitatus: Murder in the Heartland* (New York: Penguin Press, 1990); Joel Dyer, *Harvest of Rage: Why Oklahoma City Is Only the Beginning* (Boulder, Colo.: Westview Press, 1967).

engage in a racial holy war to preserve the soul of America by ridding the nation of the mud people and the Zionist Occupied Government that has become the enemy of white America.[39] How would such a race war and subversion of the government start? For some, it would begin with increased domestic terrorism such as the Oklahoma City bombing or through increased physical attacks on racial and ethnic minorities and their leaders.

A few minority writers, however, have had their own ideas about a future race war. In 1996, journalist Carl Rowan and law professor Richard Delgado independently published books warning of an impending race war in America, naming affirmative action policy as the most likely catalyst.[40] Rowan wrote that the policy is the "one explosive issue that may trigger the actual burning of America, and [it] certainly exacerbates the ever-widening divisions between and among its citizens."[41]

Broaching the same subject in a narrative approach, Delgado envisioned an interracial dialogue between two fictional law professors, one a minority professor, who inquires of his more conservative white counterpart why conservative whites oppose special programs to aid minorities. "Why do conservatives want to put an end to affirmative action?" the minority professor asks. He finds this situation particularly perplexing in view of the fact that, for minorities, the current "levels of school drop-out, unemployment, suicide, poverty, and infant mortality are the highest in the country and approaching those of the Third World." His white colleague explains that whites feel threatened by their impending minority status, and that they are lashing out at those who threaten them:

> I think they are gearing up for a race war . . . there is a general sense that it's time to pick a fight. Caucasians will cease being a majority in this country about midway in the next century. At this point, numerical and voting power should logically shift to groups of color – blacks, Asians, and Latinos. White opinion-makers don't want this to happen. So, they're

---

[39] Howard L. Bushart, John R. Craig, and Myra Barnes have written the most current comprehensive study linking these core elements together. See *Soldiers of God: White Supremacists and Their Holy War for America.* (New York: Kensington Books, 1998).

[40] Richard Delgado, *The Coming Race War* (New York: New York University Press, 1996).

[41] Carl T. Rowan, *The Coming Race War in America* (Boston: Little, Brown, 1996).

gearing up for a fight. It's one of the oldest tricks in the world – provoke your enemy until he responds, then slap him down decisively.[42]

Rowan imagines a situation of racial terrorism comprised of isolated racial conflicts in selective parts of the United States that have the overall effect of threatening everyone's security. A race war, Rowan believes, is probably unavoidable. "So many hate groups are at large that a few of them are bound to make good on their threats to make part of America, or all of it, the exclusive home of superior Aryan whites." He envisions a scenario in which whites attack blacks and blacks retaliate as they did during the 1920s. Too much rage, he says, "has built up in the minds of young blacks . . . for me to assume they will not strike out with firepower, especially if provoked. . . . Most likely to draw black retaliation of the wildest, fiercest sort would be a rash of white supremacist assassinations of prominent black leaders, a choice part of the formula in *The Turner Diaries* and other manifestos of the white supremacists."[43]

Delgado, on the other hand, envisions a situation in which governmental actions trigger insurrections among minorities, which then require them to use considerable force to suppress. His portrayal sounds eerily similar to the Los Angeles riots of 1992, in which the "not guilty" verdict reached by twelve white jurors, exonerating four Los Angeles police officers in the beating case of Rodney King, triggered three days of violence and mayhem. By the time 4,000 national guardsmen brought law and order to the riot area, 50 people had been killed, over 4,000 had been injured, 12,000 had been arrested, and over $1 billion in property damage had been caused in the worst urban rioting since the late 1960s.[44]

New York University law professor Derrick Bell has also envisioned the possibility of violent interracial conflict and extreme white reactions. Bell's futuristic essays, especially "Space Traders," raise questions for African Americans and others to ponder. Bell argues that African Americans could eventually need a twenty-first-century underground railroad to protect targeted groups from white-initiated oppression and violence. He asks: "What precisely would you do if they came for you?

[42] Delgado, 119–20.   [43] Rowan, 283.
[44] The Los Angeles Times, *Understanding the Riots: Los Angeles Before and After the Rodney King Case* (Los Angeles, Calif.: Los Angeles Times, 1992).

How would you protect your family? Where would you go? How would you get there? You have money? Could you get access to it if the government placed a hold on the assets in your checking and savings accounts?"[45]

The scenarios of Rowan, Delgado, and Bell may seem far-fetched to many. When journalist Jim Sleeper reviewed Rowan's and Delgado's books, he dismissed them as unworthy of being taken seriously, even though Rowan had gone to great lengths to document the activities of white nationalists and the growth of militias. "Neither author argues persuasively that racial injustice is worse now than ever in this century," Sleeper wrote. "Why, then, their intimations of war? Don't they risk creating self-fulfilling prophecies of doom by 'warning' about this?"[46] Whether self-fulfilling or not, Rowan's and Delgado's visions should be taken seriously by persons concerned about the future of American race relations. Although the prospect for armed racial conflict in the immediate future seems remote, the internment of the Japanese during the Second World War should at least warn us that far-fetched scenarios, under the right historical circumstances, can sometimes come to fruition.

What is most striking about the dire prognostications of Rowan, Delgado, and Bell is that none of these scholars, who have acutely observed America's deteriorating race relations, and linked part of this to affirmative action, has ever called for an end to racial preferences or a serious revamping of current preference programs. Nor have they issued any real wake-up call to black leaders to focus on addressing legitimate sources of white fear and white anger over such real issues as black-on-white crime and the deterioration of black urban neighborhoods. Black leadership, instead of being proactive and creative, continues with the same strategies developed during the last century when most of its hopes were tied to affirmative action. Black leaders often aggressively pursue public policies that alienate whites (such as racial reparations), but do little to help those blacks most in need or to improve interracial cooperation. At a time when serious conditions in the black community cry out for sustained national attention, many

[45] Derrick Bell, *Faces at the Bottom of the Well: The Permanence of Racism* (New York: Basic Books, 1992), 93–94.
[46] Jim Sleeper, "Nightmares of Rage and Destruction, *Washington Post*, Book World, November 3, 1996, p. 4.

black leaders, I believe, waste a great deal of energy championing symbolic battles – like elimination of the Confederate flag – when their energies could be channeled to much more productive enterprises.

ANTI-SEMITISM IN BLACK AND WHITE

As we have already seen, many white nationalists and white supremacists are open and unapologetic anti-Semites who see Jews as the primary source of evil in modern America. Ironically, many of their views overlap with those of black nationalists like Louis Farrakhan of the Nation of Islam, who, like his white nationalist counterparts, considers Jews to be the most dangerous members of society and a threat to the race-pure worlds that both white and black nationalists wish to create. According to Nation of Islam literature, all whites are the offspring of the demonically evil genius Yacub, and partake of his satanic evil, but the Jews are the worst of all. Jews are greedy, perfidious, ambitious, and crafty, and they seek to rule the world.[47] Blacks, by contrast, are seen as the creation of a beneficent deity. One can see here a parallel with the Christian Identity doctrine of the two different seed lines of mankind: the Adamite from which the white race descended and the Pre-Adamites from which the "mud races" descended.

Interestingly, white and black nationalists of anti-Semitic persuasion have not infrequently come together to explore areas of common ground. Michael McGhee, for instance, a former Milwaukee alderman and head of a black nationalist group called the Black Panther Militia, once invited Tom Metzger of the White Aryan Resistance to address his organization. McGhee befriended Metzger after the two met on the *Jerry Springer Show*.[48] Metzger has also held talks with Louis Farrahkan of the Nation of Islam. Similarly, black nationalists have been known to attend meetings devoted to Holocaust denial sponsored

[47] Elijah Muhammad, *Message to the Black Man in America* (Newport News, Va.: Brothers Communication System, 1992), 53, 134. On black anti-Semitism, see Anti-Defamation League of B'nai B'rith, "ADL Survey on Anti-Semitism and Prejudice in America," November 16, 1992, pp. 30–32; Jennifer Golub, "What We Know About Black Anti-Semitism," American Jewish Committee Working Paper (New York, 1990); Robert Wistrich, *Anti-Semitism: The Longest Hatred* (New York: Pantheon Books, 1991).

[48] Todd Gillman, "Panthers, Supremacists Call for U.S. Overthrow; Dallas Rally Urges Violence to Achieve Goals," *Dallas Morning News*, May 30, 1992, p. A37; D'Souza, *The End of Racism*, 400.

by the white anti-Semitic organization the Institute for Historical Review. A black professor at City College of New York, Leonard Jeffries, who is known for his hostility toward Jews, has been invited by white racists and anti-Semites to join them at conferences convened to expose the Holocaust as a Jewish fabrication.[49]

Many of the white nationalists and white supremacists we interviewed for this project – including some who would not be considered "radical" or "extreme" – expressed a degree of hatred and contempt for Jews that most will find shocking. Like Identity Christians, many white nationalists and white supremacists clearly see Jews as a much more destructive force in America than blacks or other members of the "mud races." William Pierce, for instance, echoed a common theme when he described Jews as an alien racial presence in a European America that had proved enormously destructive. The author of the *Turner Diaries* had the following exchange with our interviewer:

INTERVIEWER: Could you describe your vision for the future of America? What would the racial landscape of America look like if your vision for the future were to be realized?

PIERCE: Well . . . that's a very hypothetical question. You are asking me to describe institutions that might be developed in the future of America, and I think that's something that will require a lot of careful thought and planning as to how we want to change institutions based on the lessons we have learned from the present [racial] disaster. So about all I can really say is that we want to have a homogeneous America – a racially homogeneous America consisting of just Europeans. . . .

INTERVIEWER: Where do Jews fit in to your picture of a racially homogeneous America?

PIERCE: They don't.

INTERVIEWER: But Jews are white Europeans . . .

PIERCE: No, no [laughing].

INTERVIEWER: Why don't Jews fit into your view of a European-American society?

PIERCE: Well, Jews have lived in Europe, of course, for a while. They've had Jewish colonies in Europe since Roman times, but Jews really don't think of themselves as primarily European. They identify with the Middle East, at least the ones who are really Jewish, the ones that have a strong Jewish consciousness do. Their whole approach to life,

---

[49] D'Souza, *The End of Racism*, 400.

their whole way of relating to the people around them is entirely different from our own. They've played a very destructive role in our society and in virtually every society in which they have been a minority. We can't afford to fall into this trap again. They have to go their own way.[50]

The theme of Jews-as-Destroyers of Host-Societies is ubiquitous among the contemporary anti-Semitic right. This view is developed in an even more extensive manner by the following remarks of Lisa Turner:

> INTERVIEWER: In many of the articles that you have written and in the interviews that you have previously given, you display an intense, visceral, and many would say a truly paranoid and pathological hatred of Jews around the world. Why do you hate the Jews so much?
>
> TURNER: Well, in studying the history of the world, I've seen the way the Jews have in every place they've ever gone, invaded the territory. They have stolen, they have polluted, they have destroyed the civilizations of every place they have ever been. Many people, you know, feel that anti-Jewish feelings started with Hitler. But Hitler was a Johnny-come-lately in this area. The Jews destroyed Rome, they destroyed Egypt. If you read history, if you read the Talmud – the Talmud declares openly that the Gentiles are slaves, that they are inferior, that they are to be destroyed. One cannot look at the Jewish race and see anything but a polluter of civilization, and it certainly is not paranoid to acknowledge this. This view is based on historical fact and the actual reality of what their influence is wherever they go. To every nation they occupy, they bring economic enslavement and civilizational destruction.[51]

Anti-Semites on the contemporary racist right often point to the longstanding anti-Semitism itself as confirming evidence for their view of Jewish duplicity and destructiveness. The fact that Jews have been despised and ostracized for so long, by so many different people, and in so many different societies, is a good indication, they argue, of just how despicable Jews have been throughout history. Alternative views of the causes of anti-Semitism, such as religious rivalry or jealousy over superior economic performance, are dismissed out of hand by proponents of this view. Matthew Hale, the head of the World Church of the Creator, has articulated this position with particular clarity:

[50] William Pierce, interview.   [51] Lisa Turner, interview.

INTERVIEWER: Why do you display such hostility towards Jews in your published literature?

HALE: As far as why we have antipathy towards the Jews, it is because of their religion largely. Their religion is extremely hostile to those not Jewish. The Talmud is replete with hostility toward non-Jews, calling us cattle, saying that we're created by God so that Jews would not have to be served by beasts. The Talmud condones the rape of three-year-old girls, for that matter. It says that a girl three years of age may be violated. This is a religion that has some serious problems with it, and it's because of their religion and because of their attitude towards non-Jews that Jews have been persecuted for so many years. They have not been hated for no reason at all, and that's one of the things that I thought about when I was 11–12 years old. "Why are the Jews hated so much?" I asked. I mean, why would people seek to exterminate them? Was it for no reason? And I found in my readings that the Jews have made themselves disliked, and that's the reason.

INTERVIEWER: Don't you think that jealousy is a big factor here since the Jews have been so economically successful?

HALE: That's just a cop-out. That's the Jews trying to erect a smokescreen over what they've been doing. I'm not jealous of Jews. I don't care how much money a Jew may have. I feel I have more character and more going for me than they do, and I think it's really another kick in the teeth from the Jews for them to say that the reason why anti-Semitism exists is because we're jealous of them. The reason why anti-Semitism exists is because Semitism exists, because of Jews trying to manipulate and control the finances, the government, the laws of the people. They have done this from time immemorial. They were kicked out of Egypt because of it. Of course, the Jewish version is that they wanted to go and the Egyptians wouldn't let them go, but that's not the Egyptian version of events. They caused problems in Germany and caused the rise of Adolf Hitler. They were a problem in ancient Rome; they're been a problem throughout Europe. And it was not because of jealousy.[52]

The overall pattern among white racists is thus clear: Jews are the pariah; they are plotters and schemers out to destroy Aryan civilization; despite their European-like physical features, they are an alien and parasitic presence in America and must be expelled from any healthy white society.

---

[52] Matthew Hale, interview.

Jews as White Nationalists?

Given the extreme anti-Semitism of much of the racist right, it seems impossible to believe that white nationalist and white supremacy groups – even the more moderate ones – would attract any Jewish support. But a combination of anger at racial preferences, demographic changes, and weakening anti-Semitism among the broader white population in America have encouraged some Jews to align themselves with the white nationalist right. A strong disdain for African Americans also seems to have played a role in this development. For instance, Robert Weissberg, a highly respected Jewish political scientist, addressed the 2000 *American Renaissance* conference of white nationalists and presented a paper in which he argued that blacks and Jews are locked in an abusive relationship that is in need of dissolution. According to Weissberg, "[M]ore than half the lawyers and freedom riders assisting Southern black civil rights activists during the 1960s were Jewish."[53] However, black Americans did not return the favor, Weissberg charges, but instead repaid the Jews with anti-Semitism by supporting anti-Jewish leaders such as Louis Farrakhan and others. Jewish intellectuals such as Weissberg help supply propaganda for the white nationalist movement, and they command respect because of their academic standing and the perceived credibility of their claims.

Michael Levin and Michael H. Hart are two other Jewish academics who have affiliated with white nationalist causes in recent years. The interviewer specifically asked Levin and Hart why they would want to associate with white nationalists when so many white nationalists are anti-Semites. While disassociating themselves from anti-Semitism, both seemed to minimize the anti-Semitic threat posed by white racialists. Levin replied in the following manner:

> INTERVIEWER: You are a Jew and the views you express on race are most usually expressed by whites who dislike Jews as much as they dislike blacks. Does this make you uncomfortable?
>
> LEVIN: No, no. I get a little impatient with Jews myself. After all [racial] egalitarianism has been mostly an idea associated with Jews in the 20th century, and if you look at those who attack the current data on race

---

[53] Robert Stacy McCain, "Scholar Finds 'Abusive' Ties Between Blacks, Jews," *American Renaissance*, http://www.amren.com/washtimes.htm.

and try to sort of pooh-pooh it and dismiss it, it tends to be almost entirely Jewish.

INTERVIEWER: But those who hold your view that whites are in some sense genetically superior to blacks are most likely to be anti-Semitic whites. Doesn't that make you uncomfortable?

LEVIN: Well, you have to ask what anti-Semitism here means. People who think that whites are genetically more intelligent than blacks don't think that whites are genetically more intelligent than Jews. They don't dislike blacks and Jews in the same way. If anything, they think Jews are too clever, they're too tricky, they take over everything. They're always plotting and planning together. Obviously, that's not an attitude I have toward Jews, but the beliefs behind anti-Semitism are very different than the beliefs behind any kind of anti-black feeling.

Actually, I do get pretty disgusted sometimes with the anti-Semitism of many racialists. It disgusts me because it is so stupid. It's as if the IQs of these people drop 30 points when they hear Jews mentioned. Suddenly it all becomes Jewish conspiracies – Jews in the media, Jews inventing the Holocaust, that sort of thing. Still, their stupidity doesn't change the facts about race.[54]

Michael H. Hart, the astrophysicist who has suggested partitioning the United States into racially separate states, was even less concerned about anti-Semitism among racially conscious whites. He explained to the interviewer that white attitudes toward Jews have changed in America in recent decades, and that most whites who would be amenable to a separate white state would probably welcome Jews. Even if they didn't, he says, they would not want to kill Jews the way anti-Semites did under Hitler:

INTERVIEWER: You have suggested a division of the United States into racially separatist states. But many whites who consider themselves white separatists or white nationalists also have an animus against Jews. As a Jew yourself, how do you feel identifying or affiliating with members of the white nationalist right here?

HART: In the first place, I am not a member, nor do I affiliate with any anti-Jewish or anti-Semitic organization. I dislike them, and I assume they dislike me. But I do realize that any white separatist state will inevitably include some people who feel: "It's good that we have a country in which there are no blacks; but it would be even better if

---

[54] Michael Levin, interview, Jan. 5, 2000.

there were no Jews here either." I believe, however, that such people are a minority, and that most white Americans are not anti-Semitic and are quite willing to accept Jews as equal citizens. This is what my experience has been.

When I was a child, my parents brought me up to believe that the goyim hate the Jews and that they will never give the Jews a fair shake. Well, that might have been true at one time (and is probably true in most Arab countries today); but in my own lifetime I have not found it to be true here. On the contrary, I have generally been treated fairly by gentiles (there have been occasional exceptions); and it seems to me that most American whites are willing to judge me (and other Jews) on their individual merits (or faults), which is all I can ask.

However, suppose it turned out that within the white separatist state the prevailing opinion was different, and that the majority view there was, "No, we don't want Jews in our country," and that they therefore decided to partition the *white* state into a Christian country, a Jewish country, and an integrated (Christian and Jewish) country. I would, of course, choose to live in the integrated state and I don't think that I would be worse off because the hard-core anti-Semites were not in my country, but instead had a separate state of their own. (In fact, I would be better off.) But even if the white separatist state was only partitioned into two states, all that would mean is that American Jews like me would be forced into a small, separate, all-Jewish country. That is not what I want to happen, but it would not be an unbearable catastrophe. And it certainly bears little resemblance to Hitler's policies. Hitler did not want to give the Jews an independent state, he wanted to exterminate them, a very different policy indeed.[55]

Apparently, these Jews feel comfortable with white nationalists such as Jared Taylor and the intellectuals who write for *American Renaissance*, most of whom are far more likely to preach racial intolerance toward African Americans than anti-Semitism. There are certainly elements among the contemporary white nationalist right who see the real threat to America coming primarily from people of color. Taylor, as well as many other whites, might even be amenable to a definition of whiteness that included Jews and perhaps even a small number of Asians.

[55] Michael H. Hart, interview.

Discussion

Anti-Semitism of any kind is reprehensible, but black anti-Semitism particularly disturbs me because I recognize that African Americans owe much of their liberation to Jewish intellectuals who provided enormous support for civil rights in the past through their fund-raising, litigation, and political organizing activities on behalf of black equality.[56] More than any other group in America, liberal Jews were in the trenches with black leaders, sometimes dying for the cause of black liberation. Hasia Diner, professor of Jewish History at New York University, has accurately described the dominant Jewish attitude toward the black struggle for dignity and equality in the early decades of the civil rights struggle, when blacks had few friends among whites:

> The media of the Jewish public opinion – newspapers and magazines, in both Yiddish and English – and imaginative literature – poems, short stories, novels, dramatic works – as well as sermons, public addresses, and other forms of discourse all acknowledged that the subjugation of Blacks amounted to a "stain of shame on the American flag" (a phrase often repeated in the Yiddish press), that Jews and Blacks shared a field of understanding and a common political agenda, and that the Jew more than any other American could "plead for his stricken brother."[57]

Growing up as a black child in the rural South and frightened by the rumored presence of the Ku Klux Klan in our midst, my siblings and I would sometimes encounter hate literature filled with invectives against blacks and Jews. We always took comfort in the fact that the Klan hated Jews, too, just like they hated black folk, since the Jews, we reasoned, were rich and powerful – at least in comparison to poor blacks – and we believed in their ability to thwart the Klan. Perhaps it was irrational, but some of us felt protected by the Jewish influence

---

[56] Cheryl Greenberg, "The Southern Jewish Community and the Struggle for Civil Rights," in V. P. Franklin, Nancy L. Grant, Harold M. Kletnick, and Genna Rae McNeil, eds., *African Americans and Jews in the Twentieth Century* (Columbia: University of Missouri Press, 1998), 123.

[57] Hasia R. Diner, "Drawn Together by Self-Interest: Jewish Representation of Race and Race Relations in the Early Twentieth Century," in V. P. Franklin, Nancy L. Grant, Harold M. Kletnick, and Genna Rae McNeil, eds., *African Americans and Jews in the Twentieth Century* (Columbia: University of Missouri Press, 1998), 28.

in the South. As long as African Americans were in the same boat as Jews – objects of hatred and scorn – somehow we felt less vulnerable. For this reason it is most troubling when I see groups like Taylor's *American Renaissance* successfully seeking and finding Jewish recruits, leaving African Americans more isolated and vulnerable than ever before.

Although I comfort myself with the knowledge that the vast majority of Jews would never consciously align themselves with white nationalists, some current trends are nevertheless disturbing. White nationalists need Jewish intellectuals for the same reasons that blacks needed them before and during the civil rights movement. Jews bring intellectual depth and have great influence in America. Less than 3 percent of the population, Jews are among America's best-educated and wealthiest citizens, and hold positions in many influential fields vastly disproportionate to their small number. Jews constitute about 45 percent of the country's public intellectuals, 30 percent of its college professors, about 40 percent of its top lawyers, 26 percent of its print and broadcasting media personnel, and over 50 percent of its directors of major motion pictures.[58] Jews are prominently represented on any list of the wealthiest Americans, and this wealth is easily translated into political clout and media influence. Jews, in short, are not a group whose support African Americans can afford to lose to their adversaries and antagonists.

As the comments above show, some Jewish members of white nationalist organizations apparently believe the more extremist elements in the movement can be contained and that their place will be secure in a white separatist nation. In some ways, this seems to me utterly naive. Indeed, Jewish nationalists might consider revisiting the restaurant scene from *The Godfather*, in which Michael Corleone, played by Al Pacino, excuses himself from the table, goes to the bathroom, retrieves a hidden gun, and comes back to rid himself of unwanted friends, rather than accept their offer of truce.[59] Currently, Jewish anger over the perceived unfairness of affirmative action, over black criminality, and over perceptions of black ingratitude may be a

---

[58] Seymour Martin Lipset, *American Exceptionalism* (New York: Norton, 1996), 151–4.
[59] The scene I describe is from Mario Puzo's *The Godfather* (1972). For a full transcript of the film, see http://www.jgeoff.com/godfather/gf1/transcript/gfltranscript.html.

force driving some Jews into the same camp as white nationalists, but there is little evidence that the acceptance goes both ways.

THE GROWTH OF RACIAL HATE
GROUPS IN THE 1990S

Over the decade of the 1990s there was a substantial increase in the activities of racist "hate groups" in America, according to data collected by the Southern Poverty Law Center (SPLC), one of several public interest organizations monitoring the activities of such groups.[60] Klan organizations, neo-Nazis, racist skinheads, Christian Identity groups, the Nation of Islam, and a category of organizations composed of mostly religious groups with racist ideologies are among the groups monitored. To qualify and make the SPLC's list of racial hate groups, an entity must have engaged in documented racial hate activities during the previous year that include "marches, rallies, meetings, leafleting, publishing literature or criminal activities."[61] The SPLC does not count groups and organizations that appear to exist only in cyberspace.

Figure 3.1 shows the number of organizations classified by the SPLC as white racist or white supremacy groups for the years between 1992 and 1999. During this period, groups have risen and fallen as new groups have come and gone and consolidated their resources. In 1997

---

[60] Other private data collection agencies monitoring extremist groups and hate crimes include the Simon Wiesenthal Center, HateWatch, the Jewish Defense League, and the Anti-Defamation League. These groups can have figures either lower or higher than the Southern Poverty Law Center (SPLC), depending on how they classify a threat. Of these agencies, HateWatch monitors the broadest categories of organizations and Internet sites, and includes not only racial hate groups but those that target women and homosexuals. Most of these private watchdog groups gather their data from newspapers, law enforcement agencies, magazine articles, and Internet sites. Besides these private agencies, the FBI also monitors extremist groups and collects and publishes data on hate-related crimes. Because of criticisms of its methods of accounting, the SPLC has become especially conservative in recent years in its criteria of what counts as a hate group. While it monitors patriotic militia groups and notes associations and overlapping memberships with white supremacy groups, it carefully notes that not all these groups espouse views of racial hatred and some even contain mixed-race membership. A hatred and distrust of government (though not necessarily racism) unites many of the members of militia groups.

[61] This information about the criteria for inclusion is found on the SPLC's web page and annually in its magazine, *Intelligence Report*, published by Klanwatch.

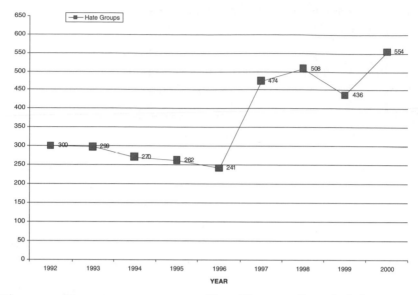

Figure 3.1 Hate groups, 1992–2000. *Note*: The 2000 figure includes 88 neo-confederate groups not counted in previous years. An effort has also been made to subtract black separatist groups and parties from the yearly totals. *Source*: Modified from data provided by the Southern Poverty Law Center, *Intelligence Report*, and personal communication.

the number of white supremacy groups jumped to a record 474 groups after a low of 241 in 1996 because of SPLC's decision to count each individual state chapter of an organization where more than one existed. Previously, the SPLC counted only one chapter per state. In 1998, the number of white supremacy groups dropped to 508, and in 1999 to 436, decreases that the SPLC attributed to efficiency moves as organizations and groups have consolidated their resources.[62] However, the number of white supremacy groups jumped to 554 in 2000, though much of this increase was the result of the SPLC decision to count neo-confederate groups as white hate groups.

Not listed in the chart are 48 black separatist and black nationalist groups. That figure is a dramatic increase over the 21 listed for 1999. Characterized as racial hate groups for their black nationalist, black

---

[62] "Report: Hate Groups Fewer in Number, but Larger in Size," http://www.cnn.com/2000/US/03/15/hate.groups.

supremacist, and anti-Semitic views, most of these groups are religious in nature, and are counterparts to Christian Identity.

Figure 3.2 shows a map of the 2000 geographical distribution of 602 racial hate groups, a number that includes 48 black separatist groups. Much hate group activity takes place in areas of the country with high minority populations. A paucity of racial hate groups in areas of the country where white nationalists have been migrating could be indicative of lower minority populations that reduce the need to organize.

Experts differ as to the seriousness of the threat posed by racial hate groups. Laird Wilcox, an expert on extremist groups such as the Ku Klux Klan and the Aryan Nations, has accused liberal watchdog agencies of exaggerating the threat posed by these groups in order to enhance their fundraising capabilities.[63] While there may be some truth in Wilcox's claim regarding specific watchdog organizations, there is still reason to believe that the number of individuals and groups in the white nationalist and white supremacy movements is most likely to be *undercounted*. Not only do individuals espousing racial hatred have other options besides joining extremist groups, but watchdog agencies are not set up to monitor groups determined to conceal themselves and their true agendas. Watchdog agencies are best able to identify groups with openly racist programs. Other groups, organizations, and journals can escape detection especially if they use coded language or express themselves through presentation of biased statistics rather than the use of traditional racial hate categories.

No watchdog agency can give accurate numbers of white Americans who sympathize with racist organizations or who might become susceptible to a white nationalist movement that used less extreme and more subtle tactics than the Ku Klux Klan and the Aryan Nations. Certainly, some potential recruits can be found among those white Americans and their offspring who embraced the racial politics of former Alabama Governor George Wallace. Running as a third-party candidate in the 1968 presidential contest with a campaign that had clear racial overtones, Wallace won five states and an impressive 9.9 million

---

[63] Robert Stacy McCain, "Researcher Says Hate 'Fringe' Isn't as Crowded as Claimed," *Washington Times*, May 9, 2000.
http://www.washtimes.com/culture/default-20005922336.htm.

Figure 3.2 Hate groups by state and type,

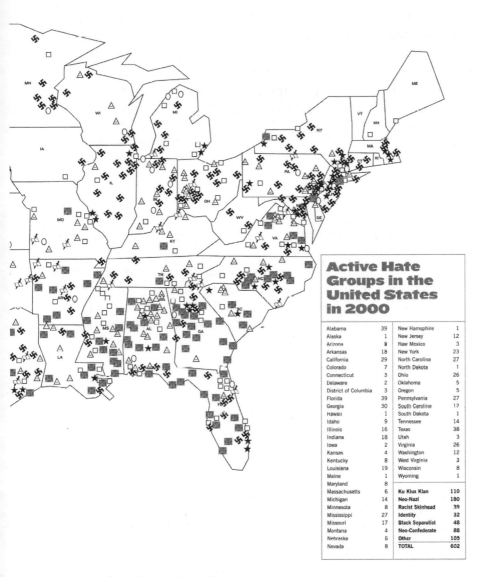

2000. Source: Southern Poverty Law Center.

votes, with only a modest campaign budget and universal hostility to his candidacy among mainstream news media.[64]

Journalists and researchers who have studied the racist right have noted that it has successfully infiltrated mainstream institutions such as school boards, state legislatures, elite branches of the military, and the halls of the United States Congress.[65] By the time of 1995's Oklahoma City bombing, members of racist militia groups had worked on political campaigns and helped to elect Helen Chenoweth (R-Idaho), Linda Smith (R-Wash.), and Steve Stockman (R-Texas). In addition, Senate Majority Leader Trent Lott (R-Miss.) had close ties with the Mississippi Chapter of the Council of Conservative Citizens, an organization that the SPLC has listed as a racial hate group because many of its members were formerly associated with the KKK and the White Citizens Council.[66]

Most important, Wilcox's assessment fails to take account of the change in strategy that has occurred among racial hate group leaders after Morris Dees, cofounder of the SPLC, successfully won a series of high-profile lawsuits against several white racist organizations. In 1987, Dees won a $7 million judgment against the United Klans of America; in 1990, a $12.5 million judgment against the White Aryan Resistance; in 1990, a $21.5 million judgment against Christian Knights KKK; and in 2000, a $6.3 million judgment against the Aryan Nations.[67] These lawsuits essentially bankrupted the organizations involved. However, from the ashes of Dees's strategy of holding the leadership of racist hate groups accountable for the violent actions of their individual members emerged a white nationalist counter-strategy

[64] Dan T. Carter, *From George Wallace to Newt Gingrich: Race in the Conservative Counterrevolution 1963–1994* (Baton Rouge: Louisiana University Press, 1996), 14–15.

[65] Jeffrey-John Nuniziata, "White Supremacy and the New World Order," http://www.impactpress.com/articles/junjul97/nazi.htm.

[66] Ridgeway, 22–6; Philip Klinkner and Rogers A. Smith report that Lott's association with the group was especially close. A column written by him ran in the CCC's newsletter alongside others that made such declarations as: "No one can deny the importance of the question of miscegnation or race-mixing. Its very essence involves the preservation of the white race as well as the Negro race. It is a matter of racial survival. Compared with future interest we have at stake in this issue, all other matters fade in significance." Quoted in *The Unsteady March: The Rise and Decline of Racial Equality in America* (Chicago: University of Chicago Press, 1999), 336.

[67] Raju Chebium, "Attorney Morris Dees Pioneer in Using 'Damage' Lit to Fight Hate Groups," CNN.com, September 8, 2000; "Morris S. Dees, Jr.," Dorothy L. Thompson Civil Rights Lecture Series, http://www.ksu.edu/dthompson/dees.html.

called "leaderless resistance." Leaderless resistance is said to have emerged out of a 1992 national conference of white supremacists held in Estes Park, Colorado, where influential leaders in the movement met to discuss SPLC lawsuits and the 1992 Ruby Ridge, Idaho, incident involving white separatist Randy Weaver.[68] At this meeting, Louis Beam of the Aryan Nations called for a strategy in which individuals were encouraged to avoid joining groups but to instead operate independently of organizations.[69] Working in small groups and using the Internet for information, individuals can participate in the white nationalist movement without formal membership in any organization.[70] There is reason to believe that leaderless resistance will significantly increase in importance in the future.[71] As I show in Chapter 5, there has been an increase in hate crimes since the FBI started collecting data in the early 1990s. Some of this activity is traceable to individuals who read hate literature or listen to racial demagogues but are not themselves members of formal organizations.

AN HISTORICAL NOTE

Although there has been a documented increase in the growth of racial hate groups and hate crimes since the FBI started collecting

---

[68] In the latter incident, federal agents seeking to arrest Weaver for his failure to appear in court shot and killed his wife and thirteen-year-old son, after his son had killed the federal marshal who shot his dog. An extensive governmental investigation concluded that the government, relying on an untrustworthy informant, had overreached its authority and violated Weaver's constitutional rights. Consequently, the Justice Department settled the case by paying Weaver and his daughters $3.1 million. The Ruby Ridge killings became a *cause célèbre* for the racist right and a source of increased recruitment. Another factor that has helped fuel a growth in militia groups was the 1993 government attack on the Branch Davidian compound in Waco, Texas. Ruby Ridge and Waco together enraged many white militia members, including Timothy McVeigh, who took out his hostilities by bombing the Alfred P. Murrah Federal Building in Oklahoma City. For more information, see Robert L. Snow, *The Militia Threat: Terrorists among Us* (New York: Plenum Trade, 1999), 13.

[69] Brent L. Smith, "Pursuing the Terrorist: Changing Legal Strategies," *Klanwatch Intelligence Report*, Winter 1997, p. 11; Dobratz and Shanks-Meile provide a summary of the factors that led to the adoption of the changed strategy of "leaderless resistance," 171–4.

[70] Stephen Sloan, "The Future of Terrorism in the U.S.," *Klanwatch Intelligence Report*, Winter 1997, p. 10.

[71] Joe Roy, "Tracking the Terror: The Most Dangerous White Supremacists Have Moved to the Patriot Underground," *Klanwatch Intelligence Report*, February 1996.

such data in the early 1990s, the presence of racial extremists on American soil is not a new phenomenon for the United States.[72] Historian Catherine McNichol Stock has traced racial hatred and racial violence on America's shores back to the 1676 uprising against Native Americans known as Bacon's Rebellion.[73] She reports that racism and nativism have waxed and waned since the Civil War. Moreover, there has been a propensity for racist organizations to attract not just the poor and powerless but many well-educated, elite members of society. At its height, the nativist American Party (or "Know Nothings," as their opponents called them), which organized largely in response to the huge influx of Irish Catholic immigrants in the late 1840s and 1850s, could boast a membership that included five U.S. senators and forty-three U.S. representatives. Know-Nothings dominated the state legislature in Massachusetts and controlled no less than six state governorships. The party declined, however, in the years following the Civil War.[74]

The post–World War I era was particularly fertile ground for the growth of white racist groups. The early 1920s witnessed the growth of the Ku Klux Klan, which at its height had as many as 3 million members that included many doctors, lawyers, judges, and university professors.[75] As a young man, future President Harry Truman almost joined the Klan, and future Supreme Court Justice Hugo Black and senator Robert F. Byrd actually did join. During this era, the racist brand of white nationalism contributed to the growth of a reactive style of black nationalism in the person of Marcus Garvey, who led a back-to-Africa movement that for a time commanded a mass following

---

[72] Chapter 5 provides more information about hate crimes and how the data was collected.

[73] Catherine McNichols Stock, *Rural Radicals: From Bacon's Rebellion to the Oklahoma City Bombing* (New York: Penguin Books, 1996), 5.

[74] John Higham's *Strangers in the Land: Patterns of American Nativism 1860–1925* (New Brunswick, N.J.: Rutgers University Press). This book provides an excellent history of nativist opposition to non-Protestant immigrants.

[75] For more information about extremist movements, see Michael Novick, *White Lies, White Power: The Fight Against White Supremacy and Reactionary Violence* (Monroe, Maine: Common Courage Press, 1995); Michael Kronenwetter, *United They Hate: White Supremacy Groups in the United States* (New York: Walker and Company, 1992); John George and Laird Wilcox, *Nazis, Communists, Klansmen, and Others on the Fringe* (Buffalo, N.Y.: Prometheus Books, 1992), 20. See also Seymour M. Lipset and Earl Rabb, *The Politics of Unreason: Right-Wing Extremism in America, 1709–1970* (New York: Harper and Row, 1970); Stock, 126.

among largely lower-class African Americans, which was also personified in the politics of Malcolm X. Today's counterpart to Garvey and Malcolm X is Nation of Islam leader Louis Farrakhan, who also favors black separatism.

CONCLUSION

This chapter has tried to present an overview of the beliefs and goals of some of the more radical elements among white nationalist and white supremacy groups, including members of the Christian Identity movement, the National Alliance, the World Church of the Creator, the Aryan Nations, and various militia organizations. Radical white nationalists believe that a race war and the fall of the American government are inevitable, that the races are created unequal, that whites are God's chosen people, and that America is the new Israel. Their propaganda is widely available, to people of any age, through the Internet and inexpensive publications.

Their efforts to attract a mass audience, however, may be limited by the fact that most Americans do not presently share their beliefs or goals and would find many of their theories extreme. The majority of Americans believe that the future of America does not include a race war or increased racial violence and that people of different races can live together peacefully. For this reason, the threat they pose to the long-term stability of America is probably less than that of the more moderate white nationalist groups and individuals discussed in the previous chapter, who subtly appeal to a more mainstream audience (and are better at disguising their true aims). Since the large and continuing influx of nonwhite immigrants in recent years is a major target of white nationalist groups, both moderate and extreme, and since opposition to this influx appears to be a source of their continuing strength, immigration issues is the topic of the next chapter.

4

DEMOGRAPHIC CHANGE AND IMMIGRATION ISSUES

If we have to take a million immigrants in, say Zulus, next year or Englishmen, and put them up in Virginia, what group would be easier to assimilate and would cause less problems for the people of Virginia [?]

> Presidential candidate Patrick Buchanan, *This Week with David Brinkley*, January 8, 1991

In this chapter, I discuss the demographic changes that have alarmed some conservatives and caused much anxiety among white nationalists. At the heart of the issue is U.S. immigration policy, both past and present, which is dramatically changing the face of our nation. What have gripped the nationalists with fear about the future of the white race are statistics from the last three decennial censuses that point toward the impending minority status of white Americans. As proof of danger, nationalists cite a combination of factors, including a white birthrate that is lower than the replacement rate, high minority birthrates, immigration from Third World nations, and interracial marriages. While the implications of such data are difficult to discern for even the most learned demographic scholars, white nationalists use distortions and inconsistencies in demographic and immigration studies to translate these dynamics into a cause for alarm for whites.[1]

Demographic data illustrate the declining majority status of white people in the United States. Most Americans are aware that racial and ethnic minorities taken together as a whole constitute a majority in cities such as Los Angeles, San Francisco, Houston, Miami, and New

---

[1] Ridgeway, 108.

York, as well as within the entire state of California. Racial and ethnic minorities will constitute at least 47 percent of the U.S. population by the year 2050.[2] In practical terms, this means that numerical strength will shift toward groups that a majority of our Founding Fathers once viewed as inferior, so much so that they instituted "systematic and self conscious efforts to make race or color a qualification for membership in the civil community."[3] For whites accustomed to being in the majority, the impending changes are likely to bring uncertainty and fear, a fear that is exacerbated by the politics of racial preferences. Moreover, the white majority appears to be left with only three clear-cut alternatives for dealing with the broad demographic changes: accepting a new American melting pot, heeding the call of white nationalism and organizing and pressuring government to slow the tide of immigration, or self-segregating by moving into whiter areas of the country.[4]

THE IMPACT OF IMMIGRATION ON AMERICAN CITIZENS

The United States has experienced a dramatic growth in immigration over the past three decades. Statistically, immigrants and their children are responsible for 90 percent of the population growth in the United States since 1995.[5] Western images convey alluring images of plush homes, immaculate lawns, and gleaming cars for all who make it to American borders. The perception of a relatively generous welfare system also increases the attractiveness of America in the immigration market, particularly for those most likely to qualify for public assistance. Confirming white nationalists' sense that numbers of immigrant populations are growing at an unparalleled rate, recent average yearly immigration levels are higher now than during the "Great Wave" of immigrants at the turn of the twentieth century.[6] Only 923,000

---

[2] David A. Bositis, "Redistricting and Minority Representation," Joint Center for Political and Economic Studies (1998): 5.

[3] George A. Fredrickson, *White Supremacy: A Comparative Study in American and South African History* (New York: Oxford University Press, 1981), xi.

[4] Ron Unz, "California and the End of White America," *Commentary*, November 1999: 12.

[5] Roy Beck, *The Case Against Immigration* (New York: Norton, 1996).

[6] Website for the Federation for American Immigration Reform, www.fairus.org.

immigrants were admitted in the years 1901–14.[7] During 1998, according to the census bureau, 660,477 immigrants legally entered and settled in the United States; in the same year, approximately 275,000 immigrants settled and stayed illegally.[8] Due to post-1970 immigration, the United States' population in 2050 is projected to be 392 million.[9]

The United States Bureau of the Census reports that over a period of ten years, the true population of Mexican-born immigrants increased to nearly 2.2 million.[10] Using reports like these, some white nationalist groups are trying to motivate potential recruits by presenting whites in the United States as people who are drowning in a sea of immigration. Whether such statistics themselves affect a nation's perception is not clear; however, it is clear that the United States has taken note of a burgeoning immigrant populace. In 1995, some 72 percent of those polled "worry that overpopulation will be a serious problem in the next 25–50 years" in the United States, up from 65 percent in 1991.[11] It is also not a coincidence that the increasing level of immigration during those years corresponds with the jump in the number of people concerned about overpopulation, although few people have spoken about this possible link directly.[12]

The impact of immigration on American citizens is real and direct. Political scientist and population researcher Virginia Abernathy identifies a decreasing quality of life and an increasing cost of living as additional indicators of overpopulation in the United States.[13] She cites the rising costs of garbage disposal, gasoline, water, and other resources as evidence that too many people consume the resources.[14] Between 1970 and 1990, per capita energy use stayed the same, yet total use increased by 24 percent. According to Abernathy, 93 percent of this increase is a product of population growth.[15] As immigrants enter the American

---

[7] Ibid.   [8] United States Census Bureau, Washington, D.C., 1999.
[9] www.fairus.org.
[10] John Abowd and Richard Freeman, eds., "Immigration, Trade, and the Labor Market," National Bureau of Economic Research Project Report (Chicago: University of Chicago Press, 1991), 79.
[11] Website for the Negative Population Growth organization, www.npg.org. Poll data is available at www.npg.org/roper.
[12] Lawrence Auster, The Path to National Suicide: An Essay on Immigration and Multiculturalism (Monterey, Va.: American Immigration Control Foundation, 1990), 7–8.
[13] Virginia Abernathy, Population Politics (New York: Plenum Press, 1993), 246.
[14] Ibid.   [15] Ibid., 252.

economy and society, they assume a highly consumption-oriented American lifestyle, and thus contribute heavily to the use of resources at an even faster rate.

Statistics, however, can sometimes be misleading. Most counties with a booming growth in the Hispanic population still have relatively small numbers of Hispanics, and they typically are a tiny fraction of the county's total population.[16] In the late 1990s, there were only twenty-one counties in the United States that could genuinely qualify as racially diverse, meaning that these counties had at least two minority groups whose percentage of the county population is greater than that of the national population and have a white population with lower than average representation.[17] Consequently, the majority of American communities lack true ethnic diversity, and the United States has only a few melting pots with a significant presence of two or more minority groups. These areas include "gateway" cities where immigrants tend to arrive and stay (e.g., Los Angeles, New York City, and San Francisco) as well as other large metropolitan areas like San Diego, Houston, Chicago, and Washington, D.C.[18]

Data on both immigrant growth and immigrant clustering suggest that statistics on this subject – especially on the effects that immigration and demographic changes have on the American population as a whole – can be confusing, unclear, and inconsistent. Different scholars of immigration can construe identical studies in completely different ways; furthermore, scholars can often point to conflicting studies that challenge the validity of any one particular study on the impact of immigration. For example, one study, by William Frey, reports that immigrant workers are markedly displacing native blue-collar workers. In contrast, David Jacobson, an editor of a labor and immigration handbook, quotes another study to make the opposite point. Frey reports that his studies consistently indicate that "poor and unskilled segments of the population . . . [are] responsive to the pressures of labor competition exerted by immigrants."[19] Jacobson asserts that "there are only modest effects of immigrants on natives' labor market

[16] William Frey, "The Diversity Myth," *American Demographics* (June 1998): 42.
[17] Ibid. [18] Ibid., 39.
[19] William Frey, "Immigration, Domestic Migration, and Demographic Balkanization in America: New Evidence for the 1990s," *Population and Development Review* 22 (December 1996): 756.

outcomes."[20] Because even scholars come to different conclusions regarding the impact of immigration in the United States, average informed citizens may not know what to believe about immigration, a position that could make some whites prime targets for the demagoguery of the more reasoned intellectuals in the white nationalist movement.

Changes in the demographics of the country have also begun to affect the strategic calculations of all major racial and ethnic groups. Americans continue to ground their identity in race and ancestry and are moving to parts of the country where that racial identity serves them best. The 1990 census showed that whites are "leaving most of the high immigration metropolitan areas."[21] In fact, "white flight" remains a documented reality in American society; indeed, it may be the most dramatic example of the demographic trends mentioned. According to demographer William Frey and journalist Jonathan Tilove, "[W]hites this time are not just fleeing the cities for the suburbs. They are leaving entire metropolitan areas and states – whole regions – for whiter destinations. . . . The whites leaving high-immigration areas are those most likely to be competing with immigrants for jobs, space, and cultural primacy."[22] Fleeing are those working-class whites who cannot afford to live in gated communities or send their children to private schools. In other words, those in direct economic competition with nonwhites are the ones moving most rapidly to whiter states. Almost naturally, a partitioning of the country is occurring as groups self-segregate.

WHITE FLIGHT

Most of the high-immigration states show negative results for internal migration during the early 1990s. Furthermore, in states where there has been an immigration inflow, there has also been a native outflow.[23] In fact, the most prominent high-immigration areas (Los Angeles, New York City, San Francisco, Chicago) show a consistent outmigration vis-

---

[20] David Jacobson, ed., *The Immigration Reader* (Malden, Mass.: Blackwell, 1998).

[21] Frey, *Population and Development Review*, 755.

[22] William Frey and Jonathan Tilove, "Immigrants in, Native Whites Out," *New York Times Magazine*, August 20, 1995, pp. 44–45.

[23] Frey, *Population and Development Review*, 755.

à-vis other parts of the country over the 1985–95 period.[24] Immigration may indeed be exerting an impact on all domestic migration, not just labor sectors. Central to our understanding of white flight is the distinction between the types of areas that are gaining from immigration and those gaining from native migration. The preference for smaller, nonmetropolitan areas in the first half of the 1990s was dominated by movements of internal migrants.[25] This white movement out of the urban center may indeed be because of the immigrant influx to these areas. There is a unique and consistent pattern of outmigration among high-school dropouts and lower income residents away from most high-immigration metropolitan areas and high-immigration states; moreover, the same pattern exists for high school and college graduates.[26]

The general pattern of outmigration shown by Frey in 1995 is unlike the "circulation of elites" characterization that has been typically applied to interstate migration.[27] Usually, states that are losing migrants because of economic downturns lose them disproportionately among their college-graduate or more well-off segments of the younger population. In like manner, states that are gaining internal migrants gain them disproportionately from these groups. The unique pattern of selective outmigration shown for most of these states during both the late 1980s and early 1990s is consistent with the explanation that links immigration to some domestic outmigration.[28]

Segregation and a reluctance to live among people of different races and cultures is a fact of life even in California, the state where whites responded to their impending minority status (since 1998, no longer impending but a reality) by passing restrictive measures such as Proposition 209, which ended affirmative action in state-supported programs, and Proposition 187, which greatly restricted services to undocumented immigrants.[29] Furthermore, according to commentator Dale Maharidge, many whites are choosing isolation and are starting to resemble Third World elites.[30] Census data also suggests that the

---

[24] Ibid. These patterns are also consistent with Garret Hardin's well-documented assertions that immigration exerts a tangible impact on domestic migration patterns. See Garrett Hardin, *Living Within Limits* (New York: Oxford, 1993).

[25] Ibid.   [26] Ibid.   [27] Ibid., 756.   [28] Ibid.   [29] Unz, 1.

[30] Dale Maharidge, *The Coming White Minority: California, Multiculturalism, and America's Future* (New York: Vintage Books, 1996).

"white islands" in California south of Sacramento and San Francisco may be the future residential patterns for other regions, as the percentage of nonwhites increases throughout America.[31]

Growing metropolitan areas across the nation suggest that whites are attracted to a different set of places than new immigrant minorities. By the year 2025, twelve states will have populations that are less than 60 percent white. At the same time, twelve states will have white populations that will exceed 85 percent. Between these extremes lie mostly southern states, which have large white and black populations.[32] Most minorities reside in metropolitan areas, so the white movement out of the urban center may be precisely because of this influx of minorities and immigrants to urban areas. As of 1996, close to 95 percent of Asians, more than 91 percent of Hispanics, and greater than 85 percent of blacks resided in metropolitan areas, and the majority of these groups were located in metropolitan areas with more than 1 million in population.[33] Cities now house disproportionate numbers of the population subgroups, which are subject to high arrest and victimization rates.[34] The cumulative redistribution of white residences and jobs out of the urban center has led to a lower quality of life for native minorities remaining in these areas.[35]

USURPING NATIVE WORKERS

There is a continued clustering of foreign-born immigrants into a few multiethnic urban areas, as native born and longer-term residents (white and black) disperse to new employment opportunities in other parts of the country. Evidence from the early 1990s indicates a continued domestic outmigration from high-immigration areas that is accentuated among low-income, less-skilled residents.[36] As demographer William Frey notes, "[b]ecause new immigration is heavily drawn from developing countries in Latin America and Asia and consists dis-

---

[31] United States Census Bureau, Washington, D.C., 1999.
[32] William Frey, "New Demographic Divide in the United States: Immigrant and Domestic 'Migrant Magnets,'" *Public Perspective* 9 (June/July 1998): 38.
[33] Frey, *American Demographics*, 43.
[34] William Frey, "Central City White Flight," *American Sociological Review* 44 (June 1979): 428, 436.
[35] Ibid., 426.
[36] Frey, *Population and Development Review*, 754.

proportionately of the less well-off and relatively unskilled, the current debate has focused on the economic consequences for native born workers, taxpayers, and government programs."[37] Relatively low-skilled immigrants provide competition for jobs with poorly educated long-term and native-born residents, and therefore serve to bid down their wages and take away employment opportunities. In Los Angeles, for example, foreign-born workers fill more than half of unskilled blue-collar jobs, but hold no more than one-fifth of the managerial and professional jobs.[38] Central city workers are more and more unable to find alternative city jobs when theirs are lost, ostensibly to growing immigrant populations. This trend seems likely to continue because a dual economy, polarized by both race and class, could make it more difficult for less well-off immigrants to follow the social mobility path taken by immigrants in an earlier era.

In "Searching for the Effect of Immigration on the Labor Market," demographic researchers George Borjas, Richard Freeman, and Lawrence Katz compared changes in native wages in an area over time, and they estimated the impact of immigrants on the earnings of natives in an area.[39] They produced evidence that comparisons by area understate the potential effect immigration-induced increases in labor supply have on lowering native wages; furthermore, in looking at the nation as a whole, rather than simply smaller metropolitan areas, they found greater depressant effects induced by the presence of immigrants.[40] They confirmed that it is primarily the less-educated natives whose lifestyles are affected negatively by immigrants; for example, immigration has been important in reducing the pay of native high school dropouts.[41]

Anger over immigrant influx and its effect on the labor market surfaced early in the development of the United States. As early as 1913, Frank Julian Warne, echoing Thomas Malthus, recognized that low standards of living would drive out higher standards of living.[42] Warne wrote, "[T]his economic law is controlled by the more recent immigrant because of his immediate necessity to secure employment and

---

[37] Ibid., 741.   [38] Ibid., 759.
[39] George Borjas, Richard Freeman, and Lawrence Katz, "Searching for the Effect of Immigration on the Labor Market," *American Economic Association Papers and Proceedings* (May 1996): 247.
[40] Ibid., 250.   [41] Ibid.   [42] www.fairus.org.

high ability to sell his labor at a low price to work for a low wage. Against the operation of this law, the native worker and the earlier immigrant are unable to defend themselves."[43] Current immigration policy gives priority to family reunification, so immigration from foreign countries occurs in "chains" to familial common destinations.[44] This is especially the case for lower-skilled immigrants, which has even more prominent implications for lower-skilled natives in these areas. Within this type of demographic dynamic, displacement is inevitable.

Direct immigrant competition with Americans for jobs affects blacks and Hispanics the most, as their rates of unemployment are above the national average; in 2000, the overall unemployment rate was 4.0 percent, the rate for whites was 3.5 percent, the rate for Hispanics was 5.7 percent, and the rate for blacks was 7.6 percent.[45] Nonunionized Hispanics and other immigrant groups have, in many areas, replaced unionized blacks. Furthermore, the presence of a large immigrant work force accustomed to conditions and wages of developing countries deflates wages and drives Americans out of entire industries.

Companies would simply rather use large numbers of immigrant laborers, willing to work long hours at lesser wages, than focus on individual worker productivity and employ fewer natives at high wages.[46] The average wage for legal migrant workers in rural areas is $9.54, while illegals make only $5.98.[47] Ironically, one of the most strident supporters of tougher immigration laws and more secure borders is the United Farm Workers Union, once led by the great labor activist César Chávez. During a 1966 Chavez-led melon worker strike to bring wages over $1 per hour, the company simply hired workers straight from Mexico.[48] This happens on a much larger scale in the entire industry, and no groups realize it more than those competing with legal and illegal immigrants for jobs. Hispanics as a whole, in fact, disproportionately support tougher immigration laws: 67 percent, according to

---

[43] Ibid.   [44] Ibid.

[45] Data is available through the Bureau of Labor Statistics Database at the United States Department of Labor, www.dol.gov.

[46] Mary Brown, *Shapers of the Great Debate on Immigration* (Westport, Conn.: Greenwood Press, 1999).

[47] George Borjas, *Friends or Strangers* (New York: Basic Books, 1990).

[48] Brown, 241.

a 1995 Roper poll.[49] An Agriculture Department study commissioned by President Bush in 1992 may help to explain why. The report found that during peak season, there were around 1 million farmworker jobs available, while 2.5 million people are farmworkers, many of them recent immigrants.[50] During the last eight years, the rate of immigration has only climbed, adding to the labor surplus. Labor economist Marshall Berry finds that now "we have three farm-workers for every farm-worker job."[51]

More recently, focus has shifted from immigrants in the agricultural sector to their "necessity" to the continued growth of the United States technology sector. Although the number of skilled immigrants pales in comparison to the number of unskilled and uneducated ones, the problem remains the same. As in the agricultural business, lax immigration policies are supported by the tech companies, and the oversupply of labor justifies their paying lower wages for longer hours. One in four research personnel at IBM's Yorktown Heights lab and two in five researchers at Bell Labs have immigrated to the United States, while many native engineers and programmers sit idle.[52] Reggie Aggarwal, the chief executive of Cvent, stated in a *Washington Post* article that one reason he hires immigrants is "they work long hours."[53] A professor of computer science at the University of California at Davis, Norman Matloff, says of the hiring policies of tech companies: "Their low hiring rates show they're not desperate. Most of them are trying to save money. They don't want to hire older workers who are perceived to cost more."[54]

In almost every sector, large companies manipulate United States immigration policy in order to maintain an oversupply of labor, much to the detriment of Americans. The new H-1B work visa program is the most recent example of this. At the present rate, 710,000 immigrants will be allowed into the United States on work visas by 2003, with the possibility of resident status and citizenship.[55] These immigrants arguably compete directly with Americans for the mostly

[49] www.npg.org/roper.
[50] Roy Beck, *The Case Against Immigration* (New York: Norton, 1996), 121.
[51] Ibid.   [52] Ibid., 138.
[53] Kenneth Bredemeier, "Work Visas Swell Area's Tech Corps," *Washington Post*, December 1, 2000.
[54] Ibid., 4.   [55] Ibid.

technical jobs they will occupy. As Representative Thomas Davis of Virginia said, "This bill may not be popular with the public, but it's popular with the CEO's."[56]

DEMOGRAPHIC BALKANIZATION

Increasingly multicultural cities, where immigrant influx and native outflow account for most of the demographic change, will differ greatly in social dimensions from the increasingly white suburbs. As a result, a clear-cut "demographic balkanization" is occurring. As William Frey notes, "[d]istinct patterns of immigration and internal migration, along with evidence that an 'immigrant push' may be operating in several high immigration areas, appear to be laying groundwork for sharper geographic disparities in demographic composition for the United States population. The post 1965 immigrants differ distinctly from such native-born United States population on characteristics such as race, age, and skill level. A continued concentration of recent immigrants and foreign-born residents, coupled with the more dispersed migration patterns of long-term residents, suggests emerging social and economic divisions between the port-of-entry metropolitan areas and other parts of the country."[57]

The old city–suburb paradigm may transform into a more regionally based distinction, in the sense that an entire area's demographics will come to define its culture, lifestyles, and political preferences. Racial and ethnic diversity may come to determine politics and policy by area. As diversity increases, a bifurcation of policy occurs. Therefore, growing numbers of racial and ethnic minority populations are having a significant effect on public policy. National policy issues such as preserving affirmative action, or ensuring that the Social Security pension funds remain solvent, are already taking on region-based constituencies. Issues that are already hotly contested become even more divisive in the context of social balkanization.

A complex regression analysis done by two scholars from the University of Colorado at Boulder, Rodney Hero and Caroline Tolbert, confirms that racial and ethnic diversity explains much of the state-by-state variation in political culture. Their findings support two conclu-

---

[56] Ibid.   [57] Frey, *Population and Development Review*, 756–7.

sions: First, that whites are moving to areas where there are more whites and less diversity and, second, that an area's politics can be defined by its race representation.[58] Therefore, based on these conclusions, one can readily see how the thriving politics of white nationalism can feed off of the growing trend of "white flight."

Such assertions are further borne out in several statistical indications of social and political balkanization that Hero and Tolbert present. One indication of this balkanization is the treatment of the poor and minorities in homogeneous states: Policies for minorities are especially poor in homogeneous states, and the disparity in the lifestyles of immigrants as compared with native whites is most pronounced in the most homogeneous states.[59] For example, infant mortality rates among minorities in such homogeneous states as Minnesota and Iowa are over twice the overall state average.[60] Furthermore, as state minority levels increase, immigrants and minorities have higher graduation rates. Homogeneous states with small minority populations generally have lower minority graduation rates and higher suspension ratios. These effects serve only to solidify notions of racial superiority among the white population and provide useful fodder for the recruitment campaigns of white nationalist groups.

So, despite the success of the civil rights movement and the passage of time, white Americans continue to show a penchant for living among themselves and avoiding ethnically diverse neighbors. What exists in California and the rest of the country is evidence that integration and multiculturalism have not worked as expected. Instead, just as historian Arthur M. Schlesinger, Jr., warned almost a decade ago, we have a country that is dividing itself into competing, rival groups. "Unless," as he argues, "a common purpose binds them together, tribal hostilities will drive them apart. Ethnic and racial conflict, it seems evident, will replace the conflict of ideologies as the explosive issue of our times."[61]

Political scientist Russell Nieli also calls into question America's policy on immigration by identifying a distinction between tribalism

---

[58] Rodney E. Hero and Caroline J. Tolbert, "A Racial/Ethnic Diversity Interpretation of Politics and Policy in the States of the U.S.," *American Journal of Political Science* 40 (August 1996): 868.

[59] Ibid., 860–1.   [60] Ibid., 864.

[61] Arthur M. Schlesinger, Jr., *The Disuniting of America: Reflections on a Multicultural Society* (New York: W. W. Norton, 1998), 10.

and personalism.[62] He defines tribalism as "that mode of consciousness that tends to view human beings, not as unique persons, but as stereotyped and depersonalized representatives of larger racial and ethnic collectives, with the collectives themselves seen as singular or homogeneous entities, rather than plural or diverse ones; in contrast, personalism is a mode of consciousness that seeks to view human beings as distinct and unique individuals ('persons'), who are capable of relating to, and communing with, others of their kind on the basis of mutual respect and equality."[63] What has happened, he argues, is that tribalism has come to dominate the country under the leadership of a national elite who has enshrined it into public policy, under the guise of furthering civil rights.[64]

After observing the migratory patterns of white Americans, white nationalists have launched a volley of criticisms against groups and individuals who continue to encourage multiculturalism. Jared Taylor points out that hypocrisy among elites is all too common:

> Just about every elected official in America, every talking head on television, every self-righteous editorial writer has chanted the mantra of integration so many times, he can recite it in his sleep. But where do these people live? Where do their children go to school? Whom do they invite to their dinner parties? Whom do they marry and urge their children to marry?
>
> They don't actually live and go to school and socialize with these wonderful black people and wonderful Mexicans and Nigerians and Pakistanis. No, integration is a splendid thing – so splendid that they insist that others should enjoy it while they nobly forgo the benefits. This is the smelly little consensus that our country's elites have quietly arrived at. Integration is our goal – but not for me, and my friends and my children.[65]

Michael Hart has made a similar observation about the disjuncture between the rhetoric of white liberals and their behavioral patterns:

> Recently, I went to a birthday party of a friend of mine in New York, a person who is very liberal and very integrationist, and one who has never

---

[62] Russell Nieli, ed., *Racial Preferences and Racial Justice* (Washington, D.C.: Ethics and Public Policy Center, 1991), 67.

[63] Ibid.   [64] Ibid., 68.

[65] Jared Taylor, ed., *The Real American Dilemma: Race, Immigration, and the Future of America* (Oakton, Va.: New Century Books, 1998), 46–7.

in his life said anything derogatory about blacks or Hispanics, and who feels no enmity against them in his heart. But I did a little counting. There were 54 people at the party, and all 54 were white! And that was in New York City, the very heartland of the melting pot. Just look at Bill and Hillary Clinton. They constantly talk about the glories of diversity. But when they moved to New York, they chose to move not to nice, diverse Manhattan, but rather to Chappaqua, one of the most lily-white towns in the whole country. But it is unfair to say that the Clintons are different than other whites in this regard. Whites of all political persuasions tend to avoid living in areas with too much "diversity."[66]

David Duke takes this theme even further with an attack on the ability of the Anti-Defamation League (ADL) to maintain respectability while essentially condoning and encouraging white supremacy amongst Jews. He argues that "the ADL supports forced integration of schools, neighborhoods, apartment complexes, clubs, churches, and communities in America, [y]et, it supports Israel which has a policy of segregated schools, neighborhoods, apartment complexes, and even whole towns for Jews and Gentiles." The ADL has been "instrumental in changing America's immigration policies that will result in European Americans becoming a minority by the middle of this century. Yet, the ADL supports Israel, which has a 'Jews Only' immigration policy."[67]

Not only have whites that can afford to do so segregated themselves into physical and cultural enclaves, some have become racial activists. This trend seems likely to continue, particularly as white nationalist groups increase their recruitment efforts. Perhaps most disturbing are the views of average Americans who increasingly traffic in stereotypes about minorities and immigrants, a practice that makes them especially receptive to the calls of white nationalist groups. Dale Maharidge reports that a constituent in a white enclave wrote the racist ditty below, which a Republican state legislator distributed to Republicans at the state capitol in Sacramento:

> Everything is mucho good.
> We own the neighborhood

---

[66] Michael H. Hart, interview.

[67] David Duke Online, "Behind the Mask of Respectability: The Truth About the Anti-Defamation League of B'nai B'rith," http://www.duke.org/adl/index.html.

We have a hobby – it's called breeding
Welfare pay for baby feeding.

The poem, purposely ungrammatical, continued, "Thanks American working dummy," and

Write to friends in motherland,
Tell them to come as fast as can.
They come in rags and Chebby trucks,
I can buy big house with welfare bucks.

As the poem went on it showed the immigrant's house packed with 14 families until

Finally, white guy moves away . . .
We think America damn good place.
Too damn good for white man race.
If they no like us, they can go.
Got lots of room in Mexico.[68]

GENERAL HOSTILITY TOWARD IMMIGRATION

Statistical proof of growing numbers of immigrants and the declining majority of white groups, coupled with social change that foretells lost jobs and lost political capital for whites, catalyzes a general hostility toward immigration among major segments of the white population. Don Black, leader of the white nationalist organization Stormfront, typifies this hostility toward immigration:

INTERVIEWER: You have expressed strong disapproval of both antidiscrimination policies on the part of the state, as well as affirmative action policies – policies of racial and ethnic preferences. Are these the government policies that you find most galling and most destructive, or are there other government policies which you find harmful . . . harmful to race relations?

BLACK: The government policy we find most detrimental in the long term, of course, is the government's immigration policy, in which Third World immigrants are allowed to come to this country, either legally or illegally. Of course, these millions of people who come here every year have resulted in many parts of the United States coming to resemble a

---

[68] Maharidge, 160–1.

Third World country. Of course, this is the kind of thing that's much more difficult to reverse than just a set of laws, such as affirmative action and other laws of that type. So immigration would be the single most destructive policy that's implemented by the government.[69]

Millions worry that immigration is rapidly transforming America into a Third World country, with crowded, violent cities, under-educated and low-skilled labor, and an ethnic spoils system replacing America's tradition of constitutionalism and individual rights. White nationalist groups may evoke comparisons to South Africa, or even Bosnia, to arouse suspicions of social tensions resulting from surges of different languages and ethnic groups. To fend off claims that immigration works in Europe, white nationalists are quick to point out that in Europe, too, immigration is often seen as a burden on welfare and a threat to national identities already threatened by globalization.

Besides removing employment opportunities for low-skilled natives, large numbers of resident Americans may hold the perception, correct or not, that the new immigrants contribute to a variety of social costs, including higher crime rates, reduced services, or increased taxes, that imply greater out-of-pocket expenses for the poor or middle class. Support for California's Proposition 187, which would restrict illegal immigrants' access to state services, showed that the perceived immigrant burden is widespread. Furthermore, this worry that recent immigrants contribute disproportionately to crime, welfare dependency, and social decay, and that their non-European origins will exacerbate America's growing ethnic strife, can eventually lead to separatist ethnic nationalism.

The building antagonism against growing minority populations and, more important, immigrants, has developed into a new generation's sentiment. When the interviewer asked Lisa Turner, Women's Information Coordinator of the World Church of the Creator, whether she grew up in a white supremacist family, she replied:

No, I did not. I would say that my family in my growing up years would probably be termed liberal – they voted for the Kennedys and that type of thing. Certainly I was never exposed to any racial views growing up. However, there was a turning point within my family in which we found

[69] Don Black, interview.

ourselves living in a neighborhood across the street from a house that was being used as an illegal alien safe house. At any given time, there might be ten or fifteen Mexican males in residence at this house, and this was when we were living in Southern California. For the first time, we realized that there was an immigration problem in this country. Prior to that time, we had no idea within our family that there was any kind of out-of-control immigration situation, and while my parents did not become, shall we say, radical prowhite activists, they did become involved in immigration reform. I went on and became, I guess in their view, more of a radical activist. But they, too, understood and recognized that there were problems in this country that needed to be recognized and faced, so I guess what you could say is that when we actually had a real-life experience in our own face, in our own family, our family did acquire a certain racial consciousness. So even though I was not raised that way, we did sort of evolve that way later on.[70]

According to a Roper Starch survey conducted in 1995, a majority of the public similarly perceives growing numbers of immigrants as threats to the stability of America; in fact, 72 percent of those surveyed said that overpopulation will pose a major problem in 25 to 50 years.[71] Additionally, 83 percent of respondents favored a reduction in immigration, 20 percent of those favored a total moratorium on immigration, and 74 percent of the total group favored a tough program to control illegal immigration.[72] In a survey of white and black Americans, 79 percent of whites and 70 percent of blacks claimed that new immigrants ought to take responsibility for working their way up without any special favors.[73] In other words, most Americans do not object to preferential treatment for veterans or for those who have disabilities, but they firmly draw the line when it comes to immigrants.

African-American citizens, in particular, feel threatened by surges of immigrants, especially because of their impact on affirmative action. Blacks in the United States interpret rising percentages of immigrants as endangering their livelihood and their access to opportunity. Ricky Gaull Silverman, vice-chairman of the Equal Employment Opportunity Commission, labeled immigrant participation in affirmative action as "the ultimate nightmare of affirmative action. It is its

---

[70] Lisa Turner, interview.   [71] www.npg.org/roper.   [72] Ibid.   [73] Ibid.

Achilles heel."[74] Hugh Graham succinctly summarizes the tensions that have emerged between African Americans and immigrants over the past two decades:

> For the Black urban poor, whose lives were largely untouched by affirmative action programs, the economic effects of large-scale immigration have been overwhelmingly negative. On balance, immigrant participation in affirmative action programs has been destabilizing. Historically, African American leaders, such as Frederick Douglass, Booker T. Washington, and W. E. B. Du Bois, had opposed importing cheap foreign-born labor to compete with native-born workers. But the 1960's encouraged a new "people of color" solidarity that paid political dividends for a generation. The immigrant success ethos, however, with its emphasis on hard work, merit, and social assimilation, clashed with hard affirmative action's emphasis on historic victimhood, reparations, and racial entitlement. These tensions were underlined in the 1990's. . . .[75]

In urban areas, these tensions between blacks and immigrants play out along economic lines, as illustrated by the experiences of George Burns, a black pastor of Christ Temple North, an inner-city church in Nashville, Tennessee. Burns notes that "Hispanics are playing the same role in the economy that African Americans once played 30 years ago. Often employers would hire blacks because blacks would work much cheaper than whites. Now Hispanics are displacing blacks in many jobs. Hispanics will work for $7.00 an hour for a job for which blacks and whites expect $12.00."[76] What Burns sees and hears in his conversations with African Americans in Nashville is an increased threat to their job security from Hispanics willing to work longer hours for less money. Even if this is the American way, the competition for jobs between blacks and Hispanics and poorly educated whites creates tensions between blacks and Hispanics and between whites and Hispanics. Moreover, it also creates incentives for employers to exploit the labor situation to no good end for blacks, whites, or Hispanics.

In addition to concerns about becoming economically disadvantaged because of immigration, many African Americans also firmly adhere to

---

[74] Hugh Graham, "Unintended Consequences: The Convergence of Affirmative Action and Immigration Policy," *American Behavioral Policy* 41 (April 1998): 899.
[75] Ibid., 910.   [76] George Burns, interview, April 11, 2001.

the belief that the U.S. government favors newly arrived immigrants over them in the administration of government benefits. Additionally, there is another source of disjunction between African-American civil rights activists and immigration advocates: opposing roles for government. Civil rights activists seek an expanded regulatory state, while immigration reformers want to dismantle a tight regulatory regime.[77]

Immigrants' mobility and relative success lead some African-American residents in low-income communities to wonder exactly who is American and who makes up the rules of the mobility gain. What is at once puzzling and disconcerting for many black residents is that immigrants often achieve economic success without having to acculturate. These feelings often boil over into antipathy and sometimes lead to black boycotts of immigrant-owned businesses. Black boycotts of Korean or Jewish businesses transcend preferences for individual retailers and become emblematic of the larger issue of whether blacks should have primary economic control over black communities.

Moreover, intergroup conflict also appears to be more prevalent in low-income black neighborhoods, where segregation and racial and ethnic inequality are more extreme. Increasing ethnic violence results from black xenophobia and criminal pathologies which exist in many black neighborhoods, in addition to black proximity to immigrant areas. Popular rap songs have focused on subjects like burning down all the Korean shops in black neighborhoods, and popular movies, such as Spike Lee's controversial *Do the Right Thing*, which featured an attempt by a black man to destroy a Korean grocery store amid a larger riot, also illustrate rising tensions between black and immigrant communities. Moreover, the media has consistently failed to report or emphasize the large numbers of rapes and murders committed by blacks against Asians, many of which look suspiciously like so-called hate crimes.

Much of the citizen anger and antigovernment sentiment that surfaced in the 1990s may be related to ethnic and racial change. A study in 1994 found that votes for H. Ross Perot in the 1992 presidential election were related to voter anger; a 1996 study then found that minority diversity was strongly correlated to a state's votes for Perot.[78] As minority diversity in a state increased, so, too, did numbers of white

[77] Graham, 901.   [78] Hero and Tolbert, 866.

votes for Perot; therefore, burgeoning diversity may induce white voter anger.

Lawrence Auster, author of *The Path to National Suicide: An Essay on Immigration and Multiculturalism*, also predicts increasing support for nascent white nationalist movements, precisely because generalized hostility toward immigration is becoming more common: "[The immigration issue] will be decided by an aroused American public who are looking at reality with their own eyes, who see their nation and way of life vanishing, and who resolve, finally, to do something about it."[79] In other words, whites who feel threatened by immigration, fueled by white nationalist rhetoric, may one day take matters into their own hands to "solve" America's immigration issues.

DISCUSSION

White nationalists are both frustrated and encouraged by policy action on immigration to the United States. Though current policies are chaotic at best, white nationalists view a regulatory freeze on immigration as one possible government solution to the problem of preserving their majority status. Using the aforementioned societal problems as the cornerstone of their platform for white domination and an end to immigration, white nationalists find agreement with their stance on immigration from a wide variety of sources. As one first-year student at a top-tier university stated in an opinion paper, "the United States would benefit greatly from a complete moratorium on immigration and a strong program to control our borders."[80] Even Peter Brimelow, a senior editor at *Forbes* magazine, has stated that "[t]he most amazing thing about current immigration policy is that it serves no economic purpose. It does nothing for Americans they could not do themselves."[81] Thus, even some of America's current and future elite agree with white nationalist leaders that immigration into the United States should be stopped.

Again, there is evidence that a similar reality existed early in America's history and that the issues arising during that history are

[79] Lawrence Auster, "Them vs. Unz," Special Letters Section, *Policy Review* (Fall 1994): 88.

[80] Aldo Dyer, "Immigration Policy: Close the Floodgates," unpublished paper, Vanderbilt University, December 5, 2000.

[81] Beck, 105.

repeating themselves today. For example, the "Anti-Alien Contract Labor Law" was passed in 1885 as a symbolic measure with which to appease domestic workers while not interfering with the labor supply. A century later, the employer sanctions provision of the Immigration Reform and Control Act repeats this pattern. In other words, the inability of Congress to respond effectively to immigration problems has less to do with the difficulties of finding a solution than it does with arriving at a consensus regarding what the true problem is.

Further confounding any attempt at a governmental solution is the nature of political debates over the immigration issue. Although controlling immigration is typically seen as a core element of the Republican Party's platform – and Republican political candidates often seize on it as an issue in high-immigration states as a way of pandering to white voters – Republican supporters are not the only political group that favors stricter immigration policies. Indeed, African Americans, union members, and even environmentalists are all generally opposed to increased immigration, and all three groups are core constituencies of the Democratic Party, especially its more liberal wing. Thus, both leading parties in the United States appear to be in tacit agreement on limiting immigration, but this political agreement has served only to prevent an open and honest dialogue on immigration and provided a political cloak under which white nationalist groups can present their views on immigration without appearing out of the mainstream.

Historically, even American Presidents have shown proclivities toward restricting immigration in the name of protecting native resources, although such rhetoric might be too politically incorrect for a President to utter today, even though his party may tacitly believe it to be true. For example, President Woodrow Wilson admonished that "America is sauntering through her resources . . . with an easy nonchalance; but presently there will come a time when she will be surprised to find herself grown old – a country crowded, strained, perplexed – when she will be obliged to pull herself together, husband her resources, concentrate her strength, steady her methods, sober her views, restrict her vagaries."[82] More recently, John F. Kennedy joined President Woodrow Wilson in his skepticism regarding our ability as

---

[82] Abernathy, 7.

a nation to grow unchecked. In *A Nation of Immigrants*, he wrote that "[t]here is, of course, a legitimate argument for some limitation upon immigration. We no longer need settlers for virgin lands, and our economy is expanding more slowly than in the nineteenth century and early twentieth centuries."[83]

Almost all critics of a more open immigration policy in America incvitably use white nationalist rhetoric in their tone and implication. They claim socially damaging policy stems from the uncontrolled influx of immigrant populations. Surges in immigration coupled with the perception of the scarce availability of political resources produce the opportunity for intergroup conflict. In other words, immigration results in political opportunities for the growing minorities, and this dynamic can initiate an outbreak of collective action from both a threatened majority and a well-entrenched already-present minority.

Critics argue that the policy that both applies to and is influenced by immigrants tends to be inextricably linked to social breakdown. Government programs that financially support immigrants bear much of the blame for rising intergroup conflict. Additionally, state-sponsored affirmative action, bilingual education, and multiculturalism are promoting dangerous levels of tensions. These tensions are fueled by white nationalists seeking to place further restrictions on immigration, and unless an appropriate outlet can be found through which to resolve immigration issues with both whites and blacks who feel threatened, violence on a national scale may ensue.

White nationalist groups equate rising immigration populations with the growth of America's welfare state. Escalating welfare costs for the foreign-born population generates pressures for Congress to respond to their constituents' concerns about an unrestrained immigrant population. Congress has alternately responded by proposing, and at times enacting, welfare reforms that share a common feature of either further severely restricting or eliminating entirely the eligibility of legal immigrants for the major means-tested federal entitlement programs. These reforms not only have fiscal implications, but they also dramatically reshape the meaning of permanent membership in United States society. As David Jacobson has noted, "[i]mminent changes in welfare policy would dramatically reorder the relationship of

[83] Ibid.

immigrants to the social welfare state. . . . If enacted, they would move the nation closer to an explicit immigrant policy, but it would be a policy of exclusion, not inclusion."[84]

Prominent political leader Barbara Jordan brought explicit national political attention to immigrant issues in 1995. As she noted in a *New York Times* editorial, her chairwomanship of the United States Commission on Immigration Reform produced bipartisan legislation to "curb illegal immigration."[85] Jordan, a former U.S. representative, touted "Americanization," the becoming a part of the American polity, as the process by which immigration could be welcomed in policy; furthermore, she argued that a common language, civic teaching, and naturalization are vital components of the steps to becoming "American."[86] Ironically, Jordan's views on immigration reform were not that different from those espoused by the far right, and the political rhetoric on this issue demonstrates how easy it is for white nationalist views to dovetail with the majority consensus, a development that could have very dangerous ramifications in the future.

In addition to concerns about welfare costs and assimilation, perhaps the strongest tension regarding immigration involves its impact on affirmative action. Alleviating the tension between policies regarding immigration and affirmative action, however, is made extremely difficult by the fact that few people agree on how Americans should be classified in their relationships to these policies. Two recent *New York Times* pieces illustrate this problem as they raise questions about the social and political interpretations of recent census data. According to an analysis by the Center on Urban and Metropolitan Policy at the Brookings Institution, non-Hispanic whites are now a minority in America's 100 largest urban centers.[87] This suggests the importance of accommodating, both socially and politically, the large influx of minorities into urban areas, especially Hispanics, whose population in the 100 largest urban areas increased 43 percent over the past

---

[84] Jacobson, *The Immigration Reader.*
[85] Barbara Jordan, "The Americanization Ideal," *New York Times* editorial, September 11, 1995.
[86] Ibid.
[87] Eric Scmitt, "Whites in Minority in Largest Cities, the Census Shows," *New York Times*, April 30, 2001.

decade.[88] It also seems to confirm white nationalist fears that whites are quickly becoming a minority population in the United States. Harvard University sociologist Orlando Patterson argues, however, that these figures are misleading because many Hispanics consider themselves to be white "in every social sense of this term."[89] The implication of Patterson's argument is twofold: Not only is the white population in the United States not headed for immediate minority status (even non-Hispanic whites are still projected as a majority by 2050), but those who are considered white, and thus not eligible for the traditional benefits of affirmative action, should be expanded to include many Hispanics. In other words, immigration policies that allow or even encourage Hispanics to move to the United States are acceptable as long as Hispanics can be grouped together with whites so that their presence does not destabilize current affirmative action policies. The tensions in these arguments – regarding who should be identified with what group and who should be entitled to which government benefit – demonstrates the fundamental incompatibility between America's current view of immigration and its historical view of affirmative action, yet political leaders seem hesitant to address this problem head-on.

The previous presidential administration did little to ameliorate the growing tension between the previous beneficiaries of affirmative action (mostly blacks) and new groups (mostly immigrants) who are claiming an entitlement to benefits under affirmative action policies. As the population of both blacks and non-Hispanic whites declines in the United States, affirmative action benefits for immigrants may need to be reconsidered. At the least, immigrant participation in affirmative action programs will become more problematic as their eligible numbers approach majority population status, especially in many metropolitan areas. It is difficult to discern any convincing arguments, on either justice or equity grounds, as to why those who voluntarily emigrated to the United States should receive preferential treatment over those with deep historical roots in the country. Indeed, in many other countries, the native-born population, and not recent immigrants or guest workers, is the one viewed as entitled to special benefits and

[88] Ibid.
[89] Orlando Patterson, "Race by the Numbers," *New York Times*, May 8, 2001.

privileges. The issue of immigrants receiving preferential treatment in education or employment is one that touches many different aspects of American life, but it is one to which few immigration policymakers have paid enough attention in recent years, to the detriment of the country as a whole.

Requiring immigration policymakers to be attentive to the concerns of citizens and local communities would be extremely useful, however, because it would bring important costs and trade-offs to the surface by providing an opportunity for public officials and citizens to educate one another. It may also give aliens a greater incentive to pursue cultural and political membership so that they may participate in a meaningful deliberative process. Finally, it may enable American political communities to respond to the needs of diverse ethnic and racial groups without diffusing the special commitments and obligations that foster attachments among members. In short, the successful resolution of American immigration issues can be accomplished only through honest communication among concerned citizens, immigrants, and public and political leaders. At the present time, such a dialogue appears to be practically nonexistent.

5

CRIME AND FEAR
OF VIOLENCE

Roslyn Jones, 28, was driving through a troubled area after attending an evening class at the University of Cincinnati when she heard someone shout a reference to a "white girl." She did not think that it was directed at her, since she is black, but she is also albino and has fair skin. The black crowd, believing that she was white, began hurling rocks and bricks at her car, shattering the windshield. She was momentarily dazed by a brick that struck her in the head. When she came to, blood was pouring from the wound as more rocks bounced off her car. Suddenly, a man began yelling "Stop. She's black! She's black!" The fusillade subsided, and the good Samaritan pulled her from the car and carried her to safety. She later told the *Cincinnati Enquirer*, "It hurts. My own people couldn't even recognize me. They didn't even look long enough to see. The first piece of white skin they saw, they hit it." Her car was looted during the night.

Robert W. Lee, *The New American*[1]

In addition to immigration issues and demographic changes, white nationalists have also utilized crime statistics to buttress their appeal to white Americans who may feel increasingly insecure because of recent demographic changes. Claiming that a white person may be in danger not only of losing his privileged, majority status but also of losing his life as well, white nationalists prey upon instinctive fears for personal safety and security in their calls to raise white consciousness about the impending "minority menace" to American society. Although personal fears for security and safety are understandable, the white nationalist solution for eliminating these concerns is nonetheless

[1] Robert W. Lee, "Police, Race and Cincinnati's Riots," *New American*, May 21, 2001.

a seductive and dangerous descent along a slippery slope that all too frequently leads from fear to violence, and in other countries around the world even to extermination.

This danger is compounded by the failure of our intellectual and political leaders to properly address the claims that white nationalists have made regarding crime. Some of their assertions are accurate and based on verifiable statistics, although they may be framed in a rhetorically exaggerated manner. Public leaders and policymakers, however, are reluctant to acknowledge their claims for fear of being portrayed as biased or even racist. But ignoring the problem of crime in general and of the white nationalists' use of it in particular will not make these problems go away. By not debating and responding to nationalist claims, our political and intellectual leaders are currently performing a great disservice to the public. Instead of denying the problem, they should be assessing those claims and how they should be handled. By encouraging ignorance and denial in the name of political correctness, our current leaders may be inadvertently fostering the kind of distrust of mainstream institutions that could provoke white citizens in the future to resort to extreme means to ensure personal safety.

In this chapter, I examine current American crime and incarceration rates and how white nationalists have used crime statistics in their efforts to raise white consciousness about minority threats to public safety. Though crime levels are significantly down since the mid-1990s, experts such as University of Pennsylvania political scientist John DiIulio, the former head of Bush's Office of Faith-Based and Community Initiatives, have raised serious questions about the accuracy of these data, which he has argued seriously undercounts crime.[2] Also in this chapter I look at the disturbing rise in hate crimes, which may present the strongest current challenge to an integrated America and may ultimately be a precursor to future racial violence. Finally, I analyze the underlying fear associated with street crime in the United States and how that fear is being fed by white nationalist propaganda,

[2] John J. DiIulio, Jr., and Anne M. Piehl, "What the Crime Statistics Don't Tell You," *Wall Street Journal*, Jan. 8, 1997; John DiIulio, Jr., "Behind the Walls of Fear: Crime Is Down Because Fear Is Causing Americans to Take Refuge Behind High Walls and Gated Communities But at What Price Does the Sense of Security Come?," *Orlando Sentinel*, September 7, 1995; John J. DiIulio, Jr., "Ten Truths about Crime," *Weekly Standard* 1 (January 15, 1996): 12.

disturbing events in other multiracial countries, and the general failure of policymakers to seriously address the racial aspects of crime in the United States. An honest and open dialogue about crime, I contend, is one of our most pressing current needs.

CRIME AND INCARCERATION RATES IN THE UNITED STATES

High rates of crime distinguish the United States from most other developed countries. Between 1945 and 1985, for all categories of serious crime, America had a combined rate three times that of other developed nations,[3] and America currently shares the dubious distinction of having the highest incarceration rate of any developed country,[4] three to five times higher than rates in other industrialized countries.[5] Moreover, as political scientist Seymour Martin Lipset reports, the "country's lead is much greater for violent crimes. As of 1993, the male homicide rate was 12.4 per 100,000, contrasted to 1.6 percent for the European Union, and only 0.9 percent for Japan."[6]

White nationalists attribute much of this disparity to the criminal activities of African-American males who, they contend, commit a vastly disproportionate share of violent street crimes (i.e., muggings, burglaries, rapes, and murders).[7] Whether one focuses on arrest rates or conviction rates, African Americans have historically accounted for a much higher proportion of criminal conduct than the 12 percent of the population which they represent.[8] According to FBI figures, since 1975, the incarceration rate for the public as a whole has more than quadrupled, from approximately 100 inmates per 100,000 residents in

---

[3] Louise I. Shelley, "American Crime: An International Anomaly?," *Comparative Social Research* 8 (1985): 81; Leon Radzinowicz and Joan King, *The Growth of Crime: The International Experience* (New York: Basic Books, 1977), 6–7, as cited in Lipset, *American Exceptionalism*, 46–7.

[4] Lipset, 17, 46–51.

[5] Ellen J. Pollock and Milo Geyelin, "U.S. Incarceration Rate Highest," *Wall Street Journal*, January 7, 1991.

[6] "The European Union," *The Economist*, October 22, 1994, survey 4 as cited in Lipset, 46.

[7] Taylor, *Paved with Good Intentions*, 10, 11, 318–23.

[8] For more information about historical trends, see Jan Chaiken, "Crunching Numbers: Crime and Incarceration at the End of the Millennium," *National Institute of Justice Journal*, January 2000, pp. 10–17.

1975 to more than 400 inmates per 100,000 residents in 1995. But the incarceration rate for African Americans, which has undergone a similarly steep rise, is of a different order of magnitude: Between 1980 and 1999, the incarceration rate for African Americans rose from an already very high rate of 1,156 inmates per 100,000 residents to a staggering 3,620 inmates per 100,000 residents.[9]

Although incarceration rates have risen starkly in the past twenty years, the violent crime rate in the United States has steadily declined over the past eight years, and it is currently 14 percent below the 1994 rate. Property crime also continues to follow a substantial decline. Between 1997 and 1998, violent crime dropped 7 percent, and property crime, 12 percent.[10] But although rates of serious violent crime have declined for both blacks and whites, blacks continue to experience the highest rates of violent crimes as both victims and perpetrators. In 1998, blacks were six times more likely to be murdered than whites and seven times more likely to kill someone. Blacks are also more likely to commit interracial crime. About 20 percent of stranger homicides are black-on-white, while only 3 percent of stranger homicides are white-on-black.[11] White nationalist professor J. Philippe Rushton of the University of Western Ontario has presented data to support his contention of a strong correlation between a state's percentage of black residents and the state's homicide rate. He attributes this correlation, which he says is evident in other countries, to higher levels of testosterone among black males.[12]

Whatever the reason, it is a fact that crime poses a serious problem for African-American communities nationally. Liberal scholars and commentators often point to racism among law enforcement personnel as the primary cause of the high incarceration and conviction rates of African Americans. But racism in the criminal justice system alone does not explain unacceptable levels of black-on-black crimes nor taint

[9] Ibid., 15.
[10] "Crime and Victim Statistics," U.S. Department of Justice, Bureau of Statistics, http://www.ojp.usdoj.gov/bjs/cvict.htm.
[11] "Homicide Trends in the U.S.," U.S. Department of Justice, Bureau of Statistics, http://www.ojp.usdoj.gov/bjs/homicide/race.htm; "Blacks Experience the Highest Rates of Violent Crime," U.S. Department of Justice, Bureau of Statistics, http://www.ojp.usdoj.gov/bjs/glance/race.htm.
[12] J. Philippe Rushton, "The American Dilemma in World Perspective," 11–30 in Taylor, *The Real Dilemma: Race, Immigration, and the Future of America.*

the eyewitness accounts found in victimization studies. A greater propensity to commit certain types of crimes has made many Americans wary of African Americans. Moreover, in unguarded moments African Americans of different social classes voice their own concerns about the matter.

According to Abigail Thernstrom and Stephan Thernstrom, a fear of the criminality of African Americans, they and others argue, affects people's behavior in numerous ways as individuals modify their lives to reduce the risk of physical harm.[13] "If the African-American crime rate suddenly dropped to the current level of the white crime rate," the Thernstroms speculate, "we would eliminate a major force that is driving blacks and whites apart and is destroying the fabric of black urban life."[14] Similarly, James Q. Wilson, one of America's leading criminologists, says that "[t]he fact that whites and blacks have different rates of crime – especially violent crime – affects the willingness of whites to live in black neighborhoods."[15] It is crucial that black political and religious leaders recognize the opportunity that black crime provides for opportunists in the white nationalists movement. There is a strong need to heighten the awareness of African Americans to their vulnerability on this particular issue.

THE WHITE NATIONALIST RESPONSE

White nationalists have seized on this issue of black crime rates and have begun a concerted effort to raise the racial awareness of white America through a series of press releases detailing the racial disparities in violent crime. As journalist Earl Ofari Hutchinson explains, "a motley collection of white supremacists and rightist extremist groups has eagerly made black-on-white violence a wedge issue in their crusade to paint blacks as the prime racial hatemongers in America. Avowed white supremacist David Duke instantly screamed that [the shooting

---

[13] Stephan Thernstrom and Abigail Thernstrom, *America in Black and White* (New York: Simon and Schuster, 1997), 259–61. Among the polls cited was the National Opinion Research Center Survey described in Thomas Edsall, "Recalling Lessons of the 1960s," *Washington Post*, May 3, 1992; George Gallup, Jr., *The Gallup Poll Public Opinion, 1993* (Wilmington, Del.: Scholarly Resources, 1994), 271.

[14] Thernstrom and Thernstrom, 285.

[15] James Q. Wilson as quoted in Robert Stacy McCain, "Hate Crimes' Not Big Problem in Race Relations, Study Finds," *Washington Times*, http://www.amren.com/crime.htm.

of five whites by a black assailant in Pittsburgh] proves that whites are under assault from lawless blacks and that the federal government won't protect them."[16]

Jared Taylor's New Century Foundation has been particularly active in drawing attention to black-on-white crime. "The Color of Crime," a report published in the spring of 1999 by Taylor's organization, analyzes FBI data from the year 1997.[17] The foundation faxed the following conclusions to major newspapers around the country:

- Blacks commit violent crimes at four to eight times the white rate. Hispanics commit violent crime at approximately three times the white rate, and Asians at one-half to three-quarters the white rate.

- Since blacks are much more violent than whites, police treat them differently. Just as police stop and question men more often than women – since men are more violent than women – they stop blacks more often than whites.

- Of the approximately 1,700,000 interracial crimes of violence involving blacks and whites, 90 percent are committed by blacks against whites. Blacks are 50 times more likely than whites to commit individual acts of interracial violence. They are up to 250 times more likely than whites to engage in multiple-offender or group interracial violence.

- Black criminals often choose white victims for their violent crimes, while white criminals rarely choose black victims. Fifty-six percent of violent crimes committed by blacks have white victims. Only two to three percent of violent crimes committed by whites have black victims.

[16] Earl Ofari Hutchinson, "Why Are Black Leaders Silent on Black Hate Crimes," Salon.com, March 6, 2000.

[17] *Criminal Victimization in the United States, 1997*, U.S. Department of Justice, Bureau of Justice Statistics (Washington, D.C.: USGPO, 1998), 3; *Crime in the United States, 1997*, U.S. Department of Justice, Bureau of Justice Statistics (Washington, D.C.: USGPO, 1998); *Hate Crime Statistics, 1997*, U.S. Department of Justice, Federal Bureau of Investigation (Washington, D.C.: USGPO, 1999); *Criminal Victimization in the United States, 1994*, U.S. Department of Justice, Bureau of Justice Statistics (Washington, D.C.: USGPO, 1997), 41, 45.

- Hispanics are a hate crime victim category in FBI reports but not a perpetrator category. Hispanic offenders are classified as whites, which inflates the white offense rate and gives the impression that Hispanics commit no hate crimes.[18]

Economist Walter Williams of George Mason University, a prominent black conservative, reanalyzed the data presented here, and provided independent verification for its soundness.[19] Data of this kind, documenting a long-term trend in racial differences in crime rates, is clearly behind the racial profiling in which police departments have regularly engaged whereby race is used as a proxy for suspected criminality. The stated goal of the analysis in "The Color of Crime," in fact, was to provide law enforcement officials with statistical evidence justifying the continuation of this practice.

Harvard law professor Randall Kennedy, an African American who has studied the problems relevant to race and crime in great depth, acknowledges that race can signal a greater statistical probability of being a criminal assailant. On this he writes: "Just as race can signal heightened risk that a black person will die younger, earn less money, reside further away from employment opportunities, experience more unpleasant encounters with the police, and possess less education than a white person, so, too, can race signal a heightened risk that a person will commit or has committed certain criminal offenses."[20]

This does not mean, Kennedy goes on to explain, that we should allow the police to routinely use race as a proxy for criminality. Such a practice is clearly unfair to the great majority of blacks, who are decent, law-abiding citizens. Kennedy draws an interesting analogy here between the arguments used by opponents of affirmative action and opponents of racial profiling. Both policies generate complaints from innocent victims who claim unfair penalization because of the misconduct of some members of their group. Innocent whites and innocent blacks suffer because of the misdeeds of others of their race. But while the Supreme Court in recent years has sought to protect innocent whites from reverse discrimination, Kennedy explains, it has avoided taking

---

[18] New Century Foundation, "Study: Blacks Commit 90% of Interracial Crime: Data Suggest That Racial Profiling May Have Scientific Basis," press release, June 2, 1999.

[19] Walter Williams, "An Ugly Conspiracy of Silence," WorldNetDaily.com, August 18, 1999.

[20] Randall Kennedy, *Race, Crime, and the Law* (New York: Pantheon Books, 1997), 145.

a decisive stance that would shield blacks from the "race-dependent decisionmaking" such as that involved in racial profiling.[21]

HATE CRIMES

Consider the following incidents:

- April 2000. A white immigration lawyer kills five racial and ethnic minorities in Pittsburgh: a Jew, an Indian, two Asians, and an African American. Before killing his Jewish victim, the man paints red swastikas on the windows of her synagogue.

- March 2000. A black man who left racist notes in his home shoots five white males, killing three.

- August 1999. A member of a white supremacist group shoots several people at a Jewish daycare center in Los Angeles and kills a Filipino mail carrier.

- July 1999. Two white men with ties to white supremacy groups kill two gay men in northern California.

- July 1999. A twenty-one-year-old college student, a member of the neo-Nazi World Church of the Creator, kills two people and shoots nine others before he commits suicide as police approach him.

- April 1999. Two white teenagers, known to hate blacks and jocks, kill twelve students and a teacher in their Littleton, Colorado, public high school before committing suicide.

- February 1999. In Alabama, two Skinheads beat a gay construction worker to death.

- October 1998. Two men lure a gay college student in Wyoming from a gay bar, pistol-whip, and murder him.

- June 1998. Three members of a white supremacy group in Texas pick up a black man in Texas, tie him to the back of a pickup truck, and drag him to death.

The above incidents are all categorized as hate crimes. What differentiates a hate crime, or a bias crime, from regular crimes is the motivation

[21] Ibid., 159–61.

of the perpetrator – the *mens rea* in criminal law – coupled with the results of the perpetrator's actions.[22] There are various formal definitions for this species of crime.[23] Law professor Frederick Lawrence explains that a racial animus, in which the perpetrator hated the victim's group or employed a discriminatory selection model to choose his victim on racial or religious group membership, underlies most hate crime statutes.[24] California, for example, defines a hate crime as any act "motivated by hatred based on race, ethnicity, religion, gender or sexual orientation."[25] Lawrence and other supporters of federal hate crime legislation argue for increased penalties for such crimes based on the depraved motivation of the perpetrator and the type of harm visited on the victim.

In 1997, President Clinton held a White House Conference on Hate Crimes and he has since endorsed federal legislation that would expand existing hate crime statutes to cover not only additional cases of racial bias but also crimes involving sexual orientation, gender, and disability. (Appendix A presents a copy of a fact sheet on hate crimes released by the White House.) [26] Existing federal hate crime legislation, enacted in 1968, does not cover sexual orientation, nor does it provide extra

---

[22] Frederick M. Lawrence, *Punishing Hate* (Cambridge, Mass.: Harvard University Press, 1999), 3.

[23] Several formal definitions of hate crimes illustrate this *mens rea* motivation:

(1) Hate Crimes Statistics Act (1990): "crimes that manifest evidence of prejudice based on race, religion, sexual orientation, or ethnicity, including where appropriate the crimes of murder, non-negligent manslaughter, forcible rape, aggravated assault, simple assault, intimidation, arson, and destruction, damage or vandalism of property." (Public Law 101–275)

(2) Bureau of Justice Administration (BJA; 1997): "hate crimes – or bias-motivated crimes – are defined as offenses motivated by hatred against a victim based on his or her race, religion, sexual orientation, ethnicity, or national origin."

(3) Anti-Defamation League (ADL): A hate crime is "any crime committed because of the victim's actual or perceived race, color, religion, ancestry, national origin, disability, gender [male or female] or sexual orientation."

(4) National Education Association (NEA): "Hate crimes and violent acts are defined as offenses motivated by hatred against a victim based on his or her beliefs or mental or physical characteristics, including race, ethnicity, and sexual orientation."

All of these definitions are listed at www.religioustolerance.org/hom_hat1.htm#of.

[24] Lawrence, 29–44.

[25] Bobby Cuza, "Hate Crimes in State Increase by 12 Percent," *Los Angeles Times*, July 28, 2000.

[26] Internet posting, Jonathan M. Young@who.eop.gov.

penalties for crimes of animus against women. Even more significant, it protects only persons engaged in one of six federally protected acts, for example, registration or voting.[27]

Newly proposed hate crime legislation that would expand these parameters was proposed by Senator Ted Kennedy as an amendment to the National Defense Authorization Act for Fiscal Year 2001.[28] Although the bill won the "support of a broad, bi-partisan majority in both chambers of Congress, the President, and 175 law enforcement, religious, civic, and civil rights groups," it was stripped from the Department of Defense Authorization bill on October 5, 2000, by a vote of 11 to 9.[29] Senator John Warner (R-Va.), chairman of the Senate Armed Services Committee, expressed concern that the controversial measure would doom the defense bill to a filibuster in the dying days of the Senate's session.[30]

In addition to federal hate crime legislation, several states have also enacted hate crime statutes. As of 1999, forty-three states plus the District of Columbia had passed some type of hate crime law, and in twenty-one of those states plus the District of Columbia, the hate crime statutes also applied to crimes against homosexuals.[31]

Despite the nationwide presence of hate crime statutes at both the state and federal level, a number of groups oppose hate crime legislation, and there is currently a vigorous debate over the constitutionality of hate crime laws. The reasons for this opposition are varied, and they include the belief that all crimes and criminals deserve equally vigorous prosecution regardless of the race of the crime victim or the motivating beliefs of the criminal. What is at issue is the decision as to whether a crime motivated by hate should be treated differently from "ordinary" crime. Additionally, some opponents of hate crime legislation believe that it trivializes atrocious acts and encourages "false, imagined, [or] frivolous" claims.[32] The constitutionality of hate crime statutes, however, remains unresolved.

[27] Elizabeth Palmer, "Senate Votes to Expand Federal Hate Crimes; Similar House Action Unlikely," *Congressional Quarterly Weekly Report*, June 24, 2000, p. 1533.

[28] Senate Amendment 3473 to Senate Bill 2549 is designed to enhance federal enforcement of hate crimes.

[29] The saga of this bill is detailed at www.religioustolerance.org/hom_hat1.htm#of.

[30] Ibid.   [31] Ibid.

[32] Dorothy Rabinowitz, "The Hate-Crimes Bandwagon," http://interactive.wsj.com/articles/SB962065107852832261.html.

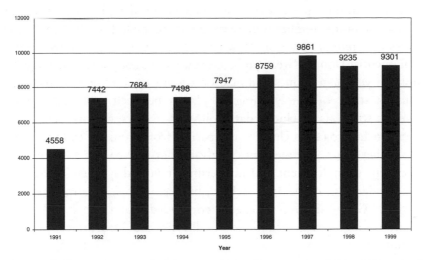

Figure 5.1 Hate crimes statistics, 1991–1999. *Data sources:* Federal Bureau of Investigations, U.S. Department of Justice Uniform Crime Reports, Hate Crime Statistics, 1991–1999.

Figure 5.1 presents statistics on hate crimes reported since the passage of the 1990 Hate Crime Statistics Act. The data show an increase in hate crimes that could represent either a real increase in the actual number of crimes or, as some critics have ventured, simply an increase in the number of crimes reported. Of the 9,861 reported hate crimes in 1997, some 6,981 involved interracial crimes, and 4,105 were classified as violent. In absolute numbers, whites commit far more hate crimes against blacks, but the disparities in the size of the two population ratios translate into figures that show blacks far more likely to attack whites than vice versa.

Some social science studies have found a relationship between adverse economic circumstances and increased racial violence, which many have attributed to increased competition for scarce goods.[33] A

---

[33] Lawrence Bobo, "Group Conflict, Prejudice, and the Paradox of Contemporary Racial Attitudes," in Phyllis A. Katz and Dalmas A. Taylor, eds., *Eliminating Racism: Profiles in Controversy* (New York: Plenum, 1998), 85–114; S. Olzak, "The Political Context of Competition: Lynching and Urban Racial Violence, 1882–1914," *Social Forces* 69 (1990): 395–421; S. Olzak and S. Shanahan, "Deprivation and Race Riots: An Extension of Spilerman's Analysis," *Social Forces* 74 (1996): 931–61; See also Donald Horowitz, *Ethnic Groups in Conflict* (Berkeley: University of California Press, 1985).

similar relationship has been observed between high unemployment and a rise in the number of hate groups, which tend to flourish during times of economic uncertainty when jobs are scarce.[34] However, political scientist Donald Green and colleagues have sought to challenge the link between hate crimes and macroeconomic factors by reanalyzing a famous study of the lynching of blacks between 1882 and 1930. Green's study also included data collected from New York City's Bias Incident Investigative Unit for the period from January 1987 through December 1995. A time series analysis that looked for a correlation between unemployment and bias crimes revealed no clear pattern in the incidence of crime against Jews, blacks, whites, Asians, or homosexuals. Green and his colleagues concluded that there is no robust relationship between economic conditions and bias attacks against minorities.[35]

Such a dismissal may be premature, however, since Green's study focused on a limited geographical area (the relatively progressive New York City), and the contemporary years were not characterized by severe economic downturns. Moreover, studies of the relationship between rates of black lynchings and economic conditions fail to capture the scope of the mass violence against blacks that occurred during mass riots.

Green and colleagues argue that demographic change is more likely to bring about racial and ethnic violence than downturns in the economy as dominant groups succumb to an impulse to defend neighborhoods and areas they consider their territory.[36] This may be the current situation in much of California. In 1999, Los Angeles, one of the most racially diverse cities in the world, recorded 12 percent more hate crimes than had occurred in the previous year. Of 1,962 statewide incidents, Los Angeles accounted for 809, or 41 percent of the total. Race motivated 60 percent of the hate crimes, with blacks most often

---

[34] "Too Busy to Hate: Racist Groups Decline as Economy Enjoys Prosperity; Patriot Movement Depleting Ranks of White Supremacists," *Klanwatch Intelligence Report* (Winter 1997): 17–18.

[35] Donald Green, Jack Glaser, and Andrew Rich, "From Lynching to Gay Bashing: The Elusive Connection Between Economic Conditions and Hate Crime," *Journal of Personality and Social Psychology* 75 (1998): 82–92.

[36] Donald P. Green, Robert P. Abelson, and Margaret Garnett, "Defended Neighborhoods, Integration, and Racially Motivated Crime," *American Journal of Sociology* 104 (1998): 372–403.

being the targets. Sexual orientation and religion accounted for, respectively, 22 percent and 17 percent of the crimes.[37]

Tensions between blacks and Latinos, two groups in competition for resources and affordable living spaces, account for some of the Los Angeles-area hate crimes. White nationalist Jared Taylor had this to say about an incident in Los Angeles in the early 1990s:

> I was particularly interested to read the remarks of the president of a black home-owners association in Los Angeles about why she didn't want Mexicans moving into her neighborhood. In 1991, she said to reporters: "It's a different culture, a different breed of people. They don't have the same values. You can't get together with them. It's like mixing oil and water." I sympathize 100 percent with that lady. When the now forgotten whites moved out of South-Central Los Angeles perhaps they said similar things about blacks.[38]

The perpetrators in most of the recent hate crimes recorded in California have been individuals not affiliated formally with hate groups. Nevertheless, a spokesperson for a watchdog agency observed that apprehended individuals are commonly saying, "Well, I'm not really a member of any group, but I found inspiration and validation for my feelings . . . and, in some cases training by going online."[39]

A surge of hate crimes committed by African Americans first received attention in 1993 when the Southern Poverty Law Centers reported a national trend in this direction.[40] Reports of an increase in the rate of black-on-white crime came weeks after Colin Ferguson, a black immigrant from Jamaica, boarded a crowded commuter train on the Long Island Railroad, selectively chose his victims by race, and ultimately killed a total of six whites and Asians while injuring another nineteen. Writings found in his apartment revealed the motivation for his crime: racial hatred.[41] No doubt the disgust of white nationalists

---

[37] Cuza, "Hate Crimes in State Increase by 12 Percent."
[38] Taylor, *The Real American Dilemma*, 45.
[39] Cuza, "Hate Crimes in State Increase by 12 Percent."
[40] "Hate Violence Not Restricted to One Group or Race," *Klanwatch Intelligence Report*, (February 1993): 6–7; Peter Applebome, "Rise Is Seen in Hate Crimes Committed by Blacks," *New York Times*, December 13, 1993.
[41] Susan Forrest and Phil Mintz, "Seething Hate Led to Rampage Aboard Train," *Buffalo News*, December 9, 1993, p. A8; Malcolm Gladwell and Rachael E. Stassen-Berger, "Slaying Blamed on Bias," *Chicago Sun-Times*, December 9, 1996.

was fueled when a prominent Jewish defense attorney, William M. Kunstler, offered to represent Ferguson, and subsequently pleaded for his innocence on grounds of insanity. Ferguson, Kunstler argued, suffered from black rage caused by a racist white society.[42] In the year following Ferguson's massacre, the Aryan Nations, the most violent of the white supremacy groups, made a comeback "reminiscent of the group's heyday in the early 1980s."[43]

Upset over the media attention generated by high-profile attacks by whites upon nonwhites and homosexuals, a number of white nationalists and white conservatives have tried to bring public attention to similar attacks by nonwhites upon whites. For instance, James Lubinskas, an affiliate of *American Renaissance* magazine, compiled a list of twenty-four especially heinous black-on-white violent crimes committed between 1990 and 1999. Similarly, conservative activist David Horowitz has recently complained on his website of a racial double standard in much crime reporting. He compared the attention generated by the Texas dragging death of a black man, James Byrd, by members of a white supremacy group, as well as that generated by the murder of gay college student Matthew Shepard in Wyoming, with the near silence of the national media about an equally heinous crime committed by blacks against whites that occurred a year before Byrd's death:

> Three white Michigan youngsters hitched a train-ride as a teenage lark. When they got off the train, they found themselves in the wrong urban neighborhood, surrounded by a gang of armed black youths. One of the teenagers, Michael Carter, aged fourteen, was killed. Dustin Kaiser, aged fifteen, who was brutally beaten, shot in the head, eventually recovered. The fourteen-year-old girl (whose name was withheld) was pistol-whipped and shot in the face after being forced to perform oral sex on her attackers. Though the six African Americans responsible for the deed were arrested and convicted, their attack was not prosecuted as a hate crime.[44]

A similar complaint comes from Larry Elder, writing for the *Jewish World Review*, in an article titled, "When the Bad Guy Is Black": "The

---

[42] As discussed in Lawrence Otis Graham, *Member of the Club: Reflections on Life in a Racially Polarized World* (New York: HarperCollins, 1995): 236.

[43] "Aryan Nations Stages Alarming Comeback in 1994," *Klanwatch Intelligence Report*, (March 1995): 1.

[44] David Horowitz, "License to Kill," FrontPageMagazine.com, July 13, 2000.

'DOUBLE STANDARD' slaps you in the face. . . . Sooner or later, the mainstream media and the white-man-done-me-wrong black leadership must face the facts. Black/white interracial crime is almost entirely committed by blacks against whites. By ignoring this, and holding black criminals to a different standard, the media heightens tensions and divisiveness."[45]

Other evidence suggests that Taylor's study of interracial crime is having its desired effect of stirring white consciousness, as well as black interest in the data. Louis Calabro, a former San Francisco police lieutenant, reacted to the report by starting his own organization called the European/American Issues Forum.[46] After interviewing Calabro, African-American journalist Clarence Page wrote that Calabro's complaints led him to "think about some of the larger biases the police, press and politicians may have about who commits hate crimes."[47]

After describing the incidents below, Page concluded that opponents of hate crimes legislation may indeed have found evidence of a harmful double standard that may alleviate racial tensions in the short run but generates inaccurate stereotypes and may have negative long-run consequences:

[A] white immigration lawyer went berserk and killed five people – a Jewish woman, an Indian man, two Asian men and a black man on a shooting spree in Pittsburgh in April. The media labeled the killings a possible hate crime within 24 hours.

But the media seemed much less eager to attach the hate-crime label to a very similar killing spree two months earlier by a black man, Ronald Taylor, who shot five white people, killing three, in a Pittsburgh suburb. In Taylor's apartment, police found "hate writings" aimed at Jews, Asians, Italians and the media, news reports said. The term hate crime was omitted from most reports.

Talk shows and Web sites have been buzzing more recently about the fatal stabbing of an 8-year-old boy by a black man while the child was playing in front of his great-grandparents' home in Alexandria, Virginia in April. Witnesses said the man made comments about killing white

---

[45] Larry Elder, "When the Bad Guy Is Black," *Jewish World Review*, March 10, 2000.
[46] Clarence Page, "Hate-Crime Laws Not for 'Whites Only,'" http://chicagotribune.com/news/columnists/page, July 16, 2000.
[47] Ibid.

people during the attack. A note was later found with the phrase "Kill them racist white kids." ... Yet more than a week after the note was found authorities were reluctant to call the crime a hate crime.[48]

Just as some black activists claim that only whites can be racists because racism requires a superior position of power in society that only whites occupy, some reporters apparently feel that only whites can commit hate crimes. One possible explanation for this is a reluctance on the part of white politicians and members of the media to label black-on-white crimes as racially motivated for fear of generating mass retaliatory racial violence. A reluctance to label black-on-white crimes as hate crimes could be reflective of a desire to prevent large-scale racial violence against racial minorities that whites could more easily accomplish given their greater numbers. Today when we think of race riots, most people recall the television images of the inner-city uprisings of the late 1960s in which minorities burnt down their own neighborhoods and stores. Interracial violence in the future may take a different form, however. As much as we might like to forget this part of our history, whites are not strangers to interracial violence. Numerous race riots occurred across the country during the period from 1880 to 1943 in which whites were the leading perpetrators of violence. Race riots then usually consisted of murderous rampages in which white mobs, often led by racist law enforcement officials, entered African-American communities to kill and pillage. These riots, sometimes more properly termed massacres, were not comparable to the riots that have occurred since the 1960s and later in which minorities perpetuated most of the violent acts.

During the riots of the nineteenth and early twentieth centuries, accusations of black crimes against white women were the pretext for the destruction of prosperous black communities, such as Rosewood, Florida, and an affluent black area in Tulsa, Oklahoma, nicknamed "Black Wall Street." Much of this history of white forays into prosperous black communities had faded from memory until revived by Hollywood in the movie *Rosewood*.[49] In recent years, more attention

---

[48] Ibid.

[49] "The Rosewood Report," http://members.aol.conv/kloveo1/rosehist.txt; C. Jeanne Bassett, "House Bill 591: Florida Compensates Rosewood Victims and Their Families for Seventy-One Year Old Injury," *Florida State University Law Review* 503 (Fall 1994).

has focused on Black Wall Street, where the losses in lives and money were considerably greater than Rosewood.[50]

In addition to concerns over provoking retaliatory racial violence, some may have other reasons for refusing to label black-on-white crimes as hate crimes. The fear of being charged with racism seems to play a part in this process, especially on the part of white law enforcement officials who are sensitive to charges of racism proceeding from their practice of racial profiling. For police departments, racial profiling of African-American males has developed as a means of protecting citizens against a group documented to commit more crimes of violence than any other group. Public attention to the routine employment of racial profiling has led to an outcry for it to stop, though white nationalists defend and encourage the practice. White law enforcement personnel may be hesitant to label the actions of black criminals as racially motivated out of fear of being accused of bias against blacks.

FEAR

Heightening white fears of African-American criminality is part of a campaign by white nationalists to stir white consciousness enough to generate new adherents to their movement. After examining a survey of the attitudes of hate crime perpetrators and white supremacists, Donald Green and his colleagues argued that discomfort with social change set the supremacists apart from the general public.[51] Demographic change, such as the impending minority status of white Americans, is a major source of this fear and discomfort.

---

[50] Michelle N. Jackson, "Black Wallstreet: Riot Destroys America's Most Affluent Black Community," WAN Black History,
http://www.wanonline.com/blackhistory/blackhistory/918.html; Scott Ellsworth and John Hope Franklin, "Death in a Promised Land: The Tulsa Race Riot of 1921," http://www.littleafrica.com; "Panel on 1921 Tulsa Race Riot Urges Reparations for Victims," *Jet*, February 21, 2000; "The Riot That Never Was," *The Economist*, April 21, 1999; Suzi Parker, "U.S. Cities Face Past Strife," *Christian Science Monitor*, March 24, 2000.

[51] Donald P. Green, Robert P. Abelson, and Margaret Garnett, "The Distinctive Political Views of Hate-Crime Perpetrators and White Supremacists," in Deborah A. Prentice and Dale T. Miller, eds., *Cultural Divides: Understanding and Overcoming Group Conflict* (New York: Russell Sage Foundation, 1999), 429–63.

Some white Americans look to other nations for clues as to what might happen here.[52] The web pages of white nationalist groups regularly feature international reports about the racial politics of countries such as South Africa and Zimbabwe. They also highlight incendiary remarks by black nationalist leaders directed at whites in America and elsewhere. For example, the *Stormfront* website produced by the white separatist leader Don Black ran as its quote of the week an excerpt from Khalid Abdul Muhammed's infamous Kean University speech in which he lambasted Jews and spoke of killing white South Africans who refused to leave the country:

> We kill the women. We kill the babies. We kill the blind. We kill the crip-
> ples. We kill them all. . . . When you get through killing them all, go to
> the Goddamn graveyard and kill them a-goddamn-again because they
> didn't die hard enough.[53]

Other reports on the nationalist web pages noted that British passport holders living in Zimbabwe who have dual citizenship were stripped of their passports and ordered to renounce their dual citizenship, an act not recognized by British law.[54] Reports of rapes, beatings, murders, and seizures of farms in America appear on the web pages of white nationalist groups, and some groups have established white refugee relief efforts.[55] Many Americans appear to be watching closely events affecting Africa's white minority, some of which have been highlighted in mainstream media. For example, the *New York Times* reported in an article titled "Bloody Harvest" that "Zimbabwe's white farmers are being held hostage, tormented and killed on their own property. They're caught in the complex politics of land and race and the machinations of a President desperate to win one more election."[56]

---

[52] For a more balanced view of how other countries deal with crime, especially in urban, multinational areas, see Hernando Gomez Buendia, ed., *Urban Crime: Global Trends and Policies* (Tokyo: United Nations University Press, 1989).

[53] Khalid Abdul Muhammad, Speech at Kean College, in Union, New Jersey, November 29, 1993.

[54] David Blair, "White Stripped of Citizenship," *London Telegraph*, May 14, 2000.

[55] Godwin, "Bloody Harvest"; "Zimbabwean Gives Account of Gang Rape," Electronic Telegraph, http://www.amren.com/zimbabwe_rape.html, April 20, 2000; "Kinsmen Redeemer/Rhodesia Project," http://www.amren.com/redeemer_proj.html.

[56] Peter Godwin, "Bloody Harvest," *New York Times Magazine*, http://www.nytimes.com/library/magazine/home/20000625mag-zimbabwe.html.

White fears of being dominated by darker races with different cultural and moral codes of behavior are also manifest in popular novels such as J. M. Coetzee's *Disgrace*.[57] The hero of this story, Professor David Lurie, helplessly witnesses the gang rape of his lesbian daughter Lucy by unknown African assailants. As he goes through his own metamorphosis, he must come to accept Lucy's decision to enter into an intimate arrangement with one of the accomplices to her rape as her only means of survival on the land she loves. In recent years, Hollywood has scrupulously avoided making films with racially incendiary plots such as this. In the future, however, one could well imagine how rising black-on-white crime rates and the impending minority status of white Americans could inspire some profit-seeking Hollywood entrepreneur to exploit the fright potential of a new version of *Birth of a Nation*, in which heroic white men and women fight for survival against swarming hordes of brown and black masses bent on revenge and redistribution.

Fear of a future race war is by no means limited to a lunatic fringe and appears to be driving some whites into the white nationalist camp. Among some white Americans, this fear of a future race war is what drives them toward nationalism, which is seen as their protection. An experience I had with a middle-aged cab driver of Jewish-Irish descent whom I will call Jerry is illustrative of what may be broader concerns of white Americans. I asked Jerry, "What do *you* think the future holds for American race relations?" As Jerry eagerly answered my question, I took copious notes that I immediately transcribed. "We're going to have a civil war," Jerry replied in a matter-of-fact tone. "It has happened in other countries and it will happen here. The Libyans and other Third World people will come over here to help the blacks. There's going to be bloodshed." He recounted a dream he had had several years earlier:

> The blacks took my family and me captive along with some other whites. They led us into a warehouse that had rows and rows of guns. I realized that the blacks were going to do to us what we had done to them. Somehow, I managed to escape. I fled that warehouse leaving behind my wife and daughter. I ran and ran giving no thoughts to their personal safety. All I could think about was how to save myself. Once I stepped outside the warehouse, I could see blacks living normal lives. I noticed a

[57] J. M. Coetzee, *Disgrace* (New York: Viking Penguin, 1999).

house across the street with an old black man and a small boy sitting on the porch. Then the realization struck me that like the runaway slaves, I had no place to go and no place to hide. My white skin would give me away immediately. The cost of returning to the camp was the loss of an eye. Two unsuccessful attempts at escape would leave a person forever in darkness. At that point, I woke up in a cold sweat. I think we are going to have a race war.[58]

When I told Jerry that many scholars think the idea of a race war on American soil is absurd, he replied, "What will cause a race war in this country are those people who say that it can't happen here. As Santayana said, those who forget their past are doomed to repeat it."[59] In the course of our conversation, Jerry admitted to occasionally finding and reading white supremacy literature.

Fear can push ordinary individuals toward extremist causes where they can become catalysts for reshaping society.[60] Loretta Williams, director of the Gustavus Myers Center for the Study of Human Rights and Bigotry, has reached the conclusion that "[t]he stuff of hatred is not the sole province of the crazies and the extremists. It is comforting but illusionary to view the perpetrators of hate crimes as sick deviants. . . . Many are ordinary folks trying to project outward their own fears and insecurities."[61] Likewise, James Ridgeway, an investigative journalist for the *Village Voice*, argues that the army of recruits for militia groups such as Timothy McVeigh and Terry Nichols consists of frustrated people whose lives have become marginalized by a changing society.

Their ranks are made up of people – mostly white men – with dead or dying American dreams: Midwestern farmers whose land was put on the auction block during the farm crisis of the 1980s, northern industrial workers whose jobs have moved overseas. They are the dispossessed, the Okies of modern America, abandoned by the times and by both political

---

[58] Author's account of conversation with a taxicab driver, March 30, 2000.

[59] A synchronicity occurred during this encounter with Jerry. He had no way of knowing that I had given several presentations before our discussion that raised the possibility of a race war in America's future.

[60] Eric Hoffer, *The True Believer: Thoughts on the Nature of Mass Movements* (New York: Harper and Row, 1951).

[61] "How Hate Strikes the Vulnerable," PBS Online, http://www.pbs.org/forgottenfires/hate_al.html.

parties. They are driven by a deep anger at their government and sometimes by strong racialist ideology, often with religious underpinnings.[62]

Many of these people have an animus toward the federal government for infringing on their rights and not protecting their interests.

A combination of factors can drive seemingly ordinary and reasonable people toward extremism. One such factor is fear for personal safety and security. If someone believes that his life or property is genuinely threatened, then he or she will seek to eliminate that threat as expeditiously as possible. White nationalists prey upon this fear in whites by focusing on crime statistics that paint African Americans as criminals. It is their sincere hope that these statistics – combined with rhetoric and hyperbole designed to exacerbate white insecurities – will raise white racial consciousness to the point where whites will seek to eliminate the perceived source of their problem: minorities. As the next section shows, white nationalists have already been successful in winning the public debate over affirmative action, so it is not farfetched to suggest that they could eventually persuade the public to adopt their viewpoints on crime as well.

The response to fear, however, does not necessarily have to be extremism; instead, it can be courage. This can include the courage to publicly debate an unpopular issue, the courage to tell the truth and stand up to extremist views, and the courage to search for responsible answers to problems like race that all Americans currently face. It would be an overstatement to suggest that many current political leaders and policymakers lack courage to genuinely face the issues that white nationalists have raised in recent years; however, unless more is done to openly and honestly address white nationalist assertions, then extremism may ultimately, and tragically, prevail over courage.

[62] Ridgeway, 9.

AFFIRMATIVE ACTION: IS THIS THE PERFECT GRIEVANCE?

6

AFFIRMATIVE ACTION: PAST AND PRESENT

Affirmative action is dividing us in ways its creators could never have intended because most Americans who do support equal opportunity and are not biased don't think it's fair to discriminate against some Americans to make up for historic discrimination against other Americans.

Senator Joseph Lieberman, Chairman of the Democratic Leadership Council, July 1995[1]

Of the various issues and controversies exploited by contemporary white nationalists, few have been more important than the issue of affirmative action. Portraying affirmative action as an unfair and illegal form of racial discrimination, white nationalists have successfully adopted a rhetoric of racial grievance that has resonated well with more mainstream elements in the American population. In the minds of many white Americans, affirmative action policies have gotten out of hand, and instead of focusing on outreach and nondiscrimination as originally conceived, they have become synonymous with quotas, reverse discrimination, and naked racial preferences, all of which are strongly opposed by the overwhelming majority of America's white population.[2]

Journalist Bob Zelnick speaks for many white Americans when he describes affirmative action as simply antiwhite discrimination. "As practiced today," Zelnick writes,

---

[1] Stephen F. Hayes, "Lieberman v. Gore: On Affirmative Action, This Ticket Is Far Apart," National Review Online, August 8, 2000.

[2] Peter Gabel, "Affirmative Action and Racial Harmony," *Tikkun* (May–June 1995): 33–6; Hacker, 118.

affirmative action discriminates on the basis of race, gender, or ethnicity against whites, males, and other unfavored groups. And yet today this official discrimination is one of the most pervasive and powerful of government policies, denying Americans jobs, career and educational opportunities, even handicapping their ability to bid on government contracts unless they fit into one of the preferred racial or ethnic categories.[3]

Although liberal critics often portray affirmative action opponents such as Zelnick as racists and reactionaries who seek to maintain the existing power relations in society, there are clearly high-minded and principled reasons for opposing many affirmative action policies. Often these reasons are connected to a genuine belief in the principles of equal rights and color-blind justice. The opening quotation from Senator Lieberman suggests such an egalitarian rationale. Lieberman, who as a young man participated in the dangerous Freedom Rides of the 1960s civil rights movement, is one of a number of white Americans formerly active in civil rights causes who has openly questioned racial and gender preferences.[4] Paul C. Roberts, a former Assistant Secretary of the Treasury during the Reagan administration, is another. During his college years, Roberts helped to organize civil rights protests on behalf of blacks but would later be appalled by the abrupt shift from the principles of equal rights to that of equal outcomes and quotas. "When I helped organize the civil rights protests as a college student," Roberts laments, "I did not expect the outcome to be racial quotas, racially gerrymandered congressional districts, government contract set-asides, or below-market interest rates on home mortgages for 'protected minorities.'"[5]

Besides the general sense of unfairness expressed by Lieberman and Zelnick, more legally minded critics of affirmative action policy often point to what they see as the clear incompatibility of racial preferences with both the letter and spirit of the 1964 Civil Rights Act, as well as with the Equal Protection Clause of the Fourteenth Amendment to the

---

[3] Bob Zelnick, *Backfire: A Reporter's Look at Affirmative Action* (Washington, D.C.: Regnery Publishing, 1996), 4.

[4] To gain the support of liberal Democrats, Lieberman during the 2000 presidential campaign softened his public pronouncements on this issue, but we have no reason to conclude that he has changed his mind in any fundamental way.

[5] Paul Craig Roberts and Lawrence M. Stratton, *The New Color Line: How Quotas and Privilege Destroy Democracy* (Washington, D.C.: Regnery Publishing, 1995), i.

United States Constitution. The clear wording of these documents would seem to support their claim. "No state," the Fourteenth Amendment declares, "shall make or enforce any law which shall abridge the privileges or immunities of citizens of the United States; nor shall any State deprive any person of life, liberty, or property, without due process of law; nor deny any person within its jurisdiction the equal protection of the laws."[6]

The 1964 Civil Rights Act is even more explicit:

No Person in the United States shall, on the ground of race, color, national origin, be excluded from participation in, be denied the benefits of, or be subjected to discrimination under any program receiving Federal financial assistance.[7]

    (a)   It shall be an unlawful employment practice for an employer –

        (1)   to fail or refuse to hire or to discharge any individual, or otherwise to discriminate against any individual with respect to his compensation, terms, conditions, or privileges of employment because of such individual's race, color, religion, sex, or national origin; or

        (2)   to limit, segregate, or classify his employees in any way which would deprive any individual of employment opportunities or otherwise adversely affect his status as an employee, because of such individual's race, color, religion, sex, or national origin.[8]

The language of both the constitutional amendment and the statutory provisions of the Civil Rights Act seems to be at odds with a policy of preference for any group since the rights discussed are framed as the protected rights of all *individuals*. Over the years, a series of Supreme Court decisions and ballot initiatives have chipped away at the policy of racial preferences, but affirmative action remains a major force in American society and it enjoys widespread support among many of America's social, economic, and political elites, including college and university presidents, business leaders, television and print media moguls, and leading politicians.[9]

---

[6] U.S. Constitution, Amendment 14, Section 1.
[7] The Civil Rights Act of 1964, 78 Statute 241, 42 U.S.C., Section 2000a.
[8] Ibid., Section 2000e.
[9] Daniel Seligman, "Affirmative Action Is Here to Stay," *Fortune*, April 19, 1982; Jennifer Hochschild, "Affirmative Action as Culture War," in Michele Lamont, ed., *The Culture*

Ordinary Americans not well versed enough to understand perceived contradictions between public policy directives and the language of civil rights laws react from a gut feeling that it is wrong to advantage or disadvantage anyone on the basis of race or sex. This was confirmed in a report by a task force on affirmative action commissioned in 1996 by the National Planning Association. "The primary dilemma today," the report concluded, "is that current strategies have led to the perception that affirmative action favors some population groups at the expense of others – that in some sense it uses one form of discrimination to combat another. This appearance of inconsistency, even if unwarranted, weighs heavily on the body politic."[10]

Even staunch defenders of current policy have acknowledged the social cost. Liberal journalist Michael Kinsley, for instance, says that the actual harm done to nonminorities by affirmative action is small, yet the policy causes great anxiety among whites, who have an exaggerated fear that they may become its victims. The policy of affirmative action, he says, "has become a scapegoat for the anxieties of the white middle class. Some of those anxieties are justified; some are self-indulgent fantasies. But the actual role of affirmative action in denying opportunities to white people is small compared with its role in the public imagination and public debate."[11] To borrow a metaphor from high finance, the anxieties caused whites are highly leveraged.

What follows is the first of several chapters discussing different aspects of affirmative action policy in the United States. This chapter presents a brief overview of the policy and its politics. I argue here that different forms of discrimination call for remedies other than racial preferences, and that proponents of affirmative action need to rethink their goals and aspirations in light of the contemporary context with its changing racial demographics and socioeconomic challenges. Many forms of affirmative action, I argue, are destructive to peaceful and productive race relations in America and are not needed to combat the

Territories of Race: Black and White Boundaries (Chicago: University of Chicago Press, 1999); William G. Bowen and Derek Bok, *The Shape of the River: Long-Term Consequences of Considering Race in College and University Admissions* (Princeton: Princeton University Press, 1998).

[10] "Affirmative Action: A Course for the Future," *Looking Ahead*, August 1, 1996 (excerpt from a report commissioned by the National Planning Association).

[11] Michael Kinsley, "The Spoils of Victimhood," *New Yorker*, March 27, 1995, p. 69.

very real discrimination that racial minorities often encounter. In following chapters I discuss affirmative action in relation to framing effects and public opinion, to how different racial and ethnic groups talk about the policy among themselves, to the arguments of white nationalists, and to the evolution of the policy in higher education.

WHAT IS AFFIRMATIVE ACTION?

Affirmative action refers to a range of governmental and private initiatives that offer preferential treatment to members of designated racial or ethnic minority groups (or to other groups thought to be disadvantaged), usually as a means of compensating them for the effects of past and present discrimination or to enhance institutional and corporate diversity. In the United States the groups covered by affirmative action include Asians, blacks, Hispanics, Native Americans, women, and the disabled. Among the areas covered are hiring, promotions, admissions to colleges and universities, government contracting, and the disbursement of scholarships and grants. Some forms of affirmative action are quite acceptable to the American public, for example, policies designed to create opportunities for disadvantaged Americans on a race-neutral basis. Other forms such as racial "plus-factoring," race-norming, and numerical quotas and "goals" are far more controversial.

Equal Rights: A Brief History

When the civil rights movement began to achieve national prominence in the mid-1950s, African-American leaders did not demand reparations for slavery or preferential treatment for minorities but sought, rather, equal rights with whites and an end to discrimination. Many decades earlier, the 1919 platform of the National Association for the Advancement of Colored People (NAACP) had similarly sought as its main goal equality of rights under the law and an equal opportunity for black Americans to partake of the many rewards and responsibilities of American public life. The NAACP's platform proclaimed its dedication to the following equal opportunity principles:

1. A vote for every Negro man and woman on the same terms as for white men and women.

2. An equal chance to acquire the kind of education that will enable the Negro everywhere wisely to use his vote.

3. A fair trial in the courts for all crimes of which he is accused by judges in whose election he has participated without discrimination because of race.

4. A right [for members of his race] to sit on the jury which passes judgment on him.

5. Defense against lynching and burning at the hands of mobs.

6. Equal service on railroad and other public carriers. This to mean sleeping car service, Pullman service, at the same cost and upon the same terms as other passengers.

7. Equal right to the use of public parks, libraries, and other community services for which he is taxed.

8. An equal chance for a livelihood in public and private employment.

9. The abolition of color-hyphenation and the substitution of straight Americanism. . . . [12]

Similar goals would later be sought by the Southern Christian Leadership Conference, founded by Rev. Martin Luther King, Jr., in 1957, which worked assiduously for equal rights and the full integration of black citizens into the wider American society.

Before the passage of comprehensive civil rights legislation in the late 1950s and 1960s, blacks in the South had been systematically denied such simple pleasures and amenities as the right to eat at a lunch counter in a restaurant, to sleep in a hotel, to use public restrooms, and to vote without personal risks – rights which white Americans had always taken for granted. The civil rights leadership of the 1950s and 1960s demanded no more than that America as a nation live up to its ideal of equal rights under the law as that ideal had been embodied in both the Declaration of Independence and the post–Civil War amendments to the U.S. Constitution.

Two pieces of civil rights legislation passed in 1957 and 1960 represented modest breakthroughs for African Americans in their struggle

[12] NAACP, *Annual Report*, 1920, cited in Albert P. Blaustein, *Civil Rights and the American Negro* (New York: Washington Square Press, 1969), 338.

for equal rights. With support from President Dwight Eisenhower, and under pressure from black leaders, Congress passed the 1957 Civil Rights Act, which created a civil rights commission and authorized the Justice Department to initiate actions to counter irregularities in federal elections. A second civil rights bill in 1960 called for the use of federal referees to oversee voting procedures and to ensure the preservation of state voting records. Like the 1957 act, the 1960 bill was designed to prevent the intimidation of black voters in federal elections.

The concept of "affirmative action" was taken over from labor law, and did not become firmly associated with civil rights enforcement until 1961, the year President Kennedy issued Executive Order 10925. Kennedy's order directed all federal contractors to take "affirmative action" (the concept was not formally defined) to ensure nondiscrimination in hiring, promotions, and all other areas of private employment. While this represented considerably more progress than the 1957 and 1960 bills, it did not address many of the major concerns of the NAACP, including discrimination in public accommodations, housing, government employment, or discrimination in that sector of the private economy involving firms that did not have contracts with the federal government.

Continued pressure from the NAACP and civil rights leaders, in conjunction with the urban riots in the summer of 1963, convinced President Kennedy to take action stronger than his previous executive order. Increased white-initiated violence in the South during the same period, which shocked millions of Americans when it was displayed in all its brutality on national television, added to the sense of urgency. In the summer of 1963 Kennedy appealed to Congress to pass legislation giving all Americans equal rights and equal access to public accommodations and jobs in what some at the time hailed as "the civil rights bill of the century."

Support for such legislation among northern liberals was greatly enhanced by the ugly defiance of federal law on the part of a number of prominent southern politicians, including, perhaps most notoriously, Alabama Governor George Wallace. He had stood in the doorway of the University of Alabama in June of 1963, blocking the entry of two black students, as he defiantly proclaimed to the American public his determination to preserve the Jim Crow system as it had long existed in the South by whatever means necessary: "I draw the line in the dust and toss the gauntlet before the feet of tyranny, and I say, Segregation now! Segregation tomorrow! Segregation forever!"[13]

Passage was still difficult because the proposed legislation was seen as too extensive and too drastic for a Congress that was still to a considerable extent controlled by southern Democrats. It took the combination of sympathy generated by Kennedy's assassination in November of 1963, the formidable legislative skills of President Lyndon B. Johnson, and the pleas and reassurances of Majority Whip Hubert Humphrey (D-Minn.) to persuade Congress to pass a comprehensive civil rights act.

Some white southerners were unconvinced by Humphrey's reassurances. Because the term discrimination was left undefined in the civil rights bill, opponents of the legislation feared that it would, in fact, lead to racial quotas in employment or to discrimiantion against whites. Senator James Eastland, a Democrat from Mississippi, had argued, for instance, that

> the bill would discriminate against white people . . . I know what will happen if there is a choice between hiring a white man or hiring a Negro both having equal qualifications. I know who will get the job. It will not be the white man.[14]

Largely as a result of these fears, the 1964 Civil Rights bill was amended explicitly to ban quota hiring. At one point during the debate, Humphrey declared that if anyone could find "language [in the proposed legislation] which provides that an employer will have to hire on the basis of percentage or quota related to color, race, religion, or national origin, [I will] start eating the pages one after another, because it is not in there."[15]

The arguments of the bill's critics were discredited in the minds of many, however, by the fact that it was almost exclusively southern segregationist Democrats who advanced them. A broad coalition of northern Democrats and moderate Republicans would unite in an effective coalition that eventually ensured the bill's passage. On June 10, 1964,

---

[13] Graham, 75.

[14] Senator James Eastland, quoted in Nicholas Lemann, "Taking Affirmative Action Apart," *New York Times Magazine*, June 11, 1995, p. 40.

[15] Hubert Humphrey quoted in Justice William Rehnquist's dissent in *United Steel Workers of America v. Weber*, 443 U.S. 193 (1979) at 242, n. 20.

after months of wrangling, supporters of the bill were finally successful in invoking cloture to break a southern filibuster that had lasted 82
days and filled 63,000 pages of the *Congressional Record*.[16] The debate
over the bill had been the longest debate in the Senate's history.

Passage of the Civil Rights Act of 1964 was a major victory for
African Americans and their supporters. In addition to its employment
provisions, the legislation barred discrimination in public accommodations such as lodging, public conveyances, theaters, and restaurants,
and it authorized the government to withhold federal funds from
schools that had not desegregated in compliance with the 1954 *Brown
v. Board of Education*[17] decision. The act was truly comprehensive in
scope and contained eleven sections. Of these eleven sections, Title VI
and Title VII are most important for enhancing our understanding of
the connection between civil rights enforcement and affirmative action.
Title VI covered nondiscrimination in federally assisted programs,
while Title VII covered employment discrimination in all large- and
medium-sized private businesses. Congress created the Equal Employment Opportunity Commission (EEOC) to monitor Title VII violations, and a year later the Labor Department established the Office of
Federal Contract Compliance (subsequently reorganized and renamed
the Office of Federal Contract Compliance Programs), which was
charged with regulating federal grants, loans, and contracts. The
original legislation, however, gave the EEOC no power to enforce its
dictates.

Far from promoting racial preferences or quota hiring, as some
believe, what Title VII originally required was simply that employers
and admissions officers stop discriminating, and make special efforts
to reach out to members of previously excluded groups. If this was
done in an acceptable manner, businesses were considered compliant
with the law. By the mid-1960s, many employers were displaying equal
opportunity notices and strides were being made in bringing qualified
blacks into businesses and into educational institutions from which
they had previously been excluded because of past discriminatory practices. In addition, requirements for the mandatory advertising of jobs
once filled primarily through Old Boys Networks and a word-of-mouth

[16] Graham, 151. A cloture is a parliamentary procedure used to end debate so that a vote
can be taken. Under senate rules, three-fifths of the senators must agree to end the debate.
[17] *Brown v. Board of Education*, 347 U.S. 483 (1954).

system created new opportunities for white men and woman who might otherwise have been excluded. By 1968, federal law comported well with the original goals and aspirations of mainstream civil rights organizations and leaders.

The Shift to Preferential Treatment

Despite the explicit language of the 1964 Civil Rights Act, which stated that no distinctions were to be made on the basis of race, color, religion, or national origin in the right to vote, in provision of public services, and in the right to public and private employment, major changes would occur in the implementation of civil rights laws beginning in the early 1970s.[18] As Harvard University sociologist Nathan Glazer has pointed out, only a few years after declaring in its public law that no distinctions were to be made on the basis of race, color, or national origin, America began an extensive and unprecedented effort to document the race, color, and national origins of just about everyone in the nation who was a student, employee, or recipient of a government grant or contract, and to restructure its public policies so that these factors would be of critical importance in determining who was to benefit from a large array of public and private programs.[19] Criticizing such "affirmative discrimination" in a 1975 book by that title, Glazer argued that the country had unwisely moved from a system of color-blindness and nondiscrimination to a policy characterized by statistical goals and quotas. Arguing along lines similar to those of Glazer, Vanderbilt University historian Hugh Davis Graham contended that the net effect of this shift from color-blindness to color-consciousness was the strengthening of the economic and political base of the minority community while at the same time weakening its moral claims and its public support among the white majority.[20]

---

[18] A similar color-blind principle was embodied in both the Open Housing Act of 1968, which made it a crime to refuse to sell or rent a dwelling to any individual on account of that individual's race, ethnicity, or religion, and in the 1965 Voting Rights Act, which gave the attorney general the authority under specific circumstances to suspend the use of literacy tests, tests which had long been used in the South as a means of discriminating against black voters.

[19] Nathan Glazer, *Affirmative Discrimination: Ethnic Inequality and Public Policy* (New York: Basic Books, 1975).

[20] Hugh Graham, "Origins of Affirmative Action: Civil Rights and the Regulatory State," *Annals of American Academy of Political and Social Science* 523 (September 1992): 60.

In retrospect, it is clear that Presidents Lyndon B. Johnson and Richard M. Nixon were instrumental in moving the country away from policies of strict neutrality in regard to the treatment of minorities and women and toward policies of preferential treatment whose goals would be equal (or proportional) results, rather than equal opportunity and greater efforts to achieve nondiscrimination. On the specific issue of blacks, Johnson set the stage for more aggressive, results-oriented affirmative action policy in a commencement address at Howard University given in June of 1965. It was in this address that Johnson first introduced the powerful image of a shackled runner, which would later influence much of the subsequent debate on the affirmative action issue:

> You do not take a man who, for years, has been hobbled by chains, liberate him, bring him to the starting line of a race saying, "You are free to compete with all the others," and still believe you have been fair. . . . This is the next and more profound stage of the battle for civil rights. We seek not just freedom of opportunity; not just legal equity but human ability; not just equality as a right and theory, but equality as a right and result.[21]

Also in 1965, Johnson issued Executive Order 11246, which reaffirmed support for Kennedy's 1961 order linking civil rights enforcement with affirmative action requirements (though as in Kennedy's earlier order, the concept of affirmative action was not specifically defined). Even though the executive order affirmed the basic principle of color-blind nondiscrimination, it would subsequently be reinterpreted by federal implementing agencies in the 1970s to mean something very different.

A major impetus for the move toward racial preferences came after the summer of 1963 brought the first of many urban riots to America's central cities. These were often viewed at the time by those sympathetic to the black struggle for basic dignity and civil rights as an expression of frustration over the slow pace of racial change in the black ghetto. In 1964 a riot broke out in Harlem, and in 1965 a much larger and bloodier clash occurred in the Watts section of Los Angeles. These culminated in what was called the "long hot summer" of 1967, which

[21] President Lyndon B. Johnson, "Commencement Address at Howard University." June 4, 1965. http://www.lbjlib.utexas.edu/johnson/archives.hom/speeches.hom/650604.htm.

brought riots to over 100 cities, and resulted in almost 2,000 injuries, 13,000 arrests, and at least 83 deaths, as inner-city black youths burned down many of their own neighborhoods.[22] Detroit, Cincinnati, and Newark were among the major troubled areas. In response to the riots, President Johnson issued Executive Order 11365, establishing a National Advisory Commission on Civil Disorders, which came to be known as the Kerner Commission after its chairman, Otto Kerner, then governor of Illinois.

The Kerner Commission was composed largely of white and black moderates and was directed to answer three basic questions: What happened? Why did it happen? What can be done to prevent it from happening again? The commission's report would attribute most of the problems in the black ghetto to racism among whites. Its summary conclusion read in part:

> This is our basic conclusion: our nation is moving towards two societies, one black, one white – separate and unequal. Reaction to last summer's disorders has quickened the movement and deepened the divisions. . . . What white Americans have never fully understood – but what the Negro can never forget – is that white society is deeply implicated in the ghetto. White institutions created it, white institutions maintain it, and white society condones it.[23]

Following the issuance of the Kerner Commission Report, Congress passed a number of antiriot bills, but after the assassination of Martin Luther King, Jr., in the spring of 1968, more urban riots occurred with outbreaks in at least 100 cities. Washington, D.C., Chicago, and Baltimore were among the hardest hit. Historian Herman Belz has persuasively argued that racial preferences were adopted largely as a result of the riots of this period and the impact they had on high-ranking government policy planners and officials. The latter, he says, came to believe that a simple policy of race neutrality was no longer sufficient to address the deep racial divisions and inequalities that beset American society. Affirmative action, according to Belz, was "defended by government policy makers [at this time] as a transitional step towards

---

[22] *Report of the Advisory Committee on Civil Disorders* (New York: Bantam Books, 1968), chap. 2, "Patterns of Disorder."

[23] *Supplemental Studies for the National Commission on Civil Disorders. Kerner Report* (Washington: U.S. Government Printing Office, 1968), 1–13.

the ultimate goal of a color-blind society and as a necessary means of enforcing equal opportunity laws."[24]

The most aggressive governmental affirmative action came, paradoxically, in the early 1970s, during the conservative Nixon administration, when the Department of Labor issued an implementing regulation that in effect amended Johnson's Executive Order 11246 by extending the quota-like features of the earlier Philadelphia Plan to all private contractors doing business with the federal government. Contractors were now required to establish target "goals and timetables" for the hiring of "underutilized" minority group members and women, and to display "good faith efforts" to meet these hiring goals and timetables. While not a rigid quota system, the "goals and timetables" requirement was nevertheless a highly race-conscious and result-oriented group approach to employment policy that critics would charge operated in practice little different from a quota system. The new regulations read in part:

> [Affirmative Action] is a set of specific and results-oriented procedures in which a contractor commits himself to apply . . . good faith effort. The objective of these procedures plus such efforts is equal employment opportunity. . . . An acceptable affirmative action program must include an analysis of areas within which the contractor is deficient in the utilization of minority groups and women, and further, goals and time-tables to which contractors' good faith efforts must be directed to correct deficiencies and thus, to increase materially the utilization of minorities and women, at all levels and in all segments of his workforce where deficiencies exist.[25]

The "goals and timetables" approach to job discrimination that was embodied in this new regulation was very similar to the "disparate impact" theory of employment discrimination that was adopted by the U.S. Supreme Court in the important case of *Griggs v. Duke Power Co.*[26] "Disparate impact" is a technical term in employment discrimination law that refers to a situation where a given hiring practice – a requirement, for instance, of a high school or college diploma in a job

---

[24] Herman Belz, *Equality: A Quarter-Century of Affirmative Action Transformed* (New Brunswick, N.J.: Transaction Books, 1991), 234.

[25] Quoted in Paul Seabury, "HEW and the Universities," *Commentary*, February 1972, p. 39.

[26] *Griggs v. Duke Power Co.*, 401 U.S. 424 (1971).

for which it is not strictly necessary – while racially neutral on its face, may disproportionately exclude members of minority groups or women. "Disparate impact" thus views discrimination in terms of statistical racial disparities or disproportionate group outcomes that may result from otherwise neutral practices that were not necessarily intended to be discriminatory.

Explaining the Shift

As already suggested, the shift from color-blind policies of racial neutrality to color-conscious policies of racial preference has often been viewed as a direct response on the part of certain elites in the federal government to the urban riots of the mid-1960s. This view, while not the whole story, contains a very important element of the truth. It was the traumatic experience of the riots of this period that convinced many high-ranking government bureaucrats and officials of the need to do more to help the disadvantaged members of minority groups – and, particularly, disadvantaged blacks – than was being done by existing equal opportunity laws. To move the poorer and less-educated members of the African-American community into the mainstream of American life, it was believed, was a goal so important to the domestic peace and social stability of America that it required going beyond simple nondiscrimination policies. However admirable in other ways, such policies came to be viewed by many liberals as working at too slow a pace to satisfy the legitimate demands of America's disadvantaged minorities, who were no longer willing to accept peaceably and quietly the subordinate social and economic position that they had traditionally occupied. To give minorities a stake in the American system, many white policymakers came to believe, it was necessary to accelerate the pace of their social, economic, and educational advancement. A large, stable black middle-class and upper-working-class, according to this view, was the best insurance against future social turmoil.

Besides such considerations of social utility, many of those who supported affirmative action policies in the late 1960s justified them on the basis of simple justice. The decades of slavery, segregation, and oppression, many argued, had created an historical entitlement to just compensation on the part of those who had been the victims of such practices, and preferential treatment, whether in employment, education, or other areas of American life, came to be seen as a means of making up for this past deprivation. Like the return of stolen goods, giving preference to minorities, particularly blacks, was viewed by affirmative action supporters as simply returning to them what was only rightfully theirs. The dictates of compensatory justice demanded no less.

In addition to the issues of social utility and social justice, many of the early supporters of affirmative action in the federal government seem to have been swayed by arguments that racism and the kind of favoritism embodied in Old Boy Networks were so ingrained in American culture that only numerically based hiring goals closely monitored by the federal government could ensure fairness to minority members and women. Affirmative action was thus seen as a practical necessity to avoid continued discrimination and the kind of foot-dragging and concealment of discriminatory activities that many believed would persist in the absence of extraordinary enforcement measures.

Two other factors which must be taken into account in trying to explain the shift from color-blindness to color-consciousness that occurred in the late 1960s were the influence of clientele groups and the political considerations of the Nixon administration. What social scientists sometimes call "clientele control," in which interest groups come to dominate the programs and agencies that handle the policies affecting them, seems to have been an important factor shaping federal civil rights policies during this period. The establishment of contract-compliance offices in federal agencies, and the creation of affirmative action positions in government as well as private industry, created a situation in which groups representing the interests of blacks, Hispanics, and women were able to gain considerable influence over the formation of public policy. The combination of a receptive white liberal political establishment and an aggressively importuning array of clientele groups appears to have been a major cause of the rapid movement away from the older color-blind and gender-blind ideals that had dominated the civil rights movement in the period before the riots.[27]

Political considerations of the Nixon administration may also have contributed to this process. Some have speculated that the Nixon

----

[27] Lemann, 54.

administration's approval of the Philadelphia Plan, which involved the direct imposition of hiring quotas in the building trades industry, and its extension of numerically based hiring goals to all federal contractors through the Office of Federal Contract Compliance, may have been motivated in part by a desire to sow dissention among core Democratic constituency groups. Whether this was Nixon's intention or not, affirmative action policy during this period most certainly did weaken the already fragile black-Jewish relationship and drove a wedge between blacks and labor unions.[28] Suspicion of the motives of the Nixon administration would seem appropriate on this matter, since Nixon himself had shown little inclination in the past to support black causes or to stand up for civil rights. Nixon had, after all, run for election in 1968 on a tough law-and-order platform that many interpreted as an appeal to the white backlash vote against black progress. While in office during his first term, he opposed the 1971 extension of the Voting Rights Act, and he fought vigorously throughout his years as President to block busing for school integration.[29] If his administration's embrace of affirmative action appears to skeptical outsiders as a Machiavellian ploy, there is certainly good reason for this.

The Stirrings of the White Backlash

Since the 1970s, affirmative action has been steeped in controversy. Its conservative opponents have argued and continue to argue that the policy is "unmeritocratic, leads to reverse discrimination, and is an un-American guarantee of equal results instead of equal opportunity."[30] According to sociologist John D. Skrentny, the position of today's conservative critics of affirmative action is not far from the dominant view of the liberals, both black and white, who supported the 1964 Civil Rights Act.[31] Leading African-American proponents of the civil rights legislation such as Martin Luther King, Jr., sought a

---

[28] Ibid., 54; Thomas Sowell, "Affirmative Action Reconsidered," *Public Interest* (Winter 1976), cited in Barry Gross, *Reverse Discrimination* (New York: Prometheus Books, 1977), 113.

[29] Rowland Evans and Robert Novak, *Nixon in the White House* (New York: Random House, 1975).

[30] John David Skrentny, *The Ironies of Affirmative Action: Politics, Culture, and Justice in America* (Chicago: University of Chicago Press, 1996), 1.

[31] Ibid., 2.

policy of color blindness, and they carefully and strategically avoided any demands that would resemble racial preferences. Skrentny argues that in the political climate of the 1960s, the "advocacy of racial preferences was one of those 'third rails' of American politics. Touch it, you die."[32]

Unlike most other developments in the area of race relations, affirmative action became official public policy enshrined in public law without any organized civil rights lobbying in its favor. As Skrentny explains, this contentious policy, so racially divisive in its effects, was not the offspring of the black civil rights groups (however much they may have applauded the actual policy once implemented), but "the construction of white male elites who traditionally have dominated government and business."[33] According to Skrentny and other scholars, it was crisis management in the wake of the urban riots of the 1960s that led many government leaders, corporate executives, and heads of government administrative agencies – almost all of them white males – to seek a more aggressive remedy for the problems plaguing blacks than simply outreach and recruitment.[34] Affirmative action, says Skrentny, represents an instance in which powerful elites ignored the express wishes of the majority of white Americans and carved out a policy designed to jump-start the success of African Americans, who were seen as "one of the most marginalized and politically weak groups in society."[35] And white male elites continue to be among affirmative action's strongest supporters today. Indeed, affirmative action policy is so firmly entrenched in white elite–dominated corporate structures and academic institutions that many believe changing its existing mode of operation would require a major upheaval. The resentment of those whites who are not in the elite, however, remains unabated.

Central to understanding the divisiveness of affirmative action policies in the United States is the widespread, underlying belief among many white Americans that African Americans are unworthy of special treatment (see Chapter 7). This contrasts with white attitudes toward other groups in America such as veterans and alumni children, who, as Skrentny points out, at least under certain circumstances are

---

[32] Ibid., 3.

[33] Ibid., 5–6; Graham, *Civil Rights Era*. For a specific example of this, see Bowen and Bok, *The Shape of the River*.

[34] Skrentny, 99–116; Graham, *Civil Rights Era*.   [35] Skrentny, 5–6.

considered fair targets of special treatment even if this means compromising otherwise meritocratic systems of decision making. According to sociologist Seymour Martin Lipset, many whites believe that there has already been a great deal of effort on the part of American society to help blacks, and that blacks have not taken good advantage of the enhanced opportunities that have been made available to them. Many white Americans, Lipset says, believe that blacks do not work hard enough to get ahead, and have only themselves to blame for lack of progress. "Americans," says Lipset, "believe that what determines success or failure is hard work, regardless of whether a person is white or black. Hence if blacks fail, it follows that it is largely their own fault."[36] Whites, he says, "increasingly seem to believe that they, or their officials, have done a great deal for blacks, but since the situation does not appear to be improving there must be something wrong with them."[37] Lipset believes that black leaders have unwittingly contributed to this negative white perception by their failure to acknowledge the great progress that blacks have actually made over the past fifty years. Whatever the reason, whites seem increasingly disinclined to support policies that are perceived as granting special privileges to blacks.

The white backlash against policies designed to help African Americans was seen almost immediately after the issuance of the Kerner Report. In the political arena the backlash manifested itself in 1968 with the rise of former Alabama Governor George W. Wallace as a serious presidential candidate, and in the Republican Party's adoption of a "southern strategy" that eventually enabled it to transform itself into a majority party after decades of minority status. Running as a third-party candidate in an electoral system strongly biased against third-party entrants, Wallace managed to win five states and an impressive 9.9 million votes. Historian Dan Carter explains Wallace's impressive showing in the following terms:

> [As Wallace] looked out upon the disordered political landscape of the 1960s, he sensed that millions of Americans felt betrayed and victimized by sinister forces of change. He knew that a substantial percentage of the American electorate despised the civil rights agitators and antiwar demonstrators as symptoms of a fundamental decline in the traditional cultural

[36] Lipset, 132.   [37] Ibid., 133.

compass of God, family, and country, a decline reflected in rising crime rates, the legalization of abortion, the rise in out-of-wedlock pregnancies, the increase in divorce rates, and the proliferation of "obscene" literature and films. And moving always beneath the surface was the fear that blacks were moving beyond their safely encapsulated ghettos into "our" streets, "our" schools, "our" neighborhoods.[38]

Carefully studying Wallace's success was Richard Nixon, who encouraged his party to pursue the disaffected Wallace voters, whom he saw as part of the nation's "silent majority." In the 1972 election Nixon's strategy proved highly successful, garnering him 67 percent of the white vote. Given their numbers and geographical distribution, the Wallace voters were certainly worth pursuing.[39]

By 1985 focus groups and surveys had driven home to the Democrats that they had an image problem with white Americans. This was particularly true in the South, where race and affirmative action issues were most salient. For instance, in interviewing whites in Macomb, Georgia, Democratic pollster Stanley Greenberg found that opposition to what was perceived as the special privileges of blacks was a prevailing sentiment among most disaffected southern voters:

> These white Democratic defectors express a profound distaste for blacks, a sentiment that pervades almost everything they think about government and politics. . . . The special status of blacks is perceived by almost all of these individuals as a serious obstacle to their [own]

---

[38] Carter, 14–15.

[39] Some of the converts to white nationalism can be found among the millions of white Americans who supported the racially conservative public policies advocated by presidential candidates George Wallace, Richard Nixon, Ronald Reagan, and George Bush. The new rightward tilt of the Republican Party even attracted some extremist and terroristic elements. Bill Wilkinson, for instance, the national leader of the Invisible Empire KKK, publicly endorsed Ronald Reagan in 1984. "Klan Holds Voter Registration Drives, Backs Candidates," *Klanwatch Intelligence Report*, July 1984, as cited in Manning Marable, *Beyond Black and White: Rethinking Race in American Politics and Society* (New York: Verso, 1995), 40. Marable, a leftist scholar, sees Reaganite Republicanism as encouraging such extremist elements. According to Marable, "Reagan created the social space or political environment for fascist and terrorist groups to operate with relative impunity." In support of this assertion, Marable discusses a string of assaults, bomb threats, robberies, and murders related to the far right that happened after Reagan's election that has blacks, Jews, Marxist, labor leaders, and abortion clinics as primary targets. Marable, however, fails to make any kind of causal connection.

personal advancement. Indeed, discrimination against whites has become a well-assimilated and ready explanation for their status, vulnerability, and failures.[40]

Some Democratic candidates aspiring to national office would take note of these white anxieties. Bill Clinton, for instance, was elected President in 1992 largely because he presented himself as a new Democrat who was not as tightly wedded to the liberal policies of the past. His success may have been due in part to the fact that he specifically avoided a close association with Jesse Jackson and traditional civil rights leaders until well into his second term.[41]

Frustration over affirmative action programs has also been cited as a major factor in David Duke's strong showing in Louisiana Republican politics. In 1989, Duke, despite his known past as a leader of the Ku Klux Klan, was elected to the Louisiana state house on the Republican ticket. In his campaign Duke championed conservative causes that included vigorous opposition to affirmative action, a tough stance against black criminals, and opposition to liberal welfare policies that allegedly encouraged black freeloading. In 1990, Duke nearly defeated the incumbent Democratic U.S. Senator, Bennett Johnston, winning 59 percent of the white vote, and in the following year, he won 55 percent of the white vote in the state gubernatorial runoff election.[42] Political analyst Gary Esolen explains that Duke's message was essentially the same throughout his campaigns:

> Why do reporters and politicians pick on me and say hateful things about me when anyone can see I'm a nice guy and reasonable fellow? Besides, even if I did say and do extreme things once or twice that's all over with now. The real reason they pick on me is that they are afraid of my message on the issues, which is that affirmative action has gone too far and become racism in the reverse, the black underclass is dragging us down, we can't afford welfare, and it's time white people had some rights again.[43]

---

[40] Edsall and Edsall, *Chain Reaction: The Impact of Race, Rights, and Taxes on American Politics* (New York: W. W. Norton, 1991, 1992), 87.

[41] Klinkner and Smith, 308–11.

[42] Tyler Bridges, *The Rise of David Duke* (Jackson: University Press of Mississippi, 1994), 193, 236–7.

[43] Gary Esolen, "David Duke's Use of Television," in Douglas Rose, ed., *The Emergence of David Duke and the Politics of Race* (Chapel Hill: University of North Carolina Press, 1992), 137–8.

It would be comforting to believe that Duke's supporters were atypical of most white Americans, but this does not seem to be the case. Indeed, a study of his supporters showed that they did not differ substantially from the general public in their attitudes about race and African Americans.[44] Moreover, on the specific question of affirmative action, polling data suggest that Duke's anti–affirmative action message resonated very well with whites in other parts of the country.[45]

During the Reagan administration, Republicans continued the pattern that Nixon started by attacking affirmative action, quotas, racial preferences, set-asides, timetables, and racial norming of test scores. But once in power they failed to change the status quo, which caused some whites to look elsewhere for representation. A 1990s Populist Party platform complained that a "vengeful civil rights industry, together with the media and the government, has institutionalized 'affirmative action,' quotas, racial preferences in educational admissions and job promotions and other racist programs."[46]

By the mid-1990s, a backlash against affirmative action was gaining momentum in unexpected places. In California, for instance, Governor Pete Wilson, who had earlier in his career supported affirmative action measures, convinced a majority of the members of the Board of Regents of the University of California to ban all racial, gender, and ethnic preferences in both admissions and employment at all UC campuses. A development of even greater national significance emerged when Glynn Custred and Thomas Wood, two California university professors, started the California Civil Rights Initiative, a ballot proposal that sought to outlaw affirmative action in state-supported programs. The initiative, which was officially listed on the ballot as Proposition 209, cleverly adopted the color-blind language of the 1964 Civil Rights Act.[47] By a vote of 54 percent to 46 percent, California voters approved

---

[44] Susan E. Howell and Sylvia Warren, "Public Opinion and David Duke," in Rose, ed., *The Emergence of David Duke and the Politics of Race*, 80–93.

[45] For data on the attitudes of whites in other parts of the country, see Howell and Warren.

[46] Leonard Zeskin, *It's Not Populism, America's New Populist Party: A Fraud by Racists and Anti-Semites* (Atlanta, Ga.: Center for Democratic Renewal and the Southern Poverty Law Center, 1984), 1–2, as cited in Dobratz and Shanks-Meile, 220.

[47] B. Drummond Ayres, Jr., "Conservatives Forge New Strategy to Challenge Affirmative Action," *New York Times*, February 16, 1995. Upon passage in 1996, Proposition 209 was immediately challenged by the American Civil Liberties Union, but was upheld by decisions handed down in 1997 by the U.S. Ninth Circuit Court of Appeals and the U.S. Supreme Court.

the initiative in November of 1996.[48] Two years after the passage of Proposition 209, voters in Washington State passed a similar referendum by a vote of 59 percent to 41 percent.[49] Although one could speculate that white Californians' fears about the state's increasingly racially diverse population was a driving force behind the passage of Proposition 209 – the state had a 43 percent minority population in 1990 – this would not explain the outcome in Washington, where the minority population was only 13 percent. The Washington results showed that widespread resentment toward racial preference policies can exist even where demographic change and growing minority numbers have not created pressure on existing institutions or created fears about the impending minority status of whites. For many white Americans, policies of racial preference seem fundamentally unjust and their opposition to such policies does not always seem to be closely tied to their personal economic circumstances. When competition over jobs and fears of social or political domination by minorities is thrown into the equation, their opposition to affirmative action can become intense.

Anti–affirmative action sentiments may account, at least in part, for the 1994 Republican capture of the House of Representatives. A post-election poll showed that a clear majority of white males voted for Republicans. Newspaper and television reports repeatedly found these men to be angry over minority preferences and declining wages.[50]

In the 2000 presidential elections, the nominees of the two major parties carefully avoided serious discussion of affirmative action. Two factors might account for this. First, Republicans feared alienating

---

[48] Article I, section 31, of the California Constitution. www.leginfo.ca.gov/const_toc.html.

[49] Moreover, on November 9, 1999, Florida Governor Jeb Bush announced an executive decision to end racial preferences in university admissions and state contracting decisions, in response in part to the planned launching of a ballot initiative to eliminate racial preferences (similar to California's Proposition 209) that polls showed would probably have passed. Instead of racial preferences, the governor proposed a plan called the "One Florida Initiative" to guarantee admission to students that ranked in the top 20 percent of the state's high schools. Governor Jeb Bush, "Announcement of One Florida Initiative," *Webcast of the One Florida Press Conference*, http://www.state.fl.us/eog/one florida/remarks original.html; Deborah Sharp, "Florida Gov. Bush Plans to Dump Parts of Affirmative Action Law," *USA Today*, November 12, 1999.

[50] "The White Male Vote," CBS/*New York Times* exit polls, *USA Today*, November 11, 1994; Juan Williams, "How Black Liberal Strategy Failed Its Followers," *Washington Post National Weekly Edition*, November 28-December 4, 1994, p. 25.

moderate white voters if they were seen and perceived as the party of whites, and, second, the Republicans had in previous elections captured a significant percentage of the white vote and now wanted support from the younger, faster-growing minority populations. George W. Bush, however, while winning 54 percent of the white vote and 31 percent of the Hispanic vote, won only 8 percent of the African-American vote, despite aggressive attempts to attract more minority voters.

For the more racially conscious segment of the white population, Bush's brand of Republicanism was too solicitous of the concerns of black and Hispanic voters and not attendant enough to the real needs of whites. Samuel Francis, for instance, a former *Washington Times* correspondent with strong white nationalist sympathies, argued that Bush's meager percentage of minority votes came at the expense of white people and their interests, which conflict, he believes, with that of racial minorities. The Republican Party, he contended, should just forget about racial minorities and seek to maximize the votes of white Americans. They should do this, he says, by "supporting a long-term moratorium on legal immigration, terminating welfare and public benefits for immigrants, seeking the abolition of affirmative action, and working for the repeal of 'hate crime' laws and the end of multiculturalism." Republicans, he says, should "encourage white voters to (1) perceive that they as a group are under threat from racial and demographic trends, and to (2) believe that the Republicans will support them against this threat."[51]

Historical Antecedents

Supporters and detractors of affirmative action have developed elaborate arguments in recent years to justify their respective positions. What few of the participants in this ongoing controversy recognize, however, is just how old this debate really is in America. Neither the race-conscious policies designed to improve the life situation of African Americans nor the controversies provoked by such policies were unique to the 1960s. On the contrary, many of the themes surrounding the contemporary affirmative action debate can be traced back as far as

---

[51] Samuel Francis, "It's Race, Stupid: The Election Was Largely a Racial Headcount – Except for Whites," American Renaissance, http://www.amren.com/jan2001.htm, 8–9.

the immediate post–Civil War period, when Congress established the Freedman's Bureau to aid the newly emancipated slaves. President Andrew Johnson, who opposed creation of the bureau, explained his reasons for vetoing the congressional legislation, citing both a lack of federal authority to enter the area of housing and education and a lack of racial even-handedness in the provisions of the bill. Johnson's arguments on the latter issue bear a striking resemblance to those who cry "reverse discrimination" in the affirmative action debate today. "The Congress of the United States," Johnson declared,

> has never founded schools for any class of its own people. . . . It has never deemed itself authorized to expend the public money for rent or purchase of homes for the thousands, not to say millions of the white race who are honestly toiling from day to day for their subsistence. A system for the support of indigent persons was never contemplated by the authors of the Constitution; nor can any good reason be advanced why as a permanent establishment it should be founded for one class or color of our people more than the other.[52]

The Freedman's Bureau would, of course, be established over Johnson's veto, and Johnson himself would almost be removed from office by a hostile Republican Congress.[53] Provisions were made to aid the former black slaves even while ignoring the poor whites that had been the object of Johnson's concern.

Concern about "reverse discrimination" would become a staple of the affirmative action debate, and was evident in Senator Eastland's earlier quotation about the damage that civil rights legislation might wreak on white Americans. Liberal supporters of affirmative action policies have always seen such charges as hypocritical in view of the many instances of racial preferences for whites throughout American history. Claims of reverse discrimination and conservative tendencies to invoke Martin Luther King, Jr.'s "I Have a Dream Speech" are especially galling to such critics in view of America's racially tainted past. Racial preferences become problematic, they charge, only when they advantage racial minorities at the expense of the white majority.

[52] Richardson, *Messages and Papers of the Presidents*, vol. 2, pp. 398–405, cited in Blaustein, 215–16.
[53] Andrew Johnson and William J. Clinton are the only presidents to be impeached by the House of Representatives. Neither man was convicted by the Senate or removed from the office.

Arguments in Favor

Supporters of race-conscious programs designed to help African Americans adjust to the demands of American life often defend such programs on the grounds that the long historical oppression of black people (as well as of women and other minorities) has left them without the resources necessary to succeed in our highly competitive society.[54] This is essentially the same argument of those who favored creation of the Freedman's Bureau in the 1860s. Those employing this argument today can point to statistics showing wide disparities between the socioeconomic condition of blacks and other minorities relative to that of whites, and to the gross underrepresentation of African Americans in many leading professions including law, engineering, medicine, and journalism.[55] The black unemployment rate, they will point out, is often double and sometimes triple that of whites, and even when minorities are employed, their median income is appreciably lower than whites.[56] This remains the case despite affirmative action policies in many areas of employment, as well as in college and university admissions. In the absence of such policies, affirmative action supporters argue, the plight of African Americans would be even bleaker than it is currently.

The problem in university admissions is seen as most acute. Harvard University Law Professor Randall Kennedy, for instance, says that the adoption of race-neutral policies for admissions to the elite institutions of higher learning in America would lead to the near absence of minorities from those institutions. "Without affirmative action," Kennedy argues, "continued access for black applicants to college and professional education would be drastically narrowed."[57] Affirmative action supporters like Kennedy, who make dire predictions about the harmful consequences of abandoning race-conscious educational policies, can point to distressing statistics to support their positions. On most standardized tests, in fact, blacks perform significantly less well than whites or Asians, and this holds true at every socioeconomic level. Even black

---

[54] An excellent detailed discussion of this viewpoint can be found in Klinkner and Smith.
[55] Hacker, chap. 7.
[56] Gerald David Jaynes and Robin M. Williams, eds., *A Common Destiny: Blacks and American Society* (Washington, D.C.: National Academy Press, 1989), chap. 6.
[57] Randall Kennedy, "Persuasion and Distrust," in Russell Nieli, ed., *Racial Preference and Racial Justice* (Washington, D.C.: Ethics and Public Policy Center, 1990), 48.

children from affluent families do not do especially well on such tests. For instance, black children from families with annual incomes over $50,000 average no higher on the SAT than Asians and whites with family incomes in the $10,000 to $20,000 range.[58]

In defense of admitting minority applicants with below-average standardized test scores, supporters of affirmative action often point out that few people complain about giving special preference in college admissions to the offspring of alumni, who benefit from affirmative action on the basis of their lineage. If it is all right to give special preference to campus legacies on the basis of their family relationships, then to give similar consideration to previously oppressed racial and ethnic groups, many argue, can hardly be considered unfair.

The situation in medical schools is of particular concern to many affirmative action supporters, since the number of blacks in medical schools has shown a precipitous decline in recent years. This, it is argued, has contributed to the shortage of medical personnel in inner-city areas, where minority doctors have traditionally been far more likely to practice than whites.[59]

The situation in the corporate employment world, affirmative action supporters point out, is only marginally better than that in higher education and the professions. Once again, they have the statistics to back up their claims. Despite more than two decades of affirmative action, women and blacks lag significantly behind white men when it comes to jobs and promotions. While constituting roughly 42 percent of the labor market, white males hold almost 100 percent of senior management positions in Fortune 500 companies.[60] And while white women hold 40 percent of middle-management jobs, black women hold only 5 percent, and black men only 4 percent.[61] Some observers, such as social scientist Andrew Hacker, say that the situation in the employment world is significantly harder for black men than for black women. Given a choice between a black man and a black woman, they contend, most employers will opt for the black woman because they view her as easier to assimilate and easier to handle.[62] Some have

---

[58] Hacker, 146.   [59] Lemann, 66.

[60] Peter Kilborn, "Women and Minorities Still Face 'Glass Ceiling,'" *New York Times*, March 16, 1995.

[61] Ibid.   [62] Hacker, 116.

suggested that affirmative action needs to be targeted more toward black males.

There is also a dispute over whether affirmative action has worked to the benefit of white women. While some argue that white women have been the greatest beneficiaries of affirmative action policies, others argue that benefits to white women have been meager and slow in coming. During the 1970s, for instance, Jennie Farley found that affirmative action did little if anything to help women. Farley cites a study that compares the gender and race composition of companies that were visited by contract compliance officers and those that were not. The study suggested that affirmative action was actually helping *men* – especially, white men – but having an adverse effect on women. Other studies of university administrative posts where there was a professed commitment to hiring women showed little actual progress in the mid-1970s.[63] Only because of more aggressive enforcement of affirmative action requirements in the Carter years, some affirmative action supporters argue, did the proportion of women in certain key sectors of the work force improve. And this improvement has not been spectacular. To retreat from affirmative action policy, they claim, would set the clock back and threaten the hard-won advances women and minorities have made in the employment arena over the past twenty years.

Some black critics of current policies argue that middle-class white women have often taken affirmative action positions that should rightfully go to blacks. Law Professor Derrick Bell, for instance, points out that white women have received by far the highest percentage of jobs under affirmative action programs, and even white men, he says, have benefited from the widespread advertising of jobs and the objective selection procedures used for hiring and admissions under affirmative action programs.[64] Bell does not believe that affirmative action policies have done much to help black people, though rather than end them, he would like to see them genuinely implemented and expanded so that they really do serve the interests of blacks.

---

[63] Jennie Farley, *Affirmative Action and the Woman Worker* (New York: Amacon, 1979), 14; Carol V. Alstyne et al., "Affirmative Inaction: The Bottom Line Tells the Tale," *Change* 9 (August 1977): 39–41, cited in Farley, 15.

[64] Derrick Bell, "The Mystique of Affirmative Action," speech at Princeton University, April 1995.

When presented with data on racial and gender disparities in employment, top executives invariably attribute the low numbers of women and minorities to a lack of qualified applicants. Affirmative action supporters, however, usually reject such a claim and argue that these numbers reflect the lack of mentoring opportunities for blacks and women and the fact that members of these groups have to combat stereotypes that are not applied to white males. Labor statistics indicate that women and blacks, while making considerable progress in certain fields, are still disproportionately concentrated at the lower rungs of many occupational ladders.[65]

Many supporters of affirmative action also deny that there exist agreed-upon standards of merit that can be fairly and objectively applied in making employment decisions. Merit, says Randall Kennedy, is always politically defined, and is therefore "a malleable concept, determined not by immanent, preexisting standards but rather by the perceived needs of society."[66] If what society needs is more blacks and more women in positions of authority, many affirmative action supporters contend, then it is legitimate to consider being black or being a women as part of a job candidate's merit. Affirmative action supporters are particularly hostile to the idea that scores on standardized tests can gauge merit.

One area that affirmative action supporters insist requires the consideration of racial minority status as part of a job candidate's "merit" is the area of law enforcement. Given the hostility that exists in many minority neighborhoods against the white-dominated criminal justice system, it is only prudent, many hold, to hire police personnel of the same race or same ethnicity as the population that is being policed. Affirmative action policies have been responsible for the expansion in the number of black police officers, it is claimed, and this has been very beneficial to minority communities. Black police, says Andrew Hacker, simply have a better understanding of black people, both criminal and law-abiding, than do white police, who are often influenced by racist stereotypes. In black communities, white police, says Hacker, "cannot catch the clues that distinguish law-abiding young men from those who are up to no good."[67]

[65] Judith H. Dobrznski, "Some Action, Little Talk: Companies Embrace Diversity, But Are Reluctant to Discuss It," *New York Times*, April 20, 1995.
[66] Kennedy, 51. [67] Hacker, 128.

Other arguments in favor of affirmative action focus on the need for diversity in both the workplace and on college campuses. In a multiracial, multiethnic society, it is contended, all students and all workers benefit from personal contact with members of different racial, ethnic, religious, and gender groups. Such personal exposure, it is said, helps to break down debilitating stereotypes and shows that talent is widely distributed across racial groups.

Closely related to the diversity-enhancement argument is the claim that minorities and women need same-race or same-gender role models before they can aspire to positions of power. In the absence of such role models, it is contended, many blacks, Hispanics, and women will feel that certain jobs are "white male jobs" that are not open to them or that they could never successfully perform. Even employment in private industry, supporters of this view maintain, has an important social function that goes well beyond the technical aspects of the work itself. Raising the aspirations of the members of formerly disadvantaged minority groups, it is said, is a social goal of such tremendous importance that it is imperative to require employers to pay careful attention to the racial and gender composition of their work force.

An older but compelling argument in favor of affirmative action stresses its nature as a compensatory device. Black people never got the forty acres and a mule that was promised them after the Civil War, many argue, and affirmative action is no more than a late – and very meager – attempt to pay them back for the centuries of unrequited toil and oppression which they have faced throughout their long sojourn in America. Those who make this argument sometimes point out that as a compensatory device affirmative action should not be faulted for its failure to rescue the most disadvantaged blacks from a life of poverty and despair. Affirmative action, they contend, was never meant to be an antipoverty program, and if many who benefit from it today are middle-class blacks, this is no more unfair than any case where heirs receive debts owed to their deceased parents or grandparents. Moreover, all African Americans, it is asserted, have been disadvantaged in some way by the effects of racism both past and present, so it is not unfair to distribute affirmative action benefits even to the better-off.[68]

---

[68] Roger Wilkins, "Racism Has Its Privileges," *The Nation*, March 27, 1995; Kennedy, 51–2; Thomas Boston, *Race, Class, and Conservatism* (Boston: Unwin Hyman, 1988).

Some argue, from the fact of disproportionately large numbers of middle-class blacks among affirmative action beneficiaries, not that the policies are fundamentally flawed but that they do not go far enough. For instance, Manning Marable, a political scientist at Columbia University, argues that if affirmative action has failed to ameliorate the conditions of large numbers of poor African Americans, it is because the policies were too conservative. Affirmative action, he says, "sought to increase representative numbers of minorities and women within the existing structure and arrangements of power, rather than challenging or redefining the institutions of authority and privilege."[69] After citing a compelling battery of statistics about black representation in the labor force, and the disproportionately high discharge rate of blacks, Marable concludes that "if affirmative action is to be criticized, it should be on the grounds that it has not gone far enough in transforming the actual power relations between black and white within US society."[70] Marable would champion if not a purely socialist, at least a more economically egalitarian, society where the gap between black and white, rich and poor, was vastly reduced from current levels.

The continued presence of racial discrimination against blacks despite all the civil rights legislation on the books is a further reason to continue with current affirmative action policies, its supporters claim. Without such result-oriented policies that pressure employers and other private institutions to promote more blacks, illegal racial discrimination, it is said, will continue unabated and inequalities will be perpetuated indefinitely. Summing up the situation of African Americans, Joe Feagin and Clairece B. Feagin reached the following conclusion with data that proponents of affirmative action often cite as a basis for either continuing with current policies or for becoming even more aggressive with race-conscious solutions:

As we move into the 21st century, most African Americans live in cities, North and South. The migration of African Americans has changed; more are now moving to the South than are leaving the region. Yet wherever they live, they face continuing racial discrimination and economic inequality. The Civil Rights Acts of 1964, 1965, 1968, 1971, and 1991

---

[69] Marable, 87.   [70] Ibid., 88.

have made many formal acts of discrimination illegal, but have not ended the millions of subtle, and covert discrimination in business, jobs, housing, education, and public accommodations that African Americans face each year in the United States.[71]

Related to the compensatory justification for affirmative action is the newly invigorated demand for racial reparations for African Americans as compensation for slavery and its bloody aftermath. Since 1989, Michigan Congressman John Conyers has introduced legislation in the House to establish a commission to study the issue of reparations. In 1999, the bill was named H.R. 40, "The Commission to Study Reparations Proposals," and Conyers sought to hold public hearings on the issue. Two events breathed new life into Conyers's piece of perennial legislation that initially seemed to be purely symbolic in nature. The first event was a 1997 effort by Ohio Congressman Tony Hall to seek passage of legislation apologizing to African Americans for slavery, and the second was *The Debt* (1999), a book by Randall A. Robinson, founder and president of TransAfrica, an international lobbying firm.[72] After citing the compensation that Jews and Japanese Americans received because of their suffering, Robinson argued that no race or religious group had suffered as much as blacks. By May 1999, an organization called the National Coalition of Blacks for Reparations had started a fundraising drive to collect funds for a class action suit on behalf of blacks "for four centuries of enslavement, unpaid labor, illegal seizure of land, mass discrimination, and other brutalities."[73] In January 2001, famed black attorney Johnny Cochran officially joined the group's Reparations Assessment team to help design a legal strategy. I return to this issue in more detail later in this chapter.

---

[71] Feagin and Feagin, 290.

[72] J. Douglas Allen-Taylor, "The Price of Pain: Can Modern-Day America Pay African Americans Back for the Scars of Slavery and Discrimination? Should We Even Try?," http://metroactive.com/papers/10.02.97/cover/race-amends-9740.html; Randall Robinson, *The Debt: What America Owes Blacks* (New York: Dutton, 1999); Richard F. America, *Paying the Social Debt: What White America Owes Black America* (Westport, Conn.: Praeger, 1993); Boris I. Bittker, *The Case for Reparations* (New York: Random House, 1973).

[73] E-mail posting of Brother Jahahara Harry Armstrong, a member of the N'Cobra Board of Directors of the Western Region, http://www.branfordmarasalis.com/messages/48.html.

Arguments Against Affirmative Action

Critics of affirmative action charge that policies of racial, ethnic, and gender preference are contrary to core American values regarding fairness, equality, and respect for the worth of individuals.[74] These values, they say, find expression in our Constitution, which guarantees equal treatment to all American citizens as individual persons, not as members of racial, ethnic, or gender groups. The language of the Fourteenth Amendment and its equal protection provisions is significant, affirmative action's opponents often insist, since it speaks only of persons and personal rights, not of groups or group rights. Shortly before he became a Supreme Court Justice, Clarence Thomas expressed this view forcefully:

> I don't believe in quotas. America was founded on a philosophy of individual rights, not group rights. I believe in compensation for actual [victims of discrimination but] not for people whose only claim to victimization is that they are members of a historically oppressed group.[75]

Affirmative action is also attacked for conferring benefits primarily on the better-off members of the beneficiary groups, while treating all white males who are not of Spanish origin as privileged individuals who can legitimately be held liable for compensatory damages to women and minorities.[76] The substitution of race-testing for means-testing as the criterion for benefits is seen by critics as a fatal flaw in the policies, insofar, at least, as affirmative action is intended as an ameliorative effort to aid the disadvantaged. The lack of fairness in allocating the costs and burdens of the policy is also cited as a fatal flaw by critics. A small number of haphazardly selected individuals must pay with their jobs, promotion opportunities, or admittances to elite universities, critics argue, for a policy the costs of which should be borne by the community as a whole. Currently, there is no fair system of burden-sharing.

[74] Terry Eastland and William J. Bennett, *Counting by Race* (New York: Basic Books, 1979).
[75] Thomas, cited in the *Wall Street Journal*, July 2, 1991.
[76] Russell Nieli, "Ethnic Tribalism and Human Personhood," in Nieli, ed., *Racial Preferences and Racial Justice*, 61–103; Robert Simon, "Preferential Hiring: A Reply to Judith Jarvis Thomson," in Cohen et al., *Equality and Preferential Treatment* (Princeton: Princeton University Press, 1977), 40–8.

Some black supporters of affirmative action policies have nonetheless acknowledged that it drives a wedge between poor whites and poor blacks, while doing little to help the "truly disadvantaged" blacks in America's urban ghettos. William Julius Wilson, now a Harvard University professor, has been among the more influential proponents of this view. Structural economic changes, Wilson argues, have been the real source of many of the problems of the inner-city black poor. A deteriorating employment picture resulting from a combination of automation, deindustrialization, and the relocation of American industry offshore and to the Sunbelt are contributing to a set of problems that cannot be resolved using traditional solutions, Wilson believes. Many poor blacks have been hurt by these developments just as many poor whites have, he says, and the problems they cause can be adequately addressed only by an aggressive full-employment policy.[77] In diverting attention away from the real source of ghetto problems, and in helping mainly middle-class and affluent blacks while alienating many white Americans, affirmative action policies have been of little or no benefit to inner-city blacks, Wilson contends. More recently, Wilson has urged policymakers and national leaders to work toward coalition politics.[78]

One of the most common arguments against affirmative action in higher education – one frequently voiced by black critics – is that the politics of racial preference place minority students in institutions too competitive for their individual needs. Economist Thomas Sowell, for instance, has argued that the effect of preferential policies in college admissions is harmful because it causes a "mismatch" between students and the colleges and universities they attend. Minority students who are sufficiently qualified to attend the less competitive institutions of higher learning are admitted into much more competitive ones where, he charges, they are ill-prepared to deal with the intellectual demands thrust upon them. As a result of preferential admissions policies, minority students who might have succeeded at a state college, he says, find themselves floundering at elite institutions.[79]

---

[77] William Julius Wilson, *The Declining Significance of Race*, 2nd ed. (Chicago: University of Chicago Press, 1980), 182.

[78] William J. Wilson, *The Bridge over the Racial Divide: Rising Inequality and Coalition Politics* (Berkeley: University of California Press, 1999).

[79] Thomas Sowell, "Are Quotas Good for Blacks?," *Commentary* (June 1978): 39–43.

Another frequently voiced criticism of race-based affirmative action policy concerns its effect in allegedly reinforcing negative stigmas and stereotypes concerning the competence of those in the beneficiary groups. Affirmative action, according to this argument, degrades and stigmatizes the members of the groups that benefit from it by suggesting that they are inferior to white males and incapable of competing with them. Yale Law Professor Stephen Carter has developed some of these themes at considerable length in his widely read book, *Reflections of an Affirmative Action Baby*. Affirmative action policies, Carter contends, set up a dichotomy in which employers and admissions officers make an invidious distinction between the "best" candidate and the "best black." Although not opposing all forms of racial preference, Carter believes that these programs inevitably make the accomplishment of all blacks suspect, even those who are well qualified and high achievers.[80]

Besides reinforcing negative stereotypes, affirmative action policy is often criticized for undermining incentives to hard work on the part of those who know they will be beneficiaries of racial preferences. Boston University economist Glenn Loury, for instance, stated many years ago that affirmative action "may alter the terms on which employers and workers interact with each other so as to perpetuate, rather than eliminate, existing disparities in productivity between minority and majority populations."[81] If workers believe that they will be favored by affirmative action, Loury argues, they will have less incentive to work hard and upgrade their skills. "They may invest less," he says, "because . . . it has become easier for them to get high level positions."[82]

Thomas Sowell has advanced a final argument against affirmative action policy of particular relevance to today's situation with our growing white nationalist movement. Sowell, who has carried out extensive studies of race relations in a number of different countries that have preferential policies, found that such policies almost always breed hatred and resentment among the members of the nonbeneficiary

---

[80] Stephen Carter, *Reflections of an Affirmative Action Baby* (New York: Basic Books, 1991).
[81] Glenn Loury, *One by One from the Inside Out: Essays and Reviews on Race and Responsibility in America* (New York: Free Press, 1995), 118.
[82] Ibid., 119.

groups, who see them as fundamentally unfair. Wherever such preferential programs are instituted, he says, the net result of such policies is to increase in intergroup enmities, which in many places around the world have led to violence or even civil war.[83] Such policies are particularly pernicious, Sowell claims, because they are so difficult to remove. Once institutionalized, none of the countries he has studied had found a way of moving beyond the preference system to establish less-divisive policy substitutes.

DISCUSSION

The affirmative action issue is obviously a complex one, and both sides in the ongoing controversy make some valid arguments in support of their respective positions. Nevertheless, I believe that it should be clear to any discerning observer of the contemporary American scene that affirmative action policy has outlived whatever usefulness it may have had in the past, and that the continuation of the policy in its present form threatens the racial peace and repose of an increasingly race-conscious population that now includes an ever-expanding number of race-conscious whites. Whatever benefits affirmative action may have conferred in the past – and it can be argued that they are sizable – it now seems undeniable that, on balance, current policies of racial preference are a negative force in American society, and that they threaten to undermine public support for those principles of racial integration and racial justice that so inspired the nation during the civil rights era of the 1950s and 1960s.

It is of the utmost importance for policy planners and politicians to recognize that we are in a new situation today. As William Julius Wilson and others have pointed out, structural changes in the world economy are affecting competition for jobs and contributing to growing wage inequality throughout the American population. Many high-wage production jobs have gone overseas to Third World nations where goods are produced at a fraction of the cost in America. At the same time, the federal government has reduced social welfare programs normally available for families in need. As a result, since the 1970s,

---

[83] Thomas Sowell, *Preferential Policies: An International Perspective* (New York: William Morrow, 1990), 13.

working-class Americans of all races have faced ever greater uncertainty in their economic lives. Americans, Wilson notes, have begun "to worry about a number of factors including unemployment, job security, declining real wages, escalating medical and housing costs, the availability of affordable child care programs, the sharp decline in the quality of public education, and crime and drug trafficking in their neighborhoods."[84]

These circumstances affect poor whites in low-skill jobs no less than poor blacks. The impressive showing of Patrick Buchanan in the 1996 New Hampshire presidential primary reflected the concerns that many less-affluent whites have about these global changes. (Buchanan ran on an antiglobalization platform that combined neoprotectionist trade policies with a neoisolationist foreign policy.) When the fears over these global economic shifts are combined with anxieties over the declining majority status of white Americans, with the continued resentment over the perceived arbitrariness and injustice of current affirmative action policies, and with public concern about the scope of both legal and illegal immigration, a set of circumstances is created that could cause large numbers of whites – particularly less-affluent whites – to embrace the idea of a distinct white interest not being adequately represented by a government that endorses racial preferences for blacks and newly arrived immigrants.[85] This is a highly toxic brew and a devil's formula for future racial unrest. We might take a lesson here from Western Europe, where a similar constellation of forces has enabled right-wing demagogues to make effective racist and xenophobic appeals for ethnic solidarity among the displaced and unemployed of the majority population.[86]

If we are truly interested in helping the distressed among those in America whom we officially label "minorities" (and we should never forget that this designation is always to some degree arbitrary in a nation consisting of over 200 different racial and ethnic groups),[87] then

[84] Wilson, The Bridge over the Racial Divide, 40.
[85] Kaplan and Weinberg; Robert Reich, The Work of Nations (New York: Alfred Knopf, 1991), 171–84; Wilson, 11–43.
[86] Wilson, 40.
[87] To get a sense of the vast racial and ethnic panoramic of America, and the inherent arbitrariness of categorizing this diverse population according to a simple, two-category, minority/nonminority designation, see the various articles in Stephan Thernstrom, ed., Harvard Encyclopedia of American Ethnic Groups (Cambridge, Mass.: Harvard

we should focus on helping those who are really in need of our help. Means-tested programs like Project Head Start, which may dispropor- tionately benefit blacks and Hispanics but only because they are disproportionately among the poor, should be our model here.[88] The widespread public support for Head Start, and for President's Bush's recent efforts to improve the educational opportunities of those in the worst performing schools, should suggest something of the political feasibility of such a class-based approach. As William Julius Wilson has said recently, we need to "bridge the racial divide" by building coalitions of all those willing to help America's truly disadvantaged and by developing policies to which Americans of all races and ethnicities can positively relate.[89]

It cannot be emphasized enough here that African Americans are not all poor, nor are they all descendants of slaves. A class-based system of distributing societal rewards would be far less controversial than the present system that often pits working-class whites against middle-class African Americans.[90] Indeed, black affluence in America seems to be a carefully hidden secret. When attorney Lawrence Otis Graham sought interviews with affluent blacks for his book *Our Kind of People: Inside America's Black Upper Classes*, he identified wealthy African Ameri- cans all across the country that had lives very much like those of afflu- ent whites. Many of those he sought to interview wished to remain anonymous for fear of how outsiders would react to their wealth and

---

University Press, 1980); and Stanley Lieberson and Mary C. Waters, *From Many Strands: Ethnic and Racial Groups in Contemporary America* (New York: Russell Sage Foundation, 1988).

[88] On Head Start as a model affirmative action program, see Priya V. Rajan, "The Head Start Program: Constructive Affirmative Action," in Carol M. Swain, ed., *Race versus Class: The New Affirmative Action Debate* (Lanham, Md.: University Press of America, 1996), 247–64.

[89] Wilson, *The Bridge over the Racial Divide*.

[90] Robert Woodson, the president of the National Center for Neighborhood Enterprise, has made similar criticisms of affirmative action policy for its failure to reach the poorest segment of the American populations. "My own children and the children of most members of the Congressional Black Caucus," Woodson told a congressional commit- tee, "have better prospects for a successful future than many children, white, black, or brown, who live in impoverished communities. It should come as no surprise that when preferential treatment is offered without regard to economic circumstances, those who have the most training and resources will be the best equipped to take advantage of any opportunities offered." Robert L. Woodson, Sr., Capitol Hill Hearing Testimony, Washington, D.C., September 7, 1995.

accomplishments. Graham's interviewees included physicians, Fortune 500 executives, politicians, and businessmen whose offspring regularly attend elite institutions. Some of these blacks were proud descendants of free blacks who had accumulated social capital from several generations of college-educated descendants. Many of these African Americans wanted their wealth and connections to remain obscured. Education at the right schools was a high priority for this group that had largely abandoned their ties to historically black colleges and universities for the added prestige and social capital of an Ivy League degree. What angers some white Americans is that minorities with accumulated social and financial capital can displace higher-scoring offspring of poor and lower-middle-class whites or Asians from families who are struggling just to get by. For most Americans this is grossly unfair, and it is this sense of injustice that has largely fueled the backlash against racial preferences.

It is sometimes said by supporters of current affirmative action policies that affirmative action was never intended as a jobs program or social welfare–type measure designed to help the disadvantaged. Harvard sociologist Orlando Patterson, for instance, says that "affirmative action was never intended to help the poorest and least able members of the minority classes and women."[91] Such a contention, however, does not comport with reality, as the scholarship of Graham, Belz, Skrentny, and others has clearly shown. Affirmative action was from its very inception in the early 1970s conceived as a special kind of program to aid formerly "shackled runners" who, it was thought, were in no position to make it on their own in American society, and whose frustrations were so volatile that they could explode in ghetto riots. The Nixon-era Philadelphia Plan, one of the first applications of the new race-conscious mode of employment policy that would serve as a model for many future affirmative action programs, was specifically targeted at working-class blacks with little formal education who, it was believed, would benefit from relatively good-paying blue-collar jobs in the construction industry. The interests and needs of middle-class blacks – or of college-educated whites seeking to enhance their "diversity" exposure – was always a secondary concern, at least in the justificatory rhetoric. From the very beginning, the moral force behind

[91] Patterson, 155.

affirmative action has always been sustained by the image of the poor or working-class black or Hispanic – the "shackled runner" – pitted in a competitive struggle against middle-class or affluent whites. Without these contrasting images of the disadvantaged minority versus the privileged white, affirmative action policies would never have received even the meager degree of public support that they have enjoyed in the past, at least among those in the nonbeneficiary categories.

Some defenders of current affirmative action policies who admit that they do little to aid the least fortunate in any direct way nevertheless defend such policies on the grounds that having more blacks or Hispanics in middle-class or upper-middle-class positions indirectly helps the minority poor by showing that minority racial or ethnic status is no longer a barrier to advancement. We are now back to the old role model argument. The role model argument has always fascinated me because of my own nontraditional background as a high-school dropout and first-generation college student from an impoverished rural black family. For some strange reason I have never felt a strong need to be motivated by role models who looked like me. In fact, most of my early role models were white men who groomed me for a career in academia. By contrast, my experiences in segregated grade schools in the rural South with plenty of black teachers was mostly a negative one – neglect is the word I would use to best describe this early pedagogy. Too many minority youth, I suspect, are being told by well-meaning people to believe that they need role models that look like them before they can realistically aspire to a particular job or skills level. If Tiger Woods had shared such a view about golf, we might never have heard of him. (Throughout his youth, we learned, Jack Nicklaus, a blond-headed white man, was the person he aspired to emulate.) While I celebrate the accomplishments of minorities who have broken barriers, I believe that the role model justification for racial preferences is perhaps the weakest and most problematic of all. Other things being equal, role models of one's own race may have advantages over others, but "other things" are rarely equal. What is true is that young people need guidance, nurturance, and encouragement from qualified and caring adults who take an active interest in their future. The race of the mentor or role model seems to me to be of secondary importance, if it is of any importance at all.

The role model argument is seen by proponents to take on a particular salience in the setting of the public school. Black children, it is said, need "culturally congruent" teachers – that is, teachers who are black like themselves – who they can relate to more easily and who are more likely to understand their special backgrounds, problems, and needs. Harvard researcher Ronald Ferguson has surveyed the empirical literature on this issue and found the evidence for the cultural congruence hypothesis to be mixed, at best. Some evidence suggests that white teachers of high socioeconomic status – that is, those most lacking in cultural congruence – seem to do *better* at educating poor black children than black teachers from less affluent backgrounds.[92]

Another argument of affirmative action supporters that I find weak is the diversity rationale. To be sure, there can be concrete learning advantages from a racially, ethnically, religiously, and geographically diverse student body in an undergraduate college, and even perhaps in some professional schools like law and business. The diversity rationale becomes more strained in the case of the working world, though even here demographic diversity may have some benefits. What the proponents of the diversity rationale forget, however, is that the diversity created by a race-neutral selection process, such as that involved in a meritocracy, is fundamentally different from one created deliberately by highly race-conscious selection processes that award huge bonus points as "plus factors" to being members of an underrepresented group. Exposure to differing peoples is supposed to broaden a person's horizons and break down negative stereotypes by showing that competence and talent is widely distributed among diverse demographic groups. But in my own experience and in the experience of many other college teachers I know, the hoped-for benefits of diversity are rarely achieved. What often happens in college settings is that students segregate themselves once they arrive on campus, creating limited opportunities for the interracial contact that is supposed to destroy

[92] Ferguson writes: "Mismatches of race between teachers and students do not appear to be the central problem [in school performance]. Even black teachers need help in learning to cope with some of the special demands that black children from disadvantaged backgrounds may present." Ronald Ferguson, "Teachers' Expectations and the Test Score Gap," in Christopher Jencks and Meredith Phillips, eds., *The Black/White Test Score Gap* (Washington, D.C.: Brookings Institution Press, 1998), 299; see also 347–50.

stereotypes. Anyone who doubts this should just peek into any university cafeteria and observe the self-segregation at the dining tables. Blacks and whites do get to know each other, but there is often with both parties a certain formalism about the contact and a lack of ease.[93] While it would be absurd to attribute this situation exclusively to racial preference policies, it would also be foolish not to see that they have contributed to a heightened racial consciousness on campus that makes true interracial friendships difficult to maintain.

One of the few exceptions to this rule seems to be among recruited athletes on college sports teams, and the exception seems closely related both to the teamwork involved in sports and to the strict meritocratic nature of the recruitment process. (Perhaps, too, this is the reason why Bill Bradley and Jack Kemp, both products of the college and professional sports world, have been among the few white politicians – and in Kemp's case one of the *very* few Republicans – who genuinely feel comfortable with black people.) Black athletes and white athletes on college sports teams both know that athletes like themselves are admitted to competitive colleges regardless of race or ethnic background under much the same relaxed set of academic standards, and they both know that the sports coach has recruited them strictly on their playing ability. Within the world of sports, at least, it is a pure color-blind meritocracy, and genuine friendships often flourish. Could the same be said if high schools or colleges extended a diversity-enhancement rationale to sports and made it easier, let us say, for a white or Asian athlete to make the school's football or basketball team? How would the black athletes who made the team under such circumstances (i.e., an affirmative action program for underrepresented whites and Asians) feel toward those advanced under the lower standard? How would the white and Asian athletes who made the team because of their contributions to "diversity" feel in the presence of the black athletes who were accorded no such special consideration? It does not take any great genius to figure out the answers to these questions and to recognize

---

[93] Allan Bloom's description of college life at the University of Chicago in the late 1980s would seem to hold true for the situation on many college campuses today: "The universities are formally integrated, and blacks and whites are used to seeing each other. But the substantial human contact, indifferent to race, soul to soul, that prevails in all other aspects of student life simply does not usually exist between the two races." Bloom, *The Closing of the American Mind* (New York: Simon and Schuster, 1989), 91–2.

that a race-conscious policy of selection in which lowered standards are applied to one group and not another is a formula for enduring racial tension and discomfort.[94]

This brings us to the key issue of stigma. Virtually every black critic of affirmative action, and even many commentators such as Stephen Carter, who, with certain qualifications and misgivings, support race-conscious policies, acknowledge that affirmative action is stigmatizing to its intended beneficiaries. It is hard to see how it could be otherwise. It is, in fact, because of the obvious and undeniable stigma involved in affirmative action programs that they have been marked throughout their history not only by great controversy but secrecy and deception. No one really wants to know that they got a job or a place in a prestigious university despite the availability of much better qualified candidates because they are black, or Puerto Rican, or female. Just imagine how a new employee would feel if she were told by her employer, "Congratulations, Ms. Thompson, you have been selected as our new affirmative action trainee." Or imagine the reaction of a college-bound high school senior who received an acceptance letter from an elite college or university which began, "We have the honor to inform you that you have been accepted into the entering freshman class of Prestige U. as part of our ongoing commitment to racial diversity." Once again, it doesn't take a genius to figure out how people would react in such circumstances.

Even William Bowen and Derek Bok, whose book *The Shape of the River* has become the most influential defense in recent years of race-conscious affirmative action policies at elite universities, are forced to acknowledge that there is probably some truth to the stigma claim. "The very existence of a process that gives explicit consideration to race can raise questions about the true abilities of even the most talented minority students," Bowen and Bok write in their book. "The possibility of such costs is one reason," they go on, "why selective institutions have been reluctant to talk about the degree of preference given black students. . . . Some of these institutions may . . . be concerned that the standing of black students in the eyes of white classmates

---

[94] I am indebted to my colleague Russell Nieli for many of the points made in this and the previous paragraph.

would be lowered if differences in test scores and high school grades were publicized."[95] A policy that requires such concealment and deception is one about which we should instinctively be skeptical.

The problem, it should be emphasized, is not simply the image of blacks in the minds of white people but the self-image and self-esteem of the black students themselves. Let me weigh in again with some personal reflections. As I stated in Chapter 1, I started my own college education with a high school equivalency diploma at a junior college that had an open-door admissions policy, and I gained admission to successively higher-ranked institutions, finally culminating with an advanced degree from an Ivy League school. Who knows what my career experiences and life would have been like had I applied to and been admitted to a more selective college or university than my preparation level warranted? By starting my education at an institution for which I was fully qualified, I was able to gain self-confidence and self-esteem that enabled me to set and reach progressively higher goals at institutions for which I had previously not been qualified. The handicap of my background caused insecurities and anxieties that I believe would inevitably be present with anyone crossing a huge social class gap in a single generation, but I was able to overcome these to a significant extent by starting out at less competitive institutions, where I could achieve at levels equal to or better than the average student, and then work my way up to more challenging places. Things would have been very different, I believe, if I had been placed in institutions where most of the white and Asian students had been much better prepared than myself, and where I would have had to work hard and struggle only to wind up finishing near the bottom of the class.

---

[95] Bowen and Bok, 264–5. This book, in my opinion, displays an elitist bias that is insensitive to the needs and aspirations of poor and working-class people, white and black alike. Throughout the book there is almost no concern expressed about the poor quality of inner-city black schools, about the problem of the high-school pipeline, or about the legitimate anger and perception of unfairness that the policies defended in the book generate among poor and working-class whites. The authors readily acknowledge that the elite schools surveyed in the study "continue to contribute to social mobility . . . primarily by giving excellent educational opportunities to students from middle class backgrounds," but they do not seem to find this distressing. Rather, they seem content with a system that improves the life chances of the already privileged by preference policies targeted at the minority middle class.

The final harm of current affirmative action policy, I think, involves its effects on motivations and incentives. What is often missed in the discussion of race-conscious policies in higher education, I believe, is how changes in incentive structures affect student choices and behavior. Over the years, I have often encountered African-American students with serious aspirations to become doctors and lawyers who have expressed an unwavering belief that affirmative action would ensure their admission to professional schools of their choice. Some of these students had academic averages of less than 2.0 on a 4.0 scale. They seemed to genuinely believe that traditionally white professional schools were obligated to take them regardless of their academic profiles. I believe this perception affected how hard these students applied themselves to their studies. Factors of this kind, I believe, are at least partially responsible for the now well-documented fact that black students in college actually *underperform* their SAT scores – that is, black students with the same SAT scores as whites do considerably less well in college in terms of their grade point averages than do whites.[96]

Other African-American students I encountered seemed immobilized by the belief that they were incapable of reaching the high academic standards of the institutions. Many seemed to have internalized notions of black inferiority as well-meaning college advisors and other minor-

---

[96] In a study of over 10,000 undergraduate students who entered eleven highly select colleges and universities in 1989, Fredrick Vars and William Bowen found that controlling for SAT scores and other academic attributes, black students with academic qualifications similar to those of whites wound up in the class rankings of their schools an average of 17.4 percentile points behind their white counterparts, a huge difference. See "Scholastic Aptitude Test Scores, Race, and College Performance in Selective Colleges and Universities," in Christopher Jencks and Meredith Phillips, eds., *The Black/White Test Score Gap* (Washington, D.C.: Brookings Institution Press, 1998), 475. In the even larger study involving twenty-eight highly selective colleges and universities that participated in the College and Beyond survey, Bowen and Bok found huge black "underperformance" of their SAT scores and other academic indicators. Slightly less than half of the thirty-point difference between blacks and whites in their average rank in class (23rd percentile for blacks, 53rd percentile for whites) could be accounted for, according to Bowen and Bok's analysis, by lower black SAT scores, lower high school grades, and other variables associated with academic outcomes. The rest of the difference resulted from the underperformance factor. Blacks were, in other words, clearly not living up to their demonstrated potentials to the same degree as whites, and the degree of underperformance, once again, was huge. See Bowen and Bok, 72–90. See also on this topic the discussion in Robert Klitgaard's *Choosing Elites* (New York: Basic Books, 1985).

ity students unwittingly contributed to their insecurities. At one college I attended, a well-meaning advisor warned me during my first semester not to expect to perform there as well academically as I had in other settings. Only my "can do" personality and naivete caused me to forge ahead, undeterred by this negative expectation. I cannot see, however, how affirmative action policies which routinely place black students in institutions where whites and Asians are more academically accomplished can fail to engender this type of condescending mentality. I also find it hard not to conclude that the effect of "stereotype threat" that Claude Steele and other researchers have illuminated as a key factor in explaining black underachievement at selective universities is greatly enhanced by such race-based preferences.[97]

U. C. Berkeley linguist John McWhorter is only the most recent of many black critics who have observed the powerful disincentive effects that affirmative action policies can have on black achievement. Drawing upon his extensive personal experiences as a teacher of undergraduate students, McWhorter concludes that black college students at quality universities often work less hard and are less committed to academic excellence than their white and Asian counterparts. McWhorter attributes this fact both to an anti-intellectual strain which he says exists in Afro-American peer cultures and to a perverse incentive system created by affirmative action policies. McWhorter also finds the same processes at work at the high school level and draws upon his own high school experience to illustrate.

"The maintenance of affirmative action," he writes, "hinders the completion of the very task it was designed to accomplish, because it

---

[97] On stereotype threat, see Claude Steele and Joshua Aronson, "Stereotype Threat and the Test Performance of Academically Successful African Americans," in Christopher Jencks and Meredith Phillips, eds., *The Black/White Test Score Gap* (Washington, D.C.: Brookings Institution Press, 1998), 401–27. Steele and Aronson summarize the findings of their numerous testing experiments in these words: "Our experiments show that making African Americans more conscious of negative stereotypes about their intellectual ability as a group can depress their test performance relative to that of whites. Conditions designed to alleviate stereotype threat, in turn, can improve the performance of blacks. . . . Eliminating stereotype threat can dramatically improve blacks' performance" (422–3). It seems hard to believe and contrary to all common sense that a policy of racial preferences in university admission would lessen the consciousness of negative stereotypes concerning intellectual abilities on the part of those being favored. On the contrary, such a policy is more likely to heighten such consciousness, especially if the negative stereotypes are already deeply ingrained in the dominant culture.

deprives black students of a basic incentive to reach for that highest bar. If every black in the country knows that not even the most selective schools in the country require the very top grades or test scores of black students, that fine universities just below this level will readily admit them with even a B+/B dossier by virtue of their "leadership qualities" or "spark," and that even just a better-than-decent application file will grant them admission to solid second-tier selective schools, then what incentive is there for any but the occasional highly driven black student to devote his most deeply committed effort to school?"

McWhorter offers his own personal testimony based on his experiences as a student in a relatively high-quality middle-class high school.

> In secondary school, I quite deliberately refrained from working to my highest potential because I knew that I would be accepted to even top universities without doing so. Almost any black child knows from an early age that there is something called affirmative action which means that black students are admitted to schools under lower standards than white; I was aware of this from at least the age of ten. And so I was quite satisfied to make B+'s and A–'s rather than the A's and A+'s I could have made with a little extra time and effort. . . . In general, one could think of few better ways to depress a race's propensity for pushing itself to do its best in school than a policy ensuring that less-than-best efforts will have a disproportionately high yield.[98]

What McWhorter says here is something that could be echoed by innumerable other black students attending quality schools, and should warn us that tampering with incentive structures can have unintended

---

[98] John McWhorter, *Losing the Race: Self-Sabotage in Black America* (New York: Free Press, 2000), 232–3. McWhorter compares current affirmative action policy in higher education to the harm done by an overly protective parent: "A parent often teaches a child to ride a bicycle without training wheels by holding the bike up and pushing the child along for a while. This gives the child a sense of the basic lay of the land, but as we all remember, there comes a point when Dad pushes you down the hill to ride by yourself for the first time. Then, and only then, do you master the subtle muscular poise that allows you to stay magically balanced and rolling along. Looking back, you realize that gaining that sense would have been quite impossible without having taken that first plunge; only when the danger of falling down looms do your mind and body avidly seek the interplay to avoid it. The only way that birds learn to fly is to be nudged gently out of the nest; they keep flapping and learn how to do it right because otherwise they fall. . . . Along these same lines, black students simply cannot get beyond the average level they post today in a situation where Dad remains trotting alongside holding the bike" (235).

and perverse consequences, both practical and psychological. Such tampering is perhaps never more dangerous than in the area of race relations.

Reparations

The nascent controversy over reparations bears many of the features of the affirmative action debate, and like the current policies of racial preference, the idea of compensating black people today for the horrible crimes perpetrated against the black slave population in the past is one fraught with problems, both practical and theoretical. To begin with, the movement toward reparations seems poorly timed given white America's unease with racial preferences and its concerns about reverse discrimination. No doubt a stronger case could have been made for reparations during the early 1960s before the affirmative action issue became salient and so negatively associated with blacks. Presently, white Americans seem to feel that they have already done a great deal for blacks, with many seeing welfare and affirmative action as compensation enough for the slavery of long ago.

Thomas Sowell has argued that demanding reparations for what happened many generations in the past is a waste of everyone's time as such a proposal has no political feasibility and draws attention away from more fruitful avenues of reform. Sowell sees the call for reparations on the part of certain black leaders as motivated mainly by a desire for publicity or, in the case of black politicians, by a desire for black votes.[99]

It seems clear that the call for reparations has inflamed many white Americans. Michael Gallager, for instance, writing for NewsMax.com, described the Reparations Assessment team as "an organization of ambulance chasers that wants to collect billions of dollars from the U.S. government and business community." Angrily, he accused the team of being part of a "blatant effort to extort money from all non-black taxpayers so that an entire race of people living in America in 2001 can profit from the shameful history of slavery, a history that none of us, black OR white, has anything to do with."[100] Another white

---

[99] Thomas Sowell, Townhall.com, July 14, 2000.
[100] Mike Gallagher, "I'm Leaving If Shysters Get Away with Race Scam," NewsMax.com, January 3, 2001.

columnist, Jon E. Dougherty, criticized the effort as "little more than a racist attempt to gain more political favor and status at the expense of civility in this country. Black bigots are attempting to convince you (or more appropriately, *browbeat you*) into believing you 'owe' them money for something you never did, condoned, or supported."[101] These angry reactions are from opinion leaders not associated with white nationalism, and are one indicator of how white Americans might respond to the movement to make the country pay for its historical treatment of the ancestors of American blacks. Some whites argue that today's descendants of black slaves have profited greatly by virtue of the fact that they live in America rather than any African land where the majority of the black population must contend daily with extreme poverty, misery, and disease.

Besides the moral and theoretical questions involved in the issue of compensation for crimes committed several generations in the past, there are also a number of practical problems surrounding any serious discussion of reparations. What, for instance, will policymakers do about immigrant blacks from Africa and the Caribbean, as well as descendants of free blacks, some of whom owned slaves? Jeffrey S. Passel and Barry Edmonston report that 5 percent of African Americans are immigrants from Africa and the Caribbean who have come to this country over the past thirty years.[102] Many of these immigrants are highly educated individuals who have concentrated in major cities. Concerning this population, Joe Feagin and Clairece B. Feagin state that "43 percent of those over 24 are college graduates. A higher percentage hold professional positions than one finds among whites."[103] Once in this country, black immigrants sometimes distance themselves from native blacks but not from the benefits of affirmative action programs. Their offspring compete with children of American-born blacks for jobs and college admission, all of which is frequently

---

[101] Jon E. Dougherty, "Slavery Kept Alive by Race-Baiting Blacks," WorldnetDaily, January 4, 2001.

[102] Jeffrey S. Passel and Barry Edmonston, "Immigrating and Race: Recent Trends in Immigration to the United States," in *Immigration and Ethnicity: The Integration of America's Newest Arrivals* (Washington, D.C.: Urban Institute Press, 1994), 52–3.

[103] Joe R. Feagin and Clairece B. Feagin, *Race and Ethnic Relations* (Upper Saddle River, N.J.: Prentice Hall, 1999), 281–2.

a source of considerable tension and resentment in some communities.[104] Whatever one may think of either affirmative action or the reparations idea, it would seem that newly arrived immigrant groups with differing histories and cultural backgrounds are owed nothing by America except nondiscrimination and equal protection of the laws.

The reparations debate involves many more complex issues which cannot be dealt with in the present context. What can be said here is that talk about reparations at the present time is ill-advised and can be positively harmful in terms of improving race relations and garnering support for policies to help the truly distressed. Current reparations talk inflames the white electorate, undermines the bridge-building process across racial lines, fuels white nationalist sentiments, and is insufficiently targeted in its aims to help those members of minority groups who are most in need. Sowell here is undoubtedly correct when he says that the whole matter should be dropped.

Conclusion

America was a different country fifty years ago before the passage of civil rights legislation and the gradual evolution of affirmative action from a program of outreach and nondiscrimination to the more aggressive race-conscious policy we know today. Legal and illegal immigration, structural changes in the economy, and the expansion of the beneficiary groups eligible for racial preferences have together created a situation where a majority of white Americans seem to feel as if they are the victims of racial discrimination of a kind condemned both by the Constitution and by civil rights laws initially passed to help oppressed African Americans. Supporters of equal opportunity and racial justice need to rethink their goals and aspirations in light of this new situation with its rapidly changing racial demographics and new economic challenges. They need to give serious thought to the possibility that affirmative action as practiced currently may not be the most effective remedy for the social pathologies common in inner-city communities such as drug abuse, unwed motherhood, and violent crime. Greater creativity is clearly called for in addressing the problems

[104] Ibid., 286.

of America's "truly disadvantaged" than a preference program that disproportionately benefits middle- and upper-middle-class minority recipients, often at the expense of working-class and lower-middle-class whites.

We should not forget, however, that discrimination remains a persistent problem affecting almost all African Americans and certain other racial and political minorities such as gays and lesbians. Given the increasing diversity of the United States, a major challenge for the twenty-first century is how to combat various forms of discrimination against racial, ethnic, and political minorities without exacerbating existing social tensions. If developments over the past decade have showed us anything, it is that racial preference policies are not the answer. Not only do they greatly intensify interracial enmity and ill will, but they do little to alleviate many of the real problems minorities face with discrimination. Preference policies have little effect, for instance, in solving the problem of discrimination that comes in the form of insensitive cab drivers who refuse to pick up black passengers at night, of sales clerks who serve white customers before black ones, or of real estate agents who steer potential black clients away from select white neighborhoods. Problems of this kind might better lend themselves to remedies such as the increased use of governmental audits like those used to investigate housing discrimination or the institution of hotlines with monetary incentives that encourage anonymous reporting of incidents of illegal discrimination.[105] There are many other forms of aggressive antidiscrimination tactics that could be used to combat some of the real problems minorities face with discrimination, ones which build upon consensus views of justice and fair play and which avoid the divisive and inflammatory issue of race-based preferences.

In the next chapter I try to assess in greater detail how Americans feel about various affirmative action–type initiatives. I attempt to show

---

[105] Government investigators could offer monetary awards to current or former employees who provided information leading to either a conviction or a consent decree in cases of alleged discrimination. In such high-profile racial discrimination cases as the 1994 class action case against Denny's Restaurant chain and the 1996 suit against Texaco Oil Company, white employees played a major role in identifying and supporting the allegations with insider information. Kurt Eichenwald, "The Two Faces of Texaco," *New York Times*, November 10, 1996; Rupert Cornwell, "Rocketing Cost of Race Bias in the U.S.," *The Independent*, May 28, 1994.

how public support for particular types of governmental policies affecting racial minorities is very much affected by how the media presents these issues. What is encouraging for the future of race relations, I suggest, is the fact that most Americans will support policies that comport with the original goals of affirmative action, including outreach, nondiscrimination, and remedial assistance and compensation for actual victims of proven discriminatory treatment.

7

FRAMING EFFECTS, OPINION SURVEYS, AND THE EVIDENCE FROM FOCUS GROUPS

It's an unfair system. . . . Why should someone get into Harvard with lower grades than . . . a white male. . . . Just because they're filling quotas, they're letting them go to Yale. That's not the way this country was built. This country is [one where] you're recognized for your ability, not your sex, not your color, and not your religion and that's the way it should be.

Anonymous white female, New York City, March 1995

In their study of relevant divisions in America, political scientists Donald R. Kinder and Lynn Sanders found that "many white Americans believe that affirmative action threatens their collective interests, that powerful institutions cater to black Americans, and that it is now white Americans who operate at a disadvantage."[1] There is reason to believe that such perceptions, like many other attitudes about race, are affected by how the media and other opinion-forming outlets present issues to the public. Social scientists refer to this presentational process as "framing effect." A "frame" allows individuals or groups to simplify and make sense of the world in which they live. On the basis of internalized frames, individuals and groups decide what is just and unjust about the world, what is moral and immoral, what is tolerable and intolerable, and who or what is to be blamed for their plight.[2]

---

[1] Donald R. Kinder and Lynn Sanders, *Divided by Color: Racial Politics and Democratic Ideals* (Chicago: University of Chicago Press, 1996), 263.
[2] For more information on how individual frames can become collective action frames

The effects of media framing can be very powerful, especially in the case of a policy like affirmative action, where the media is the major source of knowledge of the issue for most Americans. As Paul Kellstedt, a political scientist at Brown University explains, "most Americans do not directly experience affirmative action policies, school busing to achieve integration or other such governmental actions. Rather, these actions are experienced vicariously, through the national media."[3]

Over the years, Kellstedt says, media framing of affirmative action and other race-related issues has generally varied considerably, with the values incorporated in the media frames shifting between egalitarianism and individualism. Individualism refers to the principle that people should not rely on government but instead should pull their own weight. It is closely associated with the idea of self-reliance and self-improvement. Egalitarianism, on the other hand, emphasizes the principle of the equal value of each individual and supports the use of governmental social welfare policies to help remove perceived barriers to equality. There is a general consensus among Americans, Kellstedt explains, that African Americans have suffered a disadvantaged history, but there is no consensus as to what should be done about this. The egalitarian and individualistic prescriptions contradict each other. Whereas individualism, Kellstedt writes, "dictates that blacks, now free from the legal bonds of discrimination, must get ahead on their own without governmental assistance," egalitarianism "prescribes that all people must be given a fair chance, and therefore to the extent that blacks have been denied an equal chance, something must be done to rectify past wrongs."[4]

Similar disagreements over basic values are highlighted by the scholarship of Seymour Martin Lipset, who has argued that blacks and whites have different value systems that come into conflict on the issue of affirmative action. White Americans' preferences for a color-blind approach is consistent with their endorsement of the American Creed, Lipset says, which emphasizes social equality, respect across class lines,

---

leading to organized protest and social movements, see David A. Snow and Robert D. Benford, "Master Frames and Cycles of Protest," in Morris and McClung, eds., *Frontiers in Social Movement Theory*, 133–55; Erving Goffman, *Frame Analysis: An Essay on the Organization of Experience* (New York: Harper, 1974); Tarrow, 4–6.

[3] Paul M. Kellstedt, "Media Framing and the Dynamics of Racial Policy Preferences," *American Journal of Political Science* 44 (2000): 239–55.

[4] Ibid., 250.

meritocracy, and equality of opportunity.[5] According to Lipset, African Americans are the great exception to this creed because of their unique history and their tendency to respond to group-related rather than individual goals.

As I show in this chapter and the next, affirmative action has been widely framed by critics as illegal and unjust reverse discrimination against white Americans. After a discussion of framing effects, I present survey data on the issue and selected comments from focus groups of Asian, African-American, Latino, and white Americans talking about the policy. The cumulative impact of the focus group material will give readers a sense of the complexity of the issues involved here and the differing perceptions that members of different ethnic groups have about current affirmative action practices.

FRAMING EFFECTS

Studies of how the media have framed affirmative action since its inception in the late 1960s show several different themes, with "reverse discrimination" being among the most common. Other frames that are also common depict affirmative action policy as either harming African Americans or giving them undeserved advantages.[6] Public opinion surveys show that when unframed and asked simply about "affirmative action" without any reference to quotas or preferential treatment of minorities, there is significant public approval. Unlike the terms "quotas" and "preferential treatment," "affirmative action" apparently does not evoke an automatically hostile response. Surveys show that Americans who view affirmative action as being about outreach and equal opportunity are far more supportive of the policy than those who have internalized the view that the policy is mostly about quotas or reverse discrimination against nonfavored groups.[7] However, even fairly tolerant white Americans – Americans, for instance, who might be indifferent over the presence of blacks as neighbors or over the once hot-button issue of interracial marriage – often respond with

[5] Lipset, 113.
[6] William A. Gamson and Andre Modigliani, "The Changing Culture of Affirmative Action," *Research in Political Sociology* 3 (1987): 107–19.
[7] F. J. Crosby and D. I. Cordova, "Words Worth of Wisdom: Towards an Understanding of Affirmative Action," *Journal of Social Issues* 52 (1995): 641.

indignation at the "mere mention" of affirmative action policies that are associated with educational or employment preferences.[8]

It should be understood, however, that public opinion surveys are rarely designed in the manner that would allow them to detect interracial consensus on race-related issues even where such consensus may exist. Survey questions often employ language that is too vague, ambiguous, or emotionally charged to yield conclusive results or to determine what Americans really believe about the matters on which they are interrogated. This is perhaps nowhere more true than on controversial racial issues.[9] Because of these problems inherent to survey research, an analysis of respondents' answers to direct questions about their support or opposition to "affirmative action programs" may tell us very little about the types of public policies a person actually endorses. In fact, it has been found that those people who say that they oppose affirmative action may actually support more types of affirmative action programs than those who identify themselves as supporters.[10] Greater awareness of the definitional problems faced by affirmative action questions has led some researchers to conclude that the validity of survey results could be greatly improved if survey designers abandoned the phrase "affirmative action," as well as imprecise terms such as "preference" and "preferential treatment," and instead simply described the content of specific policies.[11]

Among the more salient factors contributing to framing effects are the context of the question, the question wording, the answer choices, the location on the survey, and the types of questions that preceded it.[12] For example, it has been shown that attitudes toward equal

[8] Paul Sniderman and Thomas Piazza, *The Scar of Race* (Cambridge, Mass.: Harvard University Press, 1993), 102–4.
[9] Carol M. Swain, "Affirmative Action: Legislative History, Judicial Interpretations, Public Consensus," in Neil Smelser, William J. Wilson, and Faith Mitchell, eds., *America Becoming: Racial Trends and Their Consequences* (Washington, D.C.: National Research Council, 2001), 318–47.
[10] Jim Norman, "America's Verdict on Affirmative Action Is Decidedly Mixed," *Public Perspective* 6 (1995): 49.
[11] Ricshawn Adkins, "Affirmative Action and Public Opinion Polls," in Carol Swain, ed., *Race versus Class: The New Affirmative Action Debate* (Lanham, Md.: University Press of America, 1996); Charlotte Steeh and Maria Krysan, "Poll Trends: Affirmative Action and the Public, 1971–1995," *Public Opinion Quarterly* 60 (1996): 128.
[12] Adkins, "Affirmative Action and Public Opinion Polls"; William A. Gamson and Andre Modigliani, *Talking Politics* (New York: Cambridge University Press, 1992); Kinder and Sanders, *Divided by Color*; Donald R. Kinder and Lynn Sanders, "Mimicking Political

opportunity questions on national survey questionnaires are influenced by whether the question has a negative or positive bias, by the specific concepts used, and by the nature of alternative choice offered.[13] Using data from the 1986 National Election Study, political scientist Terri Fine analyzed several questions and found that responses were affected by whether the question suggested that preferential treatment is wrong because it discriminates against whites, or wrong because it gives blacks advantages that they have not earned. Those who oppose preferential treatment are more likely to state that they oppose the policy because it is reverse discrimination against white Americans, rather than because it gives blacks undeserved advantages. The reverse discrimination frame, not surprisingly, is the same frame frequently employed by the media.[14]

Political scientist Laura Stoker has shown that survey questions that ignore the context in which affirmative action programs are implemented greatly misrepresent public opinion on the issue.[15] Stoker used a series of affirmative action experiments in which respondents were given three different contexts to justify the implementation of racial quotas: (1) no context or explanation, (2) underrepresentation of minorities, and (3) proven discrimination by a particular company. She found that affirmative action for purposes of overcoming underrepresentation and enriching diversity garnered little support among white Americans.[16] On the other hand, there was considerable support for compensatory measures for cases of proven discrimination, which, as she notes, is the only time that the post–Reagan era Supreme Court

Debate with Survey Questions: The Case of Affirmative Action for Blacks," *Social Cognition* 8 (Spring 1990): 73; Howard Schuman, Charlotte Steeh, Lawrence Bobo, and Maria Krystan, *Racial Attitudes in America* (Cambridge, Mass.: Harvard University Press, 1997); Lee Sigelman and Susan Welch, *Black Americans Views of Inequality: The Dream Deferred* (New York: Cambridge University Press, 1991), 144; Steeh and Krystan, "Poll Trends"; Laura Stoker, "Understanding Whites' Resistance to Affirmative Action: The Role of Principled Commitments and Racial Prejudice," in Jon Hurwitz and Mark Peffley, eds., *Perception and Prejudice: Race and Politics in the United States* (New Haven: Yale University Press, 1998).

[13] Terri Fine, "The Impact of Issue Framing on Public Opinion Toward Affirmative Action Programs," *Social Science* 9 (1992): 3.

[14] Ibid., 3.

[15] Stoker, "Understanding Whites' Resistance to Affirmative Action."

[16] Stoker's data suggest that advocates of affirmative action, in their attempts to garner greater public support, should develop and employ a more compelling reason to justify preferential treatment than the underrepresentation of minorities.

has endorsed the use of quotas.[17] Despite the fact that the diversity argument has become the primary justification for racial and gender preferences among supporters of current affirmative action policies, Stoker's research shows clearly that the diversity rationale is one in which most white Americans place little stock.

The results of recent referenda have shown clearly that who gets to frame voter initiatives – and how they are framed – can be crucial for predicting their success or failure at the polls. In California, for instance, opponents of affirmative action were able to determine the language of Proposition 209, which successfully ended affirmative action in state-supported governmental programs. Using the language of the Civil Rights Act of 1964, voters were asked to approve an initiative that proposed that "the state shall not discriminate against or grant preferential treatment to any individual or group on the basis of race, sex, color, ethnicity, or national origin." An initiative that passed in the state of Washington was similarly worded. A different outcome, however, occurred in Houston, Texas, when voters defeated an anti–affirmative action initiative after supporters of affirmative action were able to frame the issue so that voters had to decide whether to dismantle affirmative action programs for women and minorities instead of whether to ban state-supported discriminatory and preferential policies.[18] The difference between the measures that have passed in other states and the one that failed in Texas seems to have been one mainly of question wording. This interpretation is bolstered by the results of a 1996 postelection poll conducted by the *Los Angeles Times* in which 54 percent of Californians expressed support for affirmative action programs for women and minorities. Presumably, these are the same voters who had passed Proposition 209 banning racial and gender preferences in state-supported programs.[19]

PUBLIC OPINION SURVEY DATA

What are Americans' true attitudes about affirmative action? Do most Americans want all affirmative action policies abolished? After

---

[17] Ibid.

[18] For a more detailed discussion of this, see Klinkner and Smith, 313–14.

[19] See Bill Duryea, "Mister Connerly Comes to Florida," *American Spectator* (1999): 31 (quoting Lydia Chavez).

analyzing all the affirmative action questions from public opinion polls taken between 1977 and 1995, social scientists Charlotte Steeh and Maria Krysan concluded that the attitudes of most people fall somewhere between absolute color blindness and support for preferences.[20] Outreach programs to locate qualified minorities for employment opportunities, a form of "soft" affirmative action, is widely supported by an overwhelming majority of Americans, while other forms of preferential treatment of minorities, such as the use of quota programs and set-asides, garner much less support. Programs geared specifically for African Americans are the least popular among white Americans, while those that benefit women are more popular. Similarly, Americans are more supportive of governmental assistance for the disadvantaged when the programs are not targeted specifically for racial minorities.[21]

Not surprisingly, most surveys show African Americans to be much more supportive than white Americans of affirmative action programs, though a number of studies have also showed considerable black ambivalence.[22] In 1977, the Gallup Organization conducted one of the first national surveys to ask about affirmative action. The Gallup question read:

> Some people say that to make up for past discrimination, women and members of minority groups should be given preferential treatment in getting jobs and places in college. Others say that ability, as determined by test scores, should be the main consideration. Which point comes closest to how you feel on this matter?[23]

Eighty-three percent of whites responded that ability, as determined by test scores, rather than preferential treatment based on minority status or gender, should be the main consideration in employment and college admissions decisions. African Americans, too, showed great misgivings on the issue of preferential treatment in this poll. Sixty-four percent of nonwhites said ability as determined by test scores should

---

[20] Steeh and Krysan, 128. [21] Ibid., 128.

[22] Everett C. Ladd, "People, Opinion, and Polls: Affirmative Action, Welfare, and the Individual," *The Public Perspective*, Report of the Roper Center (April–May 1995): 37–40; Steven A. Tuch and Jack K. Martin, eds., *Racial Attitudes in the 1990s* (Westport, Conn.: Praeger Press, 1997), 226–37.

[23] National poll conducted March 25–27, 1977, *The Gallup Index*, June 1977, Report no. 143.

be the main focus of employment and college admissions decisions rather than preferential treatment.[24]

By 1988, however, African Americans were apparently far more supportive than they were in 1977 of preferences designed to make up for past discrimination. When asked whether "blacks and other minorities should receive preference in hiring to make up for past inequalities," whites and Hispanics overwhelmingly disagreed with the proposal. White opposition and Hispanic opposition were 85 percent and 64 percent, respectively (only 10 percent of whites supported the proposal, and 31 percent of Hispanics). Almost half of blacks, however – a full 48 percent – supported hiring preferences (44 percent opposed). A majority of each of the three groups, however, opposed preferential treatment in college admissions.[25] Similarly, a 1991 *Newsweek* poll showed 72 percent of whites opposed to preferential treatment in hiring (only 19 percent favored the idea), while blacks were more evenly split, 48 percent against compared with 42 percent in favor.[26] Other polls have shown much more support among African Americans than among whites for affirmative action and other forms of governmental assistance to minorities.[27]

The two races, however, may not be as far apart on a number of contentious issues as one might believe. A 1997 survey conducted by the Joint Center for Political and Economic Studies, for instance, found that 48 percent of blacks agreed with 53 percent of whites when asked the following question: "Blacks who can't get ahead in the U.S. are mostly responsible for their own condition."[28] Further breakdowns of the answers to this question showed that 59 percent of black Republicans and 57 percent of African Americans making over $60,000 a

---

[24] It should be noted that at least one survey has found that African-American leaders have differed from the African-American public on affirmative action framed as racial preferences. In response to a question asking whether preferential treatment or ability should be used in obtaining jobs and college placement, 77 percent of African American leaders supported preferential treatment, while only 23 percent of the black public did. Linda Lichter, "Who Speaks for Black America?," *Public Opinion Quarterly* (August/September 1985): 43.

[25] *The Polling Report*, August 22, 1988, cited in Graham, 565, n. 43.

[26] *Newsweek* poll cited in William Schneider, "In Job Quota Debate, Advantage GOP," *National Journal*, June 8, 1991, p. 1374.

[27] Ladd, 23–42.

[28] David A. Bositis, "National Opinion Poll on Race Relations," Joint Center for Political and Economic Studies, 1997.

year agreed with the 53 percent of whites who believed that blacks were mostly responsible for their own condition.[29] The same survey asked a related question: "We should make every possible effort to improve the position of blacks even if it means giving them preferential treatment."[30] A near-majority of African Americans (49 percent) joined with an overwhelming majority of white Americans (83 percent) to oppose preferential treatment of blacks simply as a means of improving the group's position in society.[31] A further demographic breakdown on that question showed that a majority of black baby boomers, of black men, of college-educated blacks, and of blacks earning greater than $15,000 per year opposed preferential treatment of minorities.[32]

Tables 7.1 and 7.2 present data from a December 2000 CBS/*New York Times* survey on race relations that summarizes major areas of agreement and disagreement between whites and blacks. As questions 1–5 of Table 7.1 show, majorities of whites and blacks endorse remedial programs to assist minorities in competing more effectively for college admissions and for job training. A majority of both races say that it is necessary to have laws to protect minorities against employment discrimination. A majority of both races (65 percent of blacks and 53 percent of whites) endorse giving a break to a person from a poor family over a rich person when the two were equally qualified. A majority of both races agree that as a result of affirmative action "less qualified people are hired and promoted at least some of the time." Note that the latter question differs from the others, in that it asks specifically about affirmative action. The responses clearly reflect media framing of the issue in which less deserving minorities are portrayed as supplanting better-qualified whites.

Table 7.2 highlights areas of disagreement between blacks and whites when asked specifically about affirmative action. As can be seen, white Americans are far more likely than African Americans to conclude that preference programs should be ended immediately or phased out over the next few years.

In 1996, I commissioned a national survey of racial attitudes that included a range of questions and issues, including questions relating directly to affirmative action in employment and promotion

---

[29] Ibid.   [30] Ibid.   [31] Ibid.   [32] Ibid.

Table 7.1. Affirmative Action: Issues Where Whites and Blacks Agree

	Black	White	Difference	Total % all Americans
1) Favor special educational programs to assist minorities in competing for college admissions	82	59	+23	63
Oppose	11	31	−20	28
2) Favor government financing for job training for minorities to help them get ahead in industries where they are underrepresented	95	64	+31	69
Oppose	3	29	−26	24
3) Necessary to have laws to protect minorities against discrimination in hiring and promotion	88	65	+23	69
Not necessary	9	31	−22	27
4) It is a good idea to select a person from a poor family over one from a middle-class or rich family if they all are equally qualified	65	53	+12	56
Not a good idea	20	28	−8	27
5) As a result of *affirmative action*, less qualified people are hired and promoted and admitted to college:				
At least some of the time	67	81	−14	79
Hardly ever or never	28	13	+15	15

Source: Based on nationwide telephone interviews with 1,258 adults including 173 black respondents, conducted December 6–9, 1997. In some questions, those with no opinion are not shown. The margin of sampling error is plus or minus three percentage points. Courtesy of *The New York Times*, Copyright 1997, The New York Times Company.

Table 7.2. Affirmative Action: Issues Where Disagreement Occurs

	Black	White	Difference	Total % all Americans
1) Necessary to have *affirmative action* programs to make sure companies have racially diverse work forces	80	38	+42	44
Not necessary	17	57	−40	51
2) Preference in hiring and promotion should be given to blacks to make up for past discrimination	62	31	+31	35
Should not be given	23	57	−34	52
3) *Affirmative action* programs should be continued	80	35	+45	41
Should be abolished	14	52	−38	47
4) *Affirmative action* programs should be: Ended now	1	13	−12	12
Phased out over the next few years	17	45	−28	40
Continued for the foreseeable future	80	35	+45	41

Source: Based on nationwide telephone interviews with 1,258 adults including 173 black respondents, conducted December 6–9, 1997. In some questions, those with no opinion are not shown. The margin of sampling error is plus or minus three percentage points. Courtesy of *The New York Times*, Copyright 1997, The New York Times Company.

situations.[33] Using computer-assisted technology, respondents were confronted with a combination of vignettes and standard survey questions designed to explore the circumstances where whites and blacks

[33] Response Analysis Corporation (RAC), a highly regarded public polling firm based in Princeton, New Jersey, conducted the national telephone survey of 1,875 English-speaking adults. RAC used two sampling strategies for the study: one to represent the general population of the continental United States as a whole and a second to collect

might agree if given a similar set of facts. The computer randomly varied whether the place of employment was described as a bank or textile factory, and whether the employees were white or black. The first employee described in the vignette always has higher seniority than the second employee, who is described as having slightly better performance on the job.

> Please suppose that two employees in a [textile factory or bank] are being considered for a promotion. One of them will be promoted to manager. I will read you brief descriptions of these two people and then ask you which one you think SHOULD be promoted. Both are hardworking and well liked by most of the people they work with. The first person is a [black or white] male who has worked for the company for 8 years and whose job performance has been average. The second person is a [black or white] male who has done above average work for the six years that he has worked for the company. Based on what I have told you about these two people, which one do you think should be promoted to the manager position?

A follow-up question asks: "Regardless of who you think should get the job, who do you think the [factory or bank] would probably promote?" The computer was programmed to randomly rotate the race of the employees and the type of job.

The results of the survey question may seem surprising to some. Regardless of whether it was the white-collar bank job or the blue-collar factory position, both whites and blacks rejected seniority over performance as promotion criteria.[34] I had expected the majority of Americans to prefer seniority to promotion in the factory job and performance for the bank job. Surprisingly, majorities of both races said that the promotion should go to the employee with the best

data on an oversample of African Americans. The survey included a nationwide random digit sample of 1,070 adults, and a second sample of 805 African Americans. Overall, the sample combined 920 whites with 900 blacks and 55 members of other races. Pretests of the questionnaire were conducted in March and April of 1996. Interviewing took place during the summer and early fall of 1996. Respondents encountered general questions before coming across vignettes designed to elicit information about their attitudes toward criteria for college admissions criteria and job promotions. The survey had a 51 percent response rate.

[34] The results for the factory situation showed that the better-performing second employee is always preferred unless the high seniority employee is black. These differences were significant at the 95 percent confidence level. Chi-square, three degrees of freedom, $P \leq .034$.

performance. This view cut across race and it was seen in different situations, for example, when the employees were the same race and when there was a black employee competing against a white employee. Americans of both races seem to support the idea that jobs should generally go to those who perform them the best. Support for performance over seniority increased with education and income. Because the results were essentially the same for the bank and the factory position, I present data for the factory condition.

In the factory condition, the majority of whites and blacks confronted with the two employees preferred performance over seniority for promotion. Interestingly, when the person with the highest seniority happens to be African American, support among whites for performance drops off slightly in favor of seniority. The drop among whites is from 82 percent in the same-race, white/white condition, to 74 percent in the mixed-race, black/white condition. Whites are slightly MORE willing to compromise the performance principle when a black is benefited over a white than when a white is benefited over a black.

When asked the follow-up question of which employee will probably get the promotion, respondents were evenly divided when both employees were members of the same racial group. Consistent with their experiences and awareness of discrimination, African Americans confronted with a black employee in competition with a white employee were more likely to believe that the promotion would go to the white employee regardless of the black employee's performance.[35] The view that the promotion would go to the white employee was shared among whites as well and it increased with the education and income of the respondents. Both races thus showed some awareness of discrimination against blacks, since they expected the black employee to fare worse when in competition for a promotion with a white employee.

---

[35] In the black/white factory treatment, 29 percent of the respondents agreed that the first employee would get the promotion, while in the white/black situation, 69 percent of all respondents said that the white would get the promotion. In the other two treatments in which there is a black/black and a white/white combination, the percentage that thought the first candidate would be promoted was around 50 percent. This difference is statistically significant at the 99 percent confidence interval. Chi-square, three degrees of freedom, $P \leq .001$ Nevertheless, the consideration of seniority does not overweigh the consideration of race.

Unexpected agreement also occurred on another question related to employment. On this question the computer randomly rotated the groups asked about so that one-third of the respondents were asked about females, another third about minorities, and the final third blacks.

> Suppose that a company that has few [female/minority/black] employees was choosing between two people who applied for a job. If both people were equally qualified for the job and one was [a woman/a minority person/a black person], and the other [a man/was not a minority person/white] do you think the company should hire the [woman/minority person/black person], hire the [man/other person/white person], or should they find some other way to choose?

Eighty-two percent of whites and 71 percent of blacks said the company should find some other way to choose. Only 20 percent of blacks and 12 percent of whites said that an underrepresented minority should be selected. This question was, of course, affected by framing. The availability of a "cop out" choice allows respondents to take the easy way out on this sensitive issue. Had "flip a coin" been a response category, no doubt large numbers of respondents would have opted for it. But the fact that many were in a quandary over the choice shows that both blacks and whites hold strongly to the ideal that in general the best qualified person should be hired for a job.

Despite a surprising amount of agreement between whites and blacks when asked about concrete situations, the familiar pattern of disagreement and polarization appears when questions ask specifically about "affirmative action" and the continued need for affirmative action programs. For instance, on the survey I commissioned in 1996, whites and blacks disagreed as to whether affluent minorities should be able to benefit from affirmative action. One question asked: "First, do you think that the children of black professionals, such as doctors and lawyers, should or should not be able to benefit from affirmative action laws in college admissions?" Sixty-eight percent of African Americans said that they should be able to benefit, compared with 59 percent of whites who said they should not.[36] The same pattern of response appeared on a second question that immediately followed: "Do you think the children of black celebrities – such as actors or

---

[36] The difference between whites and black is significant at the 99 percent confidence level. Chi-square, one degree of freedom, $P \leq .001$.

professional athletes – should or should not be able to benefit from affirmative action laws in college admissions?" Seventy-two percent of blacks said that they should benefit, compared with 57 percent of whites who said that they should not.[37] Again, these are questions that I believe are especially sensitive to question wording, and for African Americans, the inclusion of the word "laws" is particularly relevant. Given their ongoing experiences with discrimination, African Americans were not about to deny other African Americans the benefits of what the question refers to as "affirmative action laws." Political party affiliation was also a significant factor in responses to this question. When asked whether the children of black professionals should be able to benefit from affirmative action laws, 58 percent of Republicans said that they should not be able, as compared with 64 percent of Democrats who said that they should be able to benefit.[38]

Despite some significant differences, the above responses should give cause for optimism because they clearly show that Americans agree on many important issues, and where they disagree, the disagreement is often the result of a combination of framing effects and the differing pictures that different groups carry around in their heads when they discuss the policy. Black and white Americans share many values, and they are not separated by unbridgeable gaps when survey questions are concrete enough for people to understand fully the issue that they are being asked to resolve. As I show in the next section, different racial and ethnic groups have different ways of thinking and talking about affirmative action. Some of what appears to be racial polarization occurs because of the ambiguity surrounding the concept of affirmative action, what the policy is, and what it was designed to accomplish.

FOCUS GROUP RESULTS

I have discussed framing effects and some of the limitations of traditional surveys.[39] At this juncture it is useful to examine in greater depth

---

[37] The difference between whites and blacks is significant at the 99 percent confidence level. Chi-square, one degree of freedom, $P \leq .001$.

[38] The difference between parties is significant at the 99 percent confidence level. Chi-square, two degrees of freedom, $P \leq .001$.

[39] Significant portions of this section were previously published as Carol M. Swain, Kyra Greene, and Christine Min Wotipka, "Understanding Racial Polarization on Affirmative Action: The View from Focus Groups," in John D. Skrentny, ed., *Color Lines:*

how Americans of different races and ethnicities view affirmative action policy. This section contributes to our understanding by presenting focus group discussions with ordinary Americans led in conversations about race by a member of their own racial or ethnic group.[40] During the spring of 1995, when affirmative action was an especially salient issue, I commissioned six focus groups consisting of African Americans, white Americans, Latinos, and Asian Americans that met either in Edison, New Jersey, or in New York City. The groups ranged in size from ten to twelve members, most of whom had some college education and many of whom were college graduates. A moderator of the same race or ethnicity led each group in loose, semistructured questioning over a two-hour session.[41]

Although focus groups have their own limitations, they have some important advantages over standard surveys. For instance, unlike standard surveys, focus groups allow researchers to observe facial expressions and gestures, and to interact directly with participants, thus providing greater opportunities to probe for answers and to seek clarification of previously expressed ideas. Their conversational tone also makes it possible to exchange ideas and insights that would be impossible to capture otherwise.[42] Another advantage can be greater candor. Researchers are able to capture discussions in a setting where strangers converse among themselves knowing that there is little likelihood of their ever encountering their fellow discussants again, thereby alleviating some concerns about offending the norms or sensibilities of their coparticipants.

There are, of course, limitations to the focus group approach. Unlike surveys that allow researchers to make inferences about the attitudes of a group of people much larger than those actually interviewed, this

Affirmative Action, Immigration, and Civil Rights Options for America (Chicago: University of Chicago Press, 2001), 214–38.

[40] To conduct the focus groups, Focus Plus of New York City and Schlesinger Associates of Edison, New Jersey, recruited and organized participants for a total of six groups. May 8–11, 1995.

[41] Focus groups are small numbers of people brought together and paid a nominal fee to discuss an assigned topic. For more information, see David W. Stewart and Prem N. Shamdasani, *Focus Groups: Theory and Practice* (Newbury Park, Calif.: Sage Publications, 1990); E. Kolbert, "Test Marketing a President: How Focus Groups Pervade Campaign Politics," *New York Times Magazine*, August 30, 1992.

[42] David L. Morgan, *Focus Groups as Qualitative Research*, 2nd ed. (Thousand Oaks, Calif.: Sage Publications, 1997), 2.

cannot be done with either focus groups or interviews. Moreover, the interactions between the participants and the moderator can affect what people choose to say. Just like with surveys and interviews some individuals in focus groups undoubtedly give socially desirable responses rather than their actual opinions. According to political scientist Pamela Conover and her colleagues, "focus groups mirror the social context within which many people actually experience citizenship."[43] Since we always have leaders and followers in this society, I do not think we should be overly concerned if some groups have dominant members who emerge as opinion leaders, while other participants take a back seat and perhaps follow the leader in their views. Because so much of what we know about American attitudes toward affirmative action comes from national surveys, I made a conscious and deliberate decision to sacrifice generalizability for greater depth and specificity on the issue. The small group discussions presented in this chapter and the interviews of the white nationalists scattered throughout the book give us, I believe, an understanding of how different Americans perceive and react to affirmative action policies and programs richer than that which can be extracted from more broadly based national opinion surveys.

Affirmative Action Perceived as Quotas

Since quotas have been one of the dominant ways in which the media have portrayed affirmative action for the American public, it should not be surprising to learn from our focus groups that each racial group, including African Americans, has internalized the frame that characterizes it as a quota program. There were differences, however, in the way racial groups thought the quotas operated. While many nonblacks described them as the forced selection of fixed numbers of minorities for jobs and other societal goods, many African Americans actually viewed quotas as restrictions used to limit the number of blacks in a given setting. This perception seemed most common among African American participants from the business world. Quotas were seen as

[43] Pamela J. Conover, Ivor M. Crewe, and Don Searing, "The Nature of Citizenship in the United States and Great Britain: Empirical Comments on Theoretical Concerns," *Journal of Politics* 53 (1991): 805.

maintaining a ceiling or limit on the number of blacks hired and a way of establishing a kind of institutional tokenism.[44]

None of the participants seemed aware that under current constitutional interpretation, racial quotas are legally suspect unless they are court-imposed as a remedy for past discrimination. The fact that different racial groups automatically associate affirmative action with unfair quotas demonstrates how well the critics of affirmative action, and particularly those in the Republican Party, have helped to frame the issue. When George Bush vetoed the proposed Civil Rights Act of 1990, he told Americans that the bill was not about civil rights protections, but about "quotas, quotas, quotas."[45] This kind of rhetoric has apparently filtered down to the lowest strata of society, and what those in our focus groups were saying about affirmative action during the spring of 1995 immediately following the Republican takeover of the Congress may reflect the effects of this Republican rhetoric.[46]

Asian Americans' Perceptions of Affirmative Action

Some Asian Americans described affirmative action in terms of quotas but saw quotas in a benign light, that is, as a means to equalize opportunities and diversify workplaces and educational institutions. The main objective of affirmative action for these people was to ensure the

---

[44] We did not have representatives of the academic world in our focus groups, though many black academics complain about tokenism in university faculty hiring. I myself have observed academic departments that are determined to employ one or two prominently displayed blacks, but just as determined not to go beyond this number.

[45] Kinder and Sanders, 163.

[46] In the spring of 1995, the Republican-controlled Congress voted to kill the controversial tax break for companies that sold broadcast licenses and cable stations to minorities. Moreover, some of the early Republican presidential candidates, including Senator Bob Dole (R-Kans.), Senator Phil Gramm (R-Texas), former Tennessee Governor Lamar Alexander, and California Governor Pete Wilson were staking out anti–affirmative action positions. For some, including the front-runner Dole, the anti–affirmative action position represented a considerable change from their earlier stances. By summer, Dole had introduced a bill that would have terminated all race, gender, and ethnic preferences in federal programs, while Charles T. Canady (R-Fla.) introduced a similar version in the house (House Bill 2128). In announcing his bill, Dole proclaimed that "[f]or too many citizens our country is no longer the land of opportunity but a pie chart where jobs and other benefits are often awarded not because of hard work or merit but because of someone's biology." Senator Bob Dole, quoted in Steven A. Holmes, "G.O.P. Lawmakers Offer a Ban on Federal Affirmative Action," *New York Times*, July 25, 1995.

hiring of minorities when they were qualified, and they believed that occurrences of unqualified minorities being hired to fill quotas were "rare." Other Asians, however, took a less benign view and believed that lesser-qualified minorities were sometimes hired for jobs. However, regardless of whether they felt minorities were being hired with lesser qualifications, most Asian Americans did not believe that race was enough to keep someone in a job once hired. They believed that the minority employee, like any other employee, needed to develop job skills in order to retain a position. One middle-aged woman remarked, "Affirmative action will work up to a certain point, if you want to get the job. But there's also performance. You also have to prove yourself. You can't stay in a company just because of your color."

One Asian-American male stated a view more commonly expressed among blacks, that racial quotas are used by companies to restrict rather than to expand the number of minorities. Using the Adolph Coors company as his example, he said that the company was reluctant to hire minorities until a group of homosexuals in San Francisco was able to get the bars in that city to agree to stop selling Coors beer until the company changed its employment practices. "The point is," he explained, "[quotas] were good, but not good. Because now . . . different people work for [the company]," but, he stated, "do you know what? They're still just meeting their quota. They're still just hiring just enough [minorities] to meet their quota." Although no one in the Asian-American group made the connection, this participant's example of the negative uses of quotas coincides with the claim by many Asian Americans that, since the early 1980s, ceilings have been placed on the number of Asians admitted to top universities.[47]

Latino Americans' Perceptions of Affirmative Action

Latinos in our focus groups were less supportive of affirmative action than the Asian Americans. Like many of the whites, a number of Latinos described affirmative action as a program involving quotas and set-asides, programs that allot a certain percentage of contracts to minority-owned businesses. The majority of Latino participants agreed that lower standards were being used to select minorities for employ-

[47] Dana Y. Takagi, *The Retreat from Race: Asian American Admissions and Racial Politics* (New Brunswick, N.J.: Rutgers University Press, 1992).

ment and for admission to institutions of higher education and that this was unfair. One Latino man gave an example of the use of racial preferences that other members of his group agreed was unfair. In his hypothetical example of race norming, two candidates applied for a job and took an examination. Even though the white applicant scored a 90 on the exam, the Latino, with a score of 75, was offered the job. Latinos in our focus groups expressed opposition to affirmative action that operated in this manner. One Latina woman declared, "I don't think quotas should be [used] or standards . . . lowered. It should be the same for everybody whether you're black, white, green, or yellow. There should be one level [for everyone to reach]." Another woman stated that using job-related quotas to lower the standards for minorities in competition with white people is racism.[48]

The Latino Americans in our focus groups also seemed to feel that affirmative action quotas harmed minorities by stigmatizing them as less competent than white Americans. Many articulated some of the same concerns as those of black conservatives when they discussed the stereotypes and stigmas attached to the beneficiaries of affirmative action programs. A foreign-born Latino man gave an example that he offered as proof of the negative assumptions that whites made about successful minorities:

> The messenger comes in the morning; he's American, Anglo-Saxon. He comes and he says to me, "What are you doing here?" [I say,] "I work here. I work in the computer room." He says, "I don't understand. They give the better jobs to people who come from other countries." I got very upset. I said, "Look, I went to school. I educated myself and I'm working here. You can do the same thing if you want to. [But] if you want to stay down and be a messenger all your life, it's your problem."

Of course, this exchange may demonstrate how easily two people may perceive the reality of employment in America very differently and may talk past one another. The white American may think that the newly

---

[48] Unknown to this participant, race norming in which the scores of minority candidates are grouped and compared only with the scores of other members of their group has been illegal in the employment context since the passage of the 1991 Civil Rights Act. Our participants were generally unaware of this and almost invariably assumed that race quotas and race norming were essential elements of affirmative action programs. No doubt perceptions were fueled by media depictions of programs that appear to openly use dual admission standards in higher education.

arrived Latino is a possible beneficiary of racial preferences, whereas the Latino's image of himself is of a person who has worked hard to earn his job and is more eager to get ahead than the white messenger. This exchange also shows the entanglement of immigration policy and affirmative action, which is partially responsible for the hostility that some whites and blacks express toward immigrants who compete for benefits under existing programs.

African Americans' Perceptions of Affirmative Action

The African Americans in our focus group never defined affirmative action in terms of preferential treatment, and as we have seen, they understood the concept of quotas differently from most whites and members of other groups. Rather than sources of opportunity, quotas were seen as potentially harmful restrictions used to limit the number of minorities in a given setting. An African-American male commented that employment quotas ensure that "only a certain number of blacks can succeed, or benefit from affirmative action, when maybe there's a whole cluster of people that are qualified. Maybe affirmative action says . . . you have to have three . . . [blacks]. What about the rest of those people?" In other words, they felt that affirmative action quotas could harm blacks overall by limiting the number who are offered positions. To them, the possibility existed that qualified African Americans would be overlooked once a certain threshold was reached at a given institution.

A majority of the African Americans in our focus groups believed that quotas exist and are reflected in the makeup of institutions. Although African Americans saw quotas as potentially harmful restrictions, they did not oppose their use entirely, since they saw them as assuring a minimal level of protection against discrimination. What our black focus group members seemed to want is for employment quotas to be expanded so that more than a token number of minorities would be hired, and they displayed little interest in whether there might be times when there were not enough qualified minorities to meet the demands of these expanded numerical goals. African Americans' acceptance of numerical quotas seems to follow from their fear of leaving their fate to the goodwill and subjective decision-making process of white Americans.

Some of our African-American focus group members thought affirmative action may cause employers to forego the hiring of the most qualified minorities in the interest of meeting quotas expediently. One man stated, "If you have a quota to hire four blacks, white employers may [run out and] just grab four blacks who may not be qualified for the job." According to this view, in the minds of many white Americans, African Americans are essentially interchangeable. Thus a fear existed that some employers will not consider the differential qualifications of blacks in the same manner as they would for white applicants.

White Americans' Perceptions of Affirmative Action

White Americans were clearly the most skeptical about affirmative action. A young white college-educated teacher explained her understanding of how affirmative action operates in the following words: "If you are the hiring boss and one applicant is white and the other black, you have to select the quota. . . . You have to fill the quota and hire the black." An older white man agreed: "Employers will not take white males when they have to take blacks, Hispanic, and Chinese. . . . Otherwise, they are going to be called racist. The government has put this policy in place and rammed it down our throats – this affirmative action."

When White Americans discussed affirmative action, they often spoke as if it were a relief program that required people to simply go in and sign up for public benefits. For example, some whites prefaced their comments with statements such as, "When people are in this affirmative action. . . ." Their comments suggested a belief that most, if not all, minority hires or college admits are unqualified beneficiaries of some kind of government largesse. Consistent with the "affirmative action hurts blacks" frame, a few white Americans expressed concern that the policy unfairly maligned qualified minorities. One white man viewed affirmative action in the manner found among our African-American critics, that is, as a form of ceiling quota that kept minority hiring within certain bounds. He stated:

> I think that affirmative action gives a person the right to be choosy in discrimination. [In other words,] I filled my quota, so now I don't have to hire any more blacks, Latinos or Asians. . . . Now I can hire whoever

I want, because my quota's already been met. . . . [Once quotas are met] somebody can come to the office who is a qualified black or Latino or Asian or whatever, and they could say, "Well. . . . we don't have to [hire this person]."

More typically, whites believed that affirmative action gave African Americans better opportunities than white Americans in both employment and education. Although the white Americans in Edison, New Jersey, were less hostile than the New Yorkers, one woman nevertheless complained to the nods of others that having African Americans in her work group meant that she had to perform her duties and theirs, too. There was a general belief among whites that once African Americans were hired under affirmative action they knew that they could not be fired easily and, as a result, often neglected their duties. All in all, the whites in our focus groups did not associate affirmative action with equal opportunities for all or with anything else positive.

THE GOALS OF AFFIRMATIVE ACTION
THROUGH DIFFERENT EYES

Some Americans confuse the procedures used in affirmative action programs with the stated goals of the programs. The confusion of goals with methods has implications for survey research, since researchers often ask respondents whether they think affirmative action programs have been successful in accomplishing their goals. Responses to survey questions can often leave us with more questions than answers because racial groups shared neither a common definition of affirmative action nor a uniform idea of its goals. The data suggest that respondents' opinions can be influenced by vastly different conceptual understandings of the policy.

The perceived goals of affirmative action varied across racial and ethnic groups. In all, the most commonly stated goals among our focus group members were: (1) promoting equal opportunity in employment and education, (2) eradicating racial discrimination, (3) diversifying workplaces and other institutions, (4) maintaining quotas, (5) assisting the poor, and (6) assisting people with disabilities. These are indeed the most frequently quoted reasons for maintaining and promoting affirmative action programs.

The Asian Americans in our focus groups discussed affirmative action in terms of its equal opportunity and diversification goals. They believed the policy has been instrumental in increasing the number of African Americans in a work force traditionally dominated by white Americans. One Asian American man saw the issue purely in numerical terms. He stated, "I think equalization or parity is the key word in affirmative action in that the government looks at the ratios of people [who are] minorities . . . as well as the majority, and then by that they set their quotas." In addition, the majority of Asians stated that affirmative action programs are still needed because of the discrimination that blacks continue to face. One woman said, "If I were a black person and if I [went] to an interview, even if I [had] the educational background, I think I'd have to work harder to reach or to meet their expectation, because of what . . . employers are thinking, expecting [of] black people."

Despite their strongly stated misgivings about the policy, many Latino Americans spoke in terms of affirmative action being a vehicle for increasing opportunities in education, employment, and minority-owned businesses. One Latino man stated that "a lot of people have gotten to go to school that wouldn't be able to. A lot of people have gotten jobs based on their knowledge, and their standing, that before [affirmative action] they might have never been able to." Significantly, however, no one in this group mentioned diversity enhancement or the remediation of past and present discrimination as either a justification or goal of affirmative action. Also, unlike other groups, Latino Americans believed that affirmative action should address issues relating to bilingual education and discrimination against people with Spanish surnames.

African Americans mostly described the goals of affirmative action programs as that of combating racial discrimination in employment and education. One black man stated: "[Affirmative action] is mostly based on federal positions, and it mostly looked to education. And it looked at ways to remedy past discrimination and ways to recruit more African Americans and bring more African Americans into the work force and into the mainstream." African Americans also described affirmative action policy as targeted at getting interviews and entry-level jobs. Like many other focus group members, however, they believed that while affirmative action might help in getting one's foot in the door, promotions were based on merit. Although blacks acknowledged enhanced opportunities in education brought about by race-specific grants and scholarships, unlike other groups, they did not seem to consider such programs to be affirmative action.

One elderly black man said that affirmative action was established to pacify blacks. He stated, "It says if we hire three whites, we should hire two blacks, because we don't want blacks to overrun the place. We don't want them in charge, so we have to have some whites in there to keep it balanced." Similarly, a Jamaican male commented, "What I see in offices in corporate America is one African-American reception-ist or secretary at the front desk, an African-American supply manager who fixes the copy machine, and that is the structure of corporate America." However, a more favorable assessment of corporate affir-mative action policies came from a young black female who stated, "I see affirmative action as positive because black people who are qualified get a chance. Otherwise, they would not be seen." Affirma-tive action, she said, "allows for an opportunity that otherwise would not have been had."

White Americans generally believed that affirmative action programs are used to give preferences to less qualified minorities. They also saw affirmative action as covering a much denser network and wider scope of activities than members of our other groups thought. Their examples, for instance, frequently mentioned affirmative action poli-cies not only in hiring decisions but in promotion decisions as well. They believed that affirmative action programs were common in higher education both in admissions to colleges and universities and in the granting of scholarships, and they drew attention to affirmative action programs in government contracting and loans. While mentioning several types of affirmative action programs, whites made no real dis-tinction between quotas, goals, and special efforts at recruitment and outreach.

It seems likely that part of the racial polarization in public opinion on affirmative action issues arises because groups possess different understandings about the policy. Whites clearly believe that a major goal of affirmative action is to give preference to lesser-qualified min-orities who cannot compete on their own merits, whereas many blacks believe that the primary goal of the policy is to eradicate otherwise intractable discrimination through the use of numerical goals which they also call quotas. African Americans see attacks on affirmative action as attacks on their lifeblood, because to them affirmative action is the only policy that addresses the effects of persistent and ongoing white discrimination against blacks. For many African Americans the alternative is seen as either mandatory numerical goals and quotas or the denial of jobs and promotions in businesses and governmental agencies from continued racial discrimination. Encompassed within African Americans' support for affirmative action is fear of discrimination. Some of the discrimination they fear is clearly illegal under existing civil rights law. Their attitudes toward affirmative action as antidiscrimination protection can help explain why a majority of African Americans in the 1996 national survey said that the children of black celebrities and black professionals should be able to benefit from "affirmative action laws" in admissions. For them, all blacks need and deserve protection against persistent discrimination. This suggests that any policy modifications of affirmative action must include a substantial and convincing means of addressing antiblack discrimination if it is to win the trust of blacks.

Between these poles are Asian Americans and Latinos. Like African Americans, both Latinos and Asian Americans see some forms of affirmative action as necessary. However, Asian Americans see the program as one that benefits blacks and angers whites. They were unclear as to the impact of affirmative action on their own life chances and opportunities. Latinos, on the other hand, see affirmative action as having a direct impact on their lives, but as a group they are ambivalent about whether the programs affect them in a positive or negative way. Latinos, more so than African Americans, are concerned that affirmative action stigmatizes them by casting doubt on their achievements. They showed a clear interest in distinguishing themselves from African Americans.

WHO ARE THE BENEFICIARIES AND HOW DO THEY BENEFIT?

African Americans and at least one Latino American argued that whites benefit from affirmative action because companies that comply with the policy gain advantages in loans and government contracts. One

Latina New Yorker stated that her employer "got extra money and they got grants that came in because they had me there."[49]

African Americans in our focus groups addressed many issues surrounding immigrant beneficiaries of affirmative action and the evolution of hostility toward the policy. More than other groups, African Americans rejected the view that all minority groups in the United States should be beneficiaries of affirmative action. They were also the only group to differentiate between native-born blacks and black immigrants. The majority of African Americans did not think that newly arrived immigrant groups should be allowed to benefit from affirmative action policies; rather, they believed that these policies should be reserved for members of historically disadvantaged groups in America. One woman stated that a "woman from India came in and took advantage of [affirmative action] and is making millions and millions of dollars. She's not the only one, it's people that are coming in from other countries and they're taking advantage of all that is here."[50]

Even though Asian Americans are protected under federal affirmative action regulations, some expressed a lack of awareness as to how their group benefits from the policy. Most Asian Americans, they argued, are uninformed about their eligibility for affirmative action.

---

[49] Using very different reasoning, Law Professor Derrick Bell has made similar claims. White women, in particular, Bell has argued, have benefited from affirmative action and have often received a greater percentage of affirmative action jobs than African Americans. Similarly, he contends that white men have benefited from the widespread advertising of jobs done pursuant to affirmative action programs. Were it not for affirmative action, he argues, these jobs would be filled by the "Old Boys Network," which restricted the opportunities of some white males situated outside of the network. Derrick Bell, "The Mystique of Affirmative Action," public address delivered at Princeton University, April 24, 1995.

[50] Jennifer Lee captures this tension between African Americans and immigrant groups in New York and Philadelphia: "As Jews move up and out of black neighborhoods, and new immigrants such as Koreans, Middle Easterners, and Asian Indians move in, blacks witness a succession of newer groups moving up and out, realizing the American dream of success. The image of immigrants (and non-blacks more generally) coming into black communities, buying the businesses, and leaving with the profits at night, is a provocative one for most blacks. Who owns the stores in the community is laden with symbolism, translating into far more than what these businesses generate in profit. Lee found that African Americans frequently suspected the government of unfairly preferring immigrant minorities for small business loans and other affirmative action programs. Jennifer Lee, "From Prosiac Routine to Racial Conflict: Individualism, Opportunity, and Group Position," in "From Civil Relations to Exploding Cauldrons: Blacks, Jews, and Koreans in Urban America," unpublished manuscript.

The group blamed a number of factors for this, including a lack of outreach into Asian American communities, complacency, citizenship status, and the poor English language skills of some newly arrived Asian immigrants.

Latinos spoke mostly of African Americans as being the beneficiaries of affirmative action policy, although they understand that they, too, are a protected group. Latinos favored class-based affirmative action because they thought that such a policy would reduce the stigmatization of beneficiary groups. Some Latinos stated that affirmative action was responsible for increased hostilities between racial and ethnic groups, especially between white Americans and Latinos and between Latinos and blacks. Latinos expressed some concern that affirmative action was harmful to some minorities because it can cause them to feel privileged and consequently not to work as hard as they might.

Similarly, white Americans saw the beneficiaries of affirmative action as being mostly undeserving African Americans. When they discussed other racial groups, their tone was softer and less hostile. Two older white women in the New York focus group acknowledged gender discrimination, but argued that they had risen in their jobs without any assistance from affirmative action. In representative national samples, white women are seen to oppose the preferential treatment of racial minorities as much as white men.[51] They are somewhat more supportive of affirmative action programs for women, as is the general population, but a majority of white women still oppose such programs. This latter fact may be related to women's concerns over the lessened opportunity for their husbands and sons.

When it comes to who should benefit from affirmative action policies, there is substantially more consensus that the disabled and the poor are truly deserving. Affirmative action for the disabled was not a major area of contention for any group. Perhaps this is because the groups were aware at some level that, unlike minority status, anyone can become disabled through accident or disease at any time

---

[51] David W. Moore, "Americans Today Are Dubious about Affirmative Action," *The Gallup Poll Monthly*, March 1995; Everett C. Ladd, "Affirmative Action: Welfare and the Individual," *Public Opinion and Polls*, April/May 1995, "Preferential Treatment for Women and Minorities," *The Gallup Monthly Poll*, December 7–10, 1989; "Affirmative Action Programs," *The Gallup Monthly Poll*, March 25–28, 1977.

in one's life. Although many of the focus group members stated the general proposition that individual merit should be used to judge applicants for jobs, when they discussed the disabled, a majority held that while people should be hired for jobs that they are physically capable of performing, they did not add the qualification that the disabled applicant should be the *most* qualified for the position. One man saw helping the disadvantaged as a positive kind of affirmative action. He stated, "As far as disabled people went, when a potential employer wants to discriminate against a disabled person because he is disabled, there are affirmative action laws to combat that and to make sure that the disabled person gets a fair shake." The moderator then asked, "So you think that the affirmative action program for disabled people is a positive program?" The man responded, "Somewhat positive, yeah ... but, you've got to use it. . . . You've got to understand your rights and you have to use it."

A majority of our focus group members in each group seemed to concur with the general public that poor people, regardless of race or ethnicity, should be among the beneficiaries of affirmative action. Those who believed that strong individuals lead to stronger communities were more likely to favor programs that benefited people in need. A Latino male stated:

> There [are] so many people that before a lot of these things [i.e., affirmative action programs] were implemented never had a chance to get an education because of their class or economic standings or their race, though people will deny that, but, yeah, that's the truth and the fact of the matter is that without an education, you're never going to get that economic growth that you need in those communities and you're always going to have – it's just a circle.[52]

While supporting some class-based affirmative action, white Americans were more ambivalent about means-tested scholarships than members of our other groups. They were concerned about those persons who would be excluded from participation. To the agreement

---

[52] The greater support for race-neutral programs has led scholars such as William J. Wilson to recommend replacing affirmative action with programs that offer "affirmative opportunity" to all Americans struggling with the changing global economy, declining wages, and low-skill jobs. See Wilson's *Bridge over River Divide*.

of others in her group, one white woman stated that "a child should be able, based on his ability, how smart he is, what he's learned in his elementary years, that if he is deserving to go to a better school, whether his parents can afford to send him to a city university or private institution, that he deserves [a scholarship] on his own merit." A Latina expressed the opposite view when she argued that the "cruel reality" is that children who attend good high schools receive a better education and have superior opportunities for going to good universities. Consequently, she concluded, scholarships based solely on merit are unfair. Another participant agreed:

> I think having a scholarship just open to everyone is probably not a good idea. There should be some other merits besides [academic achievement considered] because . . . if people anywhere are going to get at the scholarships, the majority of them are going to be either upper class kids, regardless of their race, because they get the better education. They get the better schools and everything else.

African Americans mostly favored group-based affirmative action that takes race into consideration, whereas the majority of whites in our focus groups strongly opposed such programs. Some Latino Americans were concerned that race-based affirmative action programs spoil minorities into believing that they deserve special treatment because of their minority status. To them, all people should be treated equally as individuals without regard to race and without any preferential treatment. The majority of Asian Americans in our focus groups saw a need to consider the needs of both individuals and groups. However, they, too, expressed concerns about the abuse of some of the programs, and these references were directed mostly at blacks.

Just as with the goals and the definition of affirmative action, participants did not agree on who the beneficiaries of affirmative action are or should be. Not only were there different ideas relating to which specific groups have benefited and should benefit from affirmative action programs, there were also disagreements as to whether emphasis should be given to groups who suffer from past and present discrimination or only to individuals in financial need. Group differences about who the beneficiaries are and the goals of affirmative action highlight the difficulty of interpreting previously acquired information about the policy and its level of public support.

PERCEPTIONS OF DISCRIMINATION BY RACE AND ETHNICITY

The most crucial explanatory factor for understanding differences between the racial and ethnic groups' views of affirmative action programs seems to be their disparate perceptions of the existence of discrimination in American society today. Consistent with much survey research, groups divided over whether racial discrimination against blacks and other people of color is still a common occurrence.[53] On this issue, white Americans and African Americans saw different realities as whites minimized the extent of continuing discrimination against blacks, while blacks asserted its prevalence. Asian Americans and Latino Americans expressed an awareness of continued discrimination against minorities, although these groups did not explicitly agree with blacks that affirmative action is the most appropriate remedy for discrimination. Only in one instance did a Latino American express the belief that present-day discrimination justified the need for affirmative action programs. She frequently faced discrimination, she believed, because of her physical appearance as someone of Latin descent. She stated, "It might not be all the time, but it's there, a little bit. So once you go into the job market from school, I think that [minorities] can still need that help from affirmative action."

White Americans, for their part, believed that racial discrimination against minorities was largely a thing of the past. Many, however, viewed themselves as victims of "reverse discrimination." Given the powerful media frame of reverse discrimination, it was not startling that many whites mentioned reverse discrimination and saw themselves as victims unprotected by government. In each of our minority groups, a few Asian Americans, Latinos, and African Americans acknowledged the real possibility of reverse discrimination against whites. Several Asian Americans stated that if they were white Americans, they would be resentful of affirmative action because it seems to deny white people jobs for which they are qualified. In this context, one person observed that there is a growing "reactionary movement in this country, the

---

[53] Schuman et al., *Racial Attitudes in America*; Kinder and Sanders, *Divided by Color*.

angry white male." Clearly, this participant seemed alarmed by white anger and the possibility that there might be an injustice occurring, or at least the widespread perception of injustice.

Using focus group material on a number of diverse topics including affirmative action, social scientist William Gamson identified this same sort of ambivalence and equivocation in his groups.[54] According to Gamson, racial groups may express moral outrage at perceived injustice against their group, a concept he calls "single indignation." A more complex form of indignation, which he calls "double indignation," arises when a person expresses outrage at how her group is being treated, and frustration and anger at how other groups are treated as well. With affirmative action, "double indignation" in Gamson's terms can occur when individuals, such as African Americans, acknowledge that their own group is discriminated against while also admitting that attempts to rectify the injury can have adverse impacts on others. In each ethnic group, at least one person expressed sensitivity to members of other groups. For instance, a black advocate of quotas in employment worried that unqualified minorities would sometimes be hired for jobs that more qualified individuals deserve. Another woman talked about the benefits that diversity can bring to institutions, but she nevertheless expressed fears that in some instances people are being selected because of their skin color and not their ability, a development that she thought was detrimental. Similarly, an older Asian American woman reported feeling "divided on the issue" of affirmative action. She stated, "[I] wouldn't feel good about taking [a] job if I knew that I [received] it because of [my] origins."

Asian Americans and Discrimination

The Asian American focus group members did not feel that they faced much discrimination in their everyday lives, and they discussed the benefits of being perceived as a "model minority." One man said that Asian Americans may experience some prejudice directed toward them but that they are usually not discriminated against outright. A middle-aged Asian American woman said, "Maybe [discrimination] has been

---

[54] William A. Gamson, *Talking Politics* (New York: Cambridge University Press, 1992).

directed towards me; I've never felt it." However, other research suggests that Asian Americans continue to face forms of public and private discrimination.[55] Sociologist Myrtle Bell and her colleagues, for instance, found that Asian Americans experience workplace discrimination that surpasses that of white Americans but less than Latinos and African Americans.[56] A 1989 *Los Angeles Times* poll of Southern Californians found that nearly half of all blacks, 29 percent of Latinos, and 41 percent of Asian Americans in the survey reported having experienced some discrimination in their lifetimes.[57]

Unlike our other groups, Asian-American participants openly discussed the fact that members of their group might be perpetrators of discrimination. One young man said that Asians themselves are a very discriminatory people and that they are responsible for discriminating against others, including other Asian-American subgroups. He used the company that he works for as his example. It is a Japanese company in New York City with a work force that is 85 percent Japanese and the rest mostly whites and Hispanics. "We have only one black [employee]," he complained. "[The company has 80 employees] and only one black. . . . Proportion-wise it's really strange; it's not right." Another Asian American stated that "affirmative action helps in that it forces those who cannot see beyond what they've grown up with, to take a step [forward] and hire a person that might be different from what they've been used to."

The fact that Asian American participants did not feel that they had been victims of discrimination, but had witnessed discrimination against other groups, especially African Americans, is very important. This perception may explain, in part, why Asian Americans in this study, while not seeing affirmative action as beneficial to their group, nevertheless supported the policy.

---

[55] Theodore Hsein Wang and Frank Wu, "Beyond the Model Minority Myth: Why Asian Americans Support Affirmative Action," *Guild Practioner* 53 (Winter 1996): 35–47; K. K. Narasaki, "Separate But Equal? Discrimination and the Need for Affirmative Action Legislation," in *Perspectives on Affirmative Action* (Los Angeles: Asian Pacific American Public Policy Forum, 1995), 5–8; Takagi, *The Retreat from Race.*

[56] Myrtle P. Bell, David A. Harrison, and Mary E. McLaughlin, "Asian American Attitudes Toward Affirmative Action in Employment: Implications for the Model Minority Myth," *Journal of Applied Behavioral Science* 33 (1997): 356–77.

[57] Peter Skerry, *Mexican Americans: The Ambivalent Minority* (New York: Free Press, 1993).

Latino Americans and Discrimination

Members of the Latino group provided a number of examples from their own lives that showed experiences with discrimination. Some expressed the view that the job experiences of Latinos differed significantly from those of their white American counterparts. For one bank teller, it meant that she had to stay in a particular branch location in order to accommodate the bank's Latino customers despite her request for a transfer and desire for a promotion. Others talked about the subtle and not-so-subtle reactions they received to their Spanish surnames. For example, one woman explained that since she married and began using her husband's Anglo last name, she has been treated more positively by others. Not only did Latinos encounter discrimination resulting from surnames, but they also suffered from stereotypes about their countries of origin. Much like the sensitivity that some Italian Americans hold about Mafia stereotypes, the natives of Colombia in our focus groups felt that they were looked upon by American society as drug dealers.

African Americans and Discrimination

As would be expected given their history in the United States, the African-American participants expressed the strongest emotions about the impact of discrimination in their everyday lives. Overall, blacks seemed supportive of affirmative action more because of their concerns about current discrimination than about discrimination rooted in the past. In fact, concerns about ongoing discrimination seemed to dominate African Americans' conversations about affirmative action.

African Americans supported affirmative action largely because they view its programs as their only protection against continued racial discrimination, and they looked toward it rather than other civil rights legislation to provide them with a measure of relief, which might be related to the difficulty of identifying and rooting out hidden discrimination. Yet many blacks were extremely cynical about actual affirmative action programs. One young black male complained that even with affirmative action blacks have fewer opportunities to get ahead in business than whites. He asked, "[Why] do blacks have to work twice as hard as whites? Why can't we all work at the same pace and get the same benefits?" Similarly, a middle-aged black male commented that "affirmative action is a buzzword defined by the media to suggest that we're getting remedies for past discrimination, which means that somehow a black person must take a job from a white person, which suggests that white people are foreordained to have the jobs." As long as blacks see affirmative action as their only line of defense against rampant societal discrimination, they will, of course, express strong support for the policy and view any attempts to modify or eliminate affirmative action programs as a threat to their well-being. What these African Americans were most frequently arguing in support of was nondiscrimination and equal opportunity, and not racial preferences in the form of bonus points to elevate themselves above other competitors.

White Americans and Discrimination

Other than their fears of "reverse discrimination," most whites did not express concern that racial discrimination has had any serious impact on their lives. Some of the participants in our New York group felt that whites in the city had experienced discrimination under Mayor David Dinkins's administration. One man stated that when Dinkins (who is African American) was mayor, the government did not hire white people for construction jobs. He stated:

> [A person] had to be black to get the job. They didn't have to do the job right, they didn't have to know anything, but they had to be black. Now, all these unions were protesting this. . . . Men that had experience that [could do] the job . . . couldn't get the job because they weren't black. So there it is. Reverse discrimination.

A man who otherwise seemed sympathetic toward blacks commented that "a white man is the last one hired. And in my opinion, that's the only negative thing to affirmative action." Therefore, even among those whites who view the policy favorably, there is some agreement with the sentiment that affirmative action had gone too far in helping minorities and discriminating against whites.

CONCLUDING OBSERVATIONS

From this chapter, we can see how responses to questions about affirmative action are often related to how the questions are worded, the answer choices, the context, and the pictures and frames that the media and other sources have helped to propagate. Despite the debate over affirmative action and the information presented in the previous chapter, it is inaccurate to say dogmatically that white Americans oppose all affirmative action programs, while African Americans enthusiastically support them. Survey questions that use concrete examples lend support to the view that a majority of Americans support equal opportunity, outreach, and race-neutral public policies designed to help disadvantaged Americans. When Americans disagree, especially, whites and blacks, the data in this chapter suggest that it is their differential experiences with discrimination that explain their views.

The intensity of experiences with discrimination, however, is not the only source of disagreement. Groups express different opinions about affirmative action policies because they have varying amounts of information about how these policies work and the problems that they are designed to address. Focus group comments suggest that some African Americans view affirmative action as a protection against persistent discrimination, whereas many white Americans view the policy as reverse discrimination against innocent whites. Information from the focus groups can help us interpret why blacks so readily embrace affirmative action benefits for children of black celebrities and black professionals such as lawyers and doctors. Given their experiences with discrimination, African-American respondents were not about to deny other blacks protection. All blacks, even the most affluent, are seen as possible victims of white-initiated discrimination. The response of blacks might have been different if they had been presented with a longer vignette describing two different individuals competing for scarce places in college as I show in a later chapter on college admissions.

The data from the focus groups suggest that despite their willingness to express their opinions, Americans of different races and ethnicities lack a shared vocabulary and a shared perceptual basis for evaluating affirmative action policies. Within and across groups, discussions were often confused, suggesting that Americans lack a common understanding of affirmative action policies and their goals. Ironically, none of the focus group members eagerly endorsed the diversity rationale for affirmative action in higher education, and only the Asians stressed strong support for using racial preferences to rectify past discrimination. Possibly, evidence of ongoing discrimination against racial minorities could generate support among Americans for stronger antidiscrimination laws, especially since many white Americans are themselves convinced that they are the victims of racial discrimination.

Language philosopher W. B. Gallie has described speech situations dominated by what he calls "essentially contested concepts" in which discrepant and partially shared meanings lead to empty debates, devoid of meaning.[58] The affirmative action controversy may be understood in part as just such a situation. Because Americans speak different languages and see different realities when it comes to race, we are yet to have a serious discussion about race in America and especially about racial preferences and what their fate should be as the nation becomes increasingly nonwhite. As we see in the next chapter, white nationalists frame the debate about affirmative action in a manner that emphasizes the harm done to white Americans. As shown below, our failure to deal honestly and in clear language with racial issues such as affirmative action is creating an environment that opportunistic white racialists are exploiting to their own ends.

[58] W. B. Gallie, "Essentially Contested Concepts," in Max Black, ed., *The Importance of Language* (Englewood Cliffs, N.J.: Prentice Hall, 1966), 121–46.

8

A GRIEVANCE MADE TO ORDER? WHITE NATIONALIST GROUPS ON AFFIRMATIVE ACTION AND OTHER RACE-RELATED ISSUES

The National Association for the Advancement of White People (NAAWP) was set up to get us back to the point where everyone is seen as created equal, where everyone has equal opportunity, and where everybody is judged under the same guidelines and the same set of standards. The NAAWP does not wish to convey the idea that we are a white supremacist-type of organization or that we want to advance beyond other groups. We just want to return to the ideal in which racially based policies of affirmative action and special privileges and special programs of any kind which are given to anybody, no matter what their race, are viewed as contrary to the best interests of race relations here in America.

Reno Wolfe, December 22, 1999

As the opening quotation from NAAWP president Reno Wolfe suggests, affirmative action – framed as an unfair practice of illegal racial discrimination – plays a central role in the call of white nationalists for solidarity and resistance to existing racial double standards. In their pointed references to the injustice of racial preferences and all double standards in the enforcement of civil rights laws, white nationalists are tapping into grievances that many mainstream white Americans share. For this reason, policymakers and other persons in positions of authority, it is suggested here, need to take their protests more seriously than they have. As the previous two chapters have shown, many Americans of different races oppose the use of quotas or racial preferences to achieve the goals of affirmative action policies. European Americans are among the most angered over racial preferences, and an increasing number of them could become vulnerable to the appeals of white nationalists and separatists, particularly if a downturn in the economy increases uncertainty about the future.[1]

Unfortunately, much of the current discussion of affirmative action fails to take into consideration the changing political milieu in which white Americans find themselves. Whites are rapidly becoming an aging numerical minority, surrounded by poorer, faster-growing minority populations all presently eligible for racial preferences.[2] This is bound to cause heightened anxieties, resentments, and insecurities, especially among those in the white working and lower middle classes whose economic and social position is least secure. Moreover, minority defenders of multiculturalism, in making their case for racial, ethnic, and cultural minorities to organize and celebrate group pride and self-determination, have unwittingly laid the foundation for a corresponding white-centered racial movement that celebrated the racial pride of white people. What exists in America and in much of the Western world is a growing set of circumstances that could cause large numbers of white people of European extraction to embrace the idea of a distinct white interest that is not being adequately represented by a government that endorses racial preferences for nonwhites. The end result of this development can only be heightened intergroup conflict in the nations so affected.

APPROPRIATING THE LANGUAGE OF VICTIMHOOD

Just like women's groups and gay rights groups, many white nationalist organizations have adopted the 1960s civil rights frame that condemns discrimination against individuals on the basis of their race, ethnicity, religion, national origins, or gender. White nationalists

---

[1] For information about the changing global economy and how it affects all Americans, see Robert Reich, *The Work of Nations* (New York: Alfred Knopf, 1991), 171–84; Wilson, *The Bridge over the Racial Divide*, 11–43. Kaplan and Weinberg, 14–17, specifically discuss the many ways that globalization impacts the transatlantic nature of white nationalism.

[2] Kaplan and Weinberg, 15.

believe that because of affirmative action, white people have become the group most oppressed by discrimination in America, and they have sought to claim for themselves and their racial kinsmen the status of aggrieved victim. "Discriminating against whites," an NAAWP flyer proclaims, "is certainly just as morally wrong as it is against blacks, Hispanics, Asians, or anyone else, yet when reported, whites are called racists!"[3] This is a near-universal sentiment in white nationalist literature. White nationalists thus see themselves as double victims: as victims of discrimination in jobs and education, and as victims of calumny and slander when they protest such abuse.

In response to this situation, websites have appeared in recent years specifically for the purpose of enabling whites who believe they have been victims of affirmative action programs to share their sense of grievance and outrage with a sympathetic audience of fellow whites.

An example of such a website is adversity.net. The following letter posted on one of its message boards well expresses the sense of victimization and injustice that many whites feel toward those affirmative action programs that give preference to minorities.

> I was horrified at [my father's] "Archie Bunker" persona. I thought him to be the most prejudiced person I knew and swore that I would never be like him. For over 35 years I was the exact opposite of my father. I praised civil rights and encouraged affirmative action. All of this stopped when the state agency I worked for proved to me that my father had been right all the time. I have watched as black minorities are hired with no experience and then promoted within a short time, not because they are worthy of promotion, not because they are qualified, but because they are part of a quota that the state must meet. I have watched over the past ten years as racial preferences have become prevalent throughout the United States and now I am disgusted with myself for once believing that we could all be equal. People of "color" have come to expect plush jobs, they have come to expect hefty promotions. I chose to make something of my life, I worked hard, confident that someday I would achieve success. What I got was a wall named "Affirmative Action."[4]

Besides the issue of racial preferences and "reverse discrimination," most white nationalists protest with equal vehemence what they see as

---

[3] "Does Society Penalize Whites?," http://www.naawp.com/flyers/webflyer2.htm.
[4] "Re: For the Racists," http://www.adversity.net/wwwboard/messages/72.html.

a threat to the integrity of white European culture emanating from the immigration into America of large numbers of nonwhites from the Third World. Demographic trends indicating that white Americans will become a numerical minority soon after the year 2050 are a source of great alarm, and most white nationalist organizations would like to see an immediate stop to immigration, legal as well as illegal, from all non-white countries. Most white nationalists would welcome increased immigration from Europe, however.

In what follows, I offer brief sketches of some of the leading organizations, individuals, and ideas that compose the white nationalist movement, and try to explain how the white nationalist right is using the deeply felt sense of white grievance over current affirmative action policy and other race-related issues to expand its influence into more mainstream circles. Much of the material in this chapter is taken from the telephone interviews with leading white nationalist figures that were undertaken as part of this project in late 1999 and early 2000.

THE NATIONAL ASSOCIATION FOR THE ADVANCEMENT OF WHITE PEOPLE

If black people can have an organization like the National Association for the Advancement of Colored People to champion their rights and interests, why can't white people have a comparable organization to champion their concerns? Such is the logic of Reno Wolfe, the current president of the National Association for the Advancement of White People (NAAWP), an organization that he has headed since the beginning of 1998. The original NAAWP was founded by David Duke in the early 1980s, but the Duke-founded NAAWP eventually faded from the scene and Reno Wolfe goes out of his way to distinguish his revived organization from the earlier NAAWP founded by Duke. "A lot of people confuse us with an organization that originated out of Louisiana that went defunct quite a few years ago called the NAAWP," Wolfe declares. "We are the National Association for the Advancement of White People, National, Inc., out of Florida. . . . This organization has nothing at all to do with David Duke, or his philosophy, or his goals."[5] As of December 2000, Wolfe's organization reportedly had established

---

[5] Reno Wolfe, interview, Dec. 22, 1999.

a total of fifty-two chapters, including ones in Canada and South Africa.[6]

Central to the NAAWP's efforts to influence public opinion is its web-based newsletter that provides continually updated reporting on a host of race-related issues. Its newsletter commentary is permeated by a sense of protest and grievance at many perceived racial double standards in America that discriminate against whites, particularly in the areas of employment, education, and crime reporting. The NAAWP proclaims its central purposes on its website: "We are a civil rights organization specifically founded for white people to counter reverse discrimination. We welcome all people who want to learn about us." The NAAWP sees itself as a securer and protector of the rights of a beleaguered white population against a minority-favoring government that is indifferent to the legitimate rights and concerns of white people. "We are against Affirmative Action, Job Quotas, [and] Special Rights," it declares in its promotional literature. "We are for Equal Rights, Equal Opportunity & No Special Rights!"

A perusal of the NAAWP website can be quite an adventure for the first-time explorer. Melanie Harris, a research assistant on this project, describes her own encounter with naawp.com in the spring of 2000:

> I went to www.naawp.com, the site for the National Association for the Advancement of White People. Before I can even access the site, a box flashed up with a warning sign that advised me that I will be given access to "the truth" and that all are welcome to learn the truth. The warning box also informs the web surfer that the group is committed to counter reverse discrimination. It suggests that the surfer keep "an open mind." After I clicked the "ok" button in an attempt to enter the site (I later realized that pressing the "cancel" button works the same way that the "ok" button does), another box popped up in the corner of my screen asking me to "please read [their] opening message." It was addressed: "Dear White Americans," which I found shocking since the previous note had suggested that all were welcome to the site. It seemed such an abrupt shift of audience. The opening message addressed high crime and a decreasing moral value system, which differs from the 1960's, when a high school degree was respectable, people were not in debt, man and woman lived together (with man at work and woman at home), there

---

[6] "The Year in Hate: Hate Groups Top 500, Net Sites Soar," *Intelligence Report* (Winter 1999): 7; NAAWP chapter links, http://www.naawp.com/links.html.

were no curses on TV or in movies, etc. White men created both modern society and strong values. Without saying why, the site warns these values are "melting like an ice cube in the summer." For $25 a viewer can show "courage" and "commitment" by becoming a NAAWP member.[7]

By the summer of 2000, Wolfe's organization had changed its web page to project a friendlier, more inclusive image and had removed much racially virulent material.[8] Its chat board now warns visitors not to use profanity or speak of violent actions against other racial and ethnic groups. Although the NAAWP under Wolfe often reports on black crime in a manner that tends to equate Africanness with criminality and shows little concern for the sensibilities of those who are nonwhite, his organization has moved in a much more moderate direction from the earlier organization headed by David Duke.

Wolfe, for instance, specifically rejects the goals of either white supremacy or white separatism as proclaimed by other white nationalist organizations and says his group wants only equal justice as was originally envisioned in the 1964 Civil Rights Act. His organization rails against "special privilege programs" for nonwhites, and he believes the government is not doing enough to help poor whites because of its overemphasis on the problems of racial minorities. His own organization has sponsored food drives and other charitable activities for poor whites in Appalachia and elsewhere. He complained to the interviewer for this project that America is now saturated with special privilege programs from which whites are excluded. We have now, he protested, special minority-targeted programs

> for how to take care of the young and how to raise them – special this, and special that. There are special before school programs when minority children get in elementary school, and then special tutors in the school, and then special programs for that child after school. And all the way up to high school they make special dispensation for minority students who for some reason are unable to graduate when judged by the same standards applied to others. Now that's not affirmative action itself, but those are just some of the programs that are out there that we think are unfair and we oppose.[9]

---

[7] Melanie Harris's account of her spring 2000 visit to the NAAWP's website.
[8] Reno Wolfe, personal correspondence June 12, 2000.   [9] Reno Wolfe, interview.

Wolfe's organization also seeks to combine its anti–affirmative action protest with a white pride initiative that affirms the legitimacy of white people being proud of their racial and cultural heritage just as minority group members are proud of theirs. Wolfe is especially interested in rescuing the word "white" from what he sees as its denigration by the media. "People in the media," he says, "don't like our name."

> They would hope that we would probably use another name instead of NAAWP – the National Association for the Advancement of White People. If we just called ourselves the National Association for the Advancement of European Americans, then that would be more politically correct, and probably more advantageous for us in terms of media relations. Just the word "white" scares the hell out of 'em. However, once people read and learn about our organization and learn about our goals and our concepts, about what we wish to accomplish, well then they understand where we're coming from. . . . When people get past the word "white" and start understanding the whole concept and goals and principles of the organization, well then they join: then they understand what we're doing. We are the only organization out there that fights at the grass roots level throughout this country against affirmative action and all these special programs, special minority set-asides, special scholarships. . . . Instead of bringing people together, all these programs, we believe, are really racially divisive. As long as we have these programs, this country will be forever racially divided. . . . Our adversaries have tried to make the word white a dirty word. But there's nothing dirty about it. There's nothing bad about being a white. . . . If people get upset about the word white, they have to look within themselves about what's wrong with the word white. . . . My grandparents were white. As far as I know, the whole family has been white, so, I have a white heritage, a white past. Why should I be ashamed to use the word white?[10]

NATIONAL ORGANIZATION FOR EUROPEAN AMERICAN RIGHTS

If the word "white" scares away some potential supporters to the white nationalist cause, David Duke would seem to have solved this problem with his new organization, the National Organization for

[10] Ibid.

European American Rights, whose acronym – NOFEAR – suggests that whites should not fear asserting their legitimate racial interests. NOFEAR was founded in January of 2000 and by the end of the year the organization listed twenty-six national chapters, including one in New York City (see Epilogue for update).

Like the Wolfe organization, opposition to race-based preference programs seems to have played a major role in the founding of NOFEAR. In addition, concern over the preservation of the distinct racial and cultural heritage of Europeans in America, which is believed to be threatened by the expanding size of the nonwhite population, has played an equally important role. "European-Americans," Duke told our interviewer, "face . . . pernicious racial discrimination on a multi-level basis in this country."

> There's discrimination going on in hiring and promotions, in college admissions, in scholarship programs, in university admittance, in contracting, and in many other areas of American life. It's our contention that if discrimination is indeed morally wrong when exercised against minorities, then it's just as morally reprehensible when exercised against members of the European-American majority. This organization works for what we perceive to be the overall interests of European-Americans and the preservation of our heritage and way of life in this country. So it's about civil rights, but it's also about preservation of our entity as an ethnic people, our existence, our values, our culture, our traditions, and the things that really go to make up traditional America.[11]

Continuing with the affirmative action theme, Duke complained to our interviewer that whites were specifically singled out for a form of institutional discrimination in admissions to universities, as well as in a number of other areas:

> There is an institutionalized racial discrimination going on against white Americans today. There have been some recent studies at major universities, for instance, at the University of Virginia, where they found that white students were one hundred times more unlikely to get the admission or the scholarship than minorities. I mean, it's an amazing ratio. These are better qualified whites – let's make sure that this is understood. These are better qualified whites who face racial discrimination in college admissions, in scholarship programs, in hiring for major companies, in

[11] David Duke, interview.

promotions in major companies, and also in the public sphere, such as police departments, fire departments, city government, the federal government, the United States Post Office. There's a pernicious discrimination going on against white Americans today, and I believe, as I said earlier, that civil rights must be for everyone in this country *including* white Americans.[12]

Duke is seeking to attract through his organization young white Americans of the sort who might be repelled by an older organization like the Ku Klux Klan, but could be made comfortable in a more moderate organization which, while eschewing violence, forcefully champions white rights and white identity politics. Duke's group, however, is farther removed from the mainstream than is Wolfe's group insofar as it seems to flirt with some vaguely defined ideal of racial separatism and takes an openly hostile stance toward what it sees as the pernicious influence of Jews in America, particularly in Hollywood, government, and the mass media. Wolfe's group, by contrast, has no animus against any specific "Jewish influences" in America and welcomes Jews as members.

Duke himself seems to be acquiring a reputation as something of an Al Sharpton of the white race by traveling to different sites of racial conflicts and holding press conferences to publicize injustices that racial minorities or the government are believed to have committed against white Americans. NOFEAR's website also gets in the act. For instance, on June 11, 2000, when gangs of mostly black and Hispanic men accosted several women visiting Central Park, some of whom were white, NOFEAR sprang into action issuing a policy statement condemning the assaults and prominently displaying photographs of some of the assaulted white women.

More than most other white nationalists in America, Duke has sought to spread his message abroad to like-minded whites in Europe. His travels in Europe, in fact, have been so extensive in recent times that when combined with the high demand for him as a public speaker in the United States, it proved a most difficult task to arrange an interview with him for this project. Russia has been a particularly important destination of Duke's travels, and he has warned the Russians of "the world-wide genetic catastrophe" that could follow from the

---

[12] Ibid.

"relentless and systematic destruction of the European genotype."[13] Duke believes that this catastrophe can be avoided only if white Europeans around the world wake up to the situation and begin to defend the racial integrity of their group.

STORMFRONT WEBSITE

Affirmative action is a major concern of Don Black, another white nationalist who has pioneered the use of the Internet to reach a mass audience for purposes of racial recruitment and white consciousness raising. Black, a former Klansman and onetime associate of David Duke, founded his Stormfront website in the mid-1990s with the aim of heightening white awareness of antiwhite discrimination and other governmental actions he deems detrimental to white interests. Stormfront provides web linkages to dozens more white nationalist and white supremacist websites, and has become a major source of recruitment to the white nationalist cause. Black reports that since establishing Stormfront in 1995, it has received over 3 million visitors and regularly gets over 10,000 hits per week. While many of these visitors are no doubt mere curiosity seekers – or even people hostile to the white nationalist message who want to stay informed about the enemy's activities – the large number of visitors suggests something of the potential appeal that white nationalism could have among the large Internet-connected audience.

"All kinds of people come to our [web]site," Black told our interviewer. "Some people are just curious. Some people hate us. But the majority, I think, judging from our e-mail, have some positive interest. They may not agree with most of what they read, what we say at this time, but they nevertheless find some things to agree with, and they visited our site because they are looking for answers." Black estimates that about a third of his website's visitors are full supporters who agree with most of the white nationalist stands on racial issues.

Black is more explicit than many other white nationalists in affirming his belief in the necessity of geographic separation as a necessary step in the preservation of white racial and cultural integrity. "We are

[13] David Duke, "Is Russia the Key to White Survival?," http://www.duke.org/dukereport/10–00.html.

... white nationalists," he says, "in that we want a separate white nation." However, before the creation of such a nation – which Black does not see on the immediate horizon – Black believes that whites must organize to defend their interests, both individual and collective. Like other white nationalist leaders, Black places Third World immigration and affirmative action preferences at the top of his list of government wrongs. On the issue of affirmative action, Black blames the government for forcing employers and others to hire minorities over whites. His solution is a kind of libertarian regime where government does not try to thwart the private choices that individuals make about those with whom they choose to associate or not associate:

> In the short run, we want to see the government get out of the business of race mixing, get out of the business of forcing races together, and of telling employers who they can hire, who they must hire, and who they must promote, telling schools how they have to run their business, and telling people where they have to live or who they have to live with. And I think left to their own devices, members of most races will separate naturally.[14]

Black has gotten considerable national attention for his website. Of particular importance was an October 2000 CBS/HBO special called *Hate.com*, which presented interviews with him and his fourteen-year-old son, Derek, as well as other leaders of white nationalist groups and organizations. Morris Dees of the Southern Poverty Law Center, a watchdog agency, narrated the show, which focused on the threat posed by white nationalist and white supremacy groups that use the Internet. The gripping program quoted Black praising the Internet as the technological advance that provides an alternative to a liberal news media monopoly dominated by those biased against white people. It is the Internet, he explained, which allows millions of Americans to hear the views of white nationalists like himself.

For Black, however, the documentary was a disappointment. An article posted on the Stormfront website shortly after the program aired stated that the documentary was a masterpiece of lies and half-truths. Black accused CBS of "interspersing clips from other websites and individuals who have nothing to do with Stormfront." He also complained

---

[14] Don Black, interview.

that "most of the clips came from the Whitesonly.net website, whose owner openly declares himself to be a Jew who hates 'racists' and is trying to 'parody' them with hate-filled images."[15]

Black should not have been so surprised by CBS's treatment of groups like his. He apparently hoped the broadcast would show some sympathy to white grievances. In my assessment of the program and similar ones that have aired in the last two years, the commentators never seriously discuss the issues that have angered white nationalists. Although Stormfront's web pages and articles complain about crime, affirmative action, and other social issues, the CBS/HBO special failed to cover any of these grievances or issue positions. Such documentaries, however unintentionally, tend to bolster white nationalists' claims of a media double standard: The CBS/HBO special featured no high-profile hate crimes in which minorities had attacked white Americans, nor did it mention SPLC data that show a rise in black-on-white hate crimes. The most obvious incident for inclusion would have been a March 2000 case in which a black man, Ronald Taylor, shot five white people, killing three, in a Pittsburgh suburb. In his apartment, police found "hate writings" aimed at Jews, Asians, Italians, whites, and the media.[16] The inclusion of some incidents in which minorities have attacked whites and other minorities would have provided viewers with better information with which to assess the scope of hate in America. The CBS/HBO documentary seems to be typical of media policy in such matters; indeed, even Colin Ferguson's 1993 massacre of whites on the Long Island Railroad has rarely been framed as a hate crime.

AMERICAN RENAISSANCE MAGAZINE

For those who associate white racial advocacy with the Ku Klux Klan and other organizations that draw their membership from the lower end of the socioeconomic and educational spectrum, Jared Taylor's

---

[15] The broadcast became the subject of a heated attack by David Duke, who blasted what he believed was a false and distorted presentation of the facts about Stormfront by a Jewish-dominated media. Duke advised those interested to check out Black's website for themselves. See David Duke, "The Truth About HBO's 'Hate.Com,'" www.Duke.org/library/race/hate-com.html.

[16] Earl O. Hutchinson, "Why Are Black Leaders Silent on Hate Crimes?," http://www.amren.com/salon.htm; "Fast-Food Shooting Suspect Kept 'Satan' List: Cop Find Notes Filled with Hate and Possible Targets," APBNEWS.com, March 3, 2000.

American Renaissance magazine will come as quite a surprise. Founded in 1990, *American Renaissance* has become the leading intellectual journal of contemporary white nationalism with a small but highly educated readership which sees itself as the vanguard of a new racial realism that seeks to rescue America from the harmful effects of multiculturalist dogmas and poorly conceived government policies in regard to race. What the *New Republic* was to liberalism in the 1930s, *National Review* to conservatism in the 1950s, and *Commentary* to neoconservatism in the 1980s, *American Renaissance* has become to white nationalism in the 1990s and beyond. *American Renaissance* has also been the sponsor of a number of national conferences in which the intellectual elite of the white nationalist right has gathered to share ideas and fellowship.

Taylor himself seems to have been drawn to white nationalism through a variety of factors. His early youth as an American growing up in Japan no doubt heightened his own sense of racial distinctiveness and white racial consciousness. The ethnocentric ways of the Japanese – a people whose culture and achievements Taylor greatly admires – also seem to have had an impact on his views of the innate tribal component to human nature. And like almost all white nationalists, Taylor's sense of grievance and alarm has been greatly enhanced by liberal immigration laws and racial preference policies that work to the detriment of whites. Affirmative action and other prominority policies have reinforced his belief in the necessity of white people to rediscover their racial identity and reassert their racial interests.

The purpose of *American Renaissance*, Taylor told our interviewer, "is to discuss issues that are of interest to whites." He elaborated:

> After all, every other racial group in the country has groups and media organs that speak for them, and the purpose of *American Renaissance* is to speak for whites. Its subsidiary purpose is to convince a larger number of whites that it is legitimate for an organization or for a publication to in fact speak for them. Most whites are not convinced that they have legitimate group interests, so another purpose of *American Renaissance* is to convince a larger number of whites that it's entirely legitimate for them to have group interests that may sometimes be in conflict with the interests of other groups.[17]

[17] Jared Taylor, interview.

Another major purpose of *American Renaissance*, Taylor explains, is to convince Americans of the sheer folly of trying to construct a society of such diverse racial elements as one currently sees in multicultural America. Racial and ethnic diversity, Taylor contends, far from being a source of national strength, is a source of inevitable communal conflict, division, and national weakness. This is true, he says, in virtually all multiracial societies:

> As far as *American Renaissance*'s philosophy is concerned . . . I think perhaps you could summarize it in the most economical terms by saying that the position of *American Renaissance* is that race is not a trival matter of either individual or group identity, and that it is a mistake to try to build a society – as the United States has been trying for the last forty or fifty years – to build a society in which race can be made not to matter. . . . The United States is scarcely more integrated racially today than it was in the 1950s and the 1960s, and I think that's because . . . race is a salient and significant biological and social fact. I suppose you could say that that is the major assumption that underlies the positions *American Renaissance* takes – that race is important and race matters, and it's folly to try to build a society on the assumption that it can be made not to matter.[18]

In 1992 Taylor published an impassioned book, *Paved with Good Intentions*, in which he addressed "The Failure of Race Relations in Contemporary America." His book was largely an indictment of affirmative action policies and other double standards in race relations, and was harshly critical of liberal white Americans, whom he accused of encouraging black irresponsibility and black excuse-making by teaching blacks that most of their problems are the result of continuing white wickedness and white malfeasance. "Affirmative action," Taylor wrote, "is the practice of discriminating in the name of equality, of injustice in the name of justice. Perhaps nowhere else in our society have good intentions gone so sadly wrong, and good sense been driven so completely from the field."[19]

The policy of affirmative action, Taylor stated in his book, has made amicable race relations in the United States almost impossible. The

[18] Ibid.
[19] Jared Taylor, *Paved with Good Intentions* (New York: Carol and Graf Publishers, 1992), 123.

injustice of racial preferences is bitterly resented by white victims, he contends, and leaves many whites feeling betrayed by their government:

> Affirmative action preferences for blacks are now nearly a quarter century old, but show no signs of fading away. Indeed, they are more entrenched than ever, and the hypocrisy and bitterness to which they give rise are fatal to any hope for amicable race relations. . . . White men who have suffered on account of affirmative action – and one expert has estimated that as many as one in ten have – are victims of an injustice that officially does not exist. Affirmative action is the law, it is practiced by America's most prestigious institutions, and it is praised by a chorus of media partisans. Therefore it cannot be wrong. Whites who are discriminated against know perfectly well that it is not only wrong but a cynical denial of the "equal opportunity" that America so proudly proclaims.
>
> Nothing is more demoralizing than to be wronged and then to be told that one's injury is an illusion. To be betrayed by the central pillars of society – government, employer, university – leaves a lasting bitterness and alienation. Furthermore, unlike non whites, who have well-funded organizations that spring to the defense of alleged victims, the disappearance of white solidarity means that a white man is entirely on his own.[20]

Taylor sees the rise of white consciousness and white solidarity groups, and of publications like his own *American Renaissance*, as an inevitable and legitimate response to black and Hispanic racial consciousness and the prominority bias which he sees in much of American society. He finds particularly galling affirmative action preferences for newly arrived immigrants. "Whites might have been persuaded that they owed blacks something because of slavery and Jim Crow," he writes, "but what could they possibly owe an immigrant from Guatemala or Trinidad?"[21] Taylor's position here is strangely reminiscent of the views of some of our black focus group participants mentioned in the previous chapter, who complained of immigrants starting businesses with minority loans.

WHITE NATIONALIST JEWS

Many white nationalists and white separatists, including both David Duke and Don Black, harbor hatred and ill-feelings toward Jews and

[20] Ibid., 123–4, 240. [21] Ibid., 239.

their influence in America that is at least as great as their correspond-ing antipathy toward African Americans. Indeed, anyone reading Duke's autobiographical *My Awakening*,[22] which devotes eleven chap-ters – over 250 pages – to the pernicious influences that Jews have allegedly had on the world over the centuries, would assume that its author was much more concerned with wresting power from Jews in America than in keeping white culture free from black influences. Given the prominence of anti-Semitism within many white nationalist circles, one would assume that white nationalism would be a cause with little appeal to anyone of Jewish background. This, however, is not univer-sally true. One of the great surprises of this project was to discover how the intense ill will that affirmative action and certain other race-related policies often engender among white Americans can sometimes lead educated and intelligent Jews to abandon the more typical Jewish attachment to integration and liberal-pluralistic views of race and adopt some version of the white nationalist agenda. Two outstanding examples of this are Michael Hart and Michael Levin.

Hart, a Princeton-trained astrophysicist with additional degrees in law and computer science, explained to our interviewer how he first became interested in racial issues in America as a result of a deep sense of personal injury and injustice over affirmative action preferences that discriminated against Jews. Hart, who came of age in the 1950s, says he was the victim of anti-Jewish discrimination in the early part of his working years, and then later on was a victim of antiwhite discrimi-nation in the era of affirmative action. His prestigious degrees landed him at nondistinguished colleges and universities – Trinity University in Houston and Anne Arundel Community College in Maryland – and he clearly believes that he has been hurt directly by affirmative action. His resentments over this situation are deep and bitter:

> I am Jewish, and in my earlier years I was frequently discriminated against. Some institutions had quotas against Jews; others did not hire Jews at all. But later, when I became older, I was told that in order to make up for the privileges I had in the past there should be a new set of quotas and preferences put in operation against me. Quite naturally, I grew to resent this. In addition, I resented the fact that although I had never personally discriminated in any way against blacks, Hispanics, or

---

[22] David Duke, *My Awakening* (Covington, La.: Free Speech Press, 1999).

anyone else, and although I had always tried to treat people fairly, I – and the whole group to which I belonged – was nevertheless being attacked as being relentlessly racist.[23]

Hart also complains about what he sees as a conspiracy of silence and lack of candor in the way people talk about race in America. This is particularly the case, he says, on the issue of race and intelligence. An additional source of white resentment, he states, is the existence of a double standard regarding racist remarks. Expressions of white racism, he claims, are severely censured, but comparable expressions of antiwhite prejudice by blacks go unrebuked.

> I started seeing that people were not talking honestly about race. Although it is apparent that there are large differences between the races – including differences in intelligence – everyone was scared to talk about them. After a while I saw that because people were scared to talk about racial differences, a type of censorship was falling over the country. As a scientist who is devoted to the idea of a free exchange of views, free inquiry, and an honest search for truth, this bothered me a lot. In addition, I noticed that racist remarks, attitudes, and activities by blacks were passed over and ignored, while comparable actions by whites were highly publicized and denounced. There was an obvious double standard involved, and that bothered me.[24]

As explained in Chapter 2, Hart now believes that a multinational state can never work in America because it has rarely – if ever – worked anyplace else in the world. He concludes from this that America would be better off following a policy of racial separation where the nation is divided geographically into a White State, a Black State, an Hispanic State, and a Mixed Race/Multicultural State, with the latter, perhaps, being the largest of the four divisions.

Like Hart, Michael Levin first became interested in issues of race and ethnicity as a result of the controversies surrounding issues of racial preferences and affirmative action that first emerged in the early 1970s. A philosophy professor by training, Levin was particularly interested in the compensatory justice argument used by proponents of racial preferences to defend their abandonment of the principle of colorblind justice. In examining the claim that the current distress of

---

[23] Michael H. Hart, interview.   [24] Ibid.

blacks was a direct result of past wrongs by whites, and that blacks were owed compensation in the form of job preferences and preferences in university admissions for the present effects of these past wrongs, Levin was led to explore biological explanations for black/white performance differences. Levin explained to our interviewer how he initially became interested in racial issues:

> Well, I suppose it was a convergence of two philosophical interests. First, there were questions concerning affirmative action. When I began my career, the affirmative action issue was also bubbling up, raising questions about compensatory justice, which is a standard philosophical issue. That got me into the racial area, and a lot of questions in philosophy of science are raised by the issue of the reality and testability of intelligence, so it's perhaps not that surprising that I ended up where I did.[25]

Levin's extensive studies and reflections on the issues of race, intelligence, and compensatory justice were presented in a controversial book, *Why Race Matters* (1997). Levin concluded in this study that the race problem in America was primarily the result of the black inability to compete in a modern society, and this inability, he said, was rooted in genetics. "The difficulty blacks have in competing in a white world," he wrote, "are not the legacy of past wrongs, however regrettable those wrongs may have been, but are a result of biology for which whites are not to blame."[26] Elaborating on this same theme, he told our interviewer:

> Whites do better than blacks in virtually any field of endeavor – whether it's education, making money, life span, you name it, except perhaps in athletics – and this difference in outcome is consistently blamed on white racism and white discrimination. Since the shortfall in black achievement is supposed to be the fault of whites – this is where the compensation issue enters – whites are deemed to owe blacks some sort of compensation, for instance, by lowering standards for blacks so they can compete better, or by giving them jobs for which they are not the best qualified, and the like. My central contention, which I think is pretty well documented by science, is that the reason whites do better than blacks . . . is simply that whites are more intelligent, and have certain traits of temperament which conduce to long-run success, and these differences are genetic in origin. These differences are not the fault of whites, they're not

[25] Michael Levin, *Why Race Matters* (Westport: Praeger, 1998).
[26] Michael Levin, interview.

something that whites did to blacks, and they are not something for which whites owe blacks compensation.[27]

Levin's beliefs about the genetic inferiority of African Americans have made him a pariah in some quarters. Ironically, Levin teaches at an institution – the City University of New York – that has a fairly high minority population. He told our interviewer that he gets along at CUNY because most of the students there probably have no idea "what I've been up to." However, the small number of black faculty, he says, "[probably] regard me as evil." Levin's views about black mental inferiority appear well balanced by those of Leonard Jeffries, CUNY's other controversial professor, who argues that blacks are warm "sun people," while whites are cold "ice people." Jeffries is also hostile to Jews and views the Holocaust as fabrication, yet somehow he and Levin coexist at the same university.

WHITE NATIONALISM AND BIOLOGICAL EXPLANATIONS OF HUMAN DIFFERENCES

The emphasis on biological explanations of racial differences – and the corresponding deemphasis on cultural, psychological, and historical explanations – seems to have become a central feature of the new white nationalism. Black/white differences in mental ability and other traits are inborn and intractable, white nationalists claim, and it is sheer folly to think that the situation will ever change. Here, it would seem, contemporary white nationalists are reviving, often in a more sophisticated form, the biologically based racist theories of white (or "Nordic") supremacy first propounded in the early decades of the twentieth century by writers like Madison Grant and Lothrop Stoddard. Like Grant and Stoddard, they believe that there is a "rising tide of color against white world supremacy," one that, if not checked by immigration restriction and a renewed sense of solidarity on the part of whites, will lead to "the passing of the great race."[28]

---

[27] Ibid.

[28] The phrases in quotes refer to the two most important racist books of the World War I era: Madison Grant's *The Passing of the Great Race* (New York: Charles Scribner, 1916) and Lothrop Stoddard's *The Rising Tide of Color Against White World Supremacy* (New York: Charles Scribner, 1920). On the influence of Grant and Stoddard, see Higham, 157–8, 272–7.

More generally, white nationalists warn that racial preference policies could become permanent in the United States because genetic differences in ability levels mean that minorities such as blacks and Latinos will never be able to compete with whites and Asians on an equal basis. As evidence for their propositions, they point to the research of scholars such as University of Western Ontario psychologist J. Philippe Rushton, a Guggenheim fellow, who has written six books and over 200 social science articles. Rushton argues that "equalizing opportunities cannot, in fact, remove black/white disparities in IQ" because these are genetic.[29] Racial differences, he says, are to be seen not only in IQ, but in brain size, reproductive physiology, personality, temperament, propensity to commit crime, speed of physical maturation, and longevity. According to Ruston, these differences are found internationally and have their origin in long-term evolutionary processes conditioned by the different climates and geographies in which the different races of mankind evolved. In his racial hierarchy, Asians and whites are genetically superior to blacks and Hispanics with regard to intelligence, with Asians ranked slightly ahead of whites and blacks ranked at the bottom.[30]

The most recent study along these lines to get widespread attention was *The Bell Curve* (1994), by Harvard University psychology professor Richard Herrnstein and researcher Charles Murray. *The Bell Curve* is generally credited with having spurred a new willingness among academics to propound theories of innate biological differences to explain racial outcomes.[31] The authors argue that genetic differences explain many ethnic variations in socioeconomic performance, and that some groups, such as blacks, have greater percentages of low IQ members than others. Low IQ, Murray and Herrnstein claim, is associated with child abuse, crime, delinquency, and other social pathologies, whereas high IQ is correlated with professional success and educational achieve-

---

[29] J. Philippe Rushton, "The American Dilemma in World Perspective," in Jared Taylor's *The Real American Dilemma*, 11.

[30] Ibid., 11–30.

[31] Richard Herrnstein and Charles Murray, *The Bell Curve: Intelligence and Class Structure in American Life* (New York: Free Press, 1994). Other books include J. Philippe Rushton, *Race, Evolution, and Behavior* (New Brunswick, N.J.: Transaction, 1995); Arthur Jensen, *The G-Factor* (Westport, Conn.: Praeger Press, 1998); and Jon Entine, *Why Blacks Dominate Sports and Why We Are Afraid to Talk about It* (New York: Public Relations Press, 2000).

ments. Their arguments, as one critic put it, were "not racist in the traditional sense; [they] did not argue that all blacks are inferior to all whites," and they acknowledged that about 10 percent of the white population, like the much larger portion of the black population, was "doomed to failure by low intelligence." Nevertheless, as this critic put it, for *The Bell Curve* authors, "people of color were the real threat to American society."[32]

As mainstream scholars, Herrnstein and Murray were able to get around political censorship of their politically incorrect book, which became a *New York Times* best seller. Writing for the *New York Review of Books*, political theorist Alan Ryan noted that although Charles Murray (Herrnstein died soon after the book was published) expressed concern about how racists might use their research, their findings "reflect what people already think in their heart of hearts – which is, that blacks and white trash are born irremediably dumb, that black Americans have been over promoted in the academy, [and] that smarter white workers have been displaced by incompetent black ones at the behest of the federal government."[33] In a similar vein, Harvard University sociologist Orlando Patterson remarked that "*The Bell Curve* merely updated the old eugenics scare that the average intelligence of the nation is declining because less intelligent people breed more than do members of the cognitive elite."[34] Since the publication of *The Bell Curve*, there have been several books published about biological differences between the races, and it seems undeniable that Herrnstein and Murray's book has helped to promote a new boldness among academics eager to speculate about genetic differences between human ethnic and racial groups.[35]

Some of the research in this area is funded by the Pioneer Fund, a nonprofit organization founded by two American scholars who supported Hitler's eugenic policies. In its early years, financial support for the organization was provided by a wealthy textile manufacturer named Wickliffe Draper, who once flirted with Nazism and, as late as

---

[32] Carter, 113.

[33] Alan Ryan, "Apocalypse Now?," *New York Review of Books*, November 17, 1994, p. 8, as cited in Carter, 115.

[34] Orlando Patterson, *The Ordeal of Integration: Progress and Resentment in America's "Racial" Crisis* (Washington, D.C.: Civitas/Counterpoint, 1997), 128.

[35] Barry Mehler, "Race and 'Reason': Academic Ideas a Pillar of Racist Thought," *Intelligence Report* (Winter 1999): 27–32.

the 1950s, advocated sending "genetically inferior" blacks back to Africa.[36] In addition to funding a number of studies conducted by Rushton, the Pioneer Fund has financed the research of psychologist Arthur Jensen, who has concluded that compensatory education programs for blacks have failed to raise school achievement or IQ scores, and that the reason for this is probably rooted in genetics. The Pioneer Fund states in its charter that its purpose is "to conduct or aid in conducting study and research into the problems of heredity and eugenics in the human race generally."[37]

According to political scientists Philip Klinkner and Rogers Smith, there has been a resurgence of theories about the cultural and biological inferiority of blacks which, since the end of the Cold War, have increasingly been deemed respectable. The authors point to a colloquy between former New York Democratic Senator Daniel Patrick Moynihan and West Virginia Senator Jay Rockefeller that occurred during debates over President Clinton's 1994 welfare reform bill. Speaking of the chaos in the inner cities, Moynihan stated, "I mean . . . if you were a biologist, you would find yourself talking about speciation here." Rockefeller replied, "When you were talking about a matter of potentially speciation, the creation of a new American person, so to speak, I think you're right about that." Other statements quoted involving high-profile individuals make it quite clear that some prominent mainstream Americans would agree with the white nationalists in some of their characterizations of inner-city African Americans as inferior forms of humanity.

White nationalists, already convinced of genetic differences between the races, savor the kinds of studies produced by Rushton and *The Bell Curve* authors. William Pierce of the National Alliance is a good example. Pierce, author of *The Turner Diaries*, gave a genetic spin to his response to a question by our interviewer about affirmative action:

INTERVIEWER: What do you think about current affirmative action policies in regard to race?

PIERCE: Well, I mean affirmative action is one of these issues that wouldn't exist in a healthy society.

INTERVIEWER: A healthy society in your view wouldn't even have a problem of a multiplicity of races and ethnicities?

[36] Carter, 116.   [37] The Pioneer Fund Home Page, http://www.pioneerfund.org.

PIERCE: That's correct. The problem wouldn't exist in the first place. Affirmative action is something that has come about only because we have a racially mixed society and the blacks can't compete on an equal basis. They can't do it by themselves, so they get an extra boost from the government.

INTERVIEWER: Why do you think the blacks can't compete by themselves?

PIERCE: [Because] they're biologically different.[38]

Pierce's National Alliance is considered by the SPLC to be the most dangerous hate group in America. Pierce, a former lieutenant in the American Nazi Party, owns a 350-acre compound in Hillsboro, West Virginia, where he runs a white supremacy press, and he recently purchased Resistance Records, a leading producer of white power music, to enhance his ability to reach young Americans with messages of white pride, white supremacy, and contempt for nonwhite races.[39]

Similar themes are expounded in a Pierce article titled "The Roots of Civilization," where blacks – and lower-intelligence whites – are seen as the curse of any kind of higher culture:

The level of civilization which a people can develop and maintain is a function of the biological quality, the racial quality, of that people – in particular, of its problem-solving ability. That is why Blacks and certain other races have never developed even a rudimentary civilization and are incapable of sustaining a civilization built for them by whites – despite the apparent "brightness" of many Blacks. And that is why the race which built Western civilization not only must eliminate the racially alien elements from its midst but must also change those social, political, and economic institutions which continue to result in an increasing proportion of Whites who are problem-makers rather than problem-solvers.[40]

David Duke also embraces genetic explanations for the differential school performance and arrest rates of blacks. Like Rushton and Levin, he believes it is simply an established scientific fact that blacks as a group are naturally less intelligent and more violence-prone than either whites or Asians. His beliefs on these issues would seem to be part of

---

[38] Pierce interview.

[39] Kim Murphy, "Behind All the Noise of Hate Music," http://www.latimes.com/news/front/20000330/t000029972.html.

[40] William L. Pierce, "The Roots of Civilization" (reprinted from *National Vanguard* magazine, no. 59, 1978).

an evolving dogma on the part of white nationalists. Duke explained his views at length to our interviewer:

INTERVIEWER: In your autobiographical work, *My Awakening*, you describe the formative influence upon your thinking about race of Carlton Putnam's book *Race and Reason*. It was under Putnam's influence, you say, that you first came to believe that blacks and whites differed by much more than skin color – and that blacks were intellectually less capable than whites, that this intellectual inferiority was rooted in biology and genetics, and that as a result of this, black people would never be able to attain to the high level of civilization characteristic of whites. Do you still adhere to these ideas of Putnam or have your ideas on black/white differences evolved over the years?

DUKE: Well, in that book, I'm very careful to say that I don't endorse the principle of inferiority. I think that human beings, if you talk about our differences in terms of talents or intelligence or any other area, that does not necessarily make an individual human being inferior or a race inferior. . . . So there are differences but I don't get into the game of speaking of inferior or superior human beings. But I do think there are dramatic differences between racial groups, and I think that these differences have come about through evolutionary processes that have gone on obviously for hundreds of thousands of years. I think that most scientists would agree that there's at least a one hundred forty thousand year split between Europeans and Africans, and I think these differences – the differences of climate in Europe – affected our evolutionary development different than it did in Africa, and I think that this had a tremendous impact and a tremendous influence on culture. I also believe that not only are physical characteristics such as eye color or skin color or hair color or height or body structure affected by genetics, but I also believe that such things as intelligence, and even personality traits, have a very powerful genetic component. I think science is uncovering this more and more. . . .

INTERVIEWER: What are some of the specific black/white differences that you think might be genetically influenced?

DUKE: Well, we could talk about a number of them. I think propensity to crime for one. I think that blacks on average have a higher propensity to crime than whites, and I think it has to do with a number of factors, including brain differences and also including testosterone levels. We know that men have a much higher violent crime rate than women, and we know that even among white men or among black men that men with higher testosterone levels have higher rates of violent crime, and we know that on average blacks have a higher testosterone level than whites. I mean, this is a fact.

. . . We know that there is – and this has been confirmed by literally thousands of studies – that there's almost an entire standard deviation of difference in I.Q. between whites and blacks, and obviously I.Q. has a tremendous impact on society. I.Q. in fact is a better predictor of success in life, or socio-economic success in life, than a person's family income. . . . Now the question is – and it is the big question – whether [these differences] are biological or whether they are cultural – and there's been tremendous numbers of studies I think that show beyond any reasonable doubt that they are certainly of genetic origin, the genetics overwhelmingly overriding the environment. Which is not to say that environment can't affect scores to a degree. They can. . . . [But] if there would be a ratio of genetic influence to environmental influence, I think it would be between 2:1 and 3:1 – of genetics over environment. Genetics accounts for between two-thirds and three-quarters of the observed difference.[41]

Views similar to Duke's are expressed by Florida State psychology professor Glayde Whitney. Whitney, a white nationalist who wrote the introduction to Duke's *My Awakening*, believes that the Human Genome Project will provide irrefutable evidence of the genetically based intellectual inferiority of African Americans, thus providing a final answer to the questions raised in the longstanding debate over "nature versus nurture." The question of black intellectual inferiority, he contends, has been silenced and suppressed because of the imperatives of political correctness; but such inferiority, he believes, is a fact known for decades among scientists.

For those social scientists who believe that nonwhites are genetically inferior to whites and Asians with regard to intelligence, the question for them is what to do with such a preponderance of "problem-makers" and other unwanted people. Their solution is usually some kind of eugenic engineering. Richard Lynn, a professor of psychology at the University of Ulster-Coleraine, Northern Ireland, has proposed the "phasing out" of incompetent people. In a 1994 issue of the *Irish Journal of Psychology*, Lynn wrote:

What is called for here is not genocide, the killing off of the populations of incompetent cultures. But we do need to think realistically in terms of

[41] Duke, interview.

"phasing out" of such peoples. If the world is to evolve more better humans, then obviously someone must make way for them. . . . To think otherwise is mere sentimentality.[42]

Along similar lines, Edward M. Miller, a proponent of an elaborate evolutionary theory of human racial differences similar to that of Rushton, advocates conscious efforts at birth control to restrict the number of low-intelligence citizens. "In the long run," Miller has written,

> society is faced with a choice between having the population restrained by misery, and having it restrained by conscious restrictions of births. Once the idea of preventing some births is accepted, it will then be natural to discuss the question of which births. It is very likely that decisions will be based at least partially on preventing the births that are most likely to result in what that society regards as low quality citizens.[43]

At least one important survey suggests that a belief in the biological inferiority of some races in regard to intelligence is more common than generally supposed. Smith College professor Stanley Rothman and Harvard researcher Mark Snyderman surveyed a sample of mostly scientific experts in the field of educational psychology in the late 1980s and found that 53 percent believed IQ differences between whites and African Americans were at least partly genetic in origin, while only 17 percent attributed the IQ differences to environmental factors alone (the remainder either believed the data was currently insufficient to decide the issue or refused to answer the question).[44]

DISCUSSION

It is useful at this juncture to consider some of the implications of the scientific studies that reveal persistent IQ differences between whites and blacks. White nationalists like Duke and Levin have made absurdly exaggerated claims about both the degree to which these differences can reasonably be attributed to genes and the implications for individuals and society should these genetic assumptions prove true. To

---

[42] Richard Lynn as quoted in Mehler, 28.
[43] Edward M. Miller as quoted in Mehler, 30.
[44] Michael Snyderman and Stanley Rothman, "Survey of Expert Opinion on Intelligence and Aptitude Testing," *American Psychologist* 42 (1987): 137–44.

begin with the second claim: Is IQ really destiny, as most of the white nationalists seem to believe? Does a modest IQ score condemn a person to a lifetime of failure and low achievement? Are low-IQ males likely to wind up in our nation's jails or drug rehabilitation centers?

The answer here to all these questions is an unequivocal "no"! IQ is not destiny. Most of us need only look around at the people we know to see that the correlation between school smarts of the kind that measured by IQ – the *g* factor of the psychometricians – and the ability to succeed in the world of work and achievement is only a very loose one. Even Herrnstein and Murray at one point acknowledge this. "For virtually all of the topics we will be discussing," they state in *The Bell Curve*,

> cognitive ability accounts for only small to middling proportions of the variation among people. It almost always explains less than 20 percent of the variance, to use the statistician's term, usually less than 10 percent and often less than 5 percent. What this means in English is that you cannot predict what a given person will do from his IQ score. . . . We all know people who do not seem all that smart but who handle their jobs much more effectively than colleagues who probably have more raw intelligence. . . . A wide range of IQ scores can be observed in almost any job, including complex jobs such as engineer or physician.[45]

This is a disclaimer that white nationalist champions of *The Bell Curve* (and Herrnstein and Murray themselves in places) conspicuously ignore.

There is a good deal of both folk wisdom and hard scientific fact in Thomas Edison's oft repeated adage that "genius is 1% inspiration, 99% perspiration." Not only successful inventors but people who are successful in any field usually draw more upon their persistence, determination, and clear focus on their efforts than upon any rare or unusual IQ capacities. We should never underestimate the power that an individual's determination to succeed can exert over limitations imposed by a given individual's IQ. The evidence can be found each year in the extraordinary achievements of the mentally and physically handicapped participants in Special Olympics programs. Often the person who excels in life is a hard worker who comes across to observers as being someone of average intelligence. Anyone who has

[45] Herrnstein and Murray, 67–8, 117.

dealt with students in a university context knows that having a high IQ or a high score on a standardized test does not ensure academic success or even the ability to attain a college degree. The remark of Calvin Coolidge on this matter is worth repeating:

> Nothing in the world can take the place of persistence. Talent will not; nothing is more common than unsuccessful men with talent. Genius will not; unrewarded genius is almost a proverb. Education will not; the world is full of educated derelicts. Persistence and determination alone are omnipotent.

Coolidge overstates his case here, of course – abstract reasoning ability of the kind IQ tests seek to measure does count for something – but the point he is trying to make is a valid one: Many people tend to exaggerate the value of innate talent and raw brain power to success in America, to the neglect of what are often more important factors.

Those who focus on IQ scores also tend to underestimate the importance of those "multiple intelligences" that Harvard professor Howard Gardner has written so extensively about.[46] Of particular value for success at many occupations in America is what Gardner calls "interpersonal intelligence": the ability to understand and empathize with others. An aspiring salesperson, for instance, with a winning smile and an ability to understand the needs of others would do better than one with a high IQ score. Political scientist Stanley Kelley, Jr., has noted the social skills of politicians swaying mass audiences. Among useful attributes are the ability to sympathize with the plight of others and to see issues from more than one perspective.[47] Such skills are difficult to measure, but they are not likely to be closely correlated with high IQ. Harry Truman and Ronald Reagan were very successful in politics, but by all accounts they had very modest intellects. Jimmy Carter and Richard Nixon, by contrast, were high on brain power but their lack of emotional intelligence and people-handling skills contributed to their political downfalls.[48]

---

[46] Howard Gardner, *Frames of Mind: The Theory of Multiple Intelligences* (New York: Basic Books, 1983).

[47] Stanley Kelley, Jr., "Politics as Vocation: Variations on Weber," in John Geer, ed., *Politicians and Party Politics* (Baltimore: Johns Hopkins Press, 1998), 349–50.

[48] See Fred Greenstein, *The Presidential Difference* (New York: Martin Kessler Books, 2000).

So even if there are significant and intractable IQ differences between racial groups, as white nationalists contend, it is simply false to draw the dire conclusions that most do. But are IQ differences really intractable? Arthur Jensen has devoted much of his very prolific academic career trying to demonstrate that we can't really do very much to boost IQ, or to narrow the black/white IQ gap because IQ is more a matter of fixed genetic endowment than the product of any kind of environmental factors. There is reason to believe, however, that Jensen – and those who follow in his footsteps like Murray and Herrnstein – are wrong. Not only can we boost IQ, but we have been doing it for more than two generations. Psychologist James Flynn has demonstrated that IQ scores have been rising substantially for more than half a century in virtually all countries in which useable data has been obtained.[49] In many cases, IQ gains of fifteen points or more have been observed, which is about what the black/white difference has been over much of the twentieth century. Since it is virtually impossible that changes of this magnitude in so short a period of time – in some cases little more than a single generation – could be due to genetic changes, the only conclusion is that environmental factors can boost IQ, and boost it very substantially. Likely candidates for these factors include improved nutrition and vitamin intake (which also explains the increasing height of the population over the same time period), decreased incidence of debilitating childhood diseases, increased cognitive stimulation in the home, and decreased family size.

Once again, even Herrnstein and Murray must acknowledge limitations on the IQ-is-destiny approach. Speaking of "the Flynn effect," they are forced to make a large concession:

> Indirect support for the proposition that the observed B/W difference could be the result of environmental factors is provided by the worldwide phenomenon of rising test scores. We call it "the Flynn effect" because of psychologist James Flynn's pivotal role in focusing attention on it, but the phenomenon itself was identified in the 1930s when testers began to notice that IQ scores often rose with every successive year after a test was first standardized. . . . The average person could answer more items on the old test than the new test. The tendencies for IQ scores to drift

[49] James R. Flynn, "Massive IQ Gains in 14 Nations: What IQ Tests Really Measure," *Psychological Bulletin* 101 (1987): 171–91.

upward as a function of years since standardization has now been substantiated, primarily by Flynn, in many countries and on many IQ tests besides the Stanford-Binet. In some countries, the upward drift since World War II has been as much as a point a year for some spans of years. The national averages have in fact changed by amounts that are comparable to the fifteen or so IQ points separating whites and blacks in America. To put it another way, on the average, whites today may differ in IQ from whites, say, two generations ago as much as whites today differ from blacks today. Given their size and speed, the shifts in time necessarily have been due more to changes in the environment than to changes in the genes.[50]

It remained for University of Michigan psychologist Richard E. Nisbett to draw the obvious conclusion here. In an important article entitled "Race, Genetics, and IQ," which evaluated a host of studies bearing on the nature versus nurture controversy regarding racial differences in IQ, Nisbett criticized the conclusion of gene-based theorists. The facts illuminated by Flynn, Nisbett writes, give "substantial weight to the possibility that the IQ difference between blacks and whites might be entirely due to environmental factors, since the gene pool of Western countries is not changing at a rate remotely rapid enough to produce a genotypic difference in intelligence of one standard deviation." "It seems entirely plausible," Nisbett argues, "that, with respect to factors relevant to IQ, the environments of blacks today more nearly resemble the environments of whites a generation ago than they do the present environments of whites."[51] Nisbett also says that the black/white IQ gap is narrowing and may now, in fact, be only ten points instead of fifteen points. "Rigorous interventions do affect IQ and cognitive skills at every stage of the life course," he concludes.[52] His conclusions directly contradict those who contend that black test scores and achievements are so rooted in genetic limitations that they can never improve.

[50] Herrnstein and Murray, 307–8.
[51] Richard E. Nisbett, "Race, Genetics, and IQ," in Christopher Jencks and Meredith Phillips, eds., *The Black-White Test Score Gap* (Washington, D.C.: Brookings Institution Press, 1998), 86–102.
[52] Ibid., 101.

CONCLUSION

This chapter has shown some disturbing trends in American race relations. First, white nationalists use the language of the civil rights movement to frame their demands for the abolition of racial preferences in employment and college admissions, and they use the language of multiculturalism to advocate wider acceptance of the notion of a distinct white identity, white interest, and white need for self-determination. In both cases there appears to be a clear logic to their argument.

Changing economic and demographic conditions work to the advantage of white nationalists. As the white population shrinks, white Americans can be expected to behave more and more like other racial and ethnic groups. Given the human propensity for self-interested action, it is likely that whites will increasingly tend to frame their demands around a shared group identity and group consciousness. The changing economy, racial preferences for nonwhites, the impending minority status of white Americans, and minority emphasis on multiculturalism provide white nationalists with the language and grievances needed to make effective appeals about the need for whites to organize if they are to compete effectively with the demands of racial minorities.

Left unchecked, there are forces and circumstances at work in this country that could drive millions of mainstream white Americans toward white tribalism. A majority of white Americans already share some of the ideas of white nationalist leaders and scholars. For instance, a 1991 General Social Science survey showed that an overwhelming majority of white Americans thought that black and Hispanic Americans were more likely than whites to prefer living on welfare (78 percent thought blacks more likely, 74 percent thought Hispanics more likely). Sixty-two percent thought that black Americans were less hard-working than white Americans; 56 percent thought that they were more prone to violence than whites; and 53 percent said that they were less intelligent.[53] As previously explained, the "mere mention" of affirmative action preferences causes a significant percentage of white Americans to dislike blacks and to consider negative stereotypes about them to be true.

[53] *New York Times*, January 10, 1991, p. B10.

For the sake of this country, we must take decisive steps toward the amelioration of the conditions and grievances that fuel racial distrust and racial unrest. A certain percentage of white Americans – probably less than 10 percent – will always hate nonwhites. But for the rest there is hope. What we can do as a nation is to identify and address legitimate sources of white grievance and concern so that these do not provide opportunistic means for white racial tribalists to reach into the mainstream population. Michael Lind has persuasively argued that racial preferences and multiculturalism are both frauds adopted by certain elites to give the illusion of a nonexistent integration.[54] For these elites, the economy and national politics constitute the bottom line. Since these look relatively healthy now, other things are ignored. But America is in trouble at the grass-roots level. This trouble is related to race, and we ignore it at our peril. What we need to do is to refashion a collective identity that can transcend race and therefore thwart our increasing drift toward tribalism.[55]

In the twenty-first century, a portion of our attention should be directed toward addressing issues that disproportionately affect the poor and disadvantaged. America must not allow any group to suffer disadvantage because of race. Antidiscrimination laws which guarantee race neutrality in employment and university admissions should be rigorously enforced. But we must avoid policies that confer benefits and burdens on the basis of race and contribute to the growth of the kind of racial and ethnic tribalism that has proved so destructive around the world. If we have learned anything from watching the rise and fall of other nations in the past century, it is that political stability and tranquility among racial and ethnic groups cannot be taken for granted. Because race relations can deteriorate in a relatively short period of time, we must take concrete steps toward formulating public policies that do not inflame tribal passions, that are generally perceived as fair, and that can draw support from a broad spectrum of Americans.

[54] Michael Lind, *The Next American Nation: The New Nationalism and the Fourth American Revolution* (New York: Simon and Schuster, 1995), 139–40.
[55] In addition to Lind, also see Jim Sleeper, *Liberal Racism: How Fixating on Race Subverts the American Dream* (New York: Penguin Books, 1997), and Martha Nussbaum, *For Love of Country: Debating the Limits of Patriotism* (Boston: Beacon Press, 1996).

9

THE PATH FROM DISCRIMINATION TO REVERSE DISCRIMINATION IN HIGHER EDUCATION

> The inequities are not transitional or temporary for those who lose what they deserve on the merits because of their race or sex. If a white male does not get into Yale because of his race, he does not get into Yale forever, and chances are he forever does not get into Harvard, Stanford, etc. either. . . . The damage done the individual is permanent not transitional.
>
> Robert H. Bork, *Slouching Towards Gomorrah*[1]

Affirmative action occurs in three main contexts: employment, college and university admissions, and the arena of government contracting set-asides. Programs in all of these areas have been controversial and served as the basis for an ongoing and often bitter sense of grievance on the part of many whites. However, because the new white nationalists aggressively seek the recruitment of better-educated young adults, and because competition for college and university admissions is becoming more intense, I focus in this chapter on affirmative action in higher education. Affirmative action in the higher education arena is different from other areas insofar as most college and university admissions policies are voluntary, and generally there is no rigorous governmental monitoring or regulation of their practices.[2] This has not,

---

[1] Robert H. Bork, *Slouching Towards Gomorrah* (New York: ReganBooks, 1996), 241.

[2] John David Skrentny, "The Creation and Expansion of Affirmative Action Programs," in "The Minority Rights Revolution: How War and the Black Civil Rights Movement Changed American Politics," unpublished manuscript, January 2001.

however, prevented many university administrators, especially at many of the nation's most elite institutions, from pursuing racial preference policies with persistence and determination. I explore in this chapter how racial preferences in the past have been utilized to favor the white majority in the pre–civil rights era, how this practice changed in the late 1960s and early 1970s as affirmative action policies were first implemented in many universities and professional schools, and how legal, constitutional, and political thinking on these matters has evolved over time.

THE ERA OF "SEPARATE BUT EQUAL"

Racial preferences in higher education existed long before colleges and universities began extending preferences to minority applicants. Racial preferences were firmly embedded in the admission policies of racially segregated state institutions that the National Association for the Advancement of Colored People (NAACP) challenged a decade before in *Brown v. Board of Education*.[3] During the era of "separate but equal" that followed the U.S. Supreme Court's 1896 ruling in *Plessy v. Ferguson*,[4] many qualified blacks were denied admission to state-supported colleges and universities that operated under a system which effectively accorded absolute racial preferences to whites. In the 1950s, African Americans began to use the Equal Protection Clause of the Fourteenth Amendment to challenge racially discriminatory policies in higher education.[5] During this era, African Americans were not seeking preference on the basis of race or recruitment visits from college admissions officers. Instead, they merely sought an opportunity to compete on their academic merits for admission to white institutions that had systematically excluded them.

The strategy to end racial preferences for whites in the educational realm started at the graduate and professional school level with attacks against the inequality of the separate learning facilities provided for blacks. The battle eventually reached the primary and secondary school

[3] *Brown v. Board of Education*, 349 U.S. 294 (1954).
[4] *Plessy v. Ferguson*, 163 U.S. 537 (1896).
[5] The Fourteenth Amendment, originally adopted as a restriction against state actors, had been extended by the Supreme Court to protect against discrimination by federal actors as well, through the incorporation of the Due Process Clause of the Fifth Amendment.

level (K–12), culminating with the 1954 *Brown* decision. Ironically, as we see below, the attack against racial preferences for African Americans in the educational realm has taken a similar path – it, too, started with attacks on racial preference programs in graduate and professional schools, and has culminated with attacks on preference programs at primary and secondary schools.[6]

Sweatt v. Painter,[7] the first of the attacks on invidious racial preferences for whites to reach the Supreme Court, challenged the admissions policy at the University of Texas Law School, a whites-only institution, which sought to avoid admitting the black plaintiff, Herman Sweatt. The case arose when Sweatt filed suit in 1946 alleging a Fourteenth Amendment violation and requesting a writ of mandamus compelling his admission to the law school. After the first hearing, the trial judge gave the state six months to establish a black law school, an order with which the state eventually complied with by appropriating $3 million for the establishment and maintenance of a separate institution. According to Richard Kluger, the alternative school for black students consisted of "three smallish basement rooms, three part-time faculty members who were first-year instructors . . . and a library of 10,000 books plus access to the state law library in the capitol."[8] Both the trial court and the Civil Court of Appeals concluded that the state of Texas had complied with the separate but equal legal standard established in *Plessy*. Nevertheless, given a choice between attending the newly created institution or fighting for a degree from the University of Texas Law School, Sweatt chose to fight for the more prestigious degree by appealing to the Supreme Court.

In a unanimous decision, the high court reversed the lower court decision and ordered the University of Texas to admit Sweatt after reaching the conclusion that the alternative school did not provide "substantial equality in educational opportunities."[9] While specifically declining to address the doctrine of separate but equal, the Court concluded that the educational opportunities afforded by the respective schools were not in fact equal. An empirical comparison of the number of available library volumes, the size of the student body, the number

---

[6] *Wessman v. Gittens*, 160 F. 3rd 790 (1998).
[7] *Sweatt v. Painter*, 339 U.S. 629 (1950).
[8] Richard Kluger, *Simple Justice* (New York: Vintage Books, 1975), 261.
[9] *Sweatt*, 634.

of professors, and the variety of courses revealed huge inequalities. The Court also found huge differences in intangible qualities between the schools, qualities, they said, "which are incapable of objective measurement but which make for greatness in a law school."[10]

In a parallel case, *McLaurin v. Oklahoma State Regents for Higher Education*,[11] the Court required that an African American admitted to a white graduate school be treated in a manner equal to that of other students. The Court specifically invalidated restrictions that had been placed on black graduate students' use of the library, cafeteria, and classrooms. In a unanimous decision, the Court once again described the inequity in terms of intangibles such as the inability of the restricted black student to "study, to engage in discussions and exchange views with other students, and in general to learn his profession."[12] The cases involving graduate-level education turned on the inequality of these intangible benefits offered to black students relative to whites, both at separate black schools and at predominantly white institutions where blacks were shackled with restrictions on the use of the institution's facilities.

The history of racial preferences in the pre–civil rights era shows that whites in some states fought fiercely to maintain their privileges within the segregated state educational systems. Racial preferences for white students at many state institutions were a strictly followed norm, even though, practically speaking, the admission of a handful of black applicants was unlikely to diminish the educational opportunities for very many white students or cause those on campus any major inconvenience. During this era, successful blacks were sometimes admitted to traditionally white schools on an individual basis, but in very small numbers.

Eventually, Congress opened all doors with the passage of the Civil Rights Act of 1964. Many college and universities in the mid-1960s began aggressively recruiting and seeking out well-qualified black students who previously might not have considered going to a predominantly white institution. Such affirmative action policies, involving little more than heightened recruitment and outreach, were relatively

[10] Ibid.
[11] *McLaurin v. Oklahoma State Regents for Higher Education*, 339 U.S. 637 (1950).
[12] Ibid., 641.

noncontroversial. Affirmative action in higher education became more and more controversial, however, once elite institutions began recruiting large numbers of minority students that were not academically prepared to matriculate at institutions of the caliber of those that admitted them. By the late 1970s, a fierce backlash against affirmative action of this kind had begun.

THE REVERSE DISCRIMINATION CASES: FROM *DEFUNIS* TO *GRATZ*

Since the mid-1960s, African Americans have benefited from the Civil Rights Act of 1964 and from race-conscious affirmative action policies that have greatly increased the size of the black middle class and the percentages of African Americans in colleges and universities. One study reported that the percentages of blacks enrolled in Ivy League schools grew from 2.3 percent in 1967 to 6.3 percent by 1976, and the percentages in other prestigious schools increased during the same period from 1.7 to 4.8 percent.[13] However, the growth in the percentages of blacks at top schools was destined to cause resentment among better-prepared white Americans who saw themselves as displaced by lesser-qualified African Americans at the institutions whose degrees were most valuable in the marketplace. Jews, another group that has suffered historical discrimination in higher education, also protested loudly against the policies.

The minority groups that benefited from racial preferences in higher education included blacks, Hispanics, and Native Americans – and initially Asians – who were scoring below whites on some standardized tests. Susan Welch and John Gruhl cite studies that found that "only 18 percent of the black students in first-year classes of law schools across the country in 1976–77 academic year would have been admitted if the schools had used race-blind procedures in their admissions requirements, test scores and GPAs."

Only 27 percent of Hispanics, 39 percent of the Native Americans, and 60 percent of the Asian Americans would have been admitted as well. Only 39 blacks taking the LSAT in the fall 1976 scored 600 or above (out

---

[13] Bowen and Bok, 7.

of a possible 800) and also had a GPA of 3.5 or better, while 13,151 whites did.[14]

Not surprisingly, by the mid-1970s, unsuccessful white applicants for graduate and professional schools began to complain about "reverse discrimination," in which minorities with lower grade point averages and test scores gained admission to top universities over higher-scoring whites. A few sued in federal courts, charging that racial preferences in university admissions were in violation of the Fourteenth Amendment and of Title VI of the 1964 Civil Rights Act.[15] According to the complaints, universities were in violation of the Equal Protection Clause of the Fourteenth Amendment, which guarantees that a state shall not "deny to any person within its jurisdiction the equal protection of the laws."[16] The preferential treatment of blacks, no matter how noble the goal, was increasingly seen as incompatible with fundamental constitutional principles of fairness and equal rights.

The first reverse discrimination case to reach the Court was *Defunis v. Odegaard.*[17] This case involved Marco Defunis, a Jewish applicant, who applied for admission to the University of Washington Law School and was rejected. Defunis brought suit requesting an injunction compelling his admission on grounds that the law school's admissions process was an unconstitutional violation of the Fourteenth Amendment, since it allowed the admission of lower-scoring minority students under a different set of criteria. The superior court of King County, Washington, granted the injunction allowing Defunis to enroll at the law school while the case worked itself through the legal system. By the time the case reached the U.S. Supreme Court, Defunis was entering his final quarter at the law school. After hearing oral arguments on

---

[14] Susan Welch and John Gruhl, *Affirmative Action and Minority Enrollments in Medical and Law Schools* (Ann Arbor: University of Michigan Press, 1998), 58.

[15] Title VI provides that "[n]o person in the United States shall, on the ground of race, color, or national origin, be excluded from participation in, be denied the benefits of, or subjected to discrimination under any program or activity receiving federal assistance." 42 U.S.C. §2000d (1999).

[16] U.S. Constitution, amend XIV § 1.

[17] *Defunis v. Odegaard*, 416 U.S. 312 (1974). For a rich discussion of how this case fit into the affirmative action debate, see Robert M. O'Neil, *Discriminating Against Discrimination: Preferential Admissions and the Defunis Case* (Bloomington: Indiana University Press, 1975), and Allan P. Sindler, *Bakke, Defunis, and Minority Admissions* (New York: Longman Press, 1978).

the case, the Court held in a five-member *per curiam*[18] decision that the case was moot since Defunis would be permitted to graduate from law school regardless of the Court's decision.[19]

Nevertheless, *Defunis* raised serious constitutional issues that were relevant for the larger affirmative action debate in higher education. The challenged admissions procedure at the University of Washington Law School sorted applicants into two separate, race-based applicant pools where members of minority groups competed only against other minorities.[20] In effect, the law school guaranteed admittance to a certain percentage of the best minority applicants regardless of how well they stood in academic competition with nonminority applicants. (This practice, known as race norming, is now illegal under the provisions of the Civil Rights Act of 1991.)[21] A violation of the EPC was almost certain once the school conceded that most of the minority students admitted had LSAT scores below the cutoff level for successful majority applicants.[22] Given his composite scores, a nonwhite Defunis would have easily gained admission.

The Defunis case split traditional civil rights groups and Jewish organizations over the new politics of affirmative action. The Anti-Defamation League of the B'nai B'rith and the AFL-CIO filed *amici curiae* (friend of the court) briefs supporting Defunis. The Children's Defense Fund, American Hebrew Women's Council, and the National Urban League were among the many groups that opposed him.[23]

---

[18] Latin, "by the Court as a whole."

[19] A case is considered moot if a rendered decision would have no practical consequences for the parties involved. Since Defunis had been granted his injunction and was nearing graduation, the Court could justifiably argue that the case before the Court no longer met the constitutional requirements of a case or controversy.

[20] Testimony of the Chairman of the Admissions Committee indicated that the committee was instructed to evaluate minority applicants against one another and select for admission those who appeared to have the highest probability of success. Quoted at 416 U.S. 312, 323.

[21] Race norming occurs when the test scores of a racial group, for example, African Americas, are segregated from the scores of other racial groups. In the competitive process, the test scores of an individual black are evaluated against the test scores of other blacks in the pool under consideration. The 1991 Civil Rights Act invalidated race norming and the use of explicit racial quotas.

[22] See Jim Chen, "Defunis, Defunct," *Constitution Commentary* 16 (Spring 1999): 91.

[23] Ann F. Ginger, ed., *Defunis versus Odegaard and the University of Washington, the University Admissions Case*, vol. 2: *the Record* (New York: Oceana Press, 1974). See also Ronald Dworkin, "Defunis v. Sweatt," in Marshall Cohen, Thomas Nagel, and Thomas

According to law professor Ronald Dworkin, the splits occurred because in the past, liberal groups had held to three principles that were not easily reconcilable: (1) that "race classification is an evil itself"; (2) "that every person has a right to an educational opportunity commensurate with his abilities"; and (3) "that affirmative action is proper to remedy the serious inequalities of American society."[24] Over the years, Dworkin says, some liberals had increasingly come to recognize that these propositions were really not compatible because the most effective forms of affirmative action involved racial preferences rather than mere outreach and clearly do not treat people in a racially neutral or color-blind manner. Consequently, practical considerations conflicted with powerful moral claims that held that reverse discrimination is inherently unjust because of its violations of the rights of the individual members of unprotected groups.[25] Affirmative action, therefore, became a highly charged and divisive issue among groups that had traditionally supported efforts to fight bigotry.

Besides fueling a great academic debate over affirmative action in higher education, the *Defunis* case was notable for an impassioned dissent against mooting the case by Justice William O. Douglas, one of the Court's most liberal members. Douglas wanted the Court to decide the case on its merits because of the wider significance of the issues raised.[26] Accordingly, he used his dissent as an opportunity to advocate the use of race-neutral admissions policies that would de-emphasize LSAT scores while giving greater weight to individual accomplishments, interviews, and the likelihood that the person would choose to practice law in an underserved community.[27] In addition, Douglas commented on the possibility that the LSAT might systematically disadvantage applicants from certain types of culturally divergent backgrounds. An admissions process sensitive to these concerns was legitimate, Douglas contended, but he struck out against the University of Washington for setting up, in effect, a dual-track admissions

Scanlon, eds., *Equality and Preferential Treatment* (Princeton, N.J.: Princeton University Press, 1977), 64.

[24] Dworkin, 64.
[25] See also Terry Eastland and William J. Bennett, *Counting by Race: Equality from the Founding Fathers to Bakke and Weber* (New York: Basic Books, 1979).
[26] 416 U.S. at 334.   [27] Ibid.

system that, he said, not only discriminated against Defunis but stigmatized its intended beneficiaries:

> A Defunis who is white is entitled to no advantage by virtue of that fact; nor is he subject to any disability, no matter what his race or color. Whatever his race, he had a constitutional right to have his application considered on its individual merits in a racially neutral manner. . . . A segregated admissions process creates suggestions of stigma and caste no less than a segregated classroom, and in the end it may produce that result despite its contrary intention. One other assumption must be clearly disapproved, that blacks or browns cannot make it on their individual merit. That is a stamp of inferiority that a state is not permitted to place on any lawyer.[28]

Around the time of the Defunis case, two of the nation's preeminent legal scholars, Jon Hart Ely and Richard A. Posner, wrote seminal articles that set forth almost all the important arguments that would be used on both sides of the developing affirmative action controversy.[29] Ely, supporting the idea of racial preference for minorities, argued that the white majority could constitutionally impose upon itself the costs of affirmative action. There is a fundamental difference, both morally and constitutionally, he contended, between a majority group disadvantaging a powerless minority group for its own benefit and a majority group voluntarily disadvantaging itself for the benefit of a previously disadvantaged minority group:

> When a group that controls the decision making process classifies so as to advantage a minority and disadvantage itself, the reasons for being unusually suspicious, and, consequently employing a stringent brand of review are lacking. A White majority is unlikely to be tempted to either underestimate the needs and deserts of Whites relative to those of others, or to overestimate the cost of devising an alternative classification that would extend to certain Whites the advantages generally extended to Blacks.[30]

Ely's argument did not, however, address the concerns that later scholars expressed about the costs of affirmative action being

---

[28] Ibid., 334–41.

[29] See, Jon Hart Ely, "The Constitutionality of Reverse Discrimination," *University of Chicago Review* 41 (1974): 723; Richard A. Posner, "The Defunis Case and the Constitutionality of Preferential Treatment of Racial Minorities," *Constitutional Review* 1 (1974).

[30] Ely, 735–6.

disproportionately borne by poor and working-class whites not positioned to have much say in the political system about the imposition of those costs.

Richard Posner took a view of race-based affirmative action more critical than that of Ely. While Posner agreed that the Supreme Court was correct in dismissing *Defunis* on grounds of mootness, he himself was clearly opposed to the dominant justifications put forth by supporters to defend the University of Washington's policy. He specifically rejected the view of affirmative action supporters that the antidiscrimination principles embodied in the EPC condemned only those race classifications considered by judges or others to be invidious or stigmatizing. "[The] proper constitutional principle," he wrote, "is not, no 'invidious' racial or ethnic discrimination, but no use of racial or ethnic criteria to determine the distribution of government benefits and burdens. To ask whether racial exclusion may not have overriding benefits for both races in particular circumstances is to place antidiscrimination principle at the mercy of the vagaries of empirical conjecture and thereby free the judge to enact his own personal values into constitutional doctrine."[31]

After criticizing several justifications for reverse discrimination, including culturally biased exams, race as a surrogate for nonracial attributes, and the quest for racial proportionality, Posner suggested that the articulated goals of diversity and the rectification of past wrongs might not have been the most important factors explaining the acceptance of racial preferences at institutions of higher learning such as the University of Washington. "Although university administrators justify their preferential policies in terms of increasing diversity, rectifying historical injustices, and the like," Posner wrote, "in private they often will admit that appeasing student militancy was the dominant factor in the adoption of the policies."[32]

Perhaps Robert O'Neil, who had been Chairman of the Council on Legal Education, summed up best the moral and constitutional dilemma raised by the Defunis case. "Preferential admissions," O'Neil wrote,

> has been a deeply divisive issue within the academic community as well as in the courts. Also, no other public policy question has so seriously

[31] Posner, 26.   [32] Ibid., 25–6.

perplexed the liberal Jewish scholarly and professional community. Few persons of conscience question the past deprivations of minority groups, or their exclusion from the benefits of higher education; the controversy relates to the fairness and lawfulness of the remedies for that condition. Everyone wishes it were possible to help one group, and ameliorate the injustices of the past, without disadvantaging other groups and creating new injustices. The critical issue – one of both law and public policy – is whether preferential admission meets that objective.[33]

By the time of *Defunis*, the nature of the issues surrounding racial discrimination and segregation had changed greatly since the Sweatt case. Although it took over 100 years for African Americans to successfully challenge the racial preferences that benefited whites at state-supported colleges and universities, it took only a matter of a few years for whites to file reverse discrimination claims. When one considers the egregiousness of the stark racial discrimination that blacks suffered and the nature of the remedy of nondiscrimination that came out of the 1960s and gradually became racial preferences, it is perhaps not too difficult to understand why defenders of racial preferences as compensation for the past believed they were occupying the moral high ground.

Defunis shows that the seeds of the intellectual argument over the debate about racial preferences have been around since the inception of racial preferences for nonwhites. Although the seeds of the intellectual argument against preferences have largely lain dormant, except for discussions confined mostly to policy elites and members of the scholarly community, they are now being debated on a much wider scale and, at times, twisted to fuel the growth of white nationalism among disaffected whites. White power advocates are now using the mainstream conservative argument that any form of racial preference for nonwhites is an unfair, unconstitutional violation of the interests of more deserving white Americans.

SHIFTING THE DEBATE: THE DIVERSITY RATIONALE

Perhaps the most interesting parallel between the contemporary affirmative action debate over racial preferences in higher education and the previous era's debate before the Civil Rights Revolution of the

[33] O'Neil, x.

1950s and 1960s is the current Court's recognition of the intangible benefits of diversity. In *Sweatt*, the Court viewed one of the deficiencies of the black law school as its exclusion of whites, describing it as an "academic vacuum . . . removed from the interplay of ideas and the exchange of views with which the law is concerned."[34] Here the Court based at least part of its decision on the right of a black student to be exposed to the cultural milieu of a white law school, in order to be better prepared for a world in which "most lawyers, witnesses, jurors, judges, and other officials" would be white.[35]

With *Defunis* and subsequent cases, a new kind of cultural exposure argument is made. The legal justification for race-conscious affirmative action in higher education, now under challenge, revolves around the need for educational diversity to prepare not just black students but white students, too, to function adequately in the larger society now viewed not as white but as multiethnic, multiracial, and multicultural.

Four years after *Defunis*, a second case, *Regents of the University of California v. Bakke*,[36] reached the Supreme Court, in which Justice Lewis Powell, casting the deciding vote, found that the attainment of a diverse student body is a constitutionally permissible goal for universities to pursue. *Bakke* dealt with the unsuccessful application for admission to the medical school of the University of California at Davis of white applicant Alan P. Bakke. Bakke, a thirty-two-year-old mechanical engineer, had twice sought admission to the Davis medical school and twice been rejected. After learning that his grade point average and his MCAT score were substantially higher than that of most of the minorities accepted by the school, Bakke challenged the constitutionality of the Davis admissions program by arguing that it was discriminatory for Davis to set aside sixteen of its 100 entering slots for a special admissions program open only to minority applicants. Unlike the white applicants, he argued, minorities were free to compete for all 100 seats in the entering class.[37]

In a long-awaited decision written by Justice Powell, the Court struck down the preferential admissions program at Davis as incom-

---

[34] *Sweatt*, 634.   [35] Ibid.

[36] *Regents of the University of California v. Bakke*, 438 U.S. 265 (1978).

[37] For data on the qualifications of the competing applicants, see the Record filed with the U.S. Supreme Court, Brief for the Respondent, 12–13.

patible with the EPC of the Fourteenth Amendment, and it ordered Bakke admitted. However, while ruling against Davis's quota system, Powell declared that admissions officers in institutions such as Davis could take race into account as one of many "plus" factors designed to enhance the diversity of a school's student body.

As is often the case with affirmative action decisions, the justices were not able to produce a majority opinion – no more than four justices agreed in their reasoning and six separate opinions emerged. Four justices (Stevens, Burger, Stewart, and Rehnquist) found that the quota system violated the clear language of Title VI of the 1964 Civil Rights Act.[38] Another four justices (Brennan, White, Marshall, and Blackmun) held that Title VI applies the same standard as the Fourteenth Amendment[39] and that the Davis plan passed constitutional muster under an intermediate level of scrutiny.[40]

With four justices on either side of the issue, Justice Powell was able to decide the case and write the opinion announcing the judgment of the Court. He is widely credited for crafting an opinion in the form of a Solomonic compromise, with something good for each side of the dispute.[41] Justice Powell first agreed with the Brennan group that Title VI applied a constitutional standard,[42] but then disagreed with Justice Brennan's asserted standard of review. Justice Powell ruled that *any* racial or ethnic classification, even ones for allegedly benign purposes, called for strict judicial scrutiny.[43] To survive strict scrutiny, the classification must involve a compelling state interest that is not amenable to fulfillment by other means.[44] Justice Powell held that pursuit of the educational benefits that flow from an ethnically diverse student body

---

[38] *Bakke*, 438 U.S. 421. Title VI provides that "[n]o person in the United States shall, on the ground of race, color, or national origin, be excluded from participation in, be denied the benefits of, or be subjected to discrimination under any program or activity receiving Federal financial assistance" (42 U.S.C. §2000d (1999)).

[39] Ibid.   [40] Ibid., 369, 373–4.

[41] Michael Selmi, "The Life of Bakke: An Affirmative Action Retrospective," *Georgetown Law Journal* 87 (1999): 981, 983.

[42] *Bakke*, 438 U.S. 287.

[43] Ibid., 291 ("The guarantee of equal protection cannot be one thing when applied to one individual and something else when applied to a person of another color. If both are not accorded the same protection, then it is not equal").

[44] Ibid., 305 ("to justify the use of a suspect classification, a State must show that its purpose or interest is both constitutionally permissible and substantial, and that its use of the classification is necessary to the accomplishment of its purpose or the safeguarding of its interest") (internal quotations omitted).

is a constitutionally permissible state interest grounded in the First Amendment,[45] but that a quota system is not a necessary means to that end.[46] He stated:

> [T]he diversity that furthers a compelling state interest encompasses a far broader array of qualifications and characteristics of which racial or ethnic origin is but a single though important element. Petitioners' special admissions program, focused *solely* on ethnic diversity, would hinder rather than further attainment of genuine diversity.[47]

Justice Powell concluded that while quotas and processes involving separate consideration were unconstitutional, the race of an applicant could be used as one "plus" factor out of many in the admissions process.[48]

Thus, Justice Powell joined with the Stevens group in holding that the Davis quota system violated the law, but at the same time he also joined with the Brennan group in holding that race may be considered in the admissions process. For the past twenty-plus years, the *Bakke* case has stood for the proposition that colleges and universities may not set aside any seats for minorities or use race as the dominant factor in admissions decisions, but they may consider race as one "plus" factor among many in deciding whether to admit or reject a given applicant.

The practical effect of the *Bakke* decision may not have been what Powell intended. Although *Bakke* may have caused some institutions to become more circumspect about using race in the selection of their student bodies, by the 1990s, race at most elite institutions had become more than a modest "plus" factor, but a very special condition tipping the scales heavily in favor of minority candidates.[49] George Cantor reports that at the University of Michigan, if a white student did B-minus work in high school (2.8 to 2.99 grade point average) and the student's test scores fell in the upper middle range (1100–1190 on the SAT and 27–28 on the ACT), the chances of being admitted to the university were very small: only about 11 percent during the 1994–95

---

[45] Ibid., 311–12 ("the attainment of a diverse student body . . . clearly is a constitutionally permissible goal for an institution of higher education").
[46] Ibid., 316.   [47] Ibid., 315 (emphasis in original).   [48] Ibid., 318.
[49] Stephan Thernstrom and Abigail Thernstrom, *America in Black and White: One Nation Indivisible* (New York: Simon and Schuster, 1997); Dinesh D'Souza, *Illiberal Education: The Politics of Race and Sex on Campus* (New York: Vintage Books, 1991).

academic year. But if a student with the same average and score was a member of an "underrepresented minority," defined as black, Latino, or Native American, the chances of admission were excellent. In fact, they were 100 percent in 1994–95.[50] Widely publicized stories of such racial disparities in grades, test scores, and the admissions rates of minorities have led affirmative action's opponents to renew their arguments that colleges and universities are violating the civil rights laws and the Constitution, and a few rejected applicants have brought a new wave of cases challenging the current admissions regime.[51]

The divergence of actual admissions practices from those legitimized under the diversity rationale in *Bakke* is notably visible. One scholar even states that universities use *Bakke* as a "diversity fig leaf" as they carry out admissions policies with goals and practices far different than the modest "plus" factor to achieve the diversity advocated by Justice Powell.[52] One way that universities violate *Bakke* in their admissions processes is by limiting preferences to only certain historically disadvantaged racial groups, while excluding most other diversity factors from consideration. "The weakness in the 'diversity' defense," Nathan Glazer has written, "is that college presidents are not much worried about the diversity that white working-class kids, or students of Italian or Slavic backgrounds have to offer."[53] One might add that most elite universities show no interest in fostering religious diversity by recruiting members of such underrepresented religious groups as Evangelical Christians, Pentecostals, Southern Baptists, Mormons, or non-Hispanic Catholics. Most elite institutions show an interest in geographic diversity, and students from underrepresented regions of the country are often accorded a degree of "plus factor" preference, but the degree of preference given for purposes of geographic diversity is usually very modest compared with that accorded to enhance racial diversity.

---

[50] George Cantor, "Would Policies at University of Michigan Make the Perfect Test Case on Affirmative Action?," Gannett News Service, July 13, 1996.

[51] Affirmative action opponents argue that college admissions decisions should be made primarily on the basis of academic achievement as measured by indicators such as grades, test scores, and class rank. See, e.g., Thernstrom and Thernstrom, note 8.

[52] Gabriel J. Chin, "Bakke to the Wall: The Crisis of Bakkean Diversity," *William and Mary Bill of Rights Journal* 4 (1996): 881.

[53] Glazer, however, has become a reluctant supporter of racial preferences at elite universities in the case of blacks (but no other groups). See "In Defense of Preferences," *The New Republic*, April 6, 1998, pp. 18ff.

Opponents of racial preferences in higher education ready to challenge this "fig leaf" may find a more receptive audience for their arguments sitting on the Supreme Court today than Alan Bakke did twenty-two years ago. The membership of the Supreme Court has changed through the intervening years, resulting in a more conservative court.[54] Indeed, none of the justices who concluded in *Bakke* that race may be considered in the admissions process remains on the court. Moreover, the court has taken a number of occasions to elaborate on the acceptable parameters of affirmative action programs and, in so doing, has restricted the range of constitutionally permissible affirmative action programs. Two important changes in the law of affirmative action have emerged from these decisions. First, it is now well established that *all* forms of racial classification, no matter which race is benefited or burdened, are subject to strict judicial scrutiny under the Fifth and Fourteenth amendments.[55] The Supreme Court has made it clear that constitutional guarantees make all racial classifications inherently suspect, regardless of any alleged benign or remedial motivation for the classification. Writing for a plurality of the Court in the case of *City of Richmond v. J.A. Croson Co.*, Justice O'Connor explained the need for strict scrutiny of affirmative action programs even if their beneficiaries are a previously disadvantaged minority and the intent of the program is said to be benign:

> Absent searching judicial inquiry into the justifications for such race-based measures, there is simply no way of determining what classifications are "benign" or "remedial" and what classifications are in fact motivated by illegitimate notions of racial inferiority or simple racial politics. Indeed, the purpose of strict scrutiny is to "smoke out" illegitimate uses of race by assuming that the legislative body is pursuing a goal important enough to warrant use of a highly suspect tool. The test also ensures that the means chosen "fit" this compelling goal so closely that there is

---

[54] The lower federal courts have also become more conservative with the majority of judges owing their appointments to Presidents Reagan and Bush. See "Affirmative Action in the Courts: Here's Some Reasons Why That's a Bad Place for Blacks to Be," *Journal of Blacks in Higher Education* 25 (1999): 40–41.

[55] *Adarand Constructors v. Pena*, 515 U.S. at 227; *City of Richmond v. J. A. Croson Co.*, 488 U.S. at 493 (plurality opinion of O'Connor, J.; *id.* at 520 (concurring judgment of Scalia, J.) ("I agree . . . with Justice O'Connor's conclusion that strict scrutiny must be applied to all government classifications by race"); *see also Wygant v. Jackson Bd. of Ed.*, 476 U.S. 267, 273 (1986) (plurality opinion of Powell, J.).

little or no possibility that the motive for the classification was illegitimate racial prejudice or stereotype.[56]

Justice O'Connor echoed a similar concern in writing for a majority of the Court in the case of *Adarand Constructors v. Pena*. She acknowledged "the surface appeal of holding 'benign' racial classifications to a lower standard," but expressed the fear that it may not always be clear whether "a so-called benign preference is in fact benign."[57] This apprehension led her to state that "[m]ore than good motives should be required when government seeks to allocate its resources by way of an explicit racial classification system."[58]

Strict judicial scrutiny underscores the presumptive unconstitutionality of racial classifications; indeed, many commentators have observed that the use of strict scrutiny in reviewing a government action is a death knell. To survive strict judicial scrutiny, a racial classification must (1) serve a compelling state interest and (2) be narrowly tailored to achieve that interest.[59] Although the Court has stated its "wish to dispel the notion that strict scrutiny is 'strict in theory, but fatal in fact,'"[60] this assumption loses strength because of the limited set of circumstances under which a reviewing court using the strict scrutiny standard will find a program constitutional. As the Court stated in *Adarand*, "[b]y requiring strict scrutiny of racial classifications, we require courts to make sure that a government classification based on race, which *so seldom* provides a relevant basis for disparate treatment, is legitimate, before permitting unequal treatment based on race" (emphasis added).[61]

In sum, the rise of the diversity rationale in response to the first reverse discrimination case in *Bakke*, the flouting of the actual parameters of the decision by administering institutions, and the increasing

---

[56] *Croson*, 488 U.S. at 493 (plurality opinion of O'Connor, J.).

[57] *Adarand Constructors v. Pena*, 515 U.S. at 226.   [58] Ibid.

[59] Ibid., 227 ("[racial] classifications are constitutional only if they are narrowly tailored measures that further compelling governmental interests"); see also *Bakke*, 438 U.S. at 305 ("to justify the use of a suspect classification, a State must show that its purpose or interest is both constitutionally permissible and substantial, and that its use of the classification is necessary . . . to the accomplishment of its purpose or the safeguarding of its interest").

[60] Ibid., 237 (quoting Justice Marshall's concurring judgment in *Fullilove v. Klutznick*, 448 U.S. 448, 519 (1980)).

[61] Ibid., 236.

conservatism of courts have combined with public resentment to set the stage for a spate of legal challenges to the diversity rationale more generally. In the midst of this debate, the Court has unfortunately provided white nationalists with a morally charged rhetoric that can be easily twisted to inflame white resentment for unseemly ends. The rhetoric of recent court opinions uses language that commonly invokes the need to protect whites from egregious harms and injustices.[62] Whites are said to be "individual victims" suffering a "very real injustice," who are denied "enforcement of their rights";[63] they are a people who are "harm[ed]" and "disadvantaged";[64] they are "innocent third parties"[65] and "unduly burden[ed] individuals";[66] they are people "bear[ing] the burdens of redressing grievances not of their making."[67] Proponents of racial preferences, meanwhile, are accused of trying to "even the score";[68] minorities are referred to as "favored";[69] and racial preferences are characterized as presenting "serious problems of justice."[70]

Such language, adopted by the highest court in the land, has been appropriated by white nationalists and used to promote a white sense of racial grievance.[71] White nationalist groups and their leaders have eagerly embraced the language of white victimization the Court now actively endorses. David Duke, for instance, sees affirmative action policies as discrimination against European Americans. "We believe," the National Organization for European American Rights leader told our interviewer, "that European Americans face a pernicious racial discrimination on a multi-level basis in this country." "It is our contention," he explained, "that if discrimination is indeed morally wrong

---

[62] See, e.g., Justice Scalia's concurring opinion in *Croson* 488 U.S. 469, 526–8, Justice Stevens's dissent in *Wygant* 476 U.S. at 317, Justice Powell's concurrence in *Fullilove* 448 U.S. at 514, Justice O'Connor's dissent in *Metro Broadcasting*, 497 U.S. at 630, and the majority opinion in *Bakke*, 438 U.S. at 298.

[63] *Johnson v. Transportation Agency, Santa Clara County*, 480 U.S. 616, 677 (1987) (Scalia, J., dissenting).

[64] *Wygant*, Stevens dissent 476 U.S. at 317.

[65] *Fullilove*, Powell concurrence (448 U.S. at 514).

[66] *Metro Broadcasting*, O'Connor dissent (497 U.S. at 630).

[67] *Bakke*, Majority Opinion (438 U.S. at 298).

[68] Scalia concurrence in *Croson* (488 U.S. 469, 526–8).

[69] *Bakke*, Majority Opinion (438 U.S. at 298). [70] Ibid.

[71] See, e.g., Thomas Ross, "Innocence and Affirmative Action," *Vanderbilt Law Review* 297 (March 1990): 43.

when exercised against minorities, then it's just as morally reprehensible when exercised against members of the European-American majority."[72] Similarly, Reno Wolfe of the NAAWP states that his organization's position is: "stop the discrimination, no matter what it is, and treat everybody equally, treat everybody fairly, have everybody take the same test, have everyone judged on the same standards."[73] What this shows is how adept white nationalists have become in appropriating mainstream civil rights language into their criticisms of racial preferences. In some cases the civil rights frame of nondiscrimination is being cleverly used by individuals and groups whose true aim is some form of white supremacy or white separatism.

A NEW TWIST IN THE "REVERSE DISCRIMINATION" CASES

In the mid-1990s, sensing the vulnerability of racial preferences in university admissions and borrowing heavily from the strategy that the NAACP used in its successful attack against the doctrine of "separate but equal," two conservative public interest legal organizations, the Center for Individual Rights (CIR) and the Institute of Justice, began to recruit aggrieved white students to file reverse discrimination suits against state-supported educational institutions.

The first high-profile federal case brought to fruition as a result of the recruitment efforts of CIR was *Hopwood v. Texas*, a reverse discrimination case against the very same law school that had denied admission to Herman Sweatt in 1946.[74] Cheryl Hopwood, lead plaintiff in the case, wove a personal story of individual triumph over adverse circumstances and boasted academic achievements that exceeded those of most minorities who applied that year. The admissions program that she challenged gave preferences to blacks and Mexican Americans. All applicants were, for purposes of initial sorting, assigned a Texas Index score combining undergraduate grade point and LSAT score and designated either presumptive admit, presumptive deny, or discretionary zone.[75] With a few exceptions, almost all

---

[72] David Duke, interview.   [73] Reno Wolfe, interview.
[74] *Hopwood v. Texas*, 78 F.3d 932 (5th Circuit 1996), reh'g en banc denied, 84 F. 3d 720 (1996), cert denied, 518 U.S. 1033 (1996).
[75] Ibid., 934–5.

presumptive admit students were admitted and all presumptive deny students were not.[76] Applicants falling in the discretionary zone had their applications considered with a higher degree of care by the admissions committees.

On its face, the challenged plan seems to have violated the letter and spirit of *Bakke*. Black and Mexican American applicants were treated differently in three respects. First, black and Mexican American applicants were given different numerical thresholds for being assigned to the presumptive admit, presumptive deny, or discretionary zone thresholds.[77] Second, black and Mexican American applicants were considered by a separate minority subcommittee.[78] Finally, black and Mexican American applicants were placed on separate waiting lists from nonpreferred applicants.[79]

Rather than simply resolve the issue by declaring the admissions policy unconstitutional under the *Bakke* standard, in a surprising move, the Fifth Circuit Court of Appeals struck down the diversity rationale *in toto*, rejecting it as a compelling interest under the strict scrutiny standard for racial classifications, and thereby rejecting *Bakke* as a controlling precedent. As its basis for doing so, the Fifth Circuit reasoned that Justice Powell's "argument in *Bakke* garnered only his own vote and has never represented the view of the majority of the Court." The Brennan Four, the Circuit Court pointed out, had argued for intermediate scrutiny and qualified its endorsement of Justice Powell's model Harvard Plan to instances where the use of race was a compensatory device "necessitated by the lingering effects of past discrimination" and designed to bring disadvantaged persons up to par.[80] The Circuit Court then completed its dismissal of the diversity rationale with the observation that "[w]ithin the general principles of the Fourteenth Amendment, the use of race in admissions for diversity in higher education contradicts, rather than furthers, the aims of equal protection" by fostering the use of race, perpetuating the continued use of racial classifications, treating minorities as a group rather than as individuals, and promoting racial stereotypes.[81]

The Fifth Circuit reversed the lower court decision, which had held that while the specific admissions program used by the University of

[76] Ibid., 936.   [77] Ibid., 934–6.   [78] Ibid.   [79] Ibid., 938.   [80] Ibid., 944.
[81] Ibid., 945.

Texas violated the equal protection component of the Fourteenth Amendment, the law school was justified in using racial preferences. The district court had ruled that the appropriate remedy for *Hopwood* plaintiffs was to reapply (with application fees waived) under a newly adopted and more carefully structured admissions program. Moreover, it rejected the plaintiffs' request for damages or injunctive relief, except to award them one dollar each in nominal damages.[82]

Most surprisingly, given the history of the state and Sweatt's struggle to gain admission to the University of Texas Law School in an earlier period, the Court rejected the law school's attempt to justify its admissions program on remedial grounds. The Fifth Circuit held that the law school had not proved that "there are present effects of past discrimination of the type that justify the racial classifications at issue."[83] The Fifth Circuit rejected the law school's argument that "bad reputation and hostile environment" were legitimate effects of past discrimination, noting that "knowledge of historical fact simply cannot justify current racial classifications" and that "[a]ny racial tension at the law school is most certainly the result of present societal discrimination and, if anything, is contributed to, rather than alleviated by, the overt and prevalent consideration of race in admissions."[84] The Fifth Circuit likewise rejected the underrepresentation of minorities as an effect of past discrimination throughout the Texas school system by again noting that for the purposes of remedial inquiry, the scope is limited to the state actor employing the racial preference.[85]

Ultimately, having determined that the University of Texas Law School admission program did not meet the standards for invoking the remedial justification, the Fifth Circuit directed the law school to consider the plaintiffs' applications under a system devoid of racial considerations and remanded the question of damages to the district court. While not using the term "injunction" in requiring a nonrace admission program, the concurrence notes that the majority's decision "has all of the substantive earmarks of an injunction,"[86] which is a court order commanding either the performance of or the cessation of a particular action – the Court acting in its most powerful capacity. Both the bold rejection of Supreme Court precedent and the injunction-like remedy attest that the *Hopwood* court was making a sweeping

---

[82] Ibid., 934, 938.   [83] Ibid., 950.   [84] Ibid., 952.   [85] Ibid., 953.   [86] Ibid., 966.

statement against racial preferences in admissions. The manner and flavor of the decision bespeak the strength of feeling that has always characterized the affirmative action debate.

In reaching its decision, the *Hopwood* court conducted a detailed review of the evolution of Supreme Court holdings on affirmative action. Although the holdings from *Croson*[87] to *Adarand*[88] arguably stand for the proposition that racial classifications may be employed to remedy the present effects of past racial discrimination, an attempt to assert the presence of these factors failed at an institution that had a clearly documented history of discrimination. After the Supreme Court refused to review the case, *Hopwood* became binding precedent on the states in the Fifth Circuit (Louisiana, Mississippi, and Texas). *Hopwood*, then, seems to represent the apex of legal resistance to race-conscious affirmative action policies designed to enhance racial diversity in higher education.

After *Hopwood*, it was perhaps only a matter of time before the increasing selectivity of graduate and professional schools would trickle down to affect the behavior of individuals competing at other levels of the educational chain. Before 1997, all of the challenges to racial preferences in educational institutions had been brought against graduate and professional schools. This changed when two white undergraduates, Jennifer Gratz and Patrick Hamacher, filed a racial discrimination suit against the University of Michigan and its administrators alleging discrimination in the university's undergraduate admissions program. A year later, white parents in Boston filed a successful suit ending racial preferences at the elite Boston Latin School in *Wessman v. Gittens*.[89] Moreover, in a related action, the U.S. Supreme Court in March 2000 let stand a lower court decision in *Public Schools v. Eisenberg*,[90] which had declared unconstitutional an effort by Maryland school officials to prevent a white elementary school student in a predominantly black school from transferring to a magnet school because his departure would upset the delicate racial balance at the institution.[91] The Court is clearly reluctant to use race

---

[87] *City of Richmond v. J.A. Croson Co.*, 488 U.S. 469 (1989).
[88] *Adarand Constructors v. Pena*, 515 U.S. 200 (1995).
[89] *Wessman v. Gittens*, 160 F.3d 790, (1st Cir. 1998).
[90] See *Montgomery County Public Schools v. Eisenberg*, 197 F. 3d 123 (4th Cir. 1999).
[91] Jeffrey Rosen, "The Lost Promise of School Integration," *New York Times*, April 2, 2000.

as a criterion for maintaining diversity in public schools. The Supreme Court's increasing reluctance to sanction the use of racial preferences has moved the judicial branch of government into closer alignment with public opinion on this contentious issue, an instance of a general phenomenon well documented by scholars of judicial politics with regard to an array of public policy issues.[92]

After a string of setbacks, however, affirmative action supporters saw some hopeful signs in late 2000 as some lower courts began to reassert support for the *Bakke* principle of using race as a plus factor to enhance educational diversity. On December 4, 2000, the Ninth Circuit Court of Appeals affirmed a district court ruling in *Smith v. University of Washington Law School* that diversity is a compelling governmental interest.[93] U.S. District Judge Patrick Duggan issued a ruling supportive of the University of Michigan's current use of race as a plus factor in university admissions.[94] However, he declared as unconstitutional the dual track admission system that the university had in place between 1995 and 1998 that spawned the case of *Gratz v. Bollinger*.[95]

A recent Michigan district court decision in a parallel case to *Gratz*, however, has shown that the arguments of affirmative action opponents are still persuasive to certain courts. Barbara Grutter sued the University of Michigan Law School in 1997 over its admission policy, which was similar to that of the university's undergraduate admissions policy. On March 27, 2001, federal district judge Bernard Friedman ruled that the law school's admissions policy regarding race was unconstitutional and enjoined it from using race as a factor in its admissions process. In his decision, Judge Friedman rejected the law school's diversity and

---

[92] A substantial body of scholarly work makes clear that the courts generally do not stray far from the established beliefs and norms of society due to institutional constraints. See, e.g., Gerald N. Rosenberg, *The Hollow Hope: Can Courts Bring about Social Change?* (Chicago: University of Chicago Press, 1991).

[93] *Smith v. University of Washington Law School* (Civ. No. C-97-335) (W.D. Wash. Filed March 5, 1997), interlocutory appeals filed: no. 99-35209, 9935347, 9935348 (9th Cir. December 4, 2000).

[94] See the full text of the opinion at: http://www.umich.edu/~urel/admissions/legal/gratz/gra_opin.html.

[95] See *Gratz v. Bollinger*, no. 97-75231 (E.D. Mich. Filed October 14, 1997); *Grutter v. Bollinger*, no. 97-75928 (E.D. Mich. Filed December 3, 1997). For more information on both lawsuits, see the University of Michigan's web page coverage at http://www.umich.edu/~urel/admissions.

recompensatory arguments in support of using race in its admissions decisions:

> [T]he court would make the obvious observation that, ultimately, the law school student population naturally will become racially diverse under a race-blind admissions system when the gaps in LSAT scores, undergraduate GPA's, and other measures of academic performance are eliminated by investing greater educational resources in currently underperforming primary and secondary school systems. . . . This is a social and political matter, which calls for social and political solutions. The solution is not for the law school, or any other state institution, to prefer some applicants over others because of race. Whatever solution the law school elects to pursue, it must be race neutral. The focus must be upon the merit of *individual applicants*, not upon assumed characteristics of racial groups. An admissions policy that treats any applicants differently from others on account of their race is unfair and unconstitutional. As a matter of constitutional law, such a system cannot be justified on the grounds that certain races are at a greater competitive disadvantage than others because of discrimination or other societal conditions which may have created an "uneven playing field." Nor can a race-conscious system be upheld based on the predicted consequences of moving to a race-blind system. In sum, the court must reject the arguments raised . . . in defense of the law school's current admissions policy.[96]

Judge Friedman went on to find that

> [t]he Supreme Court has often stated that "distinctions between citizens solely because of their ancestry [are] odious to a free people whose institutions are founded upon the doctrine of equality." *Wygant v. Jackson Board of Education*, 476 U.S. 267 (1986), quoting *Hirabayashi v. United States*, 320 U.S. 81, 100 (1943). In our history, such distinctions generally have been used for improper purposes. Even when used for "benign" purposes, they always have the potential for causing great divisiveness. For these reasons, all racial distinctions are inherently suspect and presumptively invalid. This presumption may be overcome only upon a showing that the distinction in question serves a compelling state interest, and that the use of race is narrowly tailored to the achievement of that interest. It does not suffice for the interest in question merely to be important, beneficial, or laudable; the interest must be *compelling*. For

---

[96] *Grutter v. Bollinger*, No. 97-75928 (E.D. Mich. Decided March 27, 2001), 88–90 of the opinion.

the reasons stated in this opinion, the court concludes that the University of Michigan Law School's use of race as a factor in its admissions decisions is unconstitutional and a violation of Title VI of the 1964 Civil Rights Act. The law school's justification for using race – to assemble a racially diverse student population – is not a compelling state interest. Even if it were, the law school has not narrowly tailored its use of race to achieve that interest. Nor may the law school's use of race be justified on the alternative grounds . . . – to "level the playing field" between applicants of minority and non-minority races – because the remedying of societal discrimination, either past or present, has not been recognized as a compelling state interest.[97]

The Sixth Circuit Court of Appeals is scheduled to hear appeals of both *Grutter* and *Gratz*, but the U.S. Supreme Court will most likely be the final arbiter of the underlying issue.[98]

The University of Michigan undergraduate admissions plan that Judge Duggan found constitutional is an improvement over the older system that accorded much greater weight to race. However, it is still likely to generate intense opposition, because on a scale that reaches a maximum of 150 points, it gives 20 points for race to African Americans, Native Americans, and Hispanics – whites and Asians get none – while it gives only 12 such additional points for a perfect SAT score and only a few points for outstanding essays, legacy status, and extracurricular activities. The system also gives up to 20 additional points to those from socioeconomically disadvantaged backgrounds. Although the new system could be potentially beneficial to poor minorities because they can now get as many as 40 additional points, it is not clear how working-class whites will benefit from a point system that gives their black, Hispanic, and Native American counterparts such a huge advantage over them.

Not surprisingly, some of the loudest complaints against racial preferences in college admissions have come from whites of relatively modest means. Jennifer Gratz's parents lacked college degrees, and

---

[97] Ibid. Emphasis in original.

[98] Closer in the lineup for a Supreme Court resolution are anticipated appeals in *Smith v. University of Washington Law School*, where the Ninth Circuit Court of Appeals concluded that diversity can be an adequate justification for using race as a plus factor in admissions. See *Smith v. University of Washington Law School* (Civ. No. C-97-335) (W.D. Wash. Filed March 5, 1997), interlocutory appeals filed: no. 99-35209, 9935347, 9935348 (9th Cir. Dec. 4, 2000).

Cheryl Hopwood, the successful lead plaintiff in *Hopwood v. Texas*, was from a disadvantaged background.[99] Unlike most of the students admitted to the University of Texas Law School, Hopwood had attended a community college and had an undergraduate degree from a nondistinguished state institution.[100] It is not clear how the University of Michigan would have handled an applicant like Hopwood, though as a white person, she surely would have been at a disadvantage competing with minority applicants similarly situated as herself, since disadvantaged minority group members would receive twice the amount of bonus points she would receive. And she would be at a disadvantage competing with minority group members from the most privileged backgrounds since they would receive as many additional points because of their race as she would for her underprivileged status.

As previously suggested, media stories like the October 2000's *60 Minutes* segment interviewing white "victims" of racial preferences have no doubt helped crystallize spoken and unspoken grievances about the perceived unfairness and possible illegality of admissions policies at selective institutions. Also fueling white dissatisfaction are the newspaper articles that feature affluent minority students seemingly boasting a glut of riches in the form of multiple offers of admissions and multiple offers of scholarships. Resentment against racial preferences by the white majority shows no inclination of abating.

Unless they are rendered moot by a prior Supreme Court ruling in *Smith v. University of Washington Law School*, appeals of *Gratz* and *Grutter* will eventually reach the Supreme Court. Given the current ideological balance on the U.S. Supreme Court, with five of the nine justices in recent years taking a skeptical view of most race-based affirmative action policies, some Americans have concluded that the handwriting is on the wall for racial preferences. Others are not so sure given the possibility of changes in court personnel or the defection of one of two swing voters (Sandra Day O'Connor, Anthony Kennedy) to the pro–affirmative action camp. As insurance, a few states have wisely started to develop admissions policies that would be less likely to be vulnerable to legal challenges. Colleges and universities are aggressively

---

[99] *Hopwood v. Texas*, 78 F. 3d 932 (5th Cir. 1996) cert. denied, 116 S. Ct. 25 (1996).
[100] Derrick Bell, "Segueing Toward 70: The Rewards and Regrets of a Race-Related Life," *Harvard Journal of African American Public Policy* 6 (Summer 2000): 147.

seeking alternative ways of ensuring demographic diversity, and some creativity is being shown.[101] Some of the racial diversity that is desired, we can see, can be achieved through class-based strategies or other policies that build upon rather than contravene the race-neutral views of basic fairness that are shared by many blacks and whites alike. To the extent that we can move beyond racial conflict in university admissions, we will all become winners in a battle that has gone on for too long and claimed too many casualties.

UNIVERSITY ATTEMPTS TO ADDRESS DIVERSITY WITHOUT USING RACIAL PREFERENCES

In an effort to combat the disadvantages that African American and Hispanic students suffer because of their lowered test scores, some colleges and universities are changing their admissions criteria in search of measures that will enhance their ability to gain a higher yield of minority students without using racial preferences.[102] Thus far, the most popular solutions are the legislative plans adopted by the states of Texas and Florida, which guarantee admission to a certain percentage of the top students at each high school in the state. In Texas, the top 10 percent of each high school's graduating class gains admission to the state universities, and Florida proposes to admit the top 20 percent. Pennsylvania is considering a plan that would admit the top 15 percent.[103] Since many blacks and Hispanics attend schools where there are few whites or Asians, under such a scheme a substantial black and Hispanic admittance to the state universities is almost guaranteed. Despite their popularity, however, there are many unanswered questions about these plans. In Texas, for example, of the approximately 34,000 black eighteen-year-olds in the state in a recent year, only 21,000 graduated from high school, and only 7,500 took the SAT.[104]

---

[101] Kenneth J. Cooper, "Colleges Testing New Diversity Initiatives," *Washington Post*, April 2, 2000; James M. O'Neill, "Colleges Consider a 15 Percent Solution," *The Inquirer*, April 1, 2000, http://www.phillynews/com/inquirer/2000/Apr/01/city/HIEDO1.html.

[102] Ibid.   [103] Ibid.

[104] "After Hopwood – The Problem Does Not Lie with Texas' Top Universities," quoted in T. Vance McMahan and Don R. Willett, "Hope from Hopwood: Charting a Positive Civil Rights Course for Texas and the Nation," *Stanford Law and Policy Review* 10 (1999): 169.

A 10 percent plan will not make a difference for the 13,000 black students who never graduated or the thousands more who graduated but did not take the SAT or intend to go to college.

Before embracing alternative admission strategies as a panacea, it is important to recognize pragmatically that "new admissions policies create new sets of winners and losers."[105] Famed sociologist Robert K. Merton has shown that all public policies come with unexpected and unanticipated consequences, some positive and others negative.[106] The new legislative proposals are not exceptions to this general rule. While race-neutral, the new proposals that take a certain portion of the high-achieving students at each state high school could lead to greater rates of attrition among minority students than the old system, especially since high schools vary so widely in how well they prepare students for college. To my knowledge, most of the new proposals are lacking in accompanying funds for remedial courses for poorly prepared top students from inferior inner-city schools. Consequently, the race-neutral solution could easily lead to greater disparities in the academic abilities of college students and to higher attrition rates once at college than the old system. The old system may have disproportionately benefited middle-class minorities from suburbia, but it is arguable that these students are most prepared for a rigorous college curriculum. A minority student ranked in the top quarter or top third of a high-performing, predominantly white suburban high school is almost certainly far better prepared academically for college than a student in the top 5 or 10 percent of a low-performing minority school. What could happen is a revolving door where minorities enter and leave quickly after having had their guaranteed opportunity to attend an elite institution. Some percentage of minorities will drop completely out of the market for higher education. And remember, of course, that white supremacists will continue to use their biological difference theories to explain high attrition rates among racial minorities as evidence of their intellectual inferiority.

On the other hand, the new proposals could have the desired effect of boosting minority enrollment and retention by decreasing

---

[105] Bowen and Bok, 273.
[106] Robert K. Merton, "The Unanticipated Consequences of Purposive Social Action," *American Sociological Review* 1 (1936): 894–904.

racial hostility toward nonwhites since whites are less likely to view the new selection process as grossly unfair. Another desired effect could be to boost the self-esteem and academic performance of nonwhites through the removal of the stigma factor (identified by social psychologist Claude Steele) that causes them to feel undervalued and leads them to disassociate themselves from their learning environment.[107] Finally, such policies could have the unanticipated, but beneficial, secondary effect of achieving better integration in secondary schools since instead of clustering around competitive, suburban schools, whites may discover a competitive edge to remaining in poorer school districts.

Interestingly, critics of racial preferences have seemingly accepted the guaranteed admission plans devised by state legislators as being nonproblematic, even though it is clear that they were adopted as a means to circumvent the anti–racial preference court decisions that these critics have fought. Even conservatives such as Edward Blum, chairman of the Campaign for a Colorblind America, has endorsed the plan in his state of Texas, although the plan will help ensure a strong minority presence at state universities. When University of Texas enrollment figures showed that the 1999 incoming freshman class would have the same percentage of blacks and Hispanics as it had in 1996, the last year of racial preferences (which defied the predictions of civil rights leaders who predicted an end to diversity), Blum attributed the results to a combination of race-neutral actions that included greater university outreach and state legislative initiatives. He, like other conservatives, has generally endorsed the new policies.[108]

---

[107] Claude M. Steele, "Race and Schooling of Black Americans," *The Atlantic Monthly*, http://www.theatlantic.com/election/connection/race/steele.htm.

[108] "Hopwood Decision Not Fatal to Minorities," Campaign for a Colorblind America, August 19, 1999. Marc Levin, the director of the Campaign for a Colorblind America, stated that "it is clear that advocates of racial preferences shamefully underestimated the ability of minority students, many of whom have shown that they need only equal opportunity, not a guarantee of equal results to reach Texas's premier institutions of higher education. Finally, we can celebrate the admission of all students to UT, since we know every single one of them was admitted based on merit rather than the color of their skin."

CONCLUSION

The hard-fought legal battle over the propriety of race-conscious admissions has left us desperately searching for alternative strategies that will help us achieve diversity in higher education. Bowen and Bok have passionately argued that racial preferences in admissions should be retained and that the majority of graduates of selective colleges and universities really value racial diversity.[109] But in a recent survey in which a randomly selected national sample of college students was asked to weigh the costs and benefits of campus diversity, the results were less than enthusiastically supportive of preferences. While 84 percent of the college sample acknowledged that ethnic diversity on campus is important, 79 percent opposed the lowering of entrance standards to achieve it, and 77 percent opposed preferential admissions for minority applicants.[110] Similarly, a 1996 survey of college faculty found 60 percent opposed racial and sexual preferences in admissions and faculty hiring.[111] Thus, although the value of diversity is apparent, there is little support for using racial preferences to realize such a goal. People may say they want diversity – an argument long used as the legal basis for race-conscious admissions – but they do not want to use racial preferences to achieve it. Fortunately, there are other alternatives that Americans can agree on, as I show in a later chapter.

[109] Bowen and Bok, 218–49.
[110] "Most U.S. Students Support Diversity but Not Affirmative Action, a Survey Finds," *Chronicle of Higher Education*, April 18, 2000. Also, "Campus Poll Tackles Race," *Boston Globe*, April 19, 2000.
[111] National Association of Scholars, Faculty Survey, Regarding the Use of Sexual and Racial Preferences in Higher Education, October 16–28, 1996.

WHAT CAN HAPPEN TO YOUNG PEOPLE IN A RACIALLY CHARGED ENVIRONMENT?

THE GROWING COMPETITIVENESS OF COLLEGE ADMISSIONS

What happens to a dream deferred? Does it dry up like a raisin in the sun? Or fester like a sore – And then run? Does it stink like rotten meat? Or crust and sugar over – like a syrupy sweet? Maybe it just sags like a heavy load. Or does it explode?

Langston Hughes[1]

Although Langston Hughes wrote his famous poem, "A Dream Deferred," to give expression to the experiences and frustrations of African Americans, we can now apply his words similarly to white Americans who feel blocked and frustrated by a system from which whites traditionally have been able to master and benefit, but now do not fully understand or control. Competition for college admissions has soared in recent decades, and is affected by a number of factors, including immigration patterns and birthrates among racial and ethnic minorities, both of which have resulted in an increasing nonwhite population.[2] When high immigration rates combine with the spurt of offspring of the last wave of the baby boom generation, the result is intense competition for scarce educational resources at top institutions. Instead of abating, this situation will worsen over the next decade as the demand for freshman seats far exceeds the available slots.[3]

[1] Langston Hughes as cited in Henry Louis Gates, Jr., and Nellie Y. McKay, eds., *The Norton Anthology of African American Literature* (New York: W. W. Norton, 1996), 1267.

[2] Richard Lamm and Gary Imhoff, *The Immigration Time Bomb* (New York: Truman Talley Books, 1985); Dale Maharidge, *The Coming White Minority: California, Multiculturalism, America's Future* (New York: Vintage Books, 1996); Ron Unz, "California and the End of White America," *Commentary*, November 1999.

[3] Ethan Bronner, "College Applicants of '99 are Facing Stiffest Competition," *New York Times*, June 12, 1999, p. A1.

In this chapter I examine the impact that living in a racially charged environment can have on young Americans. First, I present information on the growing competitiveness for college admission and how this affects everyone. Second, using case studies of three young white Americans who competed for freshman seats during the latter half of the 1990s, I illustrate different modes of adaptation for young people to the new competitive environment, including anger, disappointment, frustration, and resignation.

THE IMPACT ON WHITES AND AFRICAN AMERICANS

Record numbers of high school seniors are making the choice to continue their education at a four-year institution rather than taking a job immediately after graduation.[4] Since the number of top-rated colleges and universities remains fairly constant, this has resulted in ever-larger numbers of applicants to such institutions competing for a fixed or slowly increasing number of seats in the freshman class. As a result, the chances of gaining admission to such institutions are often small. In spring 2000, for example, Wesleyan University received 6,849 applications for its 715 freshman seats.[5] The previous year, Tufts University reported 13,500 applications for 1,200 slots, and denied admission to a third of the valedictorians who applied and to many applicants with perfect standardized test scores (SAT).[6] Other second- and third-tier institutions reported similar numbers, including institutions such as Pomona, Wabash, and Trinity College. According to admissions officials, 1999 was "the most competitive on record for students seeking admission to the nation's top colleges. Harvard rejected 9 of every 10 applicants who applied. Columbia spurned suitors at a similar rate. Wesleyan rebuffed 7 out of 10."[7] By spring 2001, competition for fall classes was shaping up to be even more competitive than 1999 or 2000.

---

[4] Bronner reports that by spring 1999, 14.8 million high school seniors had registered for fall admission at a four-year college or university, breaking the previous high of 14.6 million established in 1998. Behind those statistics are an explosion in the number of children enrolled in K–12. Although the number of high school graduates has not exceeded the record of 3.2 million set in 1977, the percentage of students expected to attend college has jumped from 50 percent to 67 percent.

[5] Jacques Steinberg, "For Gatekeepers at Colleges, a Daunting Task of Weeding," *New York Times*, February 27, 2000.

[6] Bronner.   [7] Steinberg.

At Vanderbilt University, for example, the admissions office received nearly 9,500 applications for slots in the fall 2001 freshman class, an increase of 9 percent from the previous year.[8] Moreover, of those 9,500, only 16 percent will become undergraduates at Vanderbilt.[9] Under strict application of the traditional merit system, relying mostly on indicators such as class rank, grades, and standardized test scores, top institutions could easily fill all available slots with exceptionally qualified individuals while turning away thousands of impressive applicants. Presumably, the majority of meritorious, but nonetheless rejected, applicants matriculate at lower-tier institutions where the competition is not as great.

Eventually, some of the middle-ranking institutions could become more selective as they become flooded with applications from students denied admission to more preferred universities. What will happen emotionally to young white Americans who have worked hard in high school, taken all of the right courses, achieved impressive grade point averages and standardized test scores, and excelled in extracurricular activities, yet failed to gain admission to their second- or third-choice colleges and universities? The statistics cited earlier suggest it is likely that many individuals groomed since birth to matriculate at elite private institutions and flagship state universities are destined to land on the campuses of less distinguished institutions. While most will accept their fate and move on, many will harbor a sense of having been cheated out of a birthright. Still others will file reverse discrimination suits. While there are different modes of adaptation to disappointment and different ways of explaining failure to attain what many whites have come to view as entitlements, current perceptions of the use of preferences in admissions are channeling these responses of disappointment toward unfortunate and often racist ends.

The debate over standards for college admissions and the increased competitiveness for spots in incoming classes is fueling social unrest even among the youth in secondary schools. These students are acutely aware of the role that race may play in the admissions process. In 1998,

---

[8] Brendan Ryan, "Admissions Gets Record Number of Frosh Applications," *The Vanderbilt Hustler*, January 30, 2001.

[9] Ibid. The selectivity data for Vanderbilt are consistent with that of other top-25 universities. For selectivity data for all universities, see http://www.usnews.com/usnews/edu/eduhome.htm.

following the acrimonious and public airing of the dispute over racial preferences in admissions in the Cheryl Hopwood case, 29 percent of those students accepted to the University of Texas refused to identify their race on their application. While there is no way of knowing with certainty what motivated this abstention, at a minimum, such mass resistance indicates that these students were uncomfortable with publicly identifying themselves by race and approached the designation of their race on their college applications with a sense of gravity.[10]

Because students are aware of the potential importance of race in the admissions process, they may also try to use this fraudulently for their own benefit. Instead of refusing to mark their race on the application, as the students at the University of Texas did, some applicants might mark the wrong box, hoping that this would gain them extra points during the admissions process. Universities cannot police the ethnic purity of the students who check the minority boxes, so there is reason to believe that a percentage of white students will fraudulently claim to be Hispanic, Afro-American, American Indian, or other minority designation, especially if they are ambitious and believe that racial preferences are illegal and unfair. A certain percentage of students might even view such a fraudulent action as praiseworthy because of the rhetoric in Supreme Court decisions and elsewhere emphasizing the harm that these programs cause innocent white victims.

Additionally, the application form itself sends subtle messages to applicants as to the importance of race. Drawing on personal experiences, Katrina Fischer, a law school applicant, has observed that:

> [College] applications generally request that an applicant designate his/her race or ethnicity by choosing from a provided list of options, including an "other" category that may be filled in. The race selection box is usually physically located on the application near basic background information about the candidate, including home address, birth date, etc. While applicants are encouraged in other portions of the application to provide information about extracurricular activities and given the opportunity to write a personal essay, these opportunities . . . differ qualitatively from the way in which racial data is solicited from the applicant and presented to the

[10] "After Hopwood – The Problem Does Not Lie with Texas' Top Universities," quoted in McMahan and Willett, 169.

reader. . . . Hence, applications are structured in a manner that not only differentiates race from other diversity factors, but seems to encourage the extra weighting of race.[11]

In 1999, a web link of the National Association for the Advancement of White People (NAAWP) reprinted, without the permission of the participants, selected responses from a contest that the *Detroit Free Press* sponsored to gauge young people's attitudes toward affirmative action.[12] Some 3,300 school children from 129 schools responded to this question:

> Some of Michigan's public universities give preference in admissions to qualified minorities under a policy that is commonly called "affirmative action." Do you think that universities should use such policies in deciding whether to admit some students?

Figures 10.1 and 10.2 are drawings in response to the question posed above. In each picture the youthful white males portray themselves as disadvantaged in the competitive process. In both cases the artists were appalled when they learned that their drawings were featured on a white nationalist website. Michael Shea had this reaction to the news:

> I feel "used" to discover that my cartoon about affirmative action was published on the NAAWP Website. Not only did I not give them my permission, but I strongly disagree with what that organization stands for. When I drew the cartoon, I meant to say that the world should be colorblind; that race should not matter and that all races should be created equal. However the NAAWP seems to promote segregation and causes that benefit white people only. . . . I resent the use of my cartoon to promote those positions.[13]

Similarly, Jonathan Pohl wrote a letter asking that the following quotation be included in this book: "I did not intend for this cartoon to

---

[11] Katrina Fischer, "All Hail the Diversity Rationale?," unpublished paper, Yale University Law School, May 2000.
[12] The letters and cartoon cited appeared as part of an editorial cartoon and essay contest in the *Detroit Free Press*, March 24, 1999, pp. 12A and 13A.
[13] E-mail correspondence from Michael Shea of Plymouth, Michigan, June 5, 2001. He submitted the drawing while he was a student at Pioneer Middle School, Plymouth, Michigan.

Figure 10.1 "Sorry, our limit on middle-class men has been met." Michigan school child's drawing.

Figure 10.2 Michigan school child's drawing.

reflect any white nationalist feelings, nor do I consider myself racist in general. The fact that this cartoon found its way to a white power web site is insulting to me."[14] Probably, the other students would be just as appalled to find that their letters were used to illustrate the unfairness of the policy to America's white youth.

Asked to respond to the same question, one seventh grader on the NAAWP web page began her response with a rhetorical question:

> Is it fair to let someone into a college if another person who performs better is not admitted? Of course, it isn't. Affirmative action does just that. It provides an unfair dishonest approach to trying to give minorities a boost in the economy. . . . This program is racist. Judgements shouldn't be made based on a person's race or sex, but on what the person has accomplished. If we continue to use the affirmative action program, we will drive people of different races away from each other.[15]

Another tenth grader had this to say:

> It is disgraceful that universities would ever hold different acceptance standards for different people according to their race. I cannot fathom the fact that I may fail to get into the university of my choice not because I am unqualified, but because I am of the majority race. Affirmative action is an injustice to all parties concerned. For the Caucasian population, the injustice is obvious. Affirmative action is also an injustice to racial minorities. It is offensive to be accepted to a university not because you are qualified, but because you are a certain race. Affirmative action affronts the intelligence of minority students.[16]

Obviously, many high school applicants are aware of the persistent test gap that separates blacks from whites and Asians.[17] African Americans perform significantly worse than whites and Asians on most standardized tests, and this holds true at every socioeconomic level. African American youths from families with annual incomes over

[14] Personal correspondence from Jonathan R. Pohl, June 14, 2001. Pohl submitted his drawing while he was a junior at Avondale High School, Auburn Hills, Michigan.

[15] Comment of Lindsey Martin of Van Hoosen Middle School, as cited at www.naawp.com/youth/artwork. Original source, *Detroit Free Press*, March 24, 1999.

[16] Comment of Emily Zambricki of Lahser High School, as cited at www.naawp.com/youth/artwork. Original source, *Detroit Free Press*, March 24, 1999.

[17] "National College Bound Seniors: 1994 Profile of SAT and Achievement Test Takers," The College Board, Princeton, New Jersey, 1995.

$50,000, for instance, average no better on the SAT than whites and Asians with family incomes in the $10,000 to $20,000 ranges.[18] Statistics of this kind are well known, and many whites and Asians have reason to believe that they or other members of their race will be denied admission to a prestigious college in favor of an African American applicant with significantly lower test scores. Under the right circumstances, this feeling may evolve from bitterness and resentment to outrage or hatred and perhaps ultimately to violence toward minority groups who are perceived as having an advantage in the admissions struggle not because of their academic performance but simply because of their race.

Although numerous factors affect who gets admitted to colleges and universities, white applicants often blame racial preferences for their lack of success in gaining admission to their first-choice schools.[19] William Bowen and Derek Bok, the former presidents of Princeton University and Harvard University, respectively, have tried to counter this perception and have argued passionately in favor of the continued use of racial preferences.[20] Examining data collected from five selective colleges and universities, Bowen and Bok found that the elimination of racial preferences would only modestly increase the chances of admission for the average white applicant: Their probability of admission would move from 25 to 26.5 percent.[21] The authors analogize the situation of the disappointed white applicants to that of nondisabled drivers who, upon seeing a parking space reserved for the disabled, falsely assume that they would be parked there were it not for the reserved nature of the space.[22]

Despite efforts by affirmative action supporters to change public attitudes, public opinion data discussed in earlier chapters show that the public remains overwhelmingly opposed to racial preferences.

---

[18] Andrew Hacker, *Two Nations: Black and White, Separate, Hostile, and Unequal* (New York: Random House, 1992), 146.

[19] Ethan Bronner, "Conservatives Open Drive Against Affirmative Action," *New York Times*, January 26, 1999; Martin Trow, "'The Shape of the River': California after Racial Preferences," *The Public Interest* 135 (Spring 1999); Thernstrom and Thernstrom, *America in Black and White*; Thernstrom and Thernstrom, "Reflections on the Shape of the River," *UCLA Law Review* 46 (1999): 1583.

[20] Bowen and Bok, *The Shape of the River*.

[21] Ibid.   [22] Ibid., 36–7.

Support for racial preferences in recent years has even declined among the population of people traditionally most sympathetic to the concerns of minorities.[23] For decades, social science studies have documented that well-educated Americans are more tolerant of diversity, more racially liberal, and more accepting of broad democratic values than the poorly educated.[24] Recent studies, however, show that well-educated whites are especially disapproving of racial preferences in college admissions.[25] In fact, political scientist James Glaser found this group more opposed to affirmative action than poorly educated whites, even though they are more liberal on issues such as minority representation in legislatures, hiring for public works jobs, and set-asides in public contracting.[26] Using the theory of group conflict to explain this counterintuitive finding, Glaser postulates that well-educated whites are sensitive to context and especially to racial preferences on their own turf, which in this instance is higher education. Well-educated, socially tolerant whites – the very group Bowen and Bok seek to influence – seem least receptive to the affirmative action message in the area of higher education.

Although originally adopted for African Americans, affirmative action preferences now include women, Hispanics, Asian Americans, Native Americans, Eskimos, and Aleuts.[27] Journalist John O'Sullivan

---

[23] The framing of the terms of the debate about affirmative action has affected how Americans view the policy. As I have shown in Chapter 7, how we define the concept of affirmative action and measure support for it largely determines what we find. Politicians, scholars, and the media largely control the presentation of the issue to the public and they establish the terms of the debate.

[24] See, e.g., Angus Campbell, Phillip Converse, Warren E. Miller, and Donald E. Stokes, *The American Voter* (Chicago: University of Chicago Press, 1960); V.O. Key, *Public Opinion and American Democracy* (New York: Knopf, 1961); Mary R. Jackman and Michael J. Muha, "Education and Intergroup Attitudes: Moral Enlightenment, Superficial Democratic Commitment, or Ideological Refinement?," *American Sociological Review* 49 (1984): 751–69; Herbert McClosky, "Consensus and Ideology in American Politics," *American Political Science Review* 58 (1964): 361–82; Paul M. Sniderman, Richard Brody, and Phillip E. Tetlock, *Reasoning and Choice: Explorations in Political Psychology* (Cambridge: Cambridge University Press, 1991); Schuman et al., *Racial Attitudes in America*; James M. Glaser, "A Quota on Quotas: Educational Differences in Attitudes Towards Minority Preferences," unpublished manuscript, Political Science Department, Tufts University, 1999.

[25] Schuman et al.   [26] Glaser.

[27] George R. La Noue and John C. Sullivan, "Deconstructing the Affirmative Action Categories," *American Behavioral Scientist* 41 (1998): 913–26.

argues that "one-third of the population is currently covered by race preferences – a figure that is predicted to grow to approximately 50 percent by 2050. And if we add in the effect of gender preferences, whose beneficiaries include white women, two-thirds of Americans already benefit from these legal privileges." The expanding size of the affirmative action pool, O'Sullivan argues, has harmful consequences not only for white men, but for blacks as well: "A white man is now almost three times as likely to suffer officially imposed negative discrimination as he was 30 years ago, and a Black American is about five times less likely to be the beneficiary of the white man's sacrifice."[28]

Like O'Sullivan, social scientist Hugh Graham also sees the affirmative action issue as complicated by the massive influx of foreign immigrants who can claim benefits under the policy. The existence of a large pool of potential immigrant beneficiaries, says Graham, has created greater hostility toward the policy among native whites (as evidenced in the passage of measures such as California's Proposition 187, which sought to restrict immigrant access to governmental benefits), and has limited the effect of the policy on blacks, the group for which the policy was originally instituted.[29] The list of groups that can qualify for affirmative action preferences continues to expand, and there are now ever-increasing efforts expended by some in an attempt to gauge the history and current levels of discrimination and its effects on particular racial and ethnic groups in order to justify extending affirmative action benefits.[30]

THE IMPACT ON ASIANS AND JEWS

Jews have traditionally been among the nation's most liberal Americans, often aligning themselves with marginalized groups such as African Americans. But demands for racial preferences and evidence of rampant anti-Semitism among some African Americans have weakened

[28] John O'Sullivan, "Preferences for (Almost) All: Affirmative Action Today," *National Review*, April 17, 2000.

[29] Hugh Graham, "Unintended Consequences: The Convergence of Affirmative Action and Immigration Policy," *American Behavioral Scientist* 41 (1998): 898–912.

[30] Paul Brest and Miranda Oshige, "Race and Remedy in a Multicultural Society: Affirmative Action for Whom?," *Stanford Law Review* 47 (1995): 855.

the historical black/Jewish relationship.[31] Some Jews have divorced themselves from African Americans' struggle for greater inclusion into American society, and a small number have even aligned themselves with groups of white nationalists traditionally antagonistic toward Jews.

The antipathy of many Jews toward affirmative action in college admissions, now exacerbated by increased competitiveness, has well-founded historical roots. Jews have been subject to ceiling quotas in the past that severely restricted their access to the nation's best universities. As Marcia Graham Synnott explains in her study of admissions at the three top Ivy League universities, "In the 1920s, the diversity rationale, currently used to justify affirmative action, was used by university officials to limit the number of Jews in an incoming class. The official reason for setting ceilings on the admission of Jews proffered by these officials was that if Jews were overrepresented in the student body, there wouldn't be the desired diversity, or mix of students, in a class. Harvard limited Jews to 10–16% of any given class – surprisingly, there is some evidence that such a ceiling might have persisted as late as 1942."[32]

While there are racist barriers to the recruitment of Asians into white nationalist groups, there are also strong forces opposing this group in university admissions. Not only does the percentage of Asians admitted to top tier schools continue to fall even as the number of applications from highly qualified Asian applicants is rising, but statements of some Harvard University officials indicate that Asians are suffering from the same diversity-based discrimination as Jews in the 1920s. Consider the statements of, respectively, a dean, assistant dean, and admissions officer at Harvard: "[Asian Americans are] no doubt the most over-represented group in the university"; "[F]urther increases of Asians would diminish the diversity of students for which [we] strive"; "It is the diversity element that hurts most of the Asian applicants because many who apply are pre-medical, science, technical types."[33]

---

[31] Paul Berman, ed., *Blacks and Jews: Alliances and Arguments* (New York: Delacorte Press, 1994).

[32] Marcia Graham Synnott, *The Half-Opened Door: Discrimination and Admissions at Harvard, Yale, and Princeton, 1900–1970* (Westport, Conn.: Greenwood Press, 1979).

[33] Grace W. Tsuang, "Assuring Equal Access of Asian Americans to Highly Selective Universities," *Yale Law Journal* 98 (1989): 659.

With affirmative action currently premised on a notion of increasing campus diversity, and Asian applicants being discriminated against for frustrating this diversity, it is easy to understand why an Asian applicant might harbor negative feelings toward affirmative action. Daniel Farber and Suzanna Sherry argue that the radical critique of merit that many affirmative action supporters employ implies that Asians and Jews "have obtained an unfair proportion of desirable social goods"; such a critique, they conclude, has an "unintended consequence of being anti-Semitic and possibly racist."[34]

There is no escaping the fact that institutional goals to assemble a racially diverse student body can lead to the admission of fewer numbers of Asian and Jewish applicants than there would be if institutions relied mostly on traditional admissions criteria such as grades and test scores.[35] Naturally, some members of both of these groups, including those who actually get into prestigious institutions, are sympathetic to members of their ethnic groups who seem to have been denied admission to top schools because they are of the wrong race. At Princeton University, for example, Jewish students in the spring of 1999 raised the possibility of racial discrimination by citing statistics that showed a decline in the percentage of Jews at the institution. Protests and criticism of the university's admission rate for Jews came not long after the administration issued statements announcing an increase in its yield of minority students.

Although Asians and Jews are not commonly viewed as potential recruits for white supremacy groups, members of these groups sometimes feel unfairly burdened in the college admissions contest. In extreme cases, they may even begin to support racist and nationalist groups. (White nationalists Michael Levin and Michael Hart, both Jews, cited affirmative action as the catalyst for their initial interest in the white nationalist cause.) Thus it would appear that a portion of the white nationalists' message, especially about the unfairness of affirmative action, may be attractive to some Jews and Asians who by

[34] Daniel A. Farber and Suzanna Sherry, "Is the Radical Critique of Merit Anti-Semitic?," *California Law Review* 83 (1995): 853.

[35] Goodwin Liu, "Affirmative Action in Higher Education: The Diversity Rationale and the Compelling Interest Test," *Harvard Civil Rights–Civil Liberties Law Review* 33 (1998): 58

culture and tradition would have little sympathy for any ideas emanating from the racist right.

ANYONE'S CHILD? CASE STUDIES OF THREE YOUNG, WHITE AMERICANS

In this section I present vignettes about three young, white Americans, each of whom reveals a different strategy for handling the frustrations associated with the transition from high school to college. Jennifer Gratz, Matthew Lerner, and Benjamin Smith are white students who made the national news for quite different reasons.

Jennifer Gratz is a Michigan resident who filed the first successful lawsuit challenging racial preferences in undergraduate admissions. Her case may enter the annals of important constitutional decisions. Lerner, who will perhaps not achieve as enduring a place in the history of the affirmative action controversy as Gratz, came to national attention when he was profiled in a *New York Times* article on higher education that described his difficulty in gaining admission to a top university despite having an outstanding high school record.[36] His experience is illustrative of the thousands of exceptionally well-qualified high school seniors competing each year for freshmen seats in America's most competitive universities. Benjamin Smith's story is very different from that of either Gratz or Lerner. A teenager from a typical middle-class suburban home, Smith went off to a state college and became a tireless crusader for the white power movement. He would eventually come to national attention after he went on a racially motivated shooting rampage in which two people were killed and nine wounded – a carnage which ended only with Smith's own suicide. I use Smith to illustrate the vulnerability of a small but growing segment of white youth to the strategies of extremist white nationalist groups who recruit on college campuses.

I believe that by examining each of the three people highlighted in this chapter, we can enhance our understanding of some of the pressures confronting young white Americans in a milieu where racial preferences and their resulting frustrations are familiar features of the adolescent landscape.

---

[36] Bronner, "College Applicants of '99 are Facing Stiffest Competition."

Jennifer Gratz

In 1997, Jennifer Gratz became the lead plaintiff in the first case to challenge affirmative action in undergraduate admissions. In high school, Gratz was ranked twelfth in her graduating class of 299 students, had a 3.79 grade point average (on a 4.0 scale), and scored 25 out of 36 on the ACT (which, like many other students from the Midwest, she took instead of the Scholastic Achievement Test (SAT)). She was also student council vice-president, a national Honor Society member, a competitive cheerleader, and a volunteer for numerous community projects. Overall, Gratz was a stronger candidate for admissions to the University of Michigan at Ann Arbor than most of the African-American applicants, but she was not spectacular among white or Asian applicants. Although it was her lifelong ambition to attend her state's flagship campus at Ann Arbor, Gratz landed at its less distinguished Dearborn Campus, where she blamed racial preferences for her rejection rather than competition from better-prepared white or Asian students.

Angered by her knowledge that lower-scoring minority students from her high school were in possession of the cherished Ann Arbor acceptance letters, Gratz reportedly uttered immediately upon receiving her rejection letter: "Can we sue them?"[37] By using legal means to fight the system, Gratz will go down in history as a young woman who used the institutional mechanisms available to her to fight what she saw as reverse discrimination.

In her determination to challenge Michigan's system of racial preferences, Gratz had support and assistance from Carl Cohen, a University of Michigan philosophy professor and a liberal with a long history of animosity toward racial preferences. Cohen first weighed in on the affirmative action debate shortly after the U.S. Supreme Court's decision in *United Steelworkers of America v. Weber*,[38] which was decided the same year as *Bakke*. The case arose when Brian Weber, a white working-class male, challenged the legality of Kaiser Aluminum's voluntary affirmative action policy because it maintained two senior-

---

[37] Lisa Belkin, "She Says She Was Rejected by a College for Being White," *Glamour*, November 1998.

[38] *United Steelworkers of America v. Weber*, 427 U.S. 273 (1976).

ity lists. It had one list for whites and another for blacks and it filled its vacancies by selecting a candidate from the top of each list. Weber filed suit charging that the plan was in violation of Title VII of the 1964 Civil Rights Act, which prohibited racial quotas in all areas of employment. While winning in the district court, Weber lost in the U.S. Supreme Court. The Court ruled that Title VII permitted voluntary race-conscious efforts to increase employment opportunities for previously discriminated-against groups. In reaction to the Court's decision and in recognition of the social-class implications of the policy, Cohen argued that the harm done to Brian Weber "was at least as great as that done to Allan Bakke."[39] The Court, Cohen contended, was less solicitous about the rights to equal protection of white blue-collar workers than of the better-off whites seeking a medical school education. Given his longstanding interest in the effect of racial preferences on working-class whites, it is not surprising that Cohen came to Gratz's assistance.

Relying on data that he procured under the Freedom of Information Act, Cohen provided Gratz's attorneys with a smoking gun in the form of an elaborate system of grids showing that whites and blacks were admitted to the University of Michigan under very different standards. Blacks and whites were treated the same if they had either a very strong record or a very weak record (members of both races were accepted in the first case and rejected in the second). In between, a large gray area existed, where it was greatly to one's advantage to be a minority. In the in-between grids, the university would recommend admission for minority students, while their nonminority counterparts would be wait-listed or rejected outright.

Data mentioned elsewhere in this chapter illustrate the dual admissions system that was in effect at the University of Michigan. If a white applicant, for example, performed at a B-minus level in high school and had test scores in the upper middle range of achievement tests, his chances of being admitted to the university were minuscule. But if an applicant with a similar profile was a member of an "underrepresented minority," defined as black, Latino, or Native American, his chances of admission could be as high as 100 percent. Armed with such

---

[39] Carl Cohen, "Why Racial Preference Is Illegal and Immoral," *Commentary* 67 (June 1979), 40–41.

information, Gratz filed suit in a case that is currently on appeal before the Sixth Circuit Court of Appeals and will most likely end up at the Supreme Court.[40] Already her case and other pending cases since *Hopwood* have led to a radical restructuring of university admissions policies and a search for proxies that will ensure a given racial balance.[41]

Even with the racial disparities noted, Gratz can never demonstrate definitively that she lost her seat to a racial minority rather than to a more fortunate white student with a better record or more compelling essay or even to an admissions officer in a more generous mood. While less-qualified minorities were accepted by the university, many other white students were in the same position as Gratz and they rather than she might have gained admission to the university in the absence of racial preferences. The University of Michigan has released data that shows Gratz "was evaluated in a group of 424 students with similar academic qualifications. Of these, 46 minorities and 121 whites were admitted, and the remaining 257 whites received rejection letters."[42] In the absence of racial preferences, some of these 257 whites would have been accepted to the university, but most would not. Just as the Bowen and Bok analogy of the handicapped parking space cited earlier shows, the mere existence of racial preferences in higher education causes thousands of disappointed white applicants to conclude, often mistakenly, that affirmative action is responsible for their letters of rejection. In a small number of cases this is true; in many more it is not.

---

[40] In *Gratz*, a federal district court in Michigan ruled in December 2000 that Michigan could use race as a plus factor in its current admissions process, but that Michigan's dual-track admissions policy, in place from 1995 to 1998, was unconstitutional. In March 2001, however, a different federal judge in Michigan found that the University of Michigan Law School's admissions policies, which were not too different from the university's undergraduate admissions policies at issue in *Gratz*, were wholly unconstitutional. Both cases are on appeal to the Sixth Circuit Court of Appeals, and because of the conflicting nature of the two decisions, they will likely end up before the Supreme Court. See *Gratz v. Bollinger*, no. 97-75231 (E.D. Mich. Filed October 14, 1997; *Grutter v. Bollinger*, no. 97-75928 (E.D. Mich. Filed December 3, 1997)). For more information on both lawsuits, see the University of Michigan's web page coverage at http://www.umich.edu/~urel/admissions.

[41] George Cantor, "Would Policies at University of Michigan Make the Perfect Test Case on Affirmative Action?," Gannett News Service, July 13, 1996.

[42] Kenneth J. Cooper, "Deciding Who Gets in and Who Doesn't," *Washington Post*, April 2, 2000.

Unlike Jennifer Gratz, the vast majority of white college applicants will not sue colleges or universities, but they nonetheless may harbor anger toward racial preferences. A few, however, will become angry over what they see as reverse discrimination, and some will become white supremacists for the same reasons that drove Michael Hart and Jared Taylor into white nationalism. As I have stated repeatedly, demographic changes in the racial composition of the nation and the age of its population are making it harder and harder for white applicants to gain admission to the colleges and universities of their choice.[43] Since the competition for admission to top universities will heighten over the next few years, more and more white youths who see black and brown faces on campus will conclude that racial preferences account for their failure to be admitted at the college or university of their choice.[44]

Disappointed white applicants who can demonstrate an actual injury (i.e., a failure to gain admission to an elite institution) that has a dual admissions process and a set of standards for racial minorities different from those for whites have been given "standing" to sue in federal courts. This is a very important development and portends greater litigation in the future. The notion of standing comes from the "Case or Controversy" requirement found in Article III, section 2 of the U.S. Constitution. In order to have "standing" to sue for a constitutional violation, a plaintiff must demonstrate an actual injury, traceable to the actions of a given defendant, and there must be an adequate remedy at law.[45] The nature of competition for scarce seats at top institutions makes causation difficult to prove in situations where universities have selected a diverse student body composed of individuals with widely varying academic profiles. But by readily extending standing to white plaintiffs, courts implicitly seem to be accepting the notion that qualified white applicants are rejected because lesser-qualified minority applicants have displaced them. In other words, the white applicant, the court seems to be saying, would have been admitted "but for" the existence of racial preferences. The "but for" conclusion has

---

[43] Bronner, "College Applicants of '99 Are Facing Stiffest Competition."

[44] Demographic data show that one-third of the young people in the population are a racial minority, and in the states of California, Texas, and New Mexico, minority youth are a majority of the population. See, Kelvin Pollard, "1999 United States Population Data Sheet," Population Reference Bureau, http://www.Prb.org/pubs/usds99.htm.

[45] See Geoffrey R. Stone, Louis Seidman, Cass R. Sunstein, and Mark V. Tushnet, *Constitutional Law*, 3rd ed. (Aspen Law and Business Publishers, 1996), 88–128.

seemingly become imbedded in law by the ease in which white litigants have been granted standing in cases where they can never prove conclusively why they were rejected.

To facilitate reverse discrimination suits such as Gratz's, the NAAWP has a web page that features the following public service message:

> [A] student applies to a university or college and is rejected. Sounds familiar, doesn't it? Upon further investigation, he or she discovers that a classmate, whose test scores and grades were significantly lower than theirs, was accepted at the same institution. **Is this legal?** The answer is *No*, it is not legal.
>
> The majority of Americans have no idea that naked racial preferences are illegal. The late senator from Minnesota, Hubert Humphrey, promised to **"eat the Civil Rights Act of 1964, page by page, if it were ever interpreted as permitting racial quotas or reverse discrimination."** However, as everyone knows now, reverse discrimination did become a reality and it remains this way today.
>
> Discrimination on the basis of race is illegal and has been since the Supreme Court decided the Bakke case 20 years ago. . . . A college or university is not permitted to set aside a particular number of slots in its classes for particular racial groups in order to compensate for "societal" discrimination or even to achieve "diversity." Set-asides are a lawful remedy ONLY if the institution itself discriminated in the past.[46]

Its youthful reader is urged to contact the Center for Individual Rights (CIR), the conservative public interest law firm that litigated *Hopwood* and won a partial victory in *Gratz v. Bollinger*, in which the judge upheld the University of Michigan's current admissions policy while declaring unconstitutional the dual track system in which Gratz competed.

CIR has been particularly active in encouraging anti–affirmative action litigation. In 1999, the firm took out full-page advertisements in student newspapers on fifteen campuses across the country with a headline that read, "Guilty by Admission: Nearly Every Elite College in America Violates the Law. Does Yours?"[47] In addition to other activities, CIR teaches interested parties how to use the Freedom of Infor-

---

[46] Naawp.com/youth/discrim (emphasis in original).

[47] Ethan Bronner, "Conservatives Open Drive Against Affirmative Action," *New York Times*, January 26, 1999; Kate Zernike, "Campus Affirmative Action Embattled Handbooks Encourage Student Suits," *The Boston Globe*, January 27, 1999.

mation Act to pry sensitive admission data from admissions committees. CIR also distributes a handbook warning college and university trustees of their personal liability if their institution engages in racial discrimination and they continue to participate in its governance. Besides its efforts at elite institutions, CIR has advertised on the campuses of a few less selective schools in order to reach aggrieved students refused admissions at better schools.

Matthew Lerner

Matthew Lerner is an example of the downward cascading in which applicants with exceptional qualifications find themselves competing for admission at lesser institutions than the ones that would have been available to them in past years. Lerner's high school record was by any measure outstanding: "S.A.T. scores were 750 out of 800 on the verbal section, and 700 out of 800 on mathematics. Moreover, he took all advanced placement courses [in 1999] and received the highest possible mark on his calculus test. He served as president of his school's political action club, drum major in the high school band, religious director of his synagogue youth group and was a published poet."[48] Thinking of himself as highly competitive, Lerner applied to Harvard, Brown, Georgetown, and Wesleyan universities and the honors program at the University of Massachusetts. The first three universities simply rejected him outright – he was, after all, just another bright, white student and such students are plentiful at elite institutions. The University of Massachusetts was the only institution to admit him outright on the merits of his application. Lerner was wait-listed at Wesleyan and admitted only after intense lobbying by several adults who knew him.

Lerner was fortunate enough to be well connected and well liked so that powerful people could intervene on his behalf. Other applicants, however, are not as lucky. These rejected students can end up at less prestigious institutions where they can become vulnerable to nationalistic appeals that attribute their rejection letters to racial preferences rather than to intense competition from better-prepared applicants.

[48] Matthew Lerner, interview, May 11, 2000.

Lerner himself has shown no bitterness or resentment over racial preferences. Indeed, he seems to be a model of the kind of reaction to affirmative action preferences that liberal supporters of such preferences hope would be more typical. Although his first choice was Brown University, Lerner has found himself quite happy at Wesleyan, where in May 2000 he resided in a mixed-race dormitory with a distinctive bohemian ambiance. A strong supporter of racial diversity, Lerner attributed his failure to gain admission to a more selective institution to intense competition from better-prepared students rather than racial preferences for minorities, which is essentially the conclusion of the *New York Times* article in which he was featured.[49]

Benjamin Smith

Twenty-one-year-old Benjamin Smith is a puzzle that we may never fully understand. Despite numerous newspaper articles prying into his life and telling us of his Korean high school girl friend and Jewish high school buddies, he remains an enigma whose susceptibility to the message of the racist right is difficult to grasp.

We know that Smith graduated from a highly competitive high school in an affluent neighborhood and that his principal described him as an unremarkable student with average grades and no disciplinary problems. The only unusual thing about Smith's behavior while in high school were the words he wrote for his high school yearbook: *Sic semper tyrannis* (Thus ever to tyrants). These were the same words that John Wilkes Booth shouted after shooting Abraham Lincoln and the same words on the T-shirt that Timothy McVeigh wore on the day he bombed the Murrah Federal Building in Oklahoma City, and it is the state motto of Virginia.[50]

Smith's murderous shooting spree in 1999, which was directed against blacks, Asians, and Jews, left a Korean and an African American dead and nine others injured. It is described in the following account from the *Chicago Tribune*:

[49] Ibid.

[50] Steven Beaven and Tim Starks, "Suburban Rebelliousness Escalated to Baffling Racial Violence," StarNews.com,
http://www.starnews.com/news/citystate/99/july/0706st_spree.html.

Authorities have said that Smith began his shooting spree on the evening of July 2 in Chicago's Rodgers Park neighborhood, where he fired at six Orthodox Jews who were returning from Sabbath worship. Smith then went to Skokie where he shot and killed former Northwestern University basketball coach, Ricky Birdsong, an African American, as Birdsong walked through his neighborhood with his children. Next, Smith shot at an Asian couple in a car in Northbrook. . . . The next day, authorities said, Smith shot three other people – two blacks and an Asian – in separate encounters in Springfield, Decatur, and Urbana. And on July 4th . . . he shot and killed Indiana graduate student Won Joon Yoon, a Korean outside a Bloomington Church.[51]

Recruited on the campus of the University of Illinois at Champaign-Urbana in 1998, Smith joined the World Church of the Creator, one of the fastest-growing hate groups in the nation, which by 1999 had forty-one chapters in seventeen states. Working tirelessly for the group, Smith won recognition as "Creator of the Year" for passing out more than 5,000 copies of "Facts That the Government and Media Don't Want You to Know" in a single month. Diligent at his assigned task, Smith was skillful at slipping literature under people's doors, inserting them in newspapers and otherwise reaching people who would refuse the literature if it were handed to them directly on the street.[52]

Mark Potok of the Southern Poverty Law Center has stated that while WCOTC leaders "are not building bombs, they are certainly building the bombers. . . . This is a religion for and by sociopaths."[53] The WCOTC characterizes itself in very different terms.[54] When asked to explain the goals of the organization and its underlying philosophy to the interviewer, Matthew Hale, its current leader, stated the following:

The World Church of the Creator is a pro-white, racial-religious organization which is dedicated to the survival, expansion, and advancement of the white race and the white race alone. We are not a Christian organization. Instead of basing our views, our ideology, our religion on

---

[51] Kirsten Scharnberg and Ray Long, "Killer's Parents Didn't Teach Hate," *Chicago Tribune*, August 27, 1999.

[52] Stephanie Simon, "Leader of Hate's Church Mourns 'One White Man,'" Latines.com, July 6, 1999.

[53] Mark Potok of the SPLC (quoted in Simon).

[54] A description of the WCOTC and its goals is at http://hatewatch.org/wcotc/intro.html.

Christianity, we base it on the eternal laws of nature as revealed through science, logic, history and commonsense. We believe that in a natural state each and every species looks out for its own kind. Each and every sub-species looks out for its own kind. This being the case, it follows that we as white people should look out for our own kind. We should not care about the other races – they can do what they will – but we should focus on our own. The World Church of the Creator in this respect is certainly a very radical organization, and we do not pay homage to Christianity or to the Constitution or even to America. We are an international orga-nization in scope – we consider all white people, wherever they may be, to be our brothers and sisters.[55]

By all indications, Benjamin Smith was the product of a very ordi-nary upbringing. Raised in an affluent family by professional parents, he hardly fit the ignorant-southern-redneck stereotype of a white racist. According to one account, "Smith grew up in a seemingly typ-ical suburban setting: mother, father, two younger brothers, two-car garage, three golden retrievers. His mother, Beverly, was a lawyer, a high-end real estate agent, and once a member of Wilmette's board of trustees. His father, Kenneth, was a physician in internal medicine at Northwestern Memorial Hospital who left in 1996 to sell real estate."[56]

Despite some grumbling about high school teachers who tried to evoke white guilt, Smith's racist attitudes did not fully emerge until college, even though a former classmate of his in high school had been involved in recruitment efforts for the white supremacy movement. Smith's former high school teachers, his best friend (who was a Jew), and his Korean girlfriend have told interviewers that nothing about him indicated that he would one day become a racist and anti-Semitic hatemonger bent on murder and mayhem.[57] But once in college Smith rejected his birth name of Benjamin, because it sounded too Jewish, and asked instead to be addressed as "August" Smith.[58] His descent into a world of racist fantasy and paranoia was very rapid from this point onward.

[55] Matthew Hale, interview.
[56] Kirsten Scharnberg, Evan Osnos, and David Mendell, "The Making of a Racist," *Chicago Tribune*, July 25, 1999.
[57] Ibid.
[58] Raad Cawthon and Rita Giordano, "Gunman Known for His Racist Views," *Philadel-phia Inquirer*, July 6, 1999.

After his murderous rampage, Smith's parents issued a public statement that did little to clear up the bewilderment of former friends and associates regarding his conduct. Indeed, his parents seemed to be the most bewildered of all about his behavior and were clueless in trying to explain what had induced their son to become a racial extremist:

> We deeply regret all the suffering to the families and victims in the recent events that ended with the suicide of Benjamin Nathaniel Smith. We did not share or understand the beliefs our son adopted near the end of his life. It was very painful to first lose him to a viewpoint that we found abhorrent and then lose him in such a horrible final way.[59]

Television interviews of Smith's friends and his former girlfriend reveal a portrait of a normal individual who gradually became a violent racist after repeated interactions with Matthew Hale.[60] A hint of anger about affirmative action comes from a letter that he wrote while enrolled at the University of Illinois, in which he complained about excessive governmental benefits for foreign students and foreign professors. After an encounter with the law, Smith switched universities from Illinois to the University of Indiana at Bloomington. He also switched his academic major from computer science to criminal justice with future plans to attend law school.[61] In doing so, one commentator writes that Smith "was following the example of several of the movement's younger leaders, who want to be lawyers so they can be advocates for the white race inside the nation's courtrooms."[62]

At the time of their association, Matthew Hale was engaged in a legal battle with the state of Illinois for its refusal to grant him a license to practice law. Hale had graduated from the University of Southern Illinois Law School and passed the state bar exam. But the state's Committee on Character and Fitness, part of the Illinois Board of Admissions to the Bar, refused to certify Hale, reasoning that his extreme racist views would render him incapable of abiding by the state's professional conduct rules.[63] Smith's murderous rampage followed soon after. Some speculate a direct connection between these two events:

---

[59] Scharnberg and Long.
[60] "Evil among Us: Hatred in America," Discovery Channel Broadcast, April 14, 2000.
[61] Belluck.   [62] Ibid.
[63] See "Supreme Court Declines to Hear Matthew Hale's Case" at www.westlegalstudies.com.

"Hale said that although he had told Smith he planned to appeal all the way to the United States Supreme Court, Smith might have interpreted the appeal denial as a sign that the group's rights were being so trampled upon that legitimate means to advance the group's racist agenda would not succeed."[64]

When asked by our interviewer about his relationship with Smith, Hale chose his words cautiously, but acknowledged a possible connection between Smith's violent outbursts and his own legal troubles:

> Ben Smith . . . was a member from May of '98 until April of 1999. He joined the church, to my knowledge, because he believed in the racial struggle, and he did not believe in Christianity – that was something that attracted him, that we were not a Christian group. We feel that, as much as we respect our white racist Christian comrades, that it's simply a contradiction to believe in racism and believe in Christianity. The two do not go together. Ben Smith – it's hard to say exactly why he did what he did. I have surmised all along that it was because of the denial of my law license. I will never know probably the full reason why he did commit crimes. I'm concerned, though, that as white people feel more dispossessed, feel that they are without recourse, that violence will increase.[65]

If we dismiss Smith's attraction to the racist right by attributing it to the susceptibility of a warped mind, we are failing to recognize the danger of the white nationalist movement to our society. Although Smith was a confused young man, there are many others out there like him who are ripe for exploitation. Smith, I contend, could have been the son of just about any Anglo-Saxon family. His family's values appear to have been decent and mainstream. Nevertheless, he joined the white supremacy movement and later single-handedly declared war against nonwhites. If one considers that he was reading white nationalist literature of the sort described previously, at least one of the external catalysts to his violent behavior becomes apparent.

One of Smith's first required readings was the aforementioned *White Man's Bible*, a 449-page book that provides the ideological foundation

---

[64] Ibid. When Hale's case finally reached the Supreme Court in June 2000, the Court refused to grant *certiorari*, meaning it declined to hear the case, and thereby let stand the decision to bar him from practicing law.

[65] Matthew Hale, interview.

for the organization he joined.[66] As noted previously, the book, written by WCOTC founder Ben Klassen – who, like Smith, would eventually take his own life – issues a warning against the racial peril currently confronting the white race: "The White Race is not holding its own in the battle for survival. It is shrinking, while the mud races of the world are multiplying and breeding like rats."[67] Klassen's "Bible" also blames Jews for a host of America's problems, including Third World immigration and the "nigger" problem.[68] Thoroughly versed in the doctrine of the WCOTC, Smith apparently sought to start his own racial holy war (RAHOWA) that many of the more extreme white supremacy groups advocate. Socialized to hate, Smith single-handedly struck out against the "mud people" who threaten the white race.

Since Smith's murderous rampage, the WCOTC has grown significantly, with the number of chapters jumping from forty-one to seventy-five in twenty-five states and five foreign countries.[69] Not only have its prison chapters quadrupled; it has launched under Lisa Turner's guidance two women's groups, the Sisterhood and the Women's Frontier, which have doubled from five to ten chapters.[70] Hale claims that the membership for his organization is 10,000 to 30,000, though Devin Burghart of the Center for New Community disputes this claim and estimates that the total membership is only a tiny fraction of this amount.[71] As stressed in earlier chapters, membership numbers may not always be the best guide to assessing potential influence among white nationalist groups, since such groups often advise serious activists to avoid membership lists, and much of their recruitment effort takes place electronically. Everything that any recruit needs to become a virulent racist can be downloaded on the Internet.

CONTRASTING PATHS

The above profiles have introduced us to three young white Americans that seem to be more or less typical of college applicants. Jennifer Gratz, encouraged by an organization like the Center for Individual

---

[66] Ben Klassen, *The White Man's Bible* (Lighthouse Point, Fla.: World Church of the Creator, 1981).
[67] Ibid., 23.   [68] Ibid., 275.
[69] William Claiborne, *Washington Post*, June 29, 2000.
[70] Ibid.   [71] Ibid.

Rights, led the fight on behalf of thousands of mostly working-class and poor whites against what she and others perceived as the great injustice of racial preference policies. Matthew Lerner experienced slight downward cascading and the full effects of the competitive admissions process, but he did not attribute his disappointment at not getting into Brown or Harvard to racial preferences. Benjamin Smith, for whatever reason, was fully susceptible to the recruitment tactics of a white nationalist group that he encountered on a college campus. In an earlier era, we could have imagined any one of the three youths risking their lives for other Americans, as did the courageous Freedom Riders of the 1960s who helped desegregate the Jim Crow South.[72] In our present era, however, these profiles illustrate three different ways that white youths can respond to a racially charged environment, including following in the violent footsteps of Benjamin Smith. Unfortunately, the growing competition for college admissions and the increasing uncertainty surrounding the process creates an atmosphere of anxiety and anger in a milieu where a sense of unfairness is all too common among vocal youth conditioned to express themselves using the language of political correctness and multiculturalism.

[72] Thernstrom and Thernstrom, *America in Black and White*, 125–7.

MULTICULTURALISM
AND RACIAL DOUBLE
STANDARDS ON CAMPUS

> Students now enter college with their group identities intact, and they
> expect the institution to respond accordingly. . . . People have come to
> identify themselves not only according to race, gender, or ethnic
> identity, but also by class, sexual orientation, disability, and age.
>
> Edgar Beckham, Vice President of the Ford Foundation[1]

Multiculturalism on college campuses has helped spawn the growth of
group consciousness among students, who have been encouraged by
liberal elites to think of themselves in terms of their group identities
rather than their individual characteristics. A number of scholars
have criticized the excesses of multiculturalism, and a fair number of
books have focused on the racial politics of college campuses.[2] On
many campuses, multiculturalism finds expression in the form of
special academic departments and programs, ethnic theme dorms, and
special centers where minority students and faculty can congregate
together at least part of the time to escape what is becoming an increasingly balkanized campus environment. In this chapter, I discuss possible connections between the campus milieu and the growth of white
nationalism.

[1] Edgar Beckham as quoted in Sleeper, *Liberal Racism*, 1.
[2] Culture relativism grows out of anthropology, and the concept is associated with Franz
Boas, one of the founders of American cultural anthropology. Cultural relativism treats
all groups as equal, and any inequalities between groups are explained by an examina-
tion of the history of oppression. For more information about multiculturalism on college
campuses, see David O. Sacks and Peter Thiel, *The Diversity Myth: Multiculturalism and
Political Intolerance on Campus* (Oakland, Calif.: Independent Institute, 1995); Alvin
Schmidt, *The Menace of Multiculturalism* (Westport, Conn.: Praeger, 1997); Dinesh
D'Souza, *End of Racism*; Dinesh D'Souza, *Illiberal Education: The Politics of Race and
Sex on Campus* (New York: Vintage Books, 1992).

Any serious examination of multiculturalism at major colleges and universities reveals institutional goals and practices that are confused. In addition to demands for special living quarters, official recognition, and other special arrangements, some groups – including Latinos, Asians, Native Americans, gay and lesbian organizations, and women – have started to clamor for (and, in some cases, receive) special academic departments. A few white students have, in turn, established white pride organizations, such as the European-American Student Union, the Nordic Student Association, and White Student Unions, that parallel existing minority associations at their institutions.

At its best, multiculturalism celebrates the value and uniqueness of different cultures and different peoples with all groups viewed as having equal status.[3] Such multiculturalism supports free expression by all cultures and attempts to educate people from different cultures about both similarities and differences across cultures. It is premised on the idea that all cultures have an intrinsic value and are worth further study, examination, and appreciation. Multiculturalism of this kind seeks to recognize cultural contributions from a myriad of different groups and to promote respect for a diversity of lifestyles that allows people to live in harmony with those of different cultures who may be neighbors, professors, or fellow students. In short, in its most benign form, multiculturalism seeks to achieve an equality of recognition, particularly of cultural contributions that have previously been dismissed due to racism or xenophobia.[4]

At its worst, however, multiculturalism divides Americans by separating them into numerous tribal groups with competing interests. Just as with the politics of affirmative action, multiculturalism has had some unintended and unanticipated consequences, such as the establishment of white nationalist organizations that seek recognition on campus as

---

[3] For an excellent revisionist study of the experiences of different racial and ethnic groups, see Ronald Takaki, *A Different Mirror: A History of Multicultural America* (New York: Little, Brown, 1993).

[4] For a sample of some of the broader intellectual debates regarding multiculturalism, see Charles Taylor, ed., *Multiculturalism and the Politics of Recognition* (Princeton: Princeton University Press, 1992). Beyond academia, multiculturalism has also made a strong impact on the social policy of many countries, most notably the ethnically fragmented nations of Canada and Australia. For a discussion of some of the political ramifications of multiculturalist thinking, see "Multiculturalism: A Policy Response to Diversity," presentation at the UNESCO Management of Social Transformations Conference, Sydney, Australia, 1995.

genuine cultural contributions to university life. In some cases, indeed, perhaps most, multiculturalism may have had the desired effect of sensitizing white students to minority concerns. But it has also had the countervailing effect of angering and confusing other students who sometimes suffer in silence without reputable forums to discuss what they see as inequities in student organizations.

Much of the rationale behind the use of racial preferences to create diversified campuses rests on the assumption that, once admitted, students of different races will interact with one another both within and outside the classroom. What has happened on some campuses, however, is the formation of patterns of self-segregation in which mostly African-American students retreat to special departments and dorms, at least in part to escape temporarily from the stresses of being a minority student in a predominantly white environment. Often the culture centers do provide a means for minority students from different ethnic backgrounds to meet one another – for example, Mexicans, Puerto Ricans, and Cubans meet at the University of Illinois La Casa Culture Center,[5] while many African-American culture centers around the country attract students with West African and West Indian heritages. But culture exchange at such centers is often limited to those from the same broad racial or linguistic background.

This fact is particularly disturbing since the diversity rationale for race-conscious admissions largely rests on the enrichment value that the presence of minority students supposedly brings to the educational experiences of white students. The existence of segregated learning experiences at predominantly white institutions clearly threatens the primary justification for racial preferences. As legal scholars Akhil Amar and Neil Katyal have argued, "[i]f a diversity program does not, in practice, allow all students to learn from each other, then the program is not serving the state's interest in diversity – and the school should not use the 'diversity' slogan to show how the program passes constitutional muster. . . . We would, for example, be troubled by de facto segregation in university dorms."[6] Another legal scholar insists that institutions employing racial preferences under the diversity

---

[5] Tom Kim, "Cultural House Out of Reach for Asian Americans at University of Illinois," http://new.excite.com/news/uw/000803/university-91.
[6] Akhil Amar and Neil Katyal, "Bakke's Fate," *UCLA Law Review* 43 (1996): 1745.

rationale should be forced to "demonstrate clear, consistent internal policies and practices designed to facilitate interracial contact, dialogue, and understanding on campus."[7]

On many campuses, balkanization and grouping along cultural lines has prompted some white students to self-segregate and seek their own organizations and departments. One of the first white student unions was founded in 1988 at Temple University by Michael Spletzer, who stated that he started the organization because "[w]hite people are being discriminated against by affirmative action."[8] Universities that have had white student unions or similar organizations include the University of Florida at Gainesville, the University of Nebraska at Lincoln, the University of New Orleans, and Louisiana State University.[9]

Despite its noble and admirable goal of fostering educational diversity, multiculturalism too often succumbs to a double standard. Many proponents of multiculturalism allow and encourage the expression of group pride by cultural groups deemed worthy of such expression, but any group (e.g., a college white pride group) whose ideas are viewed as outside of the mainstream or at odds with what multiculturalists themselves believe is denied both resources and forums that are generally open to other, more acceptable cultural groups.[10]

Generally speaking, white power groups and white pride groups have to flourish underground if they are to exist on college campuses. Despite the presence of faculty members sympathetic to the white racialist viewpoint, there can be an absence of faculty sponsors willing to risk the ostracism and exposure that might come from publicly advising a white pride organization. The experience of David Stennett, a student at Tacoma Community College in Washington State, is probably typical. Stennett failed to find an advisor for his proposed European American organization, even though he conceived it as a moderate group and listed as one of its central goals the creation of "a better understanding of equal rights for all races." A series of strongly

---

[7] Goodwin Liu, "Affirmative Action in Higher Education: The Diversity Rationale and the Compelling Interest Test," *Harvard Civil Rights–Critical Law Review* 33 (1998): 381.

[8] Michael Spletzer as quoted in Jared Taylor, *Paved with Good Intentions*, 241.

[9] Taylor, 241; Duke, *My Awakening*, 490–505.

[10] For an account favoring multicultural hostility toward undesirable groups, see John K. Wilson, *The Myth of Political Correctness: The Conservative Attack on Higher Education* (Durham: Duke University Press, 1995).

condemnatory letters written in reaction to Stennett's proposed organization was enough to intimidate any faculty sponsors and shows the difficulties that white student organizations can face as they fight for their First Amendment rights.[11]

While they try to discourage the creation of white pride groups, some liberal administrators and faculty members may actually be heightening white consciousness through their advocacy of the establishment of "critical white studies programs." These programs are patterned after the approach to law propagated by the "critical legal studies" movement, and are intended to dethrone whiteness as the culturally normative standard in America and elsewhere. According to Jeff Howe, the premise of such programs is simple: "White is a race like any other; the close examination of white culture will produce knowledge and understanding – a consciousness – that will contribute to the dismantling of those subtle, pervasive privileges that whites enjoy at the expense of other races."[12] In 1997 the University of California at Berkeley held a conference entitled "Whiteness Studies." The idea of the conference sponsors was to deconstruct and denigrate the concept of whiteness until it no longer holds meaning in American society.

Critics of such programs fear that studying white culture in the critical manner advocated by "whiteness studies" advocates will serve only to promote rather than impede racism and that such programs could become vulnerable to the influences of white power advocates as the programs grow and change directorships. In addition, some leaders of traditional ethnic and racial studies departments fear that "white studies" will drain funds from their own programs. Any trend toward the establishment of white student organizations could imperil traditional racial and ethnic studies programs by decreasing the limited resources available to these groups and exacerbating ethnic rivalries and tensions. On balance, many fear that "whiteness studies" – whether done from a critical perspective or a more neutral or even celebratory one – will further impede community integration and only heighten racial tensions on campus.[13]

---

[11] See Euro-American Student's Web Page. http://esu.simplenet.com/mik.htm.
[12] Jeff Howe, "Like Whites on Race,"
  http://linkmag.com/Link/oct-nov-98/981030likewhites.html.
[13] Ibid.

The presence of existing gender and ethnic-based pride organizations and academic programs makes it facially unfair and nearly impossible for universities and colleges to legitimately deny white students similar programs for the promotion of their goals. Although the creation of white pride organizations can cause some unease among those familiar with certain white racial groups in America's past, there does not seem to be any constitutional means that universities can use to legitimately deny white students the same right to establish white pride organizations as other racial and ethnic groups have to establish their cultural organizations. Thus, by encouraging the proliferation on campus of multicultural groups, departments, and theme houses, university administrators may not only be undermining the slim, legal margin upon which racial preferences in admissions are legitimated (the diversity rationale), but in addition may be placing themselves in the paradoxical situation of being forced to allow similar self-segregation and cultural grouping among racially conscious white students.

What has happened in other contexts when white racialist groups seek to be included in mainstream activities may presage what will happen on campus. In some communities, for example, white supremacy organizations have sought legitimacy for their groups by offering to sponsor the cleaning up of certain highways. Seeking to avoid constitutional issues, some cities and states have abolished whole programs rather than approve an application of sponsorship by a group such as the Ku Klux Klan or Aryan Nations seeking to exercise their basic rights of participation. One can well imagine a situation where a university, confronted with the choice of sponsoring an all-white dorm or theme house or abolishing all ethnically based dorms and theme houses, chooses the latter path.

RACE TRAITOR: "TREASON TO WHITENESS IS LOYALTY TO HUMANITY"

Liberal intellectuals, both on and off college campuses, often tolerate the public disparagement of whites in a manner in which they would never tolerate similar racial disparagement aimed at any nonwhite group. *Race Traitor* is a case in point. *Race Traitor* is a journal started in 1992 by Noel Ignatiev, Harvard University lecturer and activist, and

John Garvey, an employee of New York University. Ignatiev and Garvey argue in their journal that the key to solving the social problems of our age is "to abolish the white race," by which they mean "abolishing the privileges of white skin." "Until that task is accomplished," the editors warn, "even partial reform will prove elusive, because white influence permeates every issue, domestic and foreign, in U.S. Society."[14] *Race Traitor*, they explain, "aims to serve as an intellectual center for those seeking to abolish the white race. It will encourage dissent from the conformity that maintains it and popularize examples of defection from its ranks, analyze the forces that hold it together and those that promise to tear it apart. Part of its task will be to promote debate among abolitionists. When possible, it will support practical measures, guided by the principle, *treason to whiteness is loyalty to humanity.*"[15]

Although the goal of *Race Traitor* is to end white racism, the mere existence of this journal with its provocatively stated objective of "abolishing whiteness" fuels anger and suspicion among race-conscious whites, many of whom seem to sincerely believe that their race is headed for extinction. No matter how noble its goal of ending white racism, *Race Traitor* benefits from a racial and cultural double standard that would never tolerate a parallel effort in regard to any non-white racial or ethnic group. One can hardly imagine white liberal intellectuals on college campuses or elsewhere approving of a journal written by "blacks seeking to abolish blackness" because of the association between blackness and criminality, or of a journal written by "Hispanics seeking to abolish Hispanic culture" because of that culture's association with poor, illiterate Mexicans.

There is a double standard operating with regard to *Race Traitor*, but because whites are the dominant group – at least for now – it is apparently acceptable to seek their cultural extinction and the destruction of any pride and privilege that come with white skin. It is acceptable on some college campuses to speak of eliminating whites and whiteness, to speak derisively of the contributions of dead white men, or do as one university official did and guess incorrectly that the perpetrator of a bomb threat was probably "a white guy between 25 and

---

[14] Race Traitor, Journal of the New Abolitionism, http://www.postfun.com/racetraitor.
[15] Ibid.

55 because they're the root of most evil."[16] Similar remarks and accusations aimed at any nonwhite group would not be tolerated.

Ignatiev surely has the same First Amendment rights as Jared Taylor: *Race Traitor* has as much right to exist as *American Renaissance*. But both are disturbing because of the strong message they send to disfavored groups. (Ironically, I first learned about *Race Traitor* by perusing the web pages of the white nationalist groups. The existence of a journal aimed at "abolishing whiteness" at a point in history when whites are already being threatened with minority status must cause some whites to have an extra measure of unease and help fan the flames of discord among conspiracy theorists.)

ADDITIONAL RACIAL DOUBLE STANDARDS

Many white Americans see a host of racial double standards on college campuses and in the larger society, and ask themselves why it is acceptable to speak of having black interests and brown interests but not white interests. In an article titled "What Is Racism?," Jared Taylor, writing under the pseudonym Thomas Jackson, well expresses these concerns:

> All across the country, black, Hispanic, and Asian clubs and caucuses are thought to be fine expressions of ethnic solidarity, but any club or association expressly for whites is by definition racist. The National Association for the Advancement of Colored People (NAACP) campaigns openly for black advantage but is a respected "civil rights" organization. The National Organization for the Advancement of White People (NAAWP) campaigns merely for equal treatment of all races, but is said to be viciously racist.[17]

It is because of racial double standards of this kind that David Duke says he formed the first NAAWP to serve as a white civil rights organization.[18] According to Duke, he became upset while in college

---

[16] For more information, see Scott Hogenson, "College Official Calls White Men 'Root of Most Evil,'" CNSNEWS.com.

[17] Thomas Jackson, "What Is Racism? Is Bigotry and Racism Just a White Thing?," Stormfront, http://www.stormfront.org/whitenat/racism.htm.

[18] Over the years, Duke has used electoral politics to take his views to the white public. In 1998, he ran as a presidential candidate for the Populist Party, and later won a seat in the Louisiana state legislature. In 1990, he lost a senate race and a bid for governor of the state.

because whites were not allowed to express racial pride while blacks faced no condemnation for doing so.[19] Ever since his college days, Duke has been dedicating his life's energies to further the interests and rights of white people, which he sees threatened by government policies favoring minorities and immigrants.

Double standards also pervade the reporting of interracial crime, white nationalists charge, with black-on-white crime either being ignored or downplayed, while the much rarer white-on-black crime is given endless publicity. According to Jared Taylor, the FBI collects and reports its data on crime in a manner that deliberately obscures the fact that 90 percent of interracial crime is black on white.[20] Similarly, in an article for *Jewish World Review*, Larry Elder contends that when the bad guy committing a crime is black, the media tries to reinterpret the crime as nonracial, and black leaders and liberal democrats avoid condemning the perpetrator.[21]

Of course, any discussion of racial double standards on college campuses must acknowledge how racial profiling disproportionately affects minority students, faculty, and employees at many colleges. African-American males, for example, are routinely stopped and asked for identification as they stroll across campus en route to classes and dorms. Racial profiling happens to minority faculty and staff with regularity until campus police memorize the "safe" faces or until black employees complain and the practice subsides for a few months, usually only to reemerge a short time later. No doubt this harassment occurs because of the relatively low number of minorities on college campuses and the belief that blacks from the surrounding community are more criminally prone than others and pose a threat to the college student body.

The politics of race on college campuses have prompted some white students to verbally, and sometimes physically, harass minority students on campus, often by using graffiti or by gaining access to the institution's minority student and faculty e-mail list and sending hate-filled messages. According to Justice Department statistics, in a two-year period in the late 1990s, hate crimes on college campuses increased by

---

[19] David Duke, *My Awakening*, 607–8.
[20] Jared Taylor, *The Color of Crime* (Oakton, Va.: New Century Foundation, June 1999).
[21] Larry Elder, "When the Bad Guy Is Black," *Jewish World Review*, March 10, 2000.

more than 60 percent, rising from 1,312 reported incidents in 1997 to 2,067 incidents in 1998.[22] These statistics, however, may actually understate the problem. Because the Justice Department discloses the names of the institutions involved, university officials have an incentive not to label incidents as hate crimes (even though they are), fearing an adverse impact on future student enrollment.

Minority students in recent years, especially blacks and Asians, have reported being the targets of a number of high-profile attacks. In one incident that occurred at Brown University, a black female student was beaten by three white males who told her that she was a "quota" and did not belong at that university. At Pennsylvania State University, several racial incidents have occurred in the past few years. In 1999, some 68 black students received racist e-mails signed by "The Patriot"; in 2000, a group of black students who complained of racial problems on campus received racist letters through regular mail; and in 2001, the president of the black student caucus received a racist death threat from someone who also threatened to detonate a bomb during graduation.[23] Harvard University, Florida A&M, and Texas A&M are also among the schools where students reported victimization because of their race, ethnicity, sexual orientation, or association with minority students. "Across the nation," the Southern Poverty Law Center reports, "colleges and universities are experiencing hate – both hate crimes and less drastic incidents of bias – first hand. On and around the leafy campuses where America's 'best and brightest' get their educations . . . violent racism and homophobia are becoming frighteningly commonplace."[24]

SPEECH CODES

The early 1990s was a period in which a rash of campus speech codes was enacted across America largely in response to the increase in reported acts of racial harassment and other racially motivated acts on college and university campuses. While the U.S. Supreme Court has ruled that verbal harassment is not constitutionally protected speech,

[22] The data is from the United States Department of Justice as cited in "Campus Homicides Fall, But Some Crimes Rise," *New York Times*, January 21, 2001.
[23] Donna Leinwand, "Racist Threats Set Penn State on Edge," *USA Today*, May 3, 2000.
[24] Southern Poverty Law Center, "Hate Goes to School," http://www.splc.org/cgi-bin/pr. . .ge=/intelligenceproject/ip-4n1.html.

many of the codes enacted at public institutions have failed to survive constitutional challenges on First Amendment grounds (speech codes at private institutions have fared better).[25] In general, speech codes have been used by colleges and universities to punish racist and sexist speech, especially when that speech is seen as directly intimidating to minorities. Students also have been punished under campus speech codes for defacing posters, for sending e-mails proclaiming that only white students should be admitted to a given institution, for insensitive comments made in class, or for sexually explicit words or other comments that disparage women, gays, or lesbians. Just as with other areas of race, some whites contend that there is a pernicious double standard that allows minorities to call white students racial epithets such as "honkie" and "cracker" without fear of punishment because it has been decided by college administrators that members of the dominant racial group cannot be intimidated by epithets in the same manner as minorities.

At some colleges, confusion over what one can say in public has greatly stifled debate, muzzling students, professors, and others on campus. A syllabus for a course on speech communication at one college campus, for example, carried a warning to students that stated, "Any language that may be deemed sexist, racist, or homophobic, or may be found offensive by any minority group, is prohibited. Use of such language can result in immediate failure of the paper and possible future action."[26] According to Dale Herbeck, a professor of Communications Law at Boston College, "Universities should be places where debate thrives in raucous, freewheeling and at times impolite climate.... But in the minds of many, that desire bumps up hard against the desire to preserve a tolerant, respectful community."[27] On many college campuses an atmosphere exists that discourages open and candid debate on racial issues and restricts the freedom of speech of

[25] Speech codes have been attacked by both conservatives (as too much administrative regulation) and liberals (as infringing too much upon civil liberties). Quotation in Tom Mashberg, "Debates Rage on Campus over Free-Speech Rules," *Boston Herald*, October 31, 1999; see also Stephen Ohlemacher, "Legislators Propose Ban on Campus Speech Rules," *Plain Dealer*, January 23, 2000; Harvey A. Silverglate, "An Overdue Outrage over Speech Codes," *Boston Herald*, April 26, 1999; Alan Kors and Harvey Silvergate, *The Shadow University: The Betrayal of Liberty on America's Campuses* (New York: Free Press, 1998).

[26] Ibid.   [27] Mashberg.

race-conscious whites who dare to speak their mind on the issues that matter most to them. This is a toxic situation, since any restriction on debate serves to empower racial extremist groups, which offer a forum for whites to vent their anger on issues that they cannot discuss elsewhere. And because such forums provide no contrasting views, no disagreement, and no "Devil's Advocate" to challenge factually erroneous ideas, the distorted or one-sided views of the race-conscious whites are powerfully reinforced. Within groups of like-minded people there is a tendency for individuals to push each other toward greater extremism than would exist in an atmosphere where evenly matched intellectuals debate issues.[28]

College students especially need campus forums where unpopular ideas can be openly discussed without fear of administrative punishment or physical harm. It has been my observation that during the 1990s and beyond, many whites on college campuses felt intimidated in voicing their anger about racial preferences, even in policy courses on racial issues. Instead of expressing their views openly and candidly, many students engaged in subterfuge or introduced their own views under the guise of reporting the views of someone else. When I encouraged white college students to talk openly about race, they often prefaced their comments with words such as, "My roommate thinks . . ." or "My roommate is angry about. . . ." Usually, the roommate was angry about blacks or Hispanics who grew up in the roommate's neighborhood, attended the same schools, scored lower on standardized tests, yet got into a better college or seemingly had more opportunities for internships. These same liberal white students expressed support for programs that brought disadvantaged students into colleges and prep schools but were angry and perhaps a little confused over preferences for middle-class minorities who grew up in their own neighborhoods and attended their own middle-class schools. But these college students couldn't express their own views as their own; they had to attribute them to their angry white roommates.

While some students may be reacting to nonexistent pressures and threats, on some campuses, students and faculty are fully justified in their fears of possible retaliation for speech and attitudes that depart

---

[28] Cass Sunstein, "The Law of Group Polarization," SSRN Electronic Paper Collection, http:\\papers.ssrn.com/paper.taf?abstract_id=199668.

from the norm of political correctness, particularly in the area of race. One critic describes contemporary campus life as an intellectually hostile place where groups holding considerable power are unforgiving of speech with the wrong content about topics dear to them. Little peer and institutional protection is available for independent souls who dare to say the wrong thing, and many ideas fail to find expression in the academy for fear of offending powerful individuals and groups.[29] Such observations resonate well with my own experiences on college campuses, where a relatively unforgiving and unfriendly intellectual environment often prevails.[30]

An incident at Northwestern University is illustrative. A few months after Benjamin Smith murdered former Northwestern coach Ricky Birdsong, Matthew Hale of the WCOTC challenged campus intellectuals to debate him in a public forum. As he was being escorted off the campus where he sought to establish a chapter for his organization, he challenged his hecklers to a verbal duel. "[I]f I'm so wrong," he stated, "why can't people show me, not just black me out or attack me physically? We're going to have to talk about these issues in a public forum so we can have a reasoned resolution."[31] A student who stepped forward to identify himself as a supporter of Hale met with blows from members of the Jewish Defense League. While most liberal white administrators on college campuses do not act with the hamhandedness of the JDL, they effectively pursue the same kind of censorship in sensitive areas of race relations.

CONCLUSION

As practiced by major universities and colleges, multiculturalism coupled with restrictive attitudes toward correct speech seems to have

---

[29] Trow, 82.

[30] Regardless of individual qualifications, minority faculty at many institutions must pass a litmus test that subjects their appointments to the veto power of student groups and black and Hispanic Studies programs, and if those considered are women, sexual orientation can also become a decisive factor against the scholar depending on the ideology that surrounds it. Moreover, their selection for purposes of fulfilling what seems to be the institution's diversity needs can result in either superficial evaluations of scholarship or demands for perfection that seem to exceed the demands placed on members of the majority group.

[31] Emily Bittner and Sara Neufeld, "Hale Protest Turns Violent at Northwestern," *Daily Northwestern*, January 24, 2000.

been a failure as far as promoting racial tolerance and understanding. Moreover, it has certainly led to an atmosphere of intolerance of speech and any political ideas that are not sufficiently liberal. The incidents described above and the current conditions at America's universities highlight a critical need to open up racial dialogue. What we find so often in academia, however, are forums on controversial subjects where all the participants agree with one another.

One-sided presentations on racial issues, moreover, extend beyond academia, as President Clinton's 1997 national dialogue on Race in America demonstrated. Both Clinton's 1995 Advisory Counsel and his 1997 Race Initiative Panels were dominated by supporters of current affirmative action policy who refused to address the more controversial aspects of affirmative action and the impact of the policy on racial harmony and perceptions of governmental legitimacy.[32] One reason for the avoidance of an honest discussion on race in the political arena seems to emanate from a decision of political leaders not to offend the affluent blacks in the Democratic Party coalition. Instead of genuinely addressing the problems associated with white hostility toward racial preferences and how this is affecting the experiences of young Americans of all races, African-American leaders are spending valuable political capital on the pursuit of purely symbolic victories such as the removal of the Confederate flag from public places, an effort which, in much of the South, has increased racial polarization without producing any concrete benefits for blacks or anyone else.[33] (In January 2000, shortly after the NAACP announced a boycott of South Carolina businesses because of the flag's presence, no less than ten historically black colleges and universities across the South received letters, single-spaced and in capitals, that stated: [WE WILL] EVENTUALLY GET RID OF ALL OF YOU . . . ONE WAY OR ANOTHER. THE TOTAL DESTRUCTION OF YOUR RACE IS OUR MISSION IN LIFE.[34])

We are rapidly approaching a critical situation today on college campuses. Most of the experts on hate crime believe that the reported

---

[32] *New York Times*, November 20, 1997.

[33] See, e.g., Randall Robinson, *The Debt*; "The Repercussions of Reparations," editorial, *Chicago Tribune*, May 1, 2000.

[34] Marlon Manuel, "Hate Letter to Black Schools Says Race's Destruction Is the Goal," *The Atlanta Constitution*, January 7, 2000; Nina Willdorf, "More Black Colleges Receive Threatening Letters," *Chronicle of Higher Education*, January 14, 2000.

violence on college campuses is a reaction to increased campus diversity. Contrary to the "contact hypothesis" that some social psychologists have propounded, mere contact between people of different races and ethnicities does not necessarily reduce racism or increase tolerance and understanding. What is happening on college and university campuses across the country is a manifestation of the looming racial crisis that this nation will confront unless American leaders and concerned citizens get serious about addressing the issues that white nationalists use to recruit among mainstream Americans.[35] Ignoring the issues raised by white nationalists, dismissing such people out of hand as morons or fanatics, shutting them out of public discourse completely, and forming panels about diversity where everyone already agrees with one another will not solve this problem. Only by conscious and concerted effort on the part of both politicians and citizens to honestly and openly address the claims made by white nationalists can this looming racial crisis be averted.

[35] For a treatment of how tension over diversity in society as a whole has reached the fevered pitch that it currently has (and how this tension mirrors the tension on college campuses around the country) and perhaps how such tension may be eased, see Neil J. Smelser and Jeffrey C. Alexander, *Diversity and Its Discontents: Cultural Conflict and Common Ground in Contemporary American Society* (Princeton: Princeton University Press, 1999).

12

WHITE NATIONALIST RECRUITMENT IN AMERICA

Hello, welcome to my site, I can see by the fact that you have visited my page that you are interested in the subject of race. I will start by introducing myself, my name is Derek. I am eleven years old and I am the webmaster of kids.stormfront.org. I used to be in public school, it is a shame how many white minds are wasted in that system. I am now in home school. I no longer get beat up by *gangs* of non-whites and I spend most of my day learning, instead of tutoring the slowest kids in my class. In addition to my school work, I am also learning pride in myself, my family and my people.

White people are taught in school to be ashamed of their heritage. Teachers cram as many politically correct ideas as they can, into your head in 180 days. All the great white accomplishments throughout history are diminished. Therefore, I think that now is the time that all of the white people across the globe should rise above the lies and be proud of who we are. To take back our freedom and win for all to see our heritage in its greatest glory.

Derek Black, Kids page, Stormfront.com[1]

While I identified college campuses as an area of special vulnerability and concern with regard to white nationalist recruitment in part because of the competitive admissions processes, the legal and political rhetoric surrounding racial preferences may also be coinciding with risk factors for youth even younger than college age, since nationalistic groups are not reluctant to use such young people as conduits for spreading their message. In Illinois, just weeks after Benjamin Smith's shooting rampage, the Chicago police found a sixteen-year-old

[1] Kids page, http://kids.stormfront.org. Derek Black is the son of Don Black.

boy tossing World Church of the Creator literature into the yards of homes in his Deerfield neighborhood. He was making deliveries for the same organization that had recruited Smith into the white nationalist cause.[2]

THE INTERNET

In their efforts to recruit new faces for their movement, white nationalists are using a combination of promotional and distributional methods that include the dissemination of white power music and white power comic books, the organizing of white power marches and rallies, face-to-face solicitations, and the distribution of white nationalist leaflets and booklets. Another critically important recruitment tool is the Internet, which allows like-minded souls to find each other and communicate from the privacy of their own homes. The Internet has been particularly effective in enabling young people to explore new – and socially forbidden – identities under the protection of anonymity. For example, a college student at Wofford College in Spartan, South Carolina, born as Andrew Britt Greenbaum, denied his Jewish heritage and changed his name to Wolfgang Hawke after starting his own neo-Nazi hate group on the Internet known as the Knights of Freedom.[3]

The importance of the Internet as an information dissemination and recruitment tool for white nationalist groups can hardly be over-estimated. The Internet is a technological advancement that has opened new possibilities to groups such as white nationalists with unpopular ideas likely to be censored by mainstream organizations. In 1999, the Simon Wiesenthal Center in Los Angeles, an organization that monitors racial hate groups, found over 1,800 websites associated with white supremacy organizations and individuals espousing hate-filled rhetoric. In contrast, in 1995 there was only one such site, Don Black's Stormfront.[4] Black once told a reporter that he was "tired of the Jewish monopoly over the news media and the entertainment media" and

---

[2] Jennifer Vigil, "Literature of Hate Spewed in 2 Suburbs," *Chicago Tribune*, August 12, 1999.

[3] Davie Burgdorf, "Wofford Student Continues to Lead White Supremacy Group, *United Methodist News Service*, April 5, 1999, http://www.umc.org/umns/99/pr/182.html.

[4] Hate Group Information and History, http://www.geocities.com/athens/4747/Hgstart; Intelligence Report, Southern Poverty Law Center (Winter 1999); "The New Lexicon of Hate," Simon Wiesenthal Center Report, 1999.

looked toward the Internet to provide an alternative medium to disseminate his racially hostile views about blacks and Jews.[5] One of the white nationalists interviewed for this study, Lisa Turner, credits the Internet with her recruitment to the racist WCOTC. Other extremist groups, including the Heaven's Gate suicide cult, have successfully used the Internet to expand their membership.[6]

As a medium for fringe groups, the Internet has clearly proven its recruitment power. Testifying before a senate committee in May 1999, Howard P. Berkowitz, chairman of the Anti-Defamation League, said, "[T]he Internet is probably the greatest forum for the exchange of ideas that the world has ever seen, but the medium has also allowed extremists unprecedented access to a potential audience of millions – permitting bigots to communicate easily, anonymously, and cheaply to raise money for their activities, and to threaten and intimidate their enemies. . . . The Internet offers both propaganda and how-to manuals for those seeking to act out fantasies of intolerance and violence."[7] Echoing this theme, Mark Potok, a researcher for the SPLC, told a journalist that "the Internet is allowing the White Supremacy movement to reach into places it has never reached before – middle and upper middle-class, college bound teens. The movement is terribly interested in developing the leadership cadre of tomorrow."[8]

As Tim Jordan, author of *Cyberpower*, explains, the Internet is open to all: "Anyone can open a bulletin board, create an alternative world, post their thoughts or just exist as a 'net.lurker.'[9] Since the early 1990s,

---

[5] Julie Salamon, "The Web as Home for Racism and Hate," *New York Times*, October 23, 2000.

[6] Bosah Ebo, *Cyberghetto or Cybertopia: Race, Class, and Gender on the Internet* (Westport, Conn.: Praeger Press, 1998): 4.

[7] Howard P. Berkowitz, national chairman of the Anti-Defamation League, as quoted in "ADL to Congress: There Is a 'Virus of Hate' on the Internet," U.S. Newswire, May 20, 1999; Stacia Brown and Larry Bellinger provide an excellent discussion of hate groups on the Internet and some of their strategies, *Sojourners* 29 (September/October 2000). Stacia Brown, "Virtual Hate," *Sojourners* 29 (2000); www.sojo.net/magazine/index.cfm/action/sojourners/issue/soj0009/article/000910.htm. Larry Bellinger, "You Say You Want a Revolution," *Sojourners* 29 (2000), www.sojo.net/magazine/index.cfm/action/sojourners/issue/soj0009/article/000910a.htm.

[8] "Hate Groups on the Rise," *Jet* 95 (March 22, 1999): 19.

[9] Tim Jordan, *Cyberpower: The Culture and Politics of Cyberspace and the Internet* (New York: Routledge, 1999), 21, 49–53. Also see Ebo, *Cyberghetto or Cybertopia*; Gary Selnow, *Electronic Whistle Stops: The Impact of the Internet on American Politics* (Westport, Conn.: Praeger Press, 1998).

the growth of the medium has been exponential. By 1998, some analysts estimated that 100 million full-time users were interacting via this medium. As an international collection of computers brought together by high-speed phone lines, the Internet has exponentially increased the size of the audience that white nationalist groups can reach, and has made it possible for a wide number of people to privately peruse in the comfort and security of their homes sites with highly objectionable content. As Jonathan Beane, a student at the University of Buffalo School of Law, argues, because of the Internet, "[t]he most vulnerable and attractive new recruits for hate organizations have been unaware and ignorant youth who are disillusioned about life and have not yet developed a firm belief system."[10]

Teenagers with white nationalist leanings, many of them alienated from more mainstream society, have found through the Internet a way to link up with like-minded souls. For example, in the spring of 2000, the NAAWP's youth web page displayed a letter from a clearly troubled seventeen-year-old high school student named Jessica (see Appendix B for a full transcript):

> I am quite new to the White Power Movement, having been introduced to it a little over 2 years ago, but since then life here has become virtually unbearable. To completely empathize with my situation one must understand what a danger it is to be a White Racist in an American high school. I am completely alone and immensely passionate with my beliefs, which adds to the discomfort. Fortunately, only trusted friends know about my belief. If it became known I would surely be singled out and my life would be in danger. I have always been a radical student, very vocal with my opinions and have gained a reputation of being skilled in debate, so it is very hard to sit quietly during a "World War II / Holocaust / Bad White Men" lesson in History class. My views are becoming more and more obvious as they deepen and start to emerge in normal conversation. How couldn't they? Once your eyes are open to this, race is present in everything and everywhere about us. . . . I am sure there are many out there all too familiar with my story: With bleeding heart parents that would rather sit back and watch their daughters get raped by a black then [sic] be called racist; teachers and faculty that will punish me for disagreeing with them about a Shakespeare theme, but will ignore the

[10] Jonathan S. Beane, "Cyberhate Recruitment on the Internet," Computers and the Law Final Paper, State University of New York at Buffalo, May 1, 1997. http://wings.buffalo.edu/CompLaw/CompLawPapers/beane.htm.

black students who throw food at and expose their testicles to White female students; losing more and more friends each year to race mixing and a lot of sleepless nights.[11]

According to a report of the Southern Poverty Law Center, Jessica's home state of Pennsylvania ranks among the states with the highest number of white supremacy groups.[12] And in 2000, Jessica's state also had the distinction of being the home of two high-profile incidents of interracial violence from people who were, unfortunately, better shots than Benjamin Smith. A thirty-nine-year-old unemployed African-American man, Ron Taylor, and a thirty-four-year-old white immigration lawyer, Richard Baumhammers, engaged in separate rampages that left eight people dead (three whites and five minorities) and three wounded.[13] Before killing a Jewish victim who was his lifelong neighbor, Baumhammers shot out the windows of the victim's synagogue and painted red swastikas on the outside of the building.[14]

Over the Internet, white supremacy groups provide children much younger than Jessica with coloring books where they can color in crosses and swastikas, and they also offer comic books where white heroes and heroines battle black and brown people. Indeed, Jessica's familiarity with the Internet is evident by the preface to her letter to the NAAWP, which stated "[t]he following is an article I wrote that will never be published anywhere or read by anyone, except your readers maybe. I am a 17 year old White female and I attend a small rural school in PA. I was asked to write an article on something that I dislike about my school so I wrote 2 papers . . . a nice version for my teachers and this for myself. Jessica."[15]

One commentator writes, "These days just about every organization with an unpopular, illegal, or unpalatable creed can be found on the Net, from Aryan Brotherhood to the Ku Klux Klan to Holocaust

[11] NAAWP's youth web page. http://www.naawp.com/Youth/jessica.htm.
[12] "Active Hate Groups in the United States in 1998," *Intelligence Report* (Winter 1999): 38–39.
[13] Earl O. Hutchinson, "Why Are Black Leaders Silent on Black Hate Crimes?," http://www.amren.com/salon.htm; "Fast-Food Shooting Suspect Kept 'Satan' List: Cops Find Notes Filled with Hate and Possible Targets," APBNEWS.com, March 3, 2000.
[14] Dennis B. Roddy and Bill Heltzel, "Man on Rampage: Accused Killer Richard Baumhammers Had a History of Mental Illness and a Strong Dislike for Immigrants," Post-Gazette.com, April 30, 2000.
[15] NAAWP's youth web page.

revisionists to the neo-Nazi National Alliance."[16] The range of groups includes, of course, more moderate organizations and those that effectively disguise themselves simply as sources of "scientific information" (though that information turns out to be racially tinged). On the website of the WCOTC, there are slogans such as "Build a Whiter and Brighter World," a call for RAHOWA, excerpts from *Mein Kampf*, and a feature called "Jewatch."[17] There are hate sites that target gays and advocate violence against them, sites with videotapes of actual rapes, and a site called "Niggerwatch" that monitors white-on-black crime. In 1998, if one typed "hate niggers" into the Yahoo Search engine it would generate 65,659 hits, while "white power" and "Holocaust lie" would generate even more.[18]

Recruiting teenagers through the Internet is not legally restricted, nor is the access of minors to sites with racist or otherwise disturbing contents forbidden, although some parents may purchase blocking software for their homes. In 1999, two congressional proposals – the "Children's Internet Protection Act" (House Bill 368, 543, 896, Senate 97) and the "Child Protection Act" (a proposed amendment, House Bill 2560), which would have restricted easy access to potentially harmful sites through the use of filtering software – languished on the Hill because of concerns about their constitutionality.[19] Framing a bill that would pass constitutional muster if challenged will be a difficult standard to meet given court decisions and opposition from groups such as the American Civil Liberties Union.[20] In fact, restricting content

[16] Richard Martin, "Web of Hate: Soldiers of Bigotry March Online," http://www.pretext.com/febr98/features/story4.htm.

[17] Ibid.

[18] Jean Winegardner, "Is Hate Young and New on the Web?," Online Journalism Review, http://ojr.usc.edu/content/story.cfm?id=192.

[19] For a summary of filtering bills for the 106th Congress, see http://www.techlawjournal.com/cong106/filter/Default.htm, and "Commission on Child Online Protection Off to Slow Start," http://www.techlawjournal.com/censor/20000308.htm; John P. Lynch, "School Districts and the Internet: Practice and Model Policy," *West's Education Law Reporter* 122 (January 1998): 21–25.

[20] See *Mainstream Loudon v. Board of Trustees of Loudon County Library*, 24 F. Supp. 2d 552 (1998), a software blocking case, in which the plaintiffs alleging that the use of the software violated their First Amendment right to free speech won their case, and the library declined to appeal the case (United District Court for the Eastern District of Virginia at Alexandra, Virginia, Case number 97–2049, http://www.techlawjournal.com/courts/loudon/default.htm).

on the Internet in any capacity may prove to be a legally insurmountable challenge regardless of how dangerous a site's content is. For example, in 1995, information on the Internet included a *Terrorist's Handbook* and an *Anarchist's Cookbook* with complete instructions on how one can make a bomb similar to the one used in the Oklahoma City Bombing.[21] Yet law enforcement officials seem powerless to do much about such sites.[22]

Some knowledgeable observers, however, doubt the effectiveness of the Internet when it comes to the recruitment of racists. David Goldman, a Harvard University librarian, operates HateWatch, a group that monitors hate on the web and seeks to heighten public awareness of its nature and existence. He does not, however, believe that the Internet is an effective means of recruitment, even if it does provide information and sources to contact, because of the lack of face-to-face interaction.[23] While Goldman could be correct in this assessment, many of the hate Internet sites offer regional contact information and regularly send daily e-mails alerting interested persons of the activities of groups and speakers near their homes. We know that some white nationalist activists were recruited in this manner. Lisa Turner, for instance, reports that it was an Internet contact with Matthew Hale, the head of the WCOTC, that resulted in her joining his organization and taking on her leadership role.

WHITE POWER MUSIC

White power rock music is another aggressive avenue used to reach young people. As mentioned earlier, William Pierce of the National Alliance purchased Resistance Records specifically as a way of reaching young people. White power music, according to Pierce, is a reaction to "the Negroid filth churned out by MTV and the other Jewish

---

[21] Cass R. Sunstein, "Is Violent Speech a Right?," *American Prospect* 46 (June 23, 1995): 34–37.

[22] "A Campaign to Limit the Voices of White Supremacists on the Internet Has Defenders of the First Amendment Worried," *Time*, January 22, 1996.

[23] David Goldman, telephone interview, October 7, 1999. Goldman's view of hate groups on the web is also quite expansive, for unlike other leading monitoring organizations, such as the SPLC and the Wiesenthal Center, Goldman includes the Jewish Defense League among groups monitored because of the attitude that its leadership has toward Arabs.

promoters of anti-White music designed to demoralize, corrupt, and deracinate young Whites."[24] White power music, he argues, must evolve into "a much broader category of resistance music."[25] Although some form of white power music may have always been around, there is a new emphasis on recruiting a younger teen audience.

Journalist Brad Knickerbocker describes the content of some of this white power music:

> The sound is that of most other pop music-straight rock, heavy metal, folk ballads. But listen carefully, and the words can be disturbing, even shocking. Race war is advocated. Germany's Third Reich is glorified. Blacks and Jews are denigrated, sometimes targeted for violence and destruction. It's called "white power music" played by bands with names like "Blue Eyed Devil," "Plunder and Pillage," "Bound for Glory," "Screwdriver" and "Rahowa" (acronym for "racial holy war).[26]

Racist music may also be used as a recruiting tool directed at those beyond adolescence. Thomas J. James, a former skinhead and fifteen-year member of a white supremacy group, spoke of using hate music to recruit Marines for Tom Metzger's White Aryan Resistance during his stint at Kaneohe Bay Air Station in Hawaii. When Metzger wanted more military recruits, James stated that he "successfully recruited at least four other marines by showing them videos about the White Aryan Resistance and playing them the music of bands whose lyrics preach violence and hatred."[27]

Devin Burghart of the Center for New Community has stated that white power music "is a movement that has grown from a few bands in the late 1980s to over 100 bands in the United States today, a movement that has grown from a handful of labels and distributors to over 50 in the U.S. right now, and it has been able to move closer and closer to the mainstream."[28] According to Vincent Breeding, a former marketing director for Resistance Records, "White power music is a cultural, religious, expression of people who feel they are absolutely left

---

[24] Murphy, "Behind All the Noise of Hate Music."

[25] Ibid.

[26] Brad Knickerbocker, "White Power Winning Ears with Pop Rock," *Christian Science Monitor*, March 8, 2000.

[27] "The Making of a Skinhead," Simon Wiesenthal Center, http://www.wiesenthal.com/tj/index.html.

[28] Ibid.

out of the system and have banded together. . . . In the same way that black rap [originally] attracted . . . black gangsters, skinhead music today is about nothing but fighting against the system."[29] Indeed, the overall impact and reach of music in American life – on television, in our cars, in our homes – suggests that this medium may ultimately prove quite productive for recruiting new members into white nationalist organizations.

COMIC BOOKS

As children, many of us had comic book heroes such as Superman, Batman, and Wonder Woman. Now, members of the white supremacy movement have decided that an effective way to capture young minds is to provide them with white, racially conscious comic book heroes. Instead of entertaining young minds with thrilling stories of incredible superheroes battling cosmic villains, white nationalist comic books seek to teach white children how they can and should triumph over the "villains" in their everyday lives, namely, blacks, Jews, and other minorities.

The themes of white nationalist comic books are similar to those on the adult-oriented websites. National Vanguard Books, part of William Pierce's vast organization, carries an advertisement for a comic book named the *New World Order Comix*, which is designed to inform and spur young whites to action. Its cover shows a white couple standing apart with disdain from a background crowd that includes an interracial couple and a white male with a gold chain around his neck and a sweatshirt with "rap" blazoned across the chest (i.e., a "wannabe" black). According to the publisher, the audience for the comic strip is "15–18 year olds, but the message is a serious one":[30]

> The conditions in America's schools are out of control, because the country is out of control. If we're ever to have decent, safe, high quality schools again, we must regain control of the country, and that task will fall largely on those who are now in public schools. They can begin now by understanding the nature of the evil forces which have deliber-

---

[29] Murphy, "Behind All the Noise of Hate Music."
[30] This was among several advertisements for National Vanguard Books, included in the last few pages of the *Turner Diaries*.

ately wrecked their schools, by regaining a sense of racial identity and pride, and by organizing to oppose the enemies of their race and their civilization.[31]

Although white nationalist comic books may have only a limited readership, the importance of their primary target audience means that their impact may be disproportionate to their circulation.

FACE-TO-FACE RECRUITMENT

In addition to the Internet, white power music, and comic books, face-to-face recruitment is one of the most favored methods for recruiting young people to the white nationalist cause. This type of recruitment involves everything from holding informal conversations with people in public places and distributing to them pamphlets and informational material to giving more formal public speeches about the problems that white people face in American society. Matthew Hale says that it has been relatively easy for the WCOTC to recruit college students at elite institutions, and some of his organizational literature has appeared on bulletin boards at Harvard Square and at Northwestern University.[32] When asked about his recruitment strategies, Hale stated:

> We attract college students mainly through the Internet. Many college students use the Internet, and they are attracted to us by that manner. We also have members that go on college campuses and distribute literature, members who will also simply talk to people on campuses. They will see a group of people, and they will walk up and say, Hey, have you heard about Creativity? . . . We generally reach out to the private colleges and universities, and indeed to the best schools, not through any, intentional disregard of the other schools. We find, however, that people, many of the best private schools . . . at schools such as yours, Princeton or Harvard or Yale or Northwestern, people at these schools seem to be a little more open-minded and able to grasp more thoroughly where we are coming from. The cause that we represent is by no means a cause for dummies or a cause for those who accept things blindly. We have a lot of evidence behind our views. We have a lot of history, a lot of facts, statistics and everything else to buttress our claims. Another reason why we go after

---

[31] Ibid.
[32] James Bandler, "Racist Group's Fliers Seen in the Boston Area," *Boston Globe*, July 6, 1999.

the private schools is because we want to have the elite. We are striving for that, focusing on winning the best and the brightest of the young generation.[33]

As I have discussed elsewhere in this book, there are indeed conditions on many high school and college campuses in America that make young people particularly vulnerable to recruitment strategies from white power organizations. These conditions make whites, particularly young impressionable whites, more susceptible to the message being spread by white nationalists in all of its various guises. The presentation of this message through popular and public media within the context of a larger racially charged environment make it one that is powerfully attractive to many whites of student age. These impressionable youth may one day effect the future of race relations in America.

WHO JOINS WHITE NATIONALIST GROUPS AND WHY?

In describing his recruitment of college students for the WCOTC, Matthew Hale says that those who join his group are "rebelling against the prevalent notions of our time, notions such as that all men are created equal, notions such as that we're simply all Americans, or that we all should just get along, things of this nature. These are really notions that no one ever tries to provide any proof of or any evidence for."[34] Young whites searching for an identity can stumble on groups such as Hale's WCOTC, which can fulfill psychological needs associated with the transition from adolescence to adulthood. The natural rebelliousness of youth finds a ready outlet in groups such as Hale's.

Hale explained further to the interviewer what sort of issues and concerns draw people to his organization:

[A]ffirmative action brings more people into our cause. Blackness America pageants bring more people into our cause. Black Entertainment Television brings more people into our cause. The more that the other races obtain, the more white people feel that it's being obtained at their own expense. . . . I've had so many students say, "Hey, wait minute! Why

[33] Matthew Hale, interview.   [34] Ibid.

can't I get a scholarship because I'm white . . . there are blacks that get them because they're black?" And, of course, my answer to that is, well, the blacks don't want equality. The other races don't really want equality – they talk about equality but it's really just a smokescreen. What the blacks and other races really want is supremacy, and when I tell that to people who feel aggrieved, they are very interested and they take notice.[35]

The social milieu surrounding certain types of individuals makes them particularly vulnerable to calls from white nationalists who feel that society has changed too much and that whites are slowly losing their rights. Michael Kronenwetter, author of the book *United They Hate*, explains that "hate groups grow best in times of social change," and white nationalists have attempted to use changing demographics, increases in crime rates, and the sense of injustice over racial preference policies as ways of selling the idea that the rights of white people are currently under siege.[36]

When young whites feel frustrated, angry, and oppressed, they are vulnerable to the recruitment tactics of white nationalist groups. Some will be unable to handle the information, and a few, like Benjamin Smith, resort to deadly violence. In a *Dateline* documentary on hate, newscaster Tom Brokaw raised the question on many minds concerning individuals like Smith: "How is it an intelligent, well-educated young man, who grew up in privilege, surrounded by a diverse group of friends, would come to embrace such hatred?"[37]

One answer to Brokaw's question comes from fifty years of research on social movements. The American white nationalist movement fits the profile of many other social movements, so a consideration of the general characteristics of social movements may help to answer the questions of who joins white nationalist groups and why they join. One analysis of these questions is found in the work of social philosopher Eric Hoffer, whose influential book *The True Believer* attempted to dissect the psychology behind the mass movements of the 1920s and 1930s from a non-Freudian perspective. Although Hoffer's ideas are controversial and often criticized, I believe they provide valuable

[35] Ibid.

[36] Michael Kronenwetter, *United They Hate: White Supremacist Groups in America* (New York: Walker, 1992), 85–90.

[37] Tom Brokaw, *Dateline*, July 28, 2000.

insights into the psychology of those who join radical groups like many of those discussed in this book.[38]

Mass movements, Hoffer explains, often begin with small fringe groups, but grow and eventually become part of the mainstream. Hoffer says that successful mass movements do not arrive until the "prevailing order has been discredited" by the "deliberate work of men of words with a grievance."[39] Quoting from William Butler Yeats, Hoffer writes: "Thus when the irrelevant intellectual has done his work: The best lack all conviction, while the worst are full of passionate intensity. . . . The stage is now set for fanatics."[40] Once fringe groups have their fanatics in place, according to Hoffer, they can then count on a fervent core of believers who will help lead them into the mainstream. However, even if the move into the mainstream is unsuccessful, these core believers can also be called upon to effect the group's beliefs through whatever means are available, including the use of violence, subterfuge, and intimidation. As in the case of the Bolsheviks, success can sometimes be achieved by a very small, well-organized group of dedicated fanatics whose influence can be much greater than implied by their small numbers.

In *The True Believer*, Hoffer also notes that "all mass movements generate in their adherents a readiness to die and a proclivity for united action; all of them, irrespective of the doctrine they preach and the program they project, breed fanaticism, enthusiasm, fervent hope, hatred, and intolerance; all of them are capable of releasing a powerful flow of activity in certain departments of life; all of them demand blind faith and allegiance."[41]

Another valuable perspective on social movements is provided by sociologist Sidney Tarrow.[42] What brings individuals together in a

---

[38] Although Hoffer was both a productive scholar and a public intellectual who was appointed to the National Commission on the Causes and Prevention of Violence by President Lyndon B. Johnson and received the Presidential Medal of Freedom in 1982, the receptivity to his ideas, by both the public and the academic community, has cooled in recent years. Nevertheless, his early work on social movements does contain ideas that help to illustrate certain behavioral characteristics of those who join white nationalist groups.

[39] Eric Hoffer, *The True Believer* (New York: Harper and Brothers, 1951), 130.

[40] Ibid., 141.   [41] Ibid., xi.

[42] Tarrow, 3–4. For other contemporary work on social movements, especially regarding how such movements are constructed by their ultimate members, see Aldon Morris and Carol Mueller, eds., *Frontiers in Social Movement Theory* (New Haven: Yale University Press, 1992), and Laraña et al., *New Social Movements*.

social movement, says Tarrow, is the realization that they have common interests that have been neglected by the larger society, and identifiable opponents toward whom they can direct their anger and frustration.[43] Collective action can take on a variety of different forms, depending on the choices of key leaders and the amount and nature of the control that they exert over their followers. In the United States, Tarrow and others see a country in which Americans almost always frame their demands around individual rights derived from the constitutional protections and statutory laws of the country.[44] Not surprisingly, white nationalists follow this pattern, understanding themselves as an aggrieved population whose basic rights to fair treatment, self-determination, basic law and order, and cultural integrity are being infringed upon by the onslaught of African Americans, Jews, and the federal government.

RECRUITMENT STRATEGIES FOR SPECIFIC WHITE NATIONALIST GROUPS

Social movement theory may help explain why individuals are attracted to white nationalist ideology, but once individuals express an interest in the white power movement, they can choose to express their interest through a wide range of organizations. Groups with white power themes include the relatively moderate NAAWP, which protests what it sees as racial double standards that work to the detriment of whites without embracing white supremacy or white separatism, as well as more extreme group like the Aryan Nations and the Ku Klux Klan, which condone violence and unapologetically support white supremacy. There are dozens of groups that lie somewhere between these two extremes, many of which are accessible through Don Black's Stormfront website.

Both the Ku Klux Klan and the Aryan Nations are less of a threat today because of successful lawsuits won against them by civil rights attorney Morris Dees of the Southern Poverty Law Center. Dees won three multimillion-dollar lawsuits against the Klan, and in

---

[43] Tarrow, 5–6, 129–31.

[44] Samuel Walker, *The Rights Revolution: Rights and Community in Modern America* (New York: Oxford University Press, 1998).

September 2000, also won a lawsuit against the Aryan Nations, essentially bankrupting that organization.[45] Some white nationalist groups, however, have reacted to Dees's successful lawsuits by changing strategies, and instead of focusing on building infrastructure and consolidating their organizations, they are encouraging whites who wish to challenge society to operate as loners, or in small cells consisting of a discrete number of members. Not only does this type of dispersed organization protect mother organizations from criminal liability and infiltration by FBI officials, but it also protects the anonymity of the activists.[46]

The recruitment goals of white nationalists extend beyond the mere recruitment of young people and include increased efforts to bring more educated and affluent white adults into the movement. National Alliance founder Dr. William Pierce, author of *The Turner Diaries*, described to the interviewer the demographic diversity of his organization, which he says includes many university professors and other well-educated people in addition to more humble folks:

> We have a minimum membership age of 18. We have members from that age all the way up into their nineties. I would say the average age of our members is probably early twenties. We're probably about 80 percent male, 20 percent female in our membership. So far as socio-economic categorization is concerned, that's a little more difficult for me. I have not really made very careful studies or comparisons of our membership with the general population. Being an academic myself, I was interested in the success we had had at recruiting among other academics, university faculty people. And the last survey I did, which was about a year ago, we had seven times the percentage of academics in our membership as exist in the general population. . . . [W]e get people spread over the whole spectrum. We have university professors, writers, and artists. We have engineers and teachers, and we have unemployed truck drivers.[47]

---

[45] Snow, 228–9. In 1987 Dees won a $7 million judgment against the United Klans of American; in 1990, a $12.5 million judgment against the White Aryan Resistance (WAR); in 1990, a $21.5 million judgment against Christian Knights KKK; and in 2000, a $6.3 million judgment against the Aryan Nations. See Chebium, "Attorney Morris Dees Pioneer in Using 'Damage' Lit to Fight Hate Groups"; "Morris S. Dees, Jr.," http://www.ksu.edu/dthompson/dees.html.

[46] Sam Stanton, "For Hate Peddlers, This Might Be the Last Roundup," *Sacramento Bee*, July 16, 2000.

[47] William Pierce, interview.

Pierce also explained to the interviewer what he sees as the attractiveness of the National Alliance to those who join and the major social and political concerns of its members:

There are millions of Americans who are concerned about the way our society is going. They are not just fat and happy because the economy is good. They're concerned about the decline in moral values, about the breakdown of our society, the atomization of our society. They're concerned about things like they've seen in Washington during the Clinton Administration. They're concerned about the immigration catastrophe in this country. And they're looking for answers. They really are open to answers. And we provide answers. And I think that has a great appeal to people, that we are able to help them fit a lot of things they're concerned about into a picture where it all makes sense to them.[48]

Matthew Hale also described to the interviewer the demographics of his organization, which he says is aimed particularly at recruiting bright young college students who could form the backbone of a white nationalist leadership class in the future:

We particularly attract the youth. In fact, I can say that probably half of our members are younger than 25 years old – we are a very youth-based organization. As far as income is concerned, I would say that we attract a lot of people of higher financial status. We are considered by many in the white racial movement to be the elite. For example, we do not welcome people who are irresponsible, we do not welcome people who are prone to criminal activity. We encourage responsibility and knowledge in each and every member. Unlike other organizations, we have our own books, we expect our members to read these books, and to know them thoroughly, and certainly we have attracted a lot of college students. College students have been really the bulwark, I guess you could say, of our church, the vanguard of our church. I myself graduated from two of them, so this is the type of person that we attract. . . . We find that college students in general are more receptive to new ideas, they're more open-minded, and they are willing to get involved in our church with less worry about peer pressure or what their parents may think. In a sense, it is an act of rebellion, and even students at Princeton or other prestigious universities still have the capacity of rebelling.[49]

[48] Ibid.   [49] Matthew Hale, interview.

Both Hale and Pierce argue that they are serving a public need by providing answers to questions that are on the minds of white Americans but not addressed in mainstream forums.

Besides recruitment over the Internet, white nationalist organizations sometimes resort to more old-fashioned methods of gaining followers, including the distribution of pamphlets and printed material, and the use of the private homes of existing members to discuss ideas with potential recruits. The following description given to the interviewer by William Pierce of his organization's recruitment methods is probably typical of many other white nationalist groups:

> We have mostly recruited in a non-organizational context, which is to say, we have depended upon individuals to examine the message that we present to them and make an independent and individual decision to participate with us in our effort. The Internet is probably the single largest source of new recruits for us. People hear about our Internet site or they run into us on the Internet. They read our materials, they listen to some of my weekly broadcasts, which are on the Internet, and then they make the decision to join.
>
> But we also distribute a lot of printed materials, and some people receive these printed materials, read them, perhaps order books from us, think about, and then send in an application form. We do some recruiting in an organizational context. I encourage our members, for example, to bring groups of friends to their home or perhaps on a Saturday evening or some convenient weekend time, and then play for them one of my broadcasts, which are accessible at any time through the Internet. Our members are encouraged to have people in their living room, to play a broadcast, to serve cookies and coffee and discuss the ideas that are presented in the broadcast to get people to realize that there is an organization out there which addresses the issues that they're concerned with and has answers.[50]

Jared Taylor, editor of *American Renaissance* magazine and the president of the New Century Foundation, described his membership as primarily college-educated men with an average age of about forty to forty-five, with above-average household income. About half of his membership, he said, is Christian, while the other half do not express a religious preference. Some of his subscribers, he says, are even African Americans.

[50] William Pierce, interview.

Reno Wolfe of the NAAWP also claims to have black members in his organization, which he maintains is merely a civil rights organization, quite unlike the original NAAWP organization that David Duke started more than two decades ago. When asked why any African American would want to join a group like his, Wolfe explained to the interviewer that some blacks upset over racial preferences and black crime rates find consolation in his organization's point of view:

> Many blacks don't even like [race-based educational preferences]. The blacks who are educated and know what it is leading to, they don't like it, because when you have a well-qualified black that scored high on his tests, got himself a real nice scholarship, graduated from the university of his choice, and went on to become a successful person in life, whether it was in business or whatever, and he did that on his own, the way it is now, his achievement is undermined. When he meets or comes across white companions out there in the workforce or on the university level or wherever it is, in the back of their mind, they're going to be saying that the only reason why he's a professor at this university or the president of this company or owns this company is because he has received special privileges that were denied to others. And his reputation is always going to be tainted. Whites are going to label him saying that he really didn't earn his position. Even though he did, they're going to say that he was just given his position because of the color of his skin, and that to get to where he is he had to have all these special programs, and all this special help, and everything else down the line. This has to affect blacks negatively, which is probably why we have blacks in the organization, because they realize that policies like this hurt them as much as they do whites.[51]

Unlike Wolfe's group and Taylor's group, David Duke's NOFEAR and Dan Gayman's Church of Israel are off-limits to blacks and Jews. According to Duke, his "members and supporters . . . range everywhere from students to college professors, from truck drivers to people in politics, from housewives to corporate executives." All of these diverse European Americans, he says, are attracted to his organization by their desire for racial and cultural self-preservation:

> [T]here's a natural desire of all living things to continue themselves, and to want to see their descendents be something like themselves, and have

---

[51] Reno Wolfe, interview.

the same values that their fathers and mothers and their ancestors had. And I think that that's a natural drive, it's common to every people of the earth. That's why Israel was founded – it was founded as a place for the Jewish people to preserve their heritage and preserve their culture, and for them to flourish. All people have these same basic desires and concerns. It's surely true of the European people.[52]

Like the leaders of other groups and organizations, Duke said that the Internet had provided a boost to his organization. When we interviewed Duke, NOFEAR was less than thirty days old. Duke told us that his new organization had "members in almost every state. . . . Right now, we have chapters forming all over the United States, and we've had really literally tens of thousands of inquiries and expressions of interest, and letters of support from people all over the United States. We did C-SPAN the other day, a speech that I had in Philadelphia, which launched the organization, and the C-SPAN speech has resulted in about ten thousand e-mails. We've had a tremendous outpouring of support from around the country."[53] NOFEAR has an office in New York City that issued a press release during the summer of 2000 condemning an incident that occurred in Central Park in June 2000 in which mostly black and Hispanic men accosted women of different races. NOFEAR's press release presented photographs of white women with faces swollen from crying, describing their abuse.

Lisa Turner focuses on the recruitment of white women for the atheistic "religion" that was started by Ben Klassen, author of *The White Man's Bible*. She says her primary duty is to recruit through the Internet, but she has expanded beyond that original mandate to include publishing a newsletter called *The Women's Frontier*, which is specifically addressed to race-conscious white women. Because white males in traditional white supremacy organizations seemed to harbor very conservative ideas about the role of women in their organizations, we asked Turner about women in the WCOTC. She began by explaining the church's views on women:

[W]e view men and women as being different. We believe that nature's laws should be adhered to in that men have their own special role to play, and so do women. We believe that women's most important role is as

---

[52] David Duke, interview.   [53] Ibid.

wives and mothers to white children. We certainly, though, encourage women to take on leadership roles. . . . We encourage women to be all that they can be and do all that they can do, and we do not seek to limit women. However, this is not a feminist stance. We still recognize that women are going to look at things differently than men do and take a different approach. . . . Women within the church can become reverends, just as the men can, if they take the ministerial exam. Women can lead their own church meetings and head up Women's Frontier chapters. . . . [W]e give a woman who has leadership qualities every bit as much respect as we would a man who shows such qualities.[54]

Unlike the other white nationalists, Dan Gayman of the Church of Israel has no particular recruitment strategy other than word of mouth. The recruiting approach of Gayman's church is low-key and relies on the personal example set by its existing members to attract new members to the fold:

We have no television programs, we have no radio programs, so our basic evangelistic presupposition is John 6:44: "No man can come unto me except the father which has sent me draw him, and I will raise him up to the last day." So we are totally dependent – dependent upon the power of the Holy Spirit to draw people to our religious persuasion. We really employ very minimal technological advances to achieve evangelical goals, and so the people that are drawn to this church are basically drawn by word of mouth.[55]

CONCLUSION

Fifty years ago, Eric Hoffer warned that "[t]he superior individual, whether in politics, literature, science, commerce, or industry, plays a large role in shaping a nation, but so do individuals at the other extreme – the failures, misfits, outcasts, criminals, and all those who have lost their footing, or never had one, in the ranks of respectable humanity. The game of history is usually played by the best and the worst over the heads of the majority in the middle. The reason that the inferior elements of a nation can exert a marked influence on its course is that they are wholly without reverence toward the present."[56] The truth of this statement is evident in the styles and leadership of

[54] Lisa Turner, interview. [55] Dan Gayman, interview. [56] Hoffer, 24–25.

contemporary white nationalist groups. One of the most persistent themes in the rhetoric of white nationalists is that there is a hunger among white Americans for answers to their questions about racial double standards and racial justice. It is clear that the lack of honest public dialogue on racial issues has driven some white Americans into the camps of the nationalists. Concerted efforts by watchdog agencies and institutional elites to censor white supremacy groups have failed, and today such groups have highly developed networks and forums that allow them to take their one-sided messages to millions of Americans in contexts that lack countervailing voices. This development can be viewed only as alarming, and calls for an appropriate response.

REMEDIES

13

A SEARCH FOR
CONSENSUS IN
COLLEGE AND
UNIVERSITY
ADMISSIONS

[W]e conclude that academically selective colleges and universities
have been highly successful in using race-sensitive admissions policies to
advance educational goals important to them and societal goals important to everyone. Indeed, we regard these admissions policies as an
impressive example of how venerable institutions with established ways
of operating can adapt to serve newly perceived needs.

Derek Bok and William Bowen[1]

On December 13, 2000, U.S. District Judge Patrick Duggan issued a
ruling supportive of the University of Michigan's current use of race as
a plus factor in university admissions.[2] However, Duggan declared
as unconstitutional the dual-track admission system that the university
had in place between 1995 through 1998, which spawned the nation's
first undergraduate affirmative action suit. The case of *Gratz v.
Bollinger* was filed in 1997, when white applicants Jennifer Gratz and
Patrick Hamacher challenged the admissions policies of the undergraduate College of Literature, Sciences and Arts at the University of
Michigan at Ann Arbor.

---

[1] Bok and Bowen, 290.
[2] The vignette discussed in this chapter was previously published as Carol M. Swain,
Robert Rodgers, and Bernard Silverman, "Life after *Bakke* Where Whites and Blacks
Agree: Public Support for Fairness in Educational Opportunities," *Harvard BlackLetter
Law Journal* 16 (Spring 2000): 147–84. See also Carol M. Swain, "Race as a Plus Factor
in Undergraduate Admissions – The Public Seeks an Alternative," *Harvard Journal of
African American Public Policy* 7 (2001): 1–22.

At about the same time that white students were challenging Michigan's undergraduate admissions program, Barbara Grutter, a forty-seven-year-old white mother of two children, charged the University of Michigan Law School with racial discrimination in its admissions policies.[3] The case of *Grutter v. Bollinger* was decided in March 2001 – just three months after the *Gratz* ruling – when U.S. District Judge Bernard Friedman rejected the university's claims, and the rationale of the *Gratz* decision, that race could be used in admissions decisions under certain circumstances.[4] Both *Gratz* and *Grutter* are on appeal before the Sixth Circuit Court of Appeals, and because of the conflicting nature of the two decisions, they could end up before the United States Supreme Court.

Because competition for admissions at major universities is growing and not expected to abate in the near future, and because the decision in the Gratz case could be overturned by the U.S. Supreme Court, I argue in this chapter that it is crucial for policymakers to identify selection criteria that would be less contentious and less constitutionally vulnerable than current procedures. As in the case of employment preferences and other affirmative action programs, policymakers and opinion leaders, I believe, must diligently search for consensus among Americans on polarizing racial issues in order to avert the potential for heightened racial conflict in the future.

Focusing primarily on undergraduate admissions in this chapter, I seek to answer two interrelated questions: First, do most Americans believe that institutions of higher education should select their entering classes based upon a simple contest of who has the highest test scores and grades? And second, should academic institutions interpret past academic performance in the light of the obstacles that a disadvantaged candidate has had to overcome in life?

In this chapter, I first lay out the contours of the political debate over racial preferences in college admissions, particularly in the wake of the lawsuits against the University of Michigan. This debate provides a useful backdrop for understanding how Americans are divided over racial preferences in education, but it also allows us to see poten-

[3] See *Gratz v. Bollinger*, no. 97-75231 (E.D. Mich. Filed October 14, 1997); *Grutter v. Bollinger*, no. 97–75928 (E.D. Mich. December 3, 1997).
[4] For additional information, see the University of Michigan's web page regarding the two lawsuits: http://www.umich.edu/~urel/admissions/.

tial points of consensus. Next, I report the results of a vignette embedded in a national survey designed to allow a random sample of ordinary Americans to weigh in on the question of what criteria should be used by a competitive state university in deciding whom to admit to its undergraduate program.[5] The results of this survey show that the American public has a far more expansive definition of what constitutes merit in higher education than do the leading protagonists in the current affirmative action debate. Evident among the respondents to the national survey is a shared understanding of the criteria for merit that cuts across racial lines, implying that the public might be willing to give admission committees far more flexibility in determining the makeup of their entering classes than is commonly assumed. Americans seem to draw the line, however, on the aggressive use of race as a plus favor when socioeconomic disadvantage is not present. Using socioeconomic disadvantage as a plus factor in university admissions seems to garner substantial public support. Moreover, there is biracial support for the view that lower-scoring blacks or other minorities who come from more affluent backgrounds should not be given preference over poor or working-class whites.

Finally, at the end of this chapter and in the concluding chapter, I discuss the potential for consensus among Americans across a wide variety of racial issues, including those beyond affirmative action policies in higher education. I also argue for the necessity of American policymakers and opinion leaders – black and white, religious and secular, public and private – beginning a constructive public dialogue on racial issues that goes beyond the current strictures of political correctness and self-imposed censorship. If such a genuine dialogue is not begun and if no consensus can be achieved, then the messages of white nationalist groups, I believe, will continue to find an increasingly receptive audience and one that will not necessarily be averse to using violence to further its aims.

THE CURRENT STATE OF THE PUBLIC PERCEPTION
OF RACIAL PREFERENCES IN COLLEGE ADMISSIONS

In defense of the continued use of race as a plus factor in its admissions policies, the University of Michigan assembled an impressive team

[5] For more information about the survey, see Chapter 7, n. 33.

of researchers from a variety of different fields who conducted original studies designed to provide an empirical justification of the tangible and intangible benefits of maintaining racial diversity in institutions of higher learning. Complementing their efforts was a massive study authored by two former Ivy League university presidents, Derrick Bok of Harvard and William Bowen of Princeton, which vigorously defended "race-sensitive admission policies" as being good both for the institutions implementing them and for the long-term career success and happiness of the individuals who had been admitted under such policies over the last few decades. According to Bok and Bowen, race-conscious admission policies are "an impressive example of how venerable institutions with established ways of operating can adapt to serve newly perceived needs."[6] Indeed, leaders of public and private institutions of higher education have united to defend race-conscious admission policies, while still others have sought alternative means of boosting minority enrollment, including increased outreach and recruitment efforts.

Despite the University of Michigan's initial victory and the near-unanimous support among leaders of institutions of higher education for the continued use of race as a plus factor in university admissions, much of the media framing of the issues in the Michigan cases has focused on the perceived unfairness to white Americans and the possible illegality of racial preferences. Duggan's favorable ruling in the Gratz case will probably do nothing to change the very widespread perception of unfairness that seems to attach to the use of race in university admissions. On October 29, 2000, the very popular and influential CBS 60 Minutes program featured a segment quite sympathetic to the white plaintiffs – Gratz and Grutter were both interviewed and portrayed as victims of racial discrimination. A few months earlier, Time magazine reported on the situation of minority students in California after the passage of Proposition 209, which ended affirmative action in all state-supported programs. Although minority enrollment dropped at the most elite institutions, the article argued that the downward cascading of minority students from top-ranked programs could be beneficial for them since it might lead to higher graduation rates.

[6] Bowen and Bok, 290.

Related to the issue of academic admissions are conflicting notions of what constitutes merit.[7] Determinations of merit usually involve an examination of an individual's past actions and behaviors, which can be used to assess worthiness for future rewards. Political scientist Jeremy Waldron distinguishes backward-looking merit, which takes into consideration a person's past acts and achievements, and forward-looking merit, which focuses more on what a person might become in the future.[8] In the context of admissions, these two conceptions of merit may lead to the selection of different students. Although merit is often conflated with standardized test scores and grades, it can also be conceptualized in such a manner that would acknowledge the strategic advantages that some persons bring to the table that places them in unbalanced competition with others who may be more deserving of an opportunity and in the long run more likely to do well in their chosen field.[9] It is clear that some students enjoy special academic privileges that others cannot afford and that place them in a situation of unmerited advantage over their less-affluent competitors. A growing number of college applicants invest in test preparation courses and employ tutors for advice about their applications and essays. As this practice becomes more and more widespread, higher scores on standardized tests will increasingly be a reflection of gamesmanship and abundant financial resources. Placed at a disadvantage will be students from working-class backgrounds such as Jennifer Gratz and her numerous black and Hispanic counterparts.

This type of disadvantage raises a fundamental problem for arguments in favor of "objective," merit-based standards for college admissions and illustrates a tension that all college admissions officers must face: Should admissions officers completely ignore the circumstances surrounding an applicant's objective qualifications as these are

[7] The notion of merit comes from the Greek word *axia*, which refers "to any quality or value that is the basis for differential behavior, such as praise, rewards, and income." Louis P. Pojam and Owen McLeod, eds., *What We Deserve?: A Reader on Justice and Desert* (New York: Oxford University Press, 1999), 6–7.

[8] See Jeremy Waldron, "The Wisdom of the Multitude," *Political Theory* 23 (November 1995): 563–84.

[9] In addition to standardized test scores, another supposedly objective measure of merit is an applicant's grades in high school. But just as test cores can be manipulated through preparatory classes that not all students have access to, transcripts can be manipulated by sympathetic teachers and administrators who inflate grades simply in order to make students more attractive and more competitive in the college admissions game.

measured by test scores and grades? Does a merit-based admissions policy require university admissions officers to be oblivious to race and socioeconomic status? Should socioeconomic status be considered, but not race? Is it even possible to judge an applicant from a rural, poor, public high school objectively against an applicant from an affluent, suburban, private high school? Is there any room at all for consensus in the extremely contentious arena of college admissions?

THE COLLEGE ADMISSIONS VIGNETTE

To answer such questions, we presented a random sample of Americans with a vignette profiling two high school seniors with very different social class backgrounds and test scores who were applying for admission to a state university.[10] The vignette allows us to test the hypothesis that whites and blacks, given a similar set of circumstances, can agree on what is fair in the allocation of scarce educational opportunities. To capture the zero-sum nature often inherent in decisions involving preferences, the vignette always has the applicants competing for the very last admissions slot.

In creating the student applicant profiles, we tried to present respondents with information similar to what an admissions committee might encounter. We asked survey respondents the following question: "Please suppose that a state university is deciding between two high school seniors who have applied for admission. I will read you a brief description of these two students. Then I will ask you to decide, if the college has space for only one more student, which of these do you think they should admit?" The interviewer then explains:

The first student attends a local public high school where [he or she] has maintained a "B" average. [He or she] is a [black or white] student from

[10] The national survey included a single questionnaire that was designed to detect hidden racism and determine attitudes about affirmative action policies, discrimination, and race. The first part of the questionnaire consisted of core questions asked of all respondents. The second part, which focused on affirmative action issues, was administered to approximately half the sample, randomly chosen, while the third part, which dealt with other race-related issues, was asked of the remaining half of the sample. The survey was designed to minimize framing effects of question wording, order, and context. Respondents encountered general questions before coming across vignettes designed to elicit information about their attitudes toward criteria for college admissions and job promotions.

a low-income family and has held a job throughout high school to help support [his or her] family. [He or she] scored slightly below average on [his or her] college admission tests. The second student attends a well-respected private school, where [he or she] has been an "A" student. [He or she] comes from a prominent [white or black] family and has spent two summers studying abroad. [He or she] scored well on [his or her] college admission tests.

The interviewer next asks, "Based on what I have told you about these two students, which one do you think the college should admit?" After respondents have given their answer, they are asked, "Regardless of who you think should be admitted, which student do you think the college would probably admit?"

The vignette is deliberately complex to mirror the complexity of the real world, but the basic structure of the question remains constant.[11] Whatever specific race and gender combination is assigned, the vignette always describes one individual as a hardworking "B" student from a low-income family, with *slightly* below average college admissions scores, whereas the other student is always an "A" student from an affluent family who scored well on the college admissions test. The vignette combines the indicators of social class and academic merit so that the low-income student is always depicted as less academically prepared. The question that asks respondents which student they think the college should admit is followed by an additional question that asks which student they think the college would actually admit.

Because the indicators of academic preparation (grades and test scores) and social class are always combined in the same way, it is not possible to disentangle the two. What this means is that we cannot say how respondents would have reacted if we had designed the vignette to rotate the social backgrounds of the students so that in some cases the B student was affluent and in other cases the A student was from the poorer background. For the purposes of this study, however, there

---

[11] The races and genders of the hypothetical students were randomly varied so that the sixteen possible combinations of race and gender were presented to equal numbers of randomly assigned respondents. It was possible, therefore, to remove race from consideration in some of the scenarios to see how respondents would react to two white students or two black students competing for the last slot. Similarly, I was able to compare reactions to male and female students, as well as mixed race and sex combinations. From this design, it was also possible to assess whether respondents would be more likely to lean toward a member of their own racial group.

is no need to do so, since the goal is to determine whether whites and blacks, given a similar set of circumstances, can reach agreement on principles of fairness in admissions decisions.

We specifically chose a state university rather than a private college because state universities are supported by the tax dollars of state residents and are usually thought to be more constrained in their choice of student bodies than private institutions. Similarly, we avoided a sharp contrast in the qualifications of the students because we believe that this more closely mirrors the real-life situation. In pitting a working-class applicant against a wealthy applicant, it is likely that a given respondent's perception of the opportunities available to the respective students will affect their final selection of which applicant is the more deserving of the educational opportunity in this zero-sum situation. No doubt some respondents used a forward-looking conceptualization of merit that could easily cause them to decide that the wealthy student has more opportunities in the educational marketplace. The vignette captures some of the complexity of the real world, where students from disadvantaged backgrounds often work while in high school and they often score less well on standardized tests and other traditional indicators of merit than more affluent students.

Findings from the College Admissions Vignette

Overall, the respondents were almost equally divided over which student the college should admit, with a small majority (450 of the 850 expressing a view) favoring the admission of the "B" student over the more academically prepared "A" student. This proportion is not significantly different from 50 percent.[12] The interesting question for the purposes of this analysis is: How is the proportion in favor of admitting the "B" student affected by the particular vignette or by the char-

---

[12] The questions about college admission each have a binary response, i.e., the choice of which student should or would be admitted. Therefore, we used linear logistic modeling to assess the effects of the various factors; within this standard generalized linear model framework, the significance of any particular effect can then be assessed by an analysis of deviance. This plays the same role in the linear logistic modeling of a binary response as an analysis of variance does in the linear modeling of a continuous response. See Peter McCullagh and John A. Nelder, *Generalized Linear Models*, 2nd ed. (New York: Chapman and Hall, 1989). Only the 850 respondents who expressed a definite response (over 90% of those who were interviewed in detail on this topic) were considered in the analysis.

acteristics of the respondent? An analysis of variance reported in detail in Appendix C shows that the most significant effect (p = 0.0003) is the combination of races assigned to the hypothetical students in the vignette. The age of respondents is also a significant factor (p = 0.012). Younger respondents, especially those under twenty, generally have less sympathy for the "B" student than do their older counterparts.[13]

Further analysis of the results shows that the gender of the hypothetical students is not statistically significant.[14] Also not statistically significant are the respondent's race, income, or educational background (considered as main effects). It is remarkable that none of these characteristics of the respondents, especially race, has any significant effect on the proportion favoring the "B" student. Interactions between the races assigned to the hypothetical students and the characteristics of the respondents were also considered, and the only significant interaction (p = 0.012) that was found is with respondent's income.

Figure 13.1 presents the results broken down by the races of the hypothetical students, showing for each combination whether respondents believe that the college should admit the disadvantaged "B" student or the more affluent "A" student. The figure shows that the strongest support for the "B" student is in the case when both students are white. If both students are black, then the "B" student also receives majority support, but by a narrower margin. In the "mixed race" scenarios, support for the "B" student drops; indeed, a majority of respondents select the black "A" student over the disadvantaged white "B" student.

---

[13] It is interesting that these respondents, those closest in age to those affected by college admission policies, exhibit opinions that are apparently based more on examination performance. Nonetheless, the pattern of dependence on the races attributed to the hypothetical students is similar to that in the older population, but in every case more skewed toward preference for the "A" student.

[14] The genders of the students have no effect comparable to that of race, and the preference pattern holds constant for each of the gender combinations. Respondents' attitudes are not affected whether the hypothetical students are two females, two males, or either mixed-gender allocation. There is no mixed gender effect comparable to what we observed in the mixed race scenario. There is no significant interaction between the effect of the gender allocation and that of the race allocation (after main effects have been fitted, the deviance due to the interaction of the two factors is 10.95 with nine degrees of freedom, which is clearly insignificant), or any characteristic of the respondents. We dropped, therefore, the gender allocation from the subsequent analysis.

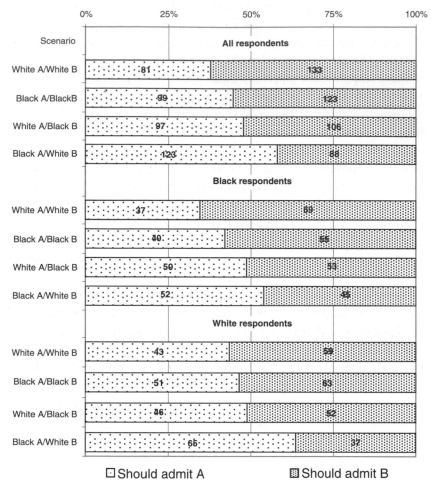

Figure 13.1 Should a college admit the student with an "A" or "B" average?

Because of the pivotal role that race plays in the study, we also broke down the choice of student by the respondent's race in Figure 13.1. The same general pattern remains for each of the scenarios. As already noted, the variation in patterns of support is not significantly different; not only is the effect of respondent's race statistically insignificant as a main effect, but there is no significant interaction between the respondent's race and the races assigned to the students. A slightly larger proportion of whites think that the college should admit the black "A" student over the economically disadvantaged white "B" student, but this is not statistically significant. Thus, not only do black and white respondents show the same overall preference pattern, but their response to the individual vignettes also shows no significant difference.

Why would respondents (particularly those over age thirty) prefer the "B" student to the "A" student? Strictly speaking, one cannot say whether they are reacting to the students' grades or indicators of social class. However, it is clear that many respondents are reacting to the individualizing factors, which have encouraged them to champion the "underdog." No doubt a few people may favor the "B" student over the "A" student simply because they believe the "B" student will get more value from the opportunity. But, more important, some respondents may have a broader definition of merit than that held by the principal actors (both opponents and proponents) in the affirmative action debate. Their definition of merit allows them to see the "B" student as being the more meritorious of the two. The "B" student has done relatively well academically while holding down a part-time job. In addition, respondents could be reacting to beliefs that the "B" student has a more limited set of options than the "A" student and that public institutions have a special obligation to create opportunities for disadvantaged state residents. The "A" student can go elsewhere, perhaps to a private institution.[15] Accordingly, respondents may be reflecting the common American belief that universities and colleges should try to "help their students transcend whatever subculture they are born and raised in, and move them out into a slightly more cosmopolitan world . . . giving young people with a yen for mobility the diplomatic passport they need to cross the borders of their racial, religious, economic, sexual or generational parish."[16]

Considering the Race Scenarios Individually

As mentioned above, income is the only characteristic of the respondents that affects the response in a way that interacts significantly with the allocation of races to the hypothetical students. To probe further,

---

[15] The notion that a state institution might have a special obligation to open doors for the disadvantaged is reflected, for example, in the University of Michigan's mission statement.

[16] Christopher Jencks and David Riesman, *The Academic Revolution* (Garden City, N.Y.: Doubleday, 1968), 26.

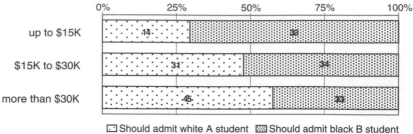

Figure 13.2 Choice between white "A" student and black "B" student by income of respondent.

we carried out individual analyses for each of the allocations separately, testing for significant effects of all five individual respondent variables: income, race, education, age, and gender. In the same-race scenarios, that is, whenever there were two white students or two black students, none of the characteristics of the respondents had a significant impact on choice. In the case where the "A" student is white and the "B" student is black, income was highly significant ($p = 0.002$),[17] but no other variables were significant. In the other mixed-race scenario, where the "A" student is black and the "B" student is white, income is not significant, but respondents' education is just barely significant at the 5 percent level.[18]

In the case of a white "A" student competing with a black "B" student, the breakdown by respondent's income is presented in Figure 13.2. By far the greatest support for the disadvantaged "B" student comes from people earning less than $15,000 per year. Although our low-income category includes more minorities than whites, and relatively more women than men, these demographic variables have no significant effect or interaction with income on the response in this case. Higher-income people favor the affluent "A" student, and their choice of the "A" student is irrespective of their race. Likewise, low-income

---

[17] Given that the effect of five factors in each of the four scenarios was assessed, a conservative approach to multiple comparisons would multiply this value by 20. It remains significant, but not overwhelmingly so.

[18] This conclusion should be treated with some care because of the large number of tests carried out, but it is investigated further below.

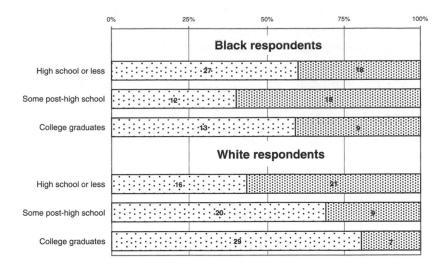

Figure 13.3 Choice between black "A" student and white "B" student by race and education of respondent.

respondents tend to favor the black "B" student, regardless of their own race or gender.[19]

The scenario in which a black "A" student competes against a white "B" student is the one in which most respondents support the "A" student. As noted above, respondent's education has a significant main effect. Furthermore, noticeable differences between respondents appear once we control for education, and in particular there is a very significant interaction between education and race in this scenario ($p = 0.008$ on an analysis of deviance based on a linear logistic model). Figure 13.3 presents the results broken down by race and educational level of the respondents. Less-educated and highly educated blacks now prefer

---

[19] To further identify this pattern, we fitted a logistic regression model that predicts the probability of preferring the "B" student: log[Prob(prefer B) / Prob(prefer A)] = 0.95 − 0.027 × (income in $000). This estimator predicts that a high-income respondent (income = $50K) would have probability 0.4 of preferring the "B" student, while a low-income respondent (income = $10K) would support the "B" student with probability 0.66. The coefficient of income in this equation has standard error 0.009, and so has a highly significant t-value.

a black "A" student to a white "B" student, but not by much. Their preference for the black "A" student is mild, and educational level has little effect among black respondents; the variations are not statistically significant. Among white respondents, however, educational level has a strong and highly significant effect. Whites with a high school education or less prefer the "B" student by a margin of 21 to 16 (57 percent), which is similar to the general population's preferences in the same-race scenarios. On the other hand, 81 percent of white college graduates (29 out of 36) select a black "A" student over a white "B" student. The behavior for moderately educated whites is intermediate.[20] It is particularly interesting that white college graduates are much more supportive of the black "A" student in this case than their black counterparts.

Why should white college graduates show such a strong preference for the black "A" student in this case? This may simply be class solidarity for one of their own. However, other explanations may be relevant here. Some whites may regard all black students as disadvantaged even if they come from privileged backgrounds. Moreover, the black "A" student has defied the stereotype of the academically challenged black student and, therefore, has earned admission to the institution based on high achievement and broad experience. Thus, the disadvantaged white student loses out to the affluent high-achieving black student. It is only in competition with a more affluent white student that the disadvantaged white student would get a break from most highly educated whites.

This discussion shows that blacks are more consistent in their support of the hardworking "B" student from the underprivileged background *even when the "B" student is white.* When preference is shown for the black "A" student as opposed to the white "B" student, the data shows that it is strongly affected by the interactive effects of the race and education of the respondents. The black student's strongest supporters are highly educated *whites*.[21] Considering the

---

[20] The chi-square cross-tabulation of preference against respondent's race and a three-level education variable is 21.6 with two degrees of freedom ($p = 0.00002$).

[21] Indeed, if we pool across all four scenarios, black college graduates are significantly more sympathetic to the "B" student (61% support) than are white college graduates (only 45%). For nongraduates, on the other hand, there are no significant differences between races.

racial polarization that is supposed to exist on the affirmative action issue, and the tendency of groups to prefer one of their own, this is truly an astounding finding; however, it becomes somewhat less so once we analyze these findings in light of other surveys.

The highly educated whites that strongly favor a black "A" student over a white "B" student are acting in accordance with their general disdain for racial preferences in higher education. For decades social science studies have documented that well-educated Americans are more tolerant of diversity, more accepting of broad democratic values than the poorly educated and more racially liberal.[22] However, recent studies show well-educated whites to be especially disapproving of minority preferences in college and university admissions.[23] In fact, James Glaser found them more opposed than poorly educated whites to preferences in higher education, even though they are more liberal on issues such as minority representation in legislatures, hiring for public works jobs, and set-asides in public contracting.[24] Using the theory of group conflict to explain his counterintuitive findings, Glaser postulates that well-educated whites are sensitive to context and especially racial preferences on their own turf, which in this instance is higher education. It is their preferences for more traditionally defined merit-based criteria that leads them to support the higher-achieving student irrespective of that student's race. Admissions criteria and practices directly affect this group, since the limited number of freshman seats at first-, second-, and third-tier institutions have meant the downward cascading of thousands of middle-class and affluent white students who have been prepared since preschool to matriculate at elite institutions.

Which Student Will the Institution Actually Admit?

We now turn to the respondents' expectations of the way the college will actually behave. The results displayed in Figure 13.4 demonstrate that the vast majority of respondents (around 90 percent in the same-race scenarios and 80 percent in the mixed-race scenarios) believe that

[22] Campbell et al., *The American Voter*; Key, *Public Opinion and American Democracy*; Jackman and Muha, "Education and Intergroup Attitudes"; McClosky, "Consensus and Ideology in American Politics"; Sniderman et al., *Reasoning and Choice*.
[23] Schuman et al., *Racial Attitudes in America*.
[24] Glaser, "A Quota on Quotas."

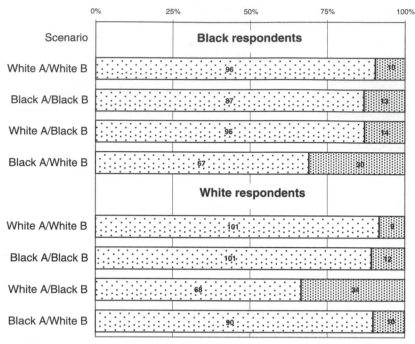

Figure 13.4 Which student will the institution admit?

the college will admit the "A" student. Although over half the respondents think that the institution should admit the low-income "B," respondents nonetheless expect the opposite to occur. They overwhelmingly expect the institution to use traditional indicators of academic merit and exclude the lower-achieving student.

The overall pattern is very similar among whites and blacks, but there is an interesting effect in the mixed-race scenarios.[25] In the "white

[25] Just as in the case of the respondents' own preferences, the genders of the hypothetical students have no effect comparable to that of their races. A female "B" student in the mixed-sex allocation "male A/female B" is given the same likelihood of admission as a male in the "male A/male B" combination. Insofar as the pattern observed in Figure 13.4 is a perception of the college's preference for the other race, there is no corresponding effect for gender. Respondents do not believe nowadays that gender is regarded by the institution as a relevant issue in a college admissions slot in a zero-sum situation.

A/black B" case, the majority of whites who believe that the "A" student will be admitted decreases from around 90 percent to around 70 percent. Exactly the converse happens in the "black A/white B" case among black respondents. This finding suggests that there is a fairly small proportion (around 20 percent of each race) who think that the college will normally select on academic merit, but will choose a "B" student of the other race against an "A" student of their own race.[26] When phrased in this way, even this finding can be seen as an example of an area where whites and blacks still agree – although this agreement exists only in a perverse sense. In any case, both groups expect the institution to place far more emphasis on grades than they themselves would.

The vast majority believes that the "A" student will be admitted, regardless of their own view as to which student should be admitted. How are the perceptions of individuals about the institution's likely behavior related to their own preferences for what it ought to do? There is a fairly small, but statistically significant, negative relationship between the two;[27] the belief that the "A" student will be admitted over the "B" student is even more overwhelming among the supporters of the "B" student. The majority of respondents do not expect that the institution will operate in the way they consider most fair. Again, whites and blacks both agree on these matters. Although a substantial number of Americans would admit the disadvantaged "B" student, they do not believe that the institution will. Instead, the majority of respondents expect the institution to reward past performance by giving greater weight to the traditional indicators of academic merit, that is, grades and test scores. And, as noted before, this expectation fits the preferences of the more highly educated white respondents who thus far seem unpersuaded by the arguments of those who strongly advocate racial preferences in admissions.

---

[26] The fact that whites give a black "B" student a much greater likelihood of admission than do blacks could be influenced by their perceptions of how affirmative action preferences might operate in higher education. Likewise, the beliefs that blacks hold about the pervasiveness of discrimination may lower their expectation of the black "A" student's chances of gaining admission.

[27] The measure of this interaction is $p < 0.005$ on a chi-square test.

HOLDING EVERYTHING CONSTANT EXCEPT RACE:
EVIDENCE FROM OTHER SURVEYS

The college admissions vignette stacked the deck so that the students were unequal in grades and social class. The depiction of the applicants perhaps elicited greater sympathy for the "underdog." In many situations, however, colleges and universities are confronted with two middle-class students with similar backgrounds. Should race then be a decisive factor? Who should get admitted to a predominantly white institution when decision-makers are confronted with two well-prepared students from different races, but similar backgrounds? Do most respondents believe that an institution should favor a black "A" student over a white "A" student if only one can be admitted to an institution that has few minorities?

New York Times/CBS polling data allow us to approach the answer to this question.[28] In December 1997, a survey asked a random sample of the U.S. population the following question: "Suppose a white student and a black student are equally qualified, but a college can admit only one of them. Do you think the college should admit the black student in order to achieve more racial balance in the college, or do you think racial balance should not be a factor?" By similar margins, blacks and whites decisively rejected the use of race as a tiebreaker between two equally qualified students competing for a single slot. Of those expressing a view, 77 percent of white respondents (644 out of 831) and 72 percent of black respondents (119 out of 156) said that the race of the student should not be a factor. Clearly, these people felt that the institution should find some other way to choose between the two applicants.

These results may seem surprising for blacks, but not for whites. Laura Stoker has shown that white Americans consider diversity enhancement a poor justification for giving preference to one racial group over another.[29] I obtained a similar result in regard to employment preferences with the following random assignment question asked on the 1996 Response Analysis Corporation (RAC) survey: "Suppose that a company that has few minority employees was choosing between

---

[28] *New York Times*/CBS News Poll, December 6–7, 1997.
[29] Stoker, "Understanding Whites' Resistance to Affirmative Action."

two people who applied for a job. If both people were equally qualified for the job and one was a minority person and the other a white,
do you think the company should hire the minority person, hire the
white person, or should they find some other way to choose?" Eighty-
two percent of whites and 71 percent of blacks said the company
should find some other way to choose. Only 20 percent of blacks and
12 percent of whites said that an underrepresented minority person
should be selected. Such agreement between whites and blacks that race
should not be a factor in college admissions and hiring decisions shows
that whites are not the only Americans uncomfortable with affirmative
action that uses race as a tie-breaker.

A second *New York Times*/CBS question asking about unequal
college applicants in an interracial scenario met with a similar response.
Using a decision rule that seems to favor objectivity, a majority of both
races preferred the admission of the most academically talented student
even when it meant less racial diversity for the college. The question
was: "Suppose there is a white student who has an A average and a
black student who has a B average, but a college can admit only one
of them. Do you think the college should admit the black student
in order to achieve more racial balance, or do you think that racial
balance should not be a factor?" A very decisive majority of both races
say that the "A" student should be admitted over the "B" student.
Among those expressing an opinion, the proportion expressing the
view that racial balance should not be a factor is over 75 percent for
black respondents (95 out of 126) and over 90 percent for whites (718
out of 793). These additional results suggest that respondents in the
College Admissions Experiment are indeed reacting to individualizing
characteristics of the two students that extended beyond their gender
and race. In the above example, however, a representative sample of
Americans presented with two students, portrayed as equal in every
respect except race, agreed that the higher-achieving student was the
one who deserved admission in the zero-sum situation described.

IMPLICATIONS OF THE PUBLIC OPINION DATA AND
THE COLLEGE ADMISSIONS VIGNETTE

These data show that the majority of Americans oppose the use of
race even as a tiebreaker between two similarly advantaged students.

However, a substantial proportion of Americans – indeed, a majority – are committed to principles that allow for a substantially broader definition of merit than that held by the leading protagonists whose views seem to dominate the affirmative action debate. The general public's broader and more forward-looking conceptualization of merit includes consideration of the obstacles and hurdles that a given person has had to overcome as part of whatever record is presented to the admissions committee. But, as we have also seen, highly educated whites are more likely to favor a backward-looking system of merit, which protects their vast accumulation of social and economic capital and their ability to transmit advantages to their offspring.

Competition for admission to elite institutions is not expected to decline over the next decade; instead, it is expected to grow even more intense.[30] How should admissions decisions be made in such an increasingly competitive milieu? One way would be for decision-makers to adopt a computer selection system that would randomly choose among the exceptionally qualified based entirely upon objective criteria of past academic performance. Or they could operate in accordance with their university mission statements by factoring in variables that go beyond grades and test scores. Or they could continue the present system of racial preferences that may require constant modification in order to avoid numerous legal challenges.

A computer program would remove some human subjectivity from the selection process, but the more mechanical process would come at the expense of the well-rounded student bodies that experienced admissions directors can assemble by actively poring over essays and letters of recommendation in search of those rare diamonds in the rough. Given the data examined, it is not too idealistic to think that a substantial percentage of Americans would favor some flexibility. Admissions based solely on grades and test scores would seem to be anathema to the widely held Horatio Alger vision of American society. Clearly, the public's general dissatisfaction with racial preferences should *not* be interpreted as a desire to award admission to the highest-scoring applicants without consideration of other factors. In addition to consideration of previous disadvantage, Americans do not seem to have any serious problems with accepting bonus points granted on a non-

[30] Bronner, "College Applicants of '99 Are Facing Stiffest Competition."

racial basis to persons with special talents, to recruited athletes, to alumni children, and to applicants from distant places.

The real debate, therefore, is not about Americans clamoring for a mass move toward a grades-and-test-score–based system that favors numbers to the exclusion of all else. If anything, the American people are asking institutions to really practice what they often purport to do in their lofty mission statements, that is, create opportunities for students of widely different social, economic, and educational backgrounds. However, the available data show that this is not what many of the nation's premier universities and colleges have done with their admissions policies. The vast majority of the nation's elite institutions have had dual admissions systems providing blanket preferences to certain minority groups while disadvantaging large numbers of nonminorities not positioned well enough in the social system to exploit other sources of preference.[31] In most instances, those minority applicants who are granted preferences are those from relatively privileged backgrounds who have had many advantages in life over their poor white, poor black, or poor Asian competitors.

Searching for a middle ground, the Educational Testing Service (ETS) has sought to identify students that it labels as "strivers" and has offered this information to colleges and universities on either a race-neutral or race-conscious basis. The experimental ETS formula uses fourteen characteristics of student background to compare a student's actual SAT score with the score that a student of this type would be expected to earn given his or her socioeconomic background and the quality of the high school attended. Any student who scores 200 points above what would be expected from someone with that background is identified as a "striver."[32] Although the Striver Index would seem to comport with the type of class-based system that the majority of Americans approve, it has come under heavy criticism because of fears that it is or will become an effort to advantage racial minorities at the expense of whites and Asians. However, the Striver Index equally disadvantages middle-class African-American students with below-average test scores and academic records, and it has

---

[31] Susan Welch and John Gruhl, *Affirmative Action and Minority Enrollments in Medical and Law Schools* (Ann Arbor: University of Michigan Press, 1998).

[32] Amy D. Marcus, "Education: New Weights Can Alter SAT Scores," *Wall Street Journal*, August 31, 1999, p. B1.

a race-neutral bias against the offspring of elite white Americans who score well on traditional measures of merit.

But the Striver Index would do little to help middle-class racial and ethnic minorities who underperform on standardized tests relative to lower-income whites and Asians.[33] Of the nearly 100,000 blacks who took the SAT in 1992, for instance, only 109 scored over 700 on the verbal section, and only 430 scored above 700 on the math section.[34] Black children from families with annual incomes over $50,000, for instance, average no higher on the SAT than Asians and whites with family incomes in the $10,000 to $20,000 range.[35] More recent work also finds similar trends:

> A 1998 study of admission applications at 28 selective American universities found that about 75 percent of white students taking the SAT scored over 1200 (out of 1600), while just over 25 percent of black students passed the 1200 mark. The poor scores cut across class and socio-economic distinctions within the African American community. According to the same study, in 1995 the average SAT score for black students from families making $50,000 or more was 849, which was the average score for white students from families earning $10,000 or less.[36]

An awareness of this persistent racial and ethnic test score gap has caused Harvard sociologist William J. Wilson to advocate the implementation of "flexible, merit-based" criteria that would encourage institutions to weight grades and test scores less by taking into consideration other factors, including an applicant's initiative and leadership abilities, ability to overcome personal hardship, self-awareness, civic and cultural awareness, honors, awards, and specialized knowledge. According to Wilson, opportunity enhancement programs can bridge racial gaps by leading to the formation of sustainable multiracial policies.[37]

---

[33] "National College Bound Seniors: 1994 Profile of SAT and Achievement Test Takers," The College Board, Princeton, New Jersey.

[34] Theodore Cross, "Suppose There Was No Affirmative Action at the Most Prestigious Colleges and Graduate Schools?," *Journal of Blacks in Higher Education* (Spring 1994): 49.

[35] Andrew Hacker, *Two Nations: Black and White, Separate, Hostile, and Unequal* (New York: Random House, 1992), 146.

[36] Hisham Aidi, "Who's Failing Black Students?," www.africana.com, January 10, 2001.

[37] Wilson, *The Bridge over the Racial Divide*, 95–110.

While public support has waned for blanket policies of racial preferences in higher education, there is support for helping persons deemed as meritorious on the basis of factors extending far beyond grades and test scores. The data in this study has shown that Americans believe that state institutions should weigh a broader set of variables when they select their students. Nevertheless, they seem to oppose the idea of racial preferences for purposes of diversity enhancement, the major justification given by universities themselves. Many Americans who value diversity broadly defined are opposed to racial preferences that seem to disadvantage other applicants who seem more deserving of admission. As Anthony Carnevale, vice-president of the Educational Testing Service, remarks, "people don't want to give the rich daughter of an African-American lawyer special treatment. But the poor African-American woman from the wrong part of town and the poor school is a different story."[38]

WHAT WILL HAPPEN TO AFRICAN-AMERICAN STUDENTS IF RACIAL PREFERENCES END?

A conservative Supreme Court decision could end racial preferences at state institutions. Does this mean that selective institutions will lose the rich diversity that African-American students add to the campus environment? Like the reports of Mark Twain's demise, I believe that reports of the demise of diversity at college campuses if uniform standards are applied are greatly exaggerated. The prognostications that campuses will become mostly white and Asian if racial preferences are ended are closer to political hyperbole than to genuine scientific forecasts. Indeed, I believe that the abolition of race-conscious admissions policies at elite institutions would have only a minor ripple effect on the participation of African Americans in higher education. There are two very good reasons for saying this. First, only a tiny percentage of institutions – those which are most competitive – are involved in the granting of significant racial preferences. The removal of racial preferences from these institutions will have little effect on most minority students, who, like most white and Asian students, attend middle-level

---

[38] Anthony Carnevale, Vice-President of Educational Testing Service, quoted in Marcus, "Education: New Weights Can Alter SAT Scores," p. B1.

or less-competitive colleges. Despite the amount of discussion that Americans devote to racial preferences in college and university admissions, it is important to keep in mind here that the overwhelming majority of college-enrolled African Americans do not attend institutions that use racial preferences. According to one survey, only the top 20 percent of colleges and universities use a "marked" degree of racial preferences; the next 20 percent uses only a very limited degree of preferences; and the remaining 60 percent of U.S. institutions use no racial preferences at all.[39]

The second reason why the elimination of racial preferences will have a much smaller effect than many believe is because of the changes it will make in the structure of incentives confronting the black middle class. There is every reason to believe that African Americans who value education at elite institutions will respond proactively to the changed circumstances and seek to improve the grades and test scores of their offspring.

On this last point it is important to understand the resilience and determination with which African Americans historically have responded to the hardships of their condition. Since the time of Reconstruction, a small number of African Americans have always gained admission to those selective white institutions that would accept them on their merits. African Americans somehow managed to maintain a toehold in these institutions despite overwhelming societal discrimination against them during a time when the black middle class was a minuscule portion of the overall black population.[40] This was true despite the absence of preferences or recruitment efforts of any kind.[41]

Today, however, the pool of middle-class and affluent African Americans that can potentially meet merit-based criteria has grown enormously. Since the early 1960s, African Americans have benefited from the civil rights movement and affirmative action policies, which have greatly increased the size of the black middle class and the percentage of African Americans in colleges and universities. Bowen and Bok cite

[39] Bowen and Bok, p. 15, n. 8.
[40] Burt Landry, *The New Black Middle Class* (Berkeley: University of California Press, 1987), 30–6; Lawrence Otis Graham, *Our Kind of People: Inside America's Black Upper Class* (New York: HarperCollins, 1999).
[41] S. A. Kendrick, "The Coming Segregation of Our Selective Colleges," College Board 66 (1967): 68.

one study that reported that the percentage of blacks enrolled in Ivy League schools grew from 2.3 percent in 1967 to 6.3 percent by 1976, and the percentage in other prestigious schools had increased from 1.7 to 4.8 percent.[42] At least two generations of African Americans have offspring that can claim alumni privileges at Princeton and Harvard.[43] By conservative estimates, the combined black middle and upper classes range anywhere from 35 to 44 percent of the total black population. More blacks today than ever before have the cultural, material, and educational resources to meet the same academic standards that white and Asian students must meet.

My main contention here is that African Americans who want to attend the most elite institutions will respond to whatever incentive structure is in place. Already, the offspring of today's African American middle class are more competitive than their parents were, and although a large gap still exists between white and black SAT scores, remedies are available to reduce that gap.[44] The *Journal of Blacks in Higher Education* cites the following reasons for lagging black scores:

> [B]lack students who take the SAT have not followed the same academic track as white students . . . white SAT test takers are more likely than black SAT takers to have completed courses in geometry. In higher level mathematics such as trigonometry and calculus, whites hold a large lead. In 1999, 52 percent of white SAT takers had taken trigonometry in high school compared to 40 percent of black test takers. A full one-quarter of white test takers had taken calculus in high school. Only 13 percent, about half as many, of black students had taken calculus.[45]

Similar discrepancies were found in the preparation for the verbal part of the SAT, where black students took fewer literature courses and honors writing courses. Moreover, far fewer blacks chose to invest in test coaching courses such as Kaplan and the Princeton Review, which can raise scores by 100 points or more. Clearly, these are areas where blacks who hope to matriculate at elite institutions can improve their preparation, and advocates of diversity can monitor black students

[42] Bowen and Bok, 7.
[43] Patterson, 22; Thernstrom and Thernstrom, *America in Black and White.*
[44] Christopher Jencks and Meredith Phillips, eds., *The Black-White Test Gap* (Washington, D.C.: Brookings Press, 1998).
[45] "This Was Not Supposed to Happen: The Black-White Test Gap Is Growing," *Journal of Blacks in Higher Education* 25 (1999): 96, 98, 99.

and schools more closely to make sure that these opportunities are provided. Foundations such as the Gates Foundation, which contributed a billion dollars to create the Gates Millennium Scholarship, can also fund test preparation courses for financially disadvantaged minorities.[46]

Before the sustained attacks on race-conscious admissions policies, little incentive existed to identify the problems responsible for the black-white test gap. There has been, however, significant progress over the past thirty years in narrowing this gap. The improvement in the scores of black high school students in math achievement has been particularly impressive. In 1978, for instance, black and white seventeen-year-olds differed in math achievement as measured by the comprehensively administered National Assessment of Educational Progress by 1.1 standard deviations. By 1990, however – just twelve years later – that gap had shrunk to 0.65 standard deviations, an impressive gain by any measure.[47] Impressive gains over this period were also seen in black SAT scores, though by the early 1990s most of this progress had come to a halt. There is every reason to believe, however, that with a proper incentive structure, and a concerted effort on the part of the black middle class to improve black test performance, these long-term upward trends can be continued anew.

Berkeley linguist John McWhorter is only the most recent of many black critics who have observed the powerful disincentive effects that current affirmative action policies can have on black achievement. "In secondary school," McWhorter writes, "I quite deliberately refrained from working to my highest potential because I knew that I would be accepted to even top universities without doing so. Almost any black child knows from an early age that there is something called affirmative action which means that black students are admitted to schools under lower standards than white; I was aware of this from at least the age of ten. And so I was quite satisfied to make B+'s and A–'s rather than the A's and A+'s I could have made with a little extra time and effort. . . . In general, one could think of few better ways to depress a race's propensity for pushing itself to do its best in school than a policy

---

[46] Theodore Cross, "Bill Gates' Gift to Racial Preferences in Higher Education," *Journal of Blacks in Higher Education* 25 (1999): 6–7.
[47] *Journal of Blacks in Higher Education* (Winter 1997/1998): 94.

ensuring that less-than-best efforts will have a disproportionately high yield."[48]

Another way to depress a race's potential to do well is to denigrate the value of standardized tests. One of the most distressing developments along these lines seems to be the increasing tendency to attack the SAT. The SAT has come under fire over the past decade as being both a poor indicator of academic potential and being biased against minorities, leading some universities to drop it altogether as a requirement for admission. Currently, approximately 280 institutions of higher learning do not require the SAT for admission, and in February 2001, Richard Atkinson, the president of the University of California, called for the California system to drop the SAT as a requirement.[49] In Atkinson's words, ". . . America's overemphasis on the SAT is compromising our educational system."[50] Although Atkinson has focused on the SAT's deleterious effects on the study habits of high school students, others seek to stop using it because it purportedly discriminates against minorities. Abandoning the SAT simply because minorities score worse than whites or Asians, however, would be a serious mistake. Minority SAT scores have increased substantially over the past three decades, and an abandonment of the SAT now would permanently stigmatize African Americans as an underachieving group. Moreover, dropping the SAT as a college entrance requirement would also detract from the accomplishments of the black students who do score well on it.

One final observation needs to be made here: A failure or unwillingness to believe in the capabilities of African American students has led to the worst kind of racism among certain white liberals, most of whom would like to believe that they are true friends of blacks. Some of this is surely due to the fact that, like white nationalists, many members of the white establishment elite believe that blacks are genetically incapable of meeting the same academic standards they set for white and Asian Americans. While they rarely admit this in public (and some do not even admit it to themselves), as journalist Jim Sleeper

---

[48] John McWhorter, *Losing the Race: Self-Sabotage in Black America* (New York: Free Press, 2000), 232–3.

[49] Mark Clayton, "Will California Lead the Way to a Post-SAT Era?," *Christian Science Monitor*, February 27, 2001.

[50] Ibid.

suggests in his controversial book, *Liberal Racism*, an unconscious belief in the genetic inferiority of African Americans paralleling those of white nationalists occasionally slips out among liberal whites when they think they are before a sympathetic audience of similar believers.[51] Rutgers University president Francis Lawrence is a case in point. At a 1995 gathering of sympathetic listeners, Lawrence, a strong proponent of affirmative action in college admissions and faculty hiring, defended racial preferences by suggesting that blacks lack the "genetic, hereditary background" to do better on standardized tests.[52] While few college presidents or admissions deans are as open as Lawrence in expressing their true views on this topic – Lawrence, in fact, subsequently came under great pressure as a result of his remarks to resign as Rutgers president, and kept his job only after apologizing profusely to all who would listen, while claiming that he had misspoke and didn't really believe that blacks were genetically less capable than whites – based on their actions, there is reason to believe that many white liberals hold convictions similar to those expressed by the Rutgers president. Most white liberals, however, know enough about current strictures of political correctness (indeed, they are the major force upholding such strictures) not to admit to such views publicly.

CONCLUSION

When it comes to the criteria for college and university admissions, Americans are not as divided as the ongoing debate over racial preferences suggests. Given a similar set of circumstances, whites and blacks can agree on flexible merit standards that take into considerations the obstacles that a given individual has overcome to compile the record that comes before the admissions committee. Neither whites nor blacks are comfortable with the use of race as a tie-breaker between students with similar backgrounds. But both races are willing to provide a helping hand for individuals from disadvantaged backgrounds. Two of the biggest problems with racial preferences in higher education as currently implemented and defended are the underlying

---

[51] Jim Sleeper, *Liberal Racism* (New York: Penguin Press, 1997).
[52] Tom Knott, "Lawrence Apology Simply Won't Do," *Washington Times*, February 10, 1995, p. B7; Richard Cohen, "Activist or Racist?," *Washington Post*, February 14, 1995, p. A15.

assumptions that all minorities are disadvantaged and that they are incapable of improving their test scores at a rate fast enough to maintain diversity at selective colleges and universities. I contend that African Americans will meet whatever standard is required of them. Clearly, the incentive structure affects how people allocate their resources, intellectual as well as financial, and African Americans are no exception to this general rule.

Since there is ample ground for black-white consensus over the extremely contentious issue of college admissions, there is reason to believe that the possibilities of consensus exist on other controversial racial issues as well. But if our national dialogue about racial policies becomes bogged down by political grandstanding, hypocritical statesmanship, and misguided leadership, then no consensus on any racial issue can be reached at a policy level. Moreover, this lack of progress toward any meaningful consensus on race will only fuel current frustrations about race relations in the United States, a situation that only plays into the current strategies of white nationalist groups. In other words, while America sleeps, white nationalist groups simply harness their resources and wait for the seemingly inevitable collapse of a constructive national dialogue. It is of utmost importance to the future of America that we not let this happen.

14

CAN RELIGION PROMOTE GREATER RACIAL AND SOCIAL HARMONY AMONG AMERICA'S DIVERSE PEOPLES?

> Deeply rooted in our religious heritage is the conviction that every man is an heir of dignity and worth. Our Judeo-Christian tradition refers to this inherent dignity of man in the Biblical term "the image of God." The image of God is universally shared in equal portions by all men. . . . Every human being has etched in his personality the indelible stamp of the Creator. Every man must be respected because God loves him. The worth of an individual does not lie in the measure of his intellect, his racial origin or his social position. Human worth lies in relatedness to God. An individual has value because he has value to God. Whenever this is recognized, "whiteness" and "blackness" pass away as determinants in a relationship and "son" and "brother" are substituted.
>
> Rev. Martin Luther King, Jr. (1967)[1]

In this chapter, I discuss the role that religious principles can play in promoting greater racial harmony in America. While focusing mostly on Christianity, I argue that spiritual leaders of different faiths have a responsibility to take a more decisive role in teaching tolerance toward others and in encouraging racial harmony and integration in their respective spheres of influence. By taking strong proactive measure now, political and spiritual leaders, I believe, can provide a counter-

---

[1] Martin Luther King, Jr., *Where Do We Go from Here: Chaos or Community* (New York: Harper and Row, 1967), 97.

weight to the growing racial and ethnic nationalism in America and help facilitate the creation of a more truly integrated society. In addition, I discuss the benefits and dangers of faith-based governmental initiatives, which have been eagerly embraced lately by some Christian organizations, and the challenge that homosexuality poses for Americans supportive of traditional religious values.

CAN RELIGION BE USED TO COMBAT RACISM?

As I was grappling with the conclusion of this book, the phone rang. At the other end was a middle-aged white insurance agent named Mike whom I had recently met after moving from Princeton, New Jersey, to Nashville, Tennessee. Mike was calling to update me about an inquiry I had made to him concerning the suspected red-lining of a property that I owned in Virginia (red-lining is an illegal practice in which agents systematically refuse home mortgages or home insurance for houses located in certain parts of town). After several unsuccessful attempts to get an insurance agent from Mike's company to visit the Virginia home and provide me with information about upgrading my insurance coverage, I called Mike with my suspicions. Within a week he was back on the phone apologizing profusely as he outlined the series of steps that he had taken since our last conversation. Mike had procured photographs of the property, confronted the agent involved, and reported him to their company's home headquarters. While I was trying to absorb all this information, Mike unexpectedly poured out his heart to me:

> I was raised to hate all African Americans, and my father still hates them and calls them niggers. I went through childhood and young adulthood hating African Americans, but all that changed on August 17, 1975 when I accepted Jesus Christ as my personal savior. Since then I have learned to practice the brotherly love that Christ commands. How can a Christian love God and hate his brother?[2]

It is obvious to anyone who converses with Mike that he is sincere in his Christian faith and speaks truthfully when he says that in accepting Jesus Christ more than twenty-five years ago, his attitude toward

---

[2] The information for this anecdote comes from a July 2000 telephone conversation with an insurance agent from a major insurer that has branch offices across the nation.

African Americans underwent a profound change, resulting in lasting friendships with some of the people he once despised. My own experience with Mike is apparently not unique. On other occasions in the past he has confronted racism among his fellow insurance agents. Much to their surprise he tells agents he catches engaging in discrimination that he will inform their victims and testify on their behalf if necessary.

Religion has been and continues to be a powerful force in the Western world. Throughout the history of Western Christendom, religion has exerted an enormous influence over the lives of ordinary people, causing them at times to engage in very praiseworthy acts like those of my insurance agent Mike, and at other times to commit the worst kinds of atrocities, all in the name of God. On a variety of indices, the United States ranks near the top of developed nations in its religious belief and practice and in recent decades, at least, has been one of the most successful in avoiding widespread bloodshed and religious intolerance.[3] Pollsters George Gallup and Jim Castelli report that 94 percent of Americans believe in God, 90 percent pray, 88 percent believe that God loves them, and 75 percent say that religious involvement has been a positive experience in their life, with 38 percent saying it has been "very positive."[4] America's religiosity, moreover, is not simply a matter of private faith and devotion but is expressed publicly in the more than 300,000 churches, synagogues, and mosques that Americans regularly attend. A 1998 Gallup poll showed that 69 percent of Americans are members of an organized religious institution – an increase over the 65 percent recorded in 1996.[5] The majority of Americans embrace a Judeo-Christian religious identity, with the overwhelming majority (80 percent) regarding the Bible as inspired scripture and not a book of fable and myth, as some critical theologians argue.[6] Moreover, millions of Christians support television evangelists such as Jesse Duplantis, Joyce Meyer, Bishop T. D. Jakes, and Marilyn Hicks, each of whom heads a worldwide, multimillion-dollar opera-

---

[3] For information about contemporary attitudes about religion in America, see: http://gallup.com/pol/indicators/indreligion.asp; George Gallup, Jr., and Jim Castelli, *The People's Religion: American Faith in the 90's* (New York: Macmillan, 1989); George Gallup, Jr., and D. Michael Lindsey, *Surveying the Religious Landscape: Trends in U.S. Beliefs* (Harrisburg, Pa.: Morehouse, 1999).
[4] Gallup and Castelli, 45.   [5] Gallup and Lindsey, 12–13.   [6] Ibid., 21–22.

tion regularly broadcast on local, national, and international cable stations.

Since ours is a nation where the vast majority of people profess to be God-fearing, prayerful individuals who believe in a loving creator, religion should contain the seeds for improved race relations, especially if people learn and apply the basic tenets of their faiths to their daily interactions with each other. Unfortunately, there is a gap between what people tell pollsters about what they believe about God and how they act toward others, a disjunction that can weaken the ability of religion to serve as an effective agent for promoting racial and social harmony.[7] To put belief into practice is the real challenge. For religion to be effective as a remedy for racial tensions and injustice, churches, synagogues, and mosques will need to adjust themselves to the special needs of the increasingly diverse twenty-first century. To become more effective, America's religious institutions will need to offer greater outreach and cultural accommodations to persons of other races and ethnicities, and their members must be willing to worship with these persons as well.[8]

In advocating a more aggressive religious response to the problems of race in America, I am aware of the unease that this recommendation will cause many people of more secular inclination. Nevertheless, I believe that a lack of competing alternatives for helping America deal with its growing racial division, coupled with the positive potentials of a religiously attuned population, justifies a faith-based approach to some of America's racial problems. The shared and overlapping religious principles found among adherents to the three great Abrahamic religions – Judaism, Christianity, Islam – potentially offer, I believe, a powerful antidote to any notions of racial superiority or racial chauvinism. The experience of my insurance agent Mike, I believe, is just one instance of the enormous power that Christian religion can exert to save us from our ingrained bigotries and prejudices.

---

[7] Gallup and Castelli, 21.

[8] George Barna is a Christian pollster who provides an excellent discussion of survey data that he uses to argue that the church is incapable of responding to the present world conditions and must reinvent itself or face oblivion during the twenty-first century. George Barna, *The Second Coming of the Church* (Nashville, Tenn.: Word Publishing, 1998).

AMERICA'S FOUNDING: CHRISTIAN AND DEIST

In the United States, Protestant religion has had a profound effect on the culture of the nation and its founding documents. Starting with George Washington, its politicians have long felt a need to profess a belief in a God that holds the nation in special esteem. Many Americans, including scholars such as David Barton, argue that the country was founded to be a Christian nation and that the First Amendment's Establishment Clause was merely designed to prevent one Christian denomination from rising above the others as the official national religion.[9] Another proponent of this view, the Baptist minister Rick Scarborough, argues that America has prospered specifically because it was founded to be a Christian nation:

> America has not been lucky; she has been blessed. She is the product of the determination of our forefathers to forge a nation built on biblical principles. As they labored to create a Christian nation, God looked with affection and favor upon their efforts and gave them supernatural guidance that enabled them to author foundational documents unlike any the world had ever seen before. The wisdom of our Declaration of Independence and Constitution can only be described as inspired. Truly the hand of God was driving the thoughts and decisions of those men.[10]

Evidence often cited in support of America being founded as a Christian nation includes statements of some of the founding fathers and the fact that nine of the thirteen colonies had official state Christian churches. The ensuing conflicts between various Christian denominations and the persecution of minority sects no doubt led the drafters of the Constitution to add a provision that in America there would be no established church at the national level. But while there was no established national church, America, according to some scholars, understood itself from the beginning as a Christian nation. Christianity, in its many denominational forms, was the unofficial if not the official religion of the nation, they contend.

---

[9] David Barton, *Original Intent: The Courts, the Constitution, and Religion* (Aledo, Tex.: Wallbuilder Press, 1997). For a contrasting viewpoint, see Mark W. Whitten, *The Myth of Christian America* (Macon, Ga.: Smyth and Helwys, 1999).

[10] Rick Scarborough, *Enough Is Enough: A Call to Christian Commitment* (Springdale, Pa.: Whitaker, 1996), 65.

Other scholars, however, dispute the "Christian nation" claim. Instead of seeing itself as a Christian nation, America, sociologist Robert Bellah has argued, developed a well-institutionalized civil religion that, while retaining certain Christian elements, is not explicitly or exclusively Christian. Borrowing the idea of a civil religion from the French philosopher Jean-Jacques Rousseau, Bellah attributed to the American civil religion the following beliefs: "the existence of God, the life to come, the reward of virtue and the punishment of vice, and the exclusion of religious intolerance."[11] He goes on to argue that the "words and acts of the founding fathers, especially the first few presidents, shaped the form and tone of the civil religion as it has been maintained ever since. Though much is selectively derived from Christianity, this religion is clearly not Christianity."[12]

There certainly is some truth in Bellah's claim here. American civil religion cannot be described as solely Christian because the God referred to again and again in our founding documents and in the speeches of our leaders is almost never referred to as Jesus Christ. While many of the members of America's founding generation were devout Christians, some of our most influential founding fathers and national leaders understood God more in a deist sense than an explicitly Christian one. God, in the deist view, is sometimes compared to a watchmaker who created the universe but later disassociated himself from his creation.[13] Some eighteenth century deists, however, did believe that God intervened in world affairs, and that certain events – like the American Revolution – could be providential. Deists, however, did not share the traditional Christian view of Christ's soteriological preeminence or uniqueness.

Ben Franklin's famous statement of faith in his *Autobiography* may be taken as a widely shared set of beliefs among many of those members of the founding generation who would have considered themselves deists or very latitudinarian Christians:

> I had been religiously educated as a Presbyterian; and tho' some of the
> dogmas of that persuasion, such as the eternal decrees of God, election,

---

[11] Robert N. Bellah, "Civil Religion in America," *Daedalus* 96 (Winter 1967): 5.
[12] Ibid., 7.
[13] "Deism" comes from the Latin word for God, "Deus," and involves a belief in the existence of God on purely rational grounds rather than on supernatural revelation.

reprobation, etc., appeared to me unintelligible, others doubtful, and I early absented myself from the public assemblies of the sect, Sunday being my studying day, I never was without some religious principles. I never doubted, for instance, the existence of the Deity; that he made the world, and govern'd it by his Providence; that the most acceptable service of God was the doing good to man; that our souls are immortal; and that all crime will be punished, and virtue rewarded, either here or hereafter. These I esteem'd the essentials of every religion; and, being to be found in all the religions we had in our country, I respected them all, tho' with different degrees of respect, as I found them more or less mix'd with other articles, which, without any tendency to inspire, promote, or confirm morality, serv'd principally to divide us, and make us unfriendly to one another. This respect to all, with an opinion that the worst had some good effects, induc'd me to avoid all discourse that might tend to lessen the good opinion another might have of his own religion; and as our province increas'd in people and new places of worship were continually wanted, and generally erected by voluntary contribution, my mite [small monetary contribution] for such purpose, whatever might be the sect, was never refused.[14]

Like Franklin, many of our founding fathers believed all major Christian denominations – or, indeed, all the major world religions – contained important elements of moral and religious truth that were universally valid and worthy of propagation.[15] Nevertheless, their positive views of religion were tempered by an acute awareness that there were some harmful, superstitious, or absurd elements to religion that needed to be eliminated or critically pruned. Among these they included any tendencies toward intolerance of other religions or the forceful imposition of one's own religion on outsiders. Consequently, they drafted a Constitution that would ensure that America would never have an established church at the national level. The religion clauses of the First Amendment guaranteed that there would never be an official national orthodoxy or official national church in the United States (Establishment Clause), while all Americans would be guaranteed the right to believe and worship as they freely chose without hindrance from the national government (Free Exercise Clause).

[14] Benjamin Franklin, *The Autobiography of Benjamin Franklin* (Mineola, N.Y.: Dover, 1996), 62–63.
[15] For an in-depth discussion of the religious views of our Founding Fathers, see Barton, chap. 6. A contrasting view can be found in Whitten, *The Myth of Christian America*.

Perhaps nowhere is the religious basis of the founders' belief system more clearly stated than in the Declaration of Independence. Basing its claim to both collective self-determination and individual liberties on a theocentric and universalist version of natural law theory, the Declaration boldly proclaims that all men are created equal by a Divine Creator, who endows men with the inalienable rights to life, liberty, and the pursuit of happiness. Natural rights are grounded in the laws of a divinely created Nature, whose sweep is universal across all boundaries of race, sect, and class. Human rights are no mere fiat of man, but God-given.

Closely related to the religious principles of the Declaration is the widespread acceptance of what social scientist Gunnar Myrdal in the 1940s called the American Creed, which included a uniquely American view of liberty, equality, and individual rights. This creed, Myrdal said, was intimately related to the American Dilemma. The "dilemma" for Myrdal involved the contradiction between the universalist principles embodied in both the Declaration of Independence and the dominant Christian belief system in America, and the actual behavior of white Americans as exemplified in their treatment of nonwhite racial and ethnic groups.[16] In more recent years, renowned black religion professor C. Eric Lincoln has picked up on Myrdal's metaphor. The "dilemma is still with us," Lincoln writes, and its ramifications, he says, can be seen in every aspect of contemporary American behavior and belief. It is, says Lincoln, "the same dilemma that produced the Black Church, which shared the birth of our nation; and it continues as the dilemma that plagues church and society alike today."[17]

Appealing to Biblical Principles

As suggested by Myrdal's and Lincoln's reflections on America's "dilemma," the belief system of a people can indict its actual behavior and, under favorable circumstances, lead to positive changes in that behavior. Some of the most positive changes in social relations among Americans have occurred because of the vigorous application of biblical principles that have pricked the consciences of some of America's

[16] Gunnar Myrdal, *An American Dilemma* (New York: Harper and Row, 1944).
[17] C. Eric Lincoln, *Race, Religion, and the Continuing American Dilemma* (New York: Hill and Wang, 1999), xviii–xix.

more morally sensitive citizens. Biblical principles undergirded both the abolitionist movement of the 1850s and the black civil rights movement of the 1950s and 1960s. Both the Old and New Testaments promote the idea of a common creator and a brotherhood of man quite inconsistent with notions of racial superiority and racial hatred. In Genesis 1:27, for instance, an account of creation is given in which all humans are depicted as descending from a single human ancestor, Adam (Hebrew for "man"), who is created "in the image of God." Similarly, in Acts 17:26, the Apostle Paul declares the peoples of all nations to be of "one blood": "And [God] hath made of one blood all nations of men for to dwell on all the face of the earth." And, finally, there is the theme of the unity of all Christians in Christ proclaimed in Galatians 3:26–29, which says that all who follow Jesus constitute one unified people regardless of caste, gender, or national origin: "There is neither Jew nor Greek, there is neither bond nor free, there is neither male nor female: for ye are all one in Christ Jesus."[18]

The Exodus story of the 400-year bondage and redemption of the Israelites was particularly important in offering hope to the enslaved blacks in America and fueled their agitation for freedom from their ungodly masters. Further evidence for the rightness of their moral position was found in Exodus 21:16, which states that "he that stealeth a man, and selleth him, or if he is found in his hand, he shall surely be put to death."

Implicit in the Christian slaves' expectation of redemption was a rejection of the interpretation of the curse of Ham and of Joshua's curse of the Gibeonites that some white slaveowners used as the scriptural basis for black enslavement.[19] Bible-believing Christians who contend

---

[18] Unless otherwise indicated, these scripture references are from the King James Version of the Bible (Nashville, Tenn.: Thomas Nelson, 1989). Genesis 1:27, 2, Acts 17: 26, 924, Galatians 3: 26–29, 973.

[19] Ham's curse comes because of an implied sexual transgression committed against his father, Noah, while the father is in a drunken state, whereas Joshua's curse against the Gibeonites is the punishment for tricking the Israelites into sparing their lives. Genesis 9:24–26: "And Noah awoke from his wine, and *knew* what his younger son had done unto him. And he said, Cursed be Canaan; a servant among servants shall he be unto his brethren," 8. Joshua 9:22–23: "And Joshua called for them, and he spake unto them, saying, Wherefore have you beguiled saying, We are very far from you; when ye dwell among us? Now therefore ye are cursed, and there shall none of you be freed from being bondsman and hewers of wood and drawers of water for the house of my God, 204."

that African Americans are the cursed descendants of Ham should also believe in the cleansing power of the blood of Jesus and the new covenant redemption. African Americans have repeatedly cited Galatians 3:28 and similar passages in the letters of the Apostle Paul to stress the universal redemptive power of Christ's mission and message.

Professor Albert Raboteau, who has written the most scholarly study of the religion of African Americans during the period of slavery, says that even before the American Revolution, black slaves in America were "declaring publicly and politically that they thought Christianity and slavery were incompatible."[20] Moreover, some slaves expected a future reversal of the power relationships in which white people would become the slaves of black people,[21] a version of the fear expressed in the dream that Jerry, the taxicab driver, related to me about blacks taking over and suppressing and imprisoning whites (Chapter 5).

Neglecting and Perverting the Biblical Message

Just as in the slavery period, the scriptural references already cited detailing curses against the sons of Ham and the Gibeonites have provided much inspiration for more recent racist religious groups such as Christian Identity, Dan Gayman's Church of Israel group, and the Ku Klux Klan, which have actively recruited in Christian churches. The Klan appropriated to its own ends the salvation symbol of the Cross, which was lighted in solemn ceremonies where devout Klansmen and Klanswomen sang beloved Christian hymns. *Amazing Grace, The Old Rugged Cross*, and *Onward Christian Soldiers* might be heard at what Klan members refer to as a "cross lighting." Biblical scriptures that are distorted beyond the recognition of most mainstream Christians provide a foundation for the Christian Identity movement's belief that Caucasians are God's "chosen people" and that Anglo-Saxons are the "true Israelites." Of course, scripture removed from context can be found to support almost any theology.[22] As part of their defense of slavery and the subordination of blacks, Christian racialists have cited

---

[20] Albert J. Raboteau, *Slave Religion: The "Invisible Institution" in the Antebellum South* (New York: Oxford University Press, 1980), 290.

[21] Ibid., 291.

[22] For brief discussions of what the Bible has to say about slavery, civil rights, abortion, and homosexuality, see Jim Hill and Rand Cheadle, *The Bible Tells Me So: Uses and Abuses of Holy Scripture* (New York: Bantam Books, 1996).

Colossians 4:1, "Masters, give unto your servants that which is just and equal; knowing that ye also have a Master in heaven," and Ephesians 6:5, which urges servants to be obedient "to them that are *your* masters according to the flesh."[23] They never explain, however, why it is whites who should always be enslaving or subordinating blacks, when slavery in the ancient world in which Paul lived was not racial (slaves could be of any race), and the New Testament proclaimed a religion that transcended racial categories.

Unfortunately, racism among Christians has not been relegated to members of white extremist groups such as Christian Identity. It has also flourished among Christians of a more moderate stripe, who profess a belief in Jesus Christ and in his principles of brotherly love and charity toward all humanity. Ralph Reed, former executive director of the Christian Coalition, has lamented how the Reverend Jerry Falwell "used his pulpit in the 1960s to condemn civil rights protesters and allowed picketers from the Congress of Racial Equality to be arrested at his church." While the Reverend Billy Graham had a friendly relationship with Martin Luther King, Jr., and conducted integrated crusades, rarely, says Reed, did he speak out against Jim Crow. Reed quotes Graham's own lament in this regard: "I must admit that in all those years it didn't cross my mind that segregation and its consequences for the human family were evil. I was blind to the reality."[24] In the past, most conservative, white evangelicals have either been indifferent to racism or they have actively or subtly opposed civil rights, integration, and interracial marriages.

Significant progress, however, has occurred in recent years. In 1995, the Southern Baptist Convention passed a resolution condemning its past pattern of racism and active involvement in slavery and the Jim Crow system. Increasingly, white southern ministers and church-

---

[23] Colossians 4:1 and Ephesians 6:5, King James Version, 144, 140.

[24] Ralph Reed, *Active Faith: How Christians Are Changing the Soul of American Politics* (New York: Free Press, 1996), 68. For more information about religion in America during the 1960s, see "Many Faiths: The '60s Reformation," in Maurice Isserman and Michael Kazin, *America Divided: The Civil War of the 1960s* (New York: Oxford University Press, 2000), 241–59. The authors draw interesting distinctions between the theologies of Billy Graham and Dr. Martin Luther King, Jr., and about the nature of American Protestantism at 244–45. For a discussion of the white Christian establishment in Mississippi during the 1960s civil rights movement, see "Inside Agitator: Ed King's Church Visits," in Marsh, 116–51.

affiliated organizations now verbally reject racism from some of the same pulpits once used to castigate civil rights activists.[25] While progress has been made, much remains to be done. As recently as 2000, Bob Jones University in South Carolina had a ban against interracial dating, repealed only after the university was heavily criticized in the national press in connection with a speech that then presidential candidate George W. Bush gave there during the late spring.

Segregated churches and segregated worship is still the norm in America, though there are many reasons for this that extend beyond racism. These reasons include different tastes in music, different styles of response during services, and different expectations about the lengths of services. Just as whites and blacks sometimes behave differently in movie theaters – with blacks sometimes engaging in a dialogue with the script – similar differences can carry over into worship styles. Some black worship styles are more interactive than what one would find in a typical white church. Blacks, for instance, often punctuate and interrupt the pastor's sermons with frequent "amens" and spontaneous acts of applause and praise. White worshipers, on the other hand, are usually more passive at church services. In addition, services in traditional black churches can last for two to three hours or longer. Often there are Sunday morning and evening services and an expectation that the most devout members will attend both sessions. By contrast, worship services at white-dominated churches are usually much shorter and more structured.

Some African-American pastors believe that there are benefits to segregated worship that outweigh any other concerns. George W. Burns has argued, "[A]s long as there are cultural differences between the races, there will be a need and a demand for separate worship services." In many ways, Burns parts company with traditional religious civil rights leaders in that he believes that biblically it is inappropriate for churches to involve themselves with political activities such as protest politics. Consequently, as a pastor for more than four decades, he avoided the civil rights protests of the 1960s, citing biblical reasons for his stance.[26] His position can be contrasted with that of Walter R. Oliver, pastor of Bible Speaks Ministries of New Haven, Connecticut, who laments the fact that his church is sometimes referred to as a black

[25] Reed, 221.   [26] George Burns, interview.

church because of its more than 90 percent black congregation. Oliver often corrects whites who make that mistake. According to Oliver, his is a church where the pastor just happens to be African American. While Burns has eschewed political protest, Oliver has embraced it, even boasting of his arrest record.

Serious efforts to integrate mainline congregations have occurred mostly in the last decade or so. In 1995, Ralph Reed urged members of the Christian Coalition to repent their legacy of racism if they wanted God's blessings on their profamily movement.[27] Reed admitted that white Christians have taken historical positions that put them on the wrong side of racism, anti-Semitism, and anti-Catholicism. Under Reed's tutelage, the Christian Coalition responded by hiring black workers. Though well-intentioned, new problems arose stemming from those efforts, such as Christian discrimination within newly integrated organizations.[28]

While Christian principles about a universal humanity and the brotherhood of man have inspired reform movements of great benefit to mankind, the practice of actual Christians throughout much of history has been one in which these principles were honored more in the breach than in observance. The checkered history of Christianity in practice worldwide gives atheists and secular humanists much fodder for ridiculing America's majority religion. Intolerance of unpopular minorities and fratricidal religious wars, they say, are the dominant legacy of Christian religious beliefs. Even some of the white nationalist groups we surveyed for this study – particularly the more extreme – share this indictment (the more moderate groups usually avoid attacking Christianity openly). For instance, Ben Klassen, founder of the atheistic World Church of the Creator and the author of *The White Man's Bible*, discusses Christianity extensively in his writings and denounces it as a religion that has brought untold horror into the world and divided the white race:

[27] Reed, 68–69.

[28] In the year 2001, the Christian Coalition had a new executive director and two pending discrimination lawsuits against the organization. In one of the suits, black employees complained about racially segregated workspaces and racial discrimination in the availability of insurance benefits and access to front door usage. The other lawsuit came from a man who alleged that he was unfairly dismissed after he refused to spy on the black workers who filed the initial discrimination suit. See George Archibald, "Bias Embroils Christian Coalition," *Washington Times*, March 5, 2001.

We indict Christianity as being the most dishonest and hypocritical of all religions. It bills itself as a religion of love and compassion when in actuality it has repeatedly used the most brutal means of both mental and physical torture against its opponents. . . . We indict Christianity as being the cause of numerous fratricidal wars between segments of the white race and the decimation and slaying of millions of our White Race Comrades. . . . We indict Christianity of conducting any number of mass murders, usually with the approval of, or at the specific direction of the highest authorities. . . . Lastly, we indict Christianity of confusing and undermining the White Man's survival instincts and having for all these centuries stood there as an impervious roadblock to formulating a racial religion for our own survival, expansion and advancement.[29]

American leaders who openly profess Christian beliefs also suffer stinging criticism and ridicule from those who have little use for Christianity. Moreover, what further harms the image of policymakers who would like to incorporate Christian principles in recent years is that it is the more conservative politicians that have promoted such ideas, and thus have conditioned the mainstream public to be cautious regarding such issues. Many make their assertions as to the Christian nature of the founding of the United States only to promote their more conservative and less culturally sensitive agendas, such as prayer in public schools. These policies are unpopular with the staunchly secular, the educated left-of-center, and non-Christians. While a large portion of the electorate continues to respect and even embrace the religious convictions of candidates for public office, the political climate seems to be departing from overt intrusions of religion into politics. Candidates who emphasize the Christian principles of the Founding Fathers are, to the extent discussed above, correct, but the public has learned to resist those who openly make such connections because of the increasing identification of such statements with the Christian Right. More moderate public figures have observed the emotional response generated by more conservative Christian politicians and have tended to shy away from showing any religious basis for their policies as a means of picking their battles. In the 2000 election, for example, the Gore/Lieberman team seemed to play both sides of the issue. The presence of a Jewish vice-presidential candidate offered more diversity and

---

[29] Klassen, 352–3.

an opportunity for a sincerely devout Lieberman to make numerous references to God, while supporting more secular policies than Gore and Lieberman's Republican opponents.

Thus, Christianity is a religion that is vulnerable to charges of hypocrisy on a number of different fronts. Its checkered past is often used by secular humanists, neopagans, and adherents of other religions as justification for dismissing biblical principles that espouse brotherly love, altruism, and charity toward others.

JUDAISM AND ISLAM

Christianity, of course, is only one of the world's many religions. Other religions popular in the United States include Judaism and Islam, both sharing some of the foundational teachings found in the Hebrew Bible, which Christians call the Old Testament. The teachings from the Bible are incompatible with the practice of racism even though adherents of all three of the Hebraic religions have participated at various times in racially inspired intolerance and violence, and have often distorted the core principles of their own faiths. For followers of Islam, Christianity, and Judaism, all mankind descended from Adam and Eve – that is, from common parents – so we are all, in a real sense, part of one and the same humanity-encompassing human family. For all their theological differences, this is an important unifying theme. Whether they call their God Jehovah, Allah, or Jesus, racism should have no place among those religious groups and people who swear their allegiance to the Abrahamic traditions. Nevertheless, racial animosities and hatreds frequently rear their ugly heads among adherents to these faiths, and it has caused the bloodshed that Klassen and others so gleefully tout as evidence of the moral bankruptcy of religion.

The Jewish holy books include the Hebrew Bible, Tanakh, which consists of the Torah (Pentateuch), Niviim (prophets), and the Kethuvim (writings), as well as the Mishnah (a collection of oral laws compiled by Rabbi Judah in the second century A.D.) and the Talmud (which contains extensive commentary on and interpretation of the Mishnah and other scripture).[30] The Torah affirms a chosen, protected

---

[30] There are actually two Talmuds. They are independent of each other, but both refer to common sources, i.e., the Mishnah and other scripture. The Yerushalma (or Talmud of the Land of Israel) does not stray too far from the Mishnah, while the more central

status for the Jewish people that most fundamentalist and conservative Christians accept and respect on the basis of their own reading of scripture. Although scriptures emphasizing brotherly love are not a central part of the Pentateuch, there are scriptures that condemn notions of racial superiority that should give reason for pause if one wants to use biblical scriptures to prove the bloodline superiority of any group. For instance, in Numbers 12:1–12, Miriam, the sister of Moses, is stricken with leprosy after she angers God by criticizing Moses' marriage to a black Ethiopian woman. Second, God blesses a marriage between Ruth, a non-Jewish Moabite woman, and Boaz, her Jewish redeemer, a union that places her in the direct family line of the Messiah. Ruth becomes a symbol of unselfish love when she tells Naomi, her aged mother-in-law: "[F]or wither thou goest, I will go; and where thou lodgest, I will lodge: thy people shall be my people, and thy God my God."[31] Whenever the Old Testament condemns interracial, interethnic marriages, it is not out of belief in any bloodline superiority or racial pride, but out of fear that nonbelievers will seduce believers into worshiping the foreign gods of pagan nations. The latter was the fate of the wise King Solomon, whose many foreign wives eventually led him into the sin of pagan worship. None of God's prohibitions against mixed marriages in the Hebrew Bible involves warnings about inferior bloodlines.

Jews, it is true, are part of an ethnic group and a religious faith, and this convergence, combined with the Chosen People doctrine, can sometimes lead to a sense of ethnic superiority or ethnic chauvinism. But the universalism in the Genesis creation story and the assertion that all human beings – not just Jews – are created in the divine image offer a powerful antidote to chauvinistic inclinations of this kind. Rabbi Avi Levine of Temple Beth Israel in Pomona, California, explains the function of the Genesis teaching in counteracting any claim to racial or ethnic superiority:

> In Judaism we believe that all human beings are created "in God's image." There is no room in Judaism for racism because in Genesis, we read that

---

work to Judaism, the Bavli (or Talmud of Babylonia) ventures into new territory. For a complete discussion of the two Talmuds, and all rabbinic literature, see Jacob Neusner, *Introduction to Rabbinic Literature* (New York: Doubleday 1994), 153–6, 183–9.

[31] Ruth 1:16.

God created the world with one person – Adam – and it was for the sake of peace among humankind that one man shouldn't say to his fellow: "My father is greater than yours." Since we all descend from the same person, no individual, no race, can claim to have a superior lineage. . . . There should be no religious racist.[32]

Like biblically oriented Jews, Muslims recognize Abraham as their progenitor and they believe in the monotheistic Allah. Can the Islamic religion reduce racism and promote social harmony? The Reverend Jerry Falwell is among a number of Christian observers who answer this question with a resounding "no." Falwell has argued that the Islamic religion teaches hatred of non-Muslims, and that whenever Muslims gain control of a nation they suppress the rights of members of other religions. Such views are fairly common among Americans, including intellectuals who display respect for Islamic cultural achievements and Islam's contribution to the European Renaissance.[33] Some white Americans also view the Islamic faith with suspicion because they associate it with Louis Farrakhan's Nation of Islam, which has called Caucasians white devils and Christianity the religion of white slavemasters.

However, there is some question as to whether the Islam-breeds-racism-and-intolerance theory can be substantiated in the United States. Indeed, as Malcolm X discovered in his pilgrimage to Mecca in the mid-1960s, Islam has been extraordinarily successful in integrating people of diverse racial, ethnic, regional, and class backgrounds. Imam Moustafa Qazwini of the Muslim Assadig Foundation of Pomona, California, makes the point that any Koran-based version of Islam is not only inconsistent with the ideology of the Nation of Islam, but with any kind of racism:

The Koran teaches us in Chapter 49:13, "Oh Mankind. We created you from a male and a female and made you into nations and tribes, that you may know one another [not despise each other]." . . . If people of faith, in particular religious leaders, open their congregations and their hearts to all people and preach the message of racial equality of God, and not

[32] "Religion Defies Racist Beliefs," January 5, 2001,
http://www.latimes.com/communities/news/inland_empire/20011010105/tivo010973.htm.
[33] Cedric Muhammad, "Religion, Theology and Self-Improvement Sundays: Many Whites Share Rev. Jerry Falwell's View on Islam,"
http://blackelectorate.com/archives/031101.asp.

make it an only black or white congregation, then the impact of their words and deeds would be clearly reflected on society and ultimately we can enjoy racial harmony and respect for each other.[34]

Malcolm X's experience in Mecca indicates at least the potential of Islam as a racially integrating force in the world. The jubilant letter he wrote home to his followers in 1964 explained how the true Islamic faith, which he saw alive for the first time among his fellow pilgrims, could break down racial barriers that otherwise divided peoples into hostile camps:

Never have I witnessed such sincere hospitality and the overwhelming spirit of true brotherhood as is practiced by people of all colors and races here in this ancient Holy Land, the home of Abraham, Muhammad, and all the other prophets of the Holy Scriptures. Over the past week, I have been utterly speechless and spellbound by the graciousness I see displayed all around me by people *of all colors.* . . . There were tens of thousands of pilgrims, from all over the world. They were of all colors, from blue-eyed blonds to black-skinned Africans. But we were all participating in the same ritual, displaying a spirit of unity and brotherhood that my experiences in America had led me to believe never could exist between the white and the non-white. . . . During the past eleven days here in the Muslim world, I have eaten from the same plate, drunk from the same glass, and slept in the same bed (or on the same rug) – while praying to the *same* God – with fellow Muslims, whose eyes were the bluest of blue, whose hair was the blondest of blond, and whose skin was whitest of white. And in the *words* and in the *actions* and in the *deeds* of the "white" Muslims, I felt the same sincerity that I felt among the black African Muslims of Nigeria, Sudan, and Ghana. We were *truly* all the same (brothers) – because their belief in one God had removed the "white" from their *minds*, the "white" from their *behavior*, and the "white" from their *attitude*. I could see from this, that perhaps if white America could accept the Oneness of God, then perhaps, too, they could accept *in reality* the Oneness of Man – and cease to measure, and hinder, and harm others in terms of their "differences" in color.[35]

Whatever criticisms one may level against the Islamic religion – and its treatment of women and its tendency at various times and places to

---

[34] "Religion Defies Racist Beliefs."
[35] Malcolm X, *The Autobiography of Malcolm X* (New York: Ballantine Books, 1996), 339–41.

veer toward unbalanced fanaticism appall almost all Westerners – Islam clearly has potential for serving a constructive role in the world in integrating people of diverse racial and ethnic backgrounds. Within the American context, as more Muslims from Africa and the Middle East immigrate to this country, there is reason to believe that the harmful aspects of the Islamic religion can be mitigated and its creative potential enhanced.

Notwithstanding this, one scholar of religion describes Islam as a religion with many contradictions:

> [E]ven as the leader of an Islamic republic issues a decree in the name of the Qur'an that all women must wear the veil, an Islamic evangelist tells a group of American students that the veil is not mandated by the Qur'an and that only in Islam are women truly liberated. While the same Muslim apologist is insisting that the Qur'an forbids violence, the terrorist group Islamic Jihad may be bombing a building, killing innocent people.[36]

Instances in which Islam has veered into fanaticism have occurred frequently in the past twenty-five years, primarily in poor, underdeveloped countries such as Afghanistan where certain ideas drawn from Islam have been selectively and self-servingly grafted onto larger political struggles. Just as some white nationalist groups use slanted interpretations of Christian beliefs to further their causes, terrorists in the Middle East and Central Asia have used slanted interpretations of Islamic beliefs to bolster their causes and to justify their deadly attacks on those, including civilians, whom they view as enemies. The September 11 attacks on the United States by operatives linked to Osama bin Laden's terrorist organization, the destruction of the Great Buddhas in Afghanistan by the extremist, fundamentalist-Islamic Taliban government, and the all-too-frequent suicide missions by Palestinians in Israel all point to some of the reasons why Americans are wary of Islam's ability to integrate peacefully people of diverse racial and ethnic backgrounds.

Ironically, the suspicions and criticisms of Islam by non-Muslims parallel those leveled at Christians by those outside the Christian Church, and those who have been hurt by practices in nominally Chris-

---

[36] Winfried Corduan, *Neighboring Faiths: A Christian Introduction to World Religions* (Downers Grove, Ill.: InterVarsity Press, 1998), 77.

tian families or surroundings. Just as many attribute some Christians' racial hatred to their connection with the church, things that are common in practice in Muslim societies are incorrectly attributed to the teachings of Islam. Cultural differences compound misunderstandings, and the truth is that the respective religious communities foster some practices even though they are not supported in the Bible or the Koran.

Further enmity is perpetuated because Christianity and Islam contain teachings that each religion is the only true religion. For Islam, one of the five pillars is a statement of faith: "There is no true god but God (Allah), and Muhammad is the Messenger (Prophet) of God." For Christians, the Nicene and Apostles' creeds express the existence of one God and His son, Jesus Christ. In addition, the verse John 14:6 states, "Jesus said, I am the way, the truth and the life; no one cometh unto the Father but by me." Cultural differences associated with given religions by those not of a particular faith and statements of the exclusiveness of one's own faith add fuel to the fire of intolerance. The practices that are most at odds with personal beliefs become magnified in order to discredit other religions or sects.

AFRICAN AMERICANS AND CHRISTIANITY

According to the Gallup International organization, African Americans are the world's most religious people. When asked to rank on a ten-point scale the importance of God in their lives African Americans recorded a mean score of 9.04, the highest of any subgroup responding to the question. Their religiosity is manifest in high rates of church membership (72 percent compared with 69 percent for other Americans), church attendance (42 percent weekly compared with 40 percent for other Americans), weekly Bible reading (48 percent compared with 22 percent for others), and daily prayer (38 percent compared with 32 percent for other Americans).[37] The vast majority of African Americans are evangelical Christians (77 percent), and they constitute 15 percent of America's Protestants.[38] Despite the high visibility of certain Muslim groups, less than 2 percent of the black population in America is Muslim, and an even smaller subset belong to the Nation of Islam,

[37] Gallup and Castelli, 122–4.   [38] Ibid., 124.

an organization that the Southern Poverty Law Center characterizes as a racial hate group.[39]

The strong black allegiance to Christianity was forged during the early days of the Atlantic slave trade, when white Christians often viewed converting Africans and Native Americans from pagan religions to Christianity as justification for slavery.[40] The Great Awakening and revivalist movements in the latter half of the eighteenth century and the early decades of the nineteenth would leave an indelible stamp on the character of African-American religiosity. The attraction of significant numbers of African Americans to the Muslim religion did not develop until the 1930s, when Elijah Poole met W. D. Fard, whose teachings provided the foundation for the black Muslim movement. (In 1978 black Muslims would split into two distinct wings, the Nation of Islam and the American Muslim Mission.)[41]

Religion has inspired in African Americans a determination and a resiliency that enabled them to survive slavery, Jim Crow segregation, and persistent racism. For countless thousands of African Americans throughout American history, religion provided the bond that helped hold families together and give black people both the courage and the strength to endure the many hardships of life in a white-dominated society that often despised them. A belief in an omnipotent, omnipresent, omniscient God who listens to prayers, blesses followers, corrects injustices, and rewards obedience enabled many African-American families to thrive despite repeated encounters with a hostile and heartless world.

There appears, however, to be a paradox here. For although African Americans are America's most religious group, they are unquestionably overrepresented today among the nation's most desperate citizens. High rates of violent crimes, drug abuse, single parenthood, illegitimacy, infant mortality, welfare dependency, and infectious diseases distinguish African Americans from other Americans. How can the nation's most religious group also be its most desperate? This is a perplexing problem that has led some to doubt the effectiveness of religion in changing peoples' lives for the better.

[39] Corduan presents an overview of Islam, which includes a discussion of the black Muslim movement. See Corduan, 77–105; Dean E. Robinson, *Black Nationalism in American Politics and Thought* (New York: Cambridge University Press, 2001), 34–50, 118–35.
[40] Raboteau, 96–150.   [41] Corduan, 103–4.

The situation, however, is much more complex than aggregate statistics about social disorganization and social dysfunction might suggest. To begin, the desperate "underclass" or "ghetto poor," who often dominate public perception about black people, represent only a minority of the African-American population – less than a third by the most expansive definitions of "underclass" or "ghetto poor," and only a sixth by more restrictive definitions. The great majority of African Americans are hard-working, law-abiding members of America's working, middle, and upper-middle classes, who have successfully avoided the most serious pathologies of the ghettos.[42]

Even among those who can be considered "ghetto poor" – that is, among poor blacks who live in urban areas where most of their neighbors are also poor – there are significant numbers of decent and law-abiding people who lead honest and upright lives despite trying circumstances. And these people are usually the most church-oriented and religious. Many of them are women who have been abandoned or otherwise abused by their men, and are struggling alone as heads of their families. Social scientists studying the black ghetto have acknowledged since at least the 1930s the importance of this church-oriented element in providing a measure of stability to lower-class urban neighborhoods. For instance, in their massive study of blacks in Chicago during the World War II era, sociologists Horace Cayton and St. Clair Drake found it was the church-oriented poor who provided a countervailing force to the otherwise chaotic forces in the poorest black areas of the city:

> The church-oriented segment of the lower class is important because it represents an element of stability in a disordered milieu. The church world is a woman's world, for less than a third of the lower-class church members are men. These lower-class church women are, on the whole, an influence for stable family relations within their social strata. As they phrase it, they are often "unequally yoked together" with men who are

---

[42] For data supportive of this position, see Patterson, 17–51; William J. Wilson, *The Truly Disadvantaged: The Inner-City, the Underclass, and Public Policy* (Chicago: University of Chicago Press, 1987), 25–26; William J. Wilson, "Studying Inner-City Social Dislocations: The Challenge of Public Agenda Research," *American Sociological Review* 56 (February 1991): 8–10; Rebecca M. Blank, *It Takes a Nation: A New Agenda for Fighting Poverty* (New York: Russell Sage Foundation and Princeton University Press, 1997), 18–20.

"sinners" and whose "sin" is reflected in a devotion to gambling, extra-marital sex relations, and "big-timing." "Respectable lowers" – male and female – are usually "church people," but they are a decided minority within the large lower class. . . . Interviews with a score of preachers in intimate contact with the lower class, as well as observation of families affiliated with lower-class churches, seem to indicate that where *both* heads of a family are "church people" the unit tends to have a pattern similar to that of the middle class.[43]

To state the matter in another way, the people who go to church regularly, who read the Bible daily, and who meet together with like-minded Christians for weekly prayer sessions are by and large not the sort of people who wind up in the statistics on crime, delinquency, drug addiction, and other ghetto pathologies. Today, just as in Cayton and Drake's time, it seems to be those among the African-American poor who most fervently practice their religious faith who do best at breaking the generational cycle of poverty, hopelessness, and self-destruction. There is a growing body of social science literature that confirms this fact.[44]

The paradox is not completely explained, however, simply by focus-ing on the religious success stories among the ghetto poor. The more stable black working class and middle class, while it has been able to avoid the most destructive pathologies of the ghetto, has been plagued in recent years by extraordinarily high rates of divorce and single parenthood that seem inconsistent with Christian norms of family life. This situation is particularly troubling since we have come to under-stand better over the past two decades through extensive social science research just how harmful it can be for children to grow up in neigh-borhoods – even middle-class ones – where both they and their friends are raised by single mothers. Summing up the results of their own and

[43] Horace Cayton and St. Clair Drake, *Black Metropolis: A Study of Negro Life in a North-ern City* (New York: Harcourt, Brace, 1945), 612, 615.

[44] E.g., see Richard B. Freeman, "Who Escapes? The Relation of Church-Going and Other Background Factors to the Socio-Economic Performance of Black Male Youths from Inner-City Poverty Tracts," Working Paper Series No. 1656 (Cambridge, Mass.: National Bureau of Economic Research, 1985); Patrick F. Fagan, "Why Religion Matters: The Impact of Religious Practice on Social Stability," Backgrounder No. 1064 (Washington, D.C.: Heritage Foundation, 1996); and David B. Larson and Byron R. Johnson, "Religion: The Forgotten Factor in Cutting Youth Crime and Saving At-Risk Urban Youth," Report 98–2 (New York: Manhattan Institute, 1998).

others' recent research on this topic, sociologists Sara McLanahan and Gary Sandefur explain the effects of widespread single parenthood in a community:

> Single parents are less able to protect their property and their children from predators. Homicide rates and robbery rates, especially among juveniles, are more common in communities with a high proportion of single-mother families, even after adjusting for factors such as income, race, age, density, and city size. . . . In sum, communities with a high proportion of single mothers have less economic power, less political power, and less social control than communities with a high proportion of two-parent families, and this affects all children in the community.[45]

Part of the African-American problem with divorce and single parenthood, it can be argued, is due simply to broader cultural changes in the dominant white society. Until the mid-1960s, divorce was relatively uncommon in white America, and at the time Lyndon Johnson assumed the presidency in 1963, only 3 percent of white babies were born out of wedlock. By the mid-1980s, however, divorce had become ubiquitous among the white middle class, and by the mid-1990s, one out of four white babies would be born to single mothers. In the wake of the hippie, yuppie, and me-generation developments of the 1965–80 period, America was indeed entering a more self-centered era that is perhaps best captured in Robert Bellah's phrase "expressive individualism." The black situation over this period was more troubling still, with rising divorce during the 1970s and 1980s on top of an out-of-wedlock birth ratio that by the mid-1990s would approach 70 percent. It looked like a variation upon an old theme where the greatest destruction is visited upon society's most fragile elements. As it was said during the Great Depression, "when white America gets a cold, black America gets pneumonia."

Besides the problems of divorce and illegitimacy, some of the seemingly intractable problems affecting African Americans such as poverty, high crime rates, high rates of welfare dependency, and high rates of infant mortality are at least partially attributable to a general moral decline in society and a culture that tolerates behaviors especially harmful to families and children. Children, of course, suffer the most

---

[45] Sara McLanahan and Gary Sandefur, *Growing Up with a Single Parent: What Hurts, What Helps* (Cambridge, Mass.: Harvard University Press, 1994), 137.

in the Faustian bargain that occurs when intellectuals and politicians defend nontraditional families as equivalent to two-parent families and when they fail to encourage responsible moral lifestyles.

The "broader cultural forces" explanation, however, goes only so far. For even if one can explain the current black situation in terms of some combination of black social and economic vulnerabilities coupled with harmful trends in the surrounding society, it is still not clear why the greater degree of black religiosity as measured by standardized surveys has not translated into more effective ways of addressing the many problems that afflict black America. A large part of the answer here would seem to lie in the quality of black religious leadership. Here an historical explanation seems necessary.

Throughout most of American history, the decision to become a religious leader in the black community has been greatly affected by the opportunity structure in black society. Because of America's legacy of slavery and Jim Crow segregation, ambitious black men and women of prior generations were limited in the types of high-prestige occupations to which they could realistically aspire. In some communities, pastor and preacher were near the top of a short list of high-status occupations that included mortician, barbershop owner, schoolteacher, beautician, shopkeeper, and post office worker. Being a pastor offered a measure of independence and gave clergy members the authority to broker deals for themselves and selected members of their community desperate for leadership. Those attracted to the ministry under such circumstances were often ambitious men seeking power, influence, money, and social status, who were not necessarily the most pious or devout members of the black community, and this fact would often stamp the overall tone of the black church. Since one of the most important elements in any Christian community is the presence of morally upright pastors and religious leaders who can serve as models of piety and clean living to the rest of the congregation, when this element is absent, as it often was from black congregations, the morality-enhancing effect of the Christian religion is correspondingly diminished.

Under such circumstances much less came to be expected of the black clergy in terms of their personal morality than was the case in most white, middle-class churches. A host of all-too-human sins and failings, including financial improprieties, sexual misconduct, and the like, would not only be more common among the black clergy, but would be more readily forgiven and forgotten by their followers. The biblical injunction to forgive sinners would be readily invoked, while the corresponding admonition "go and sin no more" would be less rigorously enforced.

It is for reasons of this kind that scandals involving immorality and marital infidelity of the sorts that have led to great public outcries in the case of white televangelists such as Jim Bakker and Jimmy Swaggart cause such relatively mild response within the black community when they occur among black religious leaders. The recent episode with Jesse Jackson is a case in point. Reverend Jackson's announcement in the spring of 2001 that he had fathered a child out of wedlock, and subsequent allegations in the press that he had given large sums of money from his national organization to set up a separate household for his mistress, do not seem to have led to any dramatic decline in his stature among significant portions of his black following.

It is this kind of leadership failure, and the acquiescence in this situation by substantial portions of black Christians, that accounts for much of the failure of religion to live up to its full promise as a transformative force in the black community. This "forgive-and-forget" attitude, moreover, has been extended not only to black religious leaders, but to black political leaders as well. When I interviewed congressional representatives for my book *Black Faces, Black Interests*, one prominent black representative said of electoral accountability, "[O]ne of the advantages and disadvantages of representing blacks is their shameless loyalty to their incumbents. You can almost get away with raping babies and be forgiven. You don't have *any* vigilance about your performance."[46]

This "forgive-and-forget" attitude toward the moral lapses of religious and political leaders can also extend to whites who are considered to be friends of blacks. This would seem to explain why African Americans were among the strongest advocates for Bill Clinton during the string of scandals that surrounded his administration. Whether justified or not, the attitude prevailed among the majority of black Americans that Bill Clinton was a true friend – "our first black president,"

---

[46] Carol M. Swain, *Black Faces, Black Interests: The Representation of African Americans in Congress* (Cambridge, Mass.: Harvard University Press, 1995), 73.

Toni Morrison called him – and as a true friend, many black people tended to overlook his many moral failings, including illicit affairs with Jennifer Flowers and Monica Lewinsky, his perjury during the Paula Jones case, Whitewater, Filegate, and a host of other questionable activities and well-publicized misdeeds. Black people were even willing to forgive and forget his decision during the 1992 presidential campaign to support the execution of a mentally retarded black man in his home state of Arkansas (Clinton did this as a way of enhancing his "tough on crime" image among conservative white voters).

Dinesh D'Souza is certainly correct when he argues that "even if racism were to disappear overnight, the worst problems facing black America would persist."[47] Black crime, illegitimacy, and single parenthood are obvious areas where an adherence to traditional Christian and Islamic principles should result in significant social improvement. The overrepresentation of African American males in criminal offender categories highlights a critical need for political and religious leaders to make family stability and crime reduction a number one priority for the race.[48]

Regrettably, however, African-American religious and political leaders have not made the reduction of single parenthood or black crime a high priority on their agendas. Rather than directly tackling these issues and concentrating their energies on the reduction of the intertwined illegitimacy and crime rates, the more prominent black leaders have concentrated their limited resources on fighting symbolic issues such as the removal of the Confederate flag or racial reparations for slavery, thereby losing allies by infuriating many moderate whites. And although black religious and political leaders have gotten the nation's attention about racial profiling – a genuine problem – they have not heightened black awareness of disproportionately high black crime rates that make racial profiling so appealing to law enforcement officials steeped in black crime statistics. Too often in their politics black leaders have used the dire conditions in urban communities to argue for more racial preferences or for increased spending for social welfare programs rather than come up with new strategies for the community and for the nation.

[47] D'Souza, *The End of Racism*, 527.
[48] "The State of Violent Crime in America," First Report of the Council on Crime in America, the New Citizenship Project, Washington, D.C., January 1996, p. 55.

Dissatisfaction with traditional black leadership has encouraged Republican leaders to form alliances with lesser-known black religious leaders with proven records of bringing results into the lives of the inner-city poor. As I discuss in the section to follow, their overtures have included both the passage of the Charitable Choice provision of the Welfare Reform Act of 1996, which allows religious organizations to compete for federal grants to fund social service programs, and the establishment of an Office of Faith-Based and Community Initiatives, which is designed to help churches, synagogues, mosques, and other religious organizations get into the business of providing services to the poor. The decision of Republican leaders to bypass the traditional black leadership is partially a reflection of their awareness that the issues that have consumed traditional black leaders, such as racial preferences in employment and university admissions, have done pitifully little for poor African Americans, most of whom vote for a political party and receive a set of policies that falls far short of their needs.

Stephen Carter, a Yale University law professor, makes a strong case for the claim that much of the black clergy has become so bound up with the fortunes of the Democratic Party that "it is no longer possible for the leaders to press ideas that their religious understanding of the world might demand."[49] What has occurred, according to Carter, is a cooptation of black religious leadership and a diversion of black Christians away from their core biblical principles toward a focus in procuring material benefits from government. As Carter points out, most black Christians are evangelicals who believe in a divinely inspired Bible and a future reward from placing Christ first. Yet the black clergy and black leadership, he charges, have focused more on worldly gains, sometimes at the expense of their Christian moral and religious principles. The prophetic voice of the outsider is compromised under such circumstances, he believes, and religion loses much of its creative and dynamic force. He gives the example of Jesse Jackson: "[T]he Reverend Jesse Jackson, having been for most of his career, passionately pro-life is forced to become pro-choice when he wants the [Democratic] party to take him seriously."[50]

---

[49] Stephen Carter, *God's Name in Vain: The Wrongs and Rights of Religion in Politics* (New York: Basic Books, 2000), 37.
[50] Ibid.

What is perhaps most disturbing about this situation is that the moral leadership vacuum created through the black clergy's cooptation by a secular political party, and the clergy's relative neglect of the traditional Christian call to personal moral and spiritual transformation, has left the moral and religious field open for radical black nationalists such as Louis Farrakhan, eager to supply the moral exhortation that is often missing from black Christianity. While black Christian leaders rarely offer any new strategies for attacking the many morally grounded problems that afflict black families and neighborhoods, black nationalists such as Farrakhan have outlined and persisted with an agenda that encourages the pursuit of black self-reliance, moral responsibility, wholesome family values, abstention from drugs and alcohol, and black independence from whites. But black nationalist rhetoric, coupled with multiculturalist arguments extolling the virtues of racial differences, potentially undermines the prospects for racial harmony in America. As political scientist Dean Robinson has warned, black nationalist rhetoric threatens to isolate blacks even further from the American mainstream. By "accepting the notion that black people constitute an organic unit," Robinson writes, "and by focusing on the goal of nation building or separate political and economic development, black nationalism inadvertently helps to produce some of the thinking and practices that created black disadvantage in the first place." Robinson continues:

> Most white Americans have thought blacks to be essentially different; and they have used this idea to justify expelling blacks, restricting black movement, and limiting the range of rights, privileges, and opportunities available to black people. It stands to reason, then, that most attempts to identify their differences from the majority population and pursue political and economic autonomy on that basis conform to one of the oldest American fantasies – what Ralph Ellison calls the desire to "get shut" of the Negro in America – to "banish [him] from the nation's bloodstream, from its social structure, and from its conscience and historical consciousness."[51]

What is obviously needed is a religiously grounded moral leadership within the black community that combines moral exhortation with a racially inclusive vision of a future integrated America. Only through

[51] Robinson, 1–2.

such a combination can the truly transformative potentials of the Christian and Muslim religions be fully realized. African-American Christian leaders' endorsement of affirmative action and their avid support for welfare benefits even for able-bodied Americans represent a contradiction of some of the biblical principles that undergird their religion. Professor J. Jorge Klor de Alva has argued that affirmative action can be viewed as a form of heresy because it conflicts so clearly with orthodox Christian principles of universalism, which stress the role of the autonomous individual, "equal to any other soul in the eyes of God," who must work out personal salvation.[52] "Rather than supporting the individual in a civil egalitarian manner, [affirmative action] favors a select few on the basis of membership in a group whose physical characteristics have been made legally significant."[53] Moreover, while supporting assistance to the poor, the Pauline letters state a clear position on the value of work. Writing to the early church at Thessalonica, the Apostle Paul admonished the new believers that "if any would not work, neither should he eat."[54] Moreover at Ephesians 4:28, Christians are told "let him that stole steal no more: but rather let him labour, working with his hands the thing which is good, that he may give to him that needeth."[55]

THE CHARITABLE CHOICE PROVISION

One of the goals of the members of the Christian Right is to see biblical principles integrated into our national laws, and to this end they have worked to elect Republican politicians, who they have found in the past to be more sympathetic to their views than Democrats. The immediate aftermath of the 2000 election resulted in tangible gains for the religious right such as the confirmation of the evangelical John Ashcroft as Attorney General and the creation of a new federal office for Faith-Based and Community Initiatives set up to coordinate and promote the work of religious and community charities. The establishment of this office is related to an earlier victory for the Christian

---

[52] J. Jorge Klor de Alva, "Is Affirmative Action a Christian Heresy?," in Robert Post and Michael Rogin, eds., *Race and Representation: Affirmative Action* (New York: Zone Books, 1998), 135–53.
[53] Ibid., 151. [54] 2 Thessalonians 3:10, King James Version, 992.
[55] Ephesians 4:28, King James Version, 979.

Right that went almost unnoticed when then Senator John Ashcroft authored the Charitable Choice provision as a rider to the 1996 Welfare Reform bill.[56] The Charitable Choice provision allows religious organizations to compete for federal dollars to provide social service programs for the poor, and is part of the privatization of welfare long advocated by Republicans. For the national government this represents a major policy shift, but not so for state governments, some of which have a long history of contracting with religious groups to provide a variety of services to disadvantaged populations (such services have included day care, GED training, literacy classes, and parenting skills).

The Charitable Choice provision is based on the premise that religious organizations should not be discriminated against as welfare service providers since many of these organizations have a proven track record of, for example, transforming former drug addicts, prostitutes, and others at the margins of society into law-abiding citizens. As framed, the law allows religious organizations to compete with private organizations on an equal basis for federal funds for social welfare programs, though states are obligated to offer secular alternatives for services to individuals who feel uncomfortable with religious providers. The religious providers cannot discriminate against individuals on the basis of religion (or several other proscribed categories, including race), though they are permitted to limit their employees to people of their own faith.

To avoid constitutional conflict, the law specifically prohibits recipients from using federal dollars for sectarian worship, religious instruction, or proselytizing.[57] Organizations that violate the rules

---

[56] The welfare reform bill named the "Personal Responsibility Act" was part of the 1994 Republican Contract with America, which enacted a major overhaul of the nation's welfare laws. This was premised on the belief that governmental programs were responsible for high illegitimacy rates, crime, poverty, and the breakup of homes. Consequently, ending welfare as it currently existed was seen as essential to helping people break free from what seemed to be a cycle of poverty and welfare dependency by strictly limiting the amount of time an individual could receive welfare assistance and by preventing pregnant teenagers from setting up their own households.

[57] For more information, see Michelle P. Ryan, "Paved with Good Intentions: The Legal Consequences of the Charitable Choice Provision," *Dickinson Law Review* 102 (1998): 383–410; Alan E. Brownstein, "Interpreting the Religion Clauses in Terms of Liberty, Equality, and Free Speech Values – A Critical Analysis of 'Neutrality Theory' and Charitable Choice," *Notre Dame Journal of Law, Ethics and Public Policy* 13 (1999):

against proselytizing and religious instruction can lose funds or be cut off from the program. This has happened in a number of cases. For example, Operation Blessing, an organization founded by Pat Robertson to provide services to homeless people, lost a $50,000 federal grant because the organization sought to evangelize the people receiving their services.[58] Other organizations have run into problems because of the clash of their religious norms with certain secular values. In 2001, for instance, there was a pending lawsuit filed by Americans United for Separation of Church and State and the American Civil Liberties Union against the state of Kentucky and Kentucky Baptist Homes for firing a counselor because she was discovered to be a lesbian.[59]

Supporters of Charitable Choice and of the Office of Faith-Based and Community Initiatives argue that religious organizations have a proven track record of meeting the needs of disadvantaged populations and a success rate that exceeds that of secular governmental programs. Moreover, many argue that interactions with the staffs and providers of religiously based programs can teach positive values to individuals at the margins of society. To deny government funding for social welfare services provided by religious groups, Charitable Choice supporters contend, would be not only discriminatory, but would hurt those most in need.

Opponents of the new alliance between the federal government and sectarian service providers claim that it forces taxpayers to subsidize religious proselytism, if not directly, then at least indirectly, since dollars to support existing programs inevitably free up resources for organizations to spend on religious services. Writing for a leading secular humanist journal, Elena Matsui and Joseph Chuman claim that the Charitable Choice programs "will turn religion against religion. It will make religion a servant of the state. It will let our government play favorites among believers, and it will destroy separation of church and

243–84; Rob Boston, "The Charitable Choice Charade," *Church and State* 51 (February 1998): 7–12; Anna Greenberg, "The Church and the Revitalization of Politics and Community," *Political Science Quarterly* 115 (2000): 377–94; James C. Geoly, "Charity Replaces Bureaucracy," *Wall Street Journal*, September 26, 1996.

[58] Robert S. Greenberger, " 'Charitable Choice' Tests Line Between Church, State," *The Wall Street Journal*, August 24, 1999.

[59] Megan Twohey, "Charitable Choice Grows, but So Do Questions," *National Journal*, October 14, 2000.

state as we have known it."[60] This view is common among secular liberals and those who are generally unsympathetic to religion. However, even some who are more religion-friendly are dubious of Charitable Choice. For instance, a writer in the influential liberal evangelical journal *Sojourners* argues that Charitable Choice opens religious organizations up to excessive governmental monitoring that may eventually work to undermine the organizations involved, causing them to change their fundamental character if they wish to maintain good governmental standing.[61] Most likely to be affected adversely, many who hold this view believe, are evangelical Christian organizations, which generally see their primary mission as spreading the Good News about Christ.

The Charitable Choice provision and the Office of Faith-Based and Community Initiatives seem to have been created with possible objections about the Establishment Clause in mind. However, as some constitutional scholars have argued, a violation of the Free Exercise Clause – which guarantees the right of an individual to practice his or her religion – is also a possible result of Charitable Choice. If, for instance, a church or an organization with a tradition of offering a prayer before meals is forced to abandon this practice at a church-run day care center or shelter for the homeless, an arguable violation of the Free Exercise Clause has occurred. The Establishment Clause and the Free Exercise Clause in this case, some argue, command conflicting outcomes, and the only way to avoid the conflict is to end government payments to religious organizations.

Charitable Choice might also have a difficult time surviving the Supreme Court's Lemon Test for unconstitutional entanglements between church and state.[62] According to this three-pronged test, to meet constitutional standards under the non-Establishment provision of the First Amendment, a legislative statute that affects religious organizations must (1) have a secular purpose; (2) have a primary effect that neither advances nor impedes religion; and (3) not foster exces-

---

[60] Elena Matsui and Joseph Chuman, "The Case Against Charitable Choice," *Humanist*, January 1, 2001.
[61] Melissa Rodgers, "Charitable Choice: Two Views: Threat to Religion," *Sojourners* 27 (July/August 1998): 29–30. See also "Conservative Churches Say They Are Wary of 'Charitable Choice,'" *Church and State*, December 2000, p. 18.
[62] Ryan, "Paved with Good Intentions," 400–4.

sive government entanglement with religion. In determining the constitutionality of a statute under the Lemon standard, the Court examines the nature of a program, the type of financial assistance it receives from the government, and the relationship between the organization and the government. Charitable Choice seems vulnerable to an "excessive entanglement" charge because of the need for governmental audits of church records and because of the need for ongoing monitoring to ensure compliance with the law.[63] Perhaps because of concerns about the potential for excessive governmental involvement in church affairs, many religious organizations have been reluctant to apply for the funds available under the Charitable Choice program, causing the Bush administration to establish a federal office to coordinate the disbursement of funds and to try to allay fears.

Besides constitutional questions, there are a number of other issues about this effort to forge more direct ties between religious organizations and the government that are troubling even for those who are otherwise supportive of religious-based groups. For instance, there is no guarantee that some of the money will not find its way into religious organizations that preach racial hatred and discrimination as part of their belief system. As long as they do not overtly discriminate in the services they provide, Christian Identity churches, for example, could receive government funds, despite their radical teachings, which include justifications for harming racial and political minorities and the overthrow of the "Zionist Occupied Government." Some Jewish organizations fear that funds will be used to support groups such as the Nation of Islam, which has been rabidly anti-Semitic over the years. To comply with the Establishment Clause, federal dollars must go to a wide range of religious groups, so taxpayers will be supporting a number of religious organizations associated with doctrines that they consider abhorrent and dangerous. Because the provision allows organizations freedom to hire employees of the same faith and because America's religious organizations are racially segregated to a large degree, governmental dollars, critics argue, could indirectly subsidize racial discrimination.

[63] Carl H. Esbeck has provided arguments in support of a constitutional case for faith-based service providers. "A Constitutional Case for Governmental Cooperation with Faith-Based Social Service Providers," http://www.law.emory.edu/ELJ/volumes/win97/esbeck.html.

Political scientist Anna Greenberg has reported that African-American churches in her study were more likely to apply for government dollars to fund outreach and other social service programs under the new partnerships.[64] Two reasons help account for this. First, African-American churches serve needier populations of the kind the 1996 legislation was designed to help, and it is therefore not surprising that they are more likely to sign on than their more affluent white counterparts. White churches have been reluctant to sign up in large numbers, not only because they have less need, but for other reasons as well. These include the nature of their constituencies and how they see their Christian mission. White evangelical churches, the fastest growing in the country, "are less likely than other churches to address, either politically or through community services, pressing social and economic problems."[65] White churches often focus on issues such as family values and abortion, and are much less likely to become involved in social needs extending beyond their congregations. For them, the focus is more on evangelism and winning souls for Jesus. Consequently, they tend to be more wary of governmental dollars and restrictions that might hamper them in these activities than some black churches.

The second reason black churches might be more inclined to sign on to programs such as those created under the Charitable Choice provision is simply more aggressive recruitment since Bush's election. The Bush administration, seeking to expand its influence among the minority population, has aggressively sought to bypass traditional black leaders by encouraging black churches to apply for federal dollars. This, however, has not gone over very well with many black Democrats. Traditional black leaders such as Reverend Jesse Jackson; Kweisi Mfume, the head of the National Association for the Advancement of Colored People; and the Congressional Black Caucus have expressed public skepticism about President Bush's efforts to encourage black ministers to participate in the programs. While their concerns are probably more political than anything else – as loyally wedded to the Democratic Party, such individuals do not want to see Republican initiatives become popular among blacks – their official statements on the issue have stressed constitutional objections.

[64] Greenberg, "The Church and the Revitalization of Politics and Community," 388–9.
[65] Ibid., 389.

Other black leaders, however, see an obvious hypocrisy in this position, given the history of black religious groups and their involvement in various aspects of the political process. For instance, Cedric Muhammad, a writer for BlackElectorate.com, has ridiculed Jackson and what he calls the civil rights establishment for their newly found constitutional reservations about mixing politics and religion: "The Rev. Jackson, actually bent over backwards to warn of the dangers of religious leaders working with politicians. This type of talk came from politicians who do *just* that for a living. . . . We found that reasoning to be peculiar, largely because most prominent leaders in the civil rights movement have the abbreviation 'Rev.' in front of their names and because these same leaders have shepherded organizations that have accepted government largesse for years. . . ."[66]

Regardless of one's partisan political leanings, it is not clear that the overtures from President Bush to black ministers will yield much in the way of additional African-American Republican votes. Instead, as a political strategy it has a real potential to backfire. If complaints from clients and irregularities in spending or bookkeeping practices result in a disproportionate number of black churches losing their federal funding, cries of white racism against governmental agencies will surely ensue. Moreover, a change in the political climate resulting in a cutback of federal funds once a dependency relationship has been created would greatly affect the operation of poor churches, causing some to go out of business. Although welfare was reformed to address what was perceived as an unhealthy dependence on governmental largesse, the push to encourage religious organizations to expand services and compete for governmental dollars runs the risk of creating a new dependency relationship equally as harmful. But as of spring 2001, the government had not provided any serious appropriation of dollars to fund the new faith-based approaches to social problems. Given cutbacks in social welfare programs, some political observers have begun to question whether there is a safety net for America's poor and whether the new partnerships can fill the void.[67]

---

[66] Muhammad, "Black Civil Rights Leaders 'Real' Concern over Bush's Meeting with Black Pastors"; "Can Religious Programs Solve America's Social Ills?," *Both Sides with Jesse Jackson*, December 24, 2000, http://www.cnn.com/transcripts/0012/24/bs.00html.

[67] Mark Murray, Marilyn Weber Serafini, and Megan Twohey, "Untested Safety Net," *National Journal* (March 1, 2001): 684–93.

HOMOSEXUALITY, WHITE NATIONALISM, AND THE BIBLE

Homosexuality is important to consider in this book because it poses a major challenge to many Christians, Jews, and Muslims, and because gays and lesbians have become targets of violence for some white nationalist groups. Jews and homosexuals are conflated in white nationalist discourse in the same manner as feminists and lesbians: All are seen as enemies of humanity in general and of the white race in particular.[68] For conservative Christians, homosexuals may not be viewed as enemies, but homosexual activity is seen as a clear violation of God's plan for the sexes. A common joke circulating among both white nationalists and conservative Christians is that God created "Adam and Eve," not "Adam and Steve." Frequently cited as proof of God's reproductive plan for mankind is Genesis 1:28, which reads: "And God blessed them [Adam and Eve], and said unto them, Be fruitful, and multiply, and replenish the earth, and subdue it."[69]

While spiritual and intellectual leaders of most Christian denominations are united in their condemnation of racism, the proper treatment of gays and lesbians is subject to much debate among people who believe in a textually based interpretation of the Bible and who favor traditional family structures. Although some Christian groups have endorsed the ordination of gay ministers and have given blessings to same-sex unions, these issues often bitterly divide many churches and denominations. The conflicts that homosexuality poses for the church are likely to grow during the twenty-first century as gays and lesbians gain power and challenge conservative ideas about what constitutes a family. Scriptures in the Old Testament, such as Leviticus 18:22, which states that "thou shalt not lie with mankind, as with womankind: it is an abomination" and Leviticus 20:18, which prescribes death for violations of this taboo, form part of the scriptural basis for the rejection of at least male homosexuality among many biblically oriented Chris-

---

[68] Jessie Daniels provides a detailed discussion of how some of the nationalist publications depict Jews as the promoters and advocates of homosexuality. See Daniels, " 'Zog' Bankers, and 'Bull Dyke' Feminists: Jewish Men and Jewish Women," in Daniels, *White Lies*, 107–32, and also 49–51.

[69] Genesis 1:28, King James Version, 2.

tians.[70] Romans 1:24–27 is usually interpreted as condemning same-sex acts among both sexes: "Wherefore God also gave them up to uncleanness through the lusts of their own hearts, to dishonor their own bodies between themselves . . . for even their women did change the natural use into that which is against nature: And likewise the men leaving the natural use of the woman, burned in their lust one toward another: men with men working that which is unseemly and receiving in themselves that recompense of their error which was meet."[71] In addition, many Christians use the story of the destruction of Sodom and Gomorrah as their basis for condemning same-sex unions.[72]

Christian proponents of gay and lesbian rights can also cite scriptures to make their case for God's acceptance of homosexuality. Most frequently quoted is the story of the relationship between David and Jonathan given in the book of Samuel. 1 Samuel 18:3 reads, "Then Jonathan and David made a covenant, because he loved him as his own soul."[73] Upon learning of Jonathan's death in battle, we are told in 2 Samuel 1:26 that David exclaimed, "I am distressed for thee, my brother Jonathan: very pleasant hast thou been unto me: thy love to me was wonderful, passing the love of women."[74] What argues against the homoerotic interpretation of this passage, however, is the context of the statement, and the reigning Mosaic law that viewed homosexuality as a perversion punishable by death. No Orthodox Jew conversant with Jewish Law could possibly read this passage in a homoerotic sense. A much more plausible interpretation of the passage is that David is sorrowfully expressing brotherly love between himself and Jonathan, the man who had pledged his abiding loyalty to David and even offered to relinquish his claim to the throne of Israel as King Saul's successor.[75]

However offensive gay rights and gay advocacy groups may find it, the simple fact of the matter is that an analysis of all relevant biblical

---

[70] Leviticus 18:22 and 20:13, King James Version, 107 and 109.
[71] Romans 1:24–7, King James Version, 937–8.
[72] Genesis 19:1–11, King James Version, 11–12.
[73] 1 Samuel 18:3, King James Version, 264.
[74] 2 Samuel 1:26, King James Version, 278.
[75] 2 Samuel 1:17–27 read in its entirety is especially useful for understanding the context of the statement. See also Leviticus 18:22 condemning homosexuality and Genesis 19:1–38 for the story of the destruction of Sodom and Gomorrah, King James Version, 11–12.

passages provides no endorsement of homosexual relationships – on the contrary, homosexual acts are condemned in the strongest possible terms. But this is not to say that Bible-believing Christians have a warrant to hate or persecute gays. Christian attitudes toward gays should be tempered by the story of Jesus and the woman caught in the act of adultery. When her accusers brought her before Jesus, he responded with characteristic love and mercy that Christians are commanded to emulate:

> Teacher, they said, This woman has been caught in the very act of adultery. Now Moses in the Law commanded us that such [women offenders] shall be stoned to death. But what do You say [to do with her – what is your sentence]? This they said to try him, hoping they might find a charge to accuse him. But Jesus stooped down and wrote on the ground with his finger. However, when they persisted with their question, He raised Himself up and said, *Let him who is without sin among you be the first to throw a stone at her.* Then he bent down and went on writing on the ground with his finger. They listened to him, and then they began going out, conscience-stricken, one by one, the oldest down to the last one of them, till Jesus was let alone, with the woman standing there before Him in the court. When Jesus raised Himself up, He said to her, *Woman, where are your accusers? Has no man condemned you?* She answered, No one Lord! And Jesus said, *I do not condemn you either. Go on your way and from now on sin no more.*[76]

The pattern here – hate the sin but love the sinner – is the Christian formula for addressing not only homosexuality, but also every other human failing listed in the Bible. As indicated by Jesus' loving advice to the woman caught in adultery, it is a distortion of the Christian message to direct hatred and violence and secular intolerance against gays and lesbians as some Christian groups have done in the past. Just as there is now an awareness of having been on the wrong side of racism and anti-Semitism, Christian groups that preach hatred toward gays and lesbians are on the wrong side of a very critical issue. Christians are expected to emulate Jesus' example of love and solicitude toward fallen humanity, and nothing in the New Testament justifies vigorous opposition to legal protections designed to protect

---

[76] John 8:4–11, *The Amplified Bible* (Grand Rapids, Mich.: Zondervan Publishing, 1987), 963.

gays and lesbians from discrimination and physical and emotional abuse.

And there is also nothing in the Gospel message that would counsel Christians to have anything but compassion for those afflicted with the terrible disease of AIDS. Those who would see homosexuality as some kind of especially heinous sin, and AIDS as God's righteous judgment on that sin, have not only ignored Jesus' message of compassion and forgiveness, but have been highly selective in their singling out of sins to condemn. For in the New Testament there is not the slightest indication that homosexuality is any different than a host of other sins that are equally condemned, including drunkenness, adultery, and slanderous accusation. In 1 Corinthians 6:9, homosexuality is only one of a number of transgressions that God singles out for dire warnings. There is no hierarchy of sins in which some sins rank greater than others:

> Do you not know that the unrighteous *and* the wrongdoers will not inherit *or* have any share in the kingdom of God? Do not be deceived: neither the impure *and* immoral, nor idolaters, nor adulterers, nor those who participate in homosexuality. Nor cheats (swindlers and thieves), nor greedy graspers, nor drunkards, nor foulmouthed revilers *and* slanderers, nor extortioners *and* robbers will inherit *or* have any share in the kingdom of heaven.[77]

In recent years, most mainstream evangelicals have softened their message toward gays and lesbians, and now often welcome them into their churches, often in the hope of turning them from their former ways. Few invoke the Old Testament law of violent punishment. The situation is very different, however, with some of the more extreme Christian Identity and white nationalist groups. Gays and lesbians are often placed alongside African Americans, Jews, Hispanics, Native Americans, and Asians by such groups, as objects of contempt and scorn.[78]

White nationalists' condemnation of gays and lesbians is based on their belief that homosexual behavior contributes to disease, is immoral and unnatural, and adds nothing to the procreation of white children. They also believe that homosexuals tend to recruit young boys and

[77] 1 Corinthians 6: 9–10, *The Amplified Bible*, 1046.
[78] Deborah Able, *Hate Groups* (Berkeley Heights, N.J.: Enslow Publishers, 1995), 40–41.

initiate them into homosexual ways. Christian Identity members often claim that the AIDS virus is God's rightful judgment on both blacks and homosexuals, who are disproportionately affected by these afflictions. The high visibility of gay and lesbian demands for political and civil rights may have increased the levels of violence against them by members of these groups.

The most extremist members of the white nationalist movement view homosexuals as deserving of the death penalty, at least in the case of white homosexuals. These extremists are alarmed because the white birthrate is below replacement levels, while minority populations are rapidly growing. The spread of homosexuality among whites, they argue, will only make this situation worse. For similar reasons, they hate abortion doctors who perform abortions on white women, and see them, too, as deserving of death.

Who do white nationalists see as responsible for the growing acceptance of homosexuality in American culture? As is usual in their literature, it is the Jews who are portrayed as responsible for most of the country's ills, including the growth in acceptance of homosexuality. A widely read article distributed by the white supremacist National Vanguard Books charges: "The Jew-controlled entertainment media have taken the lead in persuading a whole generation that homosexuality is a normal and acceptable way of life."[79] In a similar vein, one outspoken Christian Identity member explained to a researcher that the Jews were perverting the true Christian message on homosexuality:

> Now, because of the lies of the Jews and the Judeo-Christianity, we even have homosexual churches – so-called Christian churches. There is *no* such thing as a homosexual Christian! There can't be. Look up the verses for yourself . . . that's what people ought to do anyway. God hates, loathes, and despises homosexuals. Woe unto you, sodomites, there is no place for you in the Kingdom of God.[80]

Needless to say, members of Christian Identity and white nationalist groups have never understood the true loving message of the Christian Gospels, nor the fact that the God revealed in Jesus Christ is a

---

[79] *Who Rules America? The Alien Grip on Our News and Entertainment Media Must Be Broken*, National Vanguard Books, Catalog no. 13. (Hillsboro, W.Va.: National Vanguard Books, 1991), 20, as cited in Dobratz and Shanks-Meile, 129.
[80] Ibid., 156.

God who has come not to condemn, but to save sinners – a category that includes us all. The hatred and vindictiveness that has been directed at homosexual people in the past – whether by mainstream Christians or more extremist groups – simply has no place in a religion espousing universal love and forgiveness.

DISCUSSION

A number of issues affect churches, synagogues, and mosques in contemporary America, including the proper treatment of poor people, homosexuals, and racial and ethnic minorities. "Although an overwhelming majority of Americans take a positive view of religion, less than a majority are seriously observant."[81] Gallup and Castelli have found "an 'ethics gap' between Americans expressed beliefs and the state of the society they shape. While religion is highly popular in America, it is to a large extent superficial; it does not change people's lives to the degree one would expect given their level of professed faith. Related to this is a 'knowledge gap' between Americans' stated faith and the lack of the most basic knowledge about that faith. Finally, there is a gap between 'believers' and 'belongers' with millions of Americans who are nominal Christians or Jews failing to participate in the congregational lives of their denominations."[82] What is positive, however, is the fact that Americans express a large amount of tolerance for a variety of mainstream religious denominations, including Judaism.[83]

It is the case that many people, including secular humanists, atheists, and libertarian nonbelievers, lead morally upright lives without religion as an active force in their lives. Moreover, some intellectuals have argued for a secular alternative that puts its faith in Constitutional patriotism as the most obvious solution to America's race problems, because it is seen as having a potential to foster an identity transcendent of racial and ethnic group differences.[84] American

---

[81] Ibid., 23.   [82] Gallup and Castelli, 21.

[83] Gertrude Himmelfarb, "Religion in the 2000 Election," *Public Interest* 143 (Spring 2001): 25–26.

[84] Jim Sleeper, "American National Identity in a Post-National Age," in Stanley Renshon, *One America?* (Washington, D.C.: Georgetown University Press, 2001). In addition, the following books provide interesting perspectives on these issues: Eldon Eisenach,

national identity has religious roots often ignored or downplayed by those advancing its principles as a secular alternative to a Judeo-Christian America.

It is the case that some ardent white nationalists have changed their attitudes toward people of other races because of epiphanies that have caused them to develop a natural appreciation of the inherent value of a human life. Fred Cochran, a former recruiter for the Aryan Nations, renounced his racist past after an Aryan official asked him to kill his infant son because the child was born with congenital birth defects.[85] Now an activist for racial reconciliation, Cochran's conversion shows that racial and ethnic group hatred can be unlearned through an unplanned and unlikely catalyst. Although it is not discussed in the article that I cite, a religious background may have created the values that eventually led to Cochran's embrace of humanity. I believe that the potential for religious experience and for life's little epiphanies to work in conjunction to promote greater racial and social harmony in American society is greater than we presently imagine.

PERSONAL REFLECTIONS ON RELIGION

My religious views have evolved significantly over the last few years. Once a devotee to New Age religions, I have become a born-again[86] Christian water-baptized by immersion in the name of Jesus Christ

The Next Religious Establishment: National Identity and Political Theology in Post-Protestant America (Lanham, Md.: Rowman and Littlefield, 2000); Michael Lind, The Next American Nation: The New Nationalism and the Fourth American Revolution (New York: Free Press, 1995); Richard Rorty, Achieving Our Country: Leftist Thought in Twentieth Century America (Cambridge, Mass.: Harvard University Press, 1998); Kenneth Heineman, God Is a Conservative: Religion, Politics and Morality in Contemporary America (New York: New York University Press, 1998).

[85] Floyd Cochran, interview. Unlike Mike, the insurance agent, who was raised in the South to hate blacks, Cochran grew up in northern New York where he learned the same lessons:

> I lived in an all-white community. I learned to fear black men, not because of personal experiences, but because of what I saw in the media, what I heard from my parents, what I heard from teachers, law enforcement agencies. I convinced myself that I couldn't find a job. . . . I simply didn't go out to look for work. [because] I became convinced, again, through the media, through politicians, through my family that there were no jobs for white males, because of affirmative action. So, I believed in those myths, I learned those myths, again, from the society I lived in.

[86] Matthew 7:13–14, King James Version, 5.

according to the dictates of Acts 2:38.[87] I believe that it is essential for Christian leaders to teach and use as their moral guide New Testament positions on issues such as race and social tolerance within the limits established by the Bible. I firmly believe that encouraging religious practice among adherents to Abrahamic religions rather than the mere profession of faith could have a positive impact on America by facilitating greater racial and social harmony among diverse peoples. But for the church to have a major influence on our increasingly diverse and changing cultural environment, religious leaders must first connect with God in relationships real enough to attract followers. In many ways, the church in America has been a dismal failure because it has promised much and often delivered little. Frequently, there is a sharp disjuncture between church doctrines, church policies, and biblical principles, causing confusion among believers. Hypocrisy and greed among religious leaders can be a faith-destroying encounter.

Finally, I find it disconcerting that the Bible seems to be under active attack in some divinity schools and seminaries across America, attacks that sometimes seem to go beyond deconstructionism and critical scholarly analysis. In my conversations with theologians at several universities, I have found that arguments about the validity of biblical accounts are almost never counterbalanced with data from scientific studies that provide new documentation for the historical and scientific accuracy of the Bible or with analyses by more conservative theologians. The Apostle Paul, perhaps anticipating the tenor of some of today's debates about the interpretation and authenticity of biblical doctrine, in 1 Corinthians 2: 12–15 discounts the opinions of scholarly experts:

> Now we have received, not the spirit of the world, but the spirit which is of God: that we might know the things that are freely given to us of God.
>
> Which things also we speak, not in the words of which man's wisdom Teacheth, but what the Holy Ghost teacheth: comparing spiritual things with spiritual.
>
> But the natural man received not the things of the spirit of God: for they are foolishness to him: neither can he know them because they are spiritually discerned.[88]

---

[87] Acts, 86–87.   [88] 1 Corinthians 2: 12–15, King James Version, 951.

Of course, not everyone believes in the authority of any part of the Hebrew or the Christian Bible or in the existence of a Supreme Being. Consequently, religion can never be a viable solution for intellectuals who believe that religion is nonsense for the weak-minded.

15

<hr>

CONCLUDING
OBSERVATIONS
AND POLICY
RECOMMENDATIONS

And the Lord answered me and said, Write the vision, and make it plain
upon tables, that he may run who readeth it. For the vision is yet for an
appointed time, but at the end it will speak, and not lie: though it tarry,
wait for it; because it will surely come, it will not tarry.

Habbakkuk 2: 2–3

We in America, I believe, are increasingly at risk of large-scale racial
conflict unprecedented in our nation's history, which is being driven by
the simultaneous convergence of a host of powerful social forces. These
forces include changing demographics, the continued existence of racial
preference policies, the rising expectations of ethnic minorities, the
continued existence of liberal immigration policies, growing concerns
about job losses associated with globalization, the demands for multiculturalism, and the Internet's ability to enable like-minded individuals
to identify each other and to share mutual concerns and strategies
for impacting the political system. This combination of factors, in
addition to others mentioned in Chapter 1, contributes to a social
dynamic that can serve only to nourish white racial consciousness and
white nationalism, the next logical stage for identity politics in America.
There now exists an emerging white interest that is parallel with, and
structurally akin to, a black and brown interest, which increasingly
sees itself in need of protection from public and private initiatives that
are said to favor minorities at the expense of more deserving whites.

Moreover, it is not only whites who are angry or feel resentful or
threatened. A part of the future discord will come from the rising
expectations and demands of racial and ethnic minorities, which are

sure to increase as minorities become a larger portion of the American population.

The ominous tone of this book may come as a surprise to those familiar with my past research. For more than a decade I have been an unapologetic optimist on race relations who has watched with great satisfaction as my once-controversial ideas on racial redistricting and racial representation – criticized by some as wishful thinking – have become widely accepted across the political spectrum. Actually, there is no contradiction – or abrupt change – between my previous position on race relations and the views I present here. I still believe that the majority of white Americans are morally good people who do not hate members of other races or ethnicities. But the same nonquantifiable intuitions about human behavior that led me almost ten years ago to argue the optimistic claim that black politicians can represent white voters, that white voters will support suitable black candidates, and that white politicians can effectively represent black voting interests now compel me to offer a cautious warning of the potentially dangerous waters ahead that threaten our common goal of an integrated and harmonious American society.

Insights drawn from my day-to-day interactions with Americans of different races and social classes have combined with my research and personal experiences to lead me to the conclusion that in the future it will be very difficult sailing for race relations in America. New challenges present themselves that must be faced squarely if the optimistic vision for the future of America's race relations is ever to be realized.

This final chapter consists of two distinct sets of recommendations. The first set is aimed at the improvement of American society overall and the creation of greater opportunities for disadvantaged and politically powerless citizens. The policy recommendations that I make here were developed to help address lingering inequalities in American society and to help spur a vigorous debate on issues of race, ethnicity, and public policy. Some of these recommendations, I know, will be dismissed by white conservatives as partaking of the same style of Great Society social activism that allegedly failed so miserably in the past. To such critics I can say only that not all forms of policy activism are doomed to failure and that we must try to do more in the future to help the most "truly disadvantaged" members of our society, especially when their continued distress threatens the peace and repose of the entire country.

The second set of recommendations is aimed specifically at African-American leaders and intellectuals, because I believe that they have a pivotal role to play if we are to avoid more serious racial strife in the future. Some of these recommendations may be controversial, and some blacks may criticize me for washing dirty linen in public. But I believe that the issues I raise here need a public airing, and that too many black leaders seem reluctant to acknowledge some of the very real problems that currently plague black communities, not all of which can be blamed on continuing white racism.

IDEAS FOR IMPROVING AMERICAN SOCIETY

(1) Honor America's tradition of free speech by opening up political discourse on college and university campuses, in the organs of the elite news media, and in the halls of legislative bodies to provide for the inclusion of unpopular ideas on race so that they can be evaluated in open forums by individuals on opposing sides where better data and more sophisticated arguments can carry the day.

Americans need to regain control over institutions of higher learning and to restore an environment where ideas on controversial racial topics can be expressed without fear of harm or retaliation. Individuals in the white rights and white nationalist movements such as Jared Taylor and Samuel Francis occasionally raise important and legitimate public policy issues that deserve a hearing in the marketplace of ideas, whether it be the *New York Times*, Harvard University Press, Princeton University, or other mainstream venues where the dominant orthodoxy often leads to the suppression of white nationalist and white conservative views on racial issues. Hopefully, a place can be found within the academy for the presentation of unpopular ideas in forums where civility will underline the terms of debate. It bears repeating that the best way to neutralize dangerous ideas is to expose them to competing ideas and alternative explanations, ones presented in open forums characterized by reasoned dialogue and debate.

Much of the data that white nationalists present cannot be dismissed out of hand, such as the abnormally high rates of black-on-white violent crime, illegitimacy, drug abuse, and AIDS infection. But the more dubious data cited by white nationalists, including, for instance, the alleged disparities in IQ scores, can easily be challenged by the studies of mainstream scholars who report a narrowing of the gap between whites and blacks and the effects of a host of environmental factors that can lower intelligence scores. White nationalist claims about greater rates of black alcoholism and nicotine addiction can also be shown to be based on inaccurate data.

America's universities and colleges need a clear standard and a clear distinction between what should constitute hate speech and what is merely offensive because we disagree with the speaker or the speaker's claims. Unfortunately, much of what gets labeled as hate speech and picketed on university campuses falls into the latter category. Consider, for example, the spring 2001 controversy surrounding an antireparations advertisement that *Frontpage Magazine* editor David Horowitz submitted to leading colleges and universities across the country in reaction to the idea that the U.S. government should make restitution for slavery and unpaid black labor. The advertisement, titled "Ten Reasons Why Reparations for Blacks Is a Bad Idea for Blacks – and Racist Too," created a firestorm at some colleges and universities where students disagreed vehemently about the claims of the advertisement and whether its message was racist or simply an unpopular truth (see Appendix D).[1]

As Figure 15.1 shows, much of the information in the first five planks can be easily verified through historical analysis, whereas the remaining five arguments are clearly debatable and seemed designed to evoke the kind of reaction that Horowitz – and Dinesh D'Souza before him – received from black students and administrators in campuses across America. According to Horowitz, of the seventy-three college newspapers that received the paid advertisement, forty-one rejected it outright. Additionally, a number of papers that did publish the advertisement later expressed regret for poor judgment.[2]

---

[1] For a look at the image and the text of this advertisement, see
http://www.frontpagemag.com/horowitznotepad/2001/hn01-03-01.htm; Pamela Ferdinand, "Free-Speech Debate Splits Liberal Brown: Anti-Reparations Ad at Center of the Controversy," *Washington Post*, March 21, 2001.

[2] "Censorship Score Card,"
http://www.frontpagemag.com/horowitznotepad/2001/colleges.htm.

Some African-American students have reported feeling deeply wounded by the advertisement and some have protested and interfered with speeches that Horowitz has given at their campuses.[3] Instead of protest, censorship, and charges of racism, a more appropriate reaction might be for universities to sponsor debates with the bevy of lawyers and intellectuals currently pushing the reparations claim. I suspect that Horowitz's position on the reparations movement is more widely shared across America than many imagine. One of the more constructive responses to the Horowitz ad came from the Stanford University Black Students Union, which published its own detailed response to the advertisement.[4]

In contrast to the constructive response of the Black Students Union at Stanford, at Brown University student newspapers featuring the advertisement were stolen by enraged students and the school administration made little effort to apprehend or punish the perpetrators. One white student complained in a online forum about "Third World ingrates and cry babies":

SLAVERY WAS THE BEST THING THAT EVER HAPPENED TO AMERICAN BLACKS
Otherwise they might still be in Africa infested with Aids instead of pretending to be princes and princesses here in the United States . . . If I, a White, non-Jewish male, stole some periodicals which I had a "racial" problem with, I would be charged with a "HATE CRIME." If a "person of color" says "nigger," that's okay – Woah . . . there's a problem – I'm so fed up with all of this "you owe me for slavery" – I don't own a nigger and wouldn't want one in my house. SO GET A LIFE or go back to the "Africa" that you all want the title of. Us "Proud Ignorant White" folks are getting sick of the NAACP/BET/UOWEME screaming for rights that only you have . . . If you didn't have these "nigger studies," you wouldn't pass.[5]

---

[3] Sean Werely, "Horowitz Horrified: Protesters Try to Disrupt Speech by Controversial Slavery Reparations Opponent," http://www.chicagoweeklynews.com/2001s/05.10/news/horowitz_protest.shtml.

[4] Stanford Black Students Union, "Ten Reasons Why You Shouldn't Be Fooled by David Horowitz's Ad – and Why It Is Racist Too," Stanford Daily, May 2, 2001, http://www.daily.stanford.edu/dailey/serlet/story?id=5609&section=opinions&date=05-02-2001.

[5] Examples of hate speech from the Brown Daily Herald's student online forum, http://www.browndailyherald.com/stories.cfm?s=0&=4468. The same website also presents the text of a faculty letter criticizing acting President Blumstein about the publication of the Horowitz ad and the university's response to the theft of the student newspapers.

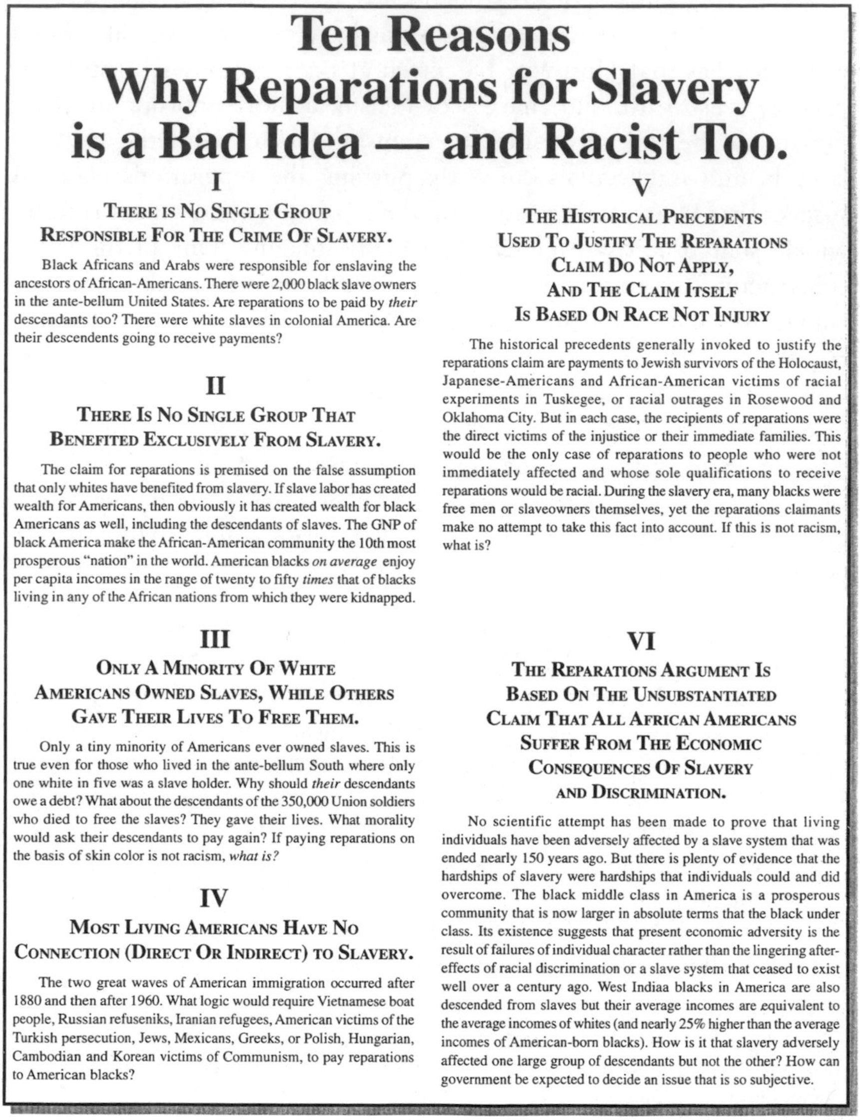

Ten Reasons Why Reparations for Slavery is a Bad Idea — and Racist Too.

I

There is No Single Group Responsible For The Crime Of Slavery.

Black Africans and Arabs were responsible for enslaving the ancestors of African-Americans. There were 2,000 black slave owners in the ante-bellum United States. Are reparations to be paid by *their* descendants too? There were white slaves in colonial America. Are their descendents going to receive payments?

II

There Is No Single Group That Benefited Exclusively From Slavery.

The claim for reparations is premised on the false assumption that only whites have benefited from slavery. If slave labor has created wealth for Americans, then obviously it has created wealth for black Americans as well, including the descendants of slaves. The GNP of black America make the African-American community the 10th most prosperous "nation" in the world. American blacks *on average* enjoy per capita incomes in the range of twenty to fifty *times* that of blacks living in any of the African nations from which they were kidnapped.

III

Only A Minority Of White Americans Owned Slaves, While Others Gave Their Lives To Free Them.

Only a tiny minority of Americans ever owned slaves. This is true even for those who lived in the ante-bellum South where only one white in five was a slave holder. Why should *their* descendants owe a debt? What about the descendants of the 350,000 Union soldiers who died to free the slaves? They gave their lives. What morality would ask their descendants to pay again? If paying reparations on the basis of skin color is not racism, *what is?*

IV

Most Living Americans Have No Connection (Direct Or Indirect) to Slavery.

The two great waves of American immigration occurred after 1880 and then after 1960. What logic would require Vietnamese boat people, Russian refuseniks, Iranian refugees, American victims of the Turkish persecution, Jews, Mexicans, Greeks, or Polish, Hungarian, Cambodian and Korean victims of Communism, to pay reparations to American blacks?

V

The Historical Precedents Used To Justify The Reparations Claim Do Not Apply, And The Claim Itself Is Based On Race Not Injury

The historical precedents generally invoked to justify the reparations claim are payments to Jewish survivors of the Holocaust, Japanese-Americans and African-American victims of racial experiments in Tuskegee, or racial outrages in Rosewood and Oklahoma City. But in each case, the recipients of reparations were the direct victims of the injustice or their immediate families. This would be the only case of reparations to people who were not immediately affected and whose sole qualifications to receive reparations would be racial. During the slavery era, many blacks were free men or slaveowners themselves, yet the reparations claimants make no attempt to take this fact into account. If this is not racism, what is?

VI

The Reparations Argument Is Based On The Unsubstantiated Claim That All African Americans Suffer From The Economic Consequences Of Slavery and Discrimination.

No scientific attempt has been made to prove that living individuals have been adversely affected by a slave system that was ended nearly 150 years ago. But there is plenty of evidence that the hardships of slavery were hardships that individuals could and did overcome. The black middle class in America is a prosperous community that is now larger in absolute terms that the black under class. Its existence suggests that present economic adversity is the result of failures of individual character rather than the lingering after-effects of racial discrimination or a slave system that ceased to exist well over a century ago. West Indiaa blacks in America are also descended from slaves but their average incomes are equivalent to the average incomes of whites (and nearly 25% higher than the average incomes of American-born blacks). How is it that slavery adversely affected one large group of descendants but not the other? How can government be expected to decide an issue that is so subjective.

Figure 15.1 Horowitz antireparations ad, 2001.

VII

The Reparations Claim Is One More Attempt To Turn African Americans Into Victims, It Sends A Damaging Message To The African-American Community And To Others

The renewed sense of grievance which is what the claim for reparations will inevitably create is not a constructive or helpful message for black leaders to send to their communities and to others. To focus the social passions of African Americans on what some other Americans may have done to their ancestors fifty or a hundred-and fifty years ago is to burden them with a crippling sense of victimhood. How are the millions of non-black refugees from tyranny and genocide who are now living in America going to receive these claims, moreover, except as demands for special treatment - and extravagant new handout that is only necessary because some blacks can't seem to locate the ladder of opportunity within reach of others, many of whom are less privileged than themselves?

VIII

Reparations To African Americans Have Already Been Paid

Since the passage of Civil Rights Acts and the advent of the Great Society in 1965, trillions of dollars in transfer payments have been made to African-Americans in the form of welfare benefits and racial preferences (in contracts, job placements and educational admissions) all under the rationale of readdressing historic racial grievances. It is said that reparations are necessary to achieve a healing between African Americans and other Americans. If trillion-dollar restitutions and a wholesale rewriting of American law (in order to accommodate racial preference) is not enough to achieve a "healing", *what is?*

IX

What About The Debt Blacks Owe To America?

Slavery existed for thousands of years before the Atlantic slave trade, and in all societies. But in the thousand years of slavery's existence, there never was an anti-slavery movement until white Anglo-Saxon Christians created one. If not for the anti-slavery beliefs and military power of white Englishmen and Americans, the slave trade would not have been brought to an end. If not for the sacrifices of white soldiers and a white American president who gave his life to sign the Emancipation Proclamation, blacks in American would *still* be slaves. If not for the dedication of Americans for all ethnicities and colors to a society based on the principle that all men are created equal, blacks in America would not enjoy the highest standard of living of blacks anywhere in the world, and indeed one of the highest standards of living of any people in the world. They would not enjoy the greatest freedoms and the most thoroughly protected individual rights anywhere. Where is the acknowledgment of black American and its leaders for *those* gifts?

X

The Reparations Claim Is A Separatist Idea That Sets African-Americans Against The Nation That Gave Them Freedom.

Blacks were here before the Mayflower. Who is more American that the descendants of African slaves? For the African-American community to isolate itself from America is to embark on a course whose implications are troubling. Yet the African-American community has had a long-running flirtation with spiritists, nationalists and the political left, who want African-Americans to be no part of American's social contract. African Americans should reject this temptation.

For all America's faults, African Americans have an enormous stake in this country and its heritage. It is this heritage that is really under attack by the reparations movement. The reparations claim is one more assault on America, conducted by racial separatists and the political left. It is an attack not only on white Americans, but on all Americans especially African Americans.

America's Africa-American citizens are the richest and most privileged black people alive, a bounty that is a direct result of the heritage that is under assault. The American idea needs the support of its African-American citizens. But African Americans also need the support of the American idea. For it is the American idea that led to the principles and created the institutions that have set African Americans and all of us free.

Racist rhetoric such as this is bound to proliferate when reasoned discussion is suppressed or discouraged.

(2) We need to address and acknowledge in appropriate venues any legitimate public policy concerns that white nationalists and white conservatives raise which governmental official and other elites presently ignore.

Some of the public policy concerns raised by white nationalists and white conservatives are shared by many ordinary Americans who would not consider themselves racists, ethnic nationalists, or even conservative. Such concerns include racial preferences, black-on-white crime, immigration policy, and racial double standards in the reporting of racial hate crimes. If American leaders seriously want to avoid a worsening of racial tension over the next several years, they must address each of these issues. Also in need of discussion is the combination of unfortunate conditions and circumstances disproportionately affecting black communities that greatly contribute to the negative perceptions that many white Americans hold of African Americans. High rates of such social ills as violent crime, single parenthood, illegitimacy, infant mortality, welfare dependency, and infectious diseases cause all African Americans to be tainted by negative stereotypes that are created by the behavioral choices of a minority of blacks.[6] These issues must be confronted honestly and constructive solutions sought to the many ills that disproportionately affect black communities.

(3) Abandon all racial and gender-based double standards, whether perpetuated by the media, by colleges and universities, by law enforcement agencies, or by individuals in positions of power.

Racial double standards are found in the reporting of black crime rates, in the public's tolerance of racial hate speech, in law enforcement's disparate treatment of criminal suspects and prisoners, and in the

[6] Patterson, 38.

handling of juvenile offenders. When it comes to the reporting of accurate data on the frequency and nature of black crime, the failure to widely publicize in the minority community the extent of African American deviance is harmful to racial minorities because it deprives them of the information that would help them better understand their predicament and the reasons why many whites and Asians are reluctant to live in minority-dominated neighborhoods. White nationalists accurately report that African Americans are responsible for an alarming proportion of the nation's violent crime, and many of the crimes they commit against whites and Asians would be labeled as racial hate crimes if similar standards were applied across races. White fear of violent crime from blacks is a rational fear supported by data showing that African Americans are far more likely than members of other racial groups to kill complete strangers.

Unacceptable racial double standards include liberties with speech that allow African Americans to verbally assault and slander whites with racial epithets and false charges without suffering any serious loss of respect or any financial or social damage in the public arena.[7] To give a few examples: During the 2000 elections the NAACP ran advertisements in Texas against presidential candidate George W. Bush that practically accused him of being an accomplice in the lynching death of James Byrd, Jr., and of being indifferent to racial hate crimes. Similarly, the Reverend Jesse Jackson campaigned for Al Gore by telling black voters that Bush's election would endanger black civil rights, and pro-Gore advertisements in New Jersey presented a picture of Bush superimposed on a Confederate flag.[8] Months earlier, Jackson inflamed passions by accusing white officials in Kokomo, Mississippi, of covering up a racial lynching after an African-American teenager, Raynard Johnson, was found hanged in his backyard. Two autopsies and a

---

[7] Larry Elder, an African-American journalist, has written some of the most compelling critiques of the criminal double standards and black racism that I have read. See "Double Criminal Standards," March 10, 2000,
http://www.frontpagemag.com/elder/leo3-13-oop.htm; "Black Racism," October 31, 2000, http://www.frontpagemag.com/elder/le10-31-oop.htm.

[8] Walter Williams, "Election 2000's Message,"
http://www.jewishworldreview.com/cols/williamso1oo1.asp; David Horowitz, "How to Deal with Racial Witch-Hunts of the Left,"
http://www.frontpagemag.com/horowitz/2001/hno2-26-01.htm.

review of the evidence by a world-renowned forensic expert hired by the family found no evidence of homicide; the medical examiner ruled suicide.[9]

Despite irresponsible claims of this nature on the part of black organizations and black leaders, rarely do those who make such charges suffer any permanent damage to their reputations. Many in fact do not even acknowledge their errors with appropriate apologies. And while there is a great reluctance by elites, both black and white, to condemn abhorrent behavior by African Americans, there is no loss of words for condemnation of anyone who dares to criticize the priorities and tactics of the major black organizations and individuals such as the NAACP and Jesse Jackson.

Unacceptable racial double standards also include the toleration of separate caucuses and clubs for racial and ethnic minorities, unless American society is ready to extend to race-conscious whites the same liberty to organize and separate themselves without risk to careers and academic standing. Presently, we have a generation of white youth on high school and college campuses who are confused by the double standards that make them racists when they question the status quo or seek to organize against racial preferences.[10]

One of the most serious racial double standards is readily evident in the different treatment of criminal suspects by law enforcement agents of all races who readily use violent and excessive force against unarmed black men, while negotiating with or nonfatally wounding white criminals who brandish deadly weapons. Whereas an unarmed Amadou Diallo was shot forty-one times outside his apartment door, a white man who was wounded in the leg by law enforcement officers was allowed to wave a gun outside the White House without any

---

[9] Earl O. Hutchinson, "Denial Is Holding Blacks Back,"
http://www.salon.com/news/feature/2000/08/03/denial/index.html; Donald V. Adderton, "Jesse Should 'Chill' Racial Rhetoric in Kokomo Death," Sun Herald Online, http://www.vh60009.vh6.infi.net/region/docs/don072200.htm; Kevin Sack, "U.S. Assures Jesse Jackson It Is Pursuing Death of Black Mississippi Youth," *New York Times on the Web*, July 13, 2000.

[10] David Duke and Jared Taylor have both complained bitterly about these double standards, and Duke has reported that they were a factor in his decision to advocate for white rights as a college student. Writing under the pseudonym of Thomas Jackson, Taylor expresses views that I believe that many whites share as he pontificates about the real racism emanating from the double standards; "What Is Racism?: Is Bigotry and Racism Just a White Thing?," http://www.stormfront.org/whitenat/racism.htm.

serious risk to his life.[11] Similarly, a suspended police officer in Nashville, Tennessee, was allowed to terrorize his girlfriend and fire "a personal pistol and a police shotgun numerous times, including taking aim at three officers and three civilians" in the open, while white police officers tarried with him for four hours before he surrendered.[12]

Past experiences with hundreds of unarmed minority men killed by police suggest that in most cases an African-American or Hispanic man who acted like the suspended Nashville cop would have been killed within minutes of brandishing a weapon. Law enforcement officials in the United States clearly exercise double standards when evaluating situations of danger and placing a cost on human life. Whereas armed or unarmed minority men are quickly killed rather than disarmed, subdued, or wounded, menacing white criminals are treated like family members gone astray. Moreover, cases like the beating and sodomizing of Haitian immigrant Abner Louima by white New York City policemen suggest that some men in uniform – both in the military and in various levels of law enforcement – hate racial minorities and use their authority to legally commit racial hate crimes under the guise of law enforcement.[13]

One other unacceptable racial double standard, most likely caused by high black crime rates, is the differing treatment of black children who commit violent crimes. Black children are far more likely than white children to be tried as adult offenders and sentenced to adult prisons.[14]

It would serve the interest of racial harmony for all American citizens to be held to the same standards for speech, news coverage,

---

[11] Deborah Feyerick, "Probe Underway into Death of New York Man, Fired upon 41 Times by Police," http:///www.cnn.com/us/9902/05/police.shooting/index.html; Bryan Robinson, "Officers Acquitted of All Charges in Diallo Shooting," http://www.courttv.com/national/diallo/022500_verdict_ctv.html; Marc Lacey and David Stout, "Armed Man Shot and Wounded Outside White House," www.nytimes.com/2001/02/07/national/07CND-WHITE.html.

[12] Leon Alligood, "Officer Surrenders, Charged After Standoff," www.tennessean.com, May 12, 2001.

[13] "Louima Verdict Sparks Disappointment, Relief, and Outrage," http://www.cnn.com/U.S.9906/08/louima.quotes/index.html; Doug Johnson, "Former Racist Reveals Ties to U.S. Military," *Denver Rocky Mountain News*, August 21, 2000.

[14] "Brazill Case Rekindles Debate on Juvenile Justice," May 18, 2001, http://www.cnn.com/2001/law/05/18/juvenile.crime.reut/index.html. A quote from the article reported, "In one study in Cook County, Illinois, 99 percent of the youth tried as adults were black or Hispanic. In another study of 2,584 cases in 18 jurisdictions, 82 percent of the juveniles tried as adults were minorities."

and treatment by law enforcement officials. There should be no exceptions. People should not be treated differently because of their race.

(4) End all racial preferences in employment and promotion situations.

Whatever benefits affirmative action may have conferred in the past – and it can be argued that they are sizable – it now seems undeniable that on balance current policies of racial preference are a negative force in American society, and that they threaten to undermine public support for those principles of racial integration and racial justice that so inspired the nation during the civil rights era of the 1950s and 1960s. It is of the utmost importance for policy planners and politicians to recognize that we are in a new situation today. As William Julius Wilson and others have pointed out, structural changes in the world economy are affecting competition for jobs and contributing to growing wage inequality throughout the American population. Many high-wage production jobs have gone overseas to Third World nations where goods are produced at a fraction of the cost as in America. At the same time, the federal government has reduced social welfare programs normally available for families in need. As a result, since the 1970s, working-class Americans of all races have faced ever greater uncertainty in their economic lives. Americans, Wilson notes, have begun "to worry about a number of factors including unemployment, job security, declining real wages, escalating medical and housing costs, the availability of affordable child care programs, the sharp decline in the quality of public education, and crime and drug trafficking in their neighborhoods."[15]

When the fears over these global economic shifts are combined with anxieties over the declining majority status of white Americans, with the continued resentment over the perceived arbitrariness and injustice of current affirmative action policies, and with public concern about the scope of both legal and illegal immigration, a set of circumstances is created that could cause large numbers of whites – and particularly the less affluent whites – to embrace the idea of a distinct white interest not being adequately represented by a govern-

[15] Wilson, *The Bridge over the Racial Divide*, 40.

ment that endorses racial preferences for blacks and newly arrived immigrants.[16]

Affirmative action policy needs a major revamping that will take into consideration the demographic changes that have occurred in the last twenty years and have dramatically reduced the percentage of whites in the population, while increasing the numbers of immigrants eligible for racial preferences. These immigrants increasingly compete against native-born Americans for educational, employment, and business opportunities. Moreover, the failure of affirmative action to reach the needs of the poorest Americans must be addressed, as well as the current practice of treating all minorities as similarly disadvantaged regardless of their family income and background. Unless the policy is modified in significant ways, affirmative action is likely to lead to increased conflict, not only between whites and people of color but between African Americans and Hispanics whose interests may be antithetical to one another.

(5) Provide public funds to ensure that all public school districts offer vocational training along with traditional academic programs so that students who do not intend to go on to college can graduate from high school with a marketable skill.

As a graduate student and mother of two school-aged boys, I lived in several different college towns and had many interactions, both positive and negative, with white-run school systems. What I found in each city was the all-too-familiar tracking of African-American students into low-level courses and a lack of vocational education for those minority youth who are not suited for college. My oldest son struggled through high school, and although it was clear that college was not a realistic option for him, he never had the opportunity to learn a marketable skill such as auto mechanics, bricklaying, barbering, or plumbing that would have enabled him to get a decent-paying job immediately after high school. Often I meet older beauticians and barbers in my travels who learned their skills while in high school, and many of them report that these options are no longer available at the schools they attended.

[16] Kaplan and Weinberg; Reich, 171–84; Wilson, 11–43.

(6) Invest public dollars such that all who seek to attend a community college are able to.

The community college route to higher education and personal advancement needs to become more widely known and available. In my own case attendance at a community college was decisive in pointing the way to a successful academic career. As a high school equivalency GED holder and a divorced mother, I found my own educational options quite limited, so I chose to attend a local community college, which opened up the opportunity that led to my subsequent degrees. A federal work-study job at Virginia Western Community College eventually led to a full-time salaried position working nights and weekends that I kept throughout my undergraduate years at nearby Roanoke College. Through such federal programs and the availability of the community college option, the American Dream became a reality for me. During my five-year affiliation with the community colleges, I met hundreds of ambitious men and women of different races whose two-year degrees opened the doors leading to a stable middle-class existence. We should invest more public funds in the community college system to allow more people to afford the expenses involved in this form of higher education.

(7) If racial preferences are to be retained, then remove from eligibility all immigrants.

There is no compelling reason, other than the self-interest of members of Congress, for foreign-born immigrants to gain preferences over native-born Americans when it comes to competition for jobs, loans, and university and college admissions. As Orlando Patterson has pointed out in a *New York Times* op-ed piece, immigrant Hispanics, who can be either white or black, compete for affirmative action benefits and contribute to the opposition that the policy receives from native-born white Americans.[17] African and Caribbean blacks admitted under affirmative action programs at colleges and universities have similarly diminished the opportunities for both white and black Americans and provoked understandable resentments. If race-based

[17] Orlando Patterson, "Race by the Numbers," *New York Times*, May 8, 2001.

affirmative action is retained, foreign-born immigrants to America should not be eligible.

The best solution, of course, would be to scrap race-based preferences entirely, and restructure affirmative action policies to give special consideration only to the socially and economically disadvantaged, where disadvantage is defined in a strictly race-neutral manner. The advantage of such a policy over our current policy can hardly be overstated. But if some form of race-conscious preferences is retained, those who have voluntarily emigrated to the United States and are no part of America's racial past have no right to special consideration.

(8) Protect racial and ethnic minorities from hidden discrimination by (a) instituting a system of monetary rewards for those who come forth to identify illegal discrimination in the organization for which they work, and (b) increasing the use and frequency of governmentally financed audit studies that seek to identify hidden discrimination by sending out pairs of comparably qualified individuals who apply for housing, loans, jobs, and entrance to competitive universities.

As suggested by the anecdote describing my insurance agent and his encounter with racism among his fellow white colleagues (Chapter 14), racial discrimination is alive and well in American society. But, as I have argued, affirmative action, aside from its perceived unfairness and its tendency to benefit the better-off, is not the most appropriate means for combating discrimination, since much of what happens in the real world is hidden from public view. A better way to address discrimination is to design an incentive structure that will encourage white Americans to identify and report the discrimination that they witness or are asked to participate in.

One possibility is to establish a national hotline and a monetary reward system for persons who provide anonymous tips about organizations that engage in discrimination or that instruct their employees to give disparate treatment to unpopular racial and political minorities. Just as white Americans concerned about racial justice sometimes infiltrate racial hate groups in order to be positioned to offer tips that might save lives, white Americans concerned about discrimination can join the battle against racism by scrutinizing the practices of the organizations and institutions with which they are affiliated.

Another possibility is to establish audit studies by government watchdog agencies that send out matched pairs of auditors to detect racial disparities in treatment. Such studies have been successfully used to detect job and housing discrimination, and they should be expanded to other agencies as well, such as college admissions and mortgage lending.

(9) Dramatically reduce the scale of current immigration and enforce more vigorously laws against hiring illegal aliens.

Any action to slow the pace of immigration will help low-skilled Americans currently being displaced by globalization and by competition from foreign-born workers willing to work longer hours for less pay. We should seriously consider the suggestion of Harvard labor economist George Borjas that America reduce its immigration to the levels of twenty-five years ago. Recent administrative decisions, however, suggest that the United States, pressured by large businesses looking for employees, is actively looking to increase immigration rather than reduce it. In addition, there seems to be a move to establish a new two-tiered system of visa processing that will further segregate potential immigrants into two distinct classes. On June 1, 2001, the Immigration and Naturalization Service (INS) implemented a new "premium processing service" whereby American businesses can pay an additional fee ($1,000) to have their visa applications for foreign workers adjudicated within fifteen business days.[18] In contrast, regular visa applications take anywhere from forty days to two years to be adjudicated. As a result, wealthy companies will be able to bypass the normal delay associated with visa applications. However, immigrants without wealthy backers are not so lucky. Indeed, the impact of this new system is likely to be further delays in processing standard visa applications and the eventual creation of a two-tiered system of immigrants, with those who can circumvent the system through their wealthy sponsors and those who must endure long waits, poor service, and uncertain processing conditions that are commonly associated with INS visa processing.

Another issue that needs to be addressed is illegal immigration and the penalties for willful violations of national laws. High-profile viola-

[18] See the INS website at www.ins.usdoj.gov for additional information.

tions suggest that the penalties for hiring and harboring illegal aliens need to be substantially increased if they are to serve as a deterrent.

(10) Politicians and media organizations should move away from the idea that minorities necessarily have a few recognized leaders who are sensitive to, and aware of, their needs and policy preferences; instead, they should explore alternative means of gathering data on the preferences of ordinary minority Americans who often are more reasonable and mainstream in their views than many of their self-appointed – or media-appointed – spokesmen.

The NAACP's campaign against the Confederate flag and in favor of racial preferences for Supreme Court clerks, together with its ongoing efforts to integrate white country clubs, are indications that something is seriously amiss in the reasoning and priorities of the black leadership class. While the NAACP pursues with vigor issues that are largely symbolic or that are of interest only to a minuscule number of the minority elite, other black leaders risk further alienation of white Americans by demanding reparations at a point in history when many whites have tired of racial preferences and have grown numb to accusations of racism. African Americans, now surpassed by less vociferous Hispanics in numbers, are hardly in a strong position to bargain with white America for much, given the high rates of black crime and the riotous attacks in recent years against white people and white and Asian-owned property. Instead of attacking the important issues of the day, which would involve heightening black awareness for the seriousness of black violations of many middle-class values and cultural norms – and of the consequences of such violations in terms of hampering full integration into mainstream society – African-American leaders, using a script from the 1960s, persist in a style of racial protest that is detrimental to the interests not only of blacks but of the nation as a whole.[19]

Policymakers concerned about black issues would do well to carry their message to ordinary black people, whose common-sense positions

---

[19] Walter Williams, "Black Politicians Fiddling Whilst Rome Burns," February 21, 2001, http://capitalismmagazine.com/2001/february/ww_black_pol.htm; Maria Elena Kennedy, "Black Group Says Jesse Jackson Does Not Represent Them," CNNNEWS.com, January 16, 2001.

on the issues of the day are a welcome alternative to the demands of racial provocateurs who are unwittingly helping white nationalists destroy the nation's fiber. The following message posted on a black website by a man named Wyatt offers good practical advice to African Americans tired of the status quo:

> We should not insist on having black or white leaders. We should have leaders of all races, but as Americans who stand on principles of human and civil rights. For me as a black man, I do not point to my leaders based on a darken hue of skin, but rather those women and men who espouse my interests and beliefs. The absurd idea that someone like, say, Randall Robinson would be a leader for me, because we are both black is crazy. He speaks of reparations, but I think reparations are ludicrous. I don't want reparations for slavery, what I want is black people being responsible for themselves in this society via working hard, cleaning their neighborhoods, fighting for safe schools, having moral lives, taking care of the children they bring into this world.[20]

(11) Replace the earned income credit with a direct monthly wage subsidy that supplements the salaries of the working poor by guaranteeing a living wage throughout the work year.

Currently, the government's biggest program for helping the working poor is the earned income credit, which reduces a person's taxes owed to the IRS in a given year. The problem is that this one-time credit provides nothing for people struggling from day to day who work at low-wage jobs and often do not earn enough money to pay the monthly rent. A direct monthly subsidy to the working poor designed to guarantee a minimum standard of living might encourage more people to work. Furthermore, allowing some of the working poor to survive above a subsistence level might reduce the frequency of certain types of crimes (such as shoplifting, prostitution, and low-level drug dealing). Extra dollars spread throughout the calendar year could make a significant difference for many people in the form of helping them procure more affordable housing and adequate food.

---

[20] Wyatt, posting on "Blacktalk" home page, December 7, 2000, http://207.201.145.199/blackleadership/-disc1/00000725.htm.

(12) Establish financial partnerships between car dealers (new and used) and governmental agencies that would allow the working poor to tap into loans and grants for automobiles that can provide them with dependable transportation.

Drawing on the experiences of family members still mired in southern poverty, I know that a working car is essential to the ability of most poor people to procure and hold jobs. Until I financed an automobile for a niece of mine, she regularly paid $12 a day in taxicab fares for transportation to her job at Kentucky Fried Chicken, where she earned $6 an hour. Other relatives and poor people that I have known have been fired or have had to quit their jobs because of a dilapidated car that broke down and was too expensive to repair. An investment in stable transportation for the working poor would reduce welfare rolls and would give individuals more dignity and more control over their lives. It could also help boost lagging automobile sales and perhaps create more jobs in the auto industry. Alternatively, governments might consider higher subsidies for public transportation systems geared toward the work schedules of major employers.

(13) Establish more humane guidelines for collecting child support from the working poor.

Often judges establish high child-support payments for uneducated, low-skill men with bleak employment options whose jobs barely pay at the subsistence level. Although as a woman I applaud the efforts to collect from deadbeat fathers, I believe that state and federal legislation has gone too far, since it often allows no flexibility for individual circumstances. Several of my brothers have had children out of wedlock by different mothers. None of these men has a high school education or a marketable job skill that would enable them to secure employment much above the minimum wage. One brother had child support payments for five illegitimate children from his teenage indiscretions deducted from his wages, which left him with take-home pay of less than $25 a week. His reaction, like that of many inner-city men, was to sell drugs to make up the difference. Another brother, who has repeatedly spent time in jail for petty offenses, had seemingly begun the process of turning his life around by getting a low-wage job at a cafeteria. Within weeks he was ordered to pay child support of $300 a month for his one son, which left him financially unable to afford a car or an apartment. He soon quit his job and within two months was incarcerated again.

In each of these cases, I believe that the unreasonably high child support payments made crime more tempting and profitable than work. High child support payments means that not enough money is left to satisfy current economic needs or to sustain the cost of raising any additional children who may be born within a marriage. Society ends up paying for the cost of the incarceration, and the unwed mother and child are worse off than they would have been if the incentive structure were different. Although I am drawing on family experiences, I know that the same issues and choices confront many other poor Americans from dysfunctional homes. Surely, our government can find a more humane means of dealing with the problem of child support than penalizing men who live at the margins of society because of low education and low skills. In some cases determinations of paternity are made without the benefit of DNA testing in situations in which uneducated and passive men waive or fail to exercise their rights to challenge the claims of the mothers of children who have several different fathers within one family.

(14) Provide audit studies of state-run social welfare agencies and monitor more closely the disbursement of funds and the prevalence of discrimination among caseworkers who provide services to uneducated and dependent individuals.

Whenever I wish to know how the welfare system is treating people, I ask my older sister Maxine, whose IQ scores placed her in the genius category and made her the talk of the predominately black school that we attended for the first five years of grade school. Like myself, Maxine dropped out of school at around the eighth grade and eventually married and divorced the father of her five children. She has been on welfare for two decades, nourishing a dream of starting a day care center for working mothers. Until the 1996 welfare reform legislation that ended the Aid to Families with Dependent Children program, she was secure with the knowledge that as long as she was the primary caretaker for one of her grandchildren and our aged mother, she would not be asked to work. Maxine has found herself dropped from the assistance rolls about every three months, asked to recertify, and forced to deal with surly workers who lost paperwork on a regular basis, cut benefits sometimes without notice, and refused to return phone calls. According to her assessment, which I have every reason to trust, the system is a mess and the caseworkers are not providing individuals with the assistance for which they qualify under current state and federal guidelines.

Although states are happy to report that welfare rolls have been drastically reduced, some individuals like Maxine are suffering abuse at the hands of poorly trained and poorly supervised social workers. Although Maxine is assertive and intelligent, years of fighting the system have worn her down. Because many welfare recipients lack the social and intellectual skills needed to demand their legal rights and because the system allows social workers much discretion, there is opportunity for abuse. It makes good political sense for oversight agencies to send in testers to conduct audit studies designed to ensure that monies are being distributed according to existing laws to all eligible potential recipients and to ensure that racial and ethnic discrimination is not a factor in the disbursement of funds. It also makes sense for agencies to survey recipients and interview articulate individuals such as Maxine, who can describe their experiences with a system that is supposedly designed to help individuals in need.

WHAT BLACK LEADERS CAN AND SHOULD DO TO HELP REDUCE RACIAL HATRED AND ANIMOSITY

The previous section focused on policy recommendations of a general nature, many of which involve actions on the part of government. In this section I address my recommendation to the black leadership class, that is, to the black politicians, preachers, civil rights leaders, doctors, university professors, entertainers, and others whose influence is so great in the black community. The first recommendation I make is perhaps the most important:

(1) Make the reduction of the black crime rate America's number one issue.

In his book *Slouching Towards Gomorrah*, former Yale University law professor Robert Bork underlines the central importance of physical safety as the *sine qua non* of a decent society:

> When physical safety becomes a major problem even for the middle classes, we must of necessity become a heavily policed, authoritarian society, a society in which middle classes live in gated and walled communities and make their places of work hardened targets.... As the killing and drugs spread to white neighborhoods and suburbs, as they are now doing, the response will be far more repressive. Both the fear of crime and the escalating harshness of the response to it will sharply reduce America's freedom of movement and peace of mind.[21]

The failure of a united black leadership to address such a central issue as black crime allows white nationalists and white conservatives to exploit the crime issue in order to polarize the races. It is important that black leaders acknowledge the legitimacy of white fears of black criminality and that they abandon the racial double standard that permits them to ignore heinous black-on-white and black-on-Asian crimes at the same time that they vigorously denounce white crimes perpetrated against blacks. Reno Wolfe of the National Association for the Advancement of White People told our interviewer that a few African Americans have joined his organization because of their dislike of such racial double standards. I have no reason to doubt Wolfe's truthfulness about this claim.

It is crucial for the future of American race relations for the black crime rate to be reduced to the point that African Americans are not seriously overrepresented among the nation's criminals. A group that constitutes less than 13 percent of the population should not be responsible for committing almost 50 percent of violent crimes. As it stands now, African-American criminals are a menace to themselves and a menace to the rest of society. Until the black crime rate is reduced so that it more closely approximates the rate of other groups, African Americans can expect racial profiling and rough police handling, as well as a more general avoidance by whites and Asians.

Most analysts agree that American crime rates have dropped in recent years. A combination of factors account for the drop, including

[21] Bork, 170.

a reduction in number of young males in the age group most likely to commit violent crimes and high black imprisonment rates, which reached record numbers during the Clinton administration. However, the nation is about to experience a spurt of young people in the population of the age groups that commit the most crimes, and thus can expect more trouble in the future. A report of the Council on Crime concluded that "recent drops in serious crime are but a lull before the coming crime storm," and that "each generation of crime-prone boys is several times more dangerous than the one before, and that over 80 percent of the most serious and frequent offenders escape detection and arrest."[22]

The overrepresentation of African-American males in the offender categories highlights the critical need for black political and religious leaders to make sure that they take their share of the responsibility for making sure that crime reduction is the number-one priority of African Americans. A serious effort to address the issue would involve expanded partnerships between churches and organizations such as the NAACP, the Urban League, and the Congressional Black Caucus, in which leaders would take the initiative to heighten black awareness of the extent of the problem and how its existence contributes to racial profiling and the rough handling of law-abiding African Americans.

Any serious discussion about strategies for reducing the black crime rate must include a recognition that its unabated continuation is sure to lead to the institution of repressive governmental measures. Author ities have already discussed serious policy proposals to use the National Guard and the army to maintain domestic security in crime-ridden areas of the country.[23] Any serious crackdown on crime is going to have a ripple effect on African Americans of all social classes much more serious than the inconvenience of racial profiling. Unabated crime could mean that the mechanisms of the state come down hard against African Americans and other groups prone to high crime rates.

One of the goals of Jared Taylor's New Century Foundation is to heighten the awareness of white Americans to their increased vulnerability to black-on-white hate crimes. Most murders occur between acquaintances, but 20 percent of homicides between strangers are now black-on-white encounters, contrasted with a white-on-black rate of

[22] "The State of Violent Crime in America," 55.   [23] Bork, 170.

just 3 percent.[24] According to the Southern Poverty Law Center, black-on-white hate crimes soared during the 1990s. Increases in black-on-white hate crimes can only have a poisonous effect on race relations in America. One can well imagine under such circumstances a kind of racial polarization where white nationalist spokesmen square off with their black counterparts – a Lisa Turner, for instance, versus Sister Souljah ("If black people kill black people every day, why not have a week to kill white people?") – in a contest for who can be the most racially offensive and incendiary.

(2) Stop treating acts of riotous behavior on the part of African Americans as opportunities to press for governmental largesse (particularly when that largesse mainly benefits the minority middle class).

The first five months of 2001 saw two significant urban uprisings which underlined racial tensions in the United States: the "Fat Tuesday" violence in Seattle and the riots in Cincinnati following the police shooting of an unarmed African-American male teenager. Both instances highlighted young black people assaulting other city residents and damaging property, sometimes with an explicitly racial motivation. In Seattle, many television and newspaper pictures revealed young black people assaulting white people in the crowd.[25] In Cincinnati, rioters targeted a "white girl" who turned out to be an albino African American, Roslyn Jones.[26] Jones was assaulted in the head with a brick and her car was damaged by rocks before rioters realized that she was black.[27] Later, she exhibited deep pain and disappointment at the racial nature of the attack: "It hurts. My own people couldn't even recognize me. They didn't even look long enough to see. The first piece of white skin they saw, they hit it."[28]

Events like those in Seattle and Cincinnati not only underscore the simmering potential for highly destructive racial violence in the United

---

[24] "Homicide Trends in the U.S.," http://www.ojp.usdoj.gov/bjs/homicide/race.htm; "Blacks Experience the Highest Rates of Violent Crime," http://www.ojp.usdoj.gov/bjs/glance/race.htm.

[25] Ian Ith, "Leaders: Fat Tuesday about Crime, Not Race," www.seattletimes.com, March 3, 2001.

[26] Dan Horn, "Civility Turned to Anarchy: How It Happened," *Cincinnati Enquirer*, April 16, 2001, p. 7.

[27] Ibid., 8.   [28] Ibid.

States, but they also create perverse incentives for black leaders to condone this type of behavior in order to extract financial concessions from city leaders. Using the potential for riotous behavior as a negotiating tool with the white power structure may have been an effective strategy in the 1960s, particularly in the development of Great Society poverty programs and affirmative action policies, but today it is a strategy that mostly benefits black leaders themselves and black middle-class businesspeople. Typically, following a racially charged urban disturbance, high-profile black leaders such as Jesse Jackson, Al Sharpton, or Kweisi Mfume flock to the scene and claim outrage at some white racist behavior that necessarily provoked the uprising. They then use the attention of the incident to negotiate with city leaders for commitments to improving minority life in that city. These commitments usually take a financial form, ostensibly to improve the lives of those who were victims of the disturbance. Yet, too often, this money is funneled to contracts and projects that end up benefiting only the minority middle class and not the inner-city residents who need it the most. Thus, black leaders gain exposure and publicity, minority middle-class businesspeople gain profits, and the victims of urban racial violence gain nothing but damaged property and empty promises.

(3) End all discussions and all demands for racial reparations for black slavery, since the continued presentation of this issue alienates potential allies of African Americans and contributes to a worsening racial climate, given white America's long expressed anger at racial preference programs.

While monetary compensation is surely due for actual losses associated with documented racial violence against blacks in places such as Tulsa, Oklahoma, and Rosewood, Florida, it is much harder to justify a compensation for the injustice of slavery. While condemning the inhumanity of slavery, many Americans believe that blacks in the United States are far better off than they would have been had they remained in African countries.[29] Likewise, some white Americans consider a whole

[29] One African-American proponent of this view is journalist Keith Richburg, the author of *Out of America: A Black Man Confronts Africa* (New York: Basic Books, 1997). Similar views were expressed two generations ago by the black writer Zora Neale Hurston, a central figure in the Harlem Renaissance.

generation of affirmative action and social welfare programs as a more than sufficient form of reparations.

What white liberals are afraid to tell African Americans is that the timing of black demands for racial reparations could not be worse, given lingering frustration among whites over racial preferences and their perceived unfairness. What many whites would like to say and what many African Americans can never admit is that perhaps blacks have been blessed by being a member of a nation that, despite all egregious flaws and shortcomings, has attained in recent years a higher level of justice, prosperity, and security for all its people, including its non-white citizens, than most other nations of the world, including virtually all African, Mideastern, and Southern Asian nations.

This great "irony of history," as the Christian theologian Reinhold Niebuhr might call it, extends to Africans in Africa as well. Given conditions in most African countries, the sale and transport of black slaves to America has all the hallmarks of what an older interpretive tradition called providence. We could draw a parallel here between the experiences of American blacks and the 400-year bondage and redemption of the Israelites in Egypt that starts with the story of Joseph being sold into slavery as part of God's divine plan to save the Israelites during a period of prolonged famine (Genesis 37). Joseph becomes a powerful leader in the Egyptian government. Years later, when he reveals his identity to the brothers who unjustly sold him into slavery, he shows true compassion for them and recognition of an underlying divine plan in which he and his brothers were merely pawns in a larger scheme.

> Now therefore be not grieved, nor angry with yourselves, that ye sold me hither: for God did send me before you to preserve life.
>
> For these two years *hath* the famine been in the land: and yet there are five years, in which there *shall* neither be eating nor harvest.
>
> And God sent me before you to preserve you a posterity in the earth, and to save your lives by great deliverance. So now it *was* not you *that* sent me hither, but God: and he hath made me a father to Pharaoh, and the lord of all his house, and a ruler throughout all the land of Egypt.[30]

Using their influence in America, black religious and political leaders are positioned to help their African brethren similar to the manner in

[30] Genesis 45:5–8, King James Version, 33.

which Joseph was able to help the starving Israelites. Whatever the African continent is today, it would be in much worse condition if there were no African Americans influential and powerful enough to help their starving brethren – many the descendents of those who sold their ancestors into slavery – in the land of their origin.

(4) Highlight the considerable progress that African Americans have made and continue to make in integrating themselves more fully into mainstream American society.

Black leaders often use the pathetic conditions in urban communities to argue for more racial preferences or for increased spending for social welfare programs. According to the standard narrative of black leaders, nothing much has changed in the circumstances of African Americans. Racism in America is worse than ever before. As this book has shown, hidden and growing racism is a problem for American society. But it is one that black leaders have themselves contributed to by their poor decisions about their allocation of time and resources. Black leaders, for example, have expended enormous social and political capital over largely symbolic issues such as the removal of the Confederate flag, reparations, and the spirited defense of black criminals, which has helped to undermine respect for their authority. Some black leaders routinely slander and malign whites for suspected crimes and affronts for which there is little evidence; for example, Steven Pagones, a white prosecutor in New York, sued Al Sharpton for libel and won a judgment for $65,000 after Sharpton falsely accused him of being involved in the rape of Tawana Brawley.[31] Among African-American leaders there is a reluctance to condemn the abhorrent behavior of other blacks, but no loss of words of condemnation and reproach for blacks who dare criticize the group.

Too often African-American leaders have been perceived by the general public as a group with constant complaints and constant demands about white racism while they themselves openly express virulent racism against members of other groups. As Journalist David Shipler writes:

---

[31] Profile of Al Sharpton as "The Power Broker," www.cbsnews.com.

African Americans do not hear themselves parroting age-old slanders against Jews and others. They do not hear themselves echoing the pernicious logic, under which they themselves have suffered, that projects one individual's faults onto an entire group. Negative imagery travels in many directions across America's ethnic lines; no group has a monopoly on malice. Unkind caricatures of African-Americans flourish among Latinos, Asians, and Jews just as they do among the majority Christian white population. And in return, such visible blacks as Louis Farrakhan, Al Sharpton, and Leonard Jeffries find license to express their prejudices acerbically, souring the atmosphere of debate and making black America appear more bigoted than it is.[32]

Many black leaders and intellectuals have convinced themselves that only whites can be racist because racism needs power to wreak harm on intended victims. Constantly blaming whites for every conceivable problem in African-American communities is a possible contributory factor for increasing black resentment and hatred of white Americans, which is manifested in black-on-white crime rates. If so, the failure to recognize and strongly condemn black racism is a form of irresponsible behavior that impedes the intellectual and cultural development of young African Americans, who seek guidance as they struggle for their own identities, just like the white youth that white nationalists have sought to recruit. Too often we forget that poor black youth experience the same adolescent confusion as young whites, and it is much less likely that there will be responsible adults around to encourage healthy, nonviolent responses to normal frustrations.

There is an additional danger here when black leaders constantly accuse whites of racism, accent the negative, and fail to acknowledge the great opportunities for personal advancement that have opened up to blacks over the past four decades. As Seymour Martin Lipset has pointed out, the failure of black leaders to acknowledge the progress that African Americans have made has led some whites to conclude that there must be something "inherent in the black situation which prevents them from getting ahead."[33] By not acknowledging the genuine progress blacks have made, black leaders play into the hands

---

[32] David K. Shipler, *A Country of Strangers: Black and Whites in America* (New York: Alfred A. Knopf, 1997), 460–1.
[33] Lipset, 132.

of those white nationalists who believe in black inferiority and black incapacity to improve themselves.

(5) Start condemning and stop contributing to the scandalously high black illegitimacy rate, and address the disproportionately high rate of AIDS and other diseases among the black population.

Some 70 percent of African-American children are born out of wedlock, and studies I cited in the previous chapter discuss the serious impact of being raised in a single-parent household on the life chances of children in comparison to those reared in two-parent families. Whether we look at drug addiction, teen pregnancy, criminal behavior, unemployment, or poor school performance, the probability of each of these social ills is greatly enhanced when children are raised in a family without a father. There is every indication that the high black crime rate – the most serious problem confronting black communities – is intimately intertwined with the high illegitimacy rate.

The Reverend Jesse Jackson has fathered one child out of wedlock with a highly educated employee of his, and NAACP president Kweisi Mfume fathered five children out of wedlock as a young man. Both of these men should know from experience the serious harm inflicted on the children of these arrangements even if the absentee father pays his child support. Roger Clegg of the Center for Equal Opportunity appeared on the CNN television program *Both Sides with Jesse Jackson* on September 17, 2000, and asked Jackson directly about the high correlation between illegitimacy and crime. Jackson, who was by then himself paying child support for an illegitimate daughter, told Clegg that illegitimacy had nothing to do with criminal justice disparities that show black youth overrepresented among criminal offenders.[34] With the exception of some ministers, mostly located in the inner city, the black family arrangement causes little concern. One wonders whether black leaders really believe the nonsense they propagate about "no real harm" in growing up in a single-parent family, or whether they are simply too embarrassed to acknowledge a painful truth.

---

[34] Roger Clegg, "Disqualifying Jesse: His Illegitimacy Problem," http://www.nationalreview.com/comment/comment012901.g.shtml.

Some successes in changing the behaviors of inner-city youths have come from efforts such as the Big Brother/Big Sister mentoring programs initiated by a nonprofit foundation called Public/Private Ventures, and from efforts to empower and mobilize black churches to fight pathologies such as drug abuse, violent crime, and high rates of illegitimacy through a combination of resources that include voluntary efforts, prayers, and private donations.[35] These successes, however, have largely been overshadowed by the many stories of crime that seem to dominate public discussion of inner-city life.

In addition to addressing the high rates of illegitimacy within the black community, black leaders also need to be more rigorous in addressing the many serious health concerns that affect blacks throughout the United States, especially AIDS. According to the Harvard University AIDS Institute, AIDS is already the leading cause of death among African Americans under age fifty-five.[36] Furthermore, nearly half of all AIDS cases in the United States are found in African Americans, and every day nearly ninety African Americans are diagnosed with HIV.[37] The need to address the onslaught of this disease within the African-American community is urgent, and black leaders must make this more of a priority in their work around the country.

What *New York Times* columnist Bob Herbert has recently said about AIDS transmission and sexual irresponsibility among black males can be said equally well about black illegitimacy and a host of other problems afflicting black communities:

> I am waiting for the so-called leaders of the black community – the politicians, the heads of civil rights organizations, the preachers – to step forward and say, in thundering tones, that it's time to bring an end to the relentlessly self-destructive behavior that has wrecked so many African American families and caused so much suffering. . . . A new and intense and creative effort – led by black Americans – will be required to reclaim the lives of the thousands upon thousands of young blacks succumbing to the ravages of destructive sexual behavior, drug use and (in so many

---

[35] Bork provides a description of the more successful programs in his book *Slouching Towards Gomorrah*, 163–5.

[36] Harvard University AIDS Institute, http://www.hsph.harvard.edu/hai/index.html.

[37] Ibid.

of these cases) the emotional pain of self-loathing, depression and despair. If ever there was a need for tough love, this is it.[38]

(6) Use African Americans' religious faith as a tool to change behavior.

As mentioned in the previous chapter, African Americans are in many ways America's most religious people, but this has not caused them to be morally better than other Americans on a host of indicators. Perhaps the reason for this is the poor examples of moral behavior set by their most revered leaders such as Dr. Martin Luther King, Jr., and the Reverend Jesse Jackson, who both had problems with marital infidelity. What is needed is a cadre of religious leaders willing not just to teach but to abide by the moral principles of biblical Christianity, principles which strongly condemn many types of behavior that have almost been normalized in many black communities.

(7) Sponsor regular informational sessions in minority communities where lawyers and judges advise convicted felons of the steps necessary to apply for pardons and the expungement of convictions that have resulted in disenfranchisement.

Forty-six states and the District of Columbia disenfranchise convicted felons while they are in prison; additionally, thirty-two of those states extend disenfranchisement to the period that a convicted felon is out on parole, and twenty-nine states extend disenfranchisement to convicted felons on probation.[39] Moreover, ten states disenfranchise convicted felons for life.[40] The impact of state felony disenfranchisement laws on African Americans is staggering. Thirteen percent of all adult black men – 1.4 million – are disenfranchised due to a felony conviction.[41] In eight states, 20 percent to 31 percent of the black men in

---

[38] Bob Herbert, "In America; A Black AIDS Epidemic," *New York Times*, June 4, 2001, p. A17.

[39] "Losing the Vote: The Impact of Felony Disenfranchisement Laws in the United States," Report of the Sentencing Project and Human Rights Watch, October 1998.

[40] Ibid. Additionally, two states disenfranchise for life those convicted of a second felony, and two other states permanently disenfranchise felons convicted prior to a specific date.

[41] Ibid.

those states are permanently disenfranchised, and in fifteen other states, at least 10 percent of the black male population is currently disenfranchised.[42]

Regaining the right to vote in those states which do not permanently disenfranchise convicted felons is generally a convoluted process that requires political or financial resources that most ex-felons, especially African-American males, do not have. To restore an ex-felon's right to vote, some states require an order from the governor, while others require an order from a parole or pardons board; in Mississippi, an ex-felon must get either an executive order or a bill passed by two-thirds of each house of the state legislature and signed by the governor in order to reclaim the right to vote.[43] Because ex-felons are not routinely informed about what is required for them to regain the right to vote, many of them incorrectly believe that they can never vote again.[44] Sponsoring informational sessions in minority communities where many ex-felons live would clear up this misconception and help many ex-felons reclaim their right to vote. In turn, this would provide ex-felons with a greater sense of connection to the larger community, which would aid their rehabilitation and reintegration into society; moreover, it would give them, and the minority community, a stronger political voice that could effectuate meaningful political changes.

(8) Institute national training programs for minority youth to instruct them on how to comport themselves in the event of a police stop so as to minimize the likelihood of a violent encounter by ensuring that no sudden moves take place and that cooperation ensues rather than cursing and threats.

The frequency of racial profiling that offends, inconveniences, and occasionally endangers the lives of hundreds of thousands of African Americans is a direct response to greater rates of criminality among blacks. Until the reduction in the black crime rate occurs, black leaders should consider holding training seminars in which blacks are taught how to conduct themselves when detained by law enforcement officials. Police departments could be invited to send officers into local communities, high schools, and churches to advise minorities of the

[42] Ibid.   [43] Ibid.   [44] Ibid.

steps to take to avoid a violent confrontation. As someone who has raised two teenage boys, I know the fear that every black mother feels when her teenage sons are stopped and questioned by the police. Properly conducted training programs can greatly alleviate fear by teaching young blacks how to act in the presence of police and other law enforcement officials.

(9) Black leaders should strategically read the books, articles, and web pages of the group's political enemies.

Martin Luther King, Jr., used to advise his associates in the Southern Christian Leadership Conference that they would do well sometimes to listen carefully to the criticisms of blacks made by their white racist detractors. Even prejudiced whites who hated blacks, he believed, might have valid observations about black problems that black leaders could find valuable. Today, African Americans would do well to read the books and articles written by white conservatives and white nationalists, as they point to issues and behaviors that cause other races to dislike and eye blacks suspiciously. For instance, a revisionist reading of Dinesh D'Souza's *The End of Racism* might focus on the value of his exposing to African Americans what other racial and ethnic groups think about the behaviors of black people and black leaders. D'Souza's book also performed an important public service for African Americans by reporting by name and by institutional affiliation some of the leading intellectuals in the white nationalist movement who attended an *American Renaissance* conference and had previously tried to disguise themselves as mainstream conservatives. Likewise, African Americans should read books like Jared Taylor's *Paved with Good Intentions: The Failure of Race Relations in Contemporary America* and log onto David Duke's web page. By studying the literature of one's opponents, one can keep abreast of what the enemy is planning and learn how to more effectively combat the harmful conclusions to which their reasoning often leads. White nationalists seem to follow a similar strategy with regard to black rivals and opponents. (Taylor, for instance, readily acknowledges reading black newspapers and black journals, and he expresses admiration for black people's degree of racial consciousness and racial organization.)

CONCLUSION

By now I hope readers of this book are convinced of the need to take white nationalism and the other challenges to American society highlighted in these pages as seriously as they would the diagnosis of cancer. Virulent racism is a malignancy that, left unchecked, will spread to healthy parts of American society where progress in race relations continues to occur. While there remain reasons for optimism in race relations discussed in the remedies section and in Chapter 7, there is much work to be done by people in positions of power and influence who too often block the policy preferences of more pragmatic-minded citizens.

I have tried to focus attention on some of the dynamics in American society that have contributed to racially charged environments that increase the vulnerability of mainstream white Americans to the subtle recruitment strategies of white nationalists. The strategic choices of white nationalists to cloak themselves in legitimate-sounding rhetoric and the intransigence of white liberals and minority group leaders who adamantly refuse to address the concerns that the white majority has expressed about the unfairness of racial preferences greatly exacerbates the situation. Woe to America if we ignore the warning signs of a nation in distress!

In 1820, Thomas Jefferson labeled the division of America over slavery as a "momentous question, [that] like a firebell in the night, awakened and filled me with terror." Today, I echo Jefferson's warning about racial divisions and tensions within the United States and the dire consequences they pose if ignored. Despite undeniable progress, a set of factors has emerged at this juncture in our history to create a potentially dangerous situation for America's future. Left unchecked, this situation could lead to unprecedented levels of racial and political unrest. The current situation is a test for all Americans, who must combat the negative forces now at work in our society through education, tolerance, understanding, and, above all, a commitment to the truth. The future alone will tell whether Americans – both black and white – are up to the challenge.

EPILOGUE

A catastrophic event has occurred since the completion of this book that warrants special consideration because of its implications for race relations, immigration policy, and the quality of American life. I am referring to the September 11, 2001, suicide attacks of the World Trade Center and the Pentagon and to the ensuing episodes of anthrax bioterrorism that have followed. These events have stolen the peace and repose of many Americans who, before September 11, 2001, rested in the confidence that such incidents occurred in other countries and found comfort in the knowledge that they could not happen here. We collectively lost our innocence on the day that nineteen Islamic militants hijacked four commercial airliners and used the planes and their human occupants as missiles of mass destruction.

Our most cherished symbols of capitalism and war were targeted. Capitalism was attacked when two airliners destroyed the twin towers of the World Trade Center in New York City with a mathematical precision that awed onlookers. Military might took a hit when the third plane took a huge chunk out of the Pentagon in Washington, D.C., while the fourth plane crashed into a rural Pennsylvania hillside after passengers forcefully resisted the hijackers' plans. Although the hijackers' intended destination for the fourth plane has not been determined, many experts have suggested that it, too, was headed toward a symbolic target in the Washington D.C., area.

In a single day, an estimated 3,000 innocent and unsuspecting Americans lost their lives in one of the worst incidents of international terrorism ever committed. The symbolism employed in these attacks was chilling. The terrorists chose planes belonging to American Airlines and United Airlines for their weapons of mass destruction, and they chose the ninth month and the eleventh day for their jihad (holy war) against America: 911. Many astute observers marveled at this diabolical symbolism and the almost supernatural precision with which these acts were rendered.

As I write on October 18, 2001, the attack on America has resulted in an international war against terrorism and in the bombing of Afghanistan, primarily by U.S. and British forces, as well as the creation of a National Office of Domestic Security, headed by former Pennsylvania Governor Tom Ridge. The object of the bombings is to destroy terrorist training camps and to persuade the Taliban government in Afghanistan to release master terrorist Osama bin Laden into U.S. custody. Bin Laden and his organization, Al-Qaeda, are believed to be behind a number of violent assaults on American interests both here and abroad, including the September 11 attacks. Additionally, he and his organization are believed to be behind the new wave of bioterrorism which includes fears of biological warfare and of contamination from deadly agents such as anthrax, a germ that has already found its way inside several American businesses and institutions, including the offices of U.S. Senator Tom Daschle and New York Governor George Pataki.

Americans have responded to terrorism with an effusive outpouring of patriotism, as well as calls for unity across racial and ethnic lines. In the aftermath of this event, blacks and whites seem much closer together. For now, the racial profiling of young black males has been surpassed by the search for suspects of Middle Eastern descent. A Newark Star-Ledger/Eagleton Rutgers poll of New Jersey residents found that 55 percent of blacks and 56 percent of whites supported restrictions on immigration from the Middle East and greater scrutiny of Middle Eastern travelers at airports. Similarly, eight of ten Floridians favor stronger curbs on immigration and more scrutiny of immigrants already in this country. Alarmed by the racial profiling, some commentators have called for a national remembrance of the circumstances that led to the internment of the Japanese during World War II.

What will be the long-term impact of these events and their fallout on the nation? We as a nation can expect a backlash against nonwhite immigrants, including an increase in hate crimes, which has already begun. As discussed in Chapter 5, hate crimes and hate groups rise during times of economic uncertainty. The closure of the U.S. stock market for several days in September combined with an already slowed economy to push the nation ever closer to a full-blown economic recession. In the aftermath of September 11, hate crimes against Americans believed to be of Middle Eastern descent have increased dramatically. At least four deaths and hundreds of acts of violence have been recorded against Arab Americans, Muslims, and Sikhs. Some of these attacks are aimed specifically at Muslims, because many Westerners view their religion as one of intolerance and terrorism.

Indeed, a critical need to reform America's immigration policies has been highlighted by the media's profiles of the terrorists, where we learned that some of them had been living in this country illegally after having overstayed their visas. Meanwhile, others lived here legally, shopping at Wal-Mart and eating at Pizza Hut, all the while planning and training for the opportunity to kill Americans. From newspaper articles and television accounts we have learned of a lax system of enforcement and tracking that has allowed thousands of foreigners to gain student visas for universities and courses that they never attended. We also learned, much to our chagrin, that America has no reliable system for tracking and apprehending thousands of foreigners who have overstayed their visas or have come for purposes other than the ones stated on immigration documents.

White nationalist David Duke (who has changed the name of his organization to the European Unity and Rights Organization because of a copyright infringement that forced him to release his acronym NOFEAR) has issued articles and press releases blaming U.S. foreign policy for the Arab hatred of America that he argues is spawned by America's pro-Israeli policies. According to Duke, "[T]he ultimate cause of this terrorism stems directly from our involvement in and support of the criminal behavior of Israel," which helps to explain why the Arabs never attack Switzerland or Sweden. Similarly, William Pierce of the National Alliance told a radio audience that "American long-term support for Israel's aggression led to the attack of September 11 in which 6,000 Americans were killed; America then launched a war to destroy Israel's enemies in the Middle East under the guise of 'fighting terrorism' and protecting America's 'freedom and democracy.'" The problem of the American people, Pierce argued, is not hijacked airliners, anthrax, or terrorists. "The problem is that we have lost control of our government. Our government no longer responds to our needs; instead it responds to the needs of an alien minority and has done this for a long time."

Pierce heads the National Alliance, an organization that the FBI considers one of the most dangerous in America. Groups such as Pierce's are likely to face increased scrutiny in the months and years to come when the war on terrorism looks inward. The heartwrenching scenes of the World Trade Center and the Pentagon in flames no doubt resurrected memories of law enforcement officials combing through the carnage left in the wake of the Oklahoma City bombing of the Murrah Federal Building. There must certainly be a heightened awareness that somewhere out there in the heartlands are other Timothy McVeighs just as capable of wasting innocent lives while referring to them as the collateral damage of war. The international war on terrorism must eventually turn toward its homegrown enemies.

In conclusion, I believe that America is more vulnerable than ever to heightened racial and ethnic tension stemming from the aftermath of September 11 and its potential for exploitation by sophisticated white nationalists who may use the events as proof that governmental officials are not doing enough to protect American interests here and abroad. In the concluding chapter of this book, written months ago, I argued that Americans "are increasingly at risk of large-scale racial conflict unprecedented in our nation's history that is being driven by the simultaneous convergence of a host of powerful social forces. These forces include changing demographics, the continued existence of racial preference policies, the rising expectations of ethnic minorities, the continued existence of liberal immigration policies, growing concerns about job losses associated with globalization, the demands for multiculturalism, and the Internet's ability to enable like-minded individuals to identify each other and to share mutual concerns and strategies for impacting the political system." In light of recent events, I would now add a growing fear of national and international terrorism to the above list of factors. Indeed, the future of America has never been more uncertain than it stands today.

APPENDIX A:
THE NEED FOR HATE
CRIMES LEGISLATION

This year, America needs action. No one should be victimized because of how they look, how they worship, or who they are. We need to work together as partners and as a national community to fight crimes fueled by hate. And we need strong federal hate crimes legislation.
President Bill Clinton, April 25, 2000

STATISTICS ON HATE CRIMES

• Nearly 60,000 hate crime incidents have been reported since 1991. According to the FBI, there have been nearly 60,000 hate crime incidents reported since 1991.

• Nearly 8,000 hate crime incidents were reported in 1998. In 1998, the latest year for which FBI figures are available, nearly 8,000 hate crime incidents were reported, nearly one hate crime every hour of every day. In 1998, there were 7,755 hate crimes incidents reported: 4,321 motivated by race (56%); 1,390 by religion (18%); and 1,260 by sexual orientation (16%).

HIGHLIGHTS OF THE NEW LOCAL LAW
ENFORCEMENT ENHANCEMENT ACT OF 2000

• The Intergovernmental Assistance Program provides technical, forensic, prosecutorial, or any other form of assistance to state and local law enforcement officials in cases that are motivated by bias based on race, color, religion, national origin, gender, disability, or sexual orientation, or that is a hate crime under state law.

- Federal Assistance and Training Grants authorize the Attorney General to make grants up to $100,000 to state, local, and Native American law enforcement officials who have incurred extraordinary expenses associated with investigating and prosecuting hate crimes. This program also authorizes grants to train local law enforcement officers in identifying, investigating, prosecuting, and preventing hate crimes, including those committed by juveniles.

- Prohibition of hate crimes.

- Gives the Justice Department jurisdiction over crimes of violence involving bodily injury, if motivated because of a person's actual or perceived race, color, religion, national origin, gender, sexual orientation, or disability. Current law does not cover sexual orientation, gender, or disability.

- Interstate Commerce Requirement. For crimes based on religion, national origin, gender, sexual orientation, or disability, a connection to interstate commerce is included for jurisdictional purposes.

- Certification Requirement. Prior to federally indicting someone, the Justice Department must certify that (1) there is reasonable cause to believe that the crime was motivated by bias, and (2) the Justice Department has consulted with state or local law enforcement officials and determined that (a) the state does not have jurisdiction or does not intend to exercise jurisdiction; (b) the state has requested that the Justice Department assume jurisdiction; (c) the state does not object to the Justice Department assuming jurisdiction; or (d) the state has completed prosecution and the Justice Department wants to initiate a subsequent prosecution.

- Amends the Hate Crimes Statistics Act to include gender. Requires the FBI to collect data from states on gender-based hate crimes in the same manner that it currently collects data for race, religion, sexual orientation, disability, or ethnicity.

KEY POINTS ABOUT THE LEGISLATION

- It is constitutional. In a letter dated June 13, 2000, to Senator Kennedy, the Department of Justice has stated unequivocally that "this statute would be constitutional under governing Supreme Court precedents."

- It maintains the primary role of state and local law enforcement in these cases. Enacting hate crimes legislation will not federalize all violent crimes. State and local law enforcement will continue to play the primary role in the investigation and prosecution of hate crimes. Building productive partnerships with state and local law enforcement will be the Department of Justice's primary goal.

- It does not threaten free speech. This legislation would punish violent acts, not beliefs or thoughts. It does not punish or prohibit in any way name-calling, verbal abuse, or expressions of bias or hatred toward any group even if such statements amount to hate speech.

APPENDIX B:
JESSICA'S LETTER

The following is an article I wrote that will never be published anywhere or read by anyone, except your readers maybe. I am a 17 year old White female and I attend a small rural school in PA. I was asked to write an article on something that I dislike about my school so I wrote 2 papers . . . a nice version for my teachers and this for myself.

Jessica

Today, like every day, I walked like a robot through the halls of my high school.

Although I was very tired due to a continuous lack of sleep, I was quickly wakened by the loud and aggressive voices of my fellow students yelling obscenities and insults in their usual incomprehensible lingo I do not wish to understand. I am familiar with their voices so there is never a need to look up to identify the source of the tumultuous shouting. Today, for a reason unknown to me (maybe so not to bump into them), I did look up and was not surprised to see the usual pack of 11 to 13 black students stomping through the hall in their oversized clothes and expensive shoes. They laughed, yelled, and pushed violently those who moved into their path.

They were of course followed by a group of adoring fans . . . the lost White students who admire and envy their dark skin, squalid unwashed hair, and awfully incorrect English.

I kept a safe distance behind this group of primates and watched with disappointment the unfortunate students and teachers who get harassed and bullied by this gang of "human beings."

This is all so routine to me I have become somewhat immune to it. Our high school is quite small and has 5 local housing projects that pour their filthy children into our overcrowded classrooms. Like so many high schools all over the country, mine is being overrun with these animals. One cannot walk to class without having to endure this chaos.

I am quite new to the White Power Movement, having been introduced to it little over 2 years ago, but since then life here has become virtually unbearable.

To completely empathize with my situation one must understand what a danger it is to be a White Racist in an American high school. I am completely alone and immensely passionate with my beliefs, which adds to the discomfort.

Fortunately, only trusted friends know about my belief. If it became known I would surely be singled out and my life would be in danger. I have always been a radical student, very vocal with my opinions and have gained a reputation of being skilled in debate, so it is very hard to sit quietly during a "World War II/Holocaust/Bad White Men" lesson in History class. My views are becoming more and more obvious as they deepen and start to emerge in normal conversation. How couldn't they? Once your eyes are open to this, race is present in everything and everywhere about us.

Knowing you are the only person in an entire school or city for that matter to feel a certain way is very painful. How divine it would be to sit back and talk with a group of intelligent people that feel the same way I do. Not the nodding of the head and the usual "Yeah, niggers are stupid" conversation I get with those I call "over the shoulder racist." I am sure you know those, they speak loudly and confidently about everything then suddenly stop and glance over their shoulder to make sure it's safe to whisper the words "nigger" or "black." One face to face conversation with a group of actual trusted racists seems like a unattainable dream to me right now.

I am sure there are many out there all too familiar with my story: With bleeding heart parents that would rather sit back and watch their daughters get raped by a black then be called racist; teachers and faculty that will punish me for disagreeing with them about a Shakespeare theme, but will ignore the black students who throw food at and expose their testicles to White female students; losing more and more friends each year to race mixing and a lot of sleepless nights. If I wasn't as strong and wise as I am I may have given up by now like so many of us already have. It is all very maddening and though I may be losing my mind, I will never lose my faith. Once your eyes are truly opened to shut them again would be more torturous than the loud and dirty blacks at school. 10:00 now, time for sleep so early in the morning I can become a robot once again and try to handle another day at my decadent American high school.[1]

---

[1] http://www.naawp.com/Youth/jessica.htm.

APPENDIX C:
STATISTICAL ANALYSIS
FOR THE COLLEGE
ADMISSIONS VIGNETTE

The data on which students the respondents thought should be admitted were treated as binary responses. The analyses reported in this appendix are all based on linear logistic models for the probability of preferring the B student. An analysis of deviance, shown in Table A.1, was carried out to test for the significance of main effects, and of interactions between attributes of the respondents and the races attributed to the two hypothetical students. The model was fitted in the S-Plus statistical language, with terms added sequentially. The linear dependence of predictor on education was on a three-point scale with 1 = high school or less, 2 = some post–high school or trade school education, and 3 = four-year college degree or higher. Income was coded in thousands of dollars to the accuracy available from the questionnaires.

The total degrees of freedom in this table is 781, because the few cases where some relevant feature of the respondents was unknown were omitted. The factor "scenario" refers to the races attributed to the hypothetical students in the study. It can be seen that the scenario has a highly significant effect, and the age of the respondent has a significant effect. The only factor that has a significant interaction with scenario is the income of the respondent, but education has an effect approaching significance at the 5 percent level. The interaction of age with scenario is remarkable for its low deviance value.

To investigate further the effect of scenario, separate analyses of deviance were carried out for the four possible allocations of race to the hypothetical students (see Table A.2). In each case reported here, income and education were considered as main effects because of their significant or near-significant interaction with the scenario described

Table A.1. Analysis of deviance for all cases

Factor	df	Deviance	p value
Scenario (race of students)	3	18.77	0.0003
Sex of students	3	0.48	0.92
Race of respondent	1	2.10	0.15
Income of respondent	1	1.41	0.23
Education of respondent	1	0.01	0.92
Sex of respondent	1	1.43	0.23
Age of respondent	1	6.27	0.012
Scenario: race	3	2.71	0.44
Scenario: income	3	11.86	0.008
Scenario: education	3	7.31	0.06
Scenario: sex	3	1.15	0.77
Scenario: age	3	0.96	0.82

Note: The notation "scenario: race" refers to interactions between the scenario and the race of the respondent, and similarly for the other factors, depending on the characteristics of the respondent.

earlier. Respondent's race was also included because of its pivotal role in this study. The interaction of age and sex with scenario was also investigated in separate tests not reported here; no significant effects were found. The only significant effects are those of income in the "white A/black B" scenario and of education and the education/race interaction in the "white B/black A" scenario. Both of these are discussed in more detail (and tested by analysis of contingency tables, which are sensitive to nonlinear effects) in the main text. In the "black A/white B" scenario, education and race together account for a deviance of 13.13 on three degrees of freedom, a value significant beyond the $p = 0.005$ level.

We now turn to logistic regression models based on the effects found to be significant in the analysis above. In each case, let $p(B)$ be the probability of preferring the B student. The logistic regression model fits a linear model to the logit of $p(B)$, that is, $\log(p(B)/(1 - p(B)))$, the log odds of preferring the B student. The logistic regression models fit to the data were as follows. For the "white A/black B" scenario, based on a sample of size 189, the model is logit $P(B) = 0.95 - 0.027I$, where I is the income in thousands of dollars, over the range

Table A.2. Analyses of deviance for subsets of the original data, according to race of hypothetical student

Scenario	Factor	df	Deviance	p value
Both students white	Income	1	0.39	0.53
	Education	1	2.03	0.15
	Race	1	1.75	0.19
	Income: education	1	0.55	0.46
	Income: race	1	2.33	0.13
	Education: race	1	0.01	0.93
Both students black	Income	1	1.21	0.22
	Education	1	0.24	0.62
	Race	1	0.13	0.72
	Income: education	1	0.39	0.53
	Income: race	1	0.15	0.70
	Education: race	1	0.48	0.49
White A student, black B student	Income	1	9.78	0.002
	Education	1	0.06	0.81
	Race	1	0.64	0.43
	Income: education	1	0.31	0.58
	Income: race	1	0.34	0.56
	Education: race	1	1.33	0.25
Black A student, white B student	Income	1	0.72	0.40
	Education	1	5.20	0.02
	Race	1	2.96	0.09
	Income: education	1	1.43	0.23
	Income: race	1	0.06	0.81
	Education: race	1	4.97	0.03

Note: The factors are all characteristics of the respondents, with ":" denoting two-factor interactions.

from \$5,000 to \$60,000. The standard error in the slope coefficient is 0.009.

In the "black A/white B" scenario, let E be the education level measured on a three-point scale, and let Wh and Bl be dummy variables for the race of the respondent (so that $Wh = 1 - Bl$). A logistic regression allowing for interactions between education and race gives the term: logit $p(B) = 0.22 Wh + 0.11(Bl \times E) - 0.86(Wh \times E)$.

APPENDIX D:
TEN REASONS WHY
REPARATIONS FOR
BLACKS IS A BAD IDEA,
AND RACIST, TOO

(1) There Is No Single Group Clearly Responsible for the Crime of Slavery
Black Africans and Arabs were responsible for enslaving the ancestors of African Americans. There were 2,000 black slaveowners in the antebellum United States. Are reparations to be paid by their descendants, too?

(2) There Is No One Group That Benefited Exclusively from Its Fruits
The claim for reparations is premised on the false assumption that only whites have benefited from slavery. If slave labor created wealth for Americans, then obviously it has created wealth for black Americans as well, including the descendants of slaves. The GNP of black America is so large that it makes the African-American community the tenth most prosperous "nation" in the world. American blacks on average enjoy per capita incomes in the range of twenty to fifty times that of blacks living in any of the African nations from which they were kidnapped.

(3) Only a Tiny Minority of White Americans Ever Owned Slaves, and Others Gave Their Lives to Free Them
Only a tiny minority of Americans ever owned slaves. This is true even for those who lived in the antebellum South, where only one white in five was a slaveholder. Why should their descendants owe a debt? What about the descendants of the 350,000 Union soldiers who died to free

the slaves? They gave their lives. What possible moral principle would ask them to pay (through their descendants) again?

(4) America Today Is a Multiethnic Nation and Most Americans Have No Connection (Direct or Indirect) to Slavery

The two great waves of American immigration occurred after 1880 and then after 1960. What rationale would require Vietnamese boat people, Russian refuseniks, Iranian refugees, Armenian victims of the Turkish persecution, Jews, Mexicans, Greeks, or Polish, Hungarian, Cambodian, and Korean victims of Communism to pay reparations to American blacks?

(5) The Historical Precedents Used to Justify the Reparations Claim Do Not Apply, and the Claim Itself Is Based on Race, Not Injury

The historical precedents generally invoked to justify the reparations claim are payments to Jewish survivors of the Holocaust, Japanese-American and African-American victims of racial experiments in Tuskegee, or racial outrages in Rosewood and Oklahoma City. But in each case, the recipients of reparations were the direct victims of the injustice or their immediate families. This would be the only case of reparations to people who were not immediately affected and whose sole qualification to receive reparations would be racial. As has already been pointed out, during the slavery era, many blacks were free men or slaveowners themselves, yet the reparations claimants make no distinction between the roles blacks actually played in the injustice itself. Randall Robinson's book on reparations, *The Debt*, which is the manifesto of the reparations movement, is pointedly subtitled, "What America Owes to Blacks." If this is not racism, what is?

(6) The Reparations Argument Is Based on the Unfounded Claim That All African-American Descendants of Slaves Suffer from the Economic Consequences of Slavery and Discrimination

No evidence-based attempt has been made to prove that living individuals have been adversely affected by a slave system that was ended over 150 years ago. But there is plenty of evidence of hardships that individuals could and did overcome. The black middle-class in America is a prosperous community that is now larger in absolute terms than

471

the black underclass. Does its existence not suggest that economic adversity is the result of failures of individual character rather than the lingering after-effects of racial discrimination and a slave system that ceased to exist well over a century ago? West Indian blacks in America are also descended from slaves, but their average incomes are equivalent to the average incomes of whites (and nearly 25% higher than the average incomes of American-born blacks). How is it that slavery adversely affected one large group of descendants but not the other? How can government be expected to decide an issue that is so subjective – and yet so critical – to the case?

(7) The Reparations Claim Is One More Attempt to Turn African-Americans into Victims, Sending a Damaging Message to the African-American Community
The renewed sense of grievance – which is what the claim for reparations will inevitably create – is neither a constructive nor a helpful message for black leaders to be sending to their communities and to others. To focus the social passions of African Americans on what some Americans may have done to their ancestors fifty or a hundred and fifty years ago is to burden them with a crippling sense of victimhood. How are the millions of refugees from tyranny and genocide who are now living in America going to receive these claims, moreover, except as demands for special treatment, an extravagant new handout that is only necessary because some blacks can't seem to locate the ladder of opportunity within reach of others, many less privileged than themselves?

(8) Reparations to African Americans Have Already Been Paid
Since the passage of the Civil Rights Act and the advent of the Great Society in 1965, trillions of dollars in transfer payments have been made to African Americans in the form of welfare benefits and racial preferences (in contracts, job placements, and educational admissions), all under the rationale of redressing historic racial grievances. It is said that reparations are necessary to achieve a healing between African Americans and other Americans. If trillion-dollar restitution and a wholesale rewriting of American law (in order to accommodate racial preferences) for African Americans is not enough to achieve a "healing," what will be enough?

(9) What About the Debt Blacks Owe to America?

Slavery existed for thousands of years before the Atlantic slave trade was born, and in all societies. But in the thousand years of its existence, there never was an antislavery movement until white Christians – Englishmen and Americans – created one. If not for the antislavery attitudes and military power of white Englishmen and Americans, the slave trade would not have been brought to an end. If not for the sacrifices of white soldiers and a white American President who gave his life to sign the Emancipation Proclamation, blacks in America would still be slaves. If not for the dedication of Americans of all ethnicities and colors to a society based on the principle that all men are created equal, blacks in America would not enjoy the highest standard of living of blacks in anywhere in the world. They would not enjoy the greatest freedoms and the most thoroughly protected individual rights anywhere. Where is the gratitude of black America and its leaders for those gifts?

(10) The Reparations Claim Is a Separatist Idea That Sets African-Americans Against the Nation That Gave Them Freedom

Blacks were here before the *Mayflower*. Who is more American than the descendants of African slaves? For the African-American community to isolate itself even further from America is to embark on a course whose implications are troubling. Yet the African-American community has had a long-running flirtation with separatists, nationalists, and the political left, who want African Americans to be no part of America's social contract. African Americans should reject this temptation.

For all America's faults, African Americans have an enormous stake in their country and their heritage. It is this heritage that is really under attack by the reparations movement. The reparations claim is one more assault on America, conducted by racial separatists and the political left. It is an attack not only on white Americans, but on all Americans, especially African Americans.

America's African-American citizens are the richest and most privileged black people alive, a bounty that is a direct result of the heritage that is under assault. The American idea needs the support of its African-American citizens. But African Americans also need the support of the American idea. For it is this idea that led to the principles and institutions that have set African-Americans – and all of us – free.

BIBLIOGRAPHY

BOOKS

Abernathy, Virginia. *Population Politics*. New York: Plenum Press, 1993.

Able, Deborah. *Hate Groups*. Berkeley Heights, N.J.: Enslow Publishers, 1995.

Ackerman, Bruce. *We the People*. Cambridge, Mass.: Harvard University Press, 1991.

America, Richard F. *Paying the Social Debt: What White America Owes Black America*. Westport, Conn.: Praeger, 1993.

The Amplified Bible. Grand Rapids, Mich.: Zondervan Publishing, 1987.

Auster, Lawrence. *The Path to National Suicide: An Essay on Immigration and Multiculturalism*. Monterey, Va.: American Immigration Control Foundation, 1990.

Barkun, Michael. *Religion and the Racist Right: The Origins of the Christian Identity Movement*. Chapel Hill: University of North Carolina Press, 1994.

Barna, George. *The Second Coming of the Church*. Nashville, Tenn.: Word Publishing, 1998.

Barton, David. *Original Intent: The Courts, the Constitution, and Religion*. Aledo, Tex.: Wallbuilder Press, 1997.

Beck, Roy. *The Case against Immigration*. New York: Norton, 1996.

Bell, Derrick. *Faces at the Bottom of the Well: The Permanence of Racism*. New York: Basic Books, 1992.

Belz, Herman. *Equality: A Quarter-Century of Affirmative Action Transformed*. New Brunswick, N.J.: Transaction Books, 1991.

Berman, Paul, ed. *Blacks and Jews: Alliances and Arguments*. New York: Delacorte Press, 1994.

Bittker, Boris I. *The Case for Reparations*. New York: Random House, 1973.

Blank, Rebecca M. *It Takes a Nation: A New Agenda for Fighting Poverty*. New York: Russell Sage Foundation and Princeton University Press, 1997.

Blaustein, Albert P. *Civil Rights and the American Negro*. New York: Washington Square Press, 1969.

Bloom, Allan. *The Closing of the American Mind*. New York: Simon and Schuster, 1989.

Borjas, George. *Friends or Strangers*. New York: Basic Books, 1990.

Bork, Robert H. *Slouching Towards Gomorrah*. New York: ReganBooks, 1996.

Boston, Thomas. *Race, Class, and Conservatism*. Boston: Unwin Hyman, 1988.

Bowen, William G., and Derek Bok. *The Shape of the River: Long-Term Consequences of Considering Race in College and University Admissions*. Princeton: Princeton University Press, 1998.

Bridges, Tyler. *The Rise of David Duke*. Jackson: University Press of Mississippi, 1994.

Brown, Mary. *Shapers of the Great Debate on Immigration*. Westport, Conn.: Greenwood Press, 1999.

Buendia, Hernando Gomez, ed. *Urban Crime: Global Trends and Policies*. Tokyo: United Nations University Press, 1989.

Bushart, Howard L., John R. Craig, and Myra Barnes. *Soldiers of God: White Supremacists and Their Holy War for America*. New York: Kensington Books, 1998.

Campbell, Angus, Phillip Converse, Warren E. Miller, and Donald E. Stokes. *The American Voter*. Chicago: University of Chicago Press, 1960.

Carter, Dan T. *From George Wallace to Newt Gingrich: Race in the Conservative Counterrevolution 1963–1994*. Baton Rouge: Louisiana University Press, 1996.

Carter, Stephen. *God's Name in Vain: The Wrongs and Rights of Religion in Politics*. New York: Basic Books, 2000.

    Reflections of an Affirmative Action Baby. New York: Basic Books, 1991.

Cayton, Horace, and St. Clair Drake. *Black Metropolis: A Study of Negro Life in a Northern City*. New York: Harcourt, Brace, 1945.

Coetzee, J. M. *Disgrace*. New York: Viking Penguin, 1999.

Corcoran, James. *Bitter Harvest, Gordon Kahl and the Posse Comitatus: Murder in the Heartland*. New York: Penguin Press, 1990.

Corduan, Winfried. *Neighboring Faiths: A Christian Introduction to World Religions*. Downers Grove, Ill.: InterVarsity Press, 1998.

Crime in the United States, 1997. U.S. Department of Justice, Bureau of Justice Statistics. Washington, D.C.: USGPO, 1998.

Criminal Victimization in the United States, 1994. U.S. Department of Justice, Bureau of Justice Statistics. Washington, D.C.: USGPO, 1997.

    1997. U.S. Department of Justice, Bureau of Justice Statistics. Washington, D.C.: USGPO, 1998.

Daniels, Jesse. *White Lies: Race, Class, Gender, and Sexuality in White Supremacist Discourse.* New York: Routledge, 1997.

Delgado, Richard. *The Coming Race War.* New York: New York University Press, 1996.

Dobratz, Betty A., and Stephanie L. Shanks-Meile. *"White Power, White Pride!": The White Separatist Movement in the United States.* New York: Twayne, 1997.

D'Souza, Dinesh. *The End of Racism: Principles for a Multiracial Society.* New York: Free Press, 1995.

    Illiberal Education: The Politics of Race and Sex on Campus. New York: Vintage Books, 1991.

Duke, David. *My Awakening.* Covington, La.: Free Speech Press, 1999.

Dyer, Joel. *Harvest of Rage: Why Oklahoma City Is Only the Beginning.* Boulder, Colo.: Westview Press, 1967.

Eastland, Terry, and William J. Bennett. *Counting by Race: Equality from the Founding Fathers to Bakke and Weber.* New York: Basic Books, 1979.

Ebo, Bosah. *Cyberghetto or Cybertopia: Race, Class, and Gender on the Internet.* Westport, Conn.: Praeger Press, 1998.

Eisenach, Eldon. *The Next Religious Establishment: National Identity and Political Theology in Post-Protestant America.* Lanham, Md.: Rowman and Littlefield, 2000.

Entine, Jon. *Why Blacks Dominate Sports and Why We Are Afraid to Talk About It.* New York: Public Relations Press, 2000.

Evans, Rowland, and Robert Novak. *Nixon in the White House.* New York: Random House, 1975.

Farley, Jennie. *Affirmative Action and the Woman Worker: Guidelines for Personnel Management.* New York: Amacom, 1979.

Feagin, Joe R., and Claircce B. Feagin. *Race and Ethnic Relations.* Upper Saddle River, N.J.: Prentice Hall, 1999.

Franklin, Benjamin. *The Autobiography of Benjamin Franklin.* Mineola, N.Y.: Dover Publications, 1996.

Fredrickson, George A. *White Supremacy: A Comparative Study in American and South African History.* New York: Oxford University Press, 1981.

The Gallup Index. Report no. 143, June 1977.

Gallup, George Jr. *The Gallup Poll Public Opinion, 1993.* Wilmington, Del.: Scholarly Resources, 1994.

Gallup, George Jr., and Jim Castelli. *The People's Religion: American Faith in the 90's.* New York: Macmillan, 1989.

Gallup, George Jr., and D. Michael Lindsey. *Surveying the Religious Landscape: Trends in U.S. Beliefs.* Harrisburg, Penn.: Morehouse Publishing, 1999.

Gamson, William A. *Talking Politics.* New York: Cambridge University Press, 1992.

Gardner, Howard. *Frames of Mind: The Theory of Multiple Intelligences*. New York: Basic Books, 1983.

Gates, Henry Louis Jr., and Nellie Y. McKay, eds. *The Norton Anthology of African American Literature*. New York: W. W. Norton, 1996.

George, John, and Laird Wilcox. *Nazis, Communists, Klansmen, and Others on the Fringe*. Buffalo, N.Y.: Prometheus Books, 1992.

Ginger, Ann F., ed. *Defunis versus Odegaard and the University of Washington, the University Admissions Case: The Record*. New York: Oceana Press, 1974.

Glazer, Nathan. *Affirmative Discrimination: Ethnic Inequality and Public Policy*. New York: Basic Books, 1975.

Goffman, Erving. *Frame Analysis: An Essay on the Organization of Experience*. New York: Harper, 1974.

Graham, Hugh D. *The Civil Rights Era: Origins and Development of a National Policy, 1960–1972*. New York: Oxford University Press, 1990.

Graham, Lawrence Otis. *Member of the Club: Reflections on Life in a Racially Polarized World*. New York: HarperCollins, 1995.

Our Kind of People: Inside America's Black Upper Class. New York: HarperCollins, 1999.

Grant, Madison. *The Passing of the Great Race*. New York: Charles Scribner, 1916.

Greenstein, Fred. *The Presidential Difference*. New York: Martin Kessler Books, 2000.

Gross, Barry. *Reverse Discrimination*. New York: Prometheus Books, 1977.

Gurr, Ted R. *Why Men Rebel*. Princeton, N.J.: Princeton University Press, 1970.

Hacker, Andrew. *Two Nations: Black and White, Separate, Hostile, and Unequal*. New York: Random House, 1992.

Hardin, Garrett. *Living Within Limits*. New York: Oxford, 1993.

Hate Crime Statistics, 1997. U.S. Department of Justice, Federal Bureau of Investigation. Washington, D.C.: USGPO, 1999.

Heineman, Kenneth. *God Is a Conservative: Religion, Politics and Morality in Contemporary America*. New York: New York University Press, 1998.

Herrnstein, Richard, and Charles Murray. *The Bell Curve: Intelligence and Class Structure in American Life*. New York: Free Press, 1994.

Higham, John. *Strangers in the Land: Patterns of American Nativism 1860–1925*. New Brunswick, N.J.: Rutgers University Press, 1955.

Hill, Jim, and Rand Cheadle. *The Bible Tells Me So: Uses and Abuses of Holy Scripture*. New York: Bantam Books, 1996.

Hoffer, Eric. *The True Believer: Thoughts on the Nature of Mass Movements*. New York: Harper & Row, 1951.

Holy Bible. King James Version. Nashville, Tenn.: Thomas Nelson, 1989.

Horowitz, Donald. *Ethnic Groups in Conflict*. Berkeley: University of California Press, 1985.

Isserman, Maurice, and Michael Kazin. *America Divided: The Civil War of the 1960s*. New York: Oxford University Press, 2000.

Jacobson, David, ed. *The Immigration Reader*. Malden, Mass.: Blackwell, 1998.

Jaynes, Gerald David, and Robin M. Williams, eds. *A Common Destiny: Blacks and American Society*. Washington, D.C.: National Academy Press, 1989.

Jencks, Christopher, and Meredith Phillips, eds. *The Black-White Test Gap*. Washington, D.C.: Brookings Press, 1998.

Jencks, Christopher, and David Riesman. *The Academic Revolution*. Garden City, N.Y.: Doubleday, 1968.

Jensen, Arthur. *The G-Factor*. Westport, Conn.: Praeger Press, 1998.

Jordan, Tim. *Cyberpower: The Culture and Politics of Cyberspace and the Internet*. New York: Routledge, 1999.

Kaplan, Jeffrey. *Encyclopedia of White Power*. Lanham, Md.: Rowman and Littlefield, 2000.

Kaplan, Jeffrey, and Leonard Weinberg. *The Emergence of a Euro-American Radical Right*. New Brunswick, N.J.: Rutgers University Press, 1999.

Kennedy, Randall. *Race, Crime, and the Law*. New York: Pantheon Books, 1997.

Kerner Report on Civil Disorders. Supplementary Studies for the National Advisory Commission on Civil Disorders. Washington, D.C.: U.S. Government Printing Office, 1968.

Key, V. O. *Public Opinion and American Democracy*. New York: Knopf, 1961.

Kinder, Donald R., and Lynn Sanders. *Divided by Color: Racial Politics and Democratic Ideals*. Chicago: University of Chicago Press, 1996.

King, Martin Luther Jr. *Where Do We Go from Here: Chaos or Community*. New York: Harper and Row, 1967.

Klassen, Ben. *The White Man's Bible*. Lighthouse Point, Fla.: World Church of the Creator, 1981.

Klinkner, Philip and Rogers A. Smith. *The Unsteady March: The Rise and Decline of Racial Equality in America*. Chicago: University of Chicago Press, 1999.

Klitgaard, Robert. *Choosing Elites*. New York: Basic Books, 1985.

Kluger, Richard. *Simple Justice*. New York: Vintage Books, 1975.

Kors, Alan, and Harvey Silvergate. *The Shadow University: The Betrayal of Liberty on America's Campuses*. New York: Free Press, 1998.

Kronenwetter, Michael. *United They Hate: White Supremacy Groups in the United States*. New York: Walker, 1992.

Lamm, Richard, and Gary Imhoff. *The Immigration Time Bomb*. New York: Truman Talley Books, 1985.

Landry, Bart. *The New Black Middle Class*. Berkeley: University of California Press, 1987.

Laraña, Enrique, Hank Johnston, and Joseph R. Gusfield, eds. *New Social Movements: From Ideology to Identity*. Philadelphia: Temple University Press, 1994.

Lawrence, Frederick M. *Punishing Hate*. Cambridge, Mass.: Harvard University Press, 1999.

Levin, Jack, and Jack McDevitt. *Hate Crimes: The Rising Tide of Bigotry and Bloodshed*. New York: Plenum Press, 1993.

Levin, Michael. *Why Race Matters: Racial Differences and What They Mean*. Westport, Conn.: Praeger, 1998.

Lieberson, Stanley, and Mary C. Waters. *From Many Strands: Ethnic and Racial Groups in Contemporary America*. New York: Russell Sage Foundation, 1988.

Lincoln, C. Eric. *Race, Religion, and the Continuing American Dilemma*. New York: Hill and Wang, 1999.

Lind, Michael. *The Next American Nation: The New Nationalism and the Fourth American Revolution*. New York: Free Press, 1995.

Lipset, Seymour M. *American Exceptionalism: A Double-Edged Sword*. New York: Norton, 1996.

Lipset, Seymour M., and Earl Rabb. *The Politics of Unreason: Right-Wing Extremism in America, 1709–1970*. New York: Harper and Row, 1970.

Los Angeles Times staff. *Understanding the Riots: Los Angeles Before and After the Rodney King Case*. Los Angeles, Calif.: Los Angeles Times, 1992.

Loury, Glenn. *One by One from the Inside Out: Essays and Reviews on Race and Responsibility in America*. New York: Free Press, 1995.

Macdonald, Andrew. *The Turner Diaries*, 2nd ed. Hillsboro, W.Va.: National Vanguard Press, 1980.

Maharidge, Dale. *The Coming White Minority: California, Multiculturalism, America's Future*. New York: Vintage Books, 1996.

Marable, Manning. *Beyond Black and White: Rethinking Race in American Politics and Society*. New York: Verso, 1995.

Marsh, Charles. *God's Long Summer: Stories of Faith and Civil Rights*. Princeton, N.J.: Princeton University Press, 1997.

McAdam, Doug, John D. McCarthy, and Mayer Zald, eds. *Comparative Perspectives on Social Movements*. New York: Cambridge University Press, 1996.

McCullagh, Peter, and John A. Nelder. *Generalized Linear Models*. 2nd ed. New York: Chapman and Hall, 1989.

McLanahan, Sara, and Gary Sandefur. *Growing Up with a Single Parent: What Hurts, What Helps.* Cambridge, Mass.: Harvard University Press, 1994.

McWhorter, John. *Losing the Race: Self-Sabotage in Black America.* New York: Free Press, 2000.

Morgan, David L. *Focus Groups as Qualitative Research.* 2nd ed. Thousand Oaks, Calif.: Sage Publications, 1997.

Morris, Aldon, and Carol Mueller, eds. *Frontiers in Social Movement Theory.* New Haven, Conn.: Yale University Press, 1992.

Muhammad, Elijah. *Message to the Black Man in America.* Newport News, Va.: Brothers Communication System, 1992.

Myrdal, Gunnar. *An American Dilemma.* New York: Harper and Row, 1944.

Neusner, Jacob. *Introduction to Rabbinic Literature.* New York: Doubleday, 1994.

Nieli, Russell, ed. *Racial Preferences and Racial Justice.* Washington, D.C.: Ethics and Public Policy Center, 1991.

Novick, Michael. *White Lies, White Power: The Fight against White Supremacy and Reactionary Violence.* Monroe, Maine: Common Courage Press, 1995.

Nussbaum, Martha. *For Love of Country: Debating the Limits of Patriotism.* Boston: Beacon Press, 1996.

O'Neil, Robert M. *Discriminating against Discrimination: Preferential Admissions and the Defunis Case.* Bloomington: Indiana University Press, 1975.

Patterson, Orlando. *The Ordeal of Integration: Progress and Resentment in America's "Racial" Crisis.* Washington, D.C.: Civitas/Counterpoint, 1997.

Perry, Bruce. *Malcolm: The Life of a Man Who Changed Black America.* Barrytown, N.Y.: Station Hill Press, 1991.

Pojam, Louis S., and Owen McLeod, eds. *What We Deserve?: A Reader on Justice and Desert.* New York: Oxford University Press, 1999.

The Polling Report. August 22, 1988.

Raboteau, Albert J. *Slave Religion: The "Invisible Institution" in the Antebellum South.* New York: Oxford University Press, 1980.

Radzinowicz, Leon, and Joan King. *The Growth of Crime: The International Experience.* New York: Basic Books, 1977.

Reed, Ralph. *Active Faith: How Christians Are Changing the Soul of American Politics.* New York: Free Press, 1996.

Reich, Robert. *The Work of Nations.* New York: Alfred Knopf, 1991.

Report of the Advisory Committee on Civil Disorders. New York: Bantam Books, 1968.

Richburg, Keith. *Out of America: A Black Man Confronts Africa.* New York: Basic Books, 1997.

Ridgeway, James. *Blood in the Face: The Ku Klux Klan, Aryan Nations, Nazi Skinheads, and the Rise of a New White Culture.* New York: Thunder's Mouth Press, 1995.

Roberts, Paul Craig, and Lawrence M. Stratton. *The New Color Line: How Quotas and Privilege Destroy Democracy.* Washington, D.C.: Regnery Publishing, 1995.

Robinson, Dean E. *Black Nationalism in American Politics and Thought.* New York: Cambridge University Press, forthcoming.

Robinson, Randall. *The Debt: What America Owes Blacks.* New York: Dutton, 2000.

Rorty, Richard. *Achieving Our Country: Leftist Thought in Twentieth Century America.* Cambridge, Mass.: Harvard University Press, 1998.

Rosenberg, Gerald N. *The Hollow Hope: Can Courts Bring about Social Change?* Chicago: University of Chicago, 1991.

Rushton, J. Philippe. *Race, Evolution, and Behavior.* New Brunswick: Transaction Books, 1995.

Sachs, David O., and Peter Thiel. *The Diversity Myth: Multiculturalism and Political Intolerance on Campus.* Oakland, Calif.: Independent Institute, 1995.

Safire, William. *Safire's New Political Dictionary: The Definitive Guide to the New Language of Politics.* New York: Random House, 1993. Pp. 76–7.

Scarborough, Rick. *Enough Is Enough: A Call to Christian Commitment.* Springdale, Penn.: Whitaker, 1996.

Schlesinger, Arthur M. Jr. *The Disuniting of America: Reflections on a Multicultural Society.* New York: W. W. Norton, 1998.

Schmidt, Alan. *The Menace of Multiculturalism.* Westport, Conn.: Praeger, 1997.

Schuman, Howard, Charlotte Steeh, Lawrence Bobo, and Maria Krystan. *Racial Attitudes in America: Trends and Interpretations,* rev. ed. Cambridge, Mass.: Harvard University Press, 1997.

Selnow, Gary. *Electronic Whistle Stops: The Impact of the Internet on American Politics.* Westport, Conn.: Praeger Press, 1998.

Shipler, David K. *A Country of Strangers: Black and Whites in America.* New York: Alfred A. Knopf, 1997.

Sigelman, Lee, and Susan Welch. *Black Americans' Views of Inequality: The Dream Deferred.* New York: Cambridge University Press, 1991.

Sindler, Allan P. *Bakke, Defunis, and Minority Admissions.* New York: Longman Press, 1978.

Skerry, Peter. *Mexican Americans: The Ambivalent Minority.* New York: Free Press, 1993.

Skrentny, John David. *The Ironies of Affirmative Action: Politics, Culture, and Justice in America.* Chicago: University of Chicago Press, 1996.

Sleeper, Jim. *Liberal Racism: How Fixating on Race Subverts the American Dream*. New York: Penguin Books, 1997.

Smelser, Neil J., and Jeffrey C. Alexander. *Diversity and Its Discontents: Cultural Conflict and Common Ground in Contemporary American Society*. Princeton: Princeton University Press, 1999.

Smoit, Albert, and Steven A. Peterson, eds. *Recent Explorations in Biology and Politics*. Greenwich, Conn.: JAI Press, 1997.

Sniderman, Paul, and Thomas Piazza. *The Scar of Race*. Cambridge, Mass.: Harvard University Press, 1993.

Sniderman, Paul M., Richard Brody, and Phillip E. Tetlock. *Reasoning and Choice: Explorations in Political Psychology*. Cambridge, Mass.: Cambridge University Press, 1991.

Snow, Robert L. *The Militia Threat: Terrorists among Us*. New York: Plenum Trade, 1999.

Sowell, Thomas. *Preferential Policies: An International Perspective*. New York: William Morrow, 1990.

Stewart, David W., and Prem N. Shamdasani. *Focus Groups: Theory and Practice*. Newbury Park, Calif.: Sage Publications, 1990.

Stock, Catherine McNichols. *Rural Radicals: From Bacon's Rebellion to the Oklahoma City Bombing*. New York: Penguin Books, 1996.

Stoddard, Lothrop. *The Rising Tide of Color against White World Supremacy*. New York: Charles Scribner, 1920.

Stone, Geoffrey R., Louis Seidman, Cass R. Sunstein, and Mark V. Tushnet. *Constitutional Law*. 3rd ed. New York: Aspen Law and Business Publishers, 1996.

Swain, Carol M. *Black Faces, Black Interests: The Representation of African Americans in Congress*. Cambridge, Mass.: Harvard University Press, 1993, 1995.

Swain, Carol M., and Russell Nieli, eds. *White Pride, White Protest: Contemporary Voices of White Nationalism*. Forthcoming, 2002.

Synnott, Marcia Graham. *The Half-Opened Door: Discrimination and Admissions at Harvard, Yale, and Princeton, 1900–1970*. Westport, Conn.: Greenwood Press, 1979.

Takagi, Dana Y. *The Retreat from Race: Asian American Admissions and Racial Politics*. New Brunswick, N.J.: Rutgers University Press, 1992.

Takaki, Ronald. *A Different Mirror: A History of Multicultural America*. New York: Little, Brown, 1993.

Tarrow, Sidney. *Power in Movement: Social Movements, Collective Action and Politics*. New York: Cambridge University Press, 1994.

Taylor, Charles, ed. *Multiculturalism and the Politics of Recognition*. Princeton: Princeton University Press, 1992.

Taylor, Jared. *The Color of Crime*. Oakton, Va.: New Century Foundation, June 1999.
  Paved with Good Intentions. New York: Carol and Graf, 1992.
Taylor, Jared, ed. *The Real Dilemma: Race, Immigration, and the Future of America*. Oakton, Va.: New Century Books, 1998.
Thernstrom, Stephan, ed. *Harvard Encyclopedia of American Ethnic Groups*. Cambridge, Mass.: Harvard University Press, 1980.
Thernstrom, Stephan, and Abigail Thernstrom. *America in Black and White: One Nation, Indivisible*. New York: Simon and Schuster, 1997.
Tuch, Steven A., and Jack K. Martin, eds. *Racial Attitudes in the 1990s: Continuity and Change*. Westport, Conn.: Praeger Press, 1997.
Walker, Samuel. *The Rights Revolution: Rights and Community in Modern America*. New York: Oxford University Press, 1998.
Welch, Susan, and John Gruhl. *Affirmative Action and Minority Enrollments in Medical and Law Schools*. Ann Arbor: University of Michigan Press, 1998.
Whitten, Mark W. *The Myth of Christian America*. Macon, Ga.: Smyth and Helwys, 1999.
Wilson, John K. *The Myth of Political Correctness: The Conservative Attack on Higher Education*. Durham, N.C.: Duke University Press, 1995.
Wilson, William Julius. *The Bridge over the Racial Divide: Rising Inequality and Coalition Politics*. Berkeley: University of California Press, 1999.
  The Declining Significance of Race: Black and Changing American Institutions, 2nd ed. Chicago: University of Chicago Press, 1980.
  The Truly Disadvantaged: The Inner-City, the Underclass, and Public Policy. Chicago: University of Chicago Press, 1987.
Wistrich, Robert. *Anti-Semitism: The Longest Hatred*. New York: Pantheon, 1991.
X, Malcolm. *The Autobiography of Malcolm X*. New York: Ballantine, 1996.
Zelnick, Bob. *Backfire: A Reporter's Look at Affirmative Action*. Washington, D.C.: Regnery Publishing, 1996.
Zeskin, Leonard. *It's Not Populism, America's New Populist Party: A Fraud by Racists and Anti-Semites*. Atlanta, Ga.: Center for Democratic Renewal and the Southern Poverty Law Center, 1984.

ARTICLES AND ESSAYS

"A Campaign to Limit the Voices of White Supremacists on the Internet Has Defenders of the First Amendment Worried," *Time*, Jan. 22, 1996.
Abowd, John, and Richard Freeman, eds. "Immigration, Trade, and the Labor Market," National Bureau of Economic Research Project Report. Chicago: University of Chicago Press, 1991.

"Active Hate Groups in the United States in 1998," *Intelligence Report* (Winter 1999): 38–9.

Adderton, Donald V. "Jesse Should 'Chill' Racial Rhetoric in Kokomo Death," Sun Herald Online, http://www.vh60009.vh6.infi.net/region/docs/don072200.htm.

Adkins, Ricshawn. "Affirmative Action and Public Opinion Polls," In Carol Swain, ed., *Race versus Class: The New Affirmative Action Debate.* Lanham, Md.: University Press of America, 1996. 101–11.

"ADL to Congress: There Is a 'Virus of Hate' on the Internet." U.S. Newswire, May 20, 1999.

"ADL Survey on Anti-Semitism and Prejudice in America." November 16, 1992.

"Affirmative Action: A Course for the Future." *Looking Ahead*, August 1, 1996.

"Affirmative Action in the Courts: Here's Some Reasons Why That's a Bad Place for Blacks to Be," *Journal of Blacks in Higher Education* 25 (1999): 40–1.

"Affirmative Action Programs," *The Gallup Monthly Poll*, March 25–8, 1977.

Aidi, Hisham. "Who's Failing Black Students?." www.africana.com, Jan. 10, 2001.

Allen-Taylor, J. Douglas. "The Price of Pain: Can Modern-Day America Pay African Americans Back for the Scars of Slavery and Discrimination? Should We Even Try?." http://metroactive.com/papers/10.02.97/cover/race-amends-9740.html.

Alligood, Leon. "Officer Surrenders, Charged After Standoff." May 12, 2001, www.tennessean.com.

Alstyne, Carol Van, et al. "Affirmative Inaction: The Bottom Line Tells the Tale," *Change* 9 (Aug. 1977): 39–41.

Amar, Akhil, and Neil Katyal. "Bakke's Fate." *UCLA Law Review* 43 (1996): 1745.

"The Americanization Ideal." Editorial, *New York Times*, Dec. 25, 2000.

"Announcement of One Florida Initiative," *Webcast of the One Florida Press Conference*, http://www.state.fl.us/eog/one florida/remarksoriginal.html.

Applebome, Peter. "Rise Is Seen in Hate Crimes Committed by Blacks." *New York Times*, December 13, 1993.

Archibald, George. "Bias Embroils Christian Coalition." *Washington Times*, March 5, 2001.

"Aryan Nations Stages Alarming Comeback in 1994." *Klanwatch Intelligence Report*, March 1995.

Auster, Lawrence. "Them vs. Unz." Special Letters Section. *Policy Review*, Fall 1994: 88–96.

Ayres, B. Drummond Jr., "Conservatives Forge New Strategy to Challenge Affirmative Action." *New York Times*, Feb. 16, 1995.

Bandler, James. "Racist Group's Fliers Seen in the Boston Area," *Boston Globe*, July 6, 1999.

Banks, William C., and Alejandro D. Carrio. "Presidential Systems in Stress: Emergency Powers in Argentina and the United States." *Michigan Journal of International Law* 15 (1993): 45–6.

Bassett, C. Jeanne. "House Bill 591: Florida Compensates *Rosewood* Victims and their Families for Seventy-One Year Old Injury." *Florida State University Law Review* 23 (1994): 503.

Beane, Jonathan S. "Cyberhate Recruitment on the Internet." Computers and the Law Final Paper, May 1, 1997,
http://wings.buffalo.edu/CompLaw/CompLawPapers/beane.htm.

Beaven, Steven, and Tim Starks. "Surburban Rebelliousness Escalated to Baffling Racial Violence."
http://www.starnews.com/news/citystate/99/july/0706st-spree.html.

"Behind the Mask of Respectability: The Truth about the Anti-Defamation League of B'nai B'rith." David Duke Online,
http://www.duke.org/adl/index.html.

Belkin, Lisa. "She Says She Was Rejected by a College for being White," *Glamour*, Nov. 1998.

Bell, Derrick. "The Mystique of Affirmative Action." Speech at Princeton University, April 25, 1995.

"Segueing Toward 70: The Rewards and Regrets of a Race-Related Life." *Harvard Journal of African American Public Policy* 6 (Summer 2000).

Bell, Myrtle P., David A. Harrison, and Mary E. McLaughlin. "Asian American Attitudes Toward Affirmative Action in Employment: Implications for the Model Minority Myth." *Journal of Applied Behavioral Science* 33 (1997): 356–77.

Bellah, Robert N. "Civil Religion in America." *Daedalus* 96 (Winter 1967): 1–21.

Bellinger, Larry. "You Say You Want a Revolution." *Sojourners* 29 (2000), www.sojo.net/magazine/index.cfm/action/sojourners/issue/soj0009/articl/000910a.htm.

Belluck, Pam. "A White Supremacist Group Seeks a New Kind of Recruit." *New York Times*, July 7, 1999.

Bittner, Emily, and Sara Neufeld. "Hale Protest Turns Violent at Northwestern." *Daily Northwestern*, Jan. 24, 2000.

"Blacks Experience the Highest Rates of Violent Crime." U.S. Department of Justice, Bureau of Statistics,
http://www.ojp.usdoj.gov/bjs/glance/race.htm.

Blair, David. "White Stripped of Citizenship." *London Telegraph*, May 14, 2000.

Bobo, Lawrence. "Group Conflict, Prejudice, and the Paradox of Contemporary Racial Attitudes." In Phyllis A. Katz and Dalmas A. Taylor, eds., *Eliminating Racism: Profiles in Controversy*. New York: Plenum, 1998. Pp. 85–114.

Borjas, George, Richard Freeman, and Lawrence Katz. "Searching for the Effect of Immigration on the Labor Market." *American Economic Association Papers and Proceedings* (May 1996): 246–51.

Bositis, David A. "National Opinion Poll on Race Relations." Washington, D.C.: Joint Center for Political and Economic Studies, 1997.

"Redistricting and Minority Representation." Washington, D.C.: Joint Center for Political and Economic Studies, 1998.

Boston, Rob. "The Charitable Choice Charade." *Church and State* 51 (Feb. 1998): 7–12.

"Brazill Case Rekindles Debate on Juvenile Justice." May 18, 2001, http://www.cnn.com/2001/law/05/18/juvenile.crime.reut/index.html.

Bredemeier, Kenneth. "Work Visas Swell Area's Tech Corps." *Washington Post*, Dec. 1, 2000.

Brest, Paul, and Miranda Oshige. "Race and Remedy in a Multicultural Society: Affirmative Action for Whom?" *Stanford Law Review* 47 (1995): 855.

Bronner, Ethan. "College Applicants of '99 Are Facing Stiffest Competition." *New York Times*, June 12, 1999.

"Conservatives Open Drive Against Affirmative Action." *New York Times*, Jan. 26, 1999.

Brown, Stacia. "Virtual Hate." *Sojourners* 29 (2000), www.sojo.net/magazine/index.cfm/action/sojourners/issue/soj0009/articl/000910.htm.

Brownstein, Alan E. "Interpreting the Religion Clauses in Terms of Liberty, Equality, and Free Speech Values – A Critical Analysis of 'Neutrality Theory' and Charitable Choice." *Notre Dame Journal of Law, Ethics and Public Policy* 13 (1999): 243–84.

Burgdorf, Davic. "Wofford Student Continues to Lead White Supremacy Group. United Methodist News Service, April 5, 1999, http://www.umc.org/umns/99/pr/182.html.

Calleros, Charles R. "Conflict, Apology, and Reconciliation at Arizona State University: A Second Case Study in Hateful Speech." *Cumberland Law Review* 27 (1996): 91.

"Campus Homicides Fall, but Some Crimes Rise." *New York Times*, Jan. 21, 2001.

"Campus Poll Tackles Race." *Boston Globe*, April 19, 2000.

Cantor, George. "Would Policies at University of Michigan Make the Perfect Test Case on Affirmative Action?" *Gannett News Service,* July 13, 1996.

Cawthon, Raad, and Rita Giordano. "Gunman Known for His Racist Views." *Philadelphia Inquirer,* July 6, p. A1.

"Censorship Score Card." *Frontpage Magazine,* http://www.frontpagemag.com/horowitzsnotepad/2001/colleges.htm.

Chaiken, Jan. "Crunching Numbers: Crime and Incarceration at the End of the Millennium." *National Institute of Justice Journal,* Jan. 2000.

Chebium, Raju. "Attorney Morris Dees Pioneer in Using 'Damage' Lit to Fight Hate Groups." CNN.com, Sept. 8, 2000.

Chen, Jim. "Defunis, Defunct." *Constitution Commentary* 16 (Spring 1999): 91.

Chin, Gabriel J. "Bakke to the Wall: The Crisis of Bakkean Diversity." *William and Mary Bill of Rights Journal* 4 (1996): 881.

Claiborne, William. "Supremacist Group Grows Nationwide." *Washington Post,* June 29, 2000.

Clayton, Mark. "Will California Lead the Way to a Post-SAT Era?" *Christian Science Monitor,* Feb. 27, 2001.

Clegg, Roger. "Disqualifying Jesse: His Illegitimacy Problem." *National Review Online,* http://www.nationalreview.com/comment/comment012901g.shtml

Clinton, William. Commencement Speech, University of California at San Diego, June 14, 1997. http://www.whitehouse.gov/Initiatives/OneAmerica/announcement.html.

Cohen, Carl. "Why Racial Preference Is Illegal and Immoral." *Commentary* 67 (June 1979): 40–1.

Cohen, Richard. "Activist or Racist?" *Washington Post,* Feb. 14, 1995.

"Commission on Child Online Protection Off to Slow Start." *Tech Law Journal,* http://www.techlawjournal.com/censor/20000308.htm.

Conover, Pamela J., Ivor M. Crewe, and Don Searing. "The Nature of Citizenship in the United States and Great Britain: Empirical Comments on Theoretical Concerns." *Journal of Politics* 53 (1991): 800–32.

"Conservative Churches Say They Are Wary of 'Charitable Choice.' " *Church and State,* Dec. 2000.

Cooper, Kenneth J. "Colleges Testing New Diversity Initiatives." *Washington Post,* April 2, 2000.

"Deciding Who Gets in and Who Doesn't." *Washington Post,* April 2, 2000.

Cornwell, Rupert. "Rocketing Cost of Race Bias in the U.S. *The Independent,* May 28, 1994.

"Crime and Victim Statistics." U.S. Department of Justice, Bureau of Statistics, http://www.ojp.usdoj.gov/bjs/cvict.htm.

Crosby, F. J., and D. I. Cordova. "Words Worth of Wisdom: Towards an Understanding of Affirmative Action." *Journal of Social Issues* 52 (1996): 33–49.

Cross, Theodore. "Bill Gates' Gift to Racial Preferences in Higher Education." *Journal of Blacks in Higher Education* 25 (Autumn 1999): 6–7.

"Suppose There Was No Affirmative Action at the Most Prestigious Colleges and Graduate Schools?" *Journal of Blacks in Higher Education* 3 (Spring 1994): 44–51.

Cuza, Bobby. "Hate Crimes Increase by 12 Percent." *Los Angeles Times*, July 28, 2000.

Daniels, Jessie. "'Zog' Bankers, and 'Bull Dyke' Feminists: Jewish Men and Jewish Women." In Jessie Daniels, *White Lies*. New York: Routledge, 1997. Pp. 107–32.

de Alva, J. Jorge Klor. "Is Affirmative Action a Christian Heresy?" In Robert Post and Michael Rogin, *Race and Representation: Affirmative Action*. New York: Zone Books, 1998.

Dedman, Bill. "Midwest Gunman Had Engaged in Racist Acts at Two Universities." *New York Times*, July 6, 1999.

DiIulio, John J. Jr., "Behind the Walls of Fear: Crime Is Down Because Fear Is Causing Americans to Take Refuge Behind High Walls and Gated Communities but at What Price Does the Sense of Security Come?" *Orlando Sentinel*, Sept. 7, 1995.

"Ten Truths about Crime." *The Weekly Standard* 1 (Jan. 15, 1996): 12.

DiIulio, John J. Jr., and Anne M. Piehl. "What the Crime Statistics Don't Tell You." *Wall Street Journal*, Jan. 8, 1997.

Diner, Hasia R. "Drawn Together by Self-Interest: Jewish Representation of Race and Race Relations in the Early Twentieth Century." In V. P. Franklin, Nancy L. Grant, Harold M. Kletnick, and Genna Rae McNeil, eds., *African Americans and Jews in the Twentieth Century*. Columbia: University of Missouri Press, 1998. Pp. 27–39.

Dobrznski, Judith H. "Some Action, Little Talk: Companies Embrace Diversity, but Are Reluctant to Discuss It." *New York Times*, April 20, 1995.

"Does Society Penalize Whites?" http://www.naawp.com/flyers/webflyer2.htm.

Dougherty, Jon E. "Slavery Kept Alive by Race-Baiting Blacks." WorldnetDaily, Jan. 4, 2001.

DuBois, W. E. B. "Back to Africa." In John Henrik Clarke, ed., *Marcus Garvey and the Vision of Africa*. New York: Random House, 1974. Pp. 105–19.

Duke, David. "America at the Crossroads." http://www.duke.org/writings/crossroads.html.

"Is Russia the Key to White Survival?"
http://www.duke.org/dukereport/10–00.html.
"The Truth about HBO's 'Hate.Com.'"
www.Duke.org/library/race/hate_com.html.
Duryea, Bill. "Mister Connerly Comes to Florida." *American Spectator* 19 (July 1999): 28–36.
Dworkin, Ronald. "Defunis v. Sweatt." In Marshall Cohen, Thomas Nagel, and Thomas Scanlon, eds., *Equality and Preferential Treatment.* Princeton, N.J.: Princeton University Press, 1977. Pp. 63–83.
Dyer, Aldo. "Immigration Policy: Close the Floodgates." Unpublished paper, Vanderbilt University, Dec. 5, 2000.
Eastman, Susan. "Divide and Conquer." Weekly Planet, http://www.weeklyplanet.com/1999/1209/cover1.html.
Edsall, Thomas B. "Clinton Stuns Rainbow Coalition." *Washington Post*, June 14, 1992.
Edsall, Thomas. "Recalling Lessons of the 1960s." *Washington Post*, May 3, 1992.
Eichenwald, Kurt. "The Two Faces of Texaco." *New York Times*, Nov. 10, 1996.
Elder, Larry. "Black Racism." Oct. 31, 2000.
http://www.frontpagemag.com/elder/le10-31-00p.htm.
"Double Criminal Standards." March 10, 2000.
http://www.frontpagemag.com/elder/le03-13-00p.htm.
"When the Bad Guy Is Black." *Jewish World Review*, March 10, 2000.
Ellsworth, Scott, and John Hope Franklin. "Death in a Promised Land: The Tulsa Race Riot of 1921." http://www.littleafrica.com.
Ely, Jon Hart. "The Constitutionality of Reverse Discrimination." *University of Chicago Review* 41 (1974): 723.
Esbeck, Carl H. "A Constitutional Case for Governmental Cooperation with Faith-Based Social Service Providers."
http://www.law.emory.edu/ELJ/volumes/win97/esbeck.html.
Esolen, Gary. "David Duke's Use of Television." In Douglas Rose, ed., *The Emergence of David Duke and the Politics of Race.* Chapel Hill: University of North Carolina Press, 1992. Pp. 136–55.
"The European Union." *The Economist*, October 22, 1994.
Fagan, Patrick F. "Why Religion Matters: The Impact of Religious Practice on Social Stability." Backgrounder no. 1064. Washington, D.C.: Heritage Foundation, 1996.
Farber, Daniel A., and Suzanna Sherry. "Is the Radical Critique of Merit Anti-Semitic?" *California Law Review* 83 (1995): 853.
"Fast-Food Shooting Suspect Kept 'Satan' List: Cop Find Notes Filled with Hate and Possible Targets." APBNEWS.com, March 3, 2000.

Ferdinand, Pamela. "Free-Speech Debate Splits Liberal Brown: Anti-Reparations Ad at Center of the Controversy." *Washington Post*, March 21, 2001.

Ferguson, Ronald. "Teachers' Expectations and the Test Score Gap." In Christopher Jencks and Meredith Phillips, eds., *The Black/White Test Score Gap*. Washington, D.C.: Brookings Institution Press, 1998. Pp. 273–317.

Feyerick, Deborah. "Probe Underway into Death of New York Man, Fired upon 41 Times by Police."
http:///www.cnn.com/us/9902/05/police.shooting/index.html.

Fine, Terri. "The Impact of Issue Framing on Public Opinion Toward Affirmative Action Programs." *Social Science* 9 (1992): 323–34.

Fischer, Katrina. "All Hail the Diversity Rationale?" Unpublished paper, Yale University Law School, May 2000.

Flynn, James R. "Massive IQ Gains in 14 Nations: What IQ Tests Really Measure." *Psychological Bulletin* 101 (1987): 171–91.

Flynn, Laurie J. "Surprising Geography of America's Digital Divide." *New York Times*, Sept. 25, 2000.

Forrest, Susan, and Phil Mintz. "Seething Hate Led to Rampage Aboard Train. *Buffalo News*, Dec. 9, 1993.

Francis, Samuel. "Equality Unmasked." In Jared Taylor, ed., *The Real American Dilemma*. Oakton, Va.: New Century Books, 1992. P. 152.

"It's Race, Stupid: The Election Was Largely a Racial Headcount – Except for Whites." American Renaissance,
http://www.amren.com/jan2001.htm.

Freeman, Richard B. "Who Escapes? The Relation of Church-Going and Other Background Factors to the Socio-Economic Performance of Black Male Youths from Inner-City Poverty Tracts." Working Paper Series No. 1656. Cambridge, Mass.: National Bureau of Economic Research, 1985.

Frey, William. "Central City White Flight." *American Sociological Review* 44 (June 1979): 425–48.

"The Diversity Myth." *American Demographics* (June 1998): 39–43.

"Immigration, Domestic Migration, and Demographic Balkanization in America: New Evidence for the 1990s." *Population and Development Review* 22 (December 1996): 741–63.

"New Demographic Divide in the United States: Immigrant and Domestic 'Migrant Magnets.'" *The Public Perspective* 9 (June/July 1998): 35–9.

Frey, William, and Jonathan Tilove. "Immigrants in, Native Whites Out." *New York Times*, Aug. 20, 1995.

Gabel, Peter. "Affirmative Action and Racial Harmony." *Tikkun* (May/June 1995): 33–36.

Gallagher, Mike. "I'm Leaving If Shysters Get Away with Race Scam." *NewsMax.com*, Jan. 3, 2001.

Gallie, W. B. "Essentially Contested Concepts." In Max Black, ed., *The Importance of Language*. Englewood Cliffs, N.J.: Prentice Hall, 1966. Pp. 121–46.

Gamson, William A., and Andre Modigliani. "The Changing Culture of Affirmative Action." *Research in Political Sociology* 3 (1987): 107–19.

Geoly, James C. "Charity Replaces Bureaucracy." *Wall Street Journal*, Sept. 26, 1996.

Gillman, Todd. "Panthers, Supremacists Call for U.S. Overthrow; Dally Rally Urges Violence to Achieve Goals." *Dallas Morning News*, May 30, 1992.

Gladwell, Malcolm, and Rachael E. Stassen-Berger. "Slaying Blamed on Bias." *Chicago Sun-Times*, Dec. 9, 1996.

Glaser, James M. "A Quota on Quotas: Educational Differences in Attitudes Towards Minority Preferences." Unpublished manuscript, Political Science Department, Tufts University, 1999.

Glazer, Nathan. "In Defense of Preferences." *The New Republic* 218 (April 6, 1998).

Godwin, Peter. "Bloody Harvest." *New York Times Magazine*, http://www.nytimes.com/library/magazine/home/20000625mag-zimbabwe.html.

Golub, Jennifer. "What We Know About Black Anti-Semitism?" American Jewish Committee Working Paper. New York, 1990.

Graham, Hugh. "Origins of Affirmative Action: Civil Rights and the Regulatory State." *Annals of American Academy of Political and Social Science* 523 (1992): 50.

"Unintended Consequences: The Convergence of Affirmative Action and Immigration Policy." *American Behavioral Scientist* 41 (1998): 898–912.

Green, Donald, Robert P. Abelson, and Margaret Garnett. "Defended Neighborhoods, Integration, and Racially Motivated Crime." *American Journal of Sociology* 104 (Sept. 1998): 372–403.

Green, Donald P., Robert P. Abelson, and Margaret Garnett. "The Distinctive Political Views of Hate-Crime Perpetrators and White Supremacists." In Deborah A. Prentice and Dale T. Miller, eds., *Cultural Divides: Understanding and Overcoming Group Conflict*. New York: Russell Sage Foundation, 1999. Pp. 429–63.

Green, Donald, Jack Glaser, and Andrew Rich. "From Lynching to Gay Bashing: The Elusive Connection Between Economic Conditions and Hate Crime." *Journal of Personality and Social Psychology* 75 (1998): 82–92.

Greenberg, Anna. "The Church and the Revitalization of Politics and Community." *Political Science Quarterly* 115 (2000): 377–94.

BIBLIOGRAPHY

Greenberg, Cheryl. "The Southern Jewish Community and the Struggle for Civil Rights." In V. P. Franklin, Nancy L. Grant, Harold M. Kletnick, and Genna Rae McNeil, eds. *African Americans and Jews in the Twentieth Century*. Columbia: University of Missouri Press, 1998. Pp. 123–64.

Greenberger, Robert S. "'Charitable Choice' Tests Line Between Church, State." *Wall Street Journal*, August 24, 1999.

Hart, Michael H. "Racial Partition of the United States." 1996. http://Irainc.com/swtaboo/taboo/mhartol.html.

"Hate Group Information and History." http://www.geocities.com/athens/4747/Hgstart.

"Hate Groups on the Rise." *Jet* 95 (March 22, 1999): 19.

"Hate Violence Not Restricted to One Group or Race." *Klanwatch Intelligence Report* (Feb. 1993): 6–7.

Hayes, Stephen F. "Lieberman v. Gore: On Affirmative Action, This Ticket is Far Apart." *National Review Online*, August 8, 2000.

Herbert, Bob. "In America; A Black AIDS Epidemic." *New York Times*, June 4, 2001.

Hero, Rodney E., and Caroline J. Tolbert. "A Racial/Ethnic Diversity Interpretation of Politics and Policy in the States of the U.S." *American Journal of Political Science* 40 (August 1996): 851–71.

Himmelfarb, Gertrude. "Religion in the 2000 Election." *The Public Interest* 143 (Spring 2001): 20–6.

Hochschild, Jennifer. "Affirmative Action as Culture War." In Michele Lamont, ed., *The Culture Territories of Race: Black and White Boundaries*. Chicago: University of Chicago Press, 1999. Pp. 343–68.

Hogenson, Scott. "College Official Calls White Men 'Root of Most Evil.'" CNSNEWS.com.

Holmes, Steven A. "G.O.P. Lawmakers Offer a Ban on Federal Affirmative Action." *New York Times*, July 25, 1995.

"Ranks of Inmates Reach One Million in a 2-Decade Rise." *New York Times*, Oct. 28, 1994.

"Homicide Trends in the U.S." U.S. Department of Justice, Bureau of Statistics, http://www.ojp.usdoj.gov/bjs/homicide/race.htm.

"Hopwood Decision Not Fatal to Minorities." Campaign for a Colorblind America, Aug. 19, 1999.

Horn, Dan. "Civility Turned to Anarchy: How It Happened." *Cincinnati Enquirer*, www.enquirer.com, April 16, 2001.

Horowitz, David. "How to Deal with Racial Witch-Hunts of the Left." http://www.frontpagemag.com/horowitz/2001/hno2-26-01.htm.

"License to Kill." *FrontPageMagazine.com*, July 13, 2000.

"How Hate Strikes the Vulnerable." *PBS Online*,
http://www.pbs.org/forgottenfires/hate_al.html.

Howe, Jeff. "Like Whites on Race."
http://linkmag.com/Link/oct-nov-98/981030likewhites.html.

Howell, Susan E., and Sylvia Warren. "Public Opinion and David Duke." In Douglas Rose, ed., *The Emergence of David Duke and the Politics of Race*. Chapel Hill: University of North Carolina Press, 1992. Pp. 80–93.

Hutchinson, Earl O. "Denial Is Holding Blacks Back."
http://www.salon.com/news/feature/2000/08/03/denial/index.html.

"Why Are Black Leaders Silent on Hate Crimes?"
http://www.amren.com/salon.htm.

"Intelligence Report." Southern Poverty Law Center, Winter 1999.

Ith, Ian. "Leaders: Fat Tuesday about Crime, Not Race."
www.seattletimes.com, March 3, 2001.

Izumi, Lance T. "Confounding the Paradigm: Asian Americans and Race Preferences." *Notre Dame Journal of Law, Ethics, and Public Policy* 11 (1997): 121–38.

Jackman, Mary R., and Michael J. Muha. "Education and Intergroup Attitudes: Moral Enlightenment, Superficial Democratic Commitment, or Ideological Refinement?" *American Sociological Review* 49 (1984): 751–69.

Jackson, Doug. "Former Racist Reveals Ties to U.S. Military." *Denver Rocky Mountain News*, Aug. 21, 2000.

Jackson, Michelle N. "Black Wallstreet: Riot Destroys America's Most Affluent Black Community." *WAN Black History*.
http://www.wanonline.com/blackhistory/blackhistory/918.html.

Jackson, Thomas. "What is Racism? Is Bigotry and Racism Just a White Thing?." *Stormfront*, http://www.stormfront.org/whitenat/racism/htm.

Johnson, Doug. "Former Racist Reveals Ties to U.S. Military." *Denver Rocky Mountain News*, Aug. 21, 2000.

Johnson, Lyndon B. "Commencement Address at Howard University." June 4, 1965. http://www.lbjlib.utexas.edu/johnson/archives.hom/speeches.hom/650604.htm.

Jordan, Barbara. "The Americanization Ideal." *New York Times,* Sept. 11, 1995.

Kelley, Stanley Jr. "Politics as Vocation: Variations on Weber." In John Geer, ed., *Politicians and Party Politics*. Baltimore, Md.: Johns Hopkins Press, 1998. Pp. 337–64.

Kellstedt, Paul M. "Media Framing and the Dynamics of Racial Policy Preferences." *American Journal of Political Science* 44 (April 2000): 239–55.

Kendrick, S. A. "The Coming Segregation of Our Selective Colleges." *College Board* 66 (1967): 68.

Kennedy, Maria Elena. "Black Group Says Jesse Jackson Does Not Represent Them." CNNNEWS.com, January 16, 2001.

Kennedy, Randall. "Persuasion and Distrust." In Russell Nieli, ed., *Racial Preference and Racial Justice*. Washington, D.C.: Ethics and Public Policy Center, 1990. Pp. 45–60.

Kilborn, Peter. "Women and Minorities Still Face 'Glass Ceiling.'" *New York Times*, March 16, 1995.

Kim, Tom. "Cultural House Out of Reach for Asian Americans at University of Illinois." http://new.excite.com/news/uw/000803/university-91.

Kinder, Donald R., and Lynn Sanders. "Mimicking Political Debate with Survey Questions: The Case of Affirmative Action for Blacks." *Social Cognition* 8 (Spring 1990): 73–4.

Kinsley, Michael. "The Spoils of Victimhood." *New Yorker* (March 27, 1995): 62–9.

"Kinsmen Redeemer/Rhodesia Project." http://www.amren.com/redeemer_proj.html.

"Klan Holds Voter Registration Drives, Backs Candidates." *Klanwatch Intelligence Report*, July 1984.

Knickerbocker, Brad. "White Power Winning Ears with Pop Rock." *Christian Science Monitor*, March 8, 2000.

Knott, Tom. "Lawrence Apology Simply Won't Do." *Washington Times*, Feb. 10, 1995.

Kolbert, E. "Test Marketing a President: How Focus Groups Pervade Campaign Politics." *New York Times Magazine*, Aug. 30, 1992.

Koniak, Susan P. "When Law Risks Madness." *Cardozo Studies in Law and Literature* 65 (Spring/Summer 1996): 65–138.

Kronenwetter, Michael. *United They Hate: White Supremacist Groups in America*. New York: Walker, 1992.

La Noue, George R., and John C. Sullivan. "Deconstructing the Affirmative Action Categories." *American Behavioral Scientist* 41 (1998): 913–26.

Lacey, Marc, and David Stout. "Armed Man Shot and Wounded Outside White House." www.nytimes.com/2001/02/07/national/07CND-WHITE.html.

Ladd, Everett C. "People, Opinion, and Polls: Affirmative Action, Welfare, and the Individual." *The Public Perspective* 6 (June/July 1995): 23.

Larson, David B., and Byron R. Johnson. "Religion: The Forgotten Factor in Cutting Youth Crime and Saving At-Risk Urban Youth." Report 98-2. New York: Manhattan Institute, 1998.

Lawson, Gary. "Symposium: Changing Images of the State: The Rise of the Administrative State." *Harvard Law Review* 107 (1994): 1231, 1233.

LeBouthillier, Arthur E. "Introduction to Nationalism." http://www.duke.org/library/potpourii/nationalism.html.

Lee, Jennifer. "From Prosiac Routine to Racial Conflict: Individualism, Opportunity, and Group Position." In "From Civil Relations to Exploding Cauldrons: Blacks, Jews, and Koreans in Urban America," unpublished manuscript.

Lee, Robert W. "Police, Race and Cincinnati's Riots." *New American,* May 21, 2001.

Lee, Thomas. "Stockton Celebrates Euro-American Heritage: The First School District to Proclaim Heritage Month." *Asian Week*, May 4, 2000. Americans Against Discrimination and Preferences, adp@dnail.com.

Leinwand, Donna. "Racist Threats Set Penn State on Edge." *USA Today*, May 3, 2000.

Lemann, Nicholas. "Taking Affirmative Action Apart." *New York Times Magazine*, June 11, 1995. Pp. 36–66.

Lichter, Linda. "Who Speaks for Black America?" *Public Opinion* 8 (Aug./Sept. 1985): 41–4, 58.

Liu, Goodwin. "Affirmative Action in Higher Education: The Diversity Rationale and the Compelling Interest Test." *Harvard Civil Rights/Civil Liberties Law Review* 33 (1998): 58.

"Losing the Vote: The Impact of Felony Disenfranchisement Laws in the United States." Report of the Sentencing Project and Human Rights Watch, Oct. 1998.

"Louima Verdict Sparks Disappointment, Relief, and Outrage." http://www.cnn.com/U.S.9906/08/louima.quotes/index.html.

Lynch, John P. "School Districts and the Internet: Practice and Model Policy." *West's Education Law Reporter* 122 (Jan. 1998): 21–5.

"The Making of a Skinhead." Simon Wiesenthal Center, http://www.wiesenthal.com/tj/index.html.

Manuel, Marlon. "Hate Letter to Black Schools Says Race's Destruction Is the Goal." *Atlanta Constitution*, Jan. 7, 2000.

Marcus, Amy D. "Education: New Weights Can Alter SAT Scores." *Wall Street Journal*, Aug. 31, 1999.

Martin, Richard. "Web of Hate: Soldiers of Bigotry March Online." http://www.pretext.com/febr98/features/story4.htm.

Mashberg, Tom. "Debates Rage On Campus Over Free-Speech Rules." *Boston Herald*, Oct. 31, 1999.

Matsui, Elena, and Joseph Chuman. "The Case Against Charitable Choice." *Humanist*, Jan. 1, 2001.

McCain, Robert Stacy. "'Hate Crimes' Not Big Problem in Race Relations, Study Finds." *Washington Times*, http://www.amren.com/crime.htm.

"Researcher Says Hate 'Fringe' Isn't as Crowded as Claimed." *Washington Times*, May 9, 2000. http://www.washtimes.com/culture/default-20005922336.htm.

"Scholar Finds 'Abusive' Ties Between Blacks, Jews." *American Renaissance*, http://www.amren.com/washtimes.htm.

McClosky, Herbert. "Consensus and Ideology in American Politics." *American Political Science Review* 58 (1964): 361–82.

McMahan, T. Vance, and Don R. Willett. "Hope from Hopwood: Charting a Positive Civil Rights Course for Texas and the Nation." *Stanford Law and Policy Review* 10 (1999): 163.

Mehler, Barry. "Race and 'Reason': Academic Ideas a Pillar of Racist Thought." *Intelligence Report* (Winter 1999): 27–32.

Merton, Robert K. "The Unanticipated Consequences of Purposive Social Action." *American Sociological Review* 1 (1936): 894–904.

Moore, David W. "Americans Today Are Dubious about Affirmative Action." *Gallup Poll Monthly*, March 1995.

"Morris S. Dees, Jr." Dorothy L. Thompson Civil Rights Lecture Series, http://www.ksu.edu/dthompson/dees.html.

"Most U.S. Students Support Diversity but Not Affirmative Action, a Survey Finds." *Chronicle of Higher Education*, April 18, 2000.

Muhammad, Cedric. "Black Civil Rights Leaders 'Real' Concern over Bush's Meeting with Black Pastors." http://blackelectorate.com/archives/031101.asp.

"Religion, Theology and Self-Improvement Sundays: Many Whites Share Rev. Jerry Falwell's View on Islam." http://blackelectorate.com/archives/031101.asp.

Muhammad, Khalid Abdul. Speech at Kean College, in Union, N.J., Nov. 29, 1993.

"Multiculturalism: A Policy Response to Diversity." Presentation at the UNESCO Management of Social Transformations Conference, Sydney, Australia, April 1995.

Murphy, Kim, "Behind All the Noise of Hate Music." http://www.latimes.com/news/front/20000330/t000029972.html.

Murray, Mark, Marilyn Weber Serafini, and Megan Twohey. "Untested Safety Net." *National Journal* (March 1, 2001): 684–93.

Narasaki, K. K. "Separate But Equal? Discrimination and the Need for Affirmative Action Legislation." In *Perspectives on Affirmative Action*. Los Angeles: Asian Pacific American Public Policy Forum, 1995.

"National College Bound Seniors: 1994 Profile of SAT and Achievement Test Takers." The College Board, Princeton, N.J.

"The New Lexicon of Hate." Simon Wiesenthal Center Report, 1999.

Nieli, Russell. "Ethnic Tribalism and Human Personhood." In Nieli, ed., *Racial Preferences and Racial Justice*. Washington, D.C.: Ethics and Public Policy Center, 1991. Pp. 61–103.

Nisbett, Richard E. "Race, Genetics, and IQ." In Christopher Jencks and Meredith Phillips, ed., *The Black-White Test Score Gap*. Washington, D.C.: Brookings Institution Press, 1998. Pp. 86–102.

Norman, Jim. "America's Verdict on Affirmative Action is Decidedly Mixed." *Public Perspective* 6 (June/July 1995): 49.

Nuniziata, Jeffrey-John. "White Supremacy and the New World Order." http://www.impactpress.com/articles/junjul97/nazi.htm.

Ohlemacher, Stephen. "Legislators Propose Ban on Campus Speech Rules." *The Plain Dealer*, January 23, 2000.

Olzak, Susan. "The Political Context of Competition: Lynching and Urban Racial Violence, 1882–1914." *Social Forces* 69 (1990): 395–421.

Olzak, Susan, and Suzanne Shanahan. "Deprivation and Race Riots: An Extension of Spilerman's Analysis." *Social Forces* 74 (1996): 931–61.

O'Neill, James M. "Colleges Consider a 15 Percent Solution." *The Inquirer*, April 1, 2000, http:/www.phillynews/com/inquirer/2000/Apr/01/city/HIEDO1.html.

O'Sullivan, John. "Preferences for (Almost) All: Affirmative Action Today." *National Review* 52 (April 17, 2000) 7: 22–4.

Page, Clarence. "Hate-Crime Laws Not for 'Whites Only.' " http://chicagotribune.come/news/columnists/page/, July 16, 2000.

Palmer, Elizabeth. "Senate Votes to Expand Federal Hate Crimes; Similar House Action Unlikely." *Congressional Quarterly Weekly Report*, June 24, 2000.

"Panel on 1921 Tulsa Race Riot Urges Reparations for Victims." *Jet*, Feb. 21, 2000.

Parker, Suzi. "U.S. Cities Face Past Strife." *Christian Science Monitor*, March 24, 2000.

Passel, Jeffrey S., and Barry Edmonston. "Immigration and Race: Recent Trends in Immigration to the United States." In *Immigration and Ethnicity: The Integration of America's Newest Arrivals*. Washington, D.C.: Urban Institute Press, 1994. Pp. 31–71.

Patterson, Orlando. "Race by the Numbers." *New York Times*, May 8, 2001.

Peffley, Mark, John Hurwitz, and Paul Sniderman. "Racial Stereotypes and Whites' Political Views of Blacks in the Context of Welfare and Crime." *American Journal of Political Science* 41 (1997): 30–60.

Pierce, William L. "The Roots of Civilization." Reprinted from *National Vanguard*, no. 59, 1978.

"Poll Finds Whites Use Stereotypes." *New York Times*, Jan. 10, 1991.

Pollard, Kelvin. "1999 United States Population Data Sheet." *Population Reference Bureau*, http://www.Prb.org/pubs/usds99.htm.

Pollock, Ellen J., and Milo Geyelin. "U.S. Incarceration Rate Highest." *Wall Street Journal*, Jan. 7, 1991.

Posner, Richard A. "The Defunis Case and the Constitutionality of Preferential Treatment of Racial Minorities." *Supreme Court Review* 1 (1974).

"Preferential Treatment for Women and Minorities." *The Gallup Monthly Poll*, December 7–10, 1989.

Rabinowitz, Dorothy. "The Hate-Crimes Bandwagon." http://interactive.wsj.com/articles/SB962065107852832261.html.

Rajan, Priya V. "The Head Start Program: Constructive Affirmative Action." In Carol M. Swain, ed., *Race versus Class: The New Affirmative Action Debate*. Lanham, Md.: University Press of America, 1996. Pp. 247–64.

"Re: For the Racists." www.adversity.net/wwwboard/messages/72.html.

Reed, Ingrid, "NJ Politics Is Nothing Short of Remarkable." *The Times*, July 3, 2001.

"Religion Defies Racist Beliefs." Jan. 5, 2001, http://www.latimes.com/communities/news/inland_empire/200110105/tivoo10973.htm.

"Report: Hate Groups Fewer in Number, but Larger in Size." http://www.cnn.com/2000/US/03/15/hate.groups.

"The Riot That Never Was." *The Economist* 351 (April 24, 1999): 29.

Robinson, Bryan. "Officers Acquitted of All Charges in Diallo Shooting." http://www.courttv.com/national/diallo/022500_verdict_ctv.html.

Roddy, Dennis B., and Bill Heltzel. "Man on Rampage: Accused Killer Richard Baumhammers Had a History of Mental Illness and a Strong Dislike for Immigrants." Post-Gazette.com, April 30, 2000.

Rogers, Melissa. "Charitable Choice: Two Views: Threat to Religion." *Sojourners* 27 (July/Aug. 1998) 4: 29–30.

Rosen, Jeffrey. "The Lost Promise of School Integration." *New York Times*, April 2, 2000.

"The Rosewood Report." http://members.aol.com/kloveo1/roschist.txt.

Ross, Loretta J. "White Supremacy in the 1990's, *The Public Eye*, http://www.publiceye.org/pra/eyes/whitsup.html.

Ross, Thomas. "Innocence and Affirmative Action." *Vanderbilt Law Review* 43 (1990): 297.

Roy, Joe. "Tracking the Terror: The Most Dangerous White Supremacists Have Moved to the Patriot Underground." *Klanwatch Intelligence Report*, Feb. 1996.

Rushton, J. Philippe. "The American Dilemma in World Perspective." In Jared Taylor, ed., *The Real American Dilemma*. Oakton, Va.: New Century Books, 1998. Pp. 11–30.

Ryan, Alan. "Apocalypse Now?" *New York Review of Books*, Nov. 17, 1994.

Ryan, Brendan. "Admissions Gets Record Number of Frosh Applications." *The Vanderbilt Hustler*, Jan. 30, 2001.

Ryan, Michelle P. "Paved with Good Intentions: The Legal Consequences of the Charitable Choice Provision." *Dickinson Law Review* 102 (1998): 383–410.

Sack, Kevin. "U.S. Assures Jesse Jackson It Is Pursuing Death of Black Mississippi Youth." New York Times On the Web, July 13, 2000.

Salamon, Julie. "The Web as Home for Racism and Hate." *New York Times*, Oct. 23, 2000.

Scharnberg, Kirsten, and Ray Long. "Killer's Parents Didn't Teach Hate." *Chicago Tribune*, Aug. 27, 1999.

Scharnberg, Kirsten, Evan Osnos, and David Mendell. "The Making of a Racist." *Chicago Tribune*, July 25, 1999.

Schmitt, Eric. "Whites in Minority in Largest Cities, the Census Shows." *New York Times*, April 30, 2001.

Schneider, Williams. "In Job Quota Debate, Advantage GOP." *National Journal*, June 8, 1991.

Seabury, Paul, "HEW and the Universities." *Commentary* 53 (Feb. 1972) 2: 38–44.

Seligman, Daniel. "Affirmative Action Is Here to Stay." *Fortune*, April 19, 1982.

Selmi, Michael. "The Life of Bakke: An Affirmative Action Retrospective." *Georgetown Law Journal* 87 (1999): 981.

Sharp, Deborah. "Florida Gov. Bush Plans to Dump Parts of Affirmative Action Law." *USA Today*, Nov. 12, 1999.

Shelley, Louise I. "American Crime: An International Anomaly?" *Comparative Social Research* 8 (1985): 81–95.

Silvergate, Harvey A. "An Overdue Outrage over Speech Codes." *Boston Herald*, April 26, 1999.

Simon, Robert. "Preferential Hiring: A Reply to Judith Jarvis Thomson." In Marshall Cohen, Thomas Nagel, and Thomas Scanlon, eds., *Equality and Preferential Treatment*. Princeton: Princeton University Press, 1977. Pp. 40–8.

Simon, Stephanie. "Leader of Hate's Church Mourns 'One White Man.'" LAtimes.com, July 6, 1999.

Skrentny, John David. "The Creation and Expansion of Affirmative Action Programs." In "The Minority Rights Revolution: How War and the Black

Civil Rights Movement Changed American Politics," unpublished book manuscript, Jan. 2001.

Sleeper, Jim. "American National Identity in a Post-National Age." In Stanley Renshon, ed., *One America?: Political Leadership, National Identity, and the Dilemmas of Diversity*. Washington, D.C.: Georgetown University Press, forthcoming.

"Nightmares of Rage and Destruction." *Washington Post*, Book World, Nov. 3, 1996.

Sloan, Stephen. "The Future of Terrorism in the U.S." *Klanwatch Intelligence Report*, Winter 1997.

Smith, Brent L. "Pursuing the Terrorist: Changing Legal Strategies." *Klanwatch Intelligence Report*, Winter 1997.

Snow, David A., and Robert D. Benford. "Master Frames and Cycles of Protest." In Aldon D. Morris and Carol McClung, *Frontiers in Social Movement Theory*. New Haven: Yale University Press, 1992. Pp. 133–55.

Snyderman, Michael, and Stanley Rothman. "Survey of Expert Opinion on Intelligence and Aptitude Testing." *American Psychologist* 42 (1987): 137–44.

Sowell, Thomas. "Are Quotas Good for Blacks?" *Commentary* (June 1978): 39–43.

Townhall.com, July 14, 2000.

Stanford Black Students Union, "Ten Reasons Why You Shouldn't Be Fooled by David Horowitz's Ad – And Why It Is Racist Too." *Stanford Daily*, May 2, 2001, http://www.daily.stanford.edu/dailey/serlet/story?id=5609&section=opinions&date=05-02-2001.

Stanton, Sam. "For Hate Peddlers, This Might Be the Last Roundup." *Sacramento Bee*, July 16, 2000.

"The State of Violent Crime in America." First Report of the Council on Crime in America, the New Citizenship Project, Washington, D.C., Jan. 1996.

Steeh, Charlotte, and Maria Krysan. "Poll Trends: Affirmative Action and the Public, 1971–1995." *Public Opinion Quarterly* 60 (1996): 128–58.

Steele, Claude M. "Race and Schooling of Black Americans." *Atlantic Monthly*, http://www.theatlantic.com/election/connection/race/steele.htm.

Steele, Claude, and Joshua Aronson. "Stereotype Threat and the Test Performance of Academically Successful African Americans." In Christopher Jencks and Meredith Phillips, eds., *The Black/White Test Score Gap*. Washington, D.C.: Brookings Institution Press, 1998. Pp. 401–27.

Steinberg, Jacques. "For Gatekeepers at Colleges, a Daunting Task of Weeding." *New York Times*, Feb. 27, 2000.

Stoker, Laura. "Understanding Whites' Resistance to Affirmative Action: The Role of Principled Commitments and Racial Prejudice." In Jon Hurwitz and Mark Peffley, eds., *Perception and Prejudice: Race and Politics in the United States*. New Haven: Yale University Press, 1998. Pp. 135–70.

"Study: Blacks Commit 90% of Interracial Crime: Data Suggest That 'Racial Profiling' May Have Scientific Basis." Press release, New Century Foundation, June 2, 1999.

Sunstein, Cass R. "Constitutionalism After the New Deal." *Harvard Law Review* 101 (1987).

"Is Violent Speech a Right?" *American Prospect* 6 (June 23, 1995): 34–7.

"The Law of Group Polarization." John M. Olin Law and Economics Working Paper No. 91. Chicago: Law School, University of Chicago, 1999. P. 1. SSRN Electronic Paper Collection.
http://papers.ssrn.com/paper.taf?abstract_id=199668.

"Supreme Court Declines to Hear Matthew Hale's Case."
www.westlegalstudies.com.

Swain, Carol M. "Affirmative Action: Legislative History, Judicial Interpretation, Public Consensus." In Neil Smelser, William J. Wilson, and Faith Mitchell, eds., *America Becoming: Racial Trends and Their Consequences*. Washington, D.C.: National Research Council, 2001. Pp. 318–47.

"Race as a Plus Factor in Undergraduate Admissions – The Public Seeks an Alternative." *Harvard Journal of African American Public Policy* 7 (2001): 1–22.

Swain, Carol M., Kyra Greene, and Christine Min Wotipka. "Understanding Racial Polarization on Affirmative Action: The View from Focus Groups." In John D. Skrentny, ed., *Color Lines: Affirmative Action, Immigration, and Civil Rights Options for America*. Chicago: University of Chicago Press, 2001. Pp. 214–38.

Swain, Carol M., Robert Rodgers, and Bernard Silverman. "Life after *Bakke* Where Whites and Blacks Agree: Public Support for Fairness in Educational Opportunities." *Harvard BlackLetter Law Journal* 16 (Spring 2000): 147–84.

Thernstrom, Stephen, and Abigail Thernstrom. "Reflections on the Shape of the River." *UCLA Law Review* 46 (1999): 1583–631.

"This Wasn't Supposed to Happen: The Black-White Test Gap Is Growing." *Journal of Blacks in Higher Education* 25 (1999): 95–100.

Tilove, Jonathan. "Don't Call Them 'White': European-Americans Demand Recognition and Respect for the Diversity of a Group That Has Been Maligned and Marginalized in the Age of Affirmative Action." *The Plain Dealer*, Dec. 31, 1995.

"White Nationalists Seek Respectability in Meeting of 'Uptown Bad Guys.'" American Renaissance, http://www.amren.com/newhous.htm.

"Too Busy to Hate: Racist Groups Decline as Economy Enjoys Prosperity; Patriot Movement Depleting Ranks of White Supremacists." *Klanwatch Intelligence Report*, Winter 1997, pp. 17–18.

Trow, Martin. "'The Shape of the River': California after Racial Preferences." *The Public Interest* 135 (Spring 1999): 64–85.

Tsuang, Grace W. "Assuring Equal Access of Asian Americans to Highly Selective Universities." *Yale Law Journal* 98 (1989): 659.

Twohey, Megan. "Charitable Choice Grows, but So Do Questions." *National Journal*, Oct. 14, 2000.

Unz, Ron. "California and the End of White America." *Commentary*, Nov. 1999.

Vars, Fredrick, and William Bowen. "Scholastic Aptitude Test Scores, Race, and College Performance in Selective Colleges and Universities." In Christopher Jencks and Meredith Phillips, eds., *The Black/White Test Score Gap*. Washington, D.C.: Brookings Institution Press, 1998. Pp. 457–79.

Vigil, Jennifer. "Literature of Hate Spewed in 2 Suburbs." *Chicago Tribune*, Aug. 12, 1999.

Waldron, Jeremy. "The Wisdom of the Multitude." *Political Theory* 23 (Nov. 1995): 563–84.

Wang, Theodore Hsein, and Frank Wu. "Beyond the Model Minority Myth: Why Asian Americans Support Affirmative Action." *Guild Practioner* 53 (Winter 1996): 35–47.

Werely, Sean. "Horowitz Horrified: Protesters Try to Disrupt Speech by Controversial Slavery Reparations Opponent." Chicago Weekly News.com, http://www.chicagoweeklynews.com/2001s/05.10/news/horowitz_protest.shtml.

Westfall, Julie. "Smith's Police Reports Detail Offenses Prior to the Shootings." http://www.uwiretoday.com/topnews072099000.html.

"The White Male Vote." CBS/*New York Times* exit polls, *USA Today*, Nov. 11, 1994.

"Who Rules America? The Alien Grip on Our News and Entertainment Media Must Be Broken." National Vanguard Books, Catalog no. 13. Hillsboro, W.Va.: National Vanguard Books, 1991.

Wilkins, Roger. "Racism Has Its Privileges." *The Nation*, March 27, 1995.

Willdorf, Nina. "More Black Colleges Receive Threatening Letters." *Chronicle of Higher Education*, Jan. 14, 2000.

Williams, Juan. "How Black Liberal Strategy Failed Its Followers." *Washington Post National Weekly Edition*, Nov. 28–Dec. 4, 1994.

Williams, Walter. "An Ugly Conspiracy of Silence." WorldNetDaily.com, Aug. 18, 1999.

"Black Politicians Fiddling Whilst Rome Burns." Feb. 21, 2001, http://capitalismmagazine.com/2001/february/ww_black_pol.htm.

"Election 2000's Message." http://www.jewishworldreview.com/cols/williams01001.asp.

Wilson, William J. "Studying Inner-City Social Dislocations: The Challenge of Public Agenda Research." *American Sociological Review* 56 (Feb. 1991): 8–10.

Winegardner, Jean. "Is Hate Young and New on the Web?" Online Journalism Review, http://ojr.usc.edu/content/story.cfm?id=192.

"The Year in Hate: Hate Groups Top 500, Net Sites Soar." *Intelligence Report*, Winter 1999.

Zerkine, Zernike. "Campus Affirmative Action Embattled Handbooks Encourage Student Suits." *Boston Globe*, Jan. 27, 1999.

"Zimbabwean Gives Account of Gang Rape." Electronic Telegraph, http://www.amren.com/zimbabwe_rape.html. April 20, 2000.

INTERVIEWS

Interviews were conducted by telephone unless otherwise noted.

Don Black, April 20, 2000.

George Burns, April 11, 2001 (interviewed in person).

David Duke, Feb. 15, 2000.

Floyd Cochran Interview with Hatewatch, Feb. 17, 1997, http://www.hatewatch.org/.

Daniel Gayman, May 24, 2000.

David Goldman, Oct. 7, 1999.

Matthew Hale, Nov. 12, 1999.

Michael H. Hart, April 14, 2000.

Matthew Lerner, May 11, 2000.

Michael Levin, Jan. 5, 2000.

William Pierce, Dec. 27, 1999.

Jared Taylor, Dec. 21, 1999.

Lisa Turner, April 28, 2000.

Reno Wolfe, Dec. 22, 1999.

STATUTES

California Constitution, www.leginfo.ca.gov/const-toc.html.

The Civil Rights Act of 1964, 78 Statute 241, 42 U.S.C.

Title 14, 42 U.S.C. §2000d (1999).

U.S. Constitution.

BIBLIOGRAPHY

COURT CASES

Adarand Constructors v. Pena, 515 U.S. 200 (1995).

Brown v. Board of Education, 347 U.S. 483 (1954).

City of Richmond v. J. A. Croson Co., 488 U.S. 469 (1989).

Defunis v. Odegaard, 416 U.S. 312 (1974).

Fullilove v. Klutznick, 448 U.S. 448, 519 (1980).

Gratz v. Bollinger, no. 97-75231 (E.D. Mich. Filed Oct. 14, 1997).

Griggs v. Duke Power Co., 401 U.S. 424 (1971).

Grutter v. Bollinger, no. 97-75928 (E.D. Mich. Dec. 3, 1997).

Grutter v. Bollinger, no. 97-75928 (E.D. Mich. Decided March 27, 2001).
    http://www.umich.edu/~urel/admissions/legal/gratz/gra_opin.html.

Johnson v. Transportation Agency, Santa Clara County, 480 U.S. 616, 677
    (1987).

Mainstream Loudon v. Board of Trustees of Loudon County Library, 24 F.
    Supp. 2d 552 (1998).

McLaurin v. Oklahoma State Regents for Higher Education, 339 U.S. 637
    (1950).

Metro Broadcasting, 497 U.S. at 630.

Plessy v. Ferguson, 163 U.S. 537 (1896).

Regents of the University of California v. Bakke, 438 U.S. 265 (1978).

Smith v. University of Washington Law School (Civ. No. C-97-335 (W.D.
    Wash. Filed March 5, 1997), interlocutory appeals filed: no. 99-35209,
    9935347, 9935348 (9th Cir Dec. 4, 2000).

Sweatt v. Painter, 339 U.S. 629 (1950).

United Steelworkers of America v. Weber, 427 U.S. 273 (1976).

Wessman v. Gittens, 160 F. 3rd 790 (1998).

Wygant v. Jackson Bd. of Ed., 476 U.S. 267, 273 (1986).

OTHER SOURCES

Brokaw, Tom. *Dateline*, July 28, 2000.

"Can Religious Programs Solve America's Social Ills?" *Both Sides with Jesse
    Jackson*, Dec. 24, 2000. www.cnn.com/transcripts/0012/24/bs.00html.

Contemporary attitudes about religion in America.
    http://gallup.com/pol/indicators/indreligion.asp.

Evil among Us: Hatred in America. Discovery Channel, April 14, 2000.

Faculty Survey, Regarding the Use of Sexual and Racial Preferences in Higher
    Education, National Association of Scholars, Oct. 16–28, 1996.

The Godfather. Paramount Pictures, 1972.

Harvard University AIDS Institute.
    http://www.hsph.harvard.edu/hai/index.html.

BIBLIOGRAPHY

Hate Group Information and History.
   http://www.geocities.com/athens/4747/Hgstart.
Hate Speech. Brown Daily Herald's student online forum,
   http://www.browndaileyherald.com/stories.cfm?s=0&=4468.
Horowitz, Donald. "Ten Reasons Why Reparations for Blacks Is a Bad Idea
   for Blacks – And Racist Too" advertisement.
   http://www.frontpagemag.com/horowitznotepad/2001/
   hn01-03-01.htm.
Ignatiev, Noel, and John Garvey. *Race Traitor, Journal of the New Abolitionism*.
   http://www.postfun.com/racetraitor.
Kids page. http://kids.stormfront.org.
NAAWP's youth web page.
   http://www.naawp.com/Youth/jessica.htm.
Profile of Al Sharpton as "The Power Broker." www.cbsnews.com.
Summary of filtering bills for the 106th Congress. *Tech Law Journal*.
   http://www.techlawjournal.com/cong106/filter/Default.htm.
Testimony of Robert L. Woodson, Sr., Capitol Hill, Washington, D.C., Sept.
   7, 1995.
United States Census Bureau, Washington, D.C., 1999.
University of Michigan's web page regarding the two lawsuits.
   http://www.umich.edu/~urel/admissions. *Gratz v. Bollinger*, no. 97-75231
   (E.D. Mich. Filed Oct. 14, 1997); *Grutter v. Bollinger*, no. 97-75928 (E.D.
   Mich. Dec. 3, 1997).
Website for the Federation for American Immigration Reform. www.fairus.org.
Website for the Negative Population Growth organization.
   www.npg.org.
Website for Religious Tolerance.
   www.religioustolerance.org/hom_hat1.htm#of.
Wolfe, Reno. Personal correspondence, June 12, 2000.
Wyatt, posting on "Blacktalk" home page, Dec. 7, 2000.
   http://207.201.145.199/blackleadership/-disc1/00000725.htm.

INDEX